Series Editors

W. Hansmann
W. Purgathofer
F. Sillion

S. J. Gortler
K. Myszkowski (eds.)

Rendering Techniques 2001

Proceedings of the Eurographics Workshop
in London, United Kingdom,
June 25–27, 2001

Eurographics

SpringerWienNewYork

Prof. Dr. Steven J. Gortler
Institute of Computer Science
Harvard University
Cambridge/Mass., USA

Professor Dr. Karol Myszkowski
Max-Planck-Institut für Informatik
Saarbrücken, Germany

© 2001 Springer-Verlag/Wien
Printed in Austria

Typesetting: Camera-ready by authors
Printing: Novographic, A-1238 Wien
Binding: Papyrus, A-1100 Wien

Printed on acid-free and chlorine-free bleached paper

SPIN: 1084676

With 198 partly coloured Figures

ISSN 0946-2767
ISBN 3-211-83709-4 Springer-Verlag Wien New York

Preface

This book contains the proceedings of the 12th Eurographics Workshop on Rendering, which took place from the 25th to the 27th of June, 2001, in London, United Kingdom. Over the past 11 years, the workshop has become the premier forum dedicated to research in rendering. Much of the work in rendering now appearing in other conferences and journals builds on ideas originally presented at the workshop.

This year we received a total of 74 submissions. Each paper was carefully reviewed by two of the 28 international programme committee members, as well as external reviewers, selected by the co-chairs from a pool of 125 individuals. In this review process, all submissions and reviews were handled electronically, with the exception of videos submitted with a few of the papers.

The overall quality of the submissions was exceptionally high. Space and time constraints forced the committee to make some difficult decisions. In the end, 29 papers were accepted, and they appear here. Almost all papers are accompanied by color images, which appear at the end of the book. The papers treat the following varied topics: methods for local and global illumination, techniques for acquisition and modeling from images, image-based rendering, new image representations, hardware assisted methods, shadow algorithms, visibility, perception, texturing, and filtering. Each year, in addition to the reviewed contributions, the workshop includes invited presentations from internationally recognized experts. This year we were pleased to have Ed Catmull (Pixar) and Michael Cohen (Microsoft Research) as invited speakers. As in previous years, we expect these proceedings to become an invaluable resource for both rendering researchers and practitioners.

We wish to thank organizing chairmen Yiorgos Chrysanthou and Mel Slater and their colleagues at the Department of Computer Science, University College London, for their help in the production of the proceedings, and for taking care of all the local organization aspects of the workshop. We also want to acknowledge Sun Microsystems, SGI-Silicon Graphics, and Electronic Arts for contributing financial support.

Finally, we wish to thank all the authors who submitted their work to the workshop, and the programme committee members and external reviewers for all the time and energy they invested in the review process. We were impressed with both the quality of the submissions and the quality of the reviews evaluating the papers. We are honored to present the results of this process in the form of this book.

Steven Gortler
Karol Myszkowski
June, 2001

Contents

Thrifty Final Gather for Radiosity

Annette Scheel†, Marc Stamminger‡, Hans-Peter Seidel†

†Max-Planck-Institut for Computer Science www.mpi-sb.mpg.de
‡iMAGIS/GRAVIR-REVES - INRIA Sophia Antipolis www-sop.inria.fr/reves/

Abstract. Finite Element methods are well suited to the computation of the light distribution in mostly diffuse scenes, but the resulting mesh is often far from optimal to accurately represent illumination. Shadow boundaries are hard to capture in the mesh, and the illumination may contain artifacts due to light transports at different mesh hierarchy levels. To render a high quality image a costly final gather reconstruction step is usually done, which re-evaluates the illumination integral for each pixel. In this paper an algorithm is presented which significantly speeds up the final gather by exploiting spatial and directional coherence information taken from the radiosity solution. Senders are classified, so that their contribution to a pixel is either interpolated from the radiosity solution or recomputed with an appropriate number of new samples. By interpolating this sampling pattern over the radiosity mesh, continuous solutions are obtained.

1 Introduction

In the past 15 years, much research has been concentrated on improvements of the radiosity method. The computation of radiosity solutions of more than one million patches is now possible on contemporary standard PCs. However, these solutions most often do not meet high-quality demands of many commercial applications. The problem is inherent to the method: because lighting detail is generated in object space, very fine tessellation is necessary to capture fine lighting detail. Thus quality is not only a time, but also a memory issue. Furthermore, the widely used linear Gouraud interpolation is prone to Mach banding, so that a human observer perceives the tessellation structure easily. In addition, long thin triangles can lead to frayed shadow boundaries, and finally the different levels at which light is transported to a patch may lead to artifacts. To some extent, these issues can be addressed by adapting subdivision to lighting discontinuities [11, 21] or by using higher-order interpolation (e.g. [6]).

Ray-based Monte-Carlo methods usually compute the illumination at independent sample positions in image space. This point sampling allows exact lighting computations, but also makes the exploitation of coherence more difficult. As a result, illumination from big light sources or indirect light make the lighting computation expensive. For stochastic sampling as a rule 500 or 1000 samples per pixel are needed in such cases, and in some cases noise is still present.

The idea of final gathering is to combine both approaches. In a view-independent preprocess a not necessarily perfect radiosity solution is computed. Then in a second view-dependent step ray tracing is performed that recomputes parts of the illumination considered critical. One common technique is to only recompute the direct light in this pass and to add the indirect light from the finite element solution (e.g. [16, 5]). Alternatively, the radiosity solution can be interpreted as a light source definition, and the last light bounce towards the eye is recomputed with ray tracing (e.g. [2]).

2

1.1 Previous Work

Compared to the huge number of publications on radiosity methods, the number of publications on a high quality rendering postprocess is surprisingly low. Often, a high quality rendering step is only a final chapter for a new radiosity algorithm, e.g. [11, 17, 2, 12], but only very few papers address the issue in detail.

In [10], Kok et al. describe a method to decrease the number of shadow samples for area light sources exploiting information from a progressive radiosity pass. Their algorithm subdivides senders adaptively in order to detect completely visible or occluded parts that can be processed quickly. With a clever shadow pattern scheme, the number of samples is reduced further. To some extent, this radiosity postprocessing step is done implicitly in the radiosity computation itself by the idea of Hierarchical Radiosity [8].

Several authors proposed the use of (hierarchical) radiosity for indirect light only, and to regenerate the usually more detailed direct illumination by ray tracing. More information from the radiosity solution is exploited in the *local pass* by Linschinski et al. [11]: Form factors are recomputed for each pixel and visibility for direct illumination only. Their approach is extended by Stürzlinger [20], where the number of samples is adapted to the relative contribution of the sources and visibility is computed in a stochastic approach. Christensen et al. [2] used a final gather step for reconstructing their radiance solutions. They gather all links with a fixed number of visibility samples, but also use the cluster hierarchy. It is pointed out that the final gather requires significant computation time and that despite their conservative resampling scheme artifacts still remain visible. Smits [17] uses a fixed number of visibility tests and analytic form factor evaluations for each point. For links carrying a relative error below a certain threshold, the estimate of the link itself is taken. To avoid bias which might occur due to the threshold, Russian Roulette is used with links whose relative error is below the threshold.

The final gather step which is very briefly described for the algorithm presented in [12] extends these ideas. For each receiver, critical senders are determined, whose contribution is to be computed exactly by final gather.

Bekaert et al. [1] use the radiosity solution for defining an importance function for a Monte-Carlo ray tracing step. A similar idea later followed in [14], where a radiosity solution is used to guide a Monte-Carlo path tracer.

Finally, the photon map approach [9] is relevant, because it is essentially a final gathering approach, however it is based on a global photon tracing pass as preprocess. From the photon hits an approximate lighting solution can be computed quickly. The high quality images, however, are then obtained from a well optimized final gather step.

1.2 Idea

The idea of this paper is to better exploit the information from the global radiosity step for a more 'thrifty' final gather. Consider the example in Fig. 1, middle, showing a coarse radiosity solution from a candle, illuminated by a big light source on the left and a smaller one on the right. Due to the different sizes of the light sources, the shadows are very different. The left shadow has a clear outline that blurs with the distance to the object; the right shadow is blurry and completely washed out after a short distance.

The radiosity solution is obtained in a few seconds and thus of poor quality, but it is clear that for a final gather step valuable information can be obtained from it. In addition to the radiosity mesh which already captures the most important changes in illumination, the link structure contains per patch hints about shadow boundaries and the light sources responsible. Furthermore, during the radiosity computation more

Fig. 1. Left: a candle stick casting a shadow from a large and a small area light source. Center: radiosity solution. Right: visibility sample numbers considered appropriate by our method.

approximate information has been computed with each link, such as the variation of the form factor or a shadow gradient.

In previous work, this information was exploited by recomputing partially visible links only, or by using a fixed number of samples per link, thus implicitly performing importance sampling guided by the link structure resulting from radiosity. We experienced severe problems with these simple approaches:

- At patch boundaries, the set of sampled senders and their hierarchy level change abruptly. Even for very precise solutions, these discontinuities, although small in size, remain visible.
- For indirect light a large fraction of links is partially occluded, so resampling all of them is very expensive. When not resampling indirect light, scenes with dominant indirect light essentially show the radiosity solution with all its artifacts.
- Taking a fixed number of samples results in bad importance sampling. It is true that hierarchical radiosity creates a mesh of links with similar errors, so using a fixed number of samples per link assigns roughly similar error to each sample. However, the error measured in HR for refinement decision is not necessarily the error we are interested in for final gather. Using a minimal area parameter also breaks the uniform error assumption, in particular for critical links with high variation. Links arrive at different levels of the hierarchy, making comparisons difficult. Furthermore, the error of a link must be seen in the context of all other links arriving at the same point.

Our new method tries to address these deficiencies. For a given receiver we extract a list of potential senders and estimate whether their contribution needs to be resampled or can be interpolated from the radiosity solution. If resampling is necessary, an appropriate sample number is determined. Both decisions can take into account the magnitude of the illumination, its relation to other contributing patches, visibility gradient estimates, perceptual issues etc.

By gathering this sampling information at the vertices and interpolating it over the patches again, we obtain a *continuous* solution without discontinuities at the patch boundaries. Nevertheless, the solution will not necessarily have a continuous derivative, so Mach banding can still appear. However, the goal of the method is to resample the solution so accurately, that this effect should also disappear.

Our final gather accuracy is (almost) independent of the radiosity accuracy. If the radiosity solution is already sufficient, the final gather will simply interpolate the radiosity values without further sampling. On the other hand a coarse solution will lead to a more expensive final gather step. However, the method can fail in detecting lighting detail that has not been captured at all by the input radiosity solution.

Note that the goal of our method is to enhance the final gather step as such. This does not exclude the use of ray-tracing acceleration methods in image space, such as adaptive progressive refinement [13]. In fact, we use directional coherence maps [7] (see also results) to exploit image space coherence.

2 Algorithm

Our method is based on the results obtained by a hierarchical radiosity algorithm with clustering. In the final radiosity solution, every object is represented by a triangle mesh with an approximate radiosity value per triangle. The link mesh contains the approximate value of the form factor, its gradient, and visibility. The HR oracle is based on an estimated radiosity change over a receiver, multiplied by the receiver's area. The goal of the final gather step is to accurately recompute the last light bounce towards the camera. For now, we will handle diffuse reflection only.

2.1 Overview of the Algorithm

First, for each vertex under consideration, a list of contributing senders is created by gathering all links arriving at all levels and at all surrounding patches (Sect. 2.2 and Fig. 2, left). Then we determine for each sender, whether its contribution can be interpolated, based on the estimated magnitude of the change in illumination it will introduce (Sect. 2.3). Furthermore, we distinguish between variations caused by the form factor and the visibility term. For a low variation the corresponding term will be interpolated, otherwise an appropriate sample number for final gathering is computed and stored with the sender (Sect. 2.4 and Fig. 2, middle).

In order to perform final gathering at a visible object point, the surrounding vertices are considered. The contributions of all senders that are marked as 'smooth' in all vertices are interpolated from the vertices to the point with its barycentric coordinates. For all other senders, samples are spawned, where the number of samples is again interpolated from the vertices (Fig. 2, right). Sect. 2.5 describes our interpolation process that leads to a continuous final gather result.

In the following, we describe the single phases of the method in more detail, discuss alternatives and justify our choices.

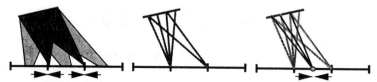

Fig. 2. Overview. Left: Collecting links from neighboring patches. Middle: Determination of sample numbers for each vertex. Right: Computation of illumination for a point inside a triangle.

2.2 Collection of Links for Vertices

In the radiosity solution links might arrive at different levels in the hierarchy at the receiver. Therefore, prior to the main algorithm, the links are 'pushed down' to leaf level on the receiver. During this push we recompute the form factor for the new links, but reuse the much more expensive visibility term. This recomputation avoids artifacts from the constant push step that typically appear when light is gathered at different hierarchy levels.

The algorithm begins by collecting the links from all patches surrounding a vertex, such that the vertex obtains a list of all senders. The information of the links is either averaged (for example for the irradiance) or the maximum is taken (for example for the visibility and form factor gradients). In this step links with visibility zero are neglected, which can be inaccurate if visibility is sampled by casting rays. However, a 'false reject' of a sender partially visible to the vertex requires that for all surrounding patches the sender was wrongly classified as completely occluded.

2.3 Classification of Senders

Usually, illumination exhibits strong coherence; hard-to-capture variations in form factor or visibility are only produced by a small portion of senders. These do not necessarily have to be light sources but can also be strongly illuminated patches creating strong indirect illumination. In either case, our algorithm tries to identify those "trouble makers" and resample them.

From the existing radiosity solution and from values computed for vertices information can be extracted to drive an **oracle** to detect senders with difficult contributions. Our oracle estimates the magnitude of the change in radiosity around a vertex due to form factor and visibility variations[1]. The threshold, which decides if this magnitude is small enough for interpolation, should respect human perception, because differences in color are not perceived equally well for all levels of illumination. In our implementation we use the CIELAB space [3] [2], because it is designed to be perceptually uniform and a color difference measure is defined which outputs JNDs (Just Noticeable Differences). Given a user specified JND, we take the radiosity values from the radiosity solution as a basis to determine which differences in illumination are acceptable.

Our first attempt was to decide according to the gradient of the illumination at the vertex. Although high gradients are a valuable hint for non-smooth illumination, the absolute difference turned out to be more significant. Additionally, it is much harder to find an intuitive threshold for gradients.

Variations in radiosity can be caused either by the form factor or the visibility term, in the diffuse case. For example, a light source could cause strong variations of the form factor, but if no occluders are present, only the form factor has to be recomputed, while visibility can be interpolated. Therefore, we estimate form factor and visibility variation separately and decide individually if form factor or visibility can be interpolated. However, the two functions depend on each other: if a patch is illuminated only weakly, shadows will be less obvious. On the other hand, a strong variation of illumination may be canceled out by a shadow. Therefore, if the variation of one term is measured the other term is kept constant.

We have developed two different oracles. The first, which compares illumination values of neighboring vertices, is more time consuming but turned out to be more reliable than the faster second, which re-uses link information from the radiosity solution.

Estimating Variation from Vertex Differences. The radiosity at a vertex c can be computed precisely using the sample distribution which will be described in Section 2.4. The radiosity of each sender is compared with the corresponding values of the neighboring vertices v_i to find out how fast the illumination changes within the neighborhood of vertex c.

---

[1]The term *variation* will be used in the following not in its mathematical meaning, but to describe *magnitude of change in radiosity*.

[2]Prior to the conversion to CIELAB a tone mapping should be applied to the color, which is not done in this implementation yet.

6

We determine the variation of the visibility term $D_s^{vis}(c)$ by computing the maximum difference between the radiosity at the center vertex due to sender s and the radiosity at all neighbor vertices v_i due to the same sender. As explained before, the form factor is kept constant for this comparison. $D_s^{vis}(c)$ is then

$$D_s^{vis}(c) = B_s F_s(c) \max_i (vis_s(c) - vis_s(v_i))\rho, \tag{1}$$

where B_s is the sender's radiosity, F_s the form factor between c and s, $vis_s(c)$ is the percentage of s which is visible from p, and ρ is the reflectivity of the receiving patch. The variation of the form factor $D_s^F(c)$ is computed analogously:

$$D_s^F(c) = B_s \max_i (F_s(c) - F_s(v_i))vis_s(c)\rho. \tag{2}$$

For both, $D_s^{vis}(c)$ and $D_s^F(c)$, a perceptual error threshold can be used. The measure can only determine if there are strong changes expected around the vertex or not, but not if the shape of the function is suited for interpolation. Consequently the measure is rather strict: it will select those contributions which can safely be interpolated, but does not detect all contributions which would also be suitable for interpolation. Of course, it is possible that features inside a triangle are missed: we can only capture what is possible with the given radiosity mesh.

Estimating Variation from Links. The links of the radiosity solution give us a cheaper estimate for the change in illumination across a receiving patch. Again, the maximum of the variation of all patches surrounding a vertex is used as estimation of the variation at a vertex.

For the hierarchical refinement an estimation of the variation of the form factor is needed anyway. For example, we use Bounded Radiosity [19], which gives a conservative lower and upper bound for the form factor. Thus, the change in radiosity due to the form factor $D_s^F(p)$ over patch p due to sender s is:

$$D_s^F(p) = B_s(F_s^{upper}(p) - F_s^{lower}(p))vis_s(p)\rho. \tag{3}$$

The vertex variation can then be computed from the maximum variation of the surrounding patches, e.g. $D_s^F(c) = \max_p(D_s^F(p))$.

If partial visibility between a sender and a receiver is detected in a link, the maximum possible change in radiosity goes from zero up to the unoccluded illumination. This gives a conservative bound on the variation due to visibility.

Additionally, we estimate the size h of the penumbra by taking into account geometric considerations (see next paragraph). With this penumbra size the bound can be tightened further: if h is larger than the patch the full cut-off will not take place inside the patch. If the visibility produces a function with gradient $B_s F_s(p)\rho/h$ then the change inside the patch with size s_r is only $B_s F_s(p)\rho s_r/h$. In summary the visibility variation $D_s^{vis}(p)$ is determined by:

$$D_s^{vis}(p) = \begin{cases} B_s F_s(p)\rho s_r/h, & h > s_r \\ B_s F_s(p)\rho, & \text{else} \end{cases} \tag{4}$$

As before, the vertex visibility variation $D_s^{vis}(x)$ is then the maximum variation of the surrounding patches. Using the maximum of all surrounding patches decreases the risk of missing an occluder.

Estimating the Size of the Penumbra. The size of the penumbra which might be produced by a sender is estimated using simplified geometric configurations. This was done before in a similar way by [18].

The size h of the penumbra can be approximated by (see Fig. 3):

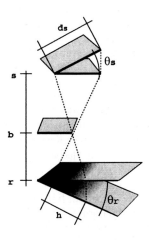

$$h = d_s \frac{\cos(\theta_s)}{\cos(\theta_r)} \frac{\|s - b\|}{\|b - r\|}, \qquad (5)$$

where d_s is the maximum diameter of the sender, $\cos(\theta_s)$ and $\cos(\theta_r)$ are the angles between the direction between the sender's and the receiver's centers and the corresponding surface normals.

During the visibility computation of the radiosity algorithm we store the occluder with hit point closest to the receiver. For this closest hit point we compute the relation between distance of the sender to the blocker $\|s - b\|$ and of the blocker to the receiver $\|b - r\|$.

Fig. 3. Size of the penumbra.

Addition of Sender Variations. So far, only single sender contributions have been investigated. But the contributions of different senders may influence each other and in the worst case several small variations may sum up and thus cause a significant variation.

To capture this worst case we select the candidates for interpolation in the following way: The variations of all senders of a vertex are sorted in decreasing order. Then, from the total sum of all variations, we subtract the single variations until the sum drops below the error threshold. The remaining contributions can then safely be interpolated, because even if they should all sum up, they will be below the error threshold. Since the highest variations are subtracted first, we ensure that the most important ones are not missed. On the other hand, this method may be too strict, because in many cases the contributions do not sum up and might even cancel out.

2.4 Number of Samples at a Vertex

If the classification procedure determines that it is better to re-compute a contribution exactly, the next step is to find the number of samples which should be used for each sender. This is not exactly true for classification by vertex comparison: the number of samples is determined first to compute the illumination at a vertex exactly in this case.

To determine the irradiance $I(x)$ at a point x the integral over all sending surfaces has to be evaluated:

$$I(x) = \sum_{Senders\, s} \int_s B(y) F(x,y) vis(x,y) dy, \qquad (6)$$

where $B(y)$ is the radiosity of the sender, $F(x,y)$ the point-to-point form factor, and $vis(x,y)$ is truc if point y is visible from point x.

We want to evaluate this integral for each vertex within a user given precision. As B we take the radiosity solution, this means the final gather recomputes the final reflection. The form factor and the visibility term are re-evaluated by randomly choosing N_s sample points on each sender.

In our algorithm, N_s is chosen in accordance to the magnitude of the irradiance at x due to this sender. From the radiosity solution we already have an estimate for this value—not for each vertex but for each patch. The relative contribution of a sender s to a receiving patch p compared to the total irradiance at this receiver is $I_s(p)/\sum_S I_s(p)$, where the irradiance $I_s(p)$ can be taken from the links, if the form factor is stored. We use the unoccluded irradiance, because the visibility term would reduce the number of samples in the presence of occluders, although this situation needs a high number of samples to capture the shadow boundary.

Given a total sample number N to approximate integral (6) the number of samples $N_s(p)$ for sender s and patch p is given by $N_s(p) = N I_s(p)/\sum_S I_s(p)$. To finally determine the number of samples N_s for a vertex x the average of the number of samples proposed by each neighboring patch sharing the vertex is taken. Only if all senders are classified as "to be re-sampled" the full sample number N will be used. In general, our algorithm manages with only 30% of N (see Sect. 3).

One could argue that it would be more efficient to use a total number of samples N which is not fixed but proportional to the aggregate irradiance, this generally means fewer samples for darker areas. In our case, we base our decision on interpolating contributions on the values computed for the vertices (see Sect. 2.3); therefore having a fixed precision for the vertices is more advantageous. Furthermore, it may be inaccurate to lower the precision for dark areas, because differences in illumination are perceived more easily there.

In many cases the sending patch will be a triangle or another primitive for which an analytic patch-to-point-form factor is known. Although this formula is also expensive to compute—it contains three arccos evaluations for a triangle for example—it might be faster than sampling if a high number of samples is used. However, our measurements (see Sect. 3) show that the time spent for form factor computation is low compared to the time spent for visibility computation.

2.5 Rendering a Triangle

After the preprocess each vertex has a list of senders with either precomputed illumination for interpolation or a set of sample positions for exact computation.

From the number of samples for the vertices the sample numbers for points inside a triangle can be determined. This is again done per sender: For a point x the number of samples for a sender s is the sum of the three vertex sample numbers for s weighted by the barycentric coordinates of point x.

Note, that we use real numbers as sample numbers to achieve smooth transitions. Having $f \in R$ samples, actually $n = \lceil f \rceil \in N$ samples will be evaluated. Each sample is weighted by one, except for the last which gets weight $f + 1 - n$. Although this results in overhead, it ensures that the sample number is continuous inside the triangle enabling a smooth representation of illumination. Furthermore, this methods works well only if the sample positions are fixed for a sender, i.e., if the i-th sample is always located at position y_i on the sender.

It is possible that a sender is classified differently by two neighboring vertices. In this case, we compute the result according to the first as well as according to the second classification and interpolate the two results, weighted by the barycentric coordinates, to obtain a continuous representation.

3 Results

3.1 Test Series

In order to test the behavior of our method, we examined the influence of different parameters on execution time and visual quality of the result. Our test scene is shown in Fig. 4(a). Three objects on a table are lit by two area light sources, a very large one and a smaller one. Both create large variations in irradiance with respect to form factor and visibility. We used the large light source as a representative for indirect light, but by making it a light source we can generate a reference solution by ray tracing.

The large penumbrae result in big problems for standard ray tracers and on final gather approaches. Obtaining an image without visible noise requires about 1000 light source samples per pixel; our reference solution was computed with Monte-Carlo ray tracing with 2000 samples in 90 minutes.[3]

(a) Test scene overview   (b) Radiosity mesh 1   (c) Radiosity mesh 2

Fig. 4. Test scene and radiosity solutions used for final gather

Fig. 5 shows three final gather results with sample number 800. The first one was obtained from the radiosity solution in Fig. 4(b) with small final gather thresholds in 578s. The result (top row) is essentially indistinguishable from the reference solution. Only the difference image (bottom row, scaled by 10) reveals errors in particular in the penumbrae. On average, visibility was resampled by 118 samples per pixel, illumination by 65 (out of 800 possible). 81% of the time were spent on the exact sampling, the remaining 19% are used for sample classification etc. (algorithm overhead).

The second column shows a less accurate solution with only 56 exact samples per pixel for visibility and 23 for the form factor on average. Artifacts become visible, but the time also decreased to 289s with an overhead of 20%. Sample numbers were determined using link information instead of the more accurate criterion (see Sect. 2.3).

For the right column, the same parameters as for the first image were used, but a coarser radiosity solution (see Fig. 4(c)) was taken as input. The resulting image has almost the same quality as the first one, but rendering time went up to 985s. The number of exact samples for visibility and form factor went up to 265 and 234, respectively. The overhead went down to 7%.

3.2 Performance for More Complex Scenes

To test the performance and behavior of the final gather for more complex environments we used three scenes with different lighting characteristics. In the first scene "office" (taken from the Radiance homepage) indirect illumination is present but not very obvious (color bleeding on the wall from the table, see color page, first row). In contrast, the

---

[3] All tests in this section were perfomed on a Linux Pentium PC with 733MHz, those in the next sections on a 1.1GHz Pentium

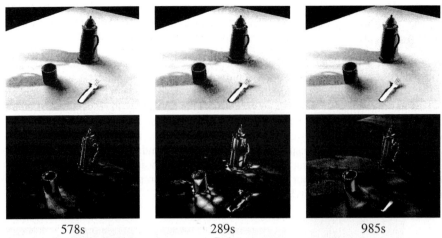

578s   289s   985s

Fig. 5. Final gather results. Left: fine radiosity solution with accurate final gather. Middle: fine radiosity solution with less accurate final gather. Right: coarse radiosity solution with accurate final gather. Lower row: difference to reference solution.

second scene "work and rest" (w.a.r.) is mostly lit indirectly including shadows from indirect light (see color page, second row). Note that, although we selected 400 (importance weighted) samples and the algorithm recomputed the highest possible sample number in these regions, still small artifacts in the indirect shadows of the plants are visible. The last scene, "public library" has raised complexity (see color page, last row). It contains 83 mostly big and lengthy area light sources, casting all kinds of sharp and blurry shadows on the floor, which causes significant problems on any Monte-Carlo and final gather approach. The HR solutions contained 7,800, 53,252, and 97,986 triangles, for office, w.a.r, and publib, respectively.

Table 1 shows the sampling statistics. The average proportion of recomputed samples for form factor and visibility varies from 25% for the office to 36% for the public library. The (v) and (l) after the scene denote whether the vertex comparison or the link information was used to find senders suitable for interpolation, respectively.

scene	total	avg. vis	avg. ff
office(v)	400	101	148
office(l)	400	130	230
w.a.r.(l)	400	126	122
publib(l)	1000	361	230

Table 1. Sample numbers for test scenes. Total: max. number of importance weighted samples per pixel, avg. vis: recomputed visibility samples, avg. ff: recomputed form factor samples.

Table 2 lists the timings for the three scenes, split up into the single computation steps. The time to classify for each sender if its contribution should be interpolated or re-sampled, depends strongly on the chosen method. As expected, reusing the link information is much faster than comparing the vertices. This is mainly because for the vertex comparison the corresponding senders for all neighbor vertices have to be found. Both methods turned out to be reliable in finding shadows and other lighting details, even for quite coarse meshes. In some cases the link information was slightly less reliable. The reliability of the link information depends also on the number of test rays used for HR. Furthermore, the bounds computed from the links on the form factor and visibility are not very tight. Therefore generally more samples are used (see Table 1), which might cancel out the time savings during the classification process.

The table column 'vertex' contains all other preprocessing steps: collection of links, determination of sample numbers, and computation of vertex irradiance. The timings here show that for highly refined radiosity solutions the vertex preprocess time slows down the algorithm.

Finally, the time for rendering the interior points was split into time for visibility and form factor computation and the remaining time which is spent for collecting the senders and interpolation. In general, by far most time is spent for visibility computation (75–80%), only a very small amount for form factors (1–10%) and the overhead is approximately 15–20%.

scene	HR	push link	classific.	vertex	interior			total
					vis	ff	rest	
office (v)	25	10	54	45	160	28	48	345
office (l)	25	10	0.1	40	217	38	52	357
w.a.r. (l)	28	3	0.1	140	518	34	51	745
publib (l)	185	37	1	405	582	15	182	1222

Table 2. Timings in seconds for test scenes (see color plates)

The images shown on the color plate were created in combination with the Directional Coherence Maps (DCM) [7]. In our case the DCMs were used to obtain anti-aliased images (36 fold oversampling) with only a moderate increase in computation time. The quality of the lighting reconstruction was not affected. The timings in Table 2 are without DCM, with DCM the whole computation took 508s, 1489s, and 4435s for office, w.a.r, and publib, respectively.

4 Conclusion and Future Work

We presented an improved, adaptive final gather step. For all pairs of receivers and senders an oracle decides whether the sender's contribution can be interpolated or needs resampling. This classification is done separately for the form factor and visibility term. The required information can be taken from the radiosity solution or it can be obtained more precisely from a full final gather at the vertices. If resampling is necessary, the number of samples is chosen adaptively. By interpolating the sample pattern, continuous solutions are obtained.

The accuracy of the final gather step is chosen independently of the radiosity solution. More sophisticated error measures can be used than in standard radiosity, for example perception based criteria, that require a more 'global view' than that of a radiosity refiner. Integration of perception is planned to be enhanced in the future, for example reducing accuracy where textures can mask out artifacts similar to [15] or for patches creating frequencies in a range where sensitivity for contrast goes down.

The performance of the final gather scales with the accuracy of its input: for accurate radiosity solutions it is usually faster than for a coarse radiosity solution. This is true as long as single patches of the radiosity solution are larger than a few image pixels. If this is not the case, the overhead of the sample classification becomes dominant. Here, a faster classification procedure which compares total illumination and not the illumination of each sender would be advantageous. For objects containing triangles in sub-pixel space it is probably necessary to switch from the polygonal mesh to a different representation (e.g. use face clusters [22] or a 3D grid bounding complex objects [4].) For very complex scenes the push step for links also might become a bottleneck both in terms of time and memory. Therefore, we would like to investigate if the final gather can work directly on the hierarchy of objects and links as created by the HR and not only at leaf level as was done in [12].

5 Acknowledgments

The first author is supported by the ESPRIT Open LTR Project 35772 "SIMULGEN", Simulation of Light for General Environments. We would also like to thank George Drettakis for fruitful discussions and proof-reading and the reviewers for their valuable comments. iMAGIS is a joint project of CNRS/INRIA/UJF/INPG.

References

[1] Philippe Bekaert, Philip Dutre, and Yves Willems. Final radiosity gather step using a monte-carlo technique with optimal importance sampling. Technical Report CW275, Katholike Univ. Leuven, 1996.

[2] Per H. Christensen, Dani Lischinski, Eric Stollnitz, and David H. Salesin. Clustering for glossy global illumination. *ACM Transactions on Graphics*, 16(1):3–33, January 1997.

[3] CIE. Recommendations on uniform color spaces–color difference equations–psychometric color terms. Technical Report 15.2, CIE, 1996.

[4] J. Dischler, L. Moustefaoui, and D. Ghazanfarpour. Radiosity including complex surfaces and geometric textures using solid irradiance and virtual surfaces. *Computers and Graphics*, 23(4), 1999.

[5] Reynald Dumont, Kadi Bouatouch, and Phillipe Gosselin. A progressive algorithm for three point transport. *Computer Graphics Forum*, 18(1):41–56, 1999.

[6] Steven J. Gortler, Peter Schröder, Michael F. Cohen, and Pat Hanrahan. Wavelet radiosity. In *Computer Graphics Proceedings, Annual Conference Series, 1993*, pages 221–230, 1993.

[7] Baining Guo. Progressive radiance evaluation using directional coherence maps. In *Computer Graphics (SIGGRAPH '98 Proceedings)*, pages 255–266, 1998.

[8] Pat Hanrahan, David Salzman, and Larry Aupperle. A rapid hierarchical radiosity algorithm. In *Computer Graphics (SIGGRAPH '91 Proceedings)*, volume 25, pages 197–206, 1991.

[9] Henrik Wann Jensen and Per H. Christensen. Efficient simulation of light transport in scenes with participating media using photon maps. In *SIGGRAPH'98 Conf. Proceedings*, pages 311–320, 1998.

[10] Arjan J. F. Kok and Frederik W. Jansen. Adaptive sampling of area light sources in ray tracing including diffuse interreflection. *Computer Graphics Forum*, 11(3):289–298, 1992.

[11] Daniel Lischinski, Filippo Tampieri, and Donald P. Greenberg. Combining hierarchical radiosity and discontinuity meshing. In *Computer Graphics (SIGGRAPH'93 Proceedings)*, pages 199–208, 1993.

[12] L. Mostefaoui, J.-M. Dischler, and D. Ghazanfarpur. Rendering inhomogeneous surfaces with radiosity. In *Rendering Techniques '99 (Proc. EG Workshop on Rendering)*, pages 283–292. Springer, 1999.

[13] James Painter and Kenneth Sloan. Antialiased ray tracing by adaptive progressive refinement. In *Computer Graphics (Proc. SIGGRAPH '89)*, volume 23, pages 281–288, 1989.

[14] F. Perez, I. Martin, X. Pueyo, and F.X. Sillion. Acceleration of monte carlo path tracing for general environments. In *Proc. Pacific Graphics 2000*, 2000.

[15] M. Ramasubramanian, S. Pattanaik, and D. P. Greenberg. A perceptually based physical error metric for realistic image synthesis. In *Computer Graphics (SIGGRAPH'99 Proceedings)*, pages 73–82, 1999.

[16] P. Shirley. *Physically Based Lighting Calculations for Computer Graphics*. PhD thesis, University of Illinois, 1991.

[17] Brian Smits. *Efficient Hierarchical Radiosity in Complex Environments*. Ph.d thesis, Cornell University, 1994.

[18] Cyril Soler and François X. Sillion. Fast calculation of soft shadow textures using convolution. In *SIGGRAPH 98 Conference Proceedings*, pages 321–332, 1998.

[19] Marc Stamminger, Philipp Slusallek, and Hans-Peter Seidel. Bounded radiosity - illumination on general surfaces and clusters. *Computer Graphics Forum (Eurographics '97)*, 16(3):309–318, 1997.

[20] W. Stürzlinger. Optimized local pass using importance sampling. In *International Conference in Central Europe of Computer Graphics and Visualization '96*, pages 342–348, 1996.

[21] V. Volevich, K. Myszkowski, A. Khodulev, and E. Kopylov. Using the visible difference predictor to improve performance of progressive global illumination computation. *ACM Transactions on Graphics*, 19(1):122–161, April 2000.

[22] Andrew J. Willmott, Paul S. Heckbert, and Michael Garland. Face cluster radiosity. In *Rendering Techniques 99 (Proceedings of EG Workshop on Rendering)*, pages 293–304. Springer, 1999.

Editors' Note: see Appendix, p. 321 for colored figure of this paper

Reflected and Transmitted Irradiance from Area Sources using Vertex Tracing

Michael M. Stark and Richard F. Riesenfeld

University of Utah
Salt Lake City, UT
mstark@cs.utah.edu

Abstract. Computing irradiance analytically from polygonal luminaires in polygonal environments has proven effective for direct lighting applications in diffuse radiosity environments. Methods for analytic integration have traditionally used edge-based solutions to the irradiance integral; our previous work presented a vertex-based analytic solution, allowing irradiance to be computed incrementally by ray tracing the apparent vertices of the luminaire. In this work we extend the vertex tracing technique to the analytic computation of irradiance from a polygonal luminaire in other indirect lighting applications: transmission through non-refractive transparent polygons, and reflection off perfectly specular polygons. Furthermore we propose an approximate method for computing transmitted irradiance through refractive polyhedra. The method remains effective in the presence of blockers.

1 Introduction

Indirect lighting, particularly specular and refractive transfer, is an important part of realistic rendering, yet continues to be a difficult problem. The literature is replete with methods for computing caustics and specular effects. For example, Arvo [1] used ray tracing from the light source to generate caustics. Monte Carlo path tracing and other stochastic techniques have also been used, but some common drawbacks are cost and sometimes noise [23]. The theory of catastrophic optics [19] has been applied to caustics from curved surfaces [33], but research has concentrated mostly on point or directional light sources. Recent research has often focused on interactive techniques [10]. More recently, Jensen's photon map technique has been used for a wide variety of global illumination problems, including specular reflection and caustics from area sources [15–17].

Our previous work in direct lighting and radiosity reconstruction in diffuse environments worked by tracing rays through the source vertices and incrementally computing irradiance [30]. The goal of this paper is to extend this work to include indirect illumination from perfectly reflective facets and through refractive objects. For the reflective effects the resulting illumination remains exact, but we employ a heuristic for refraction and use it to produce plausible caustics. Section 2 contains a brief review of the vertex tracing approach on which this work is based and extends the work to handle non-refractive transparent polygons. Section 3 shows how the approach can be extended to handle reflected irradiance, while Section 4 develops the refraction heuristic. Acceleration and efficiency issues are discussed in Section 5. Results are examined in Section 6 and future work is discussed in Section 7.

14

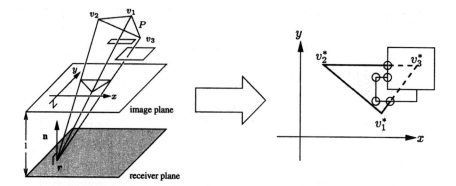

Fig. 1. To apply the vertex-based formula, the source polygon P is projected onto an image plane parallel to the receiver plane. Occluding polygons are also projected, and the apparent source is the projected source clipped against the projected occluders. The vertex tracing algorithm allows for the vertices of the apparent source to be added incrementally without actually projecting any of the polygons, or clipping the source.

2 Computing Irradiance by Tracing Vertices

We recall that the irradiance from a uniformly emitting surface S, which is not self-occluding as viewed from a point r on a receiver, can be computed from the surface integral

$$I(r) = M \int_{S} \frac{\cos\theta_0 \cos\theta}{d^2} \, dS, \tag{1}$$

where d is the distance from r to a point on S, θ_0 and θ are the angles made by the ray joining r and the point with the receiver normal at r and the surface normal at the point, respectively. The constant M is an emission constant of S [2].

If the surface is a planar polygon P with vertices $v_1, \ldots, v_n$, the irradiance may be computed from a formula attributed to Lambert:

$$I(r) = \frac{M}{2\pi} \sum_{i=1}^{n} \beta_i \cos\gamma_i, \tag{2}$$

where β_i is the angle subtended by v_i, v_{i+1} from r, and γ_i is the angle between the plane containing v_i, v_{i+1}, and r, and the normal to the receiver at r (e.g., [6]).

In polygonal environments where the source polygon can be partially occluded, the irradiance can be computed by integrating over the *apparent* source, which is the source clipped against the scene blocker polygons [7]. Applying Lambert's formula to this clipped source results in the exact irradiance, but a drawback is that the summation is over the edges, and the edges of the apparent source are more difficult to find than the vertices.

In our previous work [30] we developed a vertex-based analogue of Lambert's formula, and showed how it can be used to compute irradiance incrementally by tracing the apparent vertices of the source in the scene. The vertex-based formula is derived by projecting the polygon P through the receiver point r onto a local *image plane*, which is the plane parallel to the surface at r and one unit above as shown in Figure 1. In order for the projected polygon to be a proper bounded polygon on the image plane, the source must also be clipped against a view frustum [27]. Note this image plane is a device for computing irradiance at r, and has nothing to do with an "image plane" in a ray tracing or camera context.

The irradiance is computed by the following formula:

$$I(r) = M \sum_{v_i^*} F(x_i, y_i, m_{in}) - F(x_i, y_i, m_{out}) \qquad (3)$$

where each projected vertex v_i^* has coordinates (x_i, y_i) on the image plane, and m_{in} and m_{out} are the slopes of the incoming and outgoing edges, respectively, on the image plane. Terms where the slope is undefined are omitted from the summation. The function F is

$$F(x, y, m) = \frac{Ax}{2} \arctan(Ay) + \frac{C(y - mx)}{2} \arctan\left[C(x + my)\right] \qquad (4)$$

where

$$A = \frac{1}{\sqrt{1 + x^2}}, \qquad C = \frac{1}{\sqrt{1 + m^2 + (y - mx)^2}}. \qquad (5)$$

Equations (3), (4) and (5) provide a formula for the irradiance due to a uniformly emitting polygon in terms of the projected vertices and the local behavior of the incident edges. The sum may therefore be evaluated in any order and the formula is thus well suited for an incremental evaluation.

2.1 Vertex Tracing and Angular Spans

The incoming and outgoing edges at each vertex on the image plane can be encapsulated by an *angular span*, consisting of a position, two angles, representing the slopes of the incoming and outgoing edges, a depth, and an emission constant. From an angular span, the vertex contribution to the irradiance in (3) can be immediately computed and added to the sum. A vertex of the clipped source can be either an intrinsic vertex of the source polygon, an intrinsic blocker vertex which appears inside the source, or an *apparent* vertex caused by the intersection of two edges. The form of the angular span depends on the type of vertex.

However, actually projecting the source polygon onto the image plane and clipping defeats the purpose of the vertex-based approach. Rather, our method computes an angular span for each apparent source vertex by tracing the ray through the vertex and collecting angular spans for each polygon vertex, edge, or face the ray intersects and thereby allows the irradiance to be computed without ever projecting or clipping the source. Figure 2 illustrates the idea. The angular span algorithm handles occlusion by inserting a "full" angular span for an interior blocker intersection, and in fact cleanly handles all the "hard" cases where vertices and edges appear to coincide. Furthermore the approach generalizes easily to the situation where all the scene polygons are treated as emitters. Finding all the apparent vertices, which amounts to finding all the apparent edge intersections in the scene, tends to be the bottleneck.

The vertex-based approach provides a method for evaluating irradiance that is fundamentally different from methods based on Lambert's formula. The vertex tracing algorithm eliminates polygon clipping, an inherently unstable process, and the need to maintain polygon contours. The method continues to work well in situations when polygon clipping methods become impractical, such as when there is a great deal of fine-scale geometry, and when there are many emitting polygons such as in the problem of radiosity reconstruction.

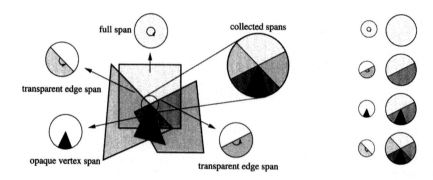

Fig. 2. A "conjunctive" vertex. Two transparent polygons and an opaque blocker appear in front of a square source. When a ray is traced through the vertex of the blocker, angular spans for the objects incident on the ray are collected (left), then sorted by distance and combined into a collection of angular spans that encodes the vertex contribution (right).

2.2 Simple Transparency

Although our previous work was concerned with uniform emission and opaque occlusion, the angular span algorithm can be extended to handle transparent (non-refracting) polygons. An angular span for a transparent polygon must be flagged to indicate it is transparent. The span combination algorithm also requires modification: when a transparent span covers an emissive span the emission is multiplied by the transparency. Furthermore, span insertion in arbitrary depth order is no longer feasible. Rather, the spans are collected as they are found along the vertex ray and then sorted by depth before they are inserted. The spans are inserted from back to front. Insertion of an opaque span involves inserting the start and end of the span, and removing all the span boundaries it covers, while insertion of a transparent span requires the emissions of the covered spans to be multiplied by the transparency of the new span. Figure 2 illustrates this for a "conjunctive" vertex.

3 Reflection

Our previous work concentrated on diffuse environments and considered only direct lighting and radiosity reconstruction. In this section we extend the vertex tracing approach to environments having perfectly reflecting polygonal surfaces.

A perfect mirror creates a *virtual image* of each object it reflects: the virtual image is the object reflected through the plane of the mirror as illustrated in Figure 3(a). Thus the radiance from a source polygon reflected off a mirror polygon is equivalent to the radiance from the virtual image clipped against the complement of the mirror polygon in the mirror plane. Equivalently, the irradiance can be computed by reflecting the receiver point in the mirror plane rather than the source—indeed this is preferable because it does not reverse the orientation of the source polygon, and it eliminates the need to reflect the source at all (Figure 3(b)). The vertex tracing algorithm may also be used provided that angular spans for edges and vertices of "negative" polygons (the complement of the mirror polygon in the mirror plane) are properly handled.

The presence of extra occluders complicates things, because they can appear in two separate places: between the source and the reflector, and between the reflector and the

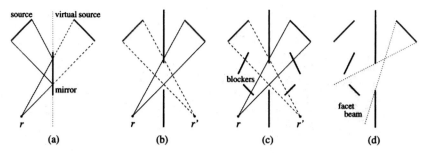

Fig. 3. Reflection in "Flatland". (a) The radiance coming from the real source reflected off a mirror is the same as the radiance coming from the virtual source, the source reflected through the mirror plane. (b) The irradiance from the virtual source clipped against the complement of the a mirror polygon is equivalent to computing the reflected irradiance, or computing the irradiance at the reflected receiver point r'. (c) Blocker polygons between the source and the mirror are most easily found by tracing from r'; those between the mirror and r are found by tracing as usual. (d) Beams can be used for efficiency

receiver point. A naive clipping approach would require the occluders to be reflected through the mirror plane, but the vertex tracing approach does not. Rather, each vertex (intrinsic or apparent) is simply traced twice, once from the actual receiver point, and once from the reflected receiver point (Figure 3(c)). From the receiver point, only vertices and intersections in front of the mirror plane are considered; from the reflected point, only those behind are considered. However, pairs of edges from both sets of occluders must be tested for apparent intersection.

Multiple reflection complicates things even more. The virtual scene requires multiple reflections of the scene in the naive approach, and the basic vertex tracing still works, but the multiple reflections must be traced separately, starting from the closest mirror surface, with the source and other blockers reflected through all but this surface, and so the process continues.

4 Refraction

Computing reflected irradiance as in the previous section works in principle by computing the irradiance from a virtual source that cannot be distinguished from the reflected real source. If such a virtual source for a refracted source polygon can be found, then the same technique applies. The refracted irradiance can be computed from the virtual source, occluded by the complement of the refractive facet. The question is, what is the virtual source? That is, what does the source look like when viewed from a receiver point through the refractive interface? This problem is more difficult than the reflective case for several reasons. First of all, lines generally appear curved under refraction, so the virtual source is not generally even a polygon. Consequently we can only approximate refracted irradiance with a polygonal virtual source. Second, accurately approximating the virtual source involves the problem of inverse ray tracing, that is, finding the ray direction which hits a particular point (*i.e.*, a source vertex) through a refractive medium. And finally, while the virtual source of a reflected polygon happens to be independent of the viewing position, this is not the case for a refracted polygon— a different virtual source is needed for each viewpoint. Figure 4 illustrates refracted virtual sources in Flatland.

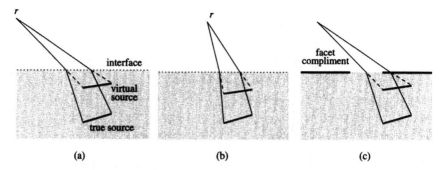

Fig. 4. Refraction in Flatland. (a) A virtual refracted source is more difficult to compute. There are many choices for the virtual source, the one illustrated is the one found by appropriately contracting the depth of the source directly toward the interface plane. (b) The virtual source changes with the viewpoint. (c) The virtual source can be clipped against a facet complement and irradiance computed as if the refractive medium were not there.

It should be made clear that the goal of this section is not to render truly focused caustics, in the sense of catastrophic optics [19]. The focusing of light by its very nature requires curved surface interfaces; indeed even the first-order behavior of refracted (and reflected) light is dependent on the surface curvature. It is therefore not reasonable to expect light transmitted through refractive surfaces to be well approximated by a macro-faceted surface approximation. We are interested in simulating how polyhedral objects transmit light, not how well this approximates a curved surface; the latter is a subject for future research. Figure 6 shows a faceted approximation to a smooth surface.

4.1 Depth Contraction

We now turn to the development of the transformation that approximates how a polygon appears when it is viewed through one, or several, refractive interfaces. This transformation can then be applied to the source, and any blocker polygons on one side of the interface so that the vertex tracing approach can be used to compute the irradiance.

Snell's law [12] governs the angle θ_2 of refraction given the angle of incidence θ_1:

$$\frac{\sin\theta_1}{\sin\theta_2} = \frac{n_2}{n_1} \tag{6}$$

where n_1 and n_2 are the indices of refraction (Figure 5(b)). The rule is well suited to ordinary ray tracing but by itself does not provide much intuition for how refraction transforms the general appearance of objects. Suppose, for example, one looks into the front face of a fish tank from across the room. The general effect is that the inside of the tank appears compressed toward the front of the tank. A similar phenomenon can be seen from a canoe or kayak in shallow still water. When the bottom is roughly flat, it always looks as if the bottom is shaped like a bowl and the observer is always above the deepest part (Figure 5(a)). Further away it tends to look more shallow. So in fact, the depth contraction is dependent on the viewing angle with respect to the surface of the water.

This apparent depth contraction phenomenon is the basis for the transformation we use for the virtual refracted source. The geometric arrangement is illustrated in Figure 5. A point q at depth d below the (flat) interface appears to be at a depth d'

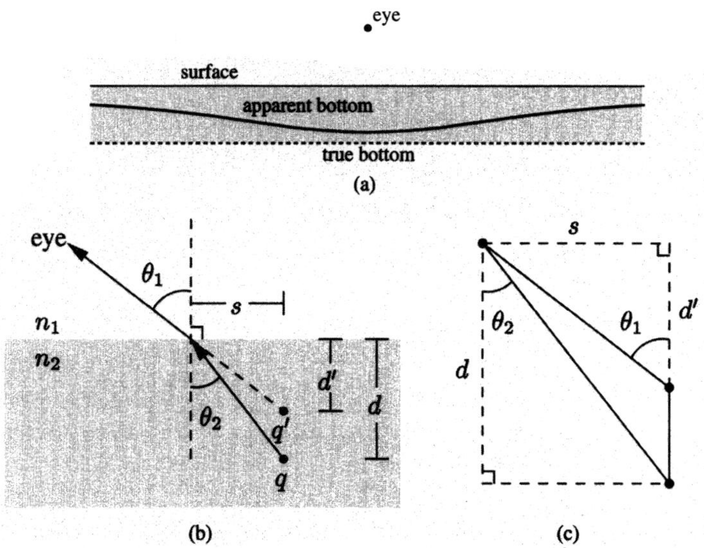

Fig. 5. Apparent depth contraction. (a) A flat bottom of a pond or pool always looks bowl-shaped, and appears deepest directly under the observer. (b) A point q at depth d appears to be at depth d' as viewed from above the interface. (c) The associated trigonometry.

below the interface. The apparent depth of the point is therefore *contracted* by the factor d'/d. From trigonometry we have

$$\tan\theta_1 = \frac{s}{d'}, \qquad \tan\theta_2 = \frac{s}{d}$$

so we have for the contraction ratio,

$$\frac{d'}{d} = \frac{\tan\theta_2}{\tan\theta_1}. \tag{7}$$

From Snell's law, the contraction ratio can be given in terms of the incident angle θ_1 or the refracted angle θ_2

$$\frac{d'}{d} = \frac{\cos\theta_1}{\sqrt{\eta^2 - \sin^2\theta_1}} = \frac{\cos\theta_2}{\sqrt{1/\eta^2 - \sin^2\theta_2}} \tag{8}$$

where $\eta = n_2/n_1$. Of course, actually computing these angles is equivalent to finding the true ray directions and thus defeats the purpose of the heuristic. But as it happens, the formulation in terms of angles is suited for approximating the virtual source, provided we make a key assumption: the apparent angular size of each refractive facet is small as seen from a receiver point, or another refractive facet (from which it can receive transmitted light). Because of this assumption, the incident and transmitted angles of any ray hitting the facet from a receiver point, or from another facet, have little variation and consequently the depth contraction ratio is nearly constant.

4.2 The Virtual Refraction Transformation

Suppose the facet with centroid c and normal $\hat{\mathbf{n}}$ lies on an interface between two regions of different optical densities and the ratio of the indices of refraction of the back side of the facet to that of the front is η. From a view point r, the cosine of the angle of incidence anywhere on the facet is approximately that of the angle of incidence at the centroid c:

$$\cos \theta_1 = \frac{(r - c) \cdot \hat{\mathbf{n}}}{\|r - c\|}.$$

A point q behind the facet has depth $d = (c - q) \cdot \hat{\mathbf{n}}$; combining this with (8) above yields a formula for the contracted point q'.

$$q' = q + (d - d')\hat{\mathbf{n}} = q + (c - q) \cdot \hat{\mathbf{n}} \left(1 - \frac{\cos \theta_1}{\sqrt{\eta^2 - 1 + \cos^2 \theta_1}} \right) \hat{\mathbf{n}}. \qquad (9)$$

If $\eta < 1$, q' will be further from the facet rather than closer, and also there is the possibility of total internal reflection, which occurs when $\cos^2 \theta_1 \leq 1 - \eta^2$.

Application of the transformation given by (9) to each vertex of the source produces a virtual source from which irradiance can be computed as if there is no refraction. Further transformations (reflections or other refractive transformations) can be applied to handle multiple reflections and refractions. The same transformation must be applied to any blocker polygons which lie between the source and the facet on the interface.

In an attenuating medium, the attenuation can be approximated from the centroid-to-centroid path length. Also, reflectance variations such as those caused by Fresnel effects can be approximated in terms of the angles between facets.

Of course, the contracted (or elongated) source is still only an approximation because the true depth contraction is a function of the position on the source and the position of the receiver, and more precise methods could be used (*e.g.*, [3]). The approximation is in the assumption that it does not vary over the source (from a fixed viewpoint). But this method does seem to produce plausible caustics both for single and multiple refractive interfaces, as shown in Figures 6 and 8.

4.3 Dispersion

Dispersion, the separation of different wavelengths of light due to variation of refractive index with wavelength [12, 17], can be simulated using our refraction method. For general dispersion computation, many different wavelengths must be included in order to achieve the smooth spectral colors often visible on the edges of caustics and such. But one advantage of using area sources as in our method is that the caustic edges are not sharp and blending occurs naturally. We have found plausible dispersion effects can be obtained by using only the three RGB channels.

5 Efficiency: Beams and Culling

A brute-force approach to vertex tracing reflective and refractive polygons can be costly, because for a particular evaluation point, every reflective and refractive polygon must be checked, and for each of these polygons, every other reflective and refractive polygon must be checked for secondary reflection and transmission, *etc.*

To reduce the cost, we propose a beam hierarchy for spatial subdivision. While this may sound similar to the beam and cone tracing and hidden surface techniques in the

---

Algorithm 1 General Beam Construction

---
for each reflective/refractive polygon **do**
   add a beam for the reflective/refractive region, with depth $d = 1$
end for

for each beam $\mathcal{B}$ in the beam list **do**
  for each scene polygon P which intersects B **do**
    add P to the occlusion list of $\mathcal{B}$
    if P is reflective/refractive and the depth d of B is less than the maximum **then**
      append a beam for P with depth $d + 1$
    end if
  end for
end for
build a hierarchy for the beams

---

literature (*e.g.*, [9, 13]), the approach is closer to the shaft culling method of Haines and Wallace [11]. In our context a *beam* is a (possibly unbounded) convex polyhedron which bounds the region in space in which a source polygon can potentially appear reflected from or refracted through another polygon, or collection of polygons. Each beam contains the following information:

- bounding planes for the polyhedron (for containment testing);
- a formula for how to create the virtual source (reflection, refraction);
- the reflective/refractive polygon;
- a depth d, indicating the number of reflections/refractions;
- a parent beam (NULL if $d = 1$);
- a list of potential occluding polygons that intersect the beam.

A beam is *primary* if its depth is 1. When a point is found to be inside a primary beam, the source can be vertex-traced along with the polygons in the occlusion list to compute the irradiance. A point inside a non-primary beam requires the multiple-interface vertex tracing described previously. The various interfaces are found by following the parent pointers to the primary beam.

There are several things worthy of note about these culling beams. First, the beam polyhedron is only a bound and nothing more—the vertex tracing algorithm handles the actual visibility. The number of beams in a scene depends on the number of reflective/refractive polygons as well as how they interact. Theoretically there is no upper limit on the number of possible inter-reflections and constructing all the beams could be very expensive. But for simple types of reflective objects, really only primary beams are required, and there will be at most one beam for each reflective polygon. For a refractive object, there will generally be only a few beams for each interior facet.

The general beam construction algorithm is shown in Algorithm 1. In our implementation, the faces and edges are stored in a bounding sphere hierarchy and this accelerates the beam-polygon intersection test. Once the beam list has been constructed, the beams themselves are stored in a hierarchy for faster containment testing. Our implementation uses a bounding volume hierarchy, but other spatial subdivision schemes could be used.

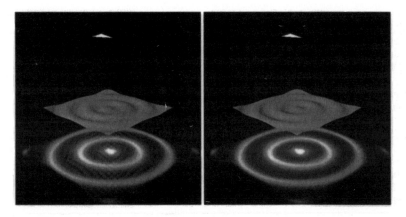

Fig. 6. Approximating caustics from a rippled water surface, using a triangulated grid of 32×32 (left, 12s) and 64×64 (right, 43s). Here the water surface is rendered as a diffuse surface for clarity; note the faceting is less noticeable under diffuse shading than in the caustics. Also note the asymmetry in the caustics due to the shape of the source.

6   Results

We have implemented our methods in the context of a standard ray tracer. When a diffuse surface is hit, the direct lighting is computed (exactly, using vertex tracing) and this is added to the reflected and transmitted light which is computed using the vertex tracing approaches discussed in this paper. The images were run on an SGI workstation using a single 400 MHz IP35 MIPS R12000 processor, and the quoted running times include setup, hierarchy construction, rendering, and output time. The images all have 512 vertical pixels.

Figure 7(a) contains the shadow of three transparent polygons, and illustrates "subtractive absorption" of light. Figure 7(b) and (c) show the shadow of a stained-glass with 171 polygons (122 leads, 49 panes) under different light sources. Note that the shape of the source has a definite effect on appearance of the shadow, and can be seen through the "pinhole" effect in various places. In Figure7(a) the top edge of the window is coplanar with a source edge and this results in the sharper C^1 discontinuities seen in the shadow.

Figures 8(a) and (b) have purely reflective objects. Figure 8(c) is a rendering of a glass icosahedron, with the surface reflectance exaggerated to more clearly show the reflected light. Figure 8(d) simulates dispersion (with a dimmer source and whiter surfaces) as described in Section 4.3. The three-color split is sufficient for the caustics due to the blurring effect, but results in color discontinuities in ray tracing the object itself. The focus of this paper is on polygonal objects, but Figure 6 shows what happens when a smooth surface is approximated with facets and the polygonal refraction is computed, in this case approximating rippled water.

7   Conclusion and Future Work

In this paper we have extended the vertex tracing approach, a general method of computing irradiance from a uniform polygonal source in a polyhedral environment, first to include transparency, then to compute exact illumination reflected from mirrored polygons, and finally to approximate transmitted irradiance. Moreover, a shaft culling technique was employed to improve the efficiency.

The caustics produced by our depth contraction heuristic are plausible, but we would like to improve the physical accuracy. In particular more attention should be paid to energy conservation, which is currently only loosely handled by our method. A better approximation to the virtual source would require a non-uniform emission to account for attenuation and reflectance variations such as Fresnel effects. Formulas such as those developed for polynomially-varying luminaires by Chen and Arvo [5] would be required. Finally, the ripple caustics suggest there might be a way to better approximate the surface rather than using flat facets, which would give a smoother irradiance distribution with far fewer surface elements.

Acknowledgments

The authors wish to thank Erik Reinhard, Peter Shirley, and William Martin for many helpful discussions. This work was supported in part by the NSF Science and Technology Center for Computer Graphics and Scientific Visualization (ASC-89-20219).

References

1. James Arvo. Backward ray tracing. In *SIGGRAPH '86 Developments in Ray Tracing seminar notes*, volume 12, August 1986.
2. James Arvo. *Analytic Methods for Simulated Light Transport.* PhD thesis, Yale University, 1995.
3. Min Chen. *Mathematical Methods for Image Synthesis.* PhD thesis, California Institute of Technology, 2001.
4. Min Chen and J. Arvo. Pertubation methods for interactive specular reflections. *IEEE Transactions on Visualization and Computer Graphics*, 6(3):253–264, July-September 2000.
5. Min Chen and James Arvo. A Closed-Form Solution for the Irradiance Due To Linearly Varying Luminaires. In B. Peroche and H. Rushmeier, editors, *Rendering Techniques 2000 (Proceedings of the Eleventh Eurographics Workshop on Rendering)*, New York, NY, 2000. Springer Wien. 137-148.
6. Michael F. Cohen and John R. Wallace. *Radiosity and Realistic Image Synthesis.* Academic Press Professional, Cambridge, MA, 1993.
7. George Dretakkis and Eugene Fiume. A fast shadow algorithm for area light sources using backprojection. In Andrew Glassner, editor, *Proceedings of SIGGRAPH '94 (Orlando, Florida, July 24–29, 1994)*, Computer Graphics Proceedings, Annual Conference Series, pages 223–230. ACM SIGGRAPH, ACM Press, July 1994. ISBN 0-89791-667-0.
8. Frédo Durand, George Drettakis, and Claude Puech. The visibility skeleton: A powerful and efficient multi-purpose global visibility tool. In Turner Whitted, editor, *SIGGRAPH 97 Conference Proceedings*, Annual Conference Series, pages 89–100. ACM SIGGRAPH, Addison Wesley, August 1997. ISBN 0-89791-896-7.
9. H. Fuchs, Z. M. Kedem, and B. F. Naylor. On visible surface generation by a priori tree structures. volume 14, pages 124–133, July 1980.
10. Xavier Granier, George Drettakis, and Bruce Walter. Fast Global Illumination Including Specular Effects. In B. Peroche and H. Rushmeier, editors, *Rendering Techniques 2000 (Proceedings of the Eleventh Eurographics Workshop on Rendering)*, pages 47–58, New York, NY, 2000. Springer Wien.
11. Eric Haines and John Wallace. Shaft culling for efficient ray-traced radiosity. In *Eurographics Workshop on Rendering*, 1991.
12. Eugene Hecht. *Optics.* Addison Wesley Longman, third edition, 1998.

13. Paul S. Heckbert and Pat Hanrahan. Beam tracing polygonal objects. In Hank Christiansen, editor, *Computer Graphics (SIGGRAPH '84 Proceedings)*, volume 18, pages 119–127, July 1984.

14. Wolfgang Heidrich, Hendrik Lensch, Michael F. Cohen, and Hans-Peter Seidel. Light Field Techniques for Reflections and Refractions. In D. Lischinski and G. W. Larson, editors, *Rendering Techniques 1999 (Proceedings of the Tenth Eurographics Workshop on Rendering)*, pages 187–196, New York, NY, 1999. Springer Wien.

15. Henrik Wann Jensen. Global illumination using photon maps. In Xavier Pueyo and Peter Schröder, editors, *Eurographics Rendering Workshop 1996*, pages 21–30, New York City, NY, June 1996. Eurographics, Springer Wien. ISBN 3-211-82883-4.

16. Henrik Wann Jensen. Rendering caustics on non-lambertian surfaces. *Computer Graphics Forum*, 16(1):57–64, 1997. ISSN 0167-7055.

17. Henrik Wann Jensen and Niels Jørgen Christensen. A practical guide to global illumination using photon maps (sigggraph 2000 course notes 8), July 2000.

18. Don P. Mitchell and Pat Hanrahan. Illumination from curved reflectors. In Edwin E. Catmull, editor, *Computer Graphics (SIGGRAPH '92 Proceedings)*, volume 26, pages 283–291, July 1992.

19. J. F. Nye. *Natural Focusing and Fine Structure of Light*. IOP Publishing Ltd, 1989.

20. H. Plantinga and C.R. Dyer. Visibility, occlusion, and the aspect graph. *International Journal of Computer Vision*, 5(2):137–160, 1990.

21. Holly E. Rushmeier and Kenneth E. Torrance. Extending the radiosity method to include specularly reflecting and translucent materials. *ACM Transactions on Graphics*, 9(1):1–27, January 1990.

22. Gernot Schauffler and Henrik Wann Jensen. Ray Tracing Point Sampled Geometry. In B. Peroche and H. Rushmeier, editors, *Rendering Techniques 2000 (Proceedings of the Eleventh Eurographics Workshop on Rendering)*, pages 319–328, New York, NY, 2000. Springer Wien.

23. Peter Shirley. A ray tracing method for illumination calculation in diffuse-specular scenes. In *Proceedings of Graphics Interface '90*, pages 205–212, May 1990.

24. Peter Shirley. *Realistic Ray Tracing*. A K Peters, Ltd, 2000.

25. François Sillion and Claude Puech. *Radiosity and Global Illumination*. Morgan Kaufmann, San Francisco, 1994.

26. Cyril Soler and François X. Sillion. Fast Calculation of Soft Shadow Textures Using Convolution. In Michael Cohen, editor, *SIGGRAPH 98 Conference Proceedings*, Annual Conference Series, pages 321–332. ACM SIGGRAPH, Addison Wesley, July 1998. ISBN 0-89791-999-8.

27. Michael M. Stark. Vertex-based formulations of irradiance from polygonal sources. Technical Report UUCS-00-012, Department of Computer Science, University of Utah, May 2000.

28. Michael M. Stark. *Analytic Illumination in Polyhedral Environments*. PhD thesis, University of Utah, 2001.

29. Michael M. Stark, Elaine Cohen, Tom Lyche, and Richard F. Riesenfeld. Computing exact shadow irradiance using splines. *Proceedings of SIGGRAPH 99*, pages 155–164, August 1999. ISBN 0-20148-560-5. Held in Los Angeles, California.

30. Michael M. Stark and Richard F. Riesenfeld. Exact Illumination in Polygonal Environments using Vertex Tracing. In B. Peroche and H. Rushmeier, editors, *Rendering Techniques 2000 (Proceedings of the Eleventh Eurographics Workshop on Rendering)*, pages 149–160, New York, NY, 2000. Springer Wien.

31. Spencer W. Thomas. Dispersive refraction in ray tracing. *The Visual Computer*, 2(1):3–8, January 1986.

32. Alan Watt and Mark Watt. *Advanced Animation and Rendering Techniques*. ACM Press, 1992.

33. Mark Watt. Light-water interaction using backward beam tracing. In Forest Baskett, editor, *Computer Graphics (SIGGRAPH '90 Proceedings)*, volume 24, pages 377–385, August 1990.

Editors' Note: see Appendix, p. 322 for colored figures of this paper

Simulating Non-Lambertian Phenomena Involving Linearly-Varying Luminaires

Min Chen   James Arvo

California Institute of Technology, Pasadena, CA

{chen,arvo}@cs.caltech.edu

Abstract. We present a new technique for exactly computing glossy reflections and transmissions of polygonal Lambertian luminaires with linearly-varying radiant exitance. To derive the underlying closed-form expressions, we introduce a rational generalization of irradiance tensors and an associated recurrence relation. The generalized tensors allow us to integrate a useful class of rational polynomials over regions of the sphere; this class of rational polynomials can simultaneously account for the linear variation of radiant exitance across a planar luminaire and simple forms of non-Lambertian scattering. Applications include the computation of irradiance at a point, view-dependent reflections from glossy surfaces, and transmissions through glossy surfaces, where the scattering is limited to Phong distributions and the incident illumination is due to linearly-varying luminaires. In polyhedral environments, the resulting expressions can be exactly evaluated in quadratic time (in the Phong exponent) using dynamic programming or efficiently approximated in linear time using standard numerical quadrature. To illustrate the use of generalized irradiance tensors, we present a greatly simplified derivation of a previously published closed-form expression for the irradiance due to linearly-varying luminaires, and simulate Phong-like scattering effects from such emitters. The validity of our algorithm is demonstrated by comparison with Monte Carlo.

Keywords: Irradiance Tensors, Illumination, Glossy Reflection, Glossy Transmission.

1   Introduction

Deterministic rendering algorithms are often quite limited in the optical effects they simulate; for the most part they are limited to diffuse and pure specular effects. A common assumption is that of a uniform luminaire with constant radiance in all directions and positions, for which a wide assortment of closed-form expressions exist for computing the radiative exchange [10, 3, 15, 17] and some Phong-like scattering effects [2]. Unfortunately, these formulas rarely apply to non-uniform luminaires, especially *inhomogeneous* (or *spatially-varying*) luminaires, that is, area light sources whose radiant exitance varies as a function of position. This limitation stems from the difficulty of computing the integrals associated with spatially-varying luminaires. Unlike uniform luminaires, they generally cannot be expressed as a polynomial integrated over regions of the sphere.

Spatially-varying luminaires constitute an important class of light sources with immediate applications to higher-order finite element methods for global illumination, both for direct lighting [9] and final gathers from coarse global solutions [13]. Few methods exist for handling this type of luminaire aside from Monte Carlo integration. DiLaura [8] and the authors [6] have addressed the problem of computing the irradiance at a point from spatially-varying luminaires with polynomially-varying radiant exitance. Both employed Stokes' theorem to convert the required surface integral to a boundary integral, and the latter approach leads to a closed-form solution for the irradiance due to a polygonal linearly-varying luminaire. As a continuation of our previous work [6], the contributions of this paper are as follows:

- A simpler derivation of the closed-form solution for the irradiance at a point due to a linearly-varying luminaire, using generalized irradiance tensors.
- The derivation of expressions for higher-order moments based on a class of rational polynomials over the sphere.
- An algorithm to evaluate these higher-order moments for simulating non-Lambertian scattering effects involving linearly-varying luminaires and non-diffuse surfaces, such as view-dependent glossy reflection and transmission.

Our approach generalizes *irradiance tensors* [2] to account for linearly-varying radiant exitance over the emitter. These new tensors are comprised of simple rational polynomials integrated over regions of the sphere. In particular, we address a limited subclass of rational polynomials corresponding to Phong distributions [12], which are shown to be well suited to simulate non-Lambertian phenomena involving linearly-varying luminaires. Using a recurrence formula derived for these *generalized irradiance tensors*, we demonstrate the exact integration of this subclass of rational polynomials in the case of polygonal emitters, and present a semi-analytical algorithm for their efficient computation. A similar approach using a tensor representation was previously used in analytically computing glossy reflection and transmission from uniform luminaires and the illumination from directional luminaires [2]. Our tensor generalization extends this previous method to handle linearly-varying luminaires as well, as shown in Figures 2a and 2b.

The remainder of the paper is organized as follows. Section 2 formulates the computation of some lighting effects involving linearly-varying luminaires and motivates our generalization of irradiance tensors in Section 3, which satisfies a recursive formula proved in Section 3.1. Based on this recurrence, we derive expressions for a simple class of rational polynomials in Section 3.2, which have immediate applications to several non-Lambertian simulations. We then discuss the exact evaluation of these expressions for polygonal emitters in Section 3.3. Finally, a semi-analytical algorithm is presented for their efficient computation in Section 3.4 and then used for image synthesis in Section 4.

2 Linearly-Varying Luminaires

In this section we examine the integrals arising in three non-Lambertian simulations involving linearly-varying luminaires; this will motivate our generalization of irradiance tensors.

Let $f(\mathbf{q}, \mathbf{u})$ denote the *radiance function* defined at all points $\mathbf{q} \in \mathbb{R}^3$ and all directions $\mathbf{u} \in \mathcal{S}^2$, the set of all unit vectors in $\mathbb{R}^3$. For fixed $\mathbf{q}$, this function simplifies to a *radiance distribution* $f(\mathbf{u})$ at $\mathbf{q}$. By default we assume that the point $\mathbf{q}$ we are interested in is at the origin. The goal of this paper is to characterize the radiance distribution function $f(\mathbf{u})$ due to a linearly-varying luminaire and to simulate various direct lighting and scattering effects from this type of emitter.

We begin with a brief recap of the formulation described in our previous work [6]. Suppose $\phi(\mathbf{x})$ is the *radiant exitance* of a luminaire at the point $\mathbf{x}$. The linearly-varying

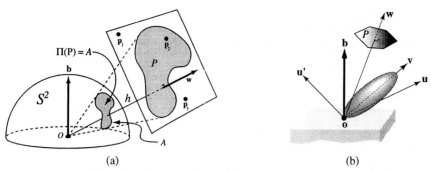

Fig. 1. *(a) The radiance distribution function $f(\mathbf{u})$ at $\mathbf{o}$ due to a planar figure P with linearly varying radiant exitance is expressed as a simple rational polynomial over its spherical projection $\Pi(P) = A$. The radiant exitance variation is uniquely determined by any three non-collinear points $\mathbf{p}_1$, $\mathbf{p}_2$, and $\mathbf{p}_3$ on the luminaire plane. (b) Given a glossy surface with a simple BRDF defined in terms of a Phong exponent around the mirror reflection $\mathbf{v}$, the reflected radiance along the view direction $\mathbf{u}'$ at $\mathbf{o}$ due to a linearly-varying luminaire P can be formulated as a simple rational polynomial integrated over regions of the sphere, that is, $\Pi(P)$.*

luminaires considered here are a class of planar emitters (not containing the origin) for which the function ϕ, mapping points on the plane to $\mathbb{R}$, is linear. Given any three non-collinear points $\mathbf{p}_1$, $\mathbf{p}_2$ and $\mathbf{p}_3$ on the luminaire with their associated radiant exitance values w_1, w_2 and w_3, the function ϕ can be expressed as

$$\phi(\mathbf{x}) = [w_1 \; w_2 \; w_3] \, [\mathbf{p}_1 \; \mathbf{p}_2 \; \mathbf{p}_3]^{-1} \, \mathbf{x}, \tag{1}$$

where $[\mathbf{p}_1 \; \mathbf{p}_2 \; \mathbf{p}_3]^{-1} \mathbf{x}$ is the barycentric coordinate vector of $\mathbf{x}$ with respect to $\mathbf{p}_1$, $\mathbf{p}_2$ and $\mathbf{p}_3$. Let h be the distance from the origin to the plane containing the luminaire and $\mathbf{w}$ denote the unit vector orthogonal to the plane, as shown in Figure 1a. We notice that the position vector $\mathbf{x}$ is related to its unit direction $\mathbf{u}$ from the origin by $\mathbf{x} = h \, \mathbf{u} / \langle \mathbf{w}, \mathbf{u} \rangle$, where $\langle \cdot, \cdot \rangle$ denotes the standard inner product. Consequently, the radiance distribution function $f(\mathbf{u})$ at the origin due to this Lambertian luminaire can be obtained by expressing $\mathbf{x}$ in equation (1) in terms of $\mathbf{u}$, yielding

$$f(\mathbf{u}) = \frac{\phi(\mathbf{x})}{\pi} = \frac{1}{\pi} \frac{\langle \mathbf{a}, \mathbf{u} \rangle}{\langle \mathbf{w}, \mathbf{u} \rangle}, \tag{2}$$

which is defined over the spherical projection of the luminaire at the origin, where the constant vector $\mathbf{a} = h \, [w_1 \; w_2 \; w_3] \, [\mathbf{p}_1 \; \mathbf{p}_2 \; \mathbf{p}_3]^{-1}$ encodes the linear variation.

Most emission and scattering effects involving linearly-varying luminaires can be formulated as weighted integrals of $f(\mathbf{u})$ given in (2) over spherical regions, which lead naturally to our tensor notion to be developed in Section 3.1. Let $\Pi(P)$ be the projection of a linearly-varying luminaire P onto the unit sphere about the origin, let $\mathbf{b}$ denote the receiver normal, and let σ measure the area on the sphere. We examine three different problems that each results in an integral with a rational integrand:

- The irradiance at the origin due to P is defined by

$$\Phi = \int_{\Pi(P)} f(\mathbf{u}) \, \langle \mathbf{b}, \mathbf{u} \rangle \, d\sigma(\mathbf{u}) = \frac{1}{\pi} \int_{\Pi(P)} \frac{\langle \mathbf{a}, \mathbf{u} \rangle \, \langle \mathbf{b}, \mathbf{u} \rangle}{\langle \mathbf{w}, \mathbf{u} \rangle} \, d\sigma(\mathbf{u}). \tag{3}$$

- Given a glossy surface with a simple BRDF defined in terms of a Phong exponent by $\rho(\mathbf{u}' \to \mathbf{u}) \equiv c\left[-\mathbf{u}^{\mathsf{T}}(\mathbf{I} - 2\mathbf{b}\mathbf{b}^{\mathsf{T}})\mathbf{u}'\right]^n$ for two directions $\mathbf{u}$ and $\mathbf{u}'$ shown in Figure 1b, the reflected radiance at a point on this surface along a view direction $\mathbf{u}'$ due to P is given by

$$f(\mathbf{u}') = \int_{\Pi(P)} \rho(\mathbf{u} \to \mathbf{u}') f(\mathbf{u}) \langle \mathbf{b}, \mathbf{u} \rangle \, d\sigma(\mathbf{u}) = \frac{c}{\pi} \int_{\Pi(P)} \frac{\langle \mathbf{v}, \mathbf{u} \rangle^n \langle \mathbf{a}, \mathbf{u} \rangle \langle \mathbf{b}, \mathbf{u} \rangle}{\langle \mathbf{w}, \mathbf{u} \rangle} \, d\sigma(\mathbf{u}),$$

where $\rho(\mathbf{u} \to \mathbf{u}') = \rho(\mathbf{u}' \to \mathbf{u})$ due to reciprocity, and $\mathbf{v} = -(\mathbf{I} - 2\mathbf{b}\mathbf{b}^{\mathsf{T}})\mathbf{u}'$ and n is the Phong exponent.

- By interpreting ρ above as a *bidirectional transmission distribution function* (BTDF) for a glossy surface, the transmitted radiance through this surface along a view direction $\mathbf{u}'$ due to P is represented by the same integral in (4), with $\mathbf{v}$ replaced by $-\mathbf{u}'$.

Note that the integrands in equations (3) and (4) are simple rational polynomials over the sphere. Simulating these non-Lambertian effects entails the computation of this type of integral.

3   Generalizing Irradiance Tensors

In this section we shall present new mathematical and computational tools for integrating some simple rational polynomials over regions of the sphere, which are required for the non-Lambertian simulations mentioned in the previous section.

3.1   Irradiance Tensors of Linearly-Varying Luminaires

As a natural generalization of the *radiation pressure tensor*, Arvo [2] introduced a tensor analogy of irradiance given by

$$\mathbf{T}^n(A) \equiv \int_A \mathbf{u} \otimes \cdots \otimes \mathbf{u} \, d\sigma(\mathbf{u}), \tag{5}$$

where $A \subset \mathcal{S}^2$ and the integrand is a n-fold tensor product. This tensor representation, known as the *irradiance tensor*, provides a useful vehicle for integrating *polynomial* functions over regions of the sphere. To concisely represent the *rational polynomial* integrals described in Section 2, we generalize the irradiance tensor shown in equation (5) to accommodate a denominator $\langle \mathbf{w}, \mathbf{u} \rangle$, resulting in a similar tensor form closely related to linearly-varying luminaires, defined as

$$\mathbf{T}^{n;1}(A, \mathbf{w}) \equiv \int_A \frac{\mathbf{u} \otimes \cdots \otimes \mathbf{u}}{\langle \mathbf{w}, \mathbf{u} \rangle} \, d\sigma(\mathbf{u}), \tag{6}$$

where we restrict $\mathbf{w}$ to be a unit vector such that $\langle \mathbf{w}, \mathbf{u} \rangle > 0$ for any $\mathbf{u} \in A$, and the orders of the numerator and the denominator are indicated respectively in the superscript $n; 1$. The elements of these tensors consist of all rational polynomials of the form $x^i y^j z^k / \langle \mathbf{w}, \mathbf{u} \rangle$ integrated over A, where $(x, y, z) \in \mathcal{S}^2$ and $i + j + k = n$.

Defined as surface integrals, the generalized irradiance tensors in equation (6) are computed by reducing them to boundary integrals, which yield closed-form solutions in polyhedral environments. Let $\mathbf{n}$ denote the outward-pointing normal of the boundary curve ∂A. Using generalized Stokes' theorem [16], we have shown (see the Appendix) that $\mathbf{T}^{n;1}$ satisfies the recurrence relation

$$\mathbf{T}^{n;1}_{Ij}(A,\mathbf{w}) = \mathbf{w}_j \mathbf{T}^{n-1}_I(A) + \frac{1}{n}\left(\delta_{jm} - \mathbf{w}_j \mathbf{w}_m\right)\left[\sum_{k=1}^{n-1}\delta_{mI_k}\mathbf{T}^{n-2;1}_{I\backslash k}(A,\mathbf{w})\right. \\ \left. - \int_{\partial A}\frac{\mathbf{u}^{n-1}_I \mathbf{n}_m}{\langle \mathbf{w},\mathbf{u}\rangle}\,ds\right] \tag{7}$$

for $n > 0$, where δ_{ij} is the Kronecker delta. The irradiance tensor $\mathbf{T}^{n-1}$ can be further expanded by [2]

$$(n+1)\mathbf{T}^n_{Ij}(A) = \sum_{k=1}^{n-1}\delta_{jI_k}\mathbf{T}^{n-2}_{I\backslash k}(A) - \int_{\partial A}\mathbf{u}^{n-1}_I \mathbf{n}_j\,ds, \tag{8}$$

with $\mathbf{T}^{-1}(A) = 0$ and $\mathbf{T}^0(A) = \sigma(A)$, which is the solid angle subtended by the spherical region A. In equations (7) and (8), I is a $(n-1)$-index $(i_1, i_2, \ldots, i_{n-1})$, where $i_k \in \{1, 2, 3\}$ for $1 \leq k \leq n-1$. We define I_k as the kth subindex of I, $I\backslash k$ to be the $(n-2)$-index obtained by deleting the kth subindex, and Ij to be the n-index obtained by appending j after I. Finally, the recurrence relation (7) is completed by the base case

$$\mathbf{T}^{0;1}(A,\mathbf{w}) = \int_{\partial A}\frac{\ln\langle \mathbf{w},\mathbf{u}\rangle}{1-\langle \mathbf{w},\mathbf{u}\rangle^2}\langle \mathbf{w},\mathbf{n}\rangle\,ds, \tag{9}$$

where the integrand is defined as 0 when $\langle \mathbf{w},\mathbf{u}\rangle = 1$. The proof of equation (9) is supplied in the Appendix.

3.2 Rational Polynomials Integrated Over the Sphere

From equation (7) we may obtain expressions for a class of rational polynomials integrated over the sphere. Although it is these individual *scalar* elements that are required for image synthesis, the tensor formulation provides a powerful tool to represent a family of rational polynomials by means of tensor composition. Given an arbitrary region $A \subset S^2$ and a sequence of axis vectors $\mathbf{v}_1, \mathbf{v}_2, \ldots$, we define a family of rational polynomials by

$$\tau^{p_1, p_2, \ldots; q}(A, \mathbf{v}_1, \mathbf{v}_2, \ldots; \mathbf{w}) \equiv \int_A \frac{\langle \mathbf{v}_1, \mathbf{u}\rangle^{p_1}\langle \mathbf{v}_2, \mathbf{u}\rangle^{p_2}\cdots}{\langle \mathbf{w},\mathbf{u}\rangle^q}\,d\sigma(\mathbf{u}) \tag{10}$$

for non-negative integers $p_1, p_2, \ldots, q$. When $q = 0$, this definition subsumes *axial moments* $\bar{\tau}^n(A, \mathbf{v})$ and *double-axis moments* $\bar{\bar{\tau}}^{n,1}(A, \mathbf{v}_1, \mathbf{v}_2)$ [2] as special cases, which correspond respectively to $\tau^{n;0}(A, \mathbf{v})$ and $\tau^{n,1;0}(A, \mathbf{v}_1, \mathbf{v}_2)$. Similarly, by specializing equation (10) to a small number of axes for $q = 1$, we may define three simple higher-order moments of $\mathbf{T}^{n;1}$, namely, $\tau^{n;1}(A, \mathbf{v}; \mathbf{w})$, $\tau^{n,1;1}(A, \mathbf{v}_1, \mathbf{v}_2; \mathbf{w})$, and $\tau^{n,1,1;1}(A, \mathbf{v}_1, \mathbf{v}_2, \mathbf{v}_3; \mathbf{w})$. For simplicity, we shall only consider the case where one factor in the numerator is raised to the power n, and all the others are of order 1. These moments can be expressed as a tensor composition of $\mathbf{T}^{n;1}$ with copies of $\mathbf{v}_1$, $\mathbf{v}_2$ or $\mathbf{v}_3$. For example, $\tau^{n;1}(A, \mathbf{v}; \mathbf{w}) = \mathbf{T}^{n;1}_I(A,\mathbf{w})(\mathbf{v}\otimes\cdots\otimes\mathbf{v})_I$. Here and throughout the paper, the summation convention is employed, where repeated subscripts imply summation from 1 to 3, including multi-indices such as I [1, p.89]. We may derive the following recurrence relations from equation (7):

$$\tau^{n;1}(A, \mathbf{v}; \mathbf{w}) = \langle \mathbf{w}, \mathbf{v} \rangle \, \bar{\tau}^{n-1}(A, \mathbf{v}) + \frac{\mathbf{v}^{\mathsf{T}}(\mathbf{I} - \mathbf{w}\mathbf{w}^{\mathsf{T}})}{n} \times$$
$$\left[(n-1)\tau^{n-2;1}(A, \mathbf{v}; \mathbf{w}) \, \mathbf{v} - \int_{\partial A} \mathbf{n} \frac{\langle \mathbf{v}, \mathbf{u} \rangle^{n-1}}{\langle \mathbf{w}, \mathbf{u} \rangle} \, ds \right] \quad (11)$$

$$\tau^{n,1;1}(A, \mathbf{v}_1, \mathbf{v}_2; \mathbf{w}) = \langle \mathbf{w}, \mathbf{v}_2 \rangle \, \bar{\tau}^{n}(A, \mathbf{v}_1) + \frac{\mathbf{v}_2^{\mathsf{T}}(\mathbf{I} - \mathbf{w}\mathbf{w}^{\mathsf{T}})}{n+1} \times$$
$$\left[n\, \tau^{n-1;1}(A, \mathbf{v}_1; \mathbf{w}) \, \mathbf{v}_1 - \int_{\partial A} \mathbf{n} \frac{\langle \mathbf{v}_1, \mathbf{u} \rangle^{n}}{\langle \mathbf{w}, \mathbf{u} \rangle} \, ds \right] \quad (12)$$

$$\tau^{n,1,1;1}(A, \mathbf{v}_1, \mathbf{v}_2, \mathbf{v}_3; \mathbf{w}) = \langle \mathbf{w}, \mathbf{v}_3 \rangle \, \bar{\bar{\tau}}^{n,1}(A, \mathbf{v}_1, \mathbf{v}_2) + \frac{\mathbf{v}_3^{\mathsf{T}}(\mathbf{I} - \mathbf{w}\mathbf{w}^{\mathsf{T}})}{n+2} \times$$
$$\left[n\tau^{n-1,1;1}(A, \mathbf{v}_1, \mathbf{v}_2; \mathbf{w}) \, \mathbf{v}_1 + \tau^{n;1}(A, \mathbf{v}_1; \mathbf{w}) \, \mathbf{v}_2 - \right.$$
$$\left. \int_{\partial A} \mathbf{n} \frac{\langle \mathbf{v}_1, \mathbf{u} \rangle^{n} \langle \mathbf{v}_2, \mathbf{u} \rangle}{\langle \mathbf{w}, \mathbf{u} \rangle} \, ds \right] \quad (13)$$

In equation (11), we have $\tau^{0;1}(A, \mathbf{v}; \mathbf{w}) = \mathbf{T}^{0;1}(A, \mathbf{w})$ and $\tau^{-1;1}(A, \mathbf{v}; \mathbf{w}) = 0$; and the double-axis moment $\bar{\bar{\tau}}^{n,1}$ in (13) can be expressed in terms of axial moments by $\left(n \langle \mathbf{v}_1, \mathbf{v}_2 \rangle \, \bar{\tau}^{n-1}(A, \mathbf{v}_1) - \int_{\partial A} \langle \mathbf{v}_1, \mathbf{u} \rangle^{n} \langle \mathbf{v}_2, \mathbf{n} \rangle \, ds \right) / (n+2)$ [2].

3.3 Exact Evaluation

Equations (11), (12) and (13) reduce the surface integrals $\tau^{n;1}$, $\tau^{n,1;1}$ and $\tau^{n,1,1;1}$ to boundary integrals of rational polynomials, and sums of axial moments and $\tau^{0;1}(= \mathbf{T}^{0;1})$. These moments can be integrated exactly whenever the resulting boundary integrals, axial moments and the base case $\tau^{0;1}$ can be. In this section we shall describe how these components can be evaluated in closed form when the region $A \subset \mathcal{S}^2$ is restricted to the spherical projection of a polygon P, which is a spherical polygon composed of segments of great arcs.

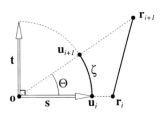

When A is a spherical polygon, the resulting boundary integrals can be evaluated along each edge ζ, which is greatly simplified due to the constant outward normal $\mathbf{n}$. We parameterize each edge ζ by $\mathbf{u}(\theta) = \mathbf{s} \cos\theta + \mathbf{t}\sin\theta$, where $\mathbf{s}$ and $\mathbf{t}$ are orthonormal vectors in the plane containing the edge and the origin, with $\mathbf{s}$ pointing toward the first vertex of the edge, as illustrated on the left. We shall define variables c and ϕ with respect to a vector $\mathbf{v}$ as:

$$c = \sqrt{\langle \mathbf{v}, \mathbf{s} \rangle^2 + \langle \mathbf{v}, \mathbf{t} \rangle^2}, \quad (\cos\phi, \sin\phi) = \left(\frac{\langle \mathbf{v}, \mathbf{s} \rangle}{c}, \frac{\langle \mathbf{v}, \mathbf{t} \rangle}{c} \right). \quad (14)$$

Exact evaluation of $\tau^{0;1}(A; \mathbf{w})$ $(= \mathbf{T}^{0;1}(A, \mathbf{w}))$ given in equation (9) requires us to integrate a scalar-valued function $\eta(\mathbf{w}, \mathbf{u})$ defined by

$$\eta(\mathbf{w}, \mathbf{u}) \equiv \frac{\ln \langle \mathbf{w}, \mathbf{u} \rangle}{1 - \langle \mathbf{w}, \mathbf{u} \rangle^2} \quad (15)$$

along each edge ζ, which has been previously elaborated by the authors [6]. The solution is *closed form* except for one special function known as the Clausen integral [11]. As for the axial moment $\bar{\tau}^n$ about a unit vector $\mathbf{v}$, Arvo [2] has shown that it reduces to a one-dimensional integral by

$$n\bar{\tau}^{n-1}(A, \mathbf{v}) \;=\; \bar{\tau}^{p-1} - \int_{\partial A} \left[\langle \mathbf{v}, \mathbf{u} \rangle^{n-2} + \langle \mathbf{v}, \mathbf{u} \rangle^{n-4} + \cdots + \langle \mathbf{v}, \mathbf{u} \rangle^{p} \right] \langle \mathbf{v}, \mathbf{n} \rangle \; ds, \quad (16)$$

where $p = 0$ when n is even, and $p = 1$ when n is odd, and $\bar{\tau}^{-1}(A) = 0$ and $\bar{\tau}^0(A) = \sigma(A)$, which can be computed either from Girard's formula [4, 2] or a boundary integral formula for $\sigma(A)$ [6, 5]. From the above edge parameterization, the complete integral in equation (16) can be evaluated exactly in $O(nk)$ time for a k-sided polygon, by computing the function $F(n, x, y) \equiv \int_x^y \cos^n \theta \, d\theta$ incrementally according to the following recurrence identity [2]:

$$F(n, x, y) \;=\; \frac{1}{n} \left[\cos^{n-1} y \sin y - \cos^{n-1} x \sin x + (n - 1) F(n - 2, x, y) \right]. \quad (17)$$

Finally, the boundary integrals appearing in formulas (11), (12) and (13) require us to compute two types of line integrals given by

$$B^n \;=\; \int_\zeta \frac{\langle \mathbf{v}_1, \mathbf{u} \rangle^n}{\langle \mathbf{w}, \mathbf{u} \rangle} \, ds, \quad \text{and} \quad B^{n,1} \;=\; \int_\zeta \frac{\langle \mathbf{v}_1, \mathbf{u} \rangle^n \langle \mathbf{v}_2, \mathbf{u} \rangle}{\langle \mathbf{w}, \mathbf{u} \rangle} \, ds,$$

which can be respectively evaluated using our edge parameterization as

$$B^n \;=\; \frac{c_1^n}{c} \int_{-\phi}^{\Theta - \phi} \frac{(\alpha_1 \cos \theta + \beta_1 \sin \theta)^n}{\cos \theta} \, d\theta, \quad (18)$$

$$B^{n,1} \;=\; \frac{c_1^n c_2}{c} \int_{-\phi}^{\Theta - \phi} \frac{(\alpha_1 \cos \theta + \beta_1 \sin \theta)^n (\alpha_2 \cos \theta + \beta_2 \sin \theta)}{\cos \theta} \, d\theta. \quad (19)$$

Here Θ is the arc length of ζ, and (c, ϕ), (c_1, ϕ_1), (c_2, ϕ_2) are variables defined for $\mathbf{w}, \mathbf{v}_1, \mathbf{v}_2$ respectively using (14), and $\alpha_1, \beta_1, \alpha_2, \beta_2$ are given by

$$\alpha_i \;=\; \cos(\phi_i - \phi), \qquad \beta_i \;=\; \sin(\phi_i - \phi) \quad (i = 1, 2).$$

Expanding the numerator using the binomial theorem, we can express B^n and $B^{n,1}$ in equations (18) and (19) in terms of integrals of the form

$$G(r, s, x, y) \;\equiv\; \int_x^y \sin^r \theta \, \cos^s \theta \, d\theta \quad (20)$$

for integers $r \geq 0$ and $s \geq -1$, yielding

$$B^n \;=\; \frac{c_1^n}{c} \sum_{k=0}^{n} \binom{n}{k} \alpha_1^{n-k} \beta_1^k \, G(k, n - k - 1, x, y), \quad (21)$$

$$B^{n,1} \;=\; \frac{c_1^n c_2}{c} \sum_{k=0}^{n} \binom{n}{k} \alpha_1^{n-k} \beta_1^k \left[\alpha_2 G(k, n - k, x, y) + \beta_2 G(k + 1, n - k - 1, x, y) \right]. \quad (22)$$

The integral in (20) can be evaluated exactly in $O(r+s)$ steps using the following recurrence relations:

$$G(r,s,x,y) = \frac{1}{r+s}\left[\sin^{r+1}y\cos^{s-1}y - \sin^{r+1}x\cos^{s-1}x + (s-1)G(r,s-2,x,y)\right]$$

$$G(r,s,x,y) = \frac{1}{r+s}\left[\sin^{r-1}x\cos^{s+1}x - \sin^{r-1}y\cos^{s+1}y + (r-1)G(r-2,s,x,y)\right]$$

where the base cases are

$$G(0,-1,x,y) = \ln\left(\frac{\tan(\pi/4+y/2)}{\tan(\pi/4+x/2)}\right), \quad G(1,0,x,y) = \cos x - \cos y,$$

$$G(1,-1,x,y) = \ln\left(\frac{\cos x}{\cos y}\right), \qquad\qquad G(0,0,x,y) = y - x.$$

Therefore, it takes $O(n^2)$ time to exactly evaluate B^n or $B^{n,1}$ over one edge using equation (21) or equation (22).

3.4 Algorithms for Efficient Evaluation

Assuming that the evaluation of $\tau^{0;1}$ using the Clausen integral takes constant time [6], it then follows from the recurrence (11) that $\tau^{n;1}$ for a k-sided polygon may be computed exactly in $O(n^3 k)$ time, since we have shown that $\bar{\tau}^{n-1}$ and $\int_{\partial A}\mathbf{n}\langle\mathbf{v},\mathbf{u}\rangle^{n-1}/\langle\mathbf{w},\mathbf{u}\rangle\,ds$ can be evaluated in $O(nk)$ and $O(n^2 k)$ respectively, by means of equations (16) and (21). However, we may reduce this complexity to $O(n^2 k)$ by reorganizing the terms obtained from the recurrence relation (11) and using dynamic programming [7, pp.301–328] to reuse many shared sub-expressions.

Let $d = \mathbf{v}^{\mathsf{T}}(\mathbf{I}-\mathbf{w}\mathbf{w}^{\mathsf{T}})\mathbf{v}$ and $k = \lfloor n/2\rfloor$, the recurrence formula (11) leads to

$$\tau^{n;1}(A,\mathbf{v};\mathbf{w}) = T_1 + \frac{1}{n}\left[\langle\mathbf{w},\mathbf{v}\rangle T_2 - \mathbf{v}^{\mathsf{T}}(\mathbf{I}-\mathbf{w}\mathbf{w}^{\mathsf{T}})T_3\right]. \tag{23}$$

Defining $q = 0$ for even n and $q = -1$ for odd n, T_1, T_2 and T_3 above are given by

$$T_1 = d^{k-q}\left(\frac{q+1}{n}\right)\left(\frac{n-1}{n-2}\right)\left(\frac{n-3}{n-4}\right)\cdots\left(\frac{q+3}{q+2}\right)\tau^{q;1}, \tag{24}$$

$$T_2 = n\bar{\tau}^{n-1}(A,\mathbf{v}) + d\left(\frac{n-1}{n-2}\right)(n-2)\bar{\tau}^{n-3}(A,\mathbf{v}) +$$
$$\cdots + d^{k-q-1}\left(\frac{n-1}{n-2}\right)\cdots\left(\frac{q+3}{q+2}\right)(q+2)\bar{\tau}^{q+1}(A,\mathbf{v}), \tag{25}$$

$$T_3 = \int_{\partial A}\frac{\mathbf{n}}{\langle\mathbf{w},\mathbf{u}\rangle}\left[\langle\mathbf{v},\mathbf{u}\rangle^{n-1} + d\left(\frac{n-1}{n-2}\right)\langle\mathbf{v},\mathbf{u}\rangle^{n-3} +\right.$$
$$\left.\cdots + d^{k-q-1}\left(\frac{n-1}{n-2}\right)\left(\frac{n-3}{n-4}\right)\cdots\left(\frac{q+3}{q+2}\right)\langle\mathbf{v},\mathbf{u}\rangle^{q+1}\right]ds. \tag{26}$$

When $\mathbf{v}$ is normalized, we may use equation (16) to express T_2 as

$$T_2 = \left[1 + d\left(\frac{n-1}{n-2}\right) + \cdots + d^{k-q-1}\left(\frac{n-1}{n-2}\right)\cdots\left(\frac{q+3}{q+2}\right)\right]\bar{\tau}^{p-1} -$$

$$\sum_{i=1}^{k} \left[\langle \mathbf{v}, \mathbf{n} \rangle \, S(n-2, c, d, -\phi, \Theta - \phi) \right], \tag{27}$$

where $\mathbf{n}$, Θ and c, ϕ given in (14) all depend on the edge ζ_i ($1 \leq i \leq k$), and p is defined as in (16). Here $S(n-2, c, d, x, y)$ is a sum of the integrals $F = \int_x^y \cos^n \theta \, d\theta$ of different exponents, given by

$$c^{n-2} F(n-2, x, y) + \left[1 + d \left(\frac{n-1}{n-2} \right) \right] c^{n-4} F(n-4, x, y) + \cdots$$

$$+ \left[1 + d \left(\frac{n-1}{n-2} \right) + \cdots + d^{k-1} \left(\frac{n-1}{n-2} \right) \cdots \left(\frac{p+3}{p+2} \right) \right] c^p F(p, x, y), \tag{28}$$

which can be computed incrementally in linear time using the identity (17). To compute the weighted sum of integrals B^n with n ranging from $q+1$ to $n-1$ required for T_3 using (21), we may precompute and cache n^2 values of $G(r, s, x, y)$ for $0 \leq r \leq n-1$ and $-1 \leq s \leq n-2$. This common technique known as *dynamic programming* reduces the cubic complexity for the exact evaluation of T_3 down to quadratic. Consequently, $\tau^{n;1}$ may be evaluated analytically using equation (23) in $O(n^2 k)$ time for a k-sided polygon. From recursive formulas (12) and (13), we may also compute $\tau^{n,1;1}$ and $\tau^{n,1,1;1}$ exactly in quadratic time, where a great deal of redundant computations involving the functions F and G may be avoided by allowing the routines for $\tau^{n;1}$ to return some additional higher-order terms in the series of T_2 and T_3. Furthermore, observing the common coefficients 1, $\frac{n-1}{n-2}$, $\frac{(n-1)(n-3)}{(n-2)(n-4)}$, $\ldots$ occurring in equations (24), (25) and (26), another optimization is to cache this series of values before evaluating T_1, T_2, T_3. All these optimizations significantly reduce the constant related to the quadratic complexity. The complete pseudo-code and details for computing $\tau^{n;1}$ and $\tau^{n,1;1}$, $\tau^{n,1,1;1}$ for a polygon are available as a technical report [5].

Another option for speeding up the computation is to approximate T_3 using numerical quadrature; this is particularly effective as T_3 has the highest computational cost, yet is typically very small in magnitude compared to T_1 and T_2. In terms of accuracy, this approach is preferable to approximating the original integral using two-dimensional quadrature, as one-dimensional quadrature rules are more robust and more amenable to higher-order methods. By computing the powers of $\langle \mathbf{v}, \mathbf{u} \rangle$ in equation (26) incrementally through repeated multiplication for each sampled $\mathbf{u}$, the complete integral (26) can be evaluated within $O(ln)$ time for each edge, where l is the number of samples used in the quadrature rule. For fixed l, this semi-analytical algorithm allows us to compute $\tau^{n;1}$ of a k-sided polygon in linear time. We have used this approach in combination with the extended trapezoidal rule to generate the images shown in Section 4.

4 Non-Lambertian Effects from Linearly-Varying Luminaires

Generalized irradiance tensors $\mathbf{T}^{n;1}$ and those moments expressed as a class of rational polynomials integrated over the sphere are well suited to the computation of emission and scattering features due to linearly-varying luminaires, especially for polygonal environments with Phong-like reflection (or transmission) distributions. Therefore, the expressions and procedures given in previous sections may be applied to the simulation of illumination, glossy reflection and glossy transmission involving linearly-varying luminaires, which will be described next.

34

4.1 Irradiance due to a Linearly-Varying Luminaire

Generalized irradiance tensors provide a more elegant means of deriving the closed-form solution for the irradiance due to a linearly-varying luminaire reported previously by the authors [6]. Our previous approach, which was based on Taylor expansion and a formula derived for *triple-axis moments*, is quite tedious.

According to definitions (10) and (6), we express the irradiance integral (3) as

$$\Phi = \frac{1}{\pi} \tau^{1,1;1}(A, \mathbf{a}, \mathbf{b}; \mathbf{w}) = \frac{1}{\pi} \mathbf{T}_{ij}^{2;1}(A, \mathbf{w}) \mathbf{a}_i \mathbf{b}_j. \tag{29}$$

Using equations (7), (8) and (9), $\mathbf{T}^{2;1}$ reduces to a boundary integral as follows:

$$\begin{aligned}
\mathbf{T}_{ij}^{2;1} &= \mathbf{w}_j \mathbf{T}_i^1 + \frac{1}{2} \left(\delta_{jm} - \mathbf{w}_j \mathbf{w}_m \right) \left[\delta_{im} \mathbf{T}^{0,1} - \int_{\partial A} \frac{\mathbf{u}_i \mathbf{n}_m}{\langle \mathbf{w}, \mathbf{u} \rangle} \, ds \right] \\
&= -\frac{1}{2} \int_{\partial A} \left[\delta_{ik} \mathbf{w}_j - \left(\delta_{jm} - \mathbf{w}_j \mathbf{w}_m \right) \left(\delta_{im} \mathbf{w}_k \, \eta - \frac{\delta_{km} \mathbf{u}_i}{\langle \mathbf{w}, \mathbf{u} \rangle} \right) \right] \mathbf{n}_k \, ds, \tag{30}
\end{aligned}$$

where η is given by equation (15). Combining equations (29) and (30), we arrive at the general boundary integral for the irradiance at the origin [6]

$$\Phi = -\frac{1}{2\pi} \int_{\partial A} \mathbf{M}_{ijk} \mathbf{a}_i \mathbf{b}_j \mathbf{n}_k \, ds, \tag{31}$$

where the 3-tensor $\mathbf{M}$, which depends on $\mathbf{w}$ and $\mathbf{u}$, is defined as

$$\mathbf{M}_{ijk}(\mathbf{w}, \mathbf{u}) = \delta_{ik} \mathbf{w}_j + \left(\delta_{jm} - \mathbf{w}_j \mathbf{w}_m \right) \left(\frac{\delta_{km} \mathbf{u}_i}{\langle \mathbf{w}, \mathbf{u} \rangle} - \delta_{im} \mathbf{w}_k \, \eta \right).$$

As we have demonstrated earlier [6], the integral (31) leads to a closed-form solution involving a single special function known as the Clausen integral for polygonal emitters.

4.2 Phong-like Glossy Reflection and Transmission

As mentioned in Section 2, the reflected radiance along the view direction $\mathbf{u}'$ on a glossy surface with Phong-like BRDF due to a linearly-varying luminaire can be formulated as a surface integral shown in equation (4), which is equivalent to $f(\mathbf{u}') = c\tau^{n,1,1;1}(A, \mathbf{v}, \mathbf{b}, \mathbf{a}; \mathbf{w})/\pi$, with n as the Phong exponent. Thus the procedures described in Section 3.4 can be implemented inside a ray tracer to simulate such glossy reflection effects. For a scene consisting of a linearly-varying luminaire P and a glossy surface Q, each pixel color is determined by the pseudo-code *GlossyReflection*, where f and n are the reflectivity and Phong exponent of Q, and Q_c, P_c, B_c denote the colors for Q, P, and the background, respectively. The technique is demonstrated in the top row of Figure 3 using a variety of exponents to simulate surfaces with varying finishes. In order to efficiently handle two color variations superimposed on the luminaire shown in Figure 3, we separate the vector $\mathbf{a}$ encoding the linear variation from equation (13) and rewrite $\tau^{n,1,1;1}$ as an inner product of $\mathbf{a}$ and a vector-valued function $\mathbf{t}(A, \mathbf{v}, \mathbf{b}, \mathbf{w})$ given by

$$\begin{aligned}
\mathbf{t}(A, \mathbf{v}, \mathbf{b}, \mathbf{w}) &= \mathbf{w} \bar{\bar{\tau}}^{n,1}(A, \mathbf{v}, \mathbf{b}) + \frac{\mathbf{I} - \mathbf{w} \mathbf{w}^{\mathsf{T}}}{n+2} \left[n\tau^{n-1,1;1}(A, \mathbf{v}, \mathbf{b}; \mathbf{w}) \, \mathbf{v} + \right. \\
&\quad \left. \tau^{n;1}(A, \mathbf{v}; \mathbf{w}) \, \mathbf{b} - \int_{\partial A} \mathbf{n} \frac{\langle \mathbf{v}, \mathbf{u} \rangle^n \langle \mathbf{b}, \mathbf{u} \rangle}{\langle \mathbf{w}, \mathbf{u} \rangle} \, ds \right], \tag{32}
\end{aligned}$$

GlossyReflection(**Eye**, Q, f, n, P, Q_c, P_c, B_c)

> **for each** pixel ξ **do**
>> **Ray** $R \leftarrow$ *ray cast from* **Eye** *to* ξ.
>> $\mathbf{q} \leftarrow$ *the first intersection point of the ray* R
>> **if** $\mathbf{q}$ is on the luminaire P
>>> $PixelColor \leftarrow P_c$
>>
>> **else if** $\mathbf{q}$ is on the glossy surface Q
>>> $\mathbf{b} \leftarrow$ *surface normal at* $\mathbf{q}$
>>> $\mathbf{u}' \leftarrow$ *direction of* R
>>> $\mathbf{v} \leftarrow (\mathbf{I} - 2\mathbf{b}\mathbf{b}^{\mathsf{T}})\mathbf{u}'$
>>> $\mathbf{w} \leftarrow$ *unit vector from* $\mathbf{q}$ *orthogonal to* P
>>> $\mathbf{a} \leftarrow$ *vector encoding the linear variation of* P
>>> $A \leftarrow$ *spherical projection of* P *at* $\mathbf{q}$
>>> $s \leftarrow \tau^{n,1,1;1}(A, \mathbf{v}, \mathbf{b}, \mathbf{a}; \mathbf{w})$ *(See Section 3.4)*
>>> $PixelColor \leftarrow f * [s * P_c + (1 - s) * B_c] + (1 - f) * Q_c$
>>
>> **else**
>>> $PixelColor \leftarrow B_c$
>>
>> **endif**
>
> **endfor**

which amortizes the computation cost for more than one color variations. In Figure 2, our analytical glossy reflection is compared with a Monte Carlo solution based on 64 samples per pixel, where the samples are stratified and distributed according to the Phong lobe (this is a form of importance sampling). The analytical solution closely matches the Monte Carlo estimate but with the advantage of eliminating statistical noise; in this example it is even slightly faster than Monte Carlo method.

Nearly the same strategy can be used to compute glossy transmission of linearly-varying luminaires by choosing $\mathbf{v}$ in equation (32) as the reversed view direction $-\mathbf{u}'$, which is now located on the other side of the transparent material. The bottom row of Figure 3 shows three images depicting a frosted glass fish tank, with different finishes specified by different Phong exponents.

The performance of our analytical approach is determined by such factors as the image resolution, the Phong exponent, and the luminaire complexity. All timings shown in Figure 2 and Figure 3 were done using a SGI Onyx2 with a 300 MHZ MIPS R12000 processor, and an image resolution of 200×200.

5   Conclusions

We have presented a number of new closed-form expressions for computing the illumination from luminaires with linearly-varying radiant exitance as well as glossy reflections and transmissions of such luminaires. These expressions are derived using a simple rational generalization of irradiance tensors, and can be evaluated analytically in $O(n^2 k)$ time for a k-sided polygonal luminaire using dynamic programming, where n is related to the glossiness of the surface. The exact solution depends on a single well-behaved special function known as the Clausen integral. We have also presented a semi-analytical algorithm for evaluating these expressions efficiently for the purpose of simulating glossy reflection and glossy transmission of linearly-varying luminaires. A similar approach is possible for general polynomials [5], although the recurrence formulas have not yet yielded a computationally tractable evaluation strategy.

36

Acknowledgements

This work was supported by a Microsoft Research Fellowship and NSF Career Award CCR9876332. Special thanks to Al Barr, Peter Schröder, Mark Meyer and Eitan Grinspun for helpful comments.

Appendix: Proofs of Equation (7) and Equation (9)

The proof of equation (7) parallels that of equation (8) shown by Arvo [1, pp. 84–87]. It is done by applying Stokes' Theorem to change the boundary integral on the right to a surface integral, which can be accomplished in four steps:

Step 1: Let $r = \|\mathbf{r}\|$. Notice that $\mathbf{n} \, ds = \mathbf{r} \times d\mathbf{r}/r^2$ and $\mathbf{u} = \mathbf{r}/r$, we may rewrite the boundary integral on the right hand side in terms of the position vector $\mathbf{r}$ and its derivatives:

$$\int_{\partial A} \frac{\mathbf{u}_I^{n-1}\mathbf{n}_m}{\langle \mathbf{w}, \mathbf{u} \rangle} \, ds = \int_{\partial A} \frac{\varepsilon_{mpl}\mathbf{r}_I^{n-1}\mathbf{r}_p \, d\mathbf{r}_l}{\langle \mathbf{w}, \mathbf{r} \rangle \, r^n} = \int_{\partial A} B_{Iml} \, d\mathbf{r}_l, \tag{33}$$

where ε_{ijk} is the permutation symbol [1, pp.69–70] and B is a $(n+1)$-order tensor B given by

$$B_{Iml} = \frac{\varepsilon_{mpl}\mathbf{r}_I^{n-1}\mathbf{r}_p}{\langle \mathbf{w}, \mathbf{r} \rangle \, r^n}.$$

Step 2: To convert the boundary integral in equation (33) into a surface integral using Stokes' theorem, we must compute the partial derivative of B_{Iml} with respect to $\mathbf{r}_s$, denoted by $B_{Iml,s}$. It follows from the chain rule that

$$B_{Iml,s} = \varepsilon_{mpl}\left(\frac{\partial}{\partial \mathbf{r}_s}\left[\frac{1}{\langle \mathbf{w}, \mathbf{r} \rangle} \right]\left[\frac{\mathbf{r}_p\mathbf{r}_I^{n-1}}{r^n} \right] + \left[\frac{1}{\langle \mathbf{w}, \mathbf{r} \rangle} \right]\frac{\partial}{\partial \mathbf{r}_s}\left[\frac{\mathbf{r}_p\mathbf{r}_I^{n-1}}{r^n} \right] \right) = \varepsilon_{mpl}[A_1 + A_2]$$

where A_1, A_2 are given by

$$A_1 = -\frac{\mathbf{w}_s\mathbf{r}_p\mathbf{r}_I^{n-1}}{\langle \mathbf{w}, \mathbf{r} \rangle^2 \, r^n}, \quad A_2 = \frac{\delta_{ps}\mathbf{r}_I^{n-1} + \mathbf{r}_p\mathbf{r}_{I,s}^{n-1}}{\langle \mathbf{w}, \mathbf{r} \rangle \, r^n} - n\frac{\mathbf{r}_s\mathbf{r}_p\mathbf{r}_I^{n-1}}{\langle \mathbf{w}, \mathbf{r} \rangle \, r^{n+2}}.$$

Thus, we have

$$\begin{aligned}
\int_{\partial A} B_{Iml} \, d\mathbf{r}_l &= \int_A B_{Iml,s} \, d\mathbf{r}_s \wedge d\mathbf{r}_l \\
&= \int_A B_{Iml,s}\left[\frac{d\mathbf{r}_s \wedge d\mathbf{r}_l - d\mathbf{r}_l \wedge d\mathbf{r}_s}{2} \right] \\
&= \int_A \varepsilon_{qsl}\varepsilon_{mpl}[A_1 + A_2]\left[\frac{\varepsilon_{qht} \, d\mathbf{r}_h \wedge d\mathbf{r}_t}{2} \right].
\end{aligned} \tag{34}$$

The transformation above follows from anti-commutativity of the wedge product [14][1, p. 68] and the tensor identity $\varepsilon_{qsl}\varepsilon_{qht} = \delta_{sh}\delta_{tl} - \delta_{st}\delta_{lh}$.

Step 3: Applying the above identity to the two terms in equation (34), we get

$$\varepsilon_{qsl}\varepsilon_{mpl}A_1 = \frac{\mathbf{r}_I^{n-1}}{\langle \mathbf{w}, \mathbf{r}\rangle^2 r^n}\left[\delta_{qm}\langle \mathbf{w}, \mathbf{r}\rangle - \mathbf{w}_m \mathbf{r}_q\right],$$

$$\varepsilon_{qsl}\varepsilon_{mpl}A_2 = \frac{1}{\langle \mathbf{w}, \mathbf{r}\rangle}\left[\frac{\delta_{qm}\mathbf{r}_I^{n-1}}{r^n} - \frac{\mathbf{r}_q \mathbf{r}_{I,m}^{n-1}}{r^n} + n\frac{\mathbf{r}_q \mathbf{r}_m \mathbf{r}_I^{n-1}}{r^{n+2}}\right].$$

Consequently, equation (34) simplifies to

$$\int_A \left[\frac{\mathbf{w}_m \mathbf{r}_I^{n-1}}{\langle \mathbf{w}, \mathbf{r}\rangle^2 r^{n-3}} - \frac{\sum_{k=1}^{n-1}\delta_{mI_k}\mathbf{r}_{I\backslash k}^{n-2}}{\langle \mathbf{w}, \mathbf{r}\rangle r^{n-3}} + n\frac{\mathbf{r}_m \mathbf{r}_I^{n-1}}{\langle \mathbf{w}, \mathbf{r}\rangle r^{n-1}}\right]\left[\frac{\varepsilon_{qht}\mathbf{r}_q \, d\mathbf{r}_h \wedge \, d\mathbf{r}_t}{2r^3}\right]. \quad (35)$$

Step 4: Multiplying equation (35) by $(\delta_{jm} - \mathbf{w}_j \mathbf{w}_m)/n$ and representing the surface integral in terms of solid angle $d\sigma(\mathbf{u}) \equiv -\varepsilon_{qst}\mathbf{r}_q \, d\mathbf{r}_s \wedge \, d\mathbf{r}_t/2r^3$ [16, p. 131], we attain

$$-\frac{1}{n}\left(\delta_{jm} - \mathbf{w}_j \mathbf{w}_m\right)\int_{\partial A} B_{Iml} \, d\mathbf{r}_l = \frac{1}{n}\left(\delta_{jm} - \mathbf{w}_j \mathbf{w}_m\right)\sum_{k=1}^{n-1}\delta_{mI_k}\mathbf{T}_{I\backslash k}^{n-2;1} + \mathbf{w}_j \mathbf{T}_I^{n-1} - \mathbf{T}_{Ij}^{n;1},$$

which verifies equation (7).

The steps to prove equation (9) are almost identical to those used in the proof of equation (7) described above, so we only show the difference here. Corresponding to equations (33) and (34), we have

$$\int_{\partial A}\frac{\ln\langle \mathbf{w}, \mathbf{u}\rangle}{1 - \langle \mathbf{w}, \mathbf{u}\rangle^2}\langle \mathbf{w}, \mathbf{n}\rangle \, ds = \int_{\partial A} B_l \, d\mathbf{r}_l = \int_A \varepsilon_{qml}B_{l,m}\left[\frac{\varepsilon_{qst} \, d\mathbf{r}_s \wedge \, d\mathbf{r}_t}{2}\right], \quad (36)$$

where the vector B is given by

$$B_l = \varepsilon_{kpl}\mathbf{w}_k\frac{\ln\langle \mathbf{w}, \mathbf{u}\rangle}{1 - \langle \mathbf{w}, \mathbf{u}\rangle^2}\cdot\frac{\mathbf{r}_p}{r^2} = \varepsilon_{kpl}\mathbf{w}_k\eta\frac{\mathbf{r}_p}{r^2},$$

and its derivative with respect to $\mathbf{r}_m$ is computed from the chain rule by

$$B_{l,m} = \varepsilon_{kpl}\mathbf{w}_k\left[\eta\frac{\partial}{\partial \mathbf{r}_m}\left(\frac{\mathbf{r}_p}{r^2}\right) + \left(\frac{\partial\eta}{\partial \mathbf{r}_m}\right)\frac{\mathbf{r}_p}{r^2}\right].$$

Here, we have

$$\frac{\partial}{\partial \mathbf{r}_m}\left(\frac{\mathbf{r}_p}{r^2}\right) = \frac{\delta_{pm}r^2 - 2\mathbf{r}_p \mathbf{r}_m}{r^4}, \quad \frac{\partial\eta}{\partial \mathbf{r}_m} = \frac{r^2 - \langle \mathbf{w}, \mathbf{r}\rangle^2 + 2\langle \mathbf{w}, \mathbf{r}\rangle^2 \ln\langle \mathbf{w}, \mathbf{u}\rangle}{\left(r^2 - \langle \mathbf{w}, \mathbf{r}\rangle^2\right)^2}\left[\frac{r^2 \mathbf{w}_m}{\langle \mathbf{w}, \mathbf{r}\rangle} - \mathbf{r}_m\right].$$

After simplification, we attain

$$\varepsilon_{qml}\varepsilon_{kpl}\mathbf{w}_k\eta\frac{\partial}{\partial \mathbf{r}_m}\left(\frac{\mathbf{r}_p}{r^2}\right) = \frac{\mathbf{r}_q}{r^3}\left[2\eta\langle \mathbf{w}, \mathbf{u}\rangle\right],$$

$$\varepsilon_{qml}\varepsilon_{kpl}\mathbf{w}_k\left(\frac{\partial\eta}{\partial \mathbf{r}_m}\right)\frac{\mathbf{r}_p}{r^2} = -\frac{\mathbf{r}_q}{r^3}\left[\frac{1}{\langle \mathbf{w}, \mathbf{u}\rangle} + 2\eta\langle \mathbf{w}, \mathbf{u}\rangle\right].$$

Equation (9) then follows easily by representing the right hand side of equation (36) in terms of solid angle $d\sigma(\mathbf{u})$, as shown in the previous derivation.

References

1. James Arvo. *Analytic Methods for Simulated Light Transport*. PhD thesis, Yale University, December 1995.
2. James Arvo. Applications of irradiance tensors to the simulation of non-Lambertian phenomena. In *Computer Graphics* Proceedings, Annual Conference Series, ACM SIGGRAPH, pages 335–342, August 1995.
3. Daniel R. Baum, Holly E. Rushmeier, and James M. Winget. Improving radiosity solutions through the use of analytically determined form-factors. *Computer Graphics*, 23(3):325–334, July 1989.
4. Marcel Berger. *Geometry*, volume 2. Springer-Verlag, New York, 1987. Translated by M. Cole and S. Levy.
5. Min Chen. *Mathematical Methods for Image Synthesis*. PhD thesis, California Institute of Technology, June 2001. http://www.cs.caltech.edu/~chen/papers/thesis/phd_thesis.ps.gz.
6. Min Chen and James Arvo. A closed-form solution for the irradiance due to linearly-varying luminaires. In B. Péroche and H. Rushmeier, editors, *Rendering Techniques 2000*. Springer-Verlag, New York, 2000.
7. Thomas H. Cormen, Charles E. Leiserson, and Ronald L. Rivest. *Introduction to Algorithms*. McGraw-Hill, New York, 1990.
8. David L. DiLaura. Non-diffuse radiative transfer 3: Inhomogeneous planar area sources and point receivers. *Journal of the Illuminating Engineering Society*, 26(1), 1997.
9. Nicholas Holzschuch and Franccois X. Sillion. Accurate computation of the radiosity gradient for constant and linear emitters. In *Proceedings of the Sixth Eurographics Workshop on Rendering*, Dublin, Eire, June 1995.
10. John R. Howell. *A Catalog of Radiation Configuration Factors*. McGraw-Hill, New York, 1982.
11. Leonard Lewin. *Dilogarithms and associated functions*. Macdonald, London, 1958.
12. Bui Tuong Phong. Illumination for computer generated pictures. *Communications of the ACM*, 18(6):311–317, June 1975.
13. Mark C. Reichert. A two-pass radiosity method driven by lights and viewer position. Master's thesis, Cornell University, January 1992.
14. M. Schreiber. *Differential Forms: A Heuristic Introduction*. Springer-Verlag, New York, 1984.
15. Peter Schröder and Pat Hanrahan. On the form factor between two polygons. In *Computer Graphics* Proceedings, Annual Conference Series, ACM SIGGRAPH, pages 163–164, August 1993.
16. Michael Spivak. *Calculus on Manifolds*. Benjamin/Cummings, Reading, Massachusetts, 1965.
17. Michael M. Stark and Richard F. Riesenfeld. Exact illumination in polygonal environments using vertex tracing. In B. Péroche and H. Rushmeier, editors, *Rendering Techniques 2000*. Springer-Verlag, New York, 2000.

Editors' Note: see Appendix, p. 323 for colored figures of this paper

An Illumination Model for a Skin Layer Bounded by Rough Surfaces

Jos Stam

Alias | wavefront
1218 Third Ave, 8th Floor,
Seattle, WA 98101

Abstract.
In this paper we present a novel illumination model that takes into account multiple anisotropic scattering in a layer bounded by two rough surfaces. We compute the model by a discrete-ordinate solution of the equation of radiative transfer. This approach is orders of magnitude faster than a Monte Carlo simulation and does not suffer from any noisy artifacts. By fitting low order splines to our results we are able to build analytical shaders. This is highly desirable since animators typically want to texture map the parameters of such a shader for higher realism. We apply our model to the important problem of rendering human skin. Our model does not seem to have appeared before in the optics literature. Most previous models did not handle rough surfaces at the skin's boundary. Also we introduce a simple analytical bidirectional transmittance distribution function (BTDF) for an isotropic rough surface by generalizing the Cook-Torrance model.

1 Introduction

This work was motivated by the desire to model the appearance of human skin. A good skin model has many obvious applications, notably in the entertainment industry, where virtual actors have to appear more life-like. Despite its importance this problem has only been marginally addressed in computer graphics. Traditional reflection models usually model the effects of subsurface scattering using a combination of a Lambert cosine term and an ambient term. Creating convincing pictures of human skin with these models is an art entirely left to the animator.

In this paper we propose a novel reflection model for a skin layer bounded by rough surfaces. Our model incorporates multiple anisotropic scattering within the skin layer. The only other model in computer graphics that is related to ours is the one proposed by Hanrahan and Krueger [5]. Their analytical model only handles skin layers bounded by perfectly smooth surfaces and they only account for single scattering. To handle multiple-scattering they use a Monte-Carlo simulation to precompute the distribution. In our experience the Monte Carlo method is too expensive to perform for all combinations of the values of the skin layer's parameters. Recently, Pharr and Hanrahan propose a generalization of the BRDF which takes into account volumetric scattering [18]. However, their technique still relies on an expensive Monte-Carlo simulation. This problem is adressed in recent work by Jensen et al. who use a diffusion approximation of the equation of radiative transfer to derive an analytical approximation for the reflection of light from a skin layer [8].

At first we expected to find an "off the shelf" solution from one of the related engineering fields. One such field, the medical sciences, studies the optics of skin for such applications as non-invasive surgery [23, 24]. Most research there either uses the

Monte Carlo method or a technique known as adding-doubling borrowed from the astronomy literature [20, 6]. Unfortunately, both techniques are too expensive for our purposes. Next we turned to the atmospheric sciences, where the reflection from the ocean is very close to that from a skin layer. There we found a very attractive model based on the discrete ordinate approximation of radiative transfer [3]. In particular, the work of Stamnes et al. solves the problem for a skin layer bounded by smooth surfaces [9, 21]. To handle rough surfaces the Monte Carlo is used [15]. We briefly mention that the discrete ordinate technique has been used in global illumination before [10, 12, 14].

Based on this extensive bibliographical search, we decided to extend Jin and Stamnes work to include rough surfaces. For this we first needed a good Bidirectional Transmittance Distribution Function (BTDF) model. We are aware of only one such model in computer graphics based on the wave theory of light [7]. Unfortunately this model is fairly complex, so we derive a simpler one in this paper for the first time. Our model is an extension of the BRDFs of Cook-Torrance [4] and of van Ginneken et al. [25]. Given the BRDF and the BTDF of the surfaces and the optical properties of skin we show how to efficiently solve the problem by a suitable "diagonalization" of the "transfer matrix." We use the machinery of Fourier transforms and eigenanalysis to perform this task. To build practical reflection models for computer graphics, we fit low-order splines to our discretized functions. Our approach is orders of magnitude faster than Monte Carlo methods, requires less memory, and does not suffer from any noisy artifacts.

The rest of the paper is organized as follows. The next section details the physics involved and introduces the equivalent discrete problem. In Section 3 we show how to solve the discrete problem efficiently. Section 4 presents a derivation of our BTDF. Section 5 clarifies many implementation issues and discusses the corresponding "skin shader". In Section 6 we present some results, while in Section 7 we conclude and discuss future research. Material of a rather technical nature is addressed in the appendices.

1.1 Notational Preliminaries

Much of the material in this paper can be presented more elegantly using a "matrix operator approach" [19]. Many relations are expressed more compactly without indices in vector and matrix form. In this paper all vectors are denoted by bold lowercase characters: $\mathbf{v}$. The elements of $\mathbf{v}$ are denoted by the corresponding italicized letter: v_i is the i-th component of $\mathbf{v}$. An element of a vector should not be confused with an indexed vector such as $\mathbf{v}_k$. A matrix is denoted by a bold upper case character such as $\mathbf{M}$ and its elements are denoted by $M_{i,j}$. The transpose of $\mathbf{M}$ is written $\mathbf{M}^T$.

2 Discretizing the Physics

2.1 Physical parameters

The basic physical quantity is the radiance u, which gives the amount of radiant power flowing from a particular position in a particular direction. Following Hanrahan and Krueger [5] we assume that the skin depth is along the z-direction and that the skin's properties are uniform in each xy-plane. We use the dimensionless optical depth $\tau = z/L$ instead of z, where L is the mean free path of a photon in the medium. Consequently, the radiance is a function of optical depth and direction. We represent a direction by an ordered pair $\pm\omega = (\pm\mu, \phi)$ where $\mu = \cos\theta$ is the cosine of the elevation angle θ and ϕ is the azimuthal angle (see Figure 1 (left)). In the following we always assume that the cosine $\mu \geq 0$. We therefore denote a downward direction by $-\omega = (-\mu, \phi)$. The use of the minus sign is purely notational in this context.

Fig. 1. Definition of a direction $\omega = (\mu, \phi)$ (left) and solid angles involved in a computing the reflection and refraction (right).

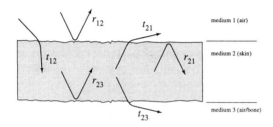

Fig. 2. Nomenclature for the BRDFs and BTDFs.

The optical properties of the skin are entirely modeled by its albedo Ω and its phase function p. The albedo gives the fraction of light that is scattered versus absorbed, while the phase function gives the probability that a photon travelling in a direction ω' is scattered in another direction ω. We rely on the *Henyey-Greenstein phase function*, a useful model frequently seen in the optics literature:

$$p(\omega', \omega) = \frac{1 - g^2}{(1 + g^2 - 2g \cos \gamma)^{3/2}}.$$

Here γ is the angle between the directions ω' and ω. The anisotropy factor $g \in [0, 1]$ models how much light is scattered forward. We associate with the phase function a linear scattering functional:

$$\mathcal{S}\{u\}(\tau, \omega) = \frac{\Omega}{4\pi} \int_{4\pi} p(\omega', \omega) u(\tau, \omega') \, d\omega', \tag{1}$$

where the integration is over all possible directions.

The reflection and refraction at the skin's boundaries are modeled as isotropic rough surfaces. In our model we assume that the skin has a uniform index of refraction n_2 and is bounded above and below by media having indices equal to n_1 and n_3, respectively. Both the transmission and reflection models depend on a roughness parameter σ. The BRDF and BTDF are denoted by $r_{ij}(\omega, \omega')$ and $t_{ij}(\omega, \omega')$, respectively, for light coming from material $i \in 1, 2, 3$ arriving at material $j \in 1, 2, 3$, where, for example, r_{12} models the reflection off of the top surface. This nomenclature is clarified in Figure 2. We associate with these distributions linear reflection and transmission operators:

$$\mathcal{R}_{ij}\{u\}(\tau, \pm\omega) = \int_{2\pi} r_{ij}(\mp\omega', \pm\omega) u(\tau, \mp\omega') \mu' \, d\omega', \tag{2}$$

$$\mathcal{T}_{ij}\{u\}(\tau, \pm\omega) \quad = \quad \int_{2\pi} t_{ij}(\pm\omega', \pm\omega)u(\tau, \pm\omega')\mu' \, d\omega', \tag{3}$$

where the integration is over the positive hemisphere and the signs depend on the BRDF or BTDF considered, e.g., r_{12} has opposite signs from r_{21} as is evident from Figure 2.

2.2 Equation of Transfer

An equation for the radiance within the skin is obtained by considering its variation in an infinitesimal cylinder aligned with the direction ω. The change is equal to the amount of light scattered into this direction minus the light absorbed and scattered out of this direction:

$$-\mu\frac{du}{d\tau} = -u + \mathcal{S}\{u\}, \tag{4}$$

where $\mathcal{S}$ is the scattering operator defined in Equation 1. To completely specify the problem, this equation requires boundary conditions at the top and the bottom of the skin layer. At the skin's surface ($\tau = 0$) the downwelling radiance is equal to the transmitted radiance plus the internal reflections of the radiance coming from the internal layer:

$$u(0, -\omega) = t_{12}(-\omega_0, -\omega) + \mathcal{R}_{21}\{u\}(0, -\omega). \tag{5}$$

Similarly, if we assume there are no sources below the skin, the upwelling radiance at the bottom of the layer ($\tau = \tau_b$) is given by

$$u(\tau_b, \omega) = \mathcal{R}_{23}\{u\}(\tau_b, \omega). \tag{6}$$

Once Equation 4 is solved using these boundary conditions, the BRDF and the BTDF due to scattering in the skin's layer are equal to

$$r_s(-\omega_0, \omega) = \mathcal{T}_{21}\{u\}(0, \omega)/\mu_0 \quad \text{and} \quad t_s(-\omega_0, -\omega) = \mathcal{T}_{23}\{u\}(\tau_b, -\omega)/\mu_0,$$

respectively. In addition, the reflection due to an ambient light source of radiance is modeled by integrating the skin's BRDF over all incident directions $-\omega_0$:

$$r_a(\omega) = \int_{2\pi} r_s(-\omega_0, \omega) \, \mu_0 \, d\mu_0.$$

The total amount of light reflected off the skin is the sum of the part directly reflected by the surface, the ambient term and the radiance leaving the subsurface layer:

$$r_{tot}(\omega) = r_{12}(-\omega_0, \omega) + r_a(\omega) + r_s(-\omega_0, \omega).$$

In Section 4 we provide a model for r_{12} (and the other r_{ij} and t_{ij}) while the next section describes a method of solution for r_s and t_s.

2.3 Angular Discretization

We discretize the angular part of Equation 4 in two steps. Because we assume that the surface roughness is isotropic and that the skin is horizontally uniform, we can decompose the azimuthal dependence of the radiance into a cosine series:

$$u(\tau, \omega) = \sum_{k=0}^{N} u_k(\tau, \mu) \cos k(\phi - \phi_0). \tag{7}$$

Next we discretize the cosines μ into $2M$ discrete samples (see Appendix A for how they are chosen):

$$\mu_1, \mu_2, \cdots, \mu_M, -\mu_1, -\mu_2, \cdots, -\mu_M. \tag{8}$$

These values are also known as "ordinates," hence the name "discrete-ordinates" to refer to this type of discretization. The corresponding values of the discretized radiances are stored in a $2M$ vector

$$\mathbf{u}_k(\tau) = (u_k(\tau, \mu_1), \cdots, u_k(\tau, -\mu_M))^T \quad k = 0, \cdots, N.$$

As shown in Appendix A, the scattering operator in Equation 4 is discretized into a collection of $N+1$ matrices $\mathbf{S}_k$ ($k = 0, \cdots, N$), each of size $2M \times 2M$. These discretizations convert the transfer equation into $N+1$ decoupled linear ordinary differential vector equations:

$$-\mathbf{W}\frac{d\mathbf{u}_k(\tau)}{d\tau} = -\mathbf{u}_k(\tau) + \mathbf{S}_k\mathbf{u}_k(\tau),$$

where $\mathbf{W}$ is a diagonal matrix containing the samples of Equation 8. The last equation can be written more compactly as

$$\frac{d\mathbf{u}_k(\tau)}{d\tau} = \mathbf{M}_k\mathbf{u}_k(\tau), \tag{9}$$

where $\mathbf{M}_k = \mathbf{W}^{-1}(\mathbf{I} - \mathbf{S}_k)$ and $\mathbf{I}$ is the identity matrix. Equation 9 is the main equation of this paper. In the next section we show how to solve it efficiently.

3 Direct Solution of the Discrete Problem

This section is inspired by the work of Jin and Stamnes [9]. However, our compact vector/matrix notation greatly simplifies the presentation. Our approach is also more general, since we consider surfaces of arbitrary roughness at the boundaries.

3.1 Diagonalization

We assume that the skin is composed of a layer with constant optical properties sandwiched between two isotropic rough surfaces. In order to simplify the notation in this section, we will drop the dependence of all quantities on the index "k". This is justified because the equations for different terms in the cosine expansion are entirely decoupled. In the skin the radiance satisfies the following equation:

$$\frac{d\mathbf{u}(\tau)}{d\tau} = \mathbf{M}\mathbf{u}(\tau).$$

Ignoring the boundary conditions for the moment, we see that this is a homogeneous vector ordinary differential equation. Such an equation is solved efficiently by putting the matrix $\mathbf{M}$ into diagonal form. Indeed, in diagonal form the equations are decoupled and can be solved analytically. Diagonalizing $\mathbf{M}$ is equivalent to computing its eigenvalues and eigenvectors: $\mathbf{M} = \mathbf{V}\mathbf{L}\mathbf{V}^{-1}$. Here $\mathbf{L}$ is a diagonal matrix containing the eigenvalues of $\mathbf{M}$:

$$\mathbf{L} = \text{diag}(\lambda_1, \cdots, \lambda_M, -\lambda_1, \cdots, -\lambda_M)$$

where $\lambda_i > 0$ for $i = 1, \cdots, M$ and $\mathbf{V}$ contains the eigenvectors stored columnwise. If we let $\mathbf{w}(\tau)$ be the transformed radiance $\mathbf{w} = \mathbf{V}^{-1}\mathbf{u}$, then

$$\frac{d\mathbf{w}(\tau)}{d\tau} = \mathbf{L}\mathbf{w}(\tau).$$

The exact solution to this differential equation is given by:

$$\mathbf{w}(\tau) = e^{\mathbf{L}\tau}\mathbf{u}_0,$$
(10)

where the exponential is simply the diagonal matrix whose elements are the exponential of the elements of $\mathbf{L}\tau$. The vector $\mathbf{u}_0$ in Equation 10 is to be determined from the boundary conditions. The radiance in the layer is then obtained by inverting our earlier transformation:

$$\mathbf{u}(\tau) = \mathbf{V}\mathbf{w}(\tau) = \mathbf{V}e^{\mathbf{L}\tau}\mathbf{u}_0.$$
(11)

Our next step is to find a vector $\mathbf{u}_0$ satisfying the boundary conditions.

3.2 Solving the Discrete Problem: Boundary conditions

We have just shown that the radiance in each layer can be solved for directly in terms of the eigenvectors and eigenvalues of the transfer matrix. We can rewrite Equation 11 separating the parts corresponding to upward and downward directions:

$$\left(\begin{array}{c} \mathbf{u}^+(\tau) \\ \mathbf{u}^-(\tau) \end{array} \right) = \left(\begin{array}{cc} \mathbf{V}^+ & \mathbf{V}^- \\ \mathbf{V}^- & \mathbf{V}^+ \end{array} \right) \left(\begin{array}{c} \mathbf{E}(\tau)\mathbf{u}_0^+ \\ \mathbf{E}(-\tau)\mathbf{u}_0^- \end{array} \right),$$
(12)

where each of the matrices $\mathbf{E}(t) = e^{\mathbf{L}^+ t}$ contains half of the exponentials. The goal in this section is to compute the unknown vectors $\mathbf{u}_0^+$ and $\mathbf{u}_0^-$ given by Equations 5 and 6. First, let $\mathbf{R}_{ij}$ and $\mathbf{T}_{ij}$ denote the discrete versions of $\mathcal{R}_{ij}$ and $\mathcal{T}_{ij}$ respectively. Since they are defined only over the positive hemisphere they are of size $M \times M$. The top and bottom boundary conditions in terms of these matrices are

$$\mathbf{u}^-(0) = \mathbf{T}_{12}\mathbf{d}_0 + \mathbf{R}_{21}\mathbf{u}^+(0) \quad \text{and}$$
(13)

$$\mathbf{u}^+(\tau_b) = \mathbf{R}_{23}\mathbf{u}^-(\tau_b).$$
(14)

The vector $\mathbf{d}_0$ represents the incident radiances, and for a directional light source is zero for each entry except for the entry corresponding to $-\mu_0$ where it is equal to one. By substituting Equations 13 and 14 into Equation 12 and rearranging,

$$\left(\begin{array}{cc} \mathbf{V}^- - \mathbf{R}_{21}\mathbf{V}^+ & \mathbf{V}^+ - \mathbf{R}_{21}\mathbf{V}^- \\ (\mathbf{V}^+ - \mathbf{R}_{23}\mathbf{V}^-)\mathbf{E}(\tau_b) & (\mathbf{V}^- - \mathbf{R}_{23}\mathbf{V}^+)\mathbf{E}(-\tau_b) \end{array} \right) \left(\begin{array}{c} \mathbf{u}_0^+ \\ \mathbf{u}_0^- \end{array} \right) = \left(\begin{array}{c} \mathbf{T}_{12}\mathbf{d}_0 \\ \mathbf{0} \end{array} \right).$$

This system, however, is ill-conditioned because the matrix $\mathbf{E}(\tau_b)$ has entries that grow exponentially with τ_b. Fortunately, we can easily fix this problem by setting $\mathbf{u}_0^+ = \mathbf{E}(-\tau_b)\tilde{\mathbf{u}}_0^+$ and solving for $(\tilde{\mathbf{u}}_0^+, \mathbf{u}_0^-)$ instead [21]. The new system becomes:

$$\left(\begin{array}{cc} (\mathbf{V}^- - \mathbf{R}_{21}\mathbf{V}^+)\mathbf{E}(-\tau_b) & \mathbf{V}^+ - \mathbf{R}_{21}\mathbf{V}^- \\ \mathbf{V}^+ - \mathbf{R}_{23}\mathbf{V}^- & (\mathbf{V}^- - \mathbf{R}_{23}\mathbf{V}^+)\mathbf{E}(-\tau_b) \end{array} \right) \left(\begin{array}{c} \tilde{\mathbf{u}}_0^+ \\ \mathbf{u}_0^- \end{array} \right) = \left(\begin{array}{c} \mathbf{T}_{12}\mathbf{d}_0 \\ \mathbf{0} \end{array} \right).$$
(15)

This linear system is well behaved and can be solved using any standard linear solver. Once the solution is obtained, the upward radiance at the top and the downward radiance at the bottom of the layer are given by:

$$\mathbf{u}^+(0) = \mathbf{V}^+\mathbf{E}(-\tau_b)\tilde{\mathbf{u}}_0^+ + \mathbf{V}^-\mathbf{u}_0^- \quad \text{and} \quad \mathbf{u}^-(\tau_b) = \mathbf{V}^-\tilde{\mathbf{u}}_0^+ + \mathbf{V}^+\mathbf{E}(-\tau_b)\mathbf{u}_0^-,$$

respectively. These are the radiances just inside the rough surfaces of the skin layer. To compute the radiances exiting the surface, we have to multiply these radiances by the transmission matrices $\mathbf{T}_{21}$ and $\mathbf{T}_{23}$, respectively:

$$\mathbf{u}_r = \mathbf{T}_{21}\mathbf{u}^+(0) \quad \text{and} \quad \mathbf{u}_t = \mathbf{T}_{23}\mathbf{u}^-(\tau_b).$$
(16)

ComputeRT:
  For $k = 0, \cdots, N$ do
    Compute the scattering matrix $\mathbf{M}_k$ (Appendix A)
    Compute the reflection and transmission matrices $\mathbf{R}_{ij}$ and $\mathbf{T}_{ij}$ (Appendix D)
    Compute eigenstructure of $\mathbf{M}_k$
    For $i = 1, \cdots, M$
      Solve linear system for incoming direction μ_i (Equation 15)
      Transmit radiances out of the layer (Equation 16)
      Set the i-th columns of $\mathbf{R}_k$ and $\mathbf{T}_k$
    next
  next

Fig. 3. Summary of our algorithm.

3.3 Summary

First we restore the subscript "k" to indicate that the radiances of Equation 16 correspond to a single term in the cosine series. Consequently, the complete description of the radiances is given by the following vectors

$$\mathbf{u}_{r,0}, \cdots, \mathbf{u}_{r,N} \quad \text{and} \quad \mathbf{u}_{t,0}, \cdots, \mathbf{u}_{t,N}.$$

These radiances are for a particular incoming direction $-\omega_0 = (-\mu_0, 0)$. To get a discrete description of the BRDF r_s of the skin layer we sample the incoming directions at the ordinates $\mu_1, \cdots, \mu_M$. The discrete representation of the BRDF is, therefore, a collection of $N + 1$ matrices $\mathbf{R}_k$ of size $M \times M$ ($k = 0, \cdots, N$). The i-th column of this matrix consists of the vector $\mathbf{u}_{r,k}$ computed for the incident direction $(-\mu_i, 0)$, $i = 1, \cdots, M$. In a similar fashion we build a set of matrices $\mathbf{T}_k$ for the BTDF t_s of the skin layer ($k = 0, \cdots, N$). A high level description of the algorithm that computes these matrices is given in Figure 3.

We have precomputed these matrices for different values of the parameters that model the skin layer. These parameters are the transparency $T = e^{-\tau b}$, the albedo Ω, the anisotropy factor g of the phase function, and the roughness σ of the surfaces bounding the skin layer. Each parameter is dimensionless and takes on values between zero and one. The ratio of the indices of refraction is kept constant throughout: it is set to 1.4, roughly that of human skin. The number of ordinates M was determined from the discretizations of the BRDF and the BTDF of the skin's surface (derived in the next section). For a roughness $\sigma = 0.1$ we neededed $M = 30$ ordinates while for other values $M = 24$ was sufficient. The number of cosine series is always set to twice the number of ordinates: $N = 2M$ [9].

Because the scattering matrix depends only on Ω and g, we first computed the eigenstructures for a set of values of the parameters. We used the RG routine from EISPACK [17] to compute the eigenvectors and eigenvalues. We encountered no numerical problems except when the albedo was exactly one. An easy fix is simply to set the albedo to a value almost equal to one, i.e., $\Omega = 0.999999$. Once the eigenstructures were available we used them to precompute the reflection r_s and transmission t_s of the skin layer. We used the routine DGESL from LINPACK to solve the linear system of Equation 15.

The precomputation generates a huge data set. Our next task was to compress the data using well chosen approximations. We first experimented with the elegant non-linear representation of Lafortune et al. [11]. We did get some good matches using three cosine lobes. However, in many cases the non-linear least square solver got stuck

46

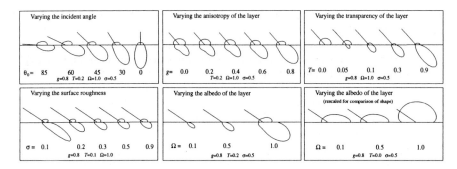

Fig. 4. Cross-sections of the reflection and transmission functions of the skin layer for different values of the parameters.

in local minima. For these reasons we adopted a less efficient but more straightforward compression scheme. First, not all cosine terms need to be included. For the reflection at the top of the layer we found that in general, 5 terms ($N = 4$) were sufficient, while for the transmission at the bottom 15 ($N = 14$) terms were required. These numbers were obtained by visually comparing the data to the approximation. We further compressed the data by fitting a cubic Bezier surface to the data stored in the reflection (resp. transmission) matrix $\mathbf{R}_k$ (resp. $\mathbf{T}_k$). We constrained the control vertices to respect the symmetry of these matrices (Helmholtz reciprocity).

In Figure 4 we demonstrate the effect of our parameters on the reflection and transmission functions. The simple shapes of the lobes first led us to believe that they might be modeled by simple analytical expressions. The variation with each parameter is, however, quite subtle and none of our analytical estimations could handle all variations at the same time. Analytical solutions are rare when multiple scattering is included. Even the simplest case of a semi-infinite constant medium with isotropic scattering does not admit an analytical solution [3]. The distributions are clearly different from a simple constant Lambert term. The simple analytical model of Hanrahan and Krueger is recovered for low albedos and smooth surfaces.

4 Reflection and Refraction from Rough Surfaces

The derivation of our BRDF and BTDF models follows the work of van Ginneken et al. [25]. We assume that our surface is an isotropic gaussian random height field [1]. The probability that a normal ω_a lies within an infinitesimal solid angle $d\omega_a = (d(\cos\theta_a), d\phi_a)$ is given by the Beckmann function [1]:

$$P(\omega_a)\, d\omega_a = \frac{1}{2\pi\sigma^2\cos^3\theta_a} \exp\left(-\frac{\tan^2\theta_a}{2\sigma^2}\right) d\omega_a, \tag{17}$$

where σ is the RMS slope of the surface. Let the surface be illuminated by a directional source of irradiance E_0 of direction $\omega_0 = (\cos\theta_0, \phi_0)$. For each direction ω_r, resp. ω_t, there is a unique normal ω_a that will reflect (resp. refract) the incoming light in the direction ω_r (resp. ω_t).

The incoming power at a surface element dA with normal ω_a is equal to:

$$\Phi_0 = E_0 \cos\theta_0'\, dA,$$

where $\cos \theta'_0$ is the cosine of the angle between the normal and the incoming direction. The amount of power that is reflected and refracted is determined by the Fresnel factor $F(\cos \theta'_0, \eta)$ [2], where η is the ratio of indices of refraction. Indeed, a fraction F of the power is reflected while a portion $(1 - F)$ is refracted. To get the total radiance reflected into direction ω_r, we multiply the radiance reflected by a point of the surface with normal ω_a by the Beckmann probability function defined in Equation 17:

$$u_r = \frac{F \, E_0 \, \cos \theta'_0 \, P(\omega_a) \, d\omega_a}{\cos \theta_r d\omega_r}.$$

The solid angles $d\omega_r$ and $d\omega_a$ are not independent. This can be understood intuitively: by varying the normal in the cone $d\omega_a$ we get a corresponding variation around the reflected direction ω_r. The size of this variation is exactly the factor which relates the two solid angles. The precise relation between them was cited by Torrance and Sparrow [22]:

$$d\omega_r = 4 \cos \theta'_0 \, d\omega_a.$$

Nayar provides an elegant geometric proof of this result [16]. In Appendix B we give an alternative proof which easily generalizes to the case of refraction to be discussed below. Consequently, our BRDF is:

$$r = \frac{F(\cos \theta'_0, \eta) \, P(\omega_a)}{4 \, \cos \theta_r \, \cos \theta_0}.$$

We now derive the BTDF in a similar fashion. As in the reflected case, the total radiance refracted into a direction ω_t is given by:

$$u_t = \frac{(1 - F) \, E_0 \, \cos \theta'_0 \, P(\omega_a) \, d\omega_a}{\cos \theta_t \, d\omega_t}.$$

The relation between the solid angles $d\omega_t$ and $d\omega_a$ is, however, very different. At first we did not pay too much attention to this relationship and simply assumed $d\omega_a = d\omega_t$. But when we compared our analytical model with a Monte Carlo simulation for validation, we found large discrepancies. Finally, after a careful analysis of other BRDF derivations [4, 25] we realized the importance of this relation. In Appendix B we prove that:

$$d\omega_t = \frac{(\cos \theta'_0 - \mu_t)^2}{\eta \mu_t} \, d\omega_a = G(\cos \theta'_0, \eta) \, \cos \theta'_0 \, d\omega_a,$$

where $\mu_t = \sqrt{\cos \theta'_0 + \eta^2 - 1}$. With this factor our BTDF is:

$$t = \frac{(1 - F(\cos \theta'_0, \eta)) \, P(\omega_a)}{\cos \theta_t \cos \theta_0 \, G(\cos \theta'_0, \eta)}.$$

We also multiply this function by the shadowing function proposed by van Ginneken et al. [25]. We prefer this shadowing function over the one used by Cook and Torrance [4] since it is consistent with the underlying model for the surface.

The BRDF and the BTDF are shown for different ratios of indices of refraction η and roughness values σ in Figure 5. The top figure corresponds to a ratio $\eta = 1.4$ which is that of skin. These plots correspond to the functions r_{12}, t_{12}, r_{21} and t_{21} of our skin model. As mentioned above we have validated our derivation using a Monte Carlo simulation. Whether this provides a good model for rough surfaces will have to be settled by experiment. At least, Cook and Torrance reported good agreement with experiment for the function r_{12} [4].

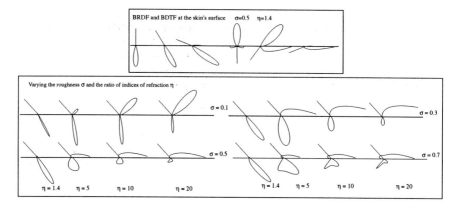

Fig. 5. Our new BRDFs and BTDFs for a rough surface. The distributions are rescaled to fit in the figure.

5   The Skin Shader

We have implemented our reflection model as a shader plugin in our animation software MAYA. The plugin is available for free on our company's web page[1]. The web page also provides more information on the parameters of our skin shader. Several of our customers have recently started to use our shader in production with good results.

Figure 6 shows several examples of human heads rendered using our new skin shader. Figure 6.(a) compares our model (right) to a Lambert shader (left) and the Hanrahan-Krueger (HK) model (center). Our model seems to be a blend between these two models, which is consistent with the plots in Figure 4. Unfortunately, the comparison is necessarily very vague. Indeed, we manually tried to find a set of parameters for both the Lambert shader and the HK model which was as close as possible to our results. In particular, we had to "brighten up" the HK model since it assumes single-scattering. Figure 6.(b) shows our model illuminated by different area light sources. Notice also that we texture mapped both the albedo and the roughness of the lips. Figure 6.(c) is similar for a male head. Finally 6.(d) demonstrates another application of our shader (notice that the surfaces have been bump mapped).

6   Conclusions and Future Work

This paper presented a novel analytical model for the reflection and transmission of light from a skin layer bounded by rough surfaces. The model includes the effects of multiple anisotropic scattering within the skin. To the best of our knowledge a model of this generality has not appeared before in the optics literature.

Our model currently lacks any form of experimental validation. The differences between our model and a simple Lambert shader are not as dramatic as we had expected. The difference is, however, noticeable. We hope to compare our model to the Cornell data [13] and possibly to other data sets from other related disciplines. Also we hope to find a better compression scheme for our computed data, most likely a simple analytical model with a few parameters which can be fit using a non-linear optimization technique.

---

[1] `http://www.aliaswavefront.com` by following "community" and "Download".

Acknowledgments

I would like to thank both Eric Stollnitz and Pamela Jackson for carefully proofreading the paper. Thanks also to Dick Rice for helping me derive a key equation.

A Details: Angular Discretization

In this appendix we provide the missing details of Section 2.3 that lead to explicit expressions for the matrices $\mathbf{M}_k$.

First, we expand the phase function into a cosine series as well:

$$p(\omega', \omega) = \sum_{k=0}^{N} p_k(\mu', \mu) \cos k(\phi - \phi'), \tag{18}$$

where the p_k are functions of the anisotropy factor g and the associated Legendre functions as shown in Appendix C. If we substitute Equations 7 and 18 into Eq. 4 we get the following $N + 1$ equations ($k = 0, \cdots, N$):

$$\mu \frac{d}{d\tau} u_k(\mu) = u_k(\mu) - \Omega_k \int_{-1}^{+1} p_k(\mu', \mu) \, u_k(\mu') \, d\mu', \tag{19}$$

where $\Omega_k = \Omega \frac{(1+\delta_{0,k})}{4}$ and $\delta_{i,j}$ is the Kronecker symbol. We now discretize the problem further by approximating the integrals in Equations 19 using a quadrature:

$$\int_{-1}^{+1} f(\mu') \, d\mu' \approx \sum_{m=1}^{M} w_m \{f(-\mu_m) + f(\mu_m)\},$$

where w_m are the weights and $\mu_m \geq 0$ are the ordinates of the quadrature. With this approximation Equation 19 becomes a set of linear equations:

$$\mu_n \frac{d}{d\tau} u_k(\mu_n) = u_k(\mu_n) - \Omega_k \sum_{m=1}^{M} w_m \left\{ p_k(-\mu_m, \mu_n) u_k(-\mu_m) + p_k(\mu_m, \mu_n) u_k(\mu_m) \right\}$$

$$-\mu_n \frac{d}{d\tau} u_k(-\mu_n) = u_k(-\mu_n) - \Omega_k \sum_{m=1}^{M} w_m \left\{ p_k(-\mu_m, -\mu_n) u_k(-\mu_m) + p_k(\mu_m, -\mu_n) u_k(\mu_m) \right\}.$$

Since $p_k(-\mu_m, \mu_n) = p_k(\mu_m, -\mu_n)$ and $p_k(\mu_m, \mu_n) = p_k(-\mu_m, -\mu_n)$ we introduce the following two $M \times M$ matrices:

$$(A_k)_{n,m} = (\Omega_k w_m p_k(\mu_m, \mu_n) - \delta_{n,m}) / \mu_n \quad \text{and}$$
$$(B_k)_{n,m} = \Omega_k w_m p_k(-\mu_m, \mu_n) / \mu_n.$$

Consequently, recalling the vector notations introduced in Section 2.3.

$$\mathbf{M}_k = \begin{pmatrix} -\mathbf{A}_k & -\mathbf{B}_k \\ \mathbf{B}_k & \mathbf{A}_k \end{pmatrix}.$$

B Relating $d\omega$ to $d\omega_a$

Computing the relationship between the two differentials $d\omega_a$ and $d\omega$ is mathematically equivalent to computing the Jacobian of the change of coordinates $\omega_a \to \omega$. In this appendix we compute the Jacobians for both the reflected and the refracted solid angles. We compute the change of coordinates in three steps:

$$\omega_a \longrightarrow (x_a, y_a) \longrightarrow (x, y) \longrightarrow \omega.$$

The relation between the spherical and cartesian coordinates is well known and given by

$$dx_a \, dy_a = \mu_a \, d\omega_a \quad \text{and} \quad dx \, dy = \mu \, d\omega.$$

Following the approach of Nayar et al. [16] we assume without loss of generality that the solid angle of the normal $d\omega_a$ is centered along the normal $(0, 0, 1)$. We also assume that the source is coming from the direction $(\mu_0, 0)$, or in cartesian coordinates $\mathbf{v}_0 = (\sqrt{1 - \mu_0^2}, 0, \mu_0)$. See Figure 1 (right). Let

$$\mathbf{n}(x_a, y_a) = (x_a, y_a, \sqrt{1 - x_a^2 - y_a^2})$$

be a normal in $dx_a \, dy_a$. Then the reflected and refracted directions are equal to

$$
\begin{aligned}
\mathbf{r} &= 2(\mathbf{n} \cdot \mathbf{v}_0)\mathbf{n} - \mathbf{v}_0 \quad \text{and} \\
\eta \mathbf{t} &= \left(\mathbf{n} \cdot \mathbf{v}_0 - \sqrt{(\mathbf{n} \cdot \mathbf{v}_0)^2 + \eta^2 - 1}\right)\mathbf{n} - \mathbf{v}_0,
\end{aligned}
$$

respectively. The transformation from the normal to the reflected vector corresponds to a change of coordinates $(x_a, y_a) \to (x, y)$, where

$$
\begin{aligned}
x &= 2(\sqrt{1 - \mu_0^2}\, x_a + \mu_0 \sqrt{1 - x_a^2 - y_a^2})x_a - \sqrt{1 - \mu_0^2} \\
y &= 2(\sqrt{1 - \mu_0^2}\, x_a + \mu_0 \sqrt{1 - x_a^2 - y_a^2})y_a.
\end{aligned}
$$

The Jacobian of this change of coordinates at $(x_a, y_a) = (0, 0)$ is easily calculated to be equal to:

$$
J = \begin{vmatrix} \frac{\partial x}{\partial x_a} & \frac{\partial x}{\partial y_a} \\ \frac{\partial y}{\partial x_a} & \frac{\partial y}{\partial y_a} \end{vmatrix} = \begin{vmatrix} 2\,\mu_0 & 0 \\ 0 & 2\,\mu_0 \end{vmatrix} = 4\,\mu_0^2.
$$

Therefore, $\mu_0 d\omega = dx dy = 4\mu_0^2 dx_a dy_a = 4\mu_0^2 d\omega_a$. In other words, $d\omega = 4\mu_0 \, d\omega_a$.

The Jacobian of the change of coordinates corresponding to the refraction at $(0, 0)$ is equal to

$$
\eta^2 J = \begin{vmatrix} \mu_0 - \mu_t & 0 \\ 0 & \mu_0 - \mu_t \end{vmatrix} = (\mu_0 - \mu_t)^2,
$$

where $\mu_t = \sqrt{\mu_0^2 + \eta^2 - 1}$ is the cosine of the refracted direction. Again we have the chain of relations

$$\frac{1}{\eta}\mu_t \, d\omega = dx dy = \frac{1}{\eta^2}(\mu_0 - \mu_t)^2 \, dx_a dy_a = \frac{1}{\eta^2}(\mu_0 - \mu_t)^2 \, d\omega_a.$$

Therefore, $d\omega = (\mu_0^2 - \mu_t)^2 (\eta \mu_t)^{-1} d\omega_a$.

C   Representation of the Phase Function

The Henyey-Greenstein Phase function has the nice property that it can be expanded explicitly in a cosine series given by Equation 18. The coefficients in the expansion are expressed in terms of the associated Legendre functions [3]. This explains why this phase function is so popular in the radiative transfer literature. The expansion follows from the following result [6]:

$$p(\cos\gamma) = \sum_{k=0}^{N} (2k+1)g^k P_k(\cos\gamma),$$

where P_k is the Legendre polynomial of degree k. From a well known relation between the Legendre polynomials and the associated ones[2], we see that the coefficients in the expansion of Equation 18 are given by:

$$p_k(\mu',\mu) = (2-\delta_{0,k}) \sum_{n=k}^{N} (2n+1)g^n \frac{(n-k)!}{(n+k)!} P_n^k(\mu')P_n^k(\mu).$$

D   Discrete Representation of the BRDF and BTDF

Let $\rho(\omega',\omega)$ be one of our BRDFs or BTDFs. We then want to compute the coefficients ρ_k in the cosine series:

$$\rho(\omega',\omega) = \sum_{k=0}^{N} \rho_k(\mu',\mu) \cos k(\phi - \phi').$$

Unlike the phase function in Appendix C, we cannot express these coefficients analytically for the BRDF and BTDF derived in Section 4. For the given set of ordinates $\mu_1, \cdots, \mu_M$ we approximate the integrals:

$$I_k(\mu_n,\mu_m) = \int_0^{2\pi} \rho(\pm\mu_n,0;\pm\mu_m,\phi)\ \cos k\phi\ d\phi,$$

for $k = 0, \cdots, N$ and $n, m = 1, \cdots, M$. The signs in the integrand depend on the BRDF/BTDF being computed. The discrete representation of the linear operators associated with ρ are then given by matrices $\mathbf{L}_k$ whose elements are

$$(L_k)_{n,m} = I_k(\mu_n,\mu_m).$$

References

1. P. Beckmann and A. Spizzichino. *The Scattering of Electromagnetic Waves from Rough Surfaces*. Pergamon, New York, 1963.
2. M. Born and E. Wolf. *Principles of Optics. Sixth (corrected) Edition*. Cambridge University Press, Cambridge, U.K., 1997.
3. S. Chandrasekhar. *Radiative Transfer*. Dover, New York, 1960.
4. R. L. Cook and K. E. Torrance. A Reflectance Model for Computer Graphics. *ACM Computer Graphics (SIGGRAPH '81)*, 15(3):307–316, August 1981.

---

[2]This relation was used in [10], for example.

52

5. P. Hanrahan and W. Krueger. Reflection from Layered Surfaces due to Subsurface Scattering. In *Proceedings of SIGGRAPH '93*, pages 165–174. Addison-Wesley Publishing Company, August 1993.

6. J. E. Hansen and L. D. Travis. Light Scattering in Planetary Atmospheres. *Space Science Reviews*, 16:527–610, 1974.

7. X. D. He. *Physically-Based Models for the Reflection, Transmission and Subsurface Scattering of Light by Smooth and Rough Surfaces, with Applications to Realistic Image Synthesis.* PhD thesis, Cornell University, Ithaca, New York, 1993.

8. H. W. Jensen, S. R. Marschner, M. Levoy, and P. Hanrahan. A Practical Model for Subsurface Light Transport. In *Computer Graphics Proceedings, Annual Conference Series, 2001*, page (to appear), August 2001.

9. Z. Jin and K. Stamnes. Radiative transfer in nonuniformly refracting layered media: atmosphere-ocean system. *Applied Optics*, 33(3):431–442, January 1994.

10. J. T. Kajiya and B. P. von Herzen. Ray Tracing Volume Densities. *ACM Computer Graphics (SIGGRAPH '84)*, 18(3):165–174, July 1984.

11. E. P. F. Lafortune, S-C. Foo, K. E. Torrance, and D. P. Greenberg. Non-Linear Approximation of Reflectance Functions. In *Computer Graphics Proceedings, Annual Conference Series, 1997*, pages 117–126, August 1997.

12. E. Languénou, K.Bouatouch, and M.Chelle. Global illumination in presence of participating media with general properties. In *Proceedings of the 5th Eurographics Workshop on Rendering*, pages 69–85, Darmstadt, Germany, June 1994.

13. S. R. Marschner, S. H. Westin, E. P. F. Lafortune, K. E. Torrance, and D. P. Greenberg. Image-based brdf measurement including human skin. *Eurographics Workshop on Rendering*, 1999.

14. N. Max. Efficient light propagation for multiple anisotropic volume scattering. In *Proceedings of the 5th Eurographics Workshop on Rendering*, pages 87–104, Darmstadt, Germany, June 1994.

15. C. D. Mobley. A numerical model for the computation of radiance distributions in natural waters with wind-roughened surfaces. *Limnology and Oceanography*, 34(8):1473–1483, 1989.

16. S. K. Nayar, K. Ikeuchi, and T. Kanade. Surface Reflection: Physical and Geometrical Perspectives. *IEEE Transactions on Pattern Analysis and Machine Intelligence*, 13(7):611–634, July 1991.

17. NETLIB. The code is publicly available from http://netlib.org.

18. M. Pharr and P. Hanrahan. Monte Carlo Evaluation of Non-Linear Scattering Equations for Subsurface Reflection. In *Computer Graphics Proceedings, Annual Conference Series, 2000*, pages 75–84, July 2000.

19. G. N. Plass, G. W. Kattawar, and F. E. Catchings. Matrix operator theory of radiative transfer. 1: Rayleigh scattering. *Applied Optics*, 12(2):314–329, February 1973.

20. A. A. Prahl, M. J. C. van Gemert, , and A. J. Welch. Determining the optical properties of turbid media by using the adding-doubling method. *Applied Optics*, 32:559–568, 1993.

21. K. Stamnes and P. Conklin. A New Multi-Layer Discrete Ordinate Approach to Radiative Transfer in Vertically Inhomogeneous Atmospheres. *Journal of Quantum Spectroscopy and Radiative Transfer*, 31(3):273–282, 1984.

22. K. E. Torrance and E. M. Sparrow. Theory for Off-Specular Reflection From Roughened Surfaces. *Journal of the Optical Society of America*, 57(9):1105–1114, September 1967.

23. V. V. Tuchin. Light scattering study of tissue. *Physics - Uspekhi*, 40(5):495–515, 1997.

24. M. J. C. van Gemert, S. L. Jacques, H. J. C. M. Sterenborg, and W. M. Star. Skin optics. *IEEE Transactions on Biomedical Engineering*, 36(12):1146–1154, December 1989.

25. B. van Ginneken, M. Stavridi, and J. J. Koenderink. Diffuse and specular reflectance from rough surfaces. *Applied Optics*, 37(1):130–139, January 1998.

Editors' Note: see Appendix, p. 324 for colored figure of this paper

Real-time, Photo-realistic, Physically Based Rendering of Fine Scale Human Skin Structure

Antonio Haro†   Brian Guenter‡   Irfan Essa†

†GVU Center / College of Computing   ‡Microsoft Research Graphics Group
Georgia Institute of Technology   Microsoft Corporation

Abstract.   Skin is noticeably bumpy in character, which is clearly visible in close-up shots in a film or game. Methods that rely on simple texture-mapping of faces lack such high frequency shape detail, which makes them look non-realistic. More specifically, this detail is usually ignored in real-time applications, or is drawn in manually by an artist. In this paper, we present techniques for capturing and rendering the fine scale structure of human skin. First, we present a method for creating normal maps of skin with a high degree of accuracy from physical data. We also present techniques inspired by texture synthesis to "grow" skin normal maps to cover the face. Finally, we demonstrate how such skin models can be rendered in real-time on consumer-end graphics hardware.

1 Introduction

Photo-realistic skin is very important in a film or a video game and is hard to render for various reasons. One reason is that humans are experts when it comes to skin realism. Another is that skin has a complicated BRDF, one that depends on many factors such as pigmentation, oiliness and dryness. Skin also possesses very fine and complicated detail. The appearance of fine scale skin structure varies smoothly across the face yet each region of skin on the human body has a very distinct appearance unique to its location. For example, forehead fine scale skin structure is distinctly different from nose fine scale structure in Figure 3. Skin that lacks fine scale structure looks unrealistic since fine scale structure is such an integral part of its appearance. In this paper, we capture fine scale structure samples, build models of fine scale structure production, and then render this detail using a measured skin BRDF. Our results show that the addition of fine scale structure adds significantly to photo-realism of facial models.

We address several problems in this paper: (1) capture of fine scale skin structure from actual skin samples, (2) approximation of the stochastic processes that generate fine scale skin structure patterns, and (3) rendering of photo-realistic skin in real-time. To capture the fine scale skin structure, we employ a material[1] used in cosmetological science to create skin imprints and measure pore size. In that field, the imprints are laser-scanned to create a range map. The resulting range map is very noisy because the samples are very small (about the size of a nickel), and hence, unsuitable for rendering, but not for the type of analysis they do. We use shape from shading [8] to get a much more accurate range map that is significantly less noisy than laser-scanning can provide. Once we produce range maps for imprints from different areas of the face,

---

[1] Silflo, manufactured by Flexico

we approximate the stochastic processes that "generated" each sample. We encode the range maps as images so that this problem reduces to texture synthesis. Since the range map for each skin sample comes from a different area of the face, and hence, a different stochastic process, separate instances of texture synthesis are started on several points on the face. Fine scale structure is "grown" in 3D until full coverage is attained. We use the result as a normal map and use it to do per-pixel bump mapping. We also approximate the BRDF of the skin, so the result approaches photo-realism.

Section 3 discusses our normal map capturing process. In Section 4, we describe how we "grow" captured normal maps. Section 5.1 discusses how we use our measured reflectance model to render fine scale structure and Section 5.2 describes our lighting model.

2 Previous Work

Traditionally, when fine scale structure is rendered, it is either drawn/produced by artists by hand, or is rendered by using layers of specialized shaders. While realistic fine scale structure can be attained by these methods, the creation of additional fine scale structure is time intensive since an artist has to manually create new fine scale structure for each desired face. If specialized shaders are used, it might not be possible to render in real-time. In both cases, some underlying properties of the stochastic process are lost since the fine scale structure might only be visually realistic at certain distances/orientations. Since we compute models of the stochastic processes that generate the skin directly from actual skin data, we can render skin that looks realistic in different lighting conditions and at different scales, without any recomputation/resynthesis.

There is much work that has been done in the area of realistic facial rendering, however, very little work has been published on capturing or synthesizing fine scale skin structure. The closest work to ours is that of Wu *et al.* [23]. In that work, fine scale skin structure is dependent on its underlying geometry. A Delaunay triangulation is done on each desired skin region to generate triangles in texture space. The edges of the triangles are then raised/lowered depending on user parameters to create a height-field which is then used as a bump map. The resulting bump map does not look very realistic because some Delaunay triangulations will not yield realistic fine scale structure. Also, a user would have to spend a lot of time selecting proper basis functions, rejecting bad triangulations, and ensuring proper fine scale structure blending from one region of the face to another in order to get fine scale structure that approaches realism. In contrast, our method implicitly takes the stochastic properties and variance across the face into account, so we achieve more realistic results with minimal user input. Nahas *et al.* [15] captured skin detail with a laser range scanner, but at a low resolution (256x256 samples). However, this resolution is too low to capture the rich detail we are able to capture using skin molds and photometric stereo.

Recent work done to capture skin reflectance properties is also worth noting. Hanrahan *et al.* [6] simulated sub-surface scattering using Monte Carlo simulations to render skin. Marschner *et al.* have done work on capturing BRDFs from images that come from a calibrated camera with subjects wearing a pattern ([13], [14]). Debevec *et al.* [3] use a more complex system to measure skin reflectance as well as surface normals and are also able to incorporate ambient lighting from different environments. All of these approaches yield high-quality renderings, however, none incorporate fine scale skin structure. Recent facial animation work has also resulted in realistic results ([5], [16]). However, since the face texture comes from images that are texture blended, high-frequency detail such as fine scale structure is lost. We use measured skin reflectance

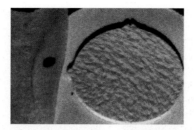

Fig. 1. Silicone mold of skin (about the size of a nickel)

models in conjunction with fine scale structure for added visual realism.

3 Normal Map Capture

We use shape from shading to capture convincing fine scale skin structure. First we make several samples of real skin texture (Figure 1) from various regions of the face using a silicone mold material. Then we apply shape from shading [8] to the silicone mold to recover the normals of the surface. Our technique is similar to the work done by others ([20], [26], [18], [19]) except that we do not require any camera calibration or structured light. In addition, we can deal with non-lambertian surfaces while using all of the pixels from each captured photograph of each sample. Throwing away pixels due to specular reflections would yield suboptimal maps due to our very simple experimental setup.

The shape from shading algorithm requires the BRDF of the surface being measured to be lambertian. We approximate this by placing polarizing filters in front of the light source and the camera and rotating them with respect to each other to eliminate all specular reflections. The remaining reflection is approximately lambertian. The illuminator we used to capture all our skin normal data, consisting of a halogen light mounted on a lazy susan, was built for $40 using materials available at any hardware store.

We take 8 photographs of the silicone mold illuminated by a point light source. The mold remains stationary, but the light position is changed in every frame by rotating the light on the lazy susan. The resulting set of images yields a set of simultaneous linear equations at each (x, y) pixel location that can be solved for the surface normal at that pixel:

$$\rho_{x,y} n_{x,y} \cdot L_i = I_{x,y} \tag{1}$$

$\rho_{x,y}$ is the diffuse albedo of the surface at pixel (x, y), $n_{x,y}$ is the normal at the pixel, and $I_{x,y}$ is the measured intensity at the pixel. L_i is the light vector for image i. $\rho_{x,y}$ is nearly constant across the silicone mold so it needs to be measured only once per image rather than at each pixel. The light intensity and position with respect to the surface is also approximately uniform over the sample so it also needs to be measured only once. This set of equations is solved at each pixel using least squares to give a normal map.

The silicone molds are not always flat, especially those taken in the nose region. This introduces a low frequency change in the surface normals that is inappropriate for bump mapping, where only the high frequency details are of interest. To eliminate the low frequency component we compute the average normal over a 50 by 50 pixel block centered at each pixel, compute the rotation that maps this normal back into

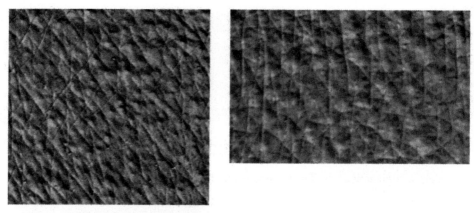

Fig. 2. *Left*: Cheek normal map, *Right*: Edge of forehead normal map

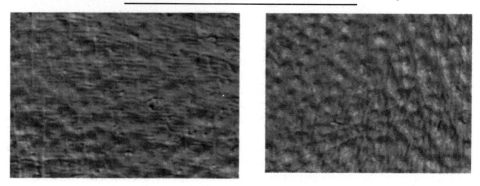

Fig. 3. *Left*: Middle of forehead normal map, *Right*: Nose normal map

the perpendicular to the normal map plane, and then apply this rotation to the normal computed from shape from shading.

Figures 2 and 3 show some example skin textures that we have captured from different regions of the face. The normal maps are encoded versions of the normals where the X, Y, Z axes map to the R, G, B channels, respectively, and the range $< -1.0, 1.0 >$ maps to $< 0, 255 >$.

4 Skin Growing

The normal maps we capture in Section 3 are of high detail, but are quite small. The molds are about 21mm in diameter. One simple way to get complete facial coverage would be to take a large amount of these molds and then to interpolate between the gaps. Samples taken from curved areas would be distorted and the process would be very inconvenient.

Another approach involves taking a small number of samples and then learning how to produce more. Fine scale skin structure varies significantly across the face (Figures 2 and 3), which is one reason it is hard to model. Since fine scale skin structure can be thought of as a stochastic process, some ideas from texture synthesis can be applied. This does not address the issue of gaps between different skin types; since skin varies

Fig. 4. Initial normal map captured from mold and synthesized map

very significantly across the face, it is not adequate to interpolate or blur the edges. Doing so would result in high-frequency discontinuities, which would be very obvious when rendered. We present our solution to this problem in Section 4.2.

4.1 Normal map synthesis

Since skin can be thought of as a stochastic process, we can apply ideas from texture synthesis to create larger regions than what we have. To create larger patches of skin, we take our normal maps that we acquired through our capture process, and encode them as images as described in Section 3. These encoded normal maps can then be thought of as small pieces of texture that we would like to synthesize.

We use the technique by Wei and Levoy[22] to synthesize larger patches. The main idea in that work was to treat texture as a Markov random field. That is, as a stochastic process that is both local and stationary, meaning that a pixel's neighborhood characterizes the process and that this characterization is the same for all pixels in the texture.

First, a histogram equalized (to the input texture) color noise image is generated for the desired dimensions needed for the skin region. Then, for each pixel in the noise image in scanline order, we assign the color of the pixel from the input texture with the most similar causal neighborhood. This is done on each level of a Gaussian pyramid starting with the topmost to ensure that the pixel that is chosen from the input texture is similar at the current and previous frequency bands. Finally, the bottom level of the pyramid is copied into the desired facial region when synthesis is complete.

Results of "growing" skin can be found in Figure 4. Recently, several texture synthesis papers ([1], [25]) have proposed copying from the source texture for some classes of texture. These approaches could yield even higher quality skin patches since larger contiguous regions from the input normal maps will exist in the synthesized skin.

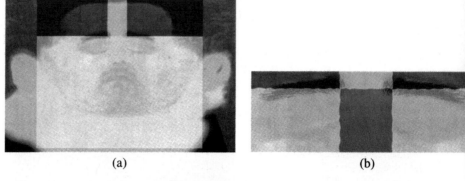

(a)   (b)

Fig. 5. (a) Each color represents a different type of fine scale skin structure to synthesize, (b) Multi-resolution splining along curves hides the boundaries between different patches

4.2 Skin stitching

Since fine scale skin structure varies across the face, we start a separate instance of texture synthesis at each different region. The regions are defined by a user by selecting a few points (7) on the albedo map (Section 5.2), specifying the forehead, nose, and cheeks as in Figure 5(a). This step is the only manual step in our pipeline, and can be done quickly.

A separate instance of texture synthesis is started at each region. When the skin in each region has grown too large for its region, the boundaries between it and its neighbors are hidden by using a modified version of multi-resolution splines [2]. Instead of performing the multi-resolution splining along a straight line along the boundary, we compute a random curve through the boundary instead, seen in Figure 5(b). We have found this looks more like the natural transitions between one type of fine scale structure to another on human skin. One major reason for this is that the boundaries are hidden more effectively along the curve; curvaceous boundaries throw the human eye off and hide seams well ([17]). We are able to generate fine scale structure for different faces rapidly with minimal user interaction using this approach.

5 Skin Rendering

To render skin realistically, we perform per-pixel bump mapping using the normal maps we have "grown". Since our mesh topologies are low ($< 15k$ vertices), storing only the normals at vertex locations loses the majority of the detail that we gain through our capture step. Instead, we store our normals in a normal map and access them on a per-pixel basis as we render the mesh. In addition, we approximate the BRDF of skin to achieve greater realism. We will discuss that further in Section 5.2.

5.1 Per-pixel Bump mapping

Our bumpmapping technique [4] is similar to the work of others ([21], [7]). The major difference between the techniques is that the per-pixel lighting calculations are done in texture space instead of object space. We perform the per-pixel lighting calculations in texture space since we would have to warp our normal map so that each normal in our map is in object space otherwise. Warping is undesirable because distortions can occur

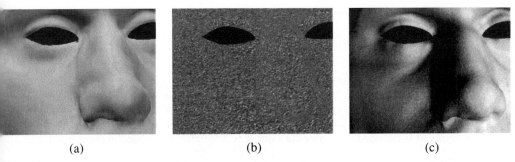

Fig. 6. (a) Encoded and transformed light vector (interpolated), (b) Normal map treated as texture (contrast enhanced), (c) $(N \cdot L')$ computed per-pixel

in the warped normal map, especially with lower resolution meshes. Also, if there are hard edges, the interpolated texture to object space transformation could be incorrect in areas between vertices.

Furthermore, if the mesh is animated, the normal map has to be re-warped each frame, which is very expensive. Working in texture space is more appealing since we only have to update the object to texture space transformation once per frame at each vertex and we have far fewer vertices than normal map pixels.

We compute transformations from object space into each vertex's texture space. At each vertex v with position $(v(x), v(y), v(z))$ and texture coordinates $(v(u), v(v))$ we form a coordinate system to perform per-pixel lighting in texture space. This coordinate system is comprised of $\delta U = (\delta u/\delta x, \delta u/\delta y, \delta u/\delta z)$, $\delta V = (\delta v/\delta x, \delta v/\delta y, \delta v/\delta z)$, and $N_{uv} = \delta U \times \delta V$, the texture space normal. The partials and N_{uv} are summed at each vertex, for all triangles, and then normalized. For a triangle T, with vertices v_0, v_1, v_2 the partials are:

$$
\begin{aligned}
\delta u/\delta x &= -B_x v_0(u)/(A_x v_0(x)), & \delta v/\delta x &= -C_x v_0(v)/(A_x v_0(x)) \\
\delta u/\delta y &= -B_y v_0(u)/(A_y v_0(y)), & \delta v/\delta y &= -C_y v_0(v)/(A_y v_0(y)) \\
\delta u/\delta z &= -B_z v_0(u)/(A_z v_0(z)), & \delta v/\delta z &= -C_z v_0(v)/(A_z v_0(z))
\end{aligned}
\tag{2}
$$

where $\langle A_x, B_x, C_x \rangle$, $\langle A_y, B_y, C_y \rangle$, $\langle A_z, B_z, C_z \rangle$ are the normals to the xuv, yuv, and zuv planes at vertex v, respectively, and are computed as:

$$
\begin{aligned}
v1_x &= (v1(x) - v0(x), v1(u) - v0(u), v1(v) - v0(v)) \\
v2_x &= (v2(x) - v0(x), v2(u) - v0(u), v2(v) - v0(v)) \\
\langle A_x, B_x, C_x \rangle &= v1_x \times v2_x
\end{aligned}
\tag{3}
$$

$$
\begin{aligned}
v1_y &= (v1(y) - v0(y), v1(u) - v0(u), v1(v) - v0(v)) \\
v2_y &= (v2(y) - v0(y), v2(u) - v0(u), v2(v) - v0(v)) \\
\langle A_y, B_y, C_y \rangle &= v1_y \times v2_y
\end{aligned}
\tag{4}
$$

$$
\begin{aligned}
v1_z &= (v1(z) - v0(z), v1(u) - v0(u), v1(v) - v0(v)) \\
v2_z &= (v2(z) - v0(z), v2(u) - v0(u), v2(v) - v0(v)) \\
\langle A_z, B_z, C_z \rangle &= v1_z \times v2_z
\end{aligned}
\tag{5}
$$

The $\delta U, \delta V$, and N_{uv} vectors form a transformation matrix at each vertex from object space into texture space:

$$M_T = \begin{bmatrix} \delta u/\delta x & \delta v/\delta x & N_{uv}(x) \\ \delta u/\delta y & \delta v/\delta y & N_{uv}(y) \\ \delta u/\delta z & \delta v/\delta z & N_{uv}(z) \end{bmatrix} \quad (6)$$

The current light position is multiplied by the inverse of the current object to world transformation matrix to bring it into object space. The light vector is then computed at each vertex in object space. It is then transformed into each vertex's texture space by using the M_T for that vertex. After the light vector has been put into texture space at a vertex, it is encoded as a color the same way normals are encoded in the normal map (Section 3) and stored as the vertex's diffuse color (Figure 6(a)).

The result of doing this is that light vectors will be linearly interpolated at all points on the mesh by the graphics card. The normal map can then be treated like a texture map (Figure 6(b)) and dotted with the encoded and interpolated light vectors, yielding per-pixel bump mapping (Figure 6(c)). This operation is equivalent to performing a per-pixel $(N \cdot L')$ where N comes from the normal map and is applied on a per-pixel instead of a per-vertex basis, and L' is the light vector in texture space at that vertex.

While the light vectors that result from this operation are normalized, the interpolated light vectors inside the triangle might not be. A solution to this problem is to use the interpolated light vectors as texture coordinates into a cube map, where each entry in the cube map is the normalized version of the index ([10]).

5.2 Lafortune Shading of Skin

Skin has a complicated BRDF that simple Gouraud or Phong shading cannot capture. We approximate the BRDF of skin with a Lafortune [11] shading model. The Lafortune model approximates the BRDF of a surface as a weighted sum of generalized cosine lobes. Each cosine lobe is parameterized by three parameters that control scaling of the dot product of the incident and exitant direction vectors along the x, y, and z directions. These parameters and the weight on each lobe comprise a non-linear approximation to the reflectance function. We use three lobes in our renderer.

We measure the parameters of each of the three specular lobes using the technique proposed by Marschner *et al.* [14]. This technique results in the parameters for each lobe as well as the albedo map, that is, the diffuse component of the skin reflectance. In practice, we use a modified version of the Lafortune model. We use the normals from the normal map and the texture space light vectors to compute the diffuse component of the model, and the normals at the vertices to compute the specular component of the model. We use the original normals instead because we do not have access to the interpolated normals at each pixel. Since most graphics cards do not support pixel shaders, we would have to render each specular lobe off-screen as many times as its corresponding exponent if we wanted to compute this per-pixel. This operation is costly since one of the lobes has a very high exponent. We have found that interpolating the specular highlights across triangles looks realistic, but with more complicated lighting, the highlights may appear slightly triangulated. There are techniques for calculating specular reflections from approximated BRDFs efficiently ([24]), and for approximating the BRDF calculations with hardware ([9], [24]), which we did not do. However, the imminent adoption of pixel shaders in upcoming consumer-end graphics cards will allow BRDFs to be calculated directly.

6 Results

Our renderer runs in real-time on a Pentium III 1GHZ with a Geforce II graphics card at 13-14 frames per second. Figure 7 shows pairs of heads shaded using the Lafortune model discussed in Section 5.2 with and without fine scale structure rendering.

The faces with fine scale structure look considerably more realistic than those without. Specular highlights such as those on the forehead and left cheek look more realistic when there is fine detail under the highlight. The skin on the faces with no fine structure simply looks too smooth, although it is shaded realistically.

All results were rendered with a high-resolution (4096x2048 pixel) bumpmap. We found that detail was still retained at 2048x1024 pixels, while most was lost at 1024x512. However, the bumpmap can be quantized as in [21] or indexed more efficiently to lower the memory requirement.

7 Conclusion

We have presented techniques to model and render realistic fine scale skin structure. Shape from shading is computed on a series of images taken of several molds of human skin under different lighting conditions. The derived normal maps are encoded as images and "grown" using texture synthesis techniques. Boundaries are hidden using a form of multi-resolution splining. Finally, an object to normal space transformation matrix is computed at each vertex so that per-pixel bump mapping can be done.

We presented results showing that fine scale structure adds significantly to the realism of rendered faces, even when the BRDF is approximated using measured lobes in a Lafortune shading model. Skin rendered without an approximated BRDF tends to look like plastic, but even with a BRDF, it looks unrealistic. Fine scale structure is something we take for granted when looking at faces, yet is extremely important for visual realism.

7.1 Future work

Rendering fine scale structure is a good first step in improving the realism of skin, but there are more things that can be done. We are interested in creating a framework to synthesize and render other types of 3D skin appearance. The addition of photorealistic 3D moles or pimples is interesting. Rendering rashes, scars, or other types of skin appearance are also intriguing. Adding hair to our fine scale structured skin via image based rendering techniques or other techniques [12] is also a promising avenue of future research. Reducing the amount of texture memory required to render fine scale structure when zoomed close to the skin is also interesting.

Acknowledgments: The authors wish to thank Sing Bing Kang for helpful discussions. We would also like to thank Greg Turk and the paper reviewers for useful comments on the paper.

References

1. M. Ashikhmin. Synthesizing natural textures. In *Symposium on Interactive 3D Graphics*, 2001.
2. P.J. Burt and E.H. Adelson. The laplacian pyramid as a compact image code. In *IEEE Transactions on Communications*, 1983.

3. P. Debevec, T. Hawkins, C. Tchou, H. Duiker, W. Sarokin, and M. Sagar. Acquiring the reflectance field of a human face. In *Computer Graphics (Proceedings of SIGGRAPH 2000)*, 145-156.

4. S. Dietrich. Texture space bumpmaps. Available from http://www.nvidia.com/.

5. B. Guenter, C. Grimm, D. Wood, H. Malvar, and F. Pighin. Making faces. In *Computer Graphics (Proceedings of SIGGRAPH 1998)*, 55-66.

6. P. Hanrahan and W. Krueger. Reflection from layered surfaces due to subsurface scattering. In *Computer Graphics (Proceedings of SIGGRAPH 1993)*, 165-174.

7. W. Heidrich and H. P. Seidel. Realistic, hardware-accellerated shading and lighting. In *Computer Graphics (Proceedings of SIGGRAPH 1999)*, 171-178.

8. B. K. P. Horn and M. J. Brooks. *Shape from Shading*. MIT Press, 1989.

9. J. Kautz and M. D. McCool. Interactive rendering with arbitrary brdfs using separable approximations. In *Proceedings of 10th Eurographics Workshop on Rendering*, 1999.

10. M. Kilgard. A practical and robust bump-mapping technique for today's gpus. Available from http://www.nvidia.com/.

11. E.P.F. Lafortune, S. Foo, K.E. Torrance, and D.P. Greenberg. Non-linear approximation of reflectance functions. In *Computer Graphics (Proceedings of SIGGRAPH 1997)*, 117-126.

12. J. Lengyel, E. Praun, A. Finkelstein, and H. Hoppe. Real-time fur over arbitrary surfaces. In *Symposium on Interactive 3D Graphics*, 145-156, 2001.

13. S. Marschner. *Inverse Rendering for Computer Graphics*. PhD thesis, Cornell University, 1998.

14. S. Marschner, B. Guenter, and S. Raghupathy. Modeling and rendering for realistic facial animation. In *Proceedings of 11th Eurographics Workshop on Rendering*, 2000.

15. M. Nahas, H. Huitric, M. Rioux, and J. Domey. Facial image synthesis using skin texture recording. *The Visual Computer*, 6(6):337–343, 1990.

16. F. Pighin, J. Hecker, D. Lischinski, R. Szeliski, and D.H. Salesin. Synthesizing realistic facial expressions from photographs. In *Computer Graphics (Proceedings of SIGGRAPH 1998)*, 75-84.

17. E. Praun, A. Finkelstein, and H. Hoppe. Lapped textures. In *Computer Graphics (Proceedings of SIGGRAPH 1998)*, 465-470.

18. H. Rushmeier and F. Bernardini. Computing consistent normals and colors from photometric data. In *2nd International Conference on 3D Digital Imaging and Modeling (3DIM)*, 1999.

19. H. Rushmeier, F. Bernardini, J. Mittleman, and G. Taubin. Acquiring input for rendering at appropriate levels of detail: Digitizing a pieta. In *Rendering Techniques*, 81-92, 1998.

20. R. Scopigno, P. Pingi, C. Rocchini, P. Cignoni, and C. Montani. 3d scanning and rendering cultural heritage artifacts on a low budget. In *European Workshop on 'High Performance Graphics Systems and Applications'*, 16-17, 2000.

21. M. Tarini, P. Cignoni, C. Rocchini, and R. Scopigno. Real time, accurate, multi-featured rendering of bump mapped surfaces. In *Eurographics*, 2000.

22. L. Wei and M. Levoy. Fast texture synthesis using tree-structured vector quantization. In *Computer Graphics (Proceedings of SIGGRAPH 2000)*, 479-488.

23. Y. Wu, P. Kalra, and N. Magnenat-Thalmann. Physically-based wrinkle simulation and skin rendering. In *Eurographics Workshop on Computer Animation and Simulation*, 1997.

24. C. Wynn. Real-time brdf-based lighting using cube-maps. Available from http://www.nvidia.com/.

25. Y. Xu., B. Guo, and H. Shum. Chaos mosaic: Fast and memory efficient texture synthesis. Technical Report MSR-TR-2000-32, Microsoft Research, 2000.

26. Yizhou Yu and Jitendra Malik. Recovering photometric properties of architectural scenes from photographs. In *Computer Graphics (Proceedings of SIGGRAPH 1998)*, 207-217.

Editors' Note: see Appendix, p. 325 for colored figure of this paper

Efficient Cloth Modeling and Rendering

Katja Daubert[†], Hendrik P. A. Lensch[†], Wolfgang Heidrich[‡], and Hans-Peter Seidel[†]

[†] Max-Planck-Institut für Informatik, [‡] The University of British Columbia [1]

Abstract. Realistic modeling and high-performance rendering of cloth and clothing is a challenging problem. Often these materials are seen at distances where individual stitches and knits can be made out and need to be accounted for. Modeling of the geometry at this level of detail fails due to sheer complexity, while simple texture mapping techniques do not produce the desired quality.
In this paper, we describe an efficient and realistic approach that takes into account view-dependent effects such as small displacements causing occlusion and shadows, as well as illumination effects. The method is efficient in terms of memory consumption, and uses a combination of hardware and software rendering to achieve high performance. It is conceivable that future graphics hardware will be flexible enough for full hardware rendering of the proposed method.

1 Introduction

One of the challenges of modeling and rendering realistic cloth or clothing is that individual stitches or knits can often be resolved from normal viewing distances. Especially with coarsely woven or knitted fabric, the surface cannot be assumed to be flat, since occlusion and self-shadowing effects become significant at grazing angles. This rules out simple texture mapping schemes as well as bump mapping. Similarly, modeling all the geometric detail is prohibitive both in terms of the memory requirements and rendering time. On the other hand, it is probably possible to compose a complex fabric surface from copies of individual weaving or knitting patterns unless the viewer gets close enough to

Fig. 1. Woolen sweater rendered using our approach (knit and perl loops).

the fabric to notice the periodicity. This leads to approaches like virtual ray-tracing [5], which are more feasible in terms of memory consumption, but still result in long rendering times.

In this paper we present a fast and memory-efficient method for modeling and rendering fabrics that is based on replicating weaving or knitting patterns. While the rendering part currently makes use of a combination of hardware and software rendering, it is conceivable that future graphics hardware will be flexible enough for full hardware rendering.

Our method assumes we have one or a small number of stitch types, which are repeated over the garment. Using a geometric model of a single stitch, we first compute

---

[1] Part of this work was done during a research visit of the first author to the University of British Columbia

the lighting (including indirect lighting and shadows) using the methods described in [3]. By sampling the stitch regularly within a plane we then generate a view dependent texture with per-pixel normals and material properties.

Before we cover the details of this representation in Section 3, we will briefly summarize related work in Section 2. We then describe acquisition and fitting of data from modeled micro-geometry in Sections 4, and 5. After discussing the rendering algorithm in Section 6 we finally present our results in Section 7.

2 Related Work

In order to efficiently render replicating patterns such as cloth without explicitly representing the geometry at the finest level, we can choose between several different representations. The first possibility is to compose global patterns of parts with precomputed illumination, such as light fields [13] and Lumigraphs [6]. However, these approaches assume fixed illumination conditions, and expanding them to arbitrary illumination yields an 8-dimensional function (which has been called the *reflectance field* [4]) that is too large to store for practical purposes.

Another possibility is to model the patterns as volumes [7, 14] or simple geometry (for example, height fields) with a spatially varying BRDF. Hardware accelerated methods for rendering shadowing and indirect illumination in height fields have been proposed recently [8, 16], as well as hardware algorithms for rendering arbitrary uniform [9, 10] and space-variant materials [11]. However, the combination of space-variant materials with bump- or displacement maps is well beyond the capabilities of current graphics hardware. This would require an excessive number of rendering passes which is neither practical in terms of performance nor in terms of numerical precision.

For high-performance rendering we therefore need to come up with more efficient representations that allow us to simulate view-dependent geometric effects (shadowing and occlusion) as well as illumination effects (specularity and interreflection) for space-variant materials in a way that is efficient both in terms of memory and rendering time.

In work parallel to ours, Xu et al. [18] developed the *lumislice*, which is a rendering method for textiles that is more tailored for high-quality, off-line rendering, whereas our method uses more precomputation to achieve near-interactive performance. In fact, the lumislice could be used as a way to precompute the data structures we use.

The method we propose is most closely related to bidirectional texture functions [2] and virtual ray-tracing [5]. As we will discuss below, our representation is, however, more compact and is easy to filter for correct anti-aliasing. Our approach is also related to image based rendering with controllable illumination, as described by Wong et al. [17]. Again, our representation is more compact, easier to filter and lends itself to partial use of graphics hardware. Future hardware is likely to have enough flexibility to eliminate the remaining software steps, making the method suitable for interactive applications.

3 Data Representation

Our representation of cloth detail is based on the composition of repeating patterns (individual weaves or knits) for which efficient data structures are used. In order to capture the variation of the optical properties across the material, we employ a spatially varying BRDF representation. The two spatial dimensions are point sampled into a 2D array. For each entry we store different parameters for a Lafortune reflection model [12], a lookup table, as well as the normal and tangent.

An entry's BRDF $f_r(\vec{l}, \vec{v})$ for the light direction $\vec{l}$ and the viewing direction $\vec{v}$ is given by the following equation:

$$f_r(\vec{l}, \vec{v}) = T(\vec{v}) \cdot f_1(\vec{l}, \vec{v}), \tag{1}$$

where $f_1(\vec{l}, \vec{v})$ denotes the Lafortune model and $T(\vec{v})$ is the lookup table[2].

The Lafortune model itself consists of a diffuse part ρ and a sum of lobes[3]:

$$f_1(\vec{l}, \vec{v}) = l_z' \cdot \left(\rho + \sum_i \left[(l_x', l_y', l_z') \cdot \begin{pmatrix} C_{x_i} & 0 & 0 \\ 0 & C_{y_i} & 0 \\ 0 & 0 & C_{z_i} \end{pmatrix} \cdot \begin{pmatrix} v_x' \\ v_y' \\ v_z' \end{pmatrix} \right]^{N_i} \right) \tag{2}$$

Each lobe's shape and size is defined by its four parameters C_x, C_y, C_z, and N. Since f_1 is wavelength dependent, we represent every parameter as a three-dimensional vector, one dimension per color channel. Before evaluating the lobe we transform the light and viewing direction into the local coordinate system given by the sampling point's average normal and tangent, yielding $\vec{l}'$ and $\vec{v}'$. In order to account for area foreshortening we multiply by l_z'.

The lookup table $T(\vec{v})$ stores color and alpha values for each of the original viewing directions. It therefore closely resembles the directional part of a light field. Values for directions not stored in the lookup table are obtained by interpolation. Although general view-dependent reflection behavior including highlights etc., could be described by a simple Lafortune BRDF, we introduce the lookup table to take more complex properties like shadowing and masking (occlusion) into account that are caused by the complex geometry of the underlying cloth model.

Like in redistribution bump mapping [1], this approach aims at simulating the occlusion effects that occur in bump maps at grazing angles. In contrast to redistribution bump mapping, however, we only need to store a single color value per viewing direction, rather than a complete normal distribution. Figure 5 demonstrates the effect of the modulation with the lookup table. The same data, acquired from the stitch model shown in the middle, was used to fit a BRDF model without a lookup table, only consisting of several cosine lobes (displayed on the left cloth in Figure 5) and a model with an additional lookup table (cf. Figure 5 on the right). Both images were rendered using the same settings for light and viewing direction. Generally, without a lookup table, the BRDF tends to blur over the single knits. Also the BRDF without the lookup table clearly is not able to capture the color shifts to red at grazing angles, which are nicely visible on the right cloth.

The alpha value stored in the lookup table is used to evaluate the transparency. It is not considered in the multiplication with f_1, but used as described in Section 6 to determine if there is a hole in the model at a certain point for a given viewing direction. The alpha values are interpolated similarly to the color values.

4   Data Acquisition

After discussing the data structure we use for representing the detail of the fabrics, we now describe how to obtain the necessary data from a given 3D model.

---

[2] Both $T(\vec{v})$ and f_1 are defined for each color channel, so $\cdot$ denotes the component-wise multiplication of the color channels.

[3] The operator a^N is defined to return zero if $a < 0$.

We model the base geometry of our knits and weaves using implicit surfaces, the skeletons of which are simple Bézier curves. By applying the Marching Cubes algorithm we generate triangle meshes, which are the input for our acquisition algorithm.

Now we can obtain the required data. As mentioned in Section 3, the spatial variations of the fabric pattern are stored as a 2D array of BRDF models. Apart from radiance samples $r(\vec{l}, \vec{v})$ for all combinations of viewing and light directions, we also need an average normal, an average tangent, and an alpha value for each viewing direction for each of these entries.

We use an extension of Heidrich et al.'s algorithm ([8]) to triangle meshes ([3]), which allows us to compute the direct and indirect illumination of a triangle mesh for a given viewing and light direction per vertex in hardware (for details see [3]). In order to account for masking and parts of the repeated geometry being visible through holes, we paste together multiple copies of the geometry.

Now we need to collect the radiance data for each sampling point. We obtain the 2D sampling locations by first defining a set of evenly spaced sampling points on the top face of the model's bounding box, as can be seen on the

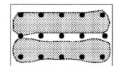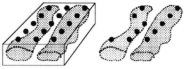

Fig. 2. Computing the sampling locations for the radiance values. Left: top view, middle: projection, right: resulting sampling locations, discarding samples at holes.

left in Figure 2. Then we project these points according to the current viewing direction (see Figure 2 in the middle) and collect the radiance samples from the surface visible through these 2D projections (see Figure 2 right), similarly to obtaining a light field.

Note that, due to parallax effects, for each entry we combine radiance samples from a number of different points on the actual geometry. Like in [17], we will use this information from different surface points to fit a BRDF for the given sampling location.

```
for each v⃗ {
  ComputeSamplingPoints();
  RepeatScene(vertex color=normals);
  StoreNormals();
  StoreAlpha();
  for each l⃗ {
    ComputeLighting();
    RepeatScene(vertex color=lighting);
    StoreRadiance();
  }
}
AverageNormals();
```

Fig. 3. Pseudo code for the acquisition procedure.

As the stitch geometry can have holes, there might be no surface visible at a sampling point for a certain viewing direction. We store this information as a boolean transparency in the alpha channel for that sample. Multiple levels of transparency values can be obtained by super-sampling, i.e. considering the neighboring pixels.

In order to compute the normals, we display the scene once for each viewing direction with the normals coded as color values. An average normal is computed by adding the normals separately for each sampling point and averaging them at the end. We can construct a tangent from the normal and the bi-normal, which in turn we define as the vector perpendicular to both the normal and the x-axis. Figure 3 shows how the steps are put together in the acquisition algorithm.

5 Fitting Process

Once we have acquired all the necessary data, we use it to find an optimal set of parameters for the Lafortune model for each entry in the array of BRDFs. This fitting procedure can be divided into two major steps which are applied alternately. At first, the parameters of the lobes are fit. Then, in the second step, the entries of the lookup table are updated. Now the lobes are fit again and so on.

Given a set of all radiance samples and the corresponding viewing and light directions acquired for one sampling point, the fitting of the parameters of the Lafortune model f_l requires a non-linear optimization method. As proposed in [12], we applied the Levenberg-Marquardt algorithm [15] for this task.

The optimization is initiated with an average gray BRDF with a moderate specular highlight and slightly anisotropic lobes, e.g. $C_x = 1.22 * C_y$ for the first and $C_y = 1.22 * C_x$ for the second lobe if two lobes are fit. For the first fitting of the BRDF the lookup table $T(\vec{v})$ is ignored, i.e. all its entries are set to white.

After fitting the lobe parameters, we need to adapt the sampling point's lookup table $T(\vec{v})$. Each entry of the table is fit separately. This time only those radiance samples of the sampling point that correspond to the viewing direction of the current entry are considered. The optimal color for one entry minimizes the following set of equations:

$$\left(r(\vec{l}_1, \vec{v}), r(\vec{l}_2, \vec{v}), \dots, r(\vec{l}_R, \vec{v}) \right)^T = T(\vec{v}) \left(f_l(\vec{l}_1, \vec{v}), f_l(\vec{l}_2, \vec{v}), \dots, f_l(\vec{l}_R, \vec{v}) \right)^T \quad (3)$$

where $r(\vec{l}_1, \vec{v}), \dots, r(\vec{l}_R, \vec{v})$ are the radiance samples of the sampling point with the common viewing direction $\vec{v}$ and the distinct light directions $\vec{l}_1, \dots, \vec{l}_R$. The currently estimated lobes are evaluated for every light direction yielding $f_l(\vec{l}_i, \vec{v})$. Treating the color channels separately, Equation 3 can be rewritten by replacing the column vector on its left side by $\vec{r}(\vec{v})$, the vector on its right side by $\vec{f}(\vec{v})$, yielding $\vec{r}(\vec{v}) = T(\vec{v}) \cdot \vec{f}(\vec{v})$. The least squares solution to this equation is given by

$$T(\vec{v}) = \frac{\langle \vec{f}(\vec{v}) | \vec{r}(\vec{v}) \rangle}{\langle \vec{f}(\vec{v}) | \vec{f}(\vec{v}) \rangle} \quad (4)$$

where $\langle \cdot | \cdot \rangle$ denotes the dot product. This is done separately for every color channel and easily extends to additional spectral components.

To further improve the result we alternately repeat the steps of fitting the lobes and fitting the lookup table. The iteration stops as soon as the average difference of the previous lookup table's entries to the new lookup table's entries is below a certain threshold.

In addition to the color, each entry in the lookup table also contains an alpha value indicating the opacity of the sample point. This value is fixed for every viewing direction and is not affected by the fitting process. Instead it is determined through ray-casting during the data acquisition phase.

Currently, we also derive the normal and tangent at each sample point directly from the geometric model. However, the result of the fitting process could probably be further improved by also computing a new normal and tangent to best fit the input data.

5.1 Mip-Map Fitting

The same fitting we have done for every single sample point can also be performed for groups of sample points. Let a sample point be a texel in a texture. Collecting all radiance samples for four neighboring sample points, averaging the normals, fitting the lobes and the entries of the lookup table then yields the BRDF corresponding to a texel on the next higher mip-map level.

By grouping even more sample points, further mip-map levels can be generated. The overall effort per level stays the same since the same number of radiance samples are involved at each level.

6 Rendering

After the fitting process has been completed for all sampling points we are ready to apply our representation of fabric patterns to a geometric model. We assume the given model has per vertex normals and valid texture coordinates $\in [0..t_N]^2$, where t_N is the number of times the pattern is to be repeated across the whole cloth geometry. Furthermore, we assume the fabric patterns are stored in a 2D array, the dimensions of which correspond to the pattern's spatial resolution $(\text{res}_x, \text{res}_y)$. Our rendering algorithm then consists of four steps:

1. Interpolate per pixel normals
2. Compute indices into the pattern array, yielding a BRDF f_r
3. Evaluate f_r with light and view mapped into geometry's local coordinate system
4. Write result to framebuffer

The goal of Step 1 is to estimate a normal for each visible point on the object. We do this by color coding the normals at the vertices and rendering the scene using Gouraud shading. Each framebuffer value with an alpha value $\neq 0$ now codes a normal.

The next step is to find out which BRDF we need to evaluate in order to obtain the color for each pixel. In order to do this we first generate a texture with the resolution $(\text{res}_x, \text{res}_y)$ in which the red and green channel of each pixel encode its position. Note that this texture has to be generated only once and can be reused for other views and light directions. Using hardware texture mapping with the above mentioned texture coordinates, the texture is replicated t_N times across the object. Now the red and green channel of each pixel in the framebuffer holds the correct indices into the 2D array of BRDFs for this specific fabric pattern.

Once we know which BRDF to evaluate, we map the light and viewing direction into the geometry's local coordinate system, using the normals obtained in Step 1 and a tangent constructed as described in Section 4. Note that two mappings need to take place: this one, which maps the world view and light to the cloth geometry's local coordinate system (yielding $\vec{l}$ and $\vec{v}$), and another when evaluating the BRDF, which transforms these values to the pattern's local coordinate system (yielding $\vec{l}'$, $\vec{v}'$).

The software evaluation of the BRDF model (see Section 3) returns three colors and an alpha value from the lookup table, which we then write to the framebuffer.

The presented rendering technique utilizes hardware as far as possible. However, the BRDF model is still evaluated in software, although mapping this onto hardware should be feasible with the next generation of graphics cards.

6.1 Mip-Mapping

As described in Section 5.1, we can generate several mip-map levels of BRDFs. We will now explain how to enhance the above algorithm to correctly use different mip-map levels, thereby exploiting OpenGL mip-mapping.

First we modify Step 2 and now generate one texture per mip-map level. Each texture's resolution corresponds to the BRDF's spatial resolution at this level. As before, the red and green channel code the pixel's location in the texture. Additionally, we now use each pixel's blue channel to code the mip-map level of the corresponding texture. For example, if we have 6 levels, all pixel's blue values are 0 in texture 0, 0.2 in texture 1, 0.4 in texture 2 and so on.

If we set up OpenGL mip-mapping with these textures specified for the correct levels, the blue channel of each pixel will tell us which texture to use, while the red and green channel still code the indices into the array of BRDFs at this level.

Blending between two mip-map levels is also possible. As we do not want to blend the texture coordinates in the red and green channels, however, we need two passes to do so. The first pass is the same as before. However, in the second pass we setup the mip-map technique to linearly interpolate between two levels. We avoid overwriting the values in the red and green channels by using a color mask. Now the value of the blue channel v_b codes between which levels to blend (in the above example between levels $l_{\min} = \lfloor v_b/0.2 \rfloor$ and $l_{\max} = \lceil v_b/0.2 \rceil$) and also tells us the blending factor (here $(v_b - l_{\min} \cdot 0.2)/0.2$).

7 Results and Applications

We implemented our algorithms on a PC with an AMD Athlon 1GHz processor and a GeForce 2 GTS graphics card. To generate the images in this paper we applied the acquired fabric patterns to cloth models we modeled with the 3D Studio Max plug-ins Garment Maker and Stitch. Our geometric models for the knit or weave patterns consist of 1300–23000 vertices and 2400–31000 triangles. The computation times of the acquisition process depend on the number of triangles, as well as the sampling density for the viewing and light directions, but generally vary from 15 minutes to about 45 minutes. We typically used 32×32 or 64×64 viewing and light directions, uniformly distributed over the hemisphere, generating up to 4096 radiance samples per sampling point on the lowest level. We found a spatial resolution of 32×32 samples to be sufficient for our detail geometry, which results in 6 mip-map levels and 1365 BRDF entries. The parameter fitting of a BRDF array of this size takes about 2.5 hours. In our implementation each BRDF in the array (including all the mip-map levels) has the same number of lobes. We found out that generally one or two lobes are sufficient to yield visually pleasing results. The threshold mentioned in Section 5 was set to 0.1 and we noted that convergence was usually achieved after 2 iterations. Once all parameters have been fit we need only 4 MB to store the complete data structure for one type of fabric, including all mip-map levels and the lookup tables with 64 entries per point.

The rendering times e.g. for Figure 1 are about 1 frame per second for a resolution of 730×400 pixels. The bulk of this time is spent on reading back the framebuffer contents in order to evaluate the BRDF for every pixel. We therefore expect that with the advent of more flexible hardware, which will allow us to implement the rendering part of this paper without such a software component, the proposed method will become feasible for interactive applications.

The dress in Figure 4(a) displays a fabric pattern computed with our method. In Figure 4(b) we compare the results of a mip-mapped BRDF to a single level one. As expected the mip-mapping nicely gets rid of the severe aliasing clearly visible in the not mip-mapped left half of the table. Figure 5 illustrates how even complex BRDFs with color shifts can be captured using our model. Figure 1 and Figure 6 show different fabric patterns displayed on the same cloth geometry.

70

8 Conclusions

In this paper we have presented a memory-efficient representation for modeling and rendering fabrics that is based on replicating individual weaving·or knitting patterns. We have demonstrated how our representation can be generated by fitting samples from a global illumination simulation to it. In a similar fashion it should be possible to acquire a fitted representation from measured image data. Our model is capable of capturing color variations due to self-shadowing and self-occlusion as well as transparency. In addition, it naturally lends itself to mip-mapping, thereby solving the filtering problem.

Furthermore we presented an efficient rendering algorithm which can be used to apply our model to any geometry, achieving near-interactive frame rates with a combination of hardware and software rendering. With the increasing flexibility of upcoming generations of graphics boards, we expect to be able to implement the rendering algorithm completely in hardware soon. This would make the approach suitable for fully interactive and even real time applications.

References

1. B. Becker and N. Max. Smooth Transitions between Bump Rendering Algorithms. In *SIGGRAPH '93 Proceedings*, pages 183–190, August 1993.
2. K. Dana, B. van Ginneken, S. Nayar, and J. Koenderink. Reflectance and Texture of Real World Surfaces. *ACM Transactions on Graphics*, 18(1):1–34, January 1999.
3. K. Daubert, W. Heidrich, J. Kautz, J.-M. Dischler, and Hans-Peter Seidel. Efficient Light Transport Using Precomputed Visibility. Technical Report MPI-I-2001-4-003, Max-Planck-Institut für Informatik, 2001.
4. P. Debevec, T. Hawkins, C. Tchou, H.-P. Duiker, W. Sarokin, and M. Sagar. Acquiring the reflectance field of a human face. In *SIGGRAPH 2000 Proceedings*, pages 145–156, July 2000.
5. J.-M. Dischler. Efficiently Rendering Macro Geometric Surface Structures with Bi-Directional Texture Functions. In *Proc. of Eurographics Workshop on Rendering*, pages 169–180, June 1998.
6. S. Gortler, R. Grzeszczuk, R. Szelinski, and M. Cohen. The Lumigraph. In *SIGGRAPH '96 Proceedings*, pages 43–54, August 1996.
7. E. Gröller, R. Rau, and W. Straßer. Modeling textiles as three dimensional textures. In *Proc. of Eurographics Workshop on Rendering*, pages 205–214, June 1996.
8. W. Heidrich, K. Daubert, J. Kautz, and H.-P. Seidel. Illuminating Micro Geometry Based on Precomputed Visibility. In *SIGGRAPH '00 Proceedings*, pages 455–464, July 2000.
9. W. Heidrich and H.-P. Seidel. Realistic, Hardware-accelerated Shading and Lighting. In *SIGGRAPH '99 Proceedings*, August 1999.
10. J. Kautz and M. McCool. Interactive Rendering with Arbitrary BRDFs using Separable Approximations. In *Proc. of Eurographics Workshop on Rendering*, pages 247 – 260, June 1999.
11. J. Kautz and H.-P. Seidel. Towards interactive bump mapping with anisotropic shift-variant BRDFs. In *2000 Eurographics/SIGGRAPH Workshop on Graphics Hardware*, pages 51–58, August 2000.
12. E. Lafortune, S. Foo, K. Torrance, and D. Greenberg. Non-Linear Approximation of Reflectance Functions. In *SIGGRAPH '97 Proceedings*, pages 117–126, August 1997.
13. M. Levoy and P. Hanrahan. Light Field Rendering. In *SIGGRAPH '96 Proceedings*, pages 31–42, August 1996.
14. F. Neyret. Modeling, Animating, and Rendering Complex Scenes Using Volumetric Textures. *IEEE Transactions on Visualization and Computer Graphics*, 4(1), January – March 1998.
15. W. Press, S. Teukolsky, W. Vetterling, and B. Flannery. *Numerical Recipes in C: The Art of Scientific Computing (2nd ed.)*. Cambridge University Press, 1992. ISBN 0-521-43108-5.
16. P. Sloan and M. Cohen. Hardware Accelerated Horizon Mapping. In *Proc. of Eurographics Workshop on Rendering*, pages 281–286, June 2000.
17. Tien-Tsin Wong, Pheng-Ann Heng, Siu-Hang Or, and Wai-Yin Ng. Image-based Rendering with Controllable Illumination. In *Proc. of Eurographics Workshop on Rendering*, pages 13–22, 1997.
18. Y.-Q. Xu, Y. Chen, S. Lin, H. Zhong, E. Wu, B. Guo, and H.-Y. Shum. Photo-realistic rendering of knitwear using the lumislice. In *Computer Graphics (SIGGRAPH '01 Proceedings)*, 2001. to be published.

Editors' Note: see Appendix, p. 326 for colored figures of this paper

Decoupling Strokes and High-Level Attributes for Interactive Traditional Drawing

Frédo Durand†, Victor Ostromoukhov†‡,
Mathieu Miller‡, François Duranleau‡, and Julie Dorsey†

†Lab for Computer Science - MIT   ‡Université de Montréal, LIGUM

Abstract. We present an interactive system, which allows the user to produce drawings in a variety of traditional styles. It takes as input an image and performs semi-automatic tonal modeling. Our system shifts tedious technical aspects to the computer side, while providing the user with freedom on the creative and aesthetic side. The user has low-level control over stroke placement, and high-level control over the tone, smudging and amount of detail. The drawing is rendered in real-time. The basic component is a thresholding model of strokes that can simulate a large class of styles (e.g. pencil, charcoal, engraving). It provides a controllable simulation of the variation of pencil pressure or stroke thickness traditionally used in tonal modeling. We introduce a novel fast equilibration approach for the resulting thresholding structure. The user can specify smudging and control the amount of detail over each part of the drawing.

1 Introduction

The broad appeal of drawing lies in its expressiveness, precision, and simplicity. The versatile role of strokes in conveying form, tone, shape, texture, and style is the source of both the richness and the difficulty of the medium. Our long-term goal is to shift the tedious technical aspects of drawing to the computer side, while providing the user with expressiveness and a new kind of freedom on the creative and aesthetic side. Our intention is not to replace traditional drawing, but to provide a fast and flexible tool to create realistic drawings. We believe our system will benefit both skilled artists due to its editing capabilities, and novices who wish create expressive drawings without tedious technical learning.

We extend the work on interactive image-based non-photorealistic rendering systems [Hae90, Ost99, PB94, SABS94, SWHS97]. As in these works, a reference photograph is used to provide both a visual aid for the user and a reference for the tones of the final image (Fig. 1). Using realistic tones as an input is not as restrictive as one may think. The control of the tone reproduction curve or burning and dodging techniques provide a large freedom [Ada95, Sch99]. Photography, slide projectors, and well before them the *camera obscura* and *camera lucida* have been used by artists as drawing aids for accurate perspective, and sometimes for tones [Kem90, Kos99, Smi87].

In our approach, we decouple the specification of strokes from higher-level attributes such as conveyed tone and precision. An attribute can be varied without affecting the others. The separation of these dimensions of drawing enables the user to experiment with a wide range of aesthetic choices.

1.1 Previous work

A variety of systems for non-photorealistic rendering [Elb95, Elb99, LS95, MKT $^+$97, ST90, WS94] construct imagery based on a 3D model. In contrast, we use a reference image to specify tones, as pioneered by Haeberli [Hae90].

Similar to our approach, Salisbury et al. [SABS94, SWHS97] generate pen-and-ink drawings starting from grey-scale images. While they capture a rich range of tonal

Fig. 1. Basic features of our interactive drawing system. The user provides a reference photograph (upper-left), edits the tones, draws strokes and specifies a precision map (lower-left) while interactively viewing the drawing (right).

and texture variations, they are limited to a specific drawing style, and in particular, to simple strokes. In their work, darker tones are obtained by adding more strokes, while our thresholding approach achieves this effect by varying the thickness and pressure of strokes. Our system shares many features with theirs, but extend it in two important respect: by providing a richer collection of strokes, and a higher degree of control, particularly in the level of detail that can be achieved. It also enhances interactivity by providing a continuous visual feedback.

Complex simulations of paper-pencil interactions have been proposed by different authors [TFN99, SB99b, SB00]. The results are impressively faithful, but their approach does not yet permit a large variety of stroke styles. However, we believe that these models could be used to generate new stroke textures for our system. Emulating traditional media is only the first step before such techniques can be applied to 3D models (as was done in [SB99a]) or to provide a user with additional features, as we propose in this paper. Our model of strokes is simpler to derive (new stroke style can be acquired using a simple scanner) and better suited for semi-automatic tonal modeling.

Our simulation of strokes is inspired by research on digital engraving [Lei94, PB94, Ost99] and, in particular, builds upon the work by Ostromoukhov [Ost99], where simple engraving strokes are simulated using a halftoning approach known as *thresholding*. Our model of strokes can handle a larger variety of media, and is included in a real-time system providing interactivity both at a high and low level. Finally, due to our new hardware-assisted thresholding, drawings can be rendered in real-time.

1.2 Overview

This paper makes the following specific contributions:
Decoupling strokes and high-level attributes: The user independently controls the placement of strokes, and higher-level properties such as tonal adjustment and preci-

sion.

Stroke model: We extend a thresholding technique to simulate a large class of styles such as pencil, charcoal, or engraving. Our model supports smudging, widely used in traditional drawing (usually by rubbing a finger or a piece of paper on the drawing).

Equilibration: Thresholding requires a matrix with a flat histogram, which can be obtained by *equilibration*. We present a new rapid probabilistic technique.

Interactive hardware implementation: Our drawing rendering algorithm is hardware-assisted and easy to implement.

2 Decoupling expressiveness and technique

We first place our work in the context of traditional drawing in order to motivate our decoupling of the user interface from image generation.

2.1 Context: the art of drawing

Inspired by different authors [Edw99, Gai96, Hal64, Men76, Spe17], we distinguish the following aspects of drawing: Gestalt, perspective, outlines, tonal modeling, and control of detail. For each category, it is important to make a distinction between the aesthetic choice and the technical achievement of this intent. It is also crucial to understand in what these aspects can be similar and different in drawing and photography.

Gestalt deals with the balance and composition of the image. Since it lies completely on the aesthetic side, our system leaves this aspect to the user. Photography has been widely used as a reference for realistic drawing [Kem90, Kos99, Smi87]. The same is true in our system, where the input image defines the perspective.

Outlines are fundamental visual components of line drawing. Similar to Salisbury et al., [SABS94], we use edge detection as a visual aid. We also offer optional outline snapping in the spirit of magic scissors [MB95]. Outline strokes are excluded from the automatic tonal modeling.

Tonal modeling in photography is surprisingly similar to the comparable process in drawing and painting. The goals are the same: reveal shape and texture, set the mood, and balance the image. Although drawing and photography usually exhibit different tonal styles, darkroom tools [Ada95, Sch99] can be used to give a photograph the tonal style of a drawing. The distinction between the choice of tones and the practical achievement of tones is crucial. Our system manages the achievement of tones, using an adapted thresholding approach. The target tones are specified by the reference image. However, the user is not limited by the initial photograph, as darkroom tools are provided to interactively alter the tones of the reference image to match the user's intent.

An often overlooked aspect of visual arts is the control of the amount of detail. In photography, it is possible to control only depth of field and use filters, while in drawing it is possible yo finely control the amount of detail over the whole image, extracting the visual essence, focusing the eye on important areas and establishing the balance between strokes and the depicted subject. Controlling the precision is a challenging and subtle task. An initial solution was proposed by Winkenbach et al. [WS94] using *detail segments*. In our system, a *precision map* locally controls the accuracy of tonal modeling and the amount of spatial detail.

2.2 A proposed decomposition of drawing

When an artist draws a stroke, all five aspects come into play, hence the difficulty for beginners. Our system attempts to decouple these aspects and to provide flexible high-level editing tools, as well as low-level stroke control. For this, we express image generation as a multidimensional mapping from a user control-space to an imaging control-space. Another benefit of this framework is a simpler implementation.

Central to our analysis is the distinction between medium simulation and user control (Fig. 2). The medium simulation is the "mechanical" imitation of (usually traditional) media. It is driven by what we call the *imaging control space*. In our thresholding-based system, the imaging control space consists of a *threshold matrix*, a *target tone* image and the amount of *smudging*. Image generation involves comparing the threshold matrix against the target tones, and uses the amount of smudging to compute a grey level for each pixel.

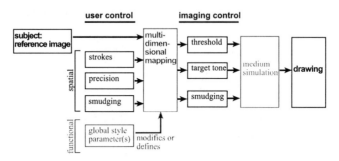

Fig. 2. Drawing generation interface as a multidimensional mapping from user control space to imaging control space. Since the user has direct control over the amount of smudging, it appears both in user and imaging control-spaces, and the sub-mapping is identity.

In contrast, the *user control space* describes the degrees of freedom of the user, which largely defines interface. The image subject is specified by an input photograph. We make a distinction between spatial input (stroke location, amount of precision, smudging), and global or functional input that affect the whole rendering *style*. Our only functional parameter specifies the influence of the precision map: whether it removes details in the target tones, or whether it favors strokes specified by the user vs. target tone accuracy.

Image generation can then be described as a multidimensional mapping from the spatial user control space to the imaging control space. Global user inputs affect or define the mappings. When the user has direct control on imaging parameters, the corresponding mapping is the identity mapping (this is the case for smudging).

2.3 Algorithm overview

The final output of our system is a pixel image, but the image generation data structures are a set of strokes and pixel maps representing target tone, precision and smudging. Unlike purely image-based systems (such as Corel Painter), the final resolution of the image need not be fixed, since the drawing is constantly regenerated from the strokes. The target tone, precision and smudging maps are scaled using the hardware. This permits device-independent interactive editing and device-specific final rendering (in the spirit of [SALS96]).

Our algorithm is summarized in Fig. 3 and will be detailed in the next sections. The strokes are used to render a raw threshold matrix. This raw matrix needs equilibration to compensate for the non-flat histogram resulting from irregular stroke placement. The amount of equilibration is affected by the precision map.

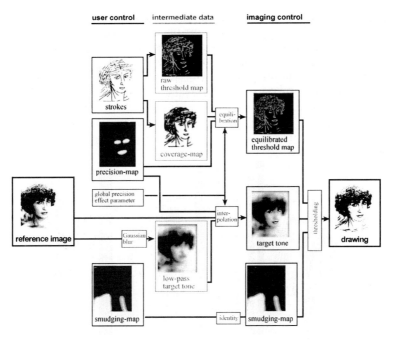

Fig. 3. Flowchart of our system. Drawing rendering is expressed as a set of 3-dimensional sub-mappings. Non-tonal strokes are not represented; they "bypass" the target tone.

The target tone image used for thresholding is a filtered version of the input image, where the amount of detail is specified by the precision map. As aforementioned, smudging is a direct parameter specified by the user.

All these mappings are implemented using the graphics hardware and the *pixel textures* [HWSE99, BM00]. This feature permits the use of the color buffer as texture coordinates for 3D texture mapping. This permits efficient mapping from a 3-dimensional space to a 3-dimensional space. Tri-linear interpolation is performed. This makes the implementation of our technique easy and fast. We render the relevant space into each channel, set the look-up-table corresponding to the desired mapping, and make a buffer-copy that performs the look-up [HWSE99, BM00].

3 Strokes and thresholding

3.1 Thresholding

In digital halftoning, tone is obtained by comparing at each pixel a threshold matrix $T(x,y)$ against the target tone of the input image $I(x,y)$. Depending on the result, the pixel is declared black or white [Uli87]. If S is the step function ($S(x) = 0$ if $x < 0$ and $S(x) = 1$ if $x \geq 0$), thresholding can be expressed as:

$$Thresh(T(x,y),I(x,y)) = S(T(x,y) - I(x,y)) \qquad (1)$$

If the histogram of the threshold matrix T is flat (all values are equally represented), faithful tone reproduction is obtained. However, the irregular placement of strokes does not result in a flat histogram. For faithful tonal rendering, an equilibration has to be performed, as will be presented in Section 4.

In our system, strokes are simulated using local threshold structures, which we call *threshold textures*. The initial principle of our rendering is simple. To render the drawing, we render all the strokes using their threshold texture, resulting in a global threshold matrix $T(x,y)$, which is then compared to the target tones $I(x,y)$ to obtain a black and white drawing. This is the key in decoupling stroke style from tonal value: the threshold texture defines the stroke style, while tone is obtained by thresholding with respect to the target tone (Fig. 4).

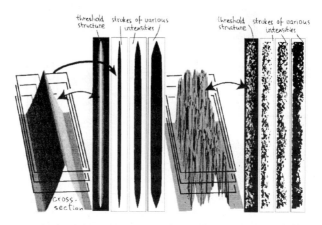

Fig. 4. Typical stroke threshold structure for etching (left) and pencil (right). We show various tonal effects conveyed by single stroke structures. The key idea is to truncate the threshold structure at a different height depending on the target tone.

When multiple strokes overlap, their merging must receive particular attention. We use the maximum blending mode, which effectively imitates the overlap of multiple traditional strokes [Ost99].

3.2 Antialiasing

Thresholding was developed for tonal rendering on high resolution devices that can only produce black dots [Uli87]. In contrast, monitors have a lower resolution but a larger gamut. We propose to modify the step function S in equation 1 to introduce smoothness, using an S-shaped function. Special care must be paid to symmetry in order to maintain tonal fidelity. The initial idea is to use a clamped sine function, with width $2w$. Using t for $T(x,y)$ and i for $I(x,y)$:

$$s(t,i,w) = \begin{cases} 1, & t-i < -w \\ 0.5 + 0.5\sin\left(-\frac{\pi(t-i)}{2w}\right), & -w \le t-i \le w \\ 0, & w < t-i \end{cases} \qquad (2)$$

This works fine for middle tone, but introduces bias for low and high tones, because the clamping to black or white obviates symmetry. We thus limit the width of the s function to the distance of the tone x to black or white $d(x) = min(1-x,x)$ and use:

$$s'(t,i,w) = s(t,i,max(w,d(i))) \qquad (3)$$

By default we use $w = 0.05$, but we will see in Section 5.3 that varying this value mimics the effect of smudging.

3.3 Stroke threshold texture

A *threshold texture* is essentially a threshold structure as described above. It has a flat histogram and is represented as a grey-level texture map. Threshold textures can be either acquired by scanning real strokes (in the spirit of e.g. [VB00]), or modeled directly. We scanned real strokes for pencil and charcoal, and modeled etching-style strokes, and then applied a simple histogram flattening algorithm.

The relevance of this model is not obvious. Clues can be found in the physical process of paper-graphite interaction [SB00]. The grey values correspond to the number of graphite particles per area, and can be seen as the probability that particles are deposited. Thresholding together with our antialiasing technique corresponds to simulating macro-graphite particles. A more phenomenological macroscopic validation is the similarity between pencil drawing and lithography, and the similarity between the threhsolding height-field and engraving [Ost99].

3.4 Individual strokes and rendering

Individual strokes are described by a skeleton, a reference to a stroke threshold texture, and a target tone for strokes excluded from automatic tonal modeling. A stroke skeleton is described by a poly-Bézier curve, along which the threshold texture is warped, as described below. The threshold textures are randomly shifted along the curve to avoid uniformity and cross-stroke correlation.

To compute the raw global threshold matrix $T(x,y)$, we transform strokes according to the Bézier skeleton using a triangle-strip band around the curve and texture mapping [GDCV98]. When rendering strokes, we use the OpenGL 1.2 blending mode MAX.

4 Equilibration

The equilibration of threshold structures is usually performed using an iterative trial-and-error approach [Ost99, OH99]. However, this is too slow for our purpose. We therefore introduce a new technique that is both direct and fast. It is not as accurate as previous techniques, but it proves sufficient for drawing. Since the histograms of our strokes are flat, we only need to compensate for overlapping strokes. We base our technique on a probability analysis of the histogram of overlapping strokes merged using the *max* mode.

4.1 Probabilistic analysis

We model the histogram of a stroke as a probability density function $p(x) = 1$ for $x \in [0,1]$. The cumulative density function (corresponding to the cumulative histogram) is $P[X \leq x] = \int_0^x p(\xi)d\xi = x$. The main assumption is that there is no correlation between strokes. This is reasonable given the texture of our strokes and their irregular placement.

The probability and cumulative density of two overlapping strokes p_1 and p_2 are:

$$
\begin{aligned}
p_{max(12)}(x) &= p_1(x) * P_2[X \leq x] + p_2(x) * P_2[X \leq x] &= 2x \\
P_{max(12)}[X \leq x] &= x^2
\end{aligned}
$$

This formula can be generalized to the histogram of n overlapping strokes:

$$
p_{max(i=1..n)}(x) = n\, x^{n-1}, \qquad P_{max(i=1..n)}[X \leq x] = x^n
$$

Experimental measurements fit this formula well (Fig. 5).

A flat histogram is then obtained by multiplying each value x by the corresponding cumulative density $P_{max(i=1..n)}(X \leq x)$ [Bov00]. Equilibration can thus be performed by applying a power function depending on the number of overlapping strokes.

78

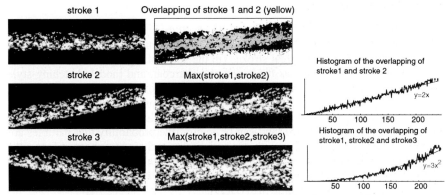

Fig. 5. Histogram of overlapping strokes under the *max* mode.

4.2 Hardware-assisted equilibration

For each pixel, we compute the number of overlapping strokes in a *coverage map* and perform the corresponding monomial mapping. The coverage map is built like the raw threshold matrix by rendering the stroke triangle strips, but using the coverage texture instead of the the threshold texture, and an additive blending mode.

A Gaussian low-pass filter is usually used to simulate the spatial integration of the visual system [Ost99, OH99, Uli87]. If we consider only straight strokes, performing a Gaussian blur in the global matrix is similar to using a Gaussian-filtered texture, which can be pre-computed. We make a linearization and neglect the effect of warping. We use coverage textures that are pre-filtered with a Gaussian (cutoff frequency is 30 cycles per degree [LO86]), and warp them like the threshold textures. We map a coverage of 1.0 to a frame-buffer value of 16, which results in a maximum number of strokes handled by pixel of 16, while providing enough dynamic for the Gaussian (quantization to 16 levels). Equilibration is performed using a look-up table and the pixel-textures hardware (Fig. 6(a)).

(a)   (b)

Fig. 6. (a) Effect of equilibration for a target tone image consisting of a grey-level ramp. (b) Hatching tool using one or two carriers (in red).

5   User control

We now discuss in more detail how the user can draw strokes and how he controls the *precision* and *smudging*.

5.1 Stroke drawing interface

The user draws free-hand strokes using the mouse or a tablet. We use a Bézier-fitting method enforcing G^1 continuity for poly-Bézier curves[Sch88]. Strokes are organized into layers to facilitate editing or selection of groups of strokes. We propose rudimentary hatching tools based on the interpolation between one or two carrier strokes and random perturbations (Fig. 6(b)).

5.2 Precision

As discussed in Section 2.1, controlling the amount of detail is a key aspect of drawing. The mastery and subtlety of this skill are unfortunately elusive and remains the prerogative of great masters. Our system however proposes a simple model of precision, controlled spatially through the precision map. We developed two mechanisms, and their respective influence is controlled through two global parameters, which can be seen as a crude attempt to introduce a notion of *style*.

The precision and smudging maps are controlled with the same interface. The user modifies them using an airbrush tool, either directly on the drawing or on the map.

Stroke saliency vs. tonal fidelity. The first precision mechanism controls the respective importance of stroke saliency and tonal fidelity. More salient strokes focus the attention on the 2D quality of the drawing, while a more faithful tone reproduction emphasizes the depicted subject.

Our system uses precision to vary the amount of equilibration. A precision of 1 corresponds to a complete equilibration and faithful tone reproduction, while a precision of 0 corresponds to no equilibration at all and more visible strokes. This mechanism is implemented by modifying the equilibration mapping presented in Section 4. The global importance of this mechanism is controlled by the weight $w_{saliency}$. Because we use the *max* merging mode, a lower precision also results in darker tones in areas covered by more than one stroke. This means that the output tone is then more ruled by the number of strokes than by the target tone.

Spatial detail. The second mechanism controls the amount of spatial detail in the target tone map. It is common artistic practice to use uniform tones for regions of little importance, and fine spatial details for regions of focus. This feature could be implemented using a non-linear blurring filter with a spatially variant Gaussian kernel size. Unfortunately this solution is too slow for real-time implementation. We therefore use a linear interpolation between the fully detailed target tone image and a low-pass version computed using a Gaussian filter (in the spirit of e.g. [KVHS00]). In practice we set the variance of the Gaussian to 5% of the image size.

5.3 Smudging

Traditional smudging softens a drawing by spreading graphite particles. In contrast to the technique by Sousa et al. [SB99b], our implementation of smudging is purely phenomenological. It is an extension of the antialiasing technique described in Section 3.2. It consists in varying the width of the s' function used for thresholding.

The user has direct control on smudging via the smudging map. It is used for imaging during the thresholding phase. The target tone is stored in the red channel, the equilibrated threshold map in the green channel, and the smudging map in the blue channel. Using the function s' defined in Eq. 3, the look-up-table is then $LUT_{thresh} = s'(r,g,b)$. Fig. 7(a) demonstrates the effect of smudging. The use of a spatially-varying bluring filter would result in a similar result, but at a higher cost.

6   Results

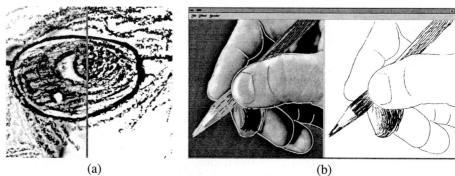

Fig. 7. (a) With (left) and without (right) smudging. (b) Snapshot of an interactive session.

Our system was implemented on Silicon Graphics workstations using the OpenGL graphics API. Fig. 7(b) presents a snapshot of an interactive session, where the drawing is refreshed at about 20Hz on an SGI Octane2 R14K.

Fig. 8(a) imitates red chalk or soft pastel. Color and background paper were added as a post-process. Fig. 8(b) uses etching strokes. Interpolation between carriers was used to generate the large number of strokes. Note the importance of outline strokes. Fig. 1 demonstrates the rich degree of economy that can be obtained, since only a dozen strokes are used for the facial features. Precision is high around the eyes and mouth.

All the examples shown in this paper were generated by a user who is not a trained illustrator. Similar or better results could be obtained by skilled artists using traditional media or a product such as *Corel Painter*. However, this is the goal of this project to make this degree of expressiveness available to a non-artist.

7   Conclusions and future work

We have presented an interactive drawing system based on a thresholding model of strokes. It permits semi-automatic tonal modeling and decouples the technical aspects of drawing from expressiveness. We have developed a fast and direct equilibration technique that is based on a probabilistic model of threshold textures. We have introduced different high-level controls, including a precision map that controls both the amount of spatial detail and the saliency of strokes. Our system provides both interactivity and high-quality output.

An important issue of future work is the introduction of higher-level textures as pioneered by Winkenbach et al. [WS94] and Salisbury et al. [SABS94] for pen-and-ink style. More elaborate hatching tools should also be provided, either using orientation textures [SWHS97] or line-integral-convolutions [TB96].

The use of a photograph restricts the drawing to a realistic perspective. Introducing warping or "carricature" tools could remove this limitation.

The introduction of color is an exciting but delicate topic; we believe that colors cannot be treated simply like tones. A better treatment of outline strokes is a challenging task as well. The complex interaction between outline and tonal strokes accounts for the elusive quality obtained by skilled artists.

The system can also be adapted for automatic drawing from 3D models. Using the discussion in Section 2.2 as a starting point, mappings from 3D properties and user control space could be defined.

(a)   (b)

Fig. 8. (a) Sanguine style (red chalk). (b) Engraving style.

Acknowledgments

We wish to thank Edouard Basilia for the photograph used in Fig. 1, and our models, Sylvie Fresco, Kari Anne Kjølaas, and Manue Brun. Many thanks to Adam Finkelstein, Justin Legakis, Joëlle Thollot, Agata Opalach and Osama Tolba for helpful discussions and suggestions about the paper. This work was supported by an NSF CISE Research Infrastructure Award (EIA-9802220) and a gift from Pixar Animation Studios. Mathieu Miller was supported by Abvent and François Duranleau by an FCAR grant (B1-03C-68966).

References

Ada95.   A. Adams. *The Negative+The Print*. Little Brown and Co, 1995.

BM00.   D. Blythe and T. McReynolds. Advanced graphics programming techniques using OpenGL. SIGGRAPH course notes, 2000.

Bov00.   A. Bovik, editor. *Handbook of Image and Video Processing*. Academic Press, 2000.

Edw99.   B. Edwards. *The New Drawing on the Right Side of the Brain*. J P Tarcher, 1999.

Elb95.   G. Elber. Line art rendering via a coverage of isoparametric curves. *IEEE Trans. on Visualization and Computer Graphics*, 1(3), September 1995.

Elb99.   G. Elber. Interactive line art rendering of free form surfaces. In *Eurographics*, 1999.

Gai96.   A. Gair, editor. *Artist's Manual: A Complete Guide to Painting and Drawing Materials and Techniques*. Chronicle Books, 1996.

GDCV98.   J. Gomes, L. Darsa, B. Costa, and L. Velho. *Warping And Morphing Of Graphical Objects*. Morgan Kaufman, 1998.

82

Hae90.   P. Haeberli. Paint by numbers: Abstract image representations. In *SIGGRAPH*, 1990.

Hal64.   R. Hale. *Drawing lessons from the great masters*. Watson Guptill, 1964.

HWSE99.   W. Heidrich, R. Westermann, H.-P. Seidel, and T. Ertl. Applications of pixel textures in visualization and realistic image synthesis. In *ACM Symp. on Interactive 3D Graphics*, 1999.

Kem90.   M. Kemp. *The Science of Art*. Yale Univ. Pr., 1990.

Kos99.   D. Kosinski. *The Artist and the Camera: Degas to Picasso*. Yale Univ. Pr., 1999.

KVHS00.   J. Kautz, P. Vazquez, W. Heidrich, and HP. Seidel. A Unified Approach to Prefiltered Environment Maps. In *Eurographics Rendering Workshop*, 2000.

Lei94.   W. Leister. Computer generated copper plates. *Computer Graphics Forum*, 13(1), 1994.

LO86.   J. Thomas L. Olzak. Seeing spatial patterns. In Boff, Kaufman, and Thomas, editors, *Handbook of Perception and Human Performance*. Wiley and Sons, 1986.

LS95.   J. Lansdown and S. Schofield. Expressive rendering: A review of nonphotorealistic techniques. *IEEE Computer Graphics and Applications*, 15(3), May 1995.

MB95.   E. Mortensen and W. Barrett. Intelligent scissors for image composition. In *SIGGRAPH*, 1995.

Men76.   D. Mendelowitz. *A Guide to Drawing*. Holt, Rinehart and Winston, 1976.

MKT$^+$97. L. Markosian, M. Kowalski, S. Trychin, L. Bourdev, D. Goldstein, and J. Hughes. Real-time nonphotorealistic rendering. In *Proc. of SIGGRAPH*, 1997.

OH99.   V. Ostromoukhov and R. Hersch. Multi-color and artistic dithering. In *Proc of SIGGRAPH*, 1999.

Ost99.   V. Ostromoukhov. Digital facial engraving. In *Proc. SIGGRAPH*, 1999.

PB94.   Y. Pnueli and A. Bruckstein. DigiDürer – a digital engraving system. *The Visual Computer*, 10(5), 1994.

SABS94.   M. Salisbury, S. Anderson, R. Barzel, and D. Salesin. Interactive pen–and–ink illustration. In *Proc. of SIGGRAPH*, 1994.

SALS96.   M. Salisbury, C. Anderson, D. Lischinski, and D. Salesin. Scale-dependent reproduction of pen-and-ink illustrations. In *Proc. of SIGGRAPH*, 1996.

SB99a.   M. Sousa and J. Buchanan. Computer-generated graphite pencil rendering of 3D polygonal models. In *Proc. of Eurographics*, 1999.

SB99b.   M. Sousa and J. Buchanan. Observational model of blenders and erasers in computer-generated pencil rendering. In *Graphics Interface*, 1999.

SB00.   M. Sousa and J. Buchanan. Observational models of graphite pencil materials. *Computer Graphics Forum*, 19(1), March 2000.

Sch88.   PJ Schneider. Phoenix: An interactive curve design system based on the automatic fitting of hand-sketched curves. Master's thesis, University of Washington, 1988.

Sch99.   G. Schaub. *The Digital Darkroom: Black-And-White Techniques Using Photoshop*. Silver Pixel Pr., 1999.

Smi87.   R. Smith. *The Artist's Handbook*. Knopf, 1987.

Spe17.   H. Speed. *The Practice and Science of Drawing*. Dover, 1917.

ST90.   T. Saito and T. Takahashi. Comprehensible rendering of 3-D shapes. In *Proc. of SIGGRAPH*, 1990.

SWHS97.   M. Salisbury, M. Wong, J. Hughes, and D. Salesin. Orientable textures for image-based pen-and-ink illustration. In *Proc. of SIGGRAPH*, 1997.

TB96.   G. Turk and D. Banks. Image-guided streamline placement. In *SIGGRAPH*, 1996.

TFN99.   S. Takagi, I. Fujishiro, and M. Nakajima. Volumetric modeling of artistic techniques in colored pencil drawing. In *SIGGRAPH 99: Conference abstracts and applications*, 1999.

Uli87.   R. Ulichney, editor. *Digital Halftoning*. MIT Press, 1987.

VB00.   O. Veryovka and J. Buchanan. Texture-based dither matrices. *Computer Graphics Forum*, 19(1), March 2000.

WS94.   G. Winkenbach and D. Salesin. Computer–generated pen–and–ink illustration. In *Proc. of SIGGRAPH*, 1994.

Editors' Note: see Appendix, p. 327 for colored figure of this paper

Artistic Composition for Image Creation

Bruce Gooch   Erik Reinhard   Chris Moulding   Peter Shirley

University of Utah

Abstract. Altering the viewing parameters of a 3D object results in computer graphics images of varying quality. One aspect of image quality is the *composition* of the image. While the esthetic properties of an image are subjective, some heuristics used by artists to create images can be approximated quantitatively. We present an algorithm based on heuristic compositional rules for finding the format, viewpoint, and layout for an image of a 3D object. Our system computes viewing parameters automatically or allows a user to explicitly manipulate them.

1   Introduction

Composition is taught to artists by showing them a few simple rules, then showing them a number of pitfalls to avoid. We apply rules from the artistic community as well as observations from the psychology literature. Perhaps it would be more systematic to extract compositional principles entirely from the psychology literature, but what is currently known in that field [15, 18, 21] is not yet specific enough to allow automation. While automation is not needed by artists who know both how to apply and when to break these rules, our system is intended for the more common non-artistic user.

Little work dealing with artistic composition has been published in the computer graphics literature. Feiner and Seligmann [9, 17] borrowed principles from technical illustration. Kawai et al. [11] automated the creation of pleasing lighting. Both He et al. [20] and Karp and Feiner [10] examined how animation sequences are developed. Kowalski et al. [12] have explored user guided composition.

2   Compositional Principles

In art, heuristics for creating images of 3D objects fall into three general categories: choosing the **format** (image size, shape, and orientation); choosing the **viewpoint**; and choosing the **layout** of the object on the image plane.

2.1   Format

The format of an image describes its shape and proportions. An image that is wider than it is tall has a *landscape* format, images that are taller than wide have a *portrait* format. Artists use the following rule of thumb [5], landscape formats should be used with horizontal objects, and portrait formats with vertical objects as in Figure 5 This allows the object to become part of the format rather than dividing it as shown in Figure 1(a).

While the proportions of the format are chosen at the whim of the artist, most art instructors agree that the format of an image should be established first [5]. Early work in psychology showed that the *golden ratio* seems to be preferred [3, 16]. The golden ratio is $(\sqrt{5}+1)/2 \approx 1.618$. Artists often use a five by eight format, which is regarded as being derived from the golden ratio.

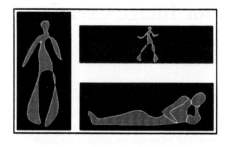 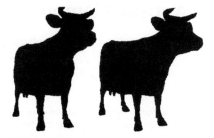

(a) The image on the left has a vertical format in accord with the subject. Likewise, in the horizontal lower image. The subject in the upper right image is out of relationship with the format and divides the image.

(b) Left: an "accidental" view where one of the cows hind legs ends up directly behind a front leg. Right: the same cow from a slightly perturbed viewing direction.

Fig. 1. Examples of some formating and viewpoint heuristics.

2.2 Viewpoint

Psychologists have studied viewers' preferences for one viewpoint over another for particular objects. A viewpoint that is preferred by most viewers is called a *canonical viewpoint*. Palmer et al. [13] found that canonical viewpoints are off-axis, while Verfaillie [19] discovered that a three-quarter view of a familiar object is preferred.

A thorough investigation of canonical views was recently carried out by Blantz et al. [6]. They found three predictors of whether a view is canonical: the significance of visible features for a given observer, the stability of the view with respect to small transformations, and the extent to which features are occluded.

Significant features for an observer may include the facial portion of a head, the handle of a tool, or the seat of a chair. In viewing objects, Blantz et al. found that people preferred views which expressed the manner in which an object was seen in its environment, i.e. chairs are viewed from above while airplanes may be viewed from above or below. They also found a distinct lack of "handedness" when humans choose preferred views. For example, when viewing a teapot a right handed viewer did not mind if the handle was placed on the left side of the image.

Image stability means that the viewpoint can be moved with little or no change in the resulting image. Many psychology researchers have shown that objects in a scene which share an edge will confuse a viewer [4, 5, 15]. For example the viewpoint that produces the "three legged cow" in Figure 1(b) is never picked as a canonical view.

When subjects in the Blantz et al. study were given the ability to choose the viewpoint for an object, it was discovered that the subjects performed an internal optimization to find a viewpoint that showed the smallest number of occlusions. This occurred for both familiar objects and artificial geometric constructs. For instance, when choosing a viewpoint for a teapot the subjects always choose a viewpoint that shows both the handle and the spout. This result agrees with Edelman et al. [8] who showed that canonical views for "nonsense" objects may also exist.

Artists have their own heuristics for choosing view directions that are consistent with the psychology results: pick an off-axis view from a natural eye height. Direct 45° angles are avoided. Another rule is to have the projections of front/side/top of the object ve areas of 4/2/1 on the canvas [2, 18] (often expressed as 55%/30%/15%). d side dimensions can be exchanged depending on the object.

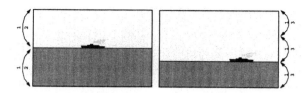

Fig. 2. *Halving the canvas creates static compositions which are peaceful and quiet, but may seem dull. Dividing the canvas into thirds yields a more dynamic image. Note that the rules are applied both horizontally and vertically (after Clifton [7]).*

2.3 Layout

The best known rule of layout is the *rule of thirds* (Figure 2). By partitioning their canvas into thirds both vertically and horizontally, and placing the strong vertical and horizontal components of the image near these lines, artists avoid equal spatial divisions of their image. Equal spatial divisions give an image balance and symmetry. However, equal divisions may also cause an image to be dull, due to the lack of any dynamic quality in the image. Artists have also found the *rule of fifths* useful. Division into quarters is to be avoided because the centerline introduces too much symmetry [7]. These rules can be mixed by dividing the canvas into thirds along one axis and fifths along the other, as in Figure 5.

There are additional, often contradictory, minor layout heuristics taught to artists which are quantifiable. Art theorists contend that the most important information in the image should be placed near the center [3, 18]. However, studies show that objects in a scene should be repelled from the corners and center of the format [2]. Having chosen a viewpoint, it is good practice to place the object in the bottom portion of the image if the viewpoint is above the object or to place the object in the top portion of the image if the viewpoint is below the object. Strong diagonal lines yield a more dynamic image. However, lines oriented toward corners tend to draw the viewers eye off of the image [7].

3 Computer Graphics Implementation

The previous section shows a method for constructing images by first choosing format based on object aspect-ratio. Then choosing the viewpoint to be both off-axis and "natural" for the object. Finally, the object is "framed" within the boundaries of the format to produce a pleasing layout. These steps lead directly to our algorithm.

Our algorithm attempts to find a good composition for a computer graphics image of a 3D object. The algorithm can be run in a fully automatic mode as long as "front" and "top" are defined for the object, but user intervention can be applied at any stage.

We first have the user select a format of either portrait or landscape for a five by eight canvas. Our default is landscape. The format could be found automatically using the principle direction of the orthographic projection of the object. We then compute an initial off axis viewpoint for the object. Finally, we use a robust optimization procedure to perturb the viewing parameters guided by heuristic rules for layout.

3.1 Viewing Parameterization

Of the many possible ways to specify viewing parameters, we choose a system with dimensions that are as intuitive as possible to help us gain insight into the optimization space. We fix two parameters to reduce the dimension of the space we search during the optimization process. The view-up vector is fixed to be parallel to the "top" direction of the model. We also fix the horizontal and vertical field-of-view parameters.

Our free variables are the two spherical coordinates of the vector from the object center to the camera, the two spherical angles of camera pan and tilt relative to that vector, and the distance of the camera to the object center. This gives five free variables, the first two corresponding to rotating position around the object, the second two controlling camera orientation relative to the object, and the last allowing the camera to move toward or away from the object.

3.2 Initial Viewpoint

As a default we choose a viewpoint above and in front of the object. We set left and right arbitrarily due to the finding of Blantz et al. [6] that viewers do not seem to have a preference for left versus right views. The specific three quarter view of the object is set according to the 4/2/1 rule described in Section 2.2. Given the octant the viewpoint resides in there is a unique direction corresponding to the proportions of the orthographic projection of the objects bounding box. Once the initial view direction is fixed, the initial distance from object center to viewpoint is set to be twice the width of the bounding box so we are certain our viewpoint is on screen. Otherwise our layout optimization could converge to a degenerate local minimum created by a blank screen.

3.3 Layout Optimization

Once we have an initial viewing direction, we would like to use a rule such as the rule of thirds, to perturb the viewing parameters into a "good" composition. We would like to detect important image features such as silhouettes, crease lines, strong illumination gradients, and important semantic features like faces. However, we have made our exploratory work as simple as possible and focus only on silhouettes. We would like our optimization procedure to move silhouette lines near third or fifth lines.

We assume that our model is polygonal, with at least a medium level of tessellation, and compute silhouettes in a brute force fashion. If the model occludes a silhouette edge we call that edge a hidden silhouette. For simplicity we do not eliminate hidden silhouettes, and use the silhouette midpoints for computation. We project each midpoints onto a target image with pixel values between zero and one (Figure 6). The target image contains a template with dark pixels near "magnet" features, and light pixels elsewhere. Minor layout heuristics can be combined with the rules of thirds or fifths by compositing their respective templates. Note that any grey scale image could be used to drive our optimization. Figure 5 shows a compositional template inspired by the famous "diamond" composition of Van Gogh's *Irises (1890)*. The objective function is the sum of the pixel values hit by silhouette midpoints. A set of silhouettes that lands mostly on dark pixels is "good", and a set that hits mostly light pixels is "bad". If a midpoint lands off-screen, it takes on the value one plus a linear distance term. This allows edges to be off screen, but encourages them to move toward the screen.

The objective function is reasonably well behaved, although with unknown gradient. This makes the downhill simplex (Nelder-Mead) [14] method well-suited because it does not require analytic derivatives for the objective function.

A concern is that the global minimum for our objective function is to move the camera far away with a pan and tilt that projects all edges onto the darkest pixel. Fortunately, there seem to be enough appealing local minima for this not to occur in practice. Our goal is a reasonable image, instead of the global minimum for the objective function, therefore a local minimum meets our needs. Another concern is that by using midpoints of segments, both short and long edges have equal weight. We could weight edges by length, but equal weighting gives extra importance to highly polygonalized regions which often correspond to preferred semantic features such as faces.

Once the layout optimization has converged, we run a secondary optimization that attempts to eliminate accidental views that arise for coincident silhouettes. A result of this secondary process is shown in Figure 1(b), where the cows hind leg becomes unoccluded. Changing the viewing distance, pan, and tilt do not affect accidental views. Therefore we fix these values and allow the secondary optimization to operate in the two dimensional space of view angles. The objective function that is minimized for this step is one over a constant term plus the sum of squared distances between all midpoints. The constant term keeps the function finite. Although this computation is quadratic on the number of silhouette edges, the objective function is only two dimensional and thus this stage is not a bottleneck. Because we are only trying to climb away from local minima where silhouette edges line up we run the secondary optimization for just 100 iterations.

3.4 Results

Our system was implemented in C on a 250MHz R10000 SGI Origin. Figure 7 shows the results of our algorithm on a 69473 triangle model of a bunny. This image converged in 272 iterations and took approximately three minutes in the initial stage of optimization. The secondary optimization to remove a possible accidental view took a few seconds. Figure 5 shows a 6272 polygon toy plane, with overlaid layout solutions from two initial viewpoints, one above and one below. The solution converged in 165 iterations and took approximately six seconds.

Figure 5 shows the initial viewpoint computed for a 5804 polygon cow model, along with three different layout solutions overlaid on their templates. The rotated template was inspired by the famous "diamond" composition of Van Gogh's *Irises (1890)*. This image layout converged in 133 iterations and took about five seconds to compute.

4   Conclusions and Future Work

We presented an overview of compositional principles and a proof-of-concept implementation that automates creation of simple images based on quantitative compositional heuristics. There are many directions to take this work. Our objective function operates on silhouette edges which may not correspond to important image features.

Our algorithms work with single objects rather than scenes. In scenes, the grouping of objects should be done in a manner which tells a story about the objects or describes their relationship with one another. There are compositional rules that can serve as guidelines in this process [4, 5, 15]. Calahan [1] explains how lighting can be used to control perceived grouping of scene elements. These processes are highly dependent on scene semantics and may thus be difficult to automate. Advanced composition will most likely remain the domain of the trained artist. However, the increasing number of computer users with no formal artistic training provides a large market for tools that assist in the aesthetic process.

88

5 Acknowledgments

We would like to thank Brian Smits and Don Nelson for their help in the initial phases of this work. This work was carried out under NSF grants NSF/STC for computer graphics EIA 8920219, NSF/ACR, NSF/MRI and by the DOE AVTC/VIEWS.

References

1. APODACA, A. A., AND GRITZ, L. *Advanced Renderman Creating CGI for Motion Pictures.* Morgan Kaufmann, 2000.
2. ARNHEIM, R. *Art and Visual Perception: A Psychology of the Creative Eye.* University of California Press, 1974.
3. ARNHEIM, R. *The Power of the Center.* University of California Press, 1988.
4. BARBOUR, C. G., AND MEYER, G. W. Visual cues and pictorial limitations in photorealistic images. *The Visual Computer 9*, 4 (1992), 151–165.
5. BETHERS, R. *Composition in Pictures.* Pitman Publishing Corporation, 1964.
6. BLANZ, V., TARR, M. J., AND BULTHOFF, H. H. What object attributes determine canonical views. *Perception 28*, 5 (1999), 575–600.
7. CLIFTON, J. *The Eye of the Artist.* North Light Publishers., 1973.
8. EDELMAN, S., AND BULTHOFF, H. Orientation dependence in the recognition of familiar and novel views of three-dimensional objects. *Vision Research 32*, 12 (1992), 2385–2400.
9. FEINER, S. Apex: an experiment in the automated creation of pictorial explanations. *IEEE Computer Graphics & Applications 5*, 11 (November 1985), 29–37.
10. KARP, P., AND FEINER, S. Issues in the automated generation of animated presentations. In *Graphics Interface* (1990), pp. 39–48.
11. KAWAI, J. K., PAINTER, J. S., AND COHEN, M. F. Radioptimization - goal based rendering. In *Proceedings of SIGGRAPH* (1993), pp. 147–154.
12. KOWALSKI, M. A., HUGHES, J. F., RUBIN, C. B., AND OHYA, J. User-guided composition effects for art-based rendering. *2001 ACM Symposium on Interactive 3D Graphics* (March 2001), 99–102. ISBN 1-58113-292-1.
13. PALMER, S., ROSCH, E., AND CHASE, P. Canonical perspective and the perception of objects. *Attention and Performance 9* (1981), 135–151.
14. PRESS, W., TEUKOLSKY, S., VETTERLING, W., AND FLANNERY, B. P. *Numerical Recipes in C*, 2nd ed. Cambridge Univ. Press, 1993.
15. RAMACHANDRAN, V., AND HIRSTEIN, W. The science of art a neurological theory of esthetic experience. *Journal of Consciousness Studies 6*, 6-7 (1999), 15–51.
16. SANDER, F. Gestaltpsychologie und kunsttheorie. ein beitrag zur psychologie der architektur. *Neue Psychologische Studien 8* (1931), 311–333.
17. SELIGMANN, D. D., AND FEINER, S. Automated generation of intent-based 3d illustrations. In *Proceedings of SIGGRAPH* (1991), pp. 123–132.
18. SOLSO, R. L. *Cognition and the Visual Arts.* MIT Press/Bradford Books Series in Cognitive Psychology, 1999.
19. VERFAILLIE, K., AND BOUTSEN, L. A corpus of 714 full-color images of depth-rotated objects. *Perception and Psychophysics 57*, 7 (1995), 925–961.
20. WEI HE, L., COHEN, M. F., AND SALESIN, D. H. The virtual cinematographer: A paradigm for automatic real-time camera control and directing. In *Proceedings of SIGGRAPH* (1996), pp. 217–224.
21. ZAKIA, R. D. *Perception and Imaging.* Focal Press Publications, 1997.

Editors' Note: see Appendix, p. 328 for colored figures of this paper

Shader Lamps:
Animating Real Objects With Image-Based Illumination

Ramesh Raskar[+]   Greg Welch[*]   Kok-Lim Low[*]   Deepak Bandyopadhyay[*]

[+]MERL, Mitsubishi Electric Research Labs
[*]University of North Carolina at Chapel Hill

Abstract

We describe a new paradigm for three-dimensional computer graphics, using projectors to graphically animate physical objects in the real world. The idea is to replace a physical object—with its inherent color, texture, and material properties—with a neutral object and projected imagery, reproducing the original (or alternative) appearance directly on the object. Because the approach is to effectively "lift" the visual properties of the object into the projector, we call the projectors *shader lamps*. We address the central issue of complete and continuous illumination of non-trivial physical objects using multiple projectors and present a set of new techniques that makes the process of illumination practical. We demonstrate the viability of these techniques through a variety of table-top applications, and describe preliminary results to reproduce life-sized virtual spaces.

Keywords: Engineering Visualization, Illumination Effects, User Interfaces, Virtual Reality.

1. Introduction

Graphics in the World. Traditionally, computer graphics techniques attempt to "capture" the real world in the computer, and then to reproduce it visually. In later years, work has been done to explore what is in effect the reversal of this relationship—to "insert" computer graphics into the real world. Primarily, this has been done for special effects in movies, and for real-time *augmented reality*. Most recently, there is a new trend to use light projectors to render imagery directly in our real physical surroundings. Examples include the *Luminous Room* [Underkoffler99] and the *Office of the Future* [Raskar98]. What we are pursuing here is a more complete extension of these ideas—the incorporation of three-dimensional computer graphics and animation directly into the real world all around us.

Stimulation and Communication of Ideas. Despite the many advances in computer graphics, architects and city planners (for example) still resort to building physical models when the time comes to seek client or constituent approval [Howard00]. The architects that we have spoken with, and many books on the subject, have noted that while it is true that designers cannot do without CAD tools anymore, "it [the computer] cannot replace the actual material experience, the physical shape and the build-up of spatial relationships." [Knoll92]. Even in this day of computer animation, animators often sculpt a physical model of a character before making computer models. This was the case with Geri in "Geri's Game" (Pixar Animation Studios). One reason for these sentiments and practices is that the human interface to a physical model is the essence of "intuitive". There are no widgets to manipulate, no sliders to move, and no displays to look through (or wear). Instead, we walk around objects, moving in and out to zoom, gazing and focusing on interesting components, all at very high visual, spatial, and temporal fidelity. We all have a lifetime of experience with this paradigm. The ambitious goal of shader lamps is to enjoy some of the advantages of this natural physical interface, in particular, the auto-stereoscopic nature of viewing physical objects, combined with the richness of computer graphics.

Figure 1: The underlying physical model of the Taj Mahal and the same model enhanced with *shader lamps*.

Image-Based Illumination. When we illuminate a real object with a white light, its surface reflects particular wavelengths of light. Because our perception of the surface attributes is dependent only on the spectrum of light that eventually reaches our eyes, we can shift or rearrange items in the optical path, as long as the spectrum of light that eventually reaches our eyes is sufficiently similar. Many physical attributes can be effectively incorporated into the light source to achieve a perceptually equivalent effect on a neutral object. Even non-realistic appearances can be realized. This concept is illustrated in Figure 2. We can use digital light projectors and computer graphics to form *shader lamps* that effectively reproduce or synthesize various surface attributes, either statically, dynamically, or interactively. While the results are theoretically equivalent for only a limited class of surfaces and attributes, our experience is that they are quite realistic and compelling for a broad range of applications.

The existence of an underlying physical model is arguably unusual for computer graphics, however, it is not for architects [Howard00], artists, and computer animators. In addition, various approaches to automatic three-dimensional fabrication are steadily becoming available, e.g. laminate object manufacturing, stereolithography, and fused deposition. It is not unreasonable to argue that three-dimensional printing and faxing are coming.

We previously presented preliminary thoughts and results in workshop settings [Raskar99b]. After further development of our ideas and methods, we are now ready to articulate the idea more completely, and to demonstrate practical methods. We present results using multiple shader lamps to animate physical objects of varying complexity—from a smooth flower vase to a relatively complex model of the Taj Mahal. We also demonstrate some applications such as small "living" dioramas, human-scale indoor models, and hand-held physical user-interface objects.

Contributions

- We introduce shader lamps as a new mode of visualizing 3D computer graphics. Our idea treats illumination basically as a 3D perspective projection from a lamp, and thus, it can be created using traditional 3D computer graphics. We present techniques that can replace not just textures, i.e. diffuse component, but can reproduce virtually any BRDF appearance.

- We present new algorithms to make the process of illumination practical. We first identify a simple radiance adjustment equation for guiding the rendering process and then present methods for the corresponding intensity correction.

- We introduce a new algorithm for determining pixel weights and computing feathering intensities across transitions in projectors' regions of influence in the presence of depth discontinuities.

2. Previous Work

Theater and entertainment. Naimark [Naimark84] used a rotating movie camera to film a living room, replete with furniture and people. The room and furniture were then painted white (neutral), and the captured imagery was projected back onto the walls using a rotating projector that was precisely registered with the original camera. This crucial co-location of the capturing and displaying devices is common to most of the current demonstrations that use pre-recorded images or image-sequences. A limited but compelling example of this idea is the projection of pre-recorded video to animate four neutral busts of singing men in the Walt Disney World "Haunted Mansion". In addition, a patented projector and fiber-optic setup animates the head of the fictional fortune teller "Madame Leota" inside a real crystal ball [Liljegren90].

Slides of modified photographs augmented with fine details are also used with very bright projectors to render imagery on a very large architectural scale. A well-known modern realization of this idea is the Son et Lumiere (light show) on the Blois castle in the Loire Valley (France). In addition, the medium is now being used elsewhere around the world. Influenced by Son et Lumiere, Marc Levoy [Levoy00] has recently experimented with projection of imagery onto small-scale fabricated statues. Instead of photographs, he first renders an image of a stored 3D model similar to our techniques and then manually positions the projector to geometrically register the projected image. The [Hypermask99], an exception in terms of automatic registration, involves projecting an animated face onto a moving mask for storytelling.

All these systems create compelling visualizations. However, the cumbersome alignment process can take several hours even for a single projector. Our technique avoids this problem by forming a 3D geometric understanding using well-known computer vision techniques described in Section 4 and then moves beyond simple image projection to reproduce reflectance properties.

Tangible luminous interfaces. The Luminous Room project treats a co-located camera-

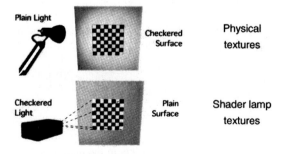

Figure 2: Concept of *shader lamps.*

projector pair as an I/O bulb to sense and inject imagery onto flat surfaces in the real physical surroundings of a room or a designated workspace [Underkoffler99]. The work we present here is distinct from, but complementary to, this work. A primary distinction is that their main focus is interaction with the information via luminous (lit) and tangible interfaces. This focus is exemplified in such applications as "Illuminating Light" and "URP" (urban planning). The latter arguably bears closest resemblance to our work, in particular the interactive simulation of building shadows from sunlight. The approach is to recognize the 2D physical objects (building "phicons") lying in a plane, track their 2D positions and orientations in the plane, and project light from overhead to reproduce the appropriate sunlight shadows. However, we are primarily interested in the use of physical objects as *truly* three-dimensional display devices for more general computer graphics, visualization and aesthetic (artistic) applications.

Modeling and rendering architecture from photographs. In the "Facade" project, a sparse set of photographs are used to model and render architectural monuments [Debevec96]. This is a good example of a hybrid approach of using geometry and images to reproduce physical human-made structures. The main challenges are related to the occlusion, sampling, and blending issues that arise when re-projecting images onto geometric models. They face these challenges with computer imagery and analytic models, while in shader lamps, we have to face them with real (light projected) imagery and physical models. It would be useful to use Facade tools to build a hybrid geometry and image model of a university campus, and then use the shader-lamp techniques to animate a scaled physical model, effectively creating a "living diorama" of the campus.

To realize the general application of this technique, one must, among other things, have a method for pre-warping the imagery to "fit" the physical object so that it appears correct to local viewers. Some limited 2D warping effects have been achieved by [Dorsey91] to model the appearance of theatrical backdrops so that they appear correct from the audience's perspective. The Office of the Future project [Raskar98] presents rendering techniques to project onto non-planar surfaces. We use techniques that build on this to illuminate potentially non-convex or a disjoint set of objects, and present new techniques to address the alignment, occlusion, sampling and blending issues.

3. The Illumination Process

We introduce the idea of rearranging the terms in the relationship between illumination and reflectance to reproduce equivalent radiance at a surface. As shown in flatland in Figure 3, the radiance in a certain direction at point (x), which has a given BRDF in the physical world (left), can be mimicked by changing the BRDF and illuminating the point with a appropriately chosen light source, e.g. a projector pixel (right). Below we identify a radiance adjustment equation for determining the necessary intensity of a projector pixel, given the position and orientation of the viewer and the virtual scene. For a more systematic rendering scheme, we describe the notion of separating the *rendering view*—the traditional virtual camera view, from the *shading view*—the position of the viewer for lighting calculations.

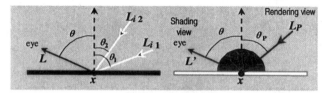

Figure 3: (Left) The radiance at a point in the direction (θ, ϕ). (Right) The radiance as a result of illumination from a projector lamp. By rearranging the parameters in the optical path, the two can be made equal.

First, let us consider the rendering equation, which is essentially a geometrical optics approximation as explained in [Kajiya86]. The radiance at a visible surface point (x) in the direction (θ,ϕ) that would reach the observer of a physical realization of the scene is

$$L(x,\theta,\phi) = g(x,\theta,\phi)(L_e(x,\theta,\phi) + h(x,\theta,\phi)) \qquad (1)$$

where

$$h(x,\theta,\phi) = \int_i F_r(x,\theta,\phi,\theta_i,\phi_i) L_i(x,\theta_i,\phi_i) \cos(\theta_i) d\omega_i \qquad (2)$$

and $g(x,\theta,\phi)$ is the geometry term (visibility and distance), $L_e(x,\theta,\phi)$ is the emitted radiance at the point (non-zero only for light sources), and $F_r(x,\theta,\phi,\theta_i,\phi_i)$ is the BRDF of the point. The integral in $h(x,\theta,\phi)$ accounts for all reflection of incident radiance $L_i(x,\theta_i,\phi_i)$ from solid angles $d\omega_i$. Radiance has dimensions of energy per unit time, area and solid angle.

Treating the projector lamp as a point emitter, the radiance due to direct projector illumination at the same surface point at distance $d(x)$ but with diffuse reflectance $k_u(x)$ is given by

$$L'(x,\theta,\phi) = g(x,\theta,\phi)k_u(x)I_p(x,\theta_p,\phi_p)\cos(\theta_p)/d(x)^2 \qquad (3)$$

where $I_p(x,\theta_p,\phi_p)$ = radiant intensity of projector in the direction (θ_p,ϕ_p) and is related to a discretized pixel value via filtering and tone representation.

We can reproduce radiance $L'(x,\theta,\phi)$ equivalent to $L(x,\theta,\phi)$ for a given viewer location, by solving Equation (3) for I_p:

$$I_p(x,\theta_p,\phi_p) = \frac{L(x,\theta,\phi)d(x)^2}{k_u(x)\cos(\theta_p)} \quad \text{for } k_u(x) > 0. \qquad (4)$$

Thus, as long as the diffuse reflectance $k_u(x)$ is nonzero for all the wavelengths represented in $L(x,\theta,\phi)$, we can effectively represent the surface attribute with appropriate pixel intensities. In practice, however, the range of values we can display are limited by the brightness, dynamic range and pixel resolution of the projector.

The rendering process here involves two viewpoints: the user's and the projector's. A simple approach would be to first render the image as seen by the user, which is represented by $L(x,\theta,\phi)$, and then use traditional image-based rendering techniques to warp this image to generate the intensity-corrected projected image, represented by $I_p(x,\theta_p,\phi_p)$ [Chen93, McMillan95]. For a changing viewer location, view-dependent shading under static lighting conditions can also be implemented [Debevec98, Levoy96, Gortler96]. However, the warping can be avoided in the case where the display medium is the same as the virtual object. For a

Figure 4: (Left) The underlying physical object is a white diffuse vase. (Middle and right) View-dependent effects, such as specular highlights, can be generated by tracking the user's location and projecting images on the vase.

single-pass rendering, we treat the moving user's viewpoint as the shading view. Then, the image synthesis process involves rendering the scene from the projector's view, by using a perspective projection matrix that matches the projector's intrinsic and extrinsic parameters, followed by radiance adjustment. The separation of the two views offers an interesting topic of study. For example, for a static projector, the visibility and view-independent shading calculations can be performed just once even when the user's viewpoint is changing.

To realize a real-time interactive implementation we use conventional 3D rendering APIs, which only approximate the general rendering equation. The BRDF computation is divided into view-dependent specular, and view-independent diffuse and ambient components. View-independent shading calculations can be performed by assuming the rendering and shading view are the same. (The virtual shadows, also view-independent, are computed using the traditional two-pass shadow-buffer technique.) For view-dependent shading, such as specular highlights (Figure 4), however, there is no existing support to separate the two views. A note in the appendix describes the required modification.

3.1 Secondary Scattering

Shader lamps are limited in the type of surface attributes that can be reproduced. In addition, since we are using neutral surfaces with (presumed) diffuse characteristics, secondary scattering is unavoidable and can potentially affect the quality of the results. When the underlying virtual object is purely diffuse, sometimes the secondary scattering can be used to our advantage. The geometric relationships, also known as form factors, among parts of the physical objects, are naturally the same as those among parts of the virtual object. Consider the radiosity solution for a patch i in a virtual scene with m light sources and n patches:

$$B_{i\text{-intended}} = k_{d_i}' \sum_j B_j F_{i,j} = k_{d_i} \left(\sum_m B_m F_{i,m} + \sum_n B_n F_{i,n} \right) \quad (5)$$

Here k_d is the diffuse reflectance, B_j is the radiance of patch j, and $F_{i,j}$ is the form factor between patches. Using shader lamps to reproduce simply the effect of direct illumination (after radiance adjustment), we are able to generate the effect of m light sources:

$$B_{i\text{-direct}} = k_{d_i} \sum_m B_m F_{i,m}. \quad (6)$$

However, due to secondary scattering, if the neutral surfaces have diffuse reflectance k_u, the perceived radiance also includes the secondary scattering due to the n patches, and that gives us

$$B_{i\text{-actual}} = B_{i\text{-direct}} + B_{i\text{-secondary}} = k_{d_i} \sum_m B_m F_{i,m} + k_u \sum_n B_n F_{i,n}. \quad (7)$$

Figure 5: (Left) A green paper illuminated with white light. (Right) The white diffuse surface on the right is illuminated with green light.

The difference between the desired and perceived radiance is

$$\left| (k_{d_i} - k_u) \sum_n B_n F_{i,n} \right|. \tag{8}$$

Thus, in scenarios where k_d and k_u are similar, we get approximate radiosity for "free"—projection of even a simple direct illumination rendering produces believable "spilling" of colors on neighboring parts of the physical objects. From the equation above, the secondary contribution from the neutral surfaces is certainly not accurate, even if we reproduce the first bounce exactly,. The difference is even larger when the virtual object has non-lambertian reflectance properties. We are currently investigating *inverse global illumination* methods so that the projected image can more accurately deliver the desired global illumination effect. Figure 5 shows a green and a white paper with spill over from natural white and projected green illumination. In this special case, the secondary scattering off the horizontal white surface below is similar for both parts.

3.2 Illumination of All Visible Surfaces

One may wonder, given a physical object, what is a good set of viewpoints for the lamps, so that every visible surface is illuminated by at least one lamp. This problem is addressed by [Stuerzlinger99], where he finds, using a hierarchical visibility algorithm, a set of camera viewpoints such that every visible part of every surface is imaged at least once. The problem of determining an optimal set of viewpoints is NP-hard and is related to the art gallery problem [O'Rourke87] known in the field of computational geometry.

4. Methods

The image-based illumination of physical objects has been explored by many. But, we believe, two main challenges have kept the previous efforts to only expensive, large scale, or one-off implementations. (a) First, the geometric registration problem, which is cast as matching the projection of a single 2D image with an object. The projection of a perspective device has up to 11 degrees of freedom (6 external and 5 internal) [Faugeras93], therefore, any effort to manually achieve the registration is likely to be extremely tedious. We propose a new simple technique in subsection 4.1 below. (b) The second problem, which appears to be unexplored, is the complete illumination of non-trivial physical objects in presence of shadows due to self occlusion. With the advent of digitally-fed projectors and real-time 3D graphics rendering, a new approach for image-based illumination is now possible. We approach these problems by creating a 3D geometric understanding of the display setup. In subsection 4.2, we describe an important intensity correction step and in subsection 4.3, we describe our solution for dealing with shadows.

4.1 Authoring and Alignment

One of the important tasks in achieving compelling visualization is to create the association between the physical objects and the graphics primitives that will enhance those objects when projected. For example, how do we specify which texture image should be used for the face of a building model, or what color distribution will look better for a physical object? We need the physical object as well as its geometric 3D representation, and real or desired surface attributes. As mentioned earlier, many hardware and software solutions are now available to scan/print 3D objects and capture/create highly detailed, textured graphics models. We demonstrate in the video how the authoring can also be done interactively by "painting" directly on top of the physical objects. We also show how the result of the user interaction can be projected on the objects and also stored on the computer. Ideally, a more sophisticated user interface would be used to create and edit graphics primitives of different shape, color and texture.

To align a projector, first we *approximately* position the projector and then *adapt* to its geometric relationship with respect to the physical object. That relationship is computed by finding projector's intrinsic parameters and the rigid transformation between the two coordinate systems. This is a classical computer vision problem [Faugeras93]. As seen in the video, we take a set of fiducials with known 3D locations on the physical object and find the corresponding projector pixels that illuminate them. This allows us to compute a 3×4 perspective projection matrix up to scale, which is decomposed to find the intrinsic and the extrinsic parameters of the projector. The rendering process uses the same internal and external parameters, so that the projected images are registered with the physical objects.

4.2 Intensity Correction

The intensity of the rendered image is modified on a per-pixel basis to take into account the reflectance of the neutral surface, the local orientation and distance with respect to the projector using Equation (4). Since the surface normals used to compute the $1/cos(\theta_P)$ correction are available only at the vertices in polygonal graphics models, we exploit the rendering pipeline for approximate interpolation. We illuminate a white diffuse version of the graphics model (or a model matching appropriate $k_u(x)$ of the physical model) with a virtual white light placed at the location of the projector lamp and render it with black fog for squared distance attenuation. The resultant intensities are smooth across curved surfaces due to shading interpolation and inversely proportional to $(d(x)^2/k_u(x)cos(\theta_P))$ factor. To use the limited dynamic range of the projectors more efficiently, we do not illuminate surfaces with $\theta_P > 60$ (since $1/cos(\theta)$ ranges from 2 to infinity). This avoids the low sampling rate of the projected pixels on oblique surfaces and also minimizes the misregistration artifacts due to any errors in geometric calibration. During the calculations to find the overlap regions (described below), highly oblique surfaces are considered not to be illuminated by that projector. See Figure 7 for an example.

4.3 Occlusions and Overlaps

For complete illumination, using additional projectors is an obvious choice. This leads to the more difficult problem of seamlessly merging images from multiple projectors. A naïve solution may involve letting only a single projector illuminate any given surface patch. But, there are two main issues when dealing with overlapping CRT, LCD or DLP projectors, which compel the use of feathering (or cross-fading) of intensities. The first is the lack of color equivalence between neighboring projectors [Majumder00], due to manufacturing process and temperature color drift during their use. The second is our desire to minimize the sensitivity to small errors in the estimated geometric calibration parameters or mechanical variations.

Feathering is commonly used to generate seamless panoramic photomosaics by combining several views from a single location [Szeliski97]. Similar techniques are exploited in multi-projector wide-field-of-view displays [Panoram, Trimensions, Raskar99], and two-dimensional arrays of flat projections. In such cases, the overlap region is typically a (well-defined) contiguous region on the display surface as well as in each projector's frame buffer. In the algorithm used in [Szeliski97, Raskar99] the intensity of a pixel is weighted proportional to the Euclidean distance to the nearest boundary (zero contribution) pixel of the (projected) image. The per-pixel weights are in the range [0, 1]. They are multiplied to the pixel intensities in the final rendered image. The pixels weights near the boundary of a source image are near zero and the pixels contribute very little, so that there is a smooth transition to the next source image. This leads to the commonly seen intensity roll-off as shown in Figure 6(a). Under ideal conditions and assuming color equivalence, the weight contribution of both projectors $A+B$ adds up to 1. Even when projector B's color response is different than that of A (say, attenuated—shown as B'), the resultant $A+B'$ (shown in blue) transitions smoothly in the overlap region.

This weight assignment strategy works well only when the target image illuminates a smooth continuous surface at and around the overlap. In our case, the physical model is usually made up of non-convex objects or a collection of disjoint objects resulting in shadows, fragmented overlap regions and, more importantly, overlap regions containing surfaces with depth discontinuities, as shown in Figure 6(c) with a simple occluder. Now, with unequal color response, the resultant weight distribution $A+B'$ has offending sharp changes, e.g. at points f and g. This situation is analogous to image-based rendering (IBR), where warping a single depth-enhanced image creates dis-occlusion artifacts. When multiple source images are warped to the target image, the color assigned to a pixel needs to be derived (from either a single image where they overwrite each other or) as a weighted combination of corresponding pixels from source images. The feathering, which actually blurs the result, is usually necessary to overcome (minor) color difference in corresponding pixels in input images and to hide ghosting effects (due to small mis-registration errors). One of the few solutions to this is proposed by [Debevec98], in which they scale the intensities by weights proportional to the angles between the target view and the source views. As mentioned in their paper, "it does not guarantee that the weights will transition smoothly across surfaces of the scene. As a result, seams can appear in the renderings where neighboring polygons are rendered with very different combinations of images." The plots in Figure 6(b) show a sample weighting scheme based on a similar idea and the corresponding problems. Below, we present a global solution using a new feathering algorithm that suits IBR as well as shader lamps. The algorithm is based on the following guidelines:

1. The sum of the intensity weights of the corresponding projector pixels is one so that the intensities are normalized;
2. The weights for pixels of a projector along a physical surface change smoothly in and near overlaps so that the inter-projector color differences do not create visible discontinuity in displayed images; and
3. The distribution of intensity weights for a projector within its framebuffer is smooth so that small errors in calibration or mechanical variations do not result in sharp edges.

In practice, it is easier to achieve (or maintain) precise geometric calibration than to ensure color equality among a set of projectors over a period of time [Majumder00]. This makes condition (2) more important than (3). But, it is not always possible to satisfy condition (2) or (3) (e.g. if the occluder moves closer to the plane so that $f = g$ in Figure 6) and hence they remain as guidelines rather than rules.

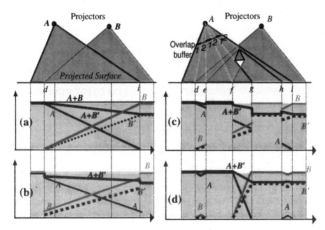

Figure 6: Intensity weights using feathering methods. The plots show the contribution of projectors A, B and B' and the resultant accumulation $A+B$ and $A+B'$ along the lit planar surface. Our technique, shown in *(d)*, creates smooth weight transitions.

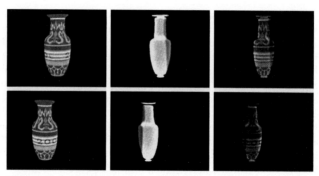

Figure 7: Illuminating a vase (Left) Rendered images (Middle) The intensity weight images, including elimination of oblique parts, and correction for surface orientation and overlap. (Right) Intensity corrected images.

The three guidelines suggest solving the feathering problem, without violating the weight constraints at depth discontinuities and shadow boundaries. Traditional feathering methods use the distance to the nearest boundary pixel to find the weight [Szeliski97, Raskar99]. Instead, we first find pixels corresponding to regions illuminated by a single projector and assign them an intensity weight of 1. Then, for each remaining pixel, the basic idea behind our technique is to find the shortest Euclidean distance to a pixel with weight 1, ignoring paths that cross depth discontinuities. The assigned weight is inversely proportional to this distance. Figure 6(d) shows the result of the new feathering algorithm in flatland for two projectors. Even under different color responses, the algorithm generates smooth transitions (see $A+B'$) on the planar surface in presence of shadows and fragmented overlaps. The algorithm can be used for 3 or more projectors without modification.

For a practical implementation, we use two buffers—an overlap buffer and a depth buffer. The depth buffer is updated by rendering the graphics model. The overlap buffer contains integer values to indicate the number of overlapping projectors for each pixel. The overlap regions (i.e. overlap count of two or more) are computed using the traditional shadow-buffer technique. The algorithm follows:

At each projector,
    Compute boundaries between regions of overlap count 1 and > 1
    Compute depth discontinuities using edge detection in depth buffer
    For each pixel in overlap region
        update shortest distance to overlap count ==1 region ignoring paths crossing depth discontinuity
At each projector,
    For each pixel in overlap region
        Find all corresponding pixels in other projectors
        Assign weights inversely proportional to the shortest distance

For some pixels in the overlap region, such as region $[h, i]$ for projector A, no nearest pixel with overlap count of 1 can be found, and so the shortest distance is set to a large value. This elegantly reduces the weight in isolated regions and also cuts down unnecessary transition zones. Figure 7 shows the set of images for the illumination of a vase, including weights and intensity corrected images.

5. Limitations

The major limitation of shader lamps is the dependence on the properties of the neutral physical surface and the controlled (dark) ambient lighting. The problem due to secondary scattering cannot be completely avoided, which makes the task of reproducing the behavior of virtual surfaces with very low reflectance very difficult. In addition, traditional projector limitations [Majumder00], such as limited depth of field, reduced dynamic range due to "black level" and non-uniformity, can affect the visual quality.

Although this type of visualization has the advantage that the user is not required to wear stereo-glasses or head-worn displays, the user-induced shadows on the projected surface can be very disturbing. In this paper, we have mainly focussed on the visualization aspect, but a more detailed study of human interaction and issues is necessary.

6. Implementation

For the setup, we used two Sony VPL6000U projectors displaying at 1024×768 resolution. The OpenGL rendering programs run on a Windows NT PC with Wildcard graphics card. The vase is made of clay and is approximately 12 cm × 12 cm × 35 cm. The Taj Mahal model is wooden and spray-painted white. Its dimensions are approximately 70 cm × 70 cm × 35 cm. Both objects were scanned, in about 30 mins each, with a 3D touch probe sensor that gives readings with an accuracy of 0.5 mm (Figure 8 left). The vase model is made up of 7,000 triangles, and the Taj Mahal model is made up of 21,000 triangles and 15 texture maps. For the specular highlight effects, we used the Origin Instruments DynaSight optical tracking system to track the viewer's location.

Each projector is calibrated by finding the pixels that illuminate a set of about 20 known 3D fiducials on the physical model. We accomplish this by moving a projected cross-hair in the projector image-space so that its center coincides with the known fiducials (Figure 8 right). The 3×4 perspective projection matrix and its decomposition into intrinsic and extrinsic parameters of the projector are computed using Matlab. The rendering process uses these parameters so that the projected images are registered with the model. It takes less than five minutes to calibrate each projector. Typically, the re-projection error is less than two pixels and the images from the two projectors appear geometrically aligned on the physical model. The intensity weights for the projector pixels are computed during preprocessing, and it takes approximately 10 seconds for each projector. During rendering, the intensities are modified using alpha-blending available in the graphics hardware. More details and high-resolution colored images are available at the website *http://www.shaderlamps.com.*

Figure 8: (Left) We use a 3D touch probe scanner to create a 3D model of the real object. (Right) The projectors are calibrated with respect to the model by finding which pixels (center of cross) illuminate the known 3D fiducials.

7. Applications

In the simplest form, shader lamps can be used to dynamically change the color of day-to-day objects or add temporary markings on them. For example, engineers can mark the areas of interest, like drilling locations, without affecting the physical surface. As seen in Figure 1, we can render virtual shadows on scaled models. City planners can move around such blocks and visualize global effects in 3D on a tabletop rather than on their computer screen. For stage shows, we can change not just the backdrops, but also simulate seasons or aging of the objects in the scene. Instead of randomly beaming laser vector images, we would like to create shapes with laser display on large buildings by calibrating the laser device with respect to a 3D model of the buildings. We can also simulate motion, as shown in the video, by projecting changing texture onto stationary rotationally symmetric objects. Interesting non-photorealistic effects can also be generated.

Tracked viewer. With simple head tracking of the viewer, we have demonstrated how a clay vase can appear to be made of metal or plastic. We could also render other view-dependent effects such as reflections. The concept can be extended to some larger setups. Sculptors often make clay models of large statues before they create the molds. It may be useful for them to visualize how the geometric forms they have created will look with different materials or under different conditions in the context of other objects. By projecting guiding points or lines (e.g. wire-frame), from the computer models, the sculptors can verify the geometric correctness of the clay models. Image-based illumination can be very effectively used in movie studios where miniature models are painstakingly built and then updated with fine details. For inserting synthetic characters into a fly-thru of a miniature set, we can project silhouette of the moving virtual character that looks perspectively correct to the tracked motion camera. This will guide the placement during post-processing because intrinsic camera parameters are not required.

Tracked Objects. We can illuminate objects so that the surface textures appear glued to the objects even as they move. In this case, we can display updated specular highlights even for a static viewer. For example, in showroom windows or on exhibition floors, one can show a rotating model of the product in changing colors or with different features enhanced. In an experimental system, a tracked "paintbrush" was used to paint on a tracked moving cuboid held by the user (Figure 9). The presence of the physical model allows natural haptic feedback. The need to attach a tracker and dynamic mis-registration due to tracker latency are the two main problems [Bandyopadhyay01].

Scaling it up. We have begun to explore extensions aimed at *walk-thru* virtual models of human-sized environments [Low01]. Instead of building an exact detailed physical replica for projection, we are using simplified versions. For example, primary structures of building interiors and mid-sized architectural objects (walls, columns, cupboards, tables, etc.), can usually be approximated with simple components (boxes, cylinders, etc.). As seen in the video, we are using construction Styrofoam blocks. The main architectural features that match the simplified physical model retain 3D auto-stereo, but the other details must be presented by projecting view-dependent images. Nevertheless, our experiment to simulate a building interior has convinced us that this setup can provide a stronger sense of immersion when compared to

Figure 9: A tracked "paintbrush" painting on a tracked cuboid.

CAVE^{TM} [Cruz-Neira93], as the user is allowed to really *walk around* in the virtual environment. However, because of large concave surfaces (e.g. corners of room), inter-reflection problem becomes more serious. Moreover, since almost all of the surfaces around the user need to be illuminated, it is now easier for the user to occlude some projectors. Strategic placement of projectors is thus more critical, and that (among other things) remains as one of the outstanding challenges.

Ideas. A shader-lamp-guided clay modeling system would be useful as a 3D version of "connect-the-dots" to provide feedback to a modeler. For example, two synchronized projectors could successively beam images of the different parts of the intended 3D model in red and green. A correct positioning of clay will be verified by a yellow illumination. After the shape is formed, the same shader lamps can be used to guide painting of the model, or the application of a real material with matching reflectance properties.

An interactive 3D touch-probe scanning system with closed-loop verification of surface reconstruction (tessellation) could be realized by continuously projecting enhanced images of the partial reconstruction on the object being scanned. This will indicate to the person scanning the required density of points, the regions that lack samples and the current deviation of the geometric model from the underlying physical object.

A useful 2-handed 3D modeling and 3D painting setup would involve tracking the user's viewpoint, input devices and a coarsely-shaped object (such as a sphere). The user can literally create and add surface properties to a virtual object that is registered with the sphere.

8. Conclusion

We have described a new mode for visualization of 3D computer graphics, which involves light projectors and physical objects to generate rich detailed images directly in the user's world. Although the method is limited when compared to traditional graphics rendered on computer screens, it offers a new way of interacting with synthetic imagery. We have presented new techniques that make image-based illumination of non-trivial objects practical. A rendering process essentially involves user's viewpoint, shape of the graphics objects, reflectance properties and illumination. Traditional computer graphics or head-mounted augmented reality generates the result for all these elements at a reduced temporal (frame rate) or spatial (pixel) resolution. With shader lamps, we attempt to keep the viewpoint and shape at the best resolution and only the added color information is at a limited resolution. We believe the visualization method is compelling for a variety of applications including training, architectural design, art and entertainment.

Acknowledgements

We thank Henry Fuchs, Anselmo Lastra and Herman Towles for their support and useful discussions. We also thank members of the "Office of the Future" group at UNC Chapel Hill and specifically Wei-Chao Chen and Sang-Uok Kum for their help.

References

[Bandyopadhyay01] D Bandyopadhyay, R Raskar, A State, H Fuchs, *Dynamic Spatially Augmented 3D Painting*. UNC Chapel Hill Tech Report TR01-006, 2001.

[Chen93] S. E. Chen, and L. Williams. *View Interpolation from Image Synthesis*. SIGGRAPH '93, pp. 279-288, July 1993.

[Cruz-Neira93] C. Cruz-Neira, D. J. Sandin, and T. A. DeFanti. *Surround-Screen Projection-Base Virtual Reality: the Design and Implementation of the CAVE*. SIGGRAPH '93, July 1993.

[Debevec96] P. Debevec, C. J. Taylor, and J. Malik. *Modeling and Rendering Architecture from Photographs*. SIGGRAPH '96, August 1996.

[Debevec98] P. Debevec, Y. Yu, and G. Borshukov. *Efficient View-Dependent Image-Based Rendering with Projective Texture-Mapping*. Proc. of 9th Eurographics Workshop on Rendering, June 1998.

[Dorsey91] J. Dorsey, F. X. Sillion, and D. Greenberg. *Design and Simulation of Opera Lighting and Projection Effects.* SIGGRAPH '91, August 1991.

[Faugeras93] O. Faugeras. *Three-Dimensional Computer Vision: A Geometric Viewpoint.* MIT Press, Cambridge, Massachusetts, 1993.

[Gortler96] S. J. Gortler, R. Grzeszczuk, R. Szeliski, and M. F. Cohen. *The Lumigraph.* SIGGRAPH '96, August 1996.

[Howard00] *HowardModels.co*m, 7944 Central Avenue, Toledo, OH 43617. *http://www.howardweb.com/model/.*

[Hypermask99] The HyperMask project. *http://www.csl.sony.co.jp/person/nielsen/HYPERMASK/.*

[Kajiya86] J. T. Kajiya. *The Rendering Equation.* Computer Graphics 20(4) (1986), pp. 143-151.

[Knoll92] W. Knoll, and M. Hechinger. *Architectural Models: Construction Techniques.* McGraw-Hill Publishing Company, ISBN 0-07-071543-2.

[Levoy96] M. Levoy, and P. Hanrahan. *Light Field Rendering.* SIGGRAPH '96, August 1996.

[Levoy00] M. Levoy. Personal communication.

[Low01] K. Low, G. Welch, A. Lastra, H. Fuchs. Life-Sized Projector-Based Dioramas: Spatially Real and Visually Virtual. To appear in Sketches & Applications, SIGGRAPH 2001.

[McMillan96] L. McMillan, and G. Bishop. *Plenoptic Modeling.* SIGGRAPH '95, August 1995.

[Liljegren90] G. E. Liljegren and E. L. Foster. *Figure with Back Projected Image Using Fiber Optics.* US Patent # 4,978.216, Walt Disney Company, USA, December 1990.

[Majumder00] A. Majumder, Z. He, H. Towles, and G. Welch. *Color Calibration of Projectors for Large Tiled Displays*, IEEE Visualization 2000.

[Naimark84] M. Naimark. *Displacements.* An exhibit at the San Francisco Museum of Modern Art, San Francisco, CA (USA), 1984.

[O'Rourke87] J. O'Rourke. *Art Gallery Theorems and Algorithms.* Oxford University Press, New York, 1987.

[Panoram] Panoram Technology. *http://www.panoramtech.com*

[Raskar98] R. Raskar, G. Welch, M. Cutts, A. Lake, L. Stesin, and H. Fuchs. *The Office of the Future: A Unified Approach to Image-Based Modeling and Spatially Immersive Displays.* SIGGRAPH '98, July 1998

[Raskar99] R. Raskar, M. Brown, R. Yang, W. Chen, G. Welch, H. Towles, B. Seales, H. Fuchs. *Multi-Projector Displays Using Camera-Based Registration.* IEEE Visualization 99, October 1999.

[Raskar99b] R. Raskar, G. Welch, W. Chen. *Tabletop Spatially Augmented Reality: Bringing Physical Models to Life using Projected Imagery.* Second Int Workshop on Augmented Reality (IWAR'99), October 1999, San Francisco, CA

[Stuerzlinger 99] W. Stuerzlinger. *Imaging all Visible Surfaces.* Graphics Interface '99, pp. 115-122, June 1999.

[Szeliski97] R. Szeliski and H. Shum. *Creating Full View Panoramic Mosaics and Environment Maps.* SIGGRAPH '97, August 1997.

[Trimensions] Trimensions. *http://www.trimensions-inc.com/*

[Underkoffler99] J. Underkoffler, B. Ullmer, and H. Ishii. *Emancipated pixels: real-world graphics in the luminous room.* SIGGRAPH '99, August 1999.

Appendix

As described in Section 3, while the rendering view defined by the projector parameters remains fixed, the shading view is specified by the head-tracked moving viewer. We show a minor modification to the traditional view setup to achieve the separation of the two views using as example OpenGL API.

```
glMatrixMode( GL_PROJECTION );
glLoadMatrix( intrinsic matrix of projector );
glMultMatrix( xform for rendering view )
glMultMatrix( inverse(xform for shading view) );
glMatrixMode( GL_MODELVIEW );
glLoadMatrix( xform for shading view );
// set virtual light position(s)
// render graphics model
```

Editors' Note: see Appendix, p. 329 for colored figures of this paper

Image-Based Reconstruction of Spatially Varying Materials

Hendrik P. A. Lensch[1]   Jan Kautz[1]   Michael Goesele[1]
Wolfgang Heidrich[2]   Hans-Peter Seidel[1]

[1] Max-Planck-Institut für Informatik   [2] The University of British Columbia
Saarbrücken, Germany   Vancouver, Canada

Abstract. The measurement of accurate material properties is an important step towards photorealistic rendering. Many real-world objects are composed of a number of materials that often show subtle changes even within a single material. Thus, for photorealistic rendering both the general surface properties as well as the spatially varying effects of the object are needed.

We present an image-based measuring method that robustly detects the different materials of real objects and fits an average bidirectional reflectance distribution function (BRDF) to each of them. In order to model the local changes as well, we project the measured data for each surface point into a basis formed by the recovered BRDFs leading to a truly spatially varying BRDF representation.

A high quality model of a real object can be generated with relatively few input data. The generated model allows for rendering under arbitrary viewing and lighting conditions and realistically reproduces the appearance of the original object.

1 Introduction

The use of realistic models for all components of image synthesis is a fundamental prerequisite for photorealistic rendering. This includes models for the geometry, light sources, and cameras, as well as materials. As more and more visual complexity is demanded, it is more and more often infeasible to generate these models manually. Automatic and semi-automatic methods for model acquisition are therefore becoming increasingly important.

In this paper we concentrate on the acquisition of realistic materials. In particular, we describe an acquisition process for spatially varying BRDFs that is efficient, reliable, and requires little manual intervention. Other methods described in the literature (see Section 2 for an overview) are either focusing on homogeneous materials, or make assumptions on the type of material to be measured (e.g. human faces). In our work, we measure spatially varying BRDFs without making any additional assumptions. In particular, our contributions are

- a robust and efficient BRDF fitting process that clusters the acquired samples into groups of similar materials and fits a Lafortune model [11] to each group,
- a method that projects every sample texel into a basis of BRDFs obtained from the clustering procedure. This projection accurately represents the material at that point and results in a compact representation of a truly spatially varying BRDF.

We require only a relatively small number of high-dynamic range photographs (about 20-25 images for one object), thereby speeding up the acquisition phase.

As a result of the fitting, clustering, and projection process, we obtain a compact representation of spatially varying materials that is well suited for rendering purposes (see Figure 5 for an example). The method works both for objects consisting of a mixture of distinct materials (e.g. paint and silver, see Figure 7), or for smooth transitions between material properties.

In the following we first review some of the previous work in this area, before we discuss the details of our own method. We start by describing the acquisition of the measurement data (Section 3), explain the resampling of this data into our data structures (Section 4), the BRDF fitting and material clustering steps (Sections 5 and 6), and finally present a method for projecting the materials into a basis of BRDFs (Section 7). Section 8 briefly describes our rendering method. In Section 9 we present our results and then we conclude in Section 10.

2 Related Work

The representation of real-world materials has recently received a lot of attention in the computer graphics community. The approaches can be grouped into three different categories: light field and image database methods with static illumination, dense sampling of the light and viewing directions to generate a tabular representation of the BRDF, and finally the fitting of reflection models, often based on a sparser set of samples. This last approach is the one we take and extend to spatially varying BRDFs.

In the first category, there has been a number of approaches ranging from a relatively sparse set of images with a geometric model [4] over the Lumigraph [7] with more images and a coarser model to the light field [13] with no geometry and a dense image database. Recently surface light fields [27, 18] have become popular, which feature both a dense sampling of the directional information and a detailed geometry. In contrast to these approaches, bidirectional texture functions [1] also work for changes in the lighting conditions, although at very high storage costs. In our work we use an algorithm similar to the function quantization approach proposed by Wood et al. [27] to resample the image data into a compact representation.

The traditional approach for dense sampling of reflectance properties is to use specialized devices (gonioreflectometers), that position both a light source and a sensor relative to the material. These devices can only obtain one sample for each pair of light and sensor position and are therefore relatively slow.

More recently, image-based approaches have been proposed. These methods are able to acquire a large number of samples at once. For example, Ward Larson [25] uses a hemispherical mirror to sample the exitant hemisphere of light with a single image. Instead of using curved mirrors, it is also possible to use curved geometry to obtain a large number of samples with a single image. This approach is taken by Lu et al [15], who assume a cylindrical surface, and Marschner et al. [17] who obtain the geometry using a range scanner. Our method is similar in spirit to the method of Marschner et al., but we are also dealing with spatially varying BRDFs and we are fitting a reflection model rather than using a tabular form in order to achieve a compact representation.

A number of researchers have also described the fitting of reflection models to the acquired sample data [2, 11, 22, 25, 28]. Of these methods, the ones by Ward Larson [25] and Lafortune et al. [11] do not consider spatial variations. Sato et al. [22] fit a Torrance-Sparrow model [24] to the data, and consider high-frequency variations for the diffuse part but only per-triangle variations for the specular part. This is also the case for the work by Yu et al. [28], which also takes indirect illumination into account. In our work, we perform the measurements in a darkened, black room, so that there is no indirect light coming from the outside of the object. Indirect light within the object is assumed to be negligible, which excludes the use of objects with extreme concavities.

Debevec et al. [2] describe a method for acquiring the reflectance field of human faces. In one part of their work they fit a specialized reflection model for human skin to the measured data (consisting of about 200 images). Both specular and diffuse parameters of the reflection model can vary rapidly across the surface, but other parameters like the de-saturation of the diffuse component at grazing angles are constant and only apply to human skin. In our work we try to avoid making assumptions on the kind of material we are measuring.

Several different representation have been used for fitting BRDF data. In addition to the models used for measured data (e.g. Koenderink et al. [10], Lafortune [11], Torrance-Sparrow [22, 28], Ward [25]), Westin et al. [26] have used spherical harmonics for projecting simulated BRDF data. In our work we use the Lafortune model because it is compact, well suited for optimization algorithms, and capable of representing interesting BRDF properties such as off-specular peaks and retro-reflection.

3 Acquisition

We obtain the 3D models with a structured light 3D scanner and a computer tomography scanner both generating dense triangle meshes. The triangle meshes are smoothed [5, 9], manually cleaned, and decimated.

All images are acquired in a measurement lab using a professional digital camera. An HMI metal halide bulb serves as point light source for the BRDF measurements. The interior of the photo studio is covered with dark and diffusely reflecting felt to reduce the influence of the environment on the measurements.

Several views of each object are captured with different camera and light source positions. For each view we acquire three sets of images: two images to recover the light source position, one image of the object's silhouette to register the 3D model with the images. We then acquire a high dynamic range image [3] of the object lit by the point light source by taking a series of photographs with varying exposure time.

In addition, a series of calibration images of a checkerboard pattern is taken whenever the lens settings are changed. The calibration method proposed by Zhang [29] is used to recover the intrinsic camera parameters. Another high dynamic range image of a gray card with known camera and light position is taken in order to compute the brightness of the light source.

To register the images with the 3D model we use a silhouette-based method [12] that yields the camera position relative to the object. The light source position is triangulated based on the reflections in a number of mirroring steel balls. The details of that approach will be described elsewhere.

4 Resampling of Radiance Values

After acquisition of the geometric model, high-dynamic range image recovery, and registration, it is necessary to merge the acquired data for further processing. For each point on the model's surface we collect all available information using two data structures.

The first one is a so called *lumitexel* denoted by $\mathcal{L}$, which is generated for every visible surface point. Each lumitexel stores the geometric and photometric data of one point, i.e. its position $\vec{x}$ and the normal $\hat{n}$ in world coordinates[1]. Linked to the lumitexel

---

[1] hats denote unit vectors and arrows denote vectors of arbitrary length.

is a list of radiance samples $\mathcal{R}_i$, each representing the outgoing radiance r of the surface point captured by one image plus the direction of the light $\hat{u}$ and the viewing direction $\hat{v}$. $\hat{u}$ and $\hat{v}$ are both given in the local coordinate frame of the surface point spanned by $\hat{n}$ and a deterministically constructed tangent and bi-normal.

A lumitexel can be seen as a very sparsely sampled BRDF. We define the error between a given BRDF f_r and a lumitexel $\mathcal{L}$ as:

$$E_{f_r}(\mathcal{L}) = \frac{1}{|\mathcal{L}|} \sum_{\mathcal{R}_i \in \mathcal{L}} s \cdot I(f_r(\hat{u}_i, \hat{v}_i)u_{i,z}, r_i) + D(f_r(\hat{u}_i, \hat{v}_i)u_{i,z}, r_i), \qquad (1)$$

where $|\mathcal{L}|$ stands for the number of radiance samples linked to the lumitexel, $I(r_1, r_2)$ is a function measuring the intensity difference, and $D(r_1, r_2)$ measures the color-difference. We introduce the weight s, to be able to compensate for noisy data (e.g. a slightly wrong normal resulting in a wrong highlight). We always set $s \leq 1$. Please note that since r represents radiance and not reflectance, the BRDF has to be multiplied by the cosine between the normal and the local light direction, which is u_z.

4.1 Assembling Lumitexels

Collecting all radiance samples for a lumitexel requires a resampling of the input images for the particular point on the surface. At first, one has to determine the set of surface points for which a lumitexel should be generated. In order to obtain the highest quality with respect to the input images, the sampling density of the surface points must match that of the images.

Every triangle of the 3D model is projected into each image using the previously determined camera parameters. The area of the projected triangle is measured in pixels and the triangle is assigned to the image I_{best} in which its projected area is largest. For every pixel within the triangle in I_{best} a lumitexel is generated.

The position $\vec{x}$ of the surface point for the lumitexel is given by the intersection of the ray from the camera through the pixel with the mesh (see Figure 1). The normal $\hat{n}$ is interpolated using the triangle's vertex normals.

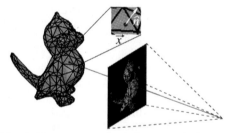

Fig. 1. *The correspondence between pixel position and point position $\vec{x}$ on the object is computed by tracing a ray through the image onto the object. At every $\vec{x}$ a local normal $\hat{n}$ can be computed from the triangle's vertex normals.*

A radiance sample $\mathcal{R}_j$ is now constructed for each image I_j in which $\vec{x}$ is visible from the camera position and the surface point is lit by the point light source. The vectors $\hat{u}_j$ and $\hat{v}_j$ can be directly calculated. The associated radiance is found by projecting $\vec{x}$ onto the image plane and retrieving the color c_j at that point using bilinear interpolation. Note, that for I_{best} no bilinear interpolation is necessary and c_{best} can be obtained without resampling since $\vec{x}$ exactly maps to the original pixel by construction. The radiance r_j of the radiance sample $\mathcal{R}_j$ is obtained by scaling c_j according to the brightness of the light source and the squared distance from the light source to $\vec{x}$.

5 BRDF Fitting

In this section we will first detail the Lafortune BRDF model [11] that we use to fit our given lumitexels. Then we will explain how this fit is performed using Levenberg-Marquardt optimization.

5.1 Lafortune Model

BRDFs are four-dimensional functions that depend on the local viewing and light direction. The dependence on wavelength is often neglected or simply three different BRDFs are used for the red, green, and blue channel. We use the latter approach.

Instead of representing a measured BRDF as a 4D table the measured samples are in our case approximated with a parameterized BRDF. This has two advantages. Firstly, the BRDF requires much less storage since only the parameters are stored and secondly, we only require a sparse set of samples that would not be sufficient to faithfully represent a complete tabular BRDF.

Many different BRDF models have been proposed (e.g. [24, 25]) with different strengths and weaknesses. Our method may be used together with any parameterized BRDF model. We have chosen the computationally simple but general and physically plausible Lafortune model [11] in its isotropic form:

$$f_r(\hat{u}, \hat{v}) = \rho_d + \sum_i [C_{x,i}(u_x v_x + u_y v_y) + C_{z,i} u_z v_z]^{N_i}, \tag{2}$$

This model uses only a handful of parameters. $\hat{u}$ and $\hat{v}$ are the local light and viewing directions, ρ_d is the diffuse component, N_i is the specular exponent, the ratio between $C_{x,i}$ and $C_{z,i}$ indicates the off-specularity of lobe i of the BRDF. The sign of $C_{x,i}$ makes the lobe i either retro-reflective (positive $C_{x,i}$) or forward-reflective (negative $C_{x,i}$). The albedo of the lobe i is given by the magnitude of the parameters $C_{x,i}$ and $C_{z,i}$. From now on we will denote the BRDF with $f_r(\vec{a}; \hat{u}, \hat{v})$, where $\vec{a}$ subsumes all the parameters of the model, i.e. ρ_d, $C_{x,i}$, $C_{z,i}$, and N_i. In the case of only one lobe $\vec{a}$ is 12-dimensional (4 parameters for each color channel).

5.2 Non-Linear Fitting

The Lafortune BRDF is non-linear in its parameters, which means that we have to use a non-linear optimization method to fit the parameters to the given data. As in the original work by Lafortune et al. [11], we use the Levenberg-Marquardt optimization [20] to determine the parameters of the Lafortune model from our measured data. This method has proven to be well-suited for fitting non-linear BRDFs.

Instead of BRDF samples we use radiance samples as our input data, which means we are not directly fitting the BRDF $f_r(\vec{a}; \hat{u}, \hat{v})$ but the radiance values $f_r(\vec{a}; \hat{u}, \hat{v}) u_z$ to the radiance samples $\mathcal{R}_i$ in order to avoid the numerically problematic division by u_z.

We also ensure that the fitting process works well and does not get stuck in undesired local minima by initializing the fitting routine with parameters that correspond to an average BRDF.

The Levenberg-Marquardt optimization outputs not only the best-fit parameter vector $\vec{a}$, but also a covariance matrix of the parameters, which provides a rough idea of the parameters that could not be fit well. This information is used in our splitting and clustering algorithm, as explained in the next section.

6 Clustering

In this section we will explain how we cluster the given lumitexels so that each cluster C_i corresponds to one material of the object. Given a set of BRDFs $\{f_i\}$, each cluster C_i consists of a list of all the lumitexels $\mathcal{L}_i$ for which f_i provides the best approximation. Determining these clusters is a problem closely related to vector quantization [6] and k-means clustering [14, 16], both of which work in affine spaces. Unfortunately, we do not have an affine space when clustering BRDF samples, and we are therefore employing a modified Lloyd [14] iteration method.

The general idea is to first fit a BRDF f_r to an initial cluster containing all the data. Then we generate two new BRDF models f_1 and f_2 using the covariance matrix from the fit (explained in more detail below) representing two new clusters. The lumitexels $\mathcal{L}_i$ from the original cluster are then distributed according to the distance $E_{f_1}(\mathcal{L}_i)$ and $E_{f_2}(\mathcal{L}_i)$ into the new clusters. We then recursively choose another cluster, split it, and redistribute the lumitexels and so on. This is repeated until the desired number of materials is reached, as detailed in Section 6.4.

6.1 Lumitexel Selection

The fitting procedure described in Section 5 performs a relatively large number of operations per radiance sample. Thus, it is expensive to fit a BRDF using all lumitexels (and all radiance samples contained in the lumitexels) generated by the assembling procedure. Instead, it is sufficient to consider only a few thousand lumitexels at the beginning. Later on, we increase the number for an accurate fit.

A first, naive approach to choosing this subset for fitting selects every n-th lumitexel regardless of its reliability or possible contribution. However, as stated in [28] and [23], for a robust estimation of the specular part of a BRDF it is very important to include radiance samples within the specular lobe of the material. Unfortunately, these brightest pixels statistically also carry the largest error.

Following these ideas we select more lumitexels in areas where a highlight is likely to occur. These areas are determined by the surface normal, the light source position and a synthetic BRDF with a broad highlight.

6.2 Splitting

Fitting just a single BRDF to the initial cluster of course is not sufficient if the concerned object consists of more than one material. In order to decide which cluster to split, we compute the following error for all clusters C_j:

$$E(C_j) = \sum_{\mathcal{L}_i \in C_j} E_{f_r}(\mathcal{L}_i) \quad \forall C_j. \tag{3}$$

The cluster C_j with the largest error will be split into two new clusters each with a different BRDF. Further materials can be extracted by further splitting the clusters.

But how do we split a cluster? The BRDF fit to a cluster represents the average material of the lumitexels in that cluster. Fitting the BRDF using the Levenberg-Marquardt algorithm (see Section 5) will also provide us with the covariance matrix of the parameters. The eigenvector belonging to the largest eigenvalue of this matrix represents the direction in which the variance of the samples is highest, and is therefore a good choice for the direction in which the parameter space is to be split.

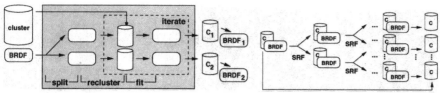

Fig. 2. *Split-recluster-fit process (SRF). The initial BRDF is split into two new BRDFs using the covariance matrix. The lumitexels from the initial cluster are distributed according to their distance to the BRDFs. Then we fit the BRDF again to each new cluster. We now iterate the reclustering and fitting until the resulting BRDFs and cluster have converged.*

Fig. 3. *The complete splitting and reclustering algorithm including the global reclustering, which is similar to the recluster-fit iteration, only that all lumitexels are distributed among all clusters.*

Let $\vec{a}$ be the fit parameter vector of the BRDF $f(\vec{a}; \hat{u}, \hat{v})$ for cluster C. $\vec{e}$ denotes the eigenvector belonging to the largest eigenvalue λ of the corresponding covariance matrix. We then construct two new BRDFs:

$$f_1(\vec{a} + \tau\lambda\vec{e}; \hat{u}, \hat{v}) \quad \text{and} \quad f_2(\vec{a} - \tau\lambda\vec{e}; \hat{u}, \hat{v}), \tag{4}$$

where τ is a scaling factor to adapt λ to a moderate value. Two new clusters C_1 and C_2 are generated by distributing every lumitexel $\mathcal{L}_i$ of cluster C either to C_1 if $E_{f_1}(\mathcal{L}_i) < E_{f_2}(\mathcal{L}_i)$, or to C_2 otherwise. In the next step, f_1 and f_2 are fit to best approximate the lumitexels in the new clusters.

6.3 Reclustering

Because the parameters of the BRDF fit to a multi-material cluster are not necessarily the center of the parameters of the contained materials and due to improper scaling of λ and other reasons like noise, the performed split will not be optimal and the two new clusters may not be clearly separated, e.g. in the case of two distinct materials some lumitexels belonging to one material may still be assigned to the cluster of the other material.

A better separation can be achieved by iterating the procedure of distributing the lumitexels $\mathcal{L}_i$ based on $E_{f_1}(\mathcal{L}_i)$ and $E_{f_2}(\mathcal{L}_i)$, and then fitting the BRDFs again. The iteration stops when the number of lumitexels in the generated cluster does not change any more. In our experiments this reclustering operation leads to a clear separation of materials and is done after each split. The split-recluster-fit (SRF) process is visualized in Figure 2.

When more than two clusters have been generated by successive binary splits and a new material is clearly distinguished, it is helpful to clean the other clusters, which were not involved in the last split, from all lumitexels belonging to the newly discovered material. This can be done in a global reclustering step by redistributing all initial lumitexels $\mathcal{L}_i$ to the cluster C_j with

$$j = \operatorname*{argmin}_k E_{f_k}(\mathcal{L}_i). \tag{5}$$

And again, the BRDFs of all involved clusters have to be refit. This global reclustering is repeated several times to clearly separate the materials. We stop this iteration when the percentage of change is smaller than some ϵ, or a maximum number of iterations is reached. The complete splitting and reclustering algorithm is depicted in Figure 3.

Fig. 4. *The clustering process at work. In every image a new cluster was created. The object was reshaded using only the single BRDFs fit to each cluster before the projection into a basis of multiple BRDFs.*

6.4 Termination of the Splitting Process

We still have to decide when to stop the splitting process. To do this we require the user to input the estimated number of materials $|M|$. We stop the splitting and clustering process after $2|M| - 1$ clusters have been created. We use this additional number of clusters to compensate for the often noisy and not absolutely accurate radiance samples (e.g. slightly wrong normals, noise in the images, misregistration, etc.).

This means that we do not have a one to one mapping between actual materials and clusters. This is not crucial since the projection, which we will present in the next section, uses a weighted sum of several BRDFs to accurately represent every lumitexel.

7 Projection

As can be seen in Figure 4 the representation of an object by a collection of only a few clusters and BRDFs make the virtual object look flat because real surface exhibit changes in the reflective properties even within a single material. These changes cannot be represented by a single BRDF per cluster since all lumitexels within the cluster would be assigned the same BRDF parameters.

To obtain truly spatially varying BRDFs we must find a specific BRDF for each lumitexel. But the sparse input data does not allow to fit a reliable or even meaningful BRDF to a single lumitexel because each lumitexel consists of only a few radiance samples. In addition, you would need to acquire a highlight in every lumitexel to reliably determine the specular part, as already explained in Section 6.1.

The solution is to project each lumitexel into a basis of BRDFs (see Section 7.1). The BRDF $f_{\pi i}$ of a lumitexel $\mathcal{L}_i$ is represented by the linear combination of m BRDFs $f_1, f_2, \ldots, f_m$:

$$f_{\pi i} = t_1 f_1 + t_2 f_2 + \ldots + t_m f_m, \tag{6}$$

with $t_1, t_2, \ldots, t_m$ being positive scalar weights. This forces the space of solutions (i.e. the possible BRDFs for a pixel) to be plausible since the basis BRDFs are already reliably fit to a large number of radiance samples.

Given the BRDFs, the weights have to be determined for each lumitexel. Let $r_{j=1\ldots|\mathcal{L}_i|}$ be the radiance values of the lumitexel $\mathcal{L}_i$. The weights are found by a least square optimization of the following system of equations using singular-value decomposition:

$$\begin{pmatrix} r_1 \\ r_2 \\ \vdots \\ r_{|\mathcal{L}_i|} \end{pmatrix} = \begin{pmatrix} \tilde{f}_1(\hat{u}_1, \hat{v}_1) & \tilde{f}_2(\hat{u}_1, \hat{v}_1) & \cdots & \tilde{f}_m(\hat{u}_1, \hat{v}_1) \\ \tilde{f}_1(\hat{u}_2, \hat{v}_2) & \tilde{f}_2(\hat{u}_2, \hat{v}_2) & \cdots & \tilde{f}_m(\hat{u}_2, \hat{v}_2) \\ \vdots & \vdots & \ddots & \vdots \\ \tilde{f}_1(\hat{u}_{|\mathcal{L}_i|}, \hat{v}_{|\mathcal{L}_i|}) & \tilde{f}_2(\hat{u}_{|\mathcal{L}_i|}, \hat{v}_{|\mathcal{L}_i|}) & \cdots & \tilde{f}_m(\hat{u}_{|\mathcal{L}_i|}, \hat{v}_{|\mathcal{L}_i|}) \end{pmatrix} \begin{pmatrix} t_1 \\ t_2 \\ \vdots \\ t_m \end{pmatrix}, \tag{7}$$

with $\tilde{f}(\hat{u},\hat{v}) := f(\hat{u},\hat{v})u_z$. Compared to the non-linear fitting of BRDF model parameters (see Section 5.2), we now have a linear problem to solve with a smaller degree of freedom and even more constraints. Above equation shows only the system for one color channel, whereas the weights t_i have to be the same for all channels. In contrast to this, BRDF parameters would require a distinct set of parameters per channel.

The least square solution may contain negative values for some t_k. But negative weights may result in an oscillating BRDF that represents only the given radiance sample accurately but will produce unpredictable values for other viewing and light directions, we therefore set t_k to zero and compute another least square solution for the remaining t's, until all t's are positive. This could also be seen as a constrained minimization problem.

7.1 Basis BRDFs

The next question is how to determine the set of basis BRDFs. Since the changes of the surface properties within one material tend to be small, a distinct set of basis BRDFs is assigned to each cluster. Therefore, it is sufficient to store just the scalar weights per lumitexel instead of the full set of BRDF parameters.

Finding the optimal set of BRDFs $f_1, f_2, \ldots, f_m$, that minimizes the error

$$E_\pi(C) = \frac{1}{|C|} \sum_{\mathcal{L}_i \in C} E_{f_{\pi i}}(\mathcal{L}_i) \tag{8}$$

for a cluster C, where $f_{\pi i}$ denotes the least square projection of the lumitexel $\mathcal{L}_i$ as defined in Equation 6, is a problem of principal function analysis (PFA) (see [27]). Principal function analysis is closely related to principal component analysis (PCA) with the important difference that functions f_m are optimized instead of vectors. Unfortunately, the PFA does not reduce to a simple eigenvalue problem as PCA does. To minimize $E_\pi(C)$, we again perform a least square optimization using the Levenberg-Marquardt method, this time fitting m BRDFs simultaneously. Within each iteration we recompute the projection $f_{\pi i}$ of lumitexel $\mathcal{L}_i$ into the currently estimated basis.

As for every optimization problem the initial parameters (BRDFs) are quite important. For a given cluster C, we use the following BRDFs as a basis:

- f_C, the BRDF fit to the cluster C,
- the BRDFs of spatially neighboring clusters to match lumitexels at cluster boundaries,
- the BRDFs of similar clusters with respect to the material,
- and two BRDFs based on f_C, one with slightly increased and one with decreased diffuse component ρ_d and exponent N.

In our experiments it turned out that this initial basis together with the projection already produces very good results with small errors. In most cases the PFA computed almost negligible changes to the initial BRDFs. This is to be expected because the initially chosen basis constructed through splitting and clustering already approximates the material properties quite well.

8 Rendering

As explained in Section 4.1 we know the position of every lumitexel, as well as the triangle it belongs to and the 2D coordinates within that triangle.

model	T	V	L	R	C	B	1-RMS	C-RMS	P-RMS	F-RMS
angels	47000	27	1606223	7.6	9	6	.2953	.1163	.1113	.1111
bird	14000	25	1917043	6.3	5	4	.1513	.0627	.0387	.0387
bust	50000	16	3627404	4.2	3	4	.1025	.0839	.0583	.0581

Table 1. *This table lists the number of triangles (T) of each model, the number of views (V) we used to reconstruct the spatially varying BRDFs, the number of acquired lumitexels (L) and the average number of radiance samples (R) per lumitexel, the number of partitioned material clusters (C), the number of basis BRDFs (B) per cluster, the RMS error for a single average BRDF (1-RMS), the RMS error when using per-cluster BRDFs, the RMS error after projecting every lumitexel into the basis of BRDFs, and finally the RMS error after doing a PFA on the basis BRDFs and projecting every lumitexel into the new basis.*

This information can then be used to generate an index texture for the full object. For every texel, that texture contains an index to the cluster it belongs to. Then we generate a weight texture map for every cluster that stores the weights resulting from the projection into the basis BRDFs. The parameters for the basis BRDFs of every cluster are stored in a small table.

Raytracing such an object is very simple, since for every point on the object that is raytraced we can simply look up the cluster the texel belongs to. Then we evaluate the basis BRDFs for the local light and viewing direction and compute the weighted sum using the weight texture map. So rendering basically reduces to evaluating a few BRDFs per pixel. Another big advantage of this representation is that mip-mapping can easily be used. Since the weighted sum is just a linear operation, the weights of neighboring texels can simply be averaged to generate the next coarser mip-map level.

If the original images are of high resolution and hence the object is sampled very densely, point sample rendering using forward projection is a viable alternative. It completely avoids the generation of texture maps and the resulting data can be used with almost no further processing. This method is used to display our results.

9 Results

We applied our algorithm to three different objects consisting of different materials with varying reflection properties in both the diffuse and the specular part. The model of the angels was generated by extracting an isosurface of a computer tomography scan. The geometry of all other models was captured using a structured light 3D scanner. Some statistics about the meshes and the number of acquired views are listed in Table 1. Acquisition of 20 views (each needing about 15 photographs) takes approx. 2.5h. The high dynamic range conversion and the registration with the 3D model takes about 5h but is a completely automated task. The clustering and the final projection takes about 1.5h.

In Figure 4 you can see how five successive split operations partition the lumitexels of the bird into its five materials. The splits were performed as described in Section 6. Only the per-cluster BRDFs determined by the clustering process are used for shading, making the object look rather flat. After performing the projection step every lumitexel is represented in a basis of four BRDFs, now resulting in a much more detailed and realistic appearance, see Figure 6.

The bust in Figure 5 shows another reconstructed object with very different reflection properties. The bronze look is very well captured.

In Figure 7 you can see a comparison between an object rendered with an acquired BRDF (using the projection method) and a photograph of the object. You can see that they are very similar, but differences can be seen in highlights and in places where not enough radiance samples were captured. Capturing more samples will increase the quality. The difference in the hair region is due to missing detail in the triangle mesh.

Another difference is due to the fact that the diffuse color of one lumitexel may not be represented in any of the constructed clusters because the number of lumitexels belonging to the same material can be so small that they nearly vanish in the mass of lumitexels of the cluster they are currently assigned to. This effect can for example be observed at the mouth of the larger angel which in reality exhibits a much more saturated red, see Figure 7.

In Table 1 we list RMS errors computed between all the radiance samples of a model and the reconstructed BRDFs. You can see that the error considerably decreases when going from one average BRDF to per-cluster BRDFs and then to per-pixel BRDFs (using projection). As already mentioned the PFA only slightly changes the RMS error.

Generally it can be said that for all the models only a few clusters were needed to accurately represent all the materials since the projection takes care of material changes. In our experiments even Lafortune BRDFs consisting of a single lobe were sufficient to form good bases for the clustering and projection.

The projection method also compensates for imprecise normals, and hence no re-fitting of the normals is needed. Using exactly reconstructed normals for example by applying a shape-from-shading approach such as the one by Rushmeier et al. [21] may yield even better results.

Due to the lack of a test object that had a single base color but varying specularity, we experimented with artificially generated data. The tests proved that our clustering algorithm is also able to clearly distinguish materials that have the same color but different specularity, even when noise was introduced in the data.

10   Conclusions and Future Work

We have presented an algorithm and demonstrated a system for reconstructing a high-quality spatially varying BRDF from complex solid objects using only a small number of images. This allows for accurately shaded, photorealistic rendering of these objects from new viewpoints and under arbitrary lighting conditions.

The output of our algorithm also allows to modify the object's geometry while preserving material properties, since the fitted BRDFs are represented on a per-texel basis and do not change with the geometry.

Both the number of input views required by our algorithm and the size of the output data (~25MB) are very small compared to previous approaches for representing real-world objects, like surface light fields or reflection fields which needed up to 600 images [27].

We have demonstrated the quality and accuracy of our approach, by applying it to different objects. The resulting spatially varying BRDFs accurately represent the original materials.

Until now interreflections within the object are not considered, but it should be easy to remove the effects of interreflections by simulating secondary reflection using the results obtained by the presented algorithm, or e.g. using techniques from [19].

We also want to investigate the possibility to do hardware accelerated rendering with the spatially varying BRDFs. Since our data can be represented as texture maps and the Lafortune model is computationally fairly simple, this should be easily possible, e.g. using techniques from [8] or from [27].

114

References

1. K. Dana, B. van Ginneken, S. Nayar, and J. Koenderink. Reflectance and texture of real-world surfaces. *ACM Transactions on Graphics*, 18(1):1–34, January 1999.
2. P. Debevec, T. Hawkins, C. Tchou, H.-P. Duiker, W. Sarokin, and M. Sagar. Acquiring the Reflectance Field of a Human Face. In *Proc. SIGGRAPH*, pages 145–156, July 2000. ISBN 1-58113-208-5.
3. P. Debevec and J. Malik. Recovering High Dynamic Range Radiance Maps from Photographs. In *Proc. SIGGRAPH*, pages 369–378, August 1997.
4. P. Debevec, C. Taylor, and J. Malik. Modeling and rendering architecture from photographs: A hybrid geometry- and image-based approach. In *Proc. SIGGRAPH*, pages 11–20, August 1996.
5. M. Garland and P. Heckbert. Surface Simplification Using Quadric Error Metrics. In *Proc. SIGGRAPH*, pages 209–216, August 1997.
6. A. Gersho and R. Gray. *Vector Quantization and Signal Compression*. Kluwer Acad. Publishers, 1992.
7. S. Gortler, R. Grzeszczuk, R. Szelinski, and M. Cohen. The Lumigraph. In *Proc. SIGGRAPH*, pages 43–54, August 1996.
8. J. Kautz and H.-P. Seidel. Towards Interactive Bump Mapping with Anisotropic Shift-Variant BRDFs. In *Eurographics/SIGGRAPH Hardware Workshop*, pages 51–58, August 2000.
9. L. Kobbelt. Discrete fairing. In *Proc. of the 7th IMA Conf. on the Mathematics of Surfaces*, pages 101–131, 1996.
10. J. Koenderink, A. van Doorn, and M. Stavridi. Bidirectional Reflection Distribution Function expressed in terms of surface scattering modes. In *Proc. 4th Europ. Conf. on Computer Vision*, pages 28–39, 1996.
11. E. Lafortune, S. Foo, K. Torrance, and D. Greenberg. Non-Linear Approximation of Reflectance Functions. In *Proc. SIGGRAPH*, pages 117–126, August 1997.
12. H. Lensch, W. Heidrich, and H.-P. Seidel. Automated Texture Registration and Stitching for Real World Models. In *Pacific Graphics '00*, pages 317–326, October 2000.
13. M. Levoy and P. Hanrahan. Light Field Rendering. In *Proc. SIGGRAPH*, pages 31–42, August 1996.
14. S. Lloyd. Least squares quantization in PCM. *IEEE Trans. on Information Theory*, IT-28:129–137, 1982.
15. R. Lu, J. Koenderink, and A. Kappers. Optical Properties (bidirectional reflectance distribution functions) of velvet. *Applied Optics*, 37(25):5974–5984, September 1998.
16. J. MacQueen. Some methods for classification and analysis of multivariate observations. In *Proc. of the 5th Berkeley Symp. on Mathematical Statistics and Probability*, volume 1, 1967.
17. S. Marschner, S. Westin, E. Lafortune, K. Torrance, and D. Greenberg. Image-based BRDF Measurement Including Human Skin. In *10th Eurographics Workshop on Rendering*, pages 131–144, June 1999.
18. G. Miller, S. Rubin, and D. Ponceleon. Lazy decompression of surface light fields for precomputed global illumination. In *9th Eurographics Workshop on Rendering*, pages 281–292, June 1998.
19. S. Nayar, K. Ikeuchi, and T. Kanade. Recovering Shape in the Presence of Interreflections. In *IEEE Int. Conf. on Robotics and Automation*, pages 1814–1819, 1991.
20. W. Press, S. Teukolsky, W. Vetterling, and B. Flannery. *Numerical Recipes in C: The Art of Scientific Computing (2nd ed.)*. Cambridge University Press, 1992. ISBN 0-521-43108-5.
21. H. Rushmeier, G. Taubin, and A. Guéziec. Applying Shape from Lighting Variation to Bump Map Capture. In *8th Eurographics Workshop on Rendering Workshop*, pages 35–44, June 1997.
22. Y. Sato, M. Wheeler, and K. Ikeuchi. Object Shape and Reflectance Modeling from Observation. In *Proc. SIGGRAPH*, pages 379–388, August 1997.
23. H. Schirmacher, W. Heidrich, M. Rubick, D. Schiron, and H.-P. Seidel. Image-Based BRDF Reconstruction. In *Proc. of the 4th VMV Conference*, pages 285–292, November 1999.
24. K. Torrance and E. Sparrow. Theory for off-specular reflection from roughened surfaces. *Journal of Optical Society of America*, 57(9), 1967.
25. G. Ward Larson. Measuring and Modeling Anisotropic Reflection. In *Proc. SIGGRAPH*, pages 265–272, July 1992.
26. S. Westin, J. Arvo, and K. Torrance. Predicting Reflectance Functions From Complex Surfaces. In *Proc. SIGGRAPH*, pages 255–264, July 1992.
27. D. Wood, D. Azuma, K. Aldinger, B. Curless, T. Duchamp, D. Salesin, and W. Stuetzle. Surface Light Fields for 3D Photography. In *Proc. SIGGRAPH*, pages 287–296, July 2000.
28. Y. Yu, P. Debevec, J. Malik, and T. Hawkins. Inverse Global Illumination: Recovering Reflectance Models of Real Scenes From Photographs. In *Proc. SIGGRAPH*, pages 215–224, August 1999.
29. Z. Zhang. Flexible Camera Calibration By Viewing a Plane From Unknown Orientations. In *Int. Conf. on Computer Vision*, pages 666–673, September 1999.

Editors' Note: see Appendix, p. 330 for colored figures of this paper

Polyhedral Visual Hulls for Real-Time Rendering

Wojciech Matusik   Chris Buehler   Leonard McMillan

MIT Laboratory for Computer Science

Abstract. We present new algorithms for creating and rendering visual hulls in real-time. Unlike voxel or sampled approaches, we compute an exact polyhedral representation for the visual hull directly from the silhouettes. This representation has a number of advantages: 1) it is a view-independent representation, 2) it is well-suited to rendering with graphics hardware, and 3) it can be computed very quickly. We render these visual hulls with a view-dependent texturing strategy, which takes into account visibility information that is computed during the creation of the visual hull. We demonstrate these algorithms in a system that asynchronously renders dynamically created visual hulls in real-time. Our system outperforms similar systems of comparable computational power.

1   Introduction

A classical approach for determining a three-dimensional model from a set of images is to compute shape-from-silhouettes. Most often, shape-from-silhouette methods employ discrete volumetric representations [12, 19]. The use of this discrete volumetric representation invariably introduces quantization and aliasing artifacts into the resulting model (i.e. the resulting model seldom projects back to the original silhouettes).

Recently, algorithms have been developed for sampling and texturing visual hulls along a discrete set of viewing rays [10]. These algorithms have been developed in the context of a real-time system for acquiring and rendering dynamic geometry. These techniques do not suffer from aliasing effects when the viewing rays correspond to the pixels in a desired output image. In addition, the algorithms address the rendering problem by view-dependently texturing the visual hull with proper visibility. However, these algorithms are only useful when a view-dependent representation of the visual hull is desired.

In this paper, we present algorithms for computing and rendering an exact polyhedral representation of the visual hull. This representation has a number of desirable properties. First, it is a view-independent representation, which implies that it only needs to be computed once for a given set of input silhouettes. Second, the representation is well-suited to rendering with graphics hardware, which is optimized for triangular mesh processing. Third, this representation can be computed and rendered just as quickly as sampled representations, and thus it is useful for real-time applications.

We demonstrate our visual hull construction and rendering algorithms in a real-time system. The system receives input from multiple video cameras and constructs visual hull meshes as quickly as possible. A separate rendering process asynchronously renders these meshes using a novel view-dependent texturing strategy with visibility.

1.1 Previous Work

Laurentini [8] introduced the *visual hull* concept to describe the maximal volume that reproduces the silhouettes of an object. Strictly, the visual hull is the maximal volume constructed from all possible silhouettes. In this paper (and in almost any practical setting) we compute the visual hull of an object with respect to a finite number of silhouettes. The silhouette seen by a pinhole camera determines a three-dimensional volume that originates from the camera's center of projection and extends infinitely while passing through the silhouette's contour on the image plane. We call this volume a silhouette cone. All silhouette cones exhibit the hull property in that they contain the actual geometry that produced the silhouette. For our purposes, a visual hull is defined as the three-dimensional intersection of silhouette cones from a set of pinhole silhouette images.

Visual hulls are most often computed using a discrete three-dimensional grid of volume elements (voxels). This technique, known as voxel carving [12, 19], proceeds by projecting each voxel onto each of the source image planes, and removing those voxels that fall completely outside of any silhouette. Octree-hierarchies are often used to accelerate this procedure. Related to voxel approaches, a recent algorithm computes discrete slices of the visual hull using graphics hardware for acceleration [9]. Other approaches improve the shape using splines [17] or color information [18].

If the primary purpose of a shape representation is to produce new renderings of that shape from different viewing conditions, then construction of an explicit model is not necessary. The image-based visual hull technique introduced in [10], renders unique views of the visual hull directly from the silhouette images, without constructing an intermediate volumetric or polyhedral model. This is accomplished by merging the cone intersection calculation with the rendering process, resulting in an algorithm similar in spirit to CSG ray casting [15].

However, sometimes an explicit three-dimensional model of the visual hull is desired. There has been work [4, 14] on general Boolean operations on 3D polyhedra. Most of these algorithms require decomposing the input polyhedra into convex polyhedra. Then, the operations are carried out on the convex polyhedra. By contrast, our algorithm makes no convexity assumptions; instead we exploit the fact that each of the intersection primitives (i.e., silhouette cones) are generalized cones with constant scaled cross-section. The algorithm in [16] also exploits the same property of silhouette cones, but exhibits performance unsuitable for real-time use.

View-dependent rendering is very popular for models that are acquired from real images (e.g., see [13]). The rendering algorithm that we use is closely related to view-dependent texture mapping (VDTM), introduced in [5] and implemented in real-time in [6]. The particular algorithm that we use is different from those two, and it is based on the unstructured lumigraph rendering (ULR) algorithm in [3]. In our implementation, we extend the ULR algorithm to handle visibility, which was not covered in the original paper.

Our real-time system is similar to previous systems. The system in [11] constructs visual hull models using voxels and uses view-dependent texture mapping for rendering, but the processing is done as an off-line process. The Virtualized Reality system [7] also constructs models of dynamic event using a variety of techniques including multi-baseline stereo.

Fig. 1. A single silhouette cone face is shown, defined by the edge in the center silhouette. Its projection in two other silhouettes is also shown.

2 Polyhedral Visual Hull Construction

We assume that each silhouette s is specified by a set of convex or non-convex 2D polygons. These polygons can have holes. Each polygon consists of a set of edges joining consecutive vertices that define its (possibly multiple) contours. Moreover, for each silhouette s we know the projection matrix associated with the imaging device (e.g., video camera) that generated the silhouette. We use a 4×4 projection matrix that maps 3D coordinates to image (silhouette) coordinates, and whose inverse maps image coordinates to 3D directions.

2.1 Algorithm Outline

In order to compute the visual hull with respect to the input silhouettes, we need to compute the intersection of the cones defined by the input silhouettes. The resulting polyhedron is described by all of its faces. Note that the faces of this polyhedron can only lie on the faces of the original cones, and the faces of the original cones are defined by the projection matrices and the edges in the input silhouettes.

Thus, a simple algorithm for computing the visual hull might do the following: For each input silhouette s_i and for each edge e in the input silhouette s_i we compute the face of the cone. Then we intersect this face with the cones of all other input silhouettes. The result of these intersections is a set of polygons that define the surface of the visual hull.

2.2 Reduction to 2D

The intersection of a face of a cone with other cones is a 3D operation (these are polygon-polyhedron intersections). It was observed by [10, 16] that these intersections can be reduced to simpler intersections in 2D. This is because each of the silhouette cones has a fixed scaled cross-section; that is, it is defined by a 2D silhouette. Reduction to 2D also allows for less complex 2D data structures to accelerate the intersections.

118

To compute the intersection of a face f of a cone $cone(s_i)$ with a cone $cone(s_j)$, we project f onto the image plane of silhouette s_j (see Figure 1). Then we compute the intersection of projected face f with silhouette s_j. Finally, we project back the resulting polygons onto the plane of face f.

2.3 Efficient Intersection of Projected Cones and Silhouettes

In the previous section, we discussed intersecting a projected cone face f with a silhouette s_j. If we repeat this operation for every projected cone face in $cone(s_i)$, then we will have intersected the entire projected silhouette cone $cone(s_i)$ with silhouette s_j. In this section we show how to efficiently compute the intersection of the projected cone $cone(s_i)$ with the silhouette s_j. We accelerate the intersection process by pre-processing the silhouettes into Edge-Bin data structures as described in [10]. The Edge-Bin structure spatially partitions a silhouette so that we can quickly compute the set of edges that a projected cone face intersects. In the following, we abbreviate $cone(s_i)$ as c_i for simplicity.

Construction of Edge-Bins. First, we observe that in case of perspective projection all rays on the surface of the cone c_i project to a pencil of lines sharing a common point p_0 (i.e., the epipole) in the image plane of s_j. We can parameterize all projected lines based on the slope α that these lines make with some reference line. Given this parameterization we partition the domain of $\alpha = (-\infty, \infty)$ into ranges such that any projected line with the slope falling inside of the given range always intersects the same set of edges of the silhouette s_j. We define a bin b_k to be a three-tuple: the start α_{start}, the end α_{end} of the range, and a corresponding set of edges S_k, $b_k = (\alpha_{start}, \alpha_{end}, S_k)$. We note that each silhouette vertex corresponds to a line that defines a range boundary.

In certain configurations, all rays project to a set of parallel epipolar lines in the image plane of s_j. When this case occurs, we use a line $p(\alpha) = p_0 + d\alpha$ to parameterize the lines, where p_0 is some arbitrary point on the line $p(\alpha)$ and d is a vector perpendicular to the direction of the projected rays. To define bins, we use the values of the parameter α at the intersection points of the line $p(\alpha)$ with the epipolar lines passing through the silhouette vertices. In this way we can describe the boundary of the bin using two values α_{start} and α_{end}, where α_{start}, α_{end} are the values of α for the lines passing through two silhouette vertices that define the region.

The Edge-Bin construction involves two steps. First, we sort the silhouette vertices based on the value of the parameter α. The lines that pass through the silhouette vertices define the bin boundaries.

Next, we observe that two consecutive slopes in the sorted list define α_{start} and α_{end} for each bin. To compute a set of edges assigned to each bin we traverse the sorted list of silhouette vertices. At the same time we maintain the list of edges in the current bin. When we visit a vertex of the silhouette we remove from the current bin an edge that ends at this vertex, and we add an edge that starts at the vertex. The start of an edge is defined as the edge endpoint that has a smaller value of parameter α. In Figure 2 we show a simple silhouette, bins, and corresponding edges for each bin.

The edges in each bin need to be sorted based on the increasing distance from the point p_0 (or the distance from parameterization line $p(\alpha)$ in case of the parallel lines). The efficient algorithm first performs a partial ordering on all the edges in the silhouette such that the edges closer to the point p_0 are first in the list. Then, when the bins are constructed the edges are inserted in the bins in the correct order.

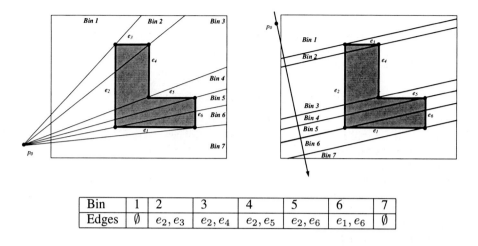

Bin	1	2	3	4	5	6	7
Edges	$\emptyset$	e_2, e_3	e_2, e_4	e_2, e_5	e_2, e_6	e_1, e_6	$\emptyset$

Fig. 2. Two example silhouettes and their corresponding Edge-Bin data structures. Two cases are shown, one with convergent bins and one with parallel bins. The edges that are stored in the bins are listed in the accompanying table.

Efficient Intersection of the Projected Cone Faces with a Silhouette. Using the edge bin data structure, we can compute efficiently the intersection of the projected cone c_i with the silhouette s_j of some other cone c_j. In order to compute the intersection we process the faces of cone c_i in consecutive order. We start by projecting the first face f_1 onto the plane of silhouette s_j. The projected face f_1 is defined by its boundary lines with the values α_{p1}, α_{p2}. First, we need to find a bin $b = \{\alpha_{start}, \alpha_{end}, S\}$ such that $\alpha_{p1} \in (\alpha_{start}, \alpha_{end})$. Then, we intersect the line α_{p1} with all the edges in S. Since the edges in S are sorted based on the increasing distance from the projected vertex of cone c_i (or distance from line $p(\alpha)$ in case of parallel lines) we can immediately compute the edges of the resulting intersection that lie on line α_{p1}. Next, we traverse the bins in the direction of the value α_{p2}. As we move across the bins we build the intersection polygons by adding the vertices that define the bins. When we get to the bin $b' = \{\alpha'_{start}, \alpha'_{end}, S'\}$ such that $\alpha_{p2} \in (\alpha'_{start}, \alpha'_{end})$ we intersect the line α_{p2} with all edges in S' and compute the remaining edges of the resulting polygons. It is important to note that the next projected face f_2 is defined by the boundary lines α_{p2}, α_{p3}. Therefore, we do not have to search for the bin α_{p2} falls into. In this manner we compute the intersection of all projected faces of cone c_i with the silhouette s_j.

2.4 Calculating Visual Hull Faces

In the previous section we described how to perform the intersection of two cones efficiently. Performing the pairwise intersection on all pairs of cones results in $k - 1$ polygon sets for each face of each cone, where k is the total number of silhouettes. The faces of the visual hull are the intersections of these polygon sets at each cone face. It is possible to perform the intersection of these polygon sets using standard algorithms for Boolean operations [1, 2], but we use a custom algorithm instead that is easy to implement and can output triangles directly.

Our polygon intersection routine works by decomposing arbitrary polygons into quadrilaterals and intersecting those. In Figure 3, we demonstrate the procedure with

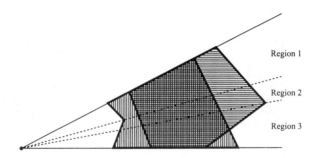

Region 1

Region 2

Region 3

Fig. 3. Our polygon intersection routine subdivides polygons into quadrilaterals for intersection.

two 5-sided polygons, one with vertical hatching and the other with horizontal hatching. We first divide the space occupied by the polygons into triangular regions based on the polygons' vertices and the apex of the silhouette cone (similar to the Edge-Bin construction process). Note that within each triangular region, the polygon pieces are quadrilaterals. Then, we intersect the quadrilaterals in each region and combine all of the results into the final polygon, shown with both horizontal and vertical hatching.

The resulting polyhedral visual hull includes redundant copies of each vertex in the polyhedron (in fact, the number of copies of each vertex is equal to the degree of the vertex divided by 2). To optionally eliminate the redundant copies, we simply merge identical vertices. Ideally, our algorithm produces a watertight triangular mesh. However, because of our non-optimal face intersection routine, our meshes may contain T-junctions which violate the watertight property.

2.5 Visibility

In order to properly texture map the visual hull we need to determine which parts of the visual hull surface are visible from which cameras.

This visibility problem is equivalent to the shadow determination problem where one places a point light source at each reference camera position, and the goal is to determine which parts of the scene are illuminated by the light and which parts lie in a shadow. Standard graphics (hardware) algorithms are directly applicable since we have a mesh representation of the visual hull surface. However, they require rendering the scene from each input camera viewpoint and reading the z-buffer or the frame-buffer. These operations can be slow (reading the frame and z-buffer can be slow) and they can suffer from the quantization artifacts of the z-buffer.

We present an alternative novel software algorithm that computes the visible parts of the visual hull surface from each of the input cameras. The algorithm has the advantages that it is simple, and it can be computed virtually at no cost at the same time that we compute the visual hull polygons.

Let us assume that we want to compute whether the faces of the visual hull that lie on the extruded edge i in silhouette s_j are visible from image k.

We observe that these faces have to be visible from the camera k if the edge i is visible from the epipole p_0 (the projection of the center of projection of image k onto the image plane of camera j). This effectively reduces the 3D visibility computation to the 2D visibility computation. Moreover, we can perform the 2D visibility computation very efficiently using the edge-bin data structures that we already computed during the

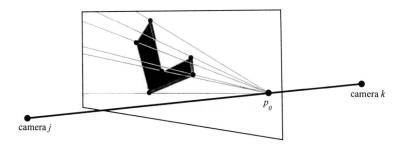

Fig. 4. We perform a conservative visibility test in 2D. In this example, the thick edges in the silhouette of camera c_j have been determined to be visible by camera c_k. These 2D edges correspond to 3D faces in the polyhedral visual hull.

visual hull computation.

First, we label all edges invisible. Then, to determine the visibility of edges in image j with respect to image k we traverse each bin in the Edge-Bin data structure. For each bin, we label the part of the first edge that lies in the bin as visible (see Figure 4). The edges in the bin are sorted in the increasing distance from the epipole; thus, the first edge in the bin corresponds to the front-most surface.

If the edge is visible in its full extent (if it is visible in all the bins in which it resides) then the edge is visible. If the edge is visible in some of its extent (if it is visible only in some bins in which it resides) then the edge is partially visible. The easiest solution in this case is to break it into the visible and invisible segments when computing the faces of the visual hull.

The visibility computation described in this section is conservative; we never label an edge visible if it is in fact invisible. However, it is often over-conservative, especially for objects whose silhouettes contains many holes.

3 View-Dependent Texturing

We have applied a novel view-dependent texturing strategy for rendering our polyhedral visual hull models in real-time. Our algorithm is based on the unstructured lumigraph rendering (ULR) algorithm detailed in [3], and we have added extensions to handle the visibility information computed during the visual hull construction.

The core idea of ULR is that the influence of a single image on the final rendering is a smoothly varying function across the desired image plane (or, equivalently, across the geometry representing the scene). These smooth weighting functions combine to form a image "blending field" that specifies how much contribution each input image makes to each pixel in the output image. The assumption of smoothness suggests an efficient rendering strategy: sparsely sample the image blending field and reconstruct it using simple basis functions (e.g., linear hat functions). The reconstructed blending field is then used to blend pixels from the input images to form the output image.

In the case of real-time rendering, the blending field can be efficiently reconstructed by triangulating the samples and using hardware alpha interpolation across the faces of

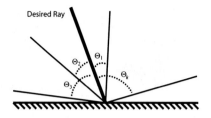

Fig. 5. Our k-nearest neighbor weighting is based on the k cameras with viewing rays closest in angle to the desired viewing ray. In this example, the desired ray is shown in bold in addition to four camera viewing rays. The angles of the k closest cameras are ordered such that $\Theta_1 \leq \Theta_2 \leq \Theta_3 \leq \ldots \leq \Theta_k$, and Θ_k is taken to be the threshold at which the weighting function falls to zero.

the triangles. The input image pixels are then blended together by projectively texturing mapping the triangles and accumulating the results in the frame buffer. The pseudocode for a multi-pass rendering version of the algorithm proceeds as follows:

> Construct a list of blending field sample locations
> **for each** input image i **do**
>   **for each** blending field sample location **do**
>   evaluate blending weight for image i and store in alpha channel
>   **end for**
>   Set current texture i
>   Set current texture matrix P_i
>   Draw triangulated samples using alpha channel blending weights
> **end for**

The sample locations are simply 3D rays along which the blending field is evaluated. In the case when a reasonably dense model of the scene is available, sampling along the rays emanating from the desired viewpoint and passing through the vertices of the model is generally sufficient to capture the variation in the blending field. In this case, the triangles that are drawn are the actual triangles of the scene model. By contrast, in the general unstructured lumigraph case, one may sample rays randomly, and the triangles that are drawn may only roughly approximate the true scene geometry.

The texture matrix P_i is simply the projection matrix associated with camera i. It is rescaled to return texture coordinates between 0 and 1. In our real-time system, these matrices are obtained from a camera calibration process.

3.1 Evaluating the Blending Weights

Our view-dependent texturing algorithm evaluates the image blending field at each vertex of the visual hull model. The weight assigned to each image is calculated to favor those cameras whose view directions most closely match that of the desired view. The weighting that we use is the k-nearest neighbor weighting used in [3] and summarized here. For each vertex of the model, we find the k cameras whose viewings rays to that vertex are closest in angle to the desired viewing ray (see Figure 5). Consider the kth ray with the largest viewing angle, Θ_k. We use this angle to define a local weighting function that maps the other angles into the range from 0 to 1: $weight(\Theta) = 1 - \frac{\Theta}{\Theta_k}$.

Applying this function to the k angles results (in general) in $k-1$ non-zero weights. We renormalize these weights to arrive at the final blending weights. In practice, we typically use $k=3$ in our four camera system, which results in two non-zero weights at each vertex.

Although other weighting schemes are possible, this one is easy to implement and does not require any pre-processing such as in [6]. It results in a (mostly) smooth blending field except in degenerate cases, such as when k (or more) input rays are equidistant from the desired ray or when less than k nearest neighbors can be found (due to visibility or some other reason).

3.2 Handling Visibility

The algorithm in [3] does not explicitly handle the problem of visibility. In our case, we have visibility information available on a per-polygon basis. We can distinguish two possible approaches to incorporating this information: one that maintains a continuous blending field reconstruction and one that does not. A continuous blending field reconstruction is one in which the blending weights for the cameras on one side of a triangle edge are the same as on the other side of the edge. A continuous reconstruction generally has less apparent visual artifacts.

A simple rule for utilizing visibility while enforcing continuous reconstruction is the following: if vertex v belongs to *any* triangle t that is not visible from camera c, then do not consider c when calculating the blending weights for v. This rule causes camera c's influence to be zero across the face of triangle t, which is expected because t is not visible from c. It also forces c's influence to fall to zero along the other sides of the edges of t (assuming that the mesh is watertight) which results in a continuous blending function.

The assumption of a watertight mesh makes the continuous visibility rule unsuitable for our non-watertight visual hull meshes. Even with a watertight mesh, the mesh must be fairly densely tessellated, or the visibility boundaries may not be well-represented.

For these reasons, we relax the requirement of reconstruction continuity in our visibility treatment. When computing blending weights, we create a separate set of blending weights for each triangle. Each set of blending weights is computed considering only those cameras that see the triangle. When rendering, we replicate vertices so that we can specify different sets of blending weights per-triangle rather than per-vertex. Although this rendering algorithm is less elegant and more complex than the continuous algorithm, it works well enough in practice.

4 Real-Time System

The current system uses four calibrated Sony DFW-V500 IEEE-1394 video cameras. Each camera is attached to a separate client (600 MHz Athlon desktop PC). The cameras are synchronized to each other using an external trigger signal. Each client captures the video stream at 15 fps and performs the following processing steps: First, it segments out the foreground object using background subtraction. Then, the silhouette and texture information are compressed and sent over a 100Mb/s network to a central server. The system typically processes video at 320×240 resolution. It can optionally process 640×480 video at a reduced frame rate.

The central server (2x933MHz Pentium III PC) performs the majority of the computations. The server application has the following three threads:

- *Network Thread* - receives and decompresses the textures and silhouettes from the clients.
- *Construction Thread* - computes the silhouette simplification, volume intersection, and visibility.
- *Rendering Thread* - performs the view-dependent texturing and display.

Each thread runs independently of the others. This allows us to efficiently utilize the multiple processors of the server. It also enables us to render the visual hull at a faster rate than we compute it. As a result, end users perceive a higher frame rate than that at which the model is actually updated.

5 Results

Our system computes polyhedral visual hull models at a peak 15 frames per second, which is the frame rate at which our cameras run. The rendering algorithm is decoupled from the model construction, and it can run up to 30 frames per second depending on the model complexity. The actual frame rates of both components, especially rendering, are dependent on the model complexity, which in turn depends on the complexity of the input silhouette contours. In order to maintain a relatively constant frame rate, we simplify the input silhouettes with a coarser polygonal approximation. The amount of simplification is controlled by the current performance of the system.

In Figure 6, we show two flat-shaded renderings of a polyhedral visual hull that was captured in real-time from our system. These images demonstrate the typical models that our system produces. The main sources of error in creating these models is poor image segmentation and a small number of input images.

Figure 7 shows the same model view-dependently textured with four video images. In Figure 7a, the model is textured using information from our novel visibility algorithm. This results in a discontinuous reconstruction of the blending field, but it more accurately captures regions of the model that were not seen by the video cameras. In Figure 7b, the model is textured without visibility information. The resulting blending field is very smooth, although some visibility errors are made near occlusions.

Figure 8 shows visualizations of the blending fields of the previous two figures. Each of the four cameras is assigned a color (red, green, blue, and yellow), and the colors are blended together using the camera blending weights. It is clear from these images that the image produced using visibility information is discontinuous while the other image is not.

6 Future Work and Conclusions

In offline testing, our algorithms are sufficiently fast to run at full 30 frames per second on reasonable computer hardware. The maximum frame rate of our current live system is limited by the fact that our cameras can only capture images at 15 frames per second in synchronized mode. Clearly, it would improve the system to use better and more cameras that can run at 30 frames per second. Additional cameras would both improve the shape of the visual hulls and the quality of the view-dependent texturing.

In the current system we compute and throw away a different mesh for each frame of video. For some applications it might be useful to derive the mesh of the next frame as a transformation of the mesh in the original frame and to store the original mesh plus the transformation function. Temporal processing such as this would also enable us to accumulate the texture (radiance) of the model as it is seen from different viewpoints. Such accumulated texture information could be used to fill in parts that are invisible in one frame with information from other frames.

In this paper we have presented novel algorithms for efficiently computing and rendering polyhedral visual hulls directly from a set of images. We implemented and tested these algorithms in a real-time system. The speed of this system and the quality of the renderings are much better than previous systems using similar resources. The primary advantage of this system is that it produces polygonal meshes of the visual hull in each frame. As we demonstrated, these meshes can be rendered quickly using view-dependent texture mapping and graphics hardware.

References

1. Balaban, I. J., "An Optimal Algorithm for Finding Segments Intersections," *Proc. 11th Annual ACM Symposium on Computational Geometry,* (1995), pp. 211-219.
2. Bentley, J. and Ottmann, T., "Algorithms for Reporting and Counting Geometric Intersections," *IEEE Trans. Comput.,* C-28, 9 (Sept. 1979), pp. 643-647.
3. Buehler, C., Bosse, M., Gortler, S., Cohen, M., McMillan, L., "Unstructured Lumigraph Rendering," To appear *SIGGRAPH 2001.*
4. Chazelle, B., "An Optimal Algorithm for Intersecting Three-Dimensional Convex Polyhedra," SIAM J. Computing, 21 (1992), pp. 671-696.
5. Debevec, P., Taylor, C., Malik. J., "Modeling and Rendering Architecture from Photographs," *SIGGRAPH 1996,* pp. 11-20.
6. Debevec, P., Yu, Y., Borshukov, G. D., "Efficient View-Dependent Image-Based Rendering with Projective Texture Mapping," *Eurographics Rendering Workshop*, (1998).
7. Kanade, T., P. W. Rander, P. J. Narayanan. "Virtualized Reality: Constructing Virtual Worlds from Real Scenes," *IEEE Multimedia,* 4, 1 (March 1997), pp. 34-47.
8. Laurentini, A., "The Visual Hull Concept for Silhouette Based Image Understanding," *IEEE PAMI,* 16, 2 (1994), pp. 150-162.
9. Lok, B., "Online Model Reconstruction for Interactive Virtual Environments," *I3D 2001.*
10. Matusik, W., Buehler, C., Raskar, R., Gortler, S., McMillan, L., "Image-Based Visual Hulls,"*SIGGRAPH 2000,* (July 2000), pp. 369-374.
11. Moezzi, S., D.Y. Kuramura, R. Jain. "Reality Modeling and Visualization from Multiple Video Sequences," *IEEE CG&A,* 16, 6 (Nov 1996), pp. 58-63.
12. Potmesil, M., "Generating Octree Models of 3D Objects from their Silhouettes in a Sequence of Images," *CVGIP,* 40 (1987), pp. 1-29.
13. Pulli, K., Cohen, M., Duchamp, T., Hoppe, H., Shapiro, L., and Stuetzle, W., "View-based Rendering: Visualizing Real Objects from Scanned Range and Color Data," *8th Eurographics Workshop on Rendering,* 1997.
14. Rappoport, A. and Spitz, S., "Interactive Boolean Operations for Conceptual Design of 3D Solids," *SIGGRAPH 1997,* pp. 269-278.
15. Roth, S. D., "Ray Casting for Modeling Solids," *Computer Graphics and Image Processing,* 18 (Feb 1982), pp. 109-144.
16. Rozenoer, M. and Shlyakhter, I., "Reconstruction of 3D Tree Models from Instrumented Photographs," M.Eng. Thesis, M.I.T., (1999).
17. Sullivan, S. and Ponce, J., "Automatic Model Construction, Pose Estimation, and Object Recognition from Photographs Using Triangular Splines," *ICCV '98,* pp. 510-516, 1998.
18. Seitz, S. and Dyer, C., "Photorealistic Scene Reconstruction by Voxel Coloring," *CVPR '97,* pp. 1067-1073, 1997.
19. Szeliski, R., "Rapid Octree Construction from Image Sequences," *CVGIP: Image Understanding,* 58, 1 (July 1993), pp. 23-32.

Editors' Note: see Appendix, p. 331 for colored figures of this paper

The Wavelet Stream:
Interactive Multi Resolution
Light Field Rendering

Ingmar Peter and Wolfgang Straßer

WSI/GRIS, University of Tübingen, Germany

`[peter|strasser]@gris.uni-tuebingen.de`

Abstract. One of the most general image based object representations is the Light Field. Unfortunately, a large amount of data is required to reconstruct high quality views from a Light Field. In this paper, we present the *wavelet stream* which employs non-standard four-dimensional wavelet decomposition for Light Field compression. It allows for progressive transmission, storage, and rendering of compressed Light Field data. Our results show that 0.8% of the original coefficients or 0.3 bits per pixel, respectively are sufficient to obtain visually pleasing new views. Additionally, the wavelet stream allows for an adaptive multi-resolution representation of the Light Field data. Furthermore, a silhouette-encoding scheme helps to reduce the number of coefficients required. Our data structure allows to store arbitrary vector-valued data like RGB- or YUV-data. The Light Field data stored in the wavelet stream can be decompressed in real time for interactive rendering. For this, the reconstruction algorithm uses supplementary caching schemes.

1 Introduction

Although the capabilities of computer graphics hardware have dramatically increased in the past years, the handling of scene complexity is still one of the most fundamental problems in computer graphics. One proposed solution for this is *image based rendering (IBR)*. Instead of constructing an exact geometry model, image based rendering uses pictorial information to describe an object. This has several advantages: The rendering time of the object is independent from its actual properties and depends only on the resolution of the data. Additionally, image based objects can be easily obtained from synthetic or real world objects, utilizing only pictures of them.

In the recent years a large number of image based approaches have been proposed. They differ from each other in generality, utilization of geometrical information, and memory requirements. One of the most general image based object representations is the *Light Field* respectively the *Lumigraph*, which were simultaneously introduced by Levoy and Hanrahan [7] and Gortler et al. [2], respectively. Although the Light Field and the Lumigraph differ in detail, in the following we will refer to both data structures uniformly as *Light Field*.

Assuming that a static object is located inside non-participating media, a four-dimensional, RGB-valued sample of the plenoptic function [1] is sufficient to describe the object's visual appearance. According to this a Light Field represents an arbitrary object by a two-dimensional array of images where all images share the same image plane. It is independent from the geometry as well the material properties of the object it represents. Furthermore a Light Field allows for reconstruction of almost arbitrary views of an object and can be used to represent synthetic as well as real world objects. Unfortunately, a large amount of data has to be stored in a Light Field to obtain new views of good quality. Therefore, various approaches were proposed for efficient compression of Light Field data.

In this paper, we present a new data structure for progressive transmission, storage, and rendering of compressed Light Field data. The *wavelet stream* employs non-standard four-dimensional wavelet decomposition to make use of the coherence in all of the four dimensions of the Light Field data. Only a small fraction of the original coefficients are sufficient to obtain visually pleasing reconstruction results. An additional *silhouette-encoding scheme* helps to reduce the number of coefficients required for encoding the Light Field. Furthermore the wavelet stream enables storing of arbitrary vector-valued data like RGB- or YUV-data. The data can be decompressed in real time and thus allows for use in interactive graphic applications. The reconstruction algorithm used during rendering is completed by supplementary caching schemes.

The remaining part of this paper is structured as follows: In the next section related work is briefly reviewed. The approach used for wavelet decomposition of Light Field data is introduced in Section 3. The wavelet stream data structure is described in detail in Section 4. Section 5 presents the results obtained. We conclude with some ideas for future research.

2 Related Work

Various approaches for Light Field data compression were proposed. Although the size of the data grows with $O(n^4)$ with respect to the resolution, the chance of obtaining high compression ratios without significant loss of quality is very good, since the sample values are highly correlated in every single dimension.

Levoy and Hanrahan [7] use vector quantization (VQ) and in a second step Lempel-Ziv encoding to compress the data. The drawback of this approach is, that the whole Light Field has to be uncompressed before it can be used, because Lempel-Ziv coding does not allow for random access. In [10] the use of Discrete Cosine Transform in combination with block coding techniques is suggested. Spherical harmonics were used by Wong et al. [18] to solve the compression problem.

Ihm et al. [4] proposed an alternative parameterization of the Light Field on the surface of a positional sphere enclosing the object. On its surface smaller directional spheres are placed which encode the directions of the samples. The directional spheres are then adaptively triangulated and the associated values are compressed using wavelet compression. Due to the fact, that only two-dimensional wavelet compression is used, the coherence in two dimensions of the data remains unused. In [5, 9] coding schemes similar to the techniques used in video compression are proposed. Prediction images are selected in two dimensions from the light field data and subdivided into blocks. The remaining data is then reconstructed applying simple operations on these blocks. Schirmacher et al. [13] uses an initial sparse Lumigraph which is interactively refined through the use of a specialized warping algorithm.

In [6, 11, 8] four-dimensional wavelet decomposition is used for compression of Light Field data. Up till now only wavelet-based compression provides a real multi resolution representation of Light Field data. Despite the use of elaborate caching schemes during data decompression, the approach of Lalonde et al. [6] reconstructs Light Fields with a resolution of 32^4 samples only in real time. In [8] high compression ratios using wavelet compression are reported. However, this approach by Magnor et al. too is not able to reconstruct the Light Field data fast enough for use in interactive applications.

These two examples [6, 8] show that two prerequisites have to be taken into account when developing a wavelet-based compression scheme for Light Field data:

- Since the generation of a specific view of an Light Field is equivalent to project- ing the four-dimensional Light Field onto a plane, particular values only of the compressed data have to be accessed and decompressed [3]. Thus random access of arbitrary values of the data has to be supported by the compression scheme.
- To enable the utilization of Light Fields in interactive applications, the data has to be uncompressed in real time.

The wavelet stream data structure as described in Section 4 archives high compres- sion ratios, while preserving a good image quality. Supplementary caching schemes allow for interactive rendering of a wavelet-compressed Light Field.

3 Wavelet Decomposition for Light Fields

Wavelets are a well-established tool for computer graphics and used in many appli- cations including image editing and compression, automatic level-of-detail control for editing, and rendering curves and surfaces or global illumination. For a comprehensive introduction into wavelets we refer to [17].

A *wavelet decomposition* transforms a signal into a collection of a *scaling coefficient* c_0^0 and *detail coefficients* d_i^j. Beside the capability of providing different level of details (LOD), while having the same storage requirements as the original signal, the wavelet decomposition of a signal allows for (lossy) compression of the signal by leaving out coefficients with low or zero value.

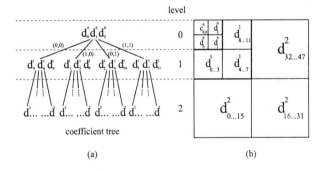

Fig. 1. Connection between structure of decomposed data (b) and corresponding tree of wavelet coefficients (a).

To meet the requirements for a fast and effective wavelet compression of Light Field data, the employed wavelet basis have to be chosen carefully. As stated in Section 2, particular values only of the Light Field data are accessed and reconstructed during ren- dering. To allow the use of wavelet compressed Light Fields in interactive applications the number of coefficients required for reconstructing a specific value should be small. Furthermore the mandatory arithmetic operations should be as simple as possible.

Both requirements are fulfilled by the Haar wavelet basis. The Haar wavelets are *tree wavelets*. This means that the wavelet functions ψ_i^j of each level j have disjunct support. Because of this, the coefficients can be organized in a *coefficient tree* as shown in Figure 1(a). In contrast to approaches from the field of image compression e.g. [12, 14] each node in the coefficient tree holds a set of coefficients which describe a contiguous subset of the Light Field data at a particular resolution. Thus for reconstruction of a particular Light Field value the coefficients stored in the nodes of the coefficient tree which relate to the respective Light Field value are sufficient only. Additionally, a value can be reconstructed from Haar wavelet coefficients using subtraction and addition only.

The *nonstandard construction* approach [17] is used to create the four-dimensional Haar wavelets and scaling functions from the one-dimensional ones. In practice, the wavelet decomposition of a data set using nonstandard Haar wavelets means to perform one step of pair wise averaging and differencing sample values in each row of the data. After doing so in each of the at most 4 dimensions of the data, the calculated coefficients are reordered separating the scaling and the detail coefficients. Then the process is repeated recursively on the scaling coefficients. At the end of the recursion, the data consists of detail coefficients d_i^j for each resolution level j and one scaling coefficient c_0^0 representing the mean value of the Light Field as shown in Figure 1 (b).

Given a threshold $\tau > 0$ the decomposed Light Field data is compressed discarding all coefficients $|d_i^j| < \tau$. The L^2 error introduced by this equals

$$\epsilon_{rms} = \sum_{|d_i| < \tau} d_i^2$$

for an orthonormal wavelet basis.

4   The Wavelet Stream Data Structure

Without loss of generality, we will use in the following for simplicity and comprehensibility two-dimensional notation and data which consists of single values in figures. All described algorithms and data structures are capable of handling four-dimensional vector-valued data sets.

4.1   Coefficient Storage

As stated in the preceding section, the Haar wavelets are tree wavelets. Therefore, the wavelet coefficients can be organized in a coefficient tree as shown in Figure 1 (a). In this tree the coefficients can be grouped disjunctly for each level j. To support progressive transmission, storage, and refinement of Light Field data, the entries of the coefficient tree are ordered in decreasing importance in the *coefficient stream*. This means to write the coefficients into the stream in the order as found in the tree when it is traversed in breadth-first order (Figure 2).

Usually the input data for wavelet compression of Light Fields consists of entries of 3×8 bit for RGB or 4×8 bit size for RGBα valued Light Fields [7]. During wavelet decomposition non-integer coefficients d_i^j are created[1]. To keep the coefficients byte-aligned for easy access only 8 bit are used to store a coefficient d_i^j. In this way some additional error is introduced due to the necessary quantization of the values.

A simple and powerful approach to reduce the quantization error significantly is to analyze all coefficients of each level j in the coefficient tree and find their absolute

---

[1]The decomposition is carried out using floating-point precision.

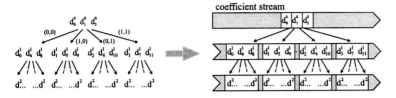

Fig. 2. Order of coefficients in the coefficient stream: The coefficients are ordered in decreasing importance by traversing the coefficient tree in breadth-first order.

minimum and maximum values min_j and max_j. These are stored in a table with floating point precision. The table is later added to the wavelet stream. For each level all coefficients are then scaled so that the maximum value range $[-128, 127]$, which can be represented using a signed byte, is exploited by the coefficients. The minimum and maximum values obtained earlier are used to correct the coefficient values during decompression. We found that this technique reduces the error introduced by quantization by a factor of approximately 3.

4.2 The Node Description Data Structure

The data stored in the wavelet stream can consist of several independent *channels* e.g. red, green, and blue or YUV. These can have different compression properties. Because of this the number of channels encoded in a node can decrease with increase of the level in the wavelet stream. We say a channel to be *active* if a node or one of its children stores information regarding to this channel. During wavelet stream traversal an array of flags is used to keep track of the channels currently active.

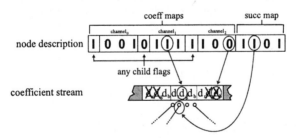

Fig. 3. Node description with the respective part of the coefficient stream. For three entries in the node description their meaning for the entries in the coefficient stream is depicted. Discarded coefficients are marked with a cross.

The coefficient tree as shown in Figure 2 can become incomplete due to the removal of coefficients during compression. Subtrees can be discarded completely if all of their coefficients are discarded. Therefore, additional meta information has to be added to the coefficient stream to encode the position of existing coefficients, active channels, and existing children of each node. As stated in Section 2, during rendering only parts of the Light Field data has to be accessed and decompressed. Unfortunately, approaches like [12, 14] do not support random access of arbitrary wavelet compressed values. Therefore, we had to develop our own approach to store the coefficients and the meta

132

information necessary for correct value reconstruction.

For each existing node N in the coefficient stream a *node description* is used, as depicted in Figure 3. For each active channel in N a single *coeff map* significance map [14] is used to encode the position of the existing coefficients.

A node N in the coefficient tree can be father of up to $2^{dim(N)}$ children, which themselves are the root nodes of up to $2^{dim(N)}$ subtrees, where $dim(N)$ is the dimension of N. If N has any children, an additional significance map, the *succ map*, is attached to the coeff maps of N's node description to encode the position of the existing children (Figure 3).

The *any child flag* (Figure 3) encodes which of N's channels are active in any of N's subtrees. If the any child flag of a channel C is set, the succ map significance map exists and in all subtrees of N information relating to C is stored. When the succ map exists, at least one of the any child flags of a node description has to be set. An unset any child flag indicates that no information which relates to the respective channel C is stored in any successors of the node. C is then said to be *deactivated* in all of the node's children.

4.3 Node Description Packing

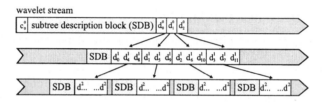

Fig. 4. Wavelet stream with subtree description blocks (SDB) in front of each group of nodes with a mutual father.

One can think of inserting a node description into the coefficient stream directly in front of the coefficients it describes. But this would waste a significant amount of memory since the wavelet coefficients are stored byte aligned for efficient access. The dimensionality of the nodes usually decreases towards the leafs of the coefficient tree. Therefore, the size of the significance maps stored in a node description can shrink to 3 bits or only 1 bit for a two-dimensional or one-dimensional node, respectively. If none of the any child flags in a node description are set which is the case for all leaf nodes, the size of a node description is $2^{dim} \times c$ bits in total, where dim denotes the dimension of the node and c the number of active channels. Since at least one byte has to be used for each node description, 4 respectively 6 bits are left unused ($c = 1$) for two- respectively one-dimensional nodes. For example, in the worst case in a wavelet stream encoding a Light Field with a resolution of $256 \times 256 \times 8 \times 8$ samples, 512 Kbytes or 8 percent of the total size of the wavelet stream would be wasted.

Instead, the node descriptions of all nodes which have the same father, are stored in a mutual *subtree description block (SDB)* in front off all coefficients they describe (Figure 4). They are packed behind each other in a single block of meta information leaving a gap of unused bits at most in the last byte of the SDB. This saves not only memory it also reduces the number of bytes necessary for efficient navigation inside the wavelet stream (Section 4.4). Behind the subtree description block all coefficients belonging to the nodes described in the SDB are stored.

After adding the subtree description blocks, the wavelet stream contains all information necessary to store, transmit, and reconstruct an incomplete coefficient tree. The scaling coefficient c_0^0 is stored at the beginning of the wavelet stream.

4.4 Value Reconstruction and Navigation

The reconstruction of a particular value from the wavelet stream is a recursive process starting at the root of the tree. It is equivalent to traverse the coefficient tree on a path which is determined by the coordinate of the requested value. During traversal the coefficients of all visited tree nodes contribute to the result.

For traversal of the tree at each node of the path a particular child has to be accessed. This means to go forward a number of bytes. Since single coefficients or complete subtrees might have been removed from the coefficient tree during compression, it is not possible to compute an offset from an arbitrary node to any of its children using a simple rule.

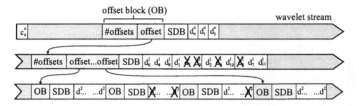

Fig. 5. Wavelet stream with offsets inserted in front of the subtree description blocks (SDB). The offsets point to the first child of each subtree described in a SDB. Discarded coefficients are marked with a cross.

To allow fast traversal along arbitrary paths, additional navigation information is added to the wavelet stream, when it is loaded into memory for rendering. For each node that has at least one child (Figure 5), an offset is inserted into the wavelet stream. This offset points to the first child of the respective node. Since all nodes with a mutual father are packed into a single block as described in Section 4.3, this means that the offset simply marks the beginning of the respective subtrees *offset block* (Figure 5). To save memory, the size of the offset representation itself is reduced to the actual needs. For each level the maximum offset and the number of bytes sufficient to encode its value are determined and stored in an additional table.

During value reconstruction a particular child of a node has to be found so that its coefficients can be used for reconstruction. Since the size of the offset block and the subtree description block (SDB) can not be known in advance, for each block an additional byte is inserted into the wavelet stream giving the number of offsets and the size of the SDB (Figure 5).

The coefficients of a particular node N can be found by parsing its SDB until the node description of N is reached. During value reconstruction the *coeff map* significance maps of N indicates which of the coefficients exist. The traversal of the wavelet stream continues if at least one *any child flag* and the corresponding bit in the *succ map* significance map is set.

4.5 Silhouette Encoding

Usually a solitary object is encoded in a Light Field. Unfortunately, due to the high frequency of the object's border, it causes the generation of a large number of detail coefficients during wavelet decomposition. If for each Light Field value its affiliation to the object is known, a number of wavelet coefficients, which is not larger than the number of pixels belonging to the object, must be sufficient to encode the object's visual appearance.

To utilize this fact the silhouette of the object is encoded. The silhouette information is stored in a *silhouette tree* as depicted in 6(a). It is fully embedded into the wavelet stream. Since the silhouette tree's subdivision scheme is identical to that used by the wavelet decomposition, we can exploit coherence in the wavelet stream and encode the silhouette tree using binary information only. In Figure 6(b) the extension of the node description data structure for silhouette encoding is depicted. Only for nodes whose Light Field values partly belong to the object and partly not, an additional *silhouette map* significance map is stored.

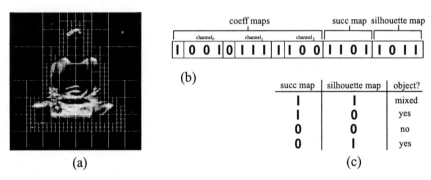

(a)

(b)

succ map	silhouette map	object?
I	I	mixed
I	0	yes
0	0	no
0	I	yes

(c)

Fig. 6. Extension of the wavelet stream for encoding of silhouette information. (a) subdivision scheme used by silhouette tree (b) extended node description data structure (c) interpretation of silhouette map and succ map entries to determine the affiliation of a particular pixel to the object.

During uncompressing the affiliation of pixels to the object is determined by interpreting the entries of the succ map and the silhouette map according to Table (c) in Figure 6.

When calculating the wavelet coefficients during decomposition using silhouette information a special approach has to be used. Since all four-dimensional Haar wavelets of a particular level have disjunct support, the entire process of reconstructing a value from the wavelet coefficients stored in a node can be described by a matrix M. The Light Field values $\vec{v} := [v_0, ..., v_{n-1}]$ can be reconstructed by multiplying wavelet coefficients $\vec{d} := [c, d_0, ..., d_{n-2}]$ with M

$$\vec{v} = M\vec{d}^T$$

with $n = 2^{dim}$ where dim is the dimension of the respective node. Since we know from the silhouette encoding that $n' \leq n$ coefficients belong to the object, $n' - 1$ wavelet coefficients are sufficient to encode the objects visual appearance. Therefore, wavelet coefficients $c', d'_0, ..., d'_{n'-2}$ have to be calculated accomplishing

$$\vec{v} = M\vec{d'}^T$$

where $\vec{d'} = [c', d'_0, ..., d'_{n'-2}, 0, ..., 0]$. Let M' be the matrix M whose last $2^{dim} - n'$ columns and the rows relating to the non-object values in $\vec{v}$ were removed. Then the new wavelet coefficients $\vec{d''}$ can be obtained with

$$\vec{d''} = M'^{-1}\vec{v'}^T$$

where $\vec{v'}$ is the vector formed of the n' Light Field values which belong to the object and $\vec{d''} = [c', d'_0, ..., d'_{n'-2}]$. Using the wavelet coefficients $\vec{d'}$ for reconstruction the Light Field values which do not belong to the object, are assigned arbitrary values. Since the usage of silhouette information allows excluding of those values this is not a problem.

For typical data sets about 10 percent of the entire data have to be spend to encode the silhouette information. On the other hand the utilization of silhouette information reduces the number of coefficients up to $20 - 30$ percent while obtaining the same compression error compared to data sets compressed without using silhouette information.

4.6 Rendering and Caching Scheme

The Light Field is rendered in a fashion similar to [16]. The retrieved Light Field values are plotted into a texture whose resolution is identical to the image plane resolution of the Light Field. This has the advantage that the coordinates for the requested Light Field values can be calculated by simple increments. The texture is then mapped onto a rectangle positioned on the image plane of the Light Field and displayed using the OpenGL.

To improve rendering speed, three different caching levels are used during Light Field rendering. The *texture cache* utilizes texture memory of the graphics hardware to store already calculated Light Field views. According to a last recently used policy a fixed number of Light Field views are stored together with the respective observer's positions. Before generating a new Light Field view the texture cache is searched for the Light Field view whose observer's position is next to that of the current observer. If the distance between current and cached observer does not exceed a user-specified limit, the Light Field view from the texture cache is used. In a background process the correct Light Field view is rendered and cross-faded onto the cached view.

If the texture cache misses, the *image based* cache is queried next. It stores for each pixel of the most recent generated Light Field view all pixel values along with their camera plane coordinates. As the image plane coordinate of each pixel is given implicitly a simple comparison of the camera coordinate is sufficient to decide whether a cached pixel value can be reused or not. This technique is only applicable if no interpolation is applied to the Light Field values as it is done during interactive Light Field rendering.

If a particular Light Field value has to be reconstructed the third-level *tree cache* is employed. Usually the coordinates of consecutive requested Light Field values differ only slightly. Therefore during traversal of the coefficient tree at every node the result calculated so far is stored together with some navigation information. When the next value is requested from the Light Field the current path is compared to the cached path and cached values are reused as long as possible.

5 Results

The wavelet stream data format as described in the previous section was implemented in C++ using a flexible framework of classes. It is possible to exchange, modify, and compare the various parts of our method. Furthermore, the class framework provides an environment for developing high-performance interactive applications.

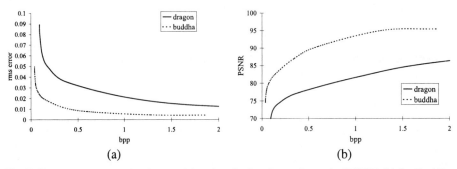

Fig. 7. Root-mean-square (rms) error (a) and peak-signal-to-noise-ratio (PSNR) (b) for Buddha and Dragon Light Field.

To measure the error introduced by compression and subsequent Light Field data reconstruction, we used the root-mean-square (rms) error ϵ_{rms} and the peak-signal-to-noise-ratio (PSNR) for relative measure. To test our approach we used the well known "Dragon" and "Buddha" Light Fields which are freely available from the Stanford Light Fields Archive [15]. Both Light Fields have a resolution of $256 \times 256 \times 32 \times 32$ 24 bit RGB values, which results in a total size of 192 Mbytes. For further improvement all Light Fields were transformed prior to compression from RGB to YUV and vice versa during Light Field rendering.

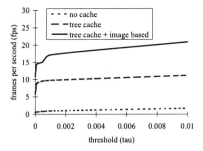

Fig. 8. Rendered frames-per-second (fps) for different caching schemes as function of compression threshold τ.

Figure 7(a) shows ϵ_{rms} for both Light Fields and different compression ratios. The results obtained from the Buddha Light Field are better because of its smooth surface. The curve showing the rms error does not intersect the x-axis, due to the fact that zero coefficients can be removed from the wavelet stream without loss of information and some error is introduced by the quantization of the non-zero coefficients. In this way an initial compression is always given when using wavelet compression. All compression ratios were measured with respect to the file size of the compressed Light Field data. The PSNR depicted in Figure 7(b) shows the good performance of wavelet-based Light Field compression as well. Again the error measurements obtained from the Buddha Light Field are better compared to the Dragon Light Field.

Figure 8 depicts the frames per second (fps) measured while rendering the Dragon light field with a resolution of 400×400 pixels on a Athlon 1200 MHz PC with

GeForce2 GTS graphics board. The frame rate increases when the threshold τ, used to discard the wavelet coefficients during compressing, is raised. This is due to the fact that the average length of the paths, on which the coefficient tree has to be traversed during reconstruction, is reduced as more of the coefficients are discarded. The acceleration caused by the texture cache (Section 4.6) is not depicted in chart 8, since on a cache hit the texture cache works as fast as the employed graphics hardware can load and display a texture. Since the speedup is archived only when a Light Field next to a previously used viewpoint in requested, this might lead to glitches in the archived frame rate.

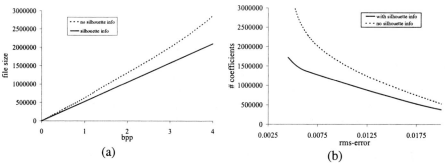

(a)

(b)

Fig. 9. Comparison of (a) the total file size and the (b) the number of coefficients of a wavelet-compressed Light Field using silhouette information and no silhouette information.

In Figure 9(a) the total file size is plotted as function of the bits per pixel (bpp) used for encoding the Light Field data when using silhouette information and not using silhouette information. Figure 9(b) shows the number of coefficients sufficient to encode a wavelet-compressed Light Field for obtaining a particular rms-error. The silhouette-encoding scheme as described in Section 4.5 works best for Light Fields with a small compression error. This is due to the fact that Light Fields compressed preserving a high image quality has to store a higher number of coefficients and thus the number of redundant coefficients due to object's border is larger.

Finally, Figure 10 (see Appendix) shows Light Fields which were compressed with different ratios. The image quality is only slightly decreased when the compression ratio increases.

6 Discussion and Future Directions

We presented a new approach for storage, transmission, and rendering of compressed Light Field data. The wavelet stream is especially well suited for progressive transmission of Light Fields over networks, because the most important parts of the data are transferred first. To decorrelate the data, 4D wavelet compression with nonstandard orthonormal Haar wavelets was used. For encoding the positions of the coefficients not discarded during compression, the new wavelet stream data format was introduced. Our approach is capable of storing arbitrary vector-valued data. The compression ratios obtained proved that only a small fraction of the original data is sufficient to obtain visually pleasing views from highly compressed Light Fields.

Since the wavelet stream can store arbitrary values, we will use this in future to investigate the visualization of Light Fields decorated with additional values, e.g. material properties or multi-dimensional pixel values. Future work will also include the implementation of the wavelet stream in Java to provide easy and fast access to Light

138

Field data over the Internet.

Acknowledgements

The authors wish to thank Stanislav Stoev and Michael Wand for valuable discussions and careful proof reading of the manuscript. We also wish to thank the anonymous reviewers who improved this work with their comments and suggestions. This work was supported by the Deutsche Forschungsgemeinschaft (DFG) and is part of the V^3D^2-project "Distributed Processing and Exchange of Digital Documents".

References

1. E. H. Adelson and J. R. Bergen. The plenoptic function and the elements of early vision. In *Computational Models of Visual Processing*, 1991.
2. Steven J. Gortler, Radek Grzeszczuk, Richard Szeliski, and Michael F. Cohen. The lumigraph. In *SIGGRAPH 96 Conference Proceedings*, pages 43–54. August 1996.
3. Xianfeng Gu, Steven J. Gortler, and Michael F. Cohen. Polyhedral geometry and the two-plane parameterization. In *Eurographics Rendering Workshop 1997*, pages 1–12, June 1997. Springer Wien.
4. Insung Ihm, Rae Kyoung Lee, and Sanghoon Park. Rendering of Spherical Light Fields. In *5th Pacific Conference on Computer Graphics and Applications*, pages 59–68, 1997.
5. Ming-Hoe Kiu, Xiao-Song Du, Robert J. Moorhead, David C. Banks, and Raghu Machiraju. Two Dimensional Sequence Compression Using MPEG. In *SPIE Vol. 3309, SPIE/IS&T Electronic Imaging '97*, San Jose, CA, January 1998.
6. Paul Lalonde and Alain Fournier. Interactive rendering of wavelet projected light fields. In *Graphics Interface*, pages 170–114, June 1999.
7. Marc Levoy and Pat Hanrahan. Light field rendering. In *SIGGRAPH 96 Conference Proceedings*, pages 31–42. August 1996.
8. M. Magnor, A. Endmann, and B. Girod. Progressive compression and rendering of light fields. In *VMV 2000*, pages 199–204, Saarbrücken, Germany.
9. Marcus Magnor and Bernd Girod. Data Compression in Image-Based Rendering. *IEEE Transactions on Circuits and Systems for Video Technology*, April 2000.
10. Gavin Miller, Steve Rubin, and Dulce Ponceleon. Lazy decompression of surface light fields for precomputer global illumination. In *Rendering Techniques '98*, pages 281–292. 1998 Springer Wien.
11. Ingmar Peter and Wolfgang Straßer. The wavelet stream: Progressive transmission of compressed light field data. In *IEEE Visualization 1999 Late Breaking Hot Topics*, pages 69–72. IEEE Computer Society, October 1999.
12. Amir Said and William A. Pearlman. A new fast and efficient image codec based on set partitioning in hierarchical trees. *IEEE Transactions on Circuits and Systems for Video Technology*, 6:243–250, June 1996.
13. Hartmut Schirmacher, Wolfgang Heidrich, and Hans-Peter Seidel. High-quality interactive lumigraph rendering through warping. In *Graphics Interface*, pages 87–94, May 2000.
14. J. M. Shapiro. Embedded image coding using zerotrees of wavelet coefficients. *IEEE Transactions on Acoustics, Speech and Signal Processing*, 41(12):3445–3462, 1993.
15. The Stanford Light Fields Archive. http://www-graphics.stanford.edu/software/lightpack/lifs.html.
16. Peter-Pike Sloan and Charles Hansen. Parallel Lumigraph Reconstruction. In *Proc. of PVG 99*, San Francisco, October 1999.
17. Eric J. Stollnitz, Tony D. DeRose, and David H. Salesin. *Wavelets for Computer Graphics: Theory and Applications*. Morgan Kaufmann, San Francisco, 1996.
18. T.-T. Wong, P.-A. Heng, S.-H. Or, and W.-Y. Ng. Illumination of image-based objects. *The Journal of Visualization and Computer Animation*, 9(3), 1998.

Editors' Note: see Appendix, p. 332 for colored figure of this paper

Differential Point Rendering

Aravind Kalaiah   Amitabh Varshney

University of Maryland[1]

Abstract.   We present a novel point rendering primitive, called *Differential Point* (DP), that captures the local differential geometry in the vicinity of a sampled point. This is a more general point representation that, for the cost of a few additional bytes, packs much more information per point than the traditional point-based models. This information is used to efficiently render the surface as a collection of local neighborhoods. The advantages to this representation are manyfold: (1) it delivers a significant reduction in the number of point primitives that represent a surface (2) it achieves robust hardware accelerated per-pixel shading – even with no connectivity information (3) it offers a novel point-based simplification technique that has a convenient and intuitive interface for the user to efficiently resolve the speed versus quality tradeoff. The number of primitives being equal, DPs produce a much better quality of rendering than a pure splat-based approach. Visual appearances being similar, DPs are about two times faster and require about 75% less disk space in comparison to splatting primitives.

1   Introduction

Point-based rendering schemes [5, 12, 13, 17, 19, 21] have evolved as a viable alternative to triangle-based representations. They offer many benefits over triangle-based models: (1) efficiency in modeling and rendering complex environments, (2) hierarchical organization to efficiently control frame-rates and visual quality, and (3) zero-connectivity for efficient streaming for remote rendering [20].

Current point primitives store only limited information about their immediate locality, such as normal, bounding ball [19], and tangent plane disk [17]. These primitives are then rasterized with flat shading and hence such representations require very high sampling to obtain a good rendering quality. In other words, the rendering algorithm dictates the sampling frequency of the modeling stage. This is clearly undesirable as it may prescribe very high sampling even in areas of low spatial frequency, causing two significant drawbacks: (1) slower rendering speed due to higher rendering computation and related CPU-memory bus activity, and (2) large disk and memory utilization.

In this work we propose an approach of storing local differential geometric information with every point. This information gives a good approximation of the surface distribution in the vicinity of each sampled point which is then used for rendering the point and its approximated vicinity. The extent of the approximated vicinity is determined by the curvature characteristics of the surface: points in a flat or a low curvature region approximate larger vicinities. Our approach has many benefits to offer:

---
[1]Graphics and Visual Informatics Laboratory, Department of Computer Science and UMIACS, University of Maryland, College Park, MD - 20742, USA, {ark,varshney}@cs.umd.edu

1. **Rendering**: Our approach achieves high rendering quality with per-pixel shading. We reduce the number of rendering primitives and push more computation into each primitive. This reduces the CPU-memory bus bandwidth and the overall amount of computation resulting in a significant speed-up. As the processor-memory speed gap increases we expect this method to get even more attractive.

2. **Storage**: The reduction in the number of primitives more than compensates for the extra bytes of information stored with each point primitive. This leads to an overall reduction in the storage requirements. This reduction also benefits faster streaming of information over the network.

3. **Generality**: The information stored with our point primitives is sufficient to derive (directly or indirectly) the requisite information for prior point primitives. Our work is primarily a focus on the efficiency of per-point rendering computation. It can potentially be used in conjunction with larger point-based organization structures - hierarchical [1, 17, 19] or otherwise [13, 21].

In the following sections, we first mention some related works and then outline the terminology from the differential geometry literature that will be used to describe our approach. This is followed by a discussion of differential points. We then describe our rendering algorithm and compare it with some splatting schemes. We conclude the paper with a discussion of this approach and its potential extensions.

2 Related Work

Classical differential geometry gives us a mathematical model for understanding the surface variation at a point. Surface curvatures can be accurately computed for parametric surfaces and can also be estimated from discrete sampled representations. Taubin [22] estimates curvature at a mesh vertex by using the eigenvalues of an approximation matrix constructed using the incident edges. Desbrun et al. [3] define discrete operators (normal, curvature, etc.) of differential geometry using Voronoi cells and finite-element/finite-volume methods.

Various hierarchical organization schemes have been used that develop lower frequency versions of the original set of point samples [1, 17, 19]. We use a simplification process that prunes an initial set of points to greatly reduce the redundancy in surface representation. Turk [23] uses a point placement approach with the point density being controlled by the local curvature properties of the surface. Witkin and Heckbert [24] use physical properties of a particle system to place points on an implicit surface.

Image-assisted organization of points [5, 13, 21] are efficient at three-dimensional transformations as they use the implicitness of relationship among pixels to achieve fast incremental computations. They are also efficient at representing complex real-world environments. The multiresolution organizations [1, 17, 19] use their hierarchical structure to achieve block culling, to control depth traversals to respect the image-quality or frame-rate constraints, and for efficient streaming of large datasets across the network [20].

Darsa et al. [2], Mark et al. [14] and Pulli et al. [18] use a triangle mesh overlaid on the image sampling plane for rendering. It can be followed by a screen space compositing process. However, such systems can be expensive in computation and storage if high resolutions are desired. Levoy and Whitted [12] introduced points as a rendering primitive. It has been used by Shade et al. [21] and Grossman and Dally [5] for synthetic environments. However, raw point primitives suffer from aliasing problems and holes. Lischinski and Rappoport [13] raytrace a point dataset. Oliveira et al. [15] use image space transformations to render point samples. Rusinkiewicz and Levoy [19] use splatting of polygonal primitives for rendering. Pfister et al. [17] follow up the splatting with a screen-space filtering process to handle holes and aliasing problems. Zwicker et al. [25] derive a screen-space formulation of the EWA filter to render high detail textured point samples with a support for transparency.

3 Differential Geometry for Surface Representation

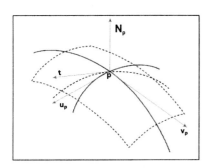

Fig. 1. Neighborhood of a Differential Point

Classical differential geometry is a study of the local properties of curves and surfaces [4]. It uses differential calculus of first and higher orders for this study. In this work we use the regular surface model which captures surface attributes such as continuity, smoothness, and degree of local surface variation. A *regular surface* is a differentiable surface which is non self-intersecting and which has a unique tangent plane at each point on the surface. Every point **p** on the regular surface has the following properties: the normal N_p, the *direction of maximum curvature* $\hat{u}_p$, the *direction of minimum curvature* $\hat{v}_p$, the *maximum normal curvature* λ_{u_p}, and the *minimum normal curvature* λ_{v_p}. They have the following relation amongst them: (1) $|\lambda_{u_p}| \geq |\lambda_{v_p}|$, (2) $\langle \hat{u}_p, \hat{v}_p \rangle = 0$, and (3) $\hat{u}_p \times \hat{v}_p = N_p$ where $\langle \cdot, \cdot \rangle$ denotes the dot product and $\times$ is the cross product operator. The differential of the normal at **p** is denoted by dN_p. Given any tangent $\hat{t}$ $(= t_u\hat{u}_p + t_v\hat{v}_p)$, $dN_p(\hat{t})$ is the first-order normal variation around **p** and is given by [4]:

$$dN_p(\hat{t}) = -(\lambda_{u_p} t_u \hat{u}_p + \lambda_{v_p} t_v \hat{v}_p) \tag{1}$$

Similarly the normal curvature along $\hat{t}$, $\lambda_p(\hat{t})$, is given by [4]:

$$\lambda_p(\hat{t}) = \lambda_{u_p} t_u^2 + \lambda_{v_p} t_v^2 \tag{2}$$

The normal variation and the normal curvature terms give us second order information about the behaviour of the regular surface around the point **p**. These properties are illustrated in Figure 1.

A salient feature of the regular surface model is that it gives complete independence to a point to describe its own neighborhood without any reliance, explicit or implicit, on the immediate sampled neighborhood or on any other global property [6, 7, 8]. Even though a surface has to be differentiable to have a regular surface representation, we need the surface to be only second-order continuous to extract properties that will be used for rendering. Discontinuities of third or higher order, in most instances, are not easily discernible and thus we do not make any effort towards reproducing them visually here. However discontinuities of the zeroth, first, and second order are visually noticeable and even important. We sample at the second-order continuous neighborhood of these points. Discontinuities are maintained implicitly by the intersection of the region of influence of the adjacent sampled points.

4 Sampling and Processing

Our fundamental rendering primitive is a point with differential geometry information. These are derived by sampling points on the surface and extracting differential geometry information per sampled point. This is followed by a simplification process that greatly reduces the redundancy in surface representation. This is a pre-process and the output is saved in a render-ready format that will be an input to our rendering algorithm outlined in Section 5.

4.1 Differential Points

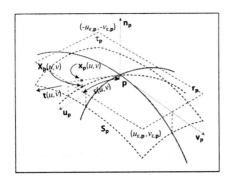

Fig. 2. Tangent plane parameterization of a Differential Point

We call our rendering primitive a *differential point* (DP). A DP, **p**, is constructed from a sample point and has the following parameters: $\mathbf{x_p}$ (the position of the point), $\lambda_{\mathbf{u_p}}$ and $\lambda_{\mathbf{v_p}}$ (the principal curvatures), and $\hat{\mathbf{u}}_{\mathbf{p}}$ and $\hat{\mathbf{v}}_{\mathbf{p}}$ (the principal directions). They derive the unit normal, $\hat{\mathbf{n}}_{\mathbf{p}}$, and the tangent plane, $\tau_{\mathbf{p}}$, of **p**. We extrapolate this information to define a surface, $\mathbf{S_p}$, that will be used to approximate the neighborhood of $\mathbf{x_p}$. The surface $\mathbf{S_p}$ is defined as follows: given any tangent $\hat{\mathbf{t}}$, the intersection of $\mathbf{S_p}$ with the normal plane of **p** that is co-planar with $\hat{\mathbf{t}}$ is a semi-circle with a radius of $\frac{1}{|\lambda_{\mathbf{p}}(\hat{\mathbf{t}})|}$ with the center of the circle being located at $\mathbf{x_p} + \frac{\hat{\mathbf{n}}_{\mathbf{p}}}{\lambda_{\mathbf{p}}(\hat{\mathbf{t}})}$ and oriented such that it is cut in half by $\mathbf{x_p}$ (if $\lambda_{\mathbf{p}}(\hat{\mathbf{t}})$ is 0, then the intersection is a line along $\hat{\mathbf{t}}$). These terms are illustrated in Figure 2.

To aid our rendering algorithms we define a coordinate system on $\tau_{\mathbf{p}}$ and $\mathbf{S_p}$. The tangent plane $\tau_{\mathbf{p}}$ is parameterized by (u, v) coordinates in the vector space of $(\hat{\mathbf{u}}_{\mathbf{p}}, \hat{\mathbf{v}}_{\mathbf{p}})$. A point on $\tau_{\mathbf{p}}$ is denoted by $\mathbf{x_p}(u, v)$ and $\hat{\mathbf{t}}(u, v)$ denotes the tangent at **p** in the direction of $\mathbf{x_p}(u, v)$. We parameterize $\mathbf{S_p}$ with the same (u, v) coordinates as $\tau_{\mathbf{p}}$, with $\mathbf{X_p}(u, v)$ denoting a point on $\mathbf{S_p}$. The points $\mathbf{X_p}(u, v)$ and $\mathbf{x_p}(u, v)$ are related by a mapping, $\mathcal{P}_{\mathbf{p}}$, with $\mathbf{x_p}(u, v)$ being the orthographic projection of $\mathbf{X_p}(u, v)$ on $\tau_{\mathbf{p}}$ along $\hat{\mathbf{n}}_{\mathbf{p}}$. The arc-length between $\mathbf{X_p}(0, 0)$ and $\mathbf{X_p}(u, v)$ is denoted by $s(u, v)$ and is measured along the semi-circle of $\mathbf{S_p}$ in the direction $\hat{\mathbf{t}}(u, v)$. The (un-normalized) normal at $\mathbf{X_p}(u, v)$ is denoted by $\mathbf{N_p}(u, v)$. Note that $\mathbf{x_p} = \mathbf{X_p}(0, 0) = \mathbf{x_p}(0, 0)$ and $\hat{\mathbf{n}}_{\mathbf{p}} = \mathbf{N_p}(0, 0)$. We use lower case characters or symbols for terms related to $\tau_{\mathbf{p}}$ and we use upper case characters or symbols for terms related to $\mathbf{S_p}$. A notable exception to this rule is $s(u, v)$.

Consider the semi-circle of $\mathbf{S_p}$ in the direction $\hat{\mathbf{t}}(u, v)$. As one moves out of $\mathbf{x_p}$ along this curve, the normal change per unit arc-length of the curve is given by the normal gradient $\mathbf{dN_p}(\hat{\mathbf{t}}(u, v))$. So, for an arc-length of $s(u, v)$, the normal at $\mathbf{X_p}(u, v)$ can be obtained by using a Taylor's expansion on each dimension to get:

$$\mathbf{N_p}(u, v) \approx \mathbf{N_p}(0, 0) + s(u, v)\, \mathbf{dN_p}(\hat{\mathbf{t}}(u, v)) \tag{3}$$

$\mathbf{S_p}$ and $\mathbf{N_p}(u, v)$ give an approximation of the spatial and the normal distribution around $\mathbf{x_p}$. (Note that $\mathbf{N_p}(u, v)$ is not the approximation of the normal of $\mathbf{S_p}$.) We use two criteria to determine the extent of the approximation:

1. *Maximum Principal Error* (ϵ): This specifies a curvature-scaled maximum ortho-graphic deviation of $\mathbf{S_p}$ along the principal directions. We lay down this constraint as: $|\lambda_{\mathbf{u_p}}(\mathbf{X_p}(u,0) - \mathbf{x_p}(u,0))| \leq \epsilon \leq 1$ and $|\lambda_{\mathbf{v_p}}(\mathbf{X_p}(0,v) - \mathbf{x_p}(0,v))| \leq \epsilon \leq 1$. Note that since $\mathbf{S_p}$ is defined by semi-circles, we have that $\|\mathbf{X_p}(u,0) - \mathbf{x_p}(u,0)\| \leq \frac{1}{|\lambda_{\mathbf{u_p}}|}$. In other words, the extrapolation is bounded by the constraints $|u| \leq u_{\epsilon,\mathbf{p}} = \frac{\sqrt{2\epsilon - \epsilon^2}}{|\lambda_{\mathbf{u_p}}|}$ and $|v| \leq v_{\epsilon,\mathbf{p}} = \frac{\sqrt{2\epsilon - \epsilon^2}}{|\lambda_{\mathbf{v_p}}|}$ as shown in Figure 2. This defines a rectangle $\mathbf{r_p}$ on $\tau_\mathbf{p}$ and bounds $\mathbf{S_p}$ accordingly since it uses the same parameterization. The ϵ constraint ensures that points of high curvature are extrapolated to a smaller area and that the "flatter" points are extrapolated to a larger area.

2. *Maximum Principal Width* (δ): If $\lambda_{\mathbf{u_p}}$ is closer to 0, then $u_{\epsilon,\mathbf{p}}$ can be very large. To deal with such cases we impose a maximum-width constraint δ. So $u_{\epsilon,\mathbf{p}}$ is computed as $\min(\delta, \frac{\sqrt{2\epsilon - \epsilon^2}}{|\lambda_{\mathbf{u_p}}|})$. Similarly, $v_{\epsilon,\mathbf{p}}$ is $\min(\delta, \frac{\sqrt{2\epsilon - \epsilon^2}}{|\lambda_{\mathbf{v_p}}|})$.

We call the surface $\mathbf{S_p}$ bounded by the ϵ and δ constraints, the normal distribution $\mathbf{N_p}(u,v)$ bounded by the ϵ and δ constraints together with the rectangle $\mathbf{r_p}$ as a Differential Point because all of these are constructed from just the second-order information at a sampled point.

4.2 Sampling and Simplification

Given a 3D model, it is first sampled by points. Currently, we sample uniformly in the parametric domain of a NURBS surface and standard techniques outlined in the differential geometry literature [4] are used to extract the differential geometry information at each sampled point. This work can be extended to triangle meshes using ideas of Taubin [22] and Desbrun et al. [3]. Alternately, a NURBS surface can be fit into the triangle mesh [11] and the points can be sampled using this representation.

Initially the surface is super-sampled so that the rectangle of each differential point overlaps sufficiently with its neighbors without leaving holes in the surface coverage. This is followed by the simplification process which prunes the redundant points that are adequately represented by its neighbors. Simplification has two main stages: (1) ordering and (2) pruning. In the first stage, we compute the *redundancy factor* of each DP: the closer it resembles its neighbors in curvature values and directions, the higher the redundancy factor. All the DPs are then ordered in a priority heap with their redundancy factor as the key. In the second stage, we iteratively pop the top of the heap (the most redundant DP of the lot) and check if the rectangles $\mathbf{r_p}$ of its neighbors cover up the surface if it is pruned: if so we prune it and re-order the heap, otherwise we mark the DP to be saved. Figure 3 illustrates the effectiveness of the simplification process. Due to page limit constraints we are unable to discuss the details of our simplification algorithm here. Full details can be found in [9].

5 Rendering

Since graphics hardware do not support $\mathbf{S_p}$ as a rendering primitive, $\mathbf{r_p}$ is used as an approximation to $\mathbf{S_p}$ when rasterizing $\mathbf{p}$. However, the shading artifacts are more readily discernible to the human eye and the screen-space normal distribution around $\mathbf{p}$ has to mimic the normal variation around $\mathbf{p}$ on the original surface. This is done by projecting the normal distribution $\mathbf{N_p}(u,v)$ onto $\mathbf{r_p}$ and rasterizing $\mathbf{r_p}$ with a normal-map of this distribution.

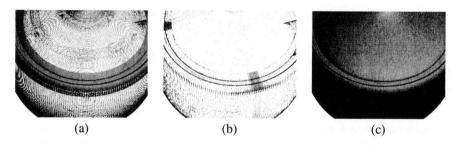

(a)   (b)   (c)

Fig. 3. Effectiveness of Simplification: (a) Rectangles of the initial set of DPs representing the teapot. (b) Rectangles of the differential points that are retained by the simplification algorithm. Simplification is currently done within a patch and not between patches. The strips of rectangles represent the differential points on the patch boundaries. (c) A rendering of the simplified model.

5.1 Normal Distribution

Consider the projection of $\mathbf{N_p}(u, v)$ onto $\tau_\mathbf{p}$ using the projection $\mathcal{P}_\mathbf{p}$ discussed in Section 4.1. The area of projection on the tangent plane is limited by the nature of the surface $\mathbf{S_p}$ and includes all (u, v) such that $\sqrt{u^2 + v^2} \leq \frac{1}{|\lambda_\mathbf{p}(\hat{\mathbf{t}}(u,v))|}$. The (un-normalized) normal distribution, $\mathbf{n_p}(u, v)$, on $\tau_\mathbf{p}$ can then be expressed using equation (3) as:

$$\mathbf{n_p}(u, v) \quad \approx \quad \mathbf{N_p}(0, 0) + s(u, v)\, \mathbf{dN_p}(\hat{\mathbf{t}}(u, v)) \tag{4}$$

where tangent $\hat{\mathbf{t}}(u, v) = \frac{(u\,\hat{\mathbf{u}}_\mathbf{p} + v\,\hat{\mathbf{v}}_\mathbf{p})}{\sqrt{u^2 + v^2}}$ and arc-length $s(u, v) = \frac{\sin^{-1}(\lambda_\mathbf{p}(\hat{\mathbf{t}}(u,v))\sqrt{u^2+v^2})}{\lambda_\mathbf{p}(\hat{\mathbf{t}}(u,v))}$ (the range of the arcsin function being $[-\frac{\pi}{2}, \frac{\pi}{2}]$). Using these terms, and equations (1) and (2) as well, equation (4) can be re-written as:

$$\mathbf{n_p}(u, v) \approx \mathbf{N_p}(0, 0) - \left[\frac{(\lambda_{\mathbf{u_p}}\, u\, \hat{\mathbf{u}}_\mathbf{p} + \lambda_{\mathbf{v_p}}\, v\, \hat{\mathbf{v}}_\mathbf{p})}{(\lambda_{\mathbf{u_p}} u^2 + \lambda_{\mathbf{v_p}} v^2)/\sqrt{u^2 + v^2}} \sin^{-1}\left(\frac{\lambda_{\mathbf{u_p}} u^2 + \lambda_{\mathbf{v_p}} v^2}{\sqrt{u^2 + v^2}} \right) \right]$$

It can be expressed in the local coordinate system $(\hat{\mathbf{e}}_x, \hat{\mathbf{e}}_y, \hat{\mathbf{e}}_z)$ of $(\hat{\mathbf{u}}_\mathbf{p}, \hat{\mathbf{v}}_\mathbf{p}, \hat{\mathbf{n}}_\mathbf{p})$ as:

$$\mathbf{n_p}(u, v) \approx \hat{\mathbf{e}}_z - \left[\frac{(\lambda_{\mathbf{u_p}}\, u\, \hat{\mathbf{e}}_x + \lambda_{\mathbf{v_p}}\, v\, \hat{\mathbf{e}}_y)}{(\lambda_{\mathbf{u_p}} u^2 + \lambda_{\mathbf{v_p}} v^2)/\sqrt{u^2 + v^2}} \sin^{-1}\left(\frac{\lambda_{\mathbf{u_p}} u^2 + \lambda_{\mathbf{v_p}} v^2}{\sqrt{u^2 + v^2}} \right) \right] \tag{5}$$

where $\hat{\mathbf{e}}_x = (1, 0, 0)$, $\hat{\mathbf{e}}_y = (0, 1, 0)$, and $\hat{\mathbf{e}}_z = (0, 0, 1)$ are the canonical basis in $\mathbb{R}^3$. Note that $\mathbf{n_p}(u, v)$ is independent of $\hat{\mathbf{u}}_\mathbf{p}$, $\hat{\mathbf{v}}_\mathbf{p}$, and $\mathbf{N_p}(0, 0)$ in the local coordinate frame. Hence DP is shaded in its local coordinate frame so that the normal distribution is computed for each combination of $\lambda_\mathbf{u}$ and $\lambda_\mathbf{v}$ and reused for all DPs with that combination.

The only hardware support to specify such a normal distribution is normal mapping. We pre-computed normal-maps in the local coordinate frame for various quantized values of $\lambda_\mathbf{u}$ and $\lambda_\mathbf{v}$. However, since $\lambda_\mathbf{u}$ and $\lambda_\mathbf{v}$ are unbounded quantities it is impossible to compute all possible normal-maps. To get around this problem we introduce a new term $\rho_\mathbf{p} = \frac{\lambda_{\mathbf{v_p}}}{\lambda_{\mathbf{u_p}}}$, and note that $-1 \leq \rho_\mathbf{p} \leq 1$ because $|\lambda_{\mathbf{u_p}}| \geq |\lambda_{\mathbf{v_p}}|$. Equation (5) can be rewritten using $\rho_\mathbf{p}$ as follows:

$$\mathbf{n_p}(u, v) \quad \approx \quad \hat{\mathbf{e}}_z - (u\,\hat{\mathbf{e}}_x + \rho_\mathbf{p}\, v\, \hat{\mathbf{e}}_y) \frac{\sin^{-1}(\lambda_{\mathbf{u_p}} \psi_\mathbf{p}(u, v))}{\psi_\mathbf{p}(u, v)} \tag{6}$$

where $\psi_{\mathbf{p}}(u,v) = (u^2 + \rho_{\mathbf{p}}v^2)/\sqrt{u^2 + v^2}$. Now consider a normal distribution for a differential point $\mathbf{m}$ whose $\lambda_{\mathbf{u_m}} = 1$: the only external parameter to $\mathbf{n_m}(u,v)$ is $\rho_{\mathbf{m}}$. Since $\rho_{\mathbf{m}}$ is bounded, we pre-compute a set, $\mathfrak{M}$, of normal distributions for discrete values of ρ and store them as normal-maps. Later, at render-time, $\mathbf{r_m}$ is normal-mapped by the normal map whose ρ value is closest to $\rho_{\mathbf{m}}$. To normal-map a general differential point $\mathbf{p}$ using the same set of normal-maps, $\mathfrak{M}$, we use the following Lemma.

Lemma 1 *When expressed in their respective local coordinate frames,* $\mathbf{n_p}(u,v) \approx \mathbf{n_m}(\lambda_{\mathbf{u_p}}u, \lambda_{\mathbf{u_p}}v)$, *where* $\mathbf{m}$ *is any DP with* $\lambda_{\mathbf{u_m}} = 1$ *and* $\rho_{\mathbf{m}} = \rho_{\mathbf{p}}$.

Proof: First, we make an observation that $\lambda_{\mathbf{u_p}}\psi_{\mathbf{p}}(u,v) = \psi_{\mathbf{p}}(\lambda_{\mathbf{u_p}}u, \lambda_{\mathbf{u_p}}v)$. Using this observation, the tangent plane normal distribution at $\mathbf{p}$ (equation (6)) becomes:

$$\begin{aligned}
\mathbf{n_p}(u,v) &\approx \hat{\mathbf{e}}_z - \left[((\lambda_{\mathbf{u_p}}u)\hat{\mathbf{e}}_x + \rho_{\mathbf{p}}(\lambda_{\mathbf{u_p}}v)\hat{\mathbf{e}}_y)\frac{\sin^{-1}(\psi_{\mathbf{p}}(\lambda_{\mathbf{u_p}}u, \lambda_{\mathbf{u_p}}v))}{\psi_{\mathbf{p}}(\lambda_{\mathbf{u_p}}u, \lambda_{\mathbf{u_p}}v)}\right] \\
&= \hat{\mathbf{e}}_z - \left[((\lambda_{\mathbf{u_p}}u)\hat{\mathbf{e}}_x + \rho_{\mathbf{m}}(\lambda_{\mathbf{u_p}}v)\hat{\mathbf{e}}_y)\frac{\sin^{-1}(\psi_{\mathbf{m}}(\lambda_{\mathbf{u_p}}u, \lambda_{\mathbf{u_p}}v))}{\psi_{\mathbf{m}}(\lambda_{\mathbf{u_p}}u, \lambda_{\mathbf{u_p}}v)}\right] \\
&\approx \mathbf{n_m}(\lambda_{\mathbf{u_p}}u, \lambda_{\mathbf{u_p}}v) \qquad\qquad\square
\end{aligned}$$

Using Lemma 1, a general $\mathbf{r_p}$ is normal-mapped with an appropriate normal map $\mathbf{n_m}(\cdot,\cdot)$ with a scaling factor of $\lambda_{\mathbf{u_p}}$.

5.2 Shading

For specular shading, apart from the local normal distribution, we also need a local half vector distribution. For this we use the cube vector mapping [10] functionality offered in the nVIDIA GeForce GPUs which allows one to specify un-normalized vectors at each vertex of a polygon and obtain linearly interpolated and normalized versions of these on a per-pixel basis. Using this feature we obtain normalized half-vectors on a per-pixel basis by specifying un-normalized half vectors at the vertices of $\mathbf{r_p}$. Per-pixel shading is achieved by using the per-pixel normal (by normal map) and half or light vector (by cube vector map) for illumination computations in the register combiners.

Let $\hat{\mathbf{h}}_{\mathbf{p}}$ denote the (normalized) half vector at $\mathbf{x_p}$ and let $\mathbf{H_p}(u,v)$ denote the (un-normalized) half vector at $\mathbf{X_p}(u,v)$ where $\mathbf{H_p}(0,0) = \hat{\mathbf{h}}_{\mathbf{p}}$. Let $\mathbf{h_p}(u,v)$ be the (un-normalized) half vector at $\mathbf{x_p}(u,v)$ obtained by applying the projection $\mathcal{P}_{\mathbf{p}}$ on $\mathbf{H_p}(u,v)$. Similarly, let $\hat{\mathbf{l}}_{\mathbf{p}}$ denote the (normalized) light vector at $\mathbf{x_p}$ and let $\mathbf{l_p}(u,v)$ and $\mathbf{L_p}(u,v)$ denote the (un-normalized) light vector distribution on $\tau_{\mathbf{p}}$ and $S_{\mathbf{p}}$ respectively with $\mathbf{L_p}(0,0) = \hat{\mathbf{l}}_{\mathbf{p}}$. Also, let $\hat{\mathbf{w}}_{\mathbf{p}}$ denote the (normalized) view vector at $\mathbf{x_p}$ and let $\mathbf{w_p}(u,v)$ and $\mathbf{W_p}(u,v)$ denote the (un-normalized) view vector distribution on $\tau_{\mathbf{p}}$ and $S_{\mathbf{p}}$ respectively with $\mathbf{W_p}(0,0) = \hat{\mathbf{w}}_{\mathbf{p}}$. Similar to equation (4), $\mathbf{h_p}(u,v)$ can be written as:

$$\begin{aligned}
\mathbf{h_p}(u,v) &\approx \mathbf{H_p}(0,0) + s(u,v)\,\mathbf{dH_p}(\hat{\mathbf{t}}(u,v)) \\
&\approx \mathbf{H_p}(0,0) + \sqrt{u^2 + v^2}\,\mathbf{dH_p}(\mathbf{t}(u,v)) \\
&= \mathbf{H_p}(0,0) + u\frac{\partial}{\partial u}\mathbf{H_p}(u,v)\Big|_{\substack{u=0\\v=0}} + v\frac{\partial}{\partial v}\mathbf{H_p}(u,v)\Big|_{\substack{u=0\\v=0}} \quad (7)
\end{aligned}$$

Let $\mathbf{a}$ be the position of the light and $\mathbf{b}$ be the position of the eye. The partial

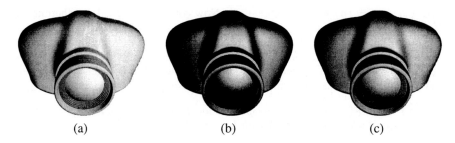

Fig. 4. Illumination and per-pixel Shading: (a) Diffuse Illumination. (b) Specular Illumination. (c) Diffuse and Specular Illumination

differential of equation (7) can then be re-written as follows:

$$
\frac{\partial}{\partial u}\mathbf{H_p}(u,v)\bigg|_{\substack{u=0\\v=0}} = \frac{\partial}{\partial u}\left(\frac{\mathbf{L_p}(u,v)}{\|\mathbf{L_p}(u,v)\|} + \frac{\mathbf{W_p}(u,v)}{\|\mathbf{W_p}(u,v)\|}\right)\bigg|_{\substack{u=0\\v=0}}
$$

$$
= \frac{((\hat{\mathbf{l}}_\mathbf{p}\cdot\hat{\mathbf{u}}_\mathbf{p})\hat{\mathbf{l}}_\mathbf{p} - \hat{\mathbf{u}}_\mathbf{p})}{\|\mathbf{a}-\mathbf{x_p}\|} + \frac{((\hat{\mathbf{w}}_\mathbf{p}\cdot\hat{\mathbf{u}}_\mathbf{p})\hat{\mathbf{w}}_\mathbf{p} - \hat{\mathbf{u}}_\mathbf{p})}{\|\mathbf{b}-\mathbf{x_p}\|}
$$

When expressed in the local coordinate frame, we get:

$$
\frac{\partial}{\partial u}\mathbf{H_p}(u,v)\bigg|_{\substack{u=0\\v=0}} = \frac{((\hat{\mathbf{l}}_\mathbf{p}\cdot\hat{\mathbf{e}}_x)\hat{\mathbf{l}}_\mathbf{p} - \hat{\mathbf{e}}_x)}{\|\mathbf{a}-\mathbf{x_p}\|} + \frac{((\hat{\mathbf{w}}_\mathbf{p}\cdot\hat{\mathbf{e}}_x)\hat{\mathbf{w}}_\mathbf{p} - \hat{\mathbf{e}}_x)}{\|\mathbf{b}-\mathbf{x_p}\|} \tag{8}
$$

the other partial differential of equation (7) can be computed similarly. The subtraction and the dot products in equation (8) are simple and fast operations. The square root and the division operations are combined together by the fast inverse square root approximation [16] which in practice causes no compromise in the visual quality. The light vector distribution on $\tau_\mathbf{p}$ can be derived similarly and is given by $\mathbf{l_p}(u,v) \approx \hat{\mathbf{l}}_\mathbf{p} - u\hat{\mathbf{e}}_x - v\hat{\mathbf{e}}_y$.

The tangent plane normal, half vector, and the light vector distribution around $\mathbf{p}$ are used for shading $\mathbf{p}$ which essentially involves two kinds of computation: (1) mapping of the relevant vectors and (2) per-pixel computation. The overall rendering algorithm is given in Figure 5. The rectangle $\mathbf{r_p}$ is mapped by the normal map and the half vector (or light vector) map. Normal mapping involves choosing the best approximation to the normal distribution from the set of pre-computed normal maps $\mathcal{M}$. Half-vector mapping involves computing un-normalized half vectors at the vertices of $\mathbf{r_p}$ using equation (7) and using them as the texture coordinates of the cube vector map that is mapped onto $\mathbf{r_p}$. Per-pixel shading is done in the hardware register combiners using the (per-pixel) normal and half vectors [10]. If both diffuse and specular shading are desired then shading is done in two passes with the accumulation buffer being used to buffer the results of the first pass. The accumulation buffer can be bypassed by disabling depth writes in the second pass, but it leads to multiple writes to a pixel due to rectangle overlaps and depth quantization which results in bright artifacts. If three textures are accessible at the combiners then both illuminations can be combined into one pass.

6 Implementation and Results

All the test cases were run on a 866MHz Pentium 3 PC with 512MB RDRAM and having a nVIDIA GeForce2 card supported by 32MB of DDR RAM. All the test win-

```
Display( )
         (Compute 𝓜 and load them into texture memory at the program start time)
1        Clear the depth and the color buffers
2        Configure the register combiners for diffuse shading
3        ∀ DP p
4            𝓜ₚ = normal-map ∈ 𝓜 whose ρ is closest to ρₚ
5            Map 𝓜ₚ onto rₚ
6            Compute the light vector, lₚ(·, ·), at the vertices of rₚ
7            Use the light vectors to map a cube vector map onto rₚ
8            Render rₚ
9        Clear the color buffer after loading it into the accumulation buffer
10       Clear the depth buffer
11       Configure the register combiners for specular shading
12       ∀ DP p
13           𝓜ₚ = normal-map ∈ 𝓜 whose ρ is closest to ρₚ
14           Map 𝓜ₚ onto rₚ (The details from the last pass can be cached)
15           Compute the half vector, hₚ(·, ·), at the vertices of rₚ
16           Use the half vectors to map a cube vector map onto rₚ
17           Render rₚ
18       Add the accumulation buffer to the color buffer
19       Swap the front and the back color buffers
```

Fig. 5. The Rendering Algorithm

dows were 800×600 in size. We used 256 normal maps ($|\mathcal{M}|=256$) corresponding to uniformly sampled values of $\rho_\mathbf{p}$ and we built a linear mip-map on each of these with a highest resolution of 32×32. The resolution of the cube vector map was $512\times512\times6$.

We demonstrate our work on three models: the Utah Teapot, a Human Head model, and a Camera prototype. The models are in the NURBS representation. The component patches are sampled uniformly in the parametric domain and simplified independent of each other. The error threshold ϵ is the main parameter of the sampling process. δ ensures that the rectangles from the low curvature region do not block the nearby rectangles in the higher curvature regions and also ensures that the rectangles do not overrun the boundary significantly. Simplification can lead to an order-of-magnitude speed-up in rendering and can save substantial storage space as reported in Table 1. In our current representation, each DP uses 62 bytes of storage: 6 bytes for the diffuse and specular colors, 12 floats (48 bytes) for the point location, principal directions and the normal, and 2 floats (8 bytes) for the two curvature values. We anticipate over 80% compression by using quantized values, delta differences, and index colors. Both the specular and diffuse shading are done at the hardware level. However, accumulation buffer is not supported in hardware by nVIDIA and is implemented in software by the OpenGL drivers. So the case of both diffuse and specular illumination can be slow.

On an average, about $330,000$ DPs can be rendered per second with diffuse illumination. The diffuse and specular illumination passes take around the same time. The main bottleneck in rendering is the bus bandwidth. This can be seen by noting that specular and diffuse illumination give around the same frame rates even though the cost of computing the half vectors is higher than the cost of computing the light vectors and that per-pixel computation is higher for specular illumination. The pixel-fill rate was not a bottleneck as the frame rates did not vary with the size of the window.

Table 1. Summary of results: NP = Number of points, SS = Storage Space, PT = Pre-processing time, FPS = Frames per second. (Illumination is done with a moving light source)

Statistical Highlights	Without Simplification			With Simplification		
	Teapot	*Head*	*Camera*	*Teapot*	*Head*	*Camera*
NP	156,800	376,400	216,712	25,713	64,042	46,077
SS (in MB)	9.19	22.06	12.69	1.51	3.75	2.70
PT (in sec)	22.5	22.2	15.25	146.5	485.5	178.17
FPS (Diffuse)	2.13	0.89	1.59	12.51	5.26	6.89
FPS (Specular)	2.04	0.88	1.52	11.76	5.13	6.67

Table 2. Comparison with Splatting Primitives: (*Test 1*) Same Number of Rendering Primitives, (*Test 2*) Approximately similar rendering quality. DP = Differential Points, SP = Square Primitive, RP = Rectangle Primitive, and EP = Elliptical Primitive.

Statistical Highlights		Rendering Primitive			
		DP	*SP*	*RP*	*EP*
	NP	156,800	156,800	156,800	156,800
Test 1	SS (in MB)	9.19	4.90	4.90	4.90
	FPS (Diffuse)	2.13	11.76	10.52	2.35
	NP	156,800	1,411,200	1,155,200	320,000
Test 2	SS (in MB)	9.19	44.10	36.10	10.01
	FPS (Diffuse)	2.13	1.61	1.49	1.16

The main focus of this paper is the rendering quality and efficiency delivered by DPs as rendering primitives. Previous works on point sample rendering have orthogonal benefits such as faster transformation [21] and multiresolution [1, 17, 19] which can potentially be extended to DPs. To demonstrate the benefits of DPs we compare the rendering performance of an unsimplified differential point representation of a teapot to the splatting of unsimplified and unstructured versions of sampled points. For the splatting test cases, we take the original point samples from which DPs were constructed and associate each of them with a bounding ball whose radius is determined by comparing its distance from its sampled neighbors. From this we consider three kinds of test rendering primitives for splatting:

1. **Square Primitive**: They are squares parallel to the view plane with a width equal to the radius of the bounding ball [19]. They are rendered without blending.

2. **Rectangle Primitive**: Consider a disc on the tangent plane of the point, with a radius equal to the radius of the bounding ball. An orthogonal projection on a plane parallel to the view plane and located at the position of the point results in an ellipse. The rectangle primitive is obtained by fitting a rectangle around the ellipse with the sides of the rectangle being parallel to the principal axes of the ellipse [17]. The rectangle primitives are rendered with Z-buffering but without any blending.

3. **Elliptical Primitive**: We initialize 256 texture maps representing ellipses (with a unit radius along the semi-major axis) varying from a sphere to a nearly "flat" ellipse. The texture maps have an alpha value of 0 in the interior of the ellipse and 1 elsewhere. At run time, the rectangle primitive is texture mapped with a scaled version of the closest approximation of its ellipsoid. The texture-mapped rectangles are then rendered with a small depth offset and blending [19]. This is implemented in hardware using the register combiners.

DPs were compared with the splatting primitives for two test cases: (*Test 1*) same number of rendering primitives and (*Test 2*) approximately similar visual quality of rendering. For *Test 1*, DPs were found to deliver a much better rendering quality for the same number of primitives as seen in Figure 6 and summarized in Table 2. DPs especially fared well in high curvature areas which are not well modeled and rendered by the splat primitives. Moreover, DPs had nearly the same frame rates as the elliptical primitives. Sample renderings of *Test 2* are shown in Figure 6 and the results are summarized in Table 2. For this test the number of square, rectangle, and elliptical primitives were increased by increasing the sampling frequency of the uniformly sampled model used for DPs. In *Test 2*, DPs clearly out-performed the splatting primitives in both criteria.

7   Conclusions and Future Work

The results and the test comparisons clearly demonstrate the efficiency of DPs as rendering primitives. The ease of simplification gives DPs an added advantage to get a significant speed up. High rendering quality is achieved because the normal distribution is fairly accurate. The rendering efficiency of DPs is attributed to the sparse surface representation that reduces bus bandwidth.

One shortcoming of DPs is that the complexity of the borders limit the maximum width of the interior DPs through the δ constraint. This leads to increased sampling in the interior even though these DPs have enough room to expand within the bounds laid down by the ϵ constraint. A width-determination approach that uses third order differential information (such as the variation of the surface curvature) should be able to deal with this more efficiently. DPs are currently implemented for a NURBS representation. The main challenge in extending them to polygonal models would be the accurate computation of curvature properties and handling of discontinuities.

In its current form DPs are not efficient when a large set of points fall onto the same pixel while rendering. We plan to explore a multiresolution scheme of DPs that will efficiently render lower frequency versions of the original surface under such instances. Texturing can be achieved by texturing the rectangles $\mathbf{r_p}$ and having a separate texture pass while rendering. The texture coordinates of the vertices of $\mathbf{r_p}$ can be computed with the aid of the object space parameterization of $\mathbf{S_p}$.

8   Acknowledgements

We would like to thank the anonymous reviewers for their constructive comments that were exceptionally detailed and insightful. We would like to thank our colleagues at the Graphics and Visual Informatics Laboratory at the University of Maryland, College Park and at the Center for Visual Computing at SUNY, Stony Brook. We would also like to thank Robert McNeel & Associates for the Head and the Camera models and for the openNURBS C++ code. Last, but not the least, we would like to acknowledge NSF funding grants IIS00-81847, ACR-98-12572 and DMI-98-00690.

References

1. C. F. Chang, G. Bishop, and A. Lastra. LDI Tree: A hierarchical representation for image-based rendering. In *Proceedings of SIGGRAPH'99*, pages 291–298, 1999.
2. L. Darsa, B. C. Silva, and A. Varshney. Navigating static environments using image-space simplification and morphing. In *1997 Symp. on Interactive 3D Graphics*, pages 25–34, 1997.

150

3. M. Desbrun, M. Meyer, P. Schröder, and A. H. Barr. Discrete differential-geometry operations in nD. *http://www.multires.caltech.edu/pubs/DiffGeoOperators.pdf*, 2000.
4. M. P. do Carmo. *Differential Geometry of Curves and Surfaces*. Prentice-Hall. Inc., Englewood Cliffs, New Jersey, 1976.
5. J. P. Grossman and William J. Dally. Point sample rendering. In *Rendering Techniques '98*, Eurographics, pages 181–192. Springer-Verlag Wien New York, 1998.
6. I. Guskov, W. Sweldens, and P. Schröder. Multiresolution signal processing for meshes. In *Proceedings of SIGGRAPH 99*, pages 325–334, 1999.
7. P. S. Heckbert and M. Garland. Optimal triangulation and quadric-based surface simplification. *Computational Geometry*, 14:49–65, 1999.
8. V. L. Interrante. Illustrating surface shape in volume data via principal direction-driven 3D line integral convolution. In *Proceedings of SIGGRAPH 97*, pages 109–116, August 1997.
9. A. Kalaiah and A. Varshney. Modeling and rendering of points with local neighborhood. In *Technical Report CS-TR-4224, Computer Science Department, University of Maryland, College Park*, March 2001 (http://www.cs.umd.edu/~ark/dpr.pdf).
10. M. J. Kilgard. A practical and robust bump-mapping technique for today's GPUs. In *Game Developers Conference*, July, 2000 (available at http://www.nvidia.com).
11. V. Krishnamurthy and M. Levoy. Fitting smooth surfaces to dense polygon meshes. In *Proceedings of SIGGRAPH 96*, pages 313–324, August 1996.
12. M. Levoy and T. Whitted. The use of points as a display primitive. In *TR 85-022, Computer Science Department, University of North Carolina at Chapel Hill*, January 1985.
13. D. Lischinski and A. Rappoport. Image-based rendering for non-diffuse synthetic scenes. In *Rendering Techniques '98*, Eurographics, pages 301–314. Springer-Verlag New York, 1998.
14. W. R. Mark, L. McMillan, and G. Bishop. Post-rendering 3D warping. In *1997 Symposium on Interactive 3D Graphics*, pages 7–16, April 1997.
15. M. M. Oliveira, G. Bishop, and D. McAllister. Relief texture mapping. In *Proceedings of SIGGRAPH 2000*, pages 359–368, July 2000.
16. A. Paeth. *Graphics Gems*, volume 5. Academic Press, 1995.
17. H. Pfister, M. Zwicker, J. van Baar, and M. Gross. Surfels: Surface elements as rendering primitives. In *Proceedings of SIGGRAPH 2000*, pages 335–342, July 2000.
18. K. Pulli, M. Cohen, T. Duchamp, H. Hoppe, L. Shapiro, and W. Stuetzle. View-based rendering: Visualizing real objects from scanned range and color data. In *Rendering Techniques '97*, pages 23–34. Springer-Verlag New York, June 1997.
19. S. Rusinkiewicz and M. Levoy. QSplat: A multiresolution point rendering system for large meshes. In *Proceedings of SIGGRAPH 2000*, pages 343–352, July 2000.
20. S. Rusinkiewicz and M. Levoy. Streaming QSplat: A viewer for networked visualization of large, dense models. In *Symposium of Interactive 3D Graphics*, pages 63–68, March 2001.
21. J. Shade, S. Gortler, L. He, and R. Szeliski. Layered depth images. In *Proceedings of SIGGRAPH 98*, pages 231–242, August 1998.
22. G. Taubin. Estimating the tensor of curvature of a surface from a polyhedral approximation. In *Fifth International Conference on Computer Vision*, pages 902–907, 1995.
23. G. Turk. Re-tiling polygonal surfaces. In *Proc. of SIGGRAPH 92*, pages 55–64, July 1992.
24. A. P. Witkin and P. S. Heckbert. Using particles to sample and control implicit surfaces. In *Proceedings of SIGGRAPH 94*, pages 269–278, July 1994.
25. M. Zwicker, H. Pfister, J. van Baar, and M. Gross. Surface splatting. In *Proceedings of SIGGRAPH 2001 (to appear)*, 2001.

Editors' Note: see Appendix, p. 333 for colored figures of this paper

Interactive Sampling and Rendering for Complex and Procedural Geometry

Marc Stamminger, George Drettakis

iMAGIS / GRAVIR - REVES - INRIA Sophia-Antipolis
2004, route de Lucioles, F-06902, Sophia-Antipolis, France.
{Marc.Stamminger|George.Drettakis}@sophia.inria.fr, http://www-sop.inria.fr/reves

Abstract. We present a new sampling method for procedural and complex geometries, which allows interactive point-based modeling and rendering of such scenes. For a variety of scenes, object-space point sets can be generated rapidly, resulting in a sufficiently dense sampling of the final image. We present an integrated approach that exploits the simplicity of the point primitive. For procedural objects a hierarchical sampling scheme is presented that adapts sample densities locally according to the projected size in the image. Dynamic procedural objects and interactive user manipulation thus become possible. The same scheme is also applied to on-the-fly generation and rendering of terrains, and enables the use of an efficient occlusion culling algorithm. Furthermore, by using points the system enables interactive rendering and simple modification of complex objects (e.g., trees). For display, hardware-accelerated 3-D point rendering is used, but our sampling method can be used by any other point-rendering approach.

1 Introduction and Motivation

The complexity of virtual environments has grown spectacularly over the recent years, with the advent of high performance, but affordable, graphics hardware. The paradox is that the majority of objects in such scenes often covers only a few, or even fractions of, pixels on the screen. The traditional advantage of polygon-based scan-line coherence is thus lost, while resources are wasted by transforming and clipping geometry which is either invisible, or is smaller than a pixel. This has led to the investigation of alternatives to pure polygon-based rendering in recent research. Several researchers have turned to ray-tracing based approaches (e.g., [14, 24]); An interesting recent alternative is *point-based rendering* [4, 16, 19], which is actually an old idea revisited [6].

Point based rendering methods represent the scene's geometry as a set of *point samples*, that is object space position, surface normal and material data. Usually, the point samples are obtained from images of the scene that include depth and material information, but they are rendered and lit as independent small polygons or oriented disks. It has been shown that such point sample representations are well suited both for fast rendering of extremely complex geometry [19] and for high-quality visualisation [16]. These methods however generate samples as a *pre-process*, thus restricting their use to static, unmodifiable scenes.

In this paper, we focus on points as a primitive well adapted for interactive applications and non static scenes. We believe that points are particularly well suited for such applications for the following reasons:

- Objects can be represented at different levels of details very efficiently, by properly choosing point densities (e.g., [19]). When we interactively modify procedural objects, sample recomputation is necessary for all levels of detail, at every

152

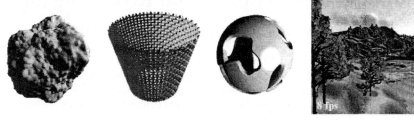

Fig. 1. Examples of our point sample generation algorithm.

frame. Most level of detail techniques create coarse levels bottom-up, resulting in computational expense proportional to the object's complexity. In contrast, point samples can be generated top-down, so coarse representations are obtained very quickly. In addition, a coarse representation of an object can be refined incrementally, for example for a closer view, by adding new points. If the object does not change, all old samples remain valid.

- Rendering procedural and dynamic objects requires adaptive refinement in critical regions. With points this can be easily achieved in a straightforward manner by adding additional points locally. Since point representations do not require the maintenance of topological information, object topology can be trivially changed. Examples are CSG models or geometry modifiers such as the wickerwork or holes modifier used in Fig.1. In contrast, the use of meshes (e.g., of triangles), to represent dynamically changing procedural objects or non-standard topologies requires intricate book-keeping when adaptively subdividing, and careful processing to avoid cracks and other artifacts. This leads to complex implementations and numerical robustness problems.
- Points representing a single object or surface are independent, so they can be generated in parallel, in contrast to polygonal meshes. As we shall see, points also lead to simple solutions for visibility culling, and can take advantage of hardware acceleration more easily than for triangles, which require the use of triangle-strips which are non-trivial to generate adaptively.

We present an integrated system which incorporates the above advantages, and can be used for applications such as interactive procedural modelling for design of outdoors or indoors scenes, or VR/game type interactive viewing and manipulation. To achieve sufficiently rapid generation of point samples in this context, we introduce $\sqrt{5}$ adaptive sampling. Our new scheme allows us to hierarchically generate new samples *locally*, in the regions they are required, according to the current viewpoint. We apply this approach to procedural models, including displacement maps and terrains. For complex objects such as trees, we use quasi-random sampling to generate points. The continuous level of detail property of points allows smooth frame rate control. Finally, the use of a hierarchical caching mechanism, parallel computation and an direct mapping to graphics hardware vectors, significantly increases the efficiency of rendering. Examples of our approach are shown in Fig. 1.

2 Related work

Levoy and Whitted [6], were the first to explicitly investigate the use of points as an alternative to traditional geometry; They treated issues of displacement mapping and texture filtering. In the last few years, there has been significant interest in point-based approaches. Grossman and Dally [4] generated point representations of objects in a preprocess, and presented efficient ways of rendering them. The Surfels approach [16], concentrates on ways to efficiently render point representations, and presents several reconstruction mechanisms. Points are also used in the Q-splat algorithm [19], whose goal is to render very large polygonal data sets. The emphasis of this work is the compactness and the flexibility of the data structure and consequent rendering quality to allow treatment of enormous databases, and in particular those that do not fit into main memory. A direct ray-tracing algorithm for point-sets has been developed by Schaufler and Wann Jensen [20]. The use of particles for modeling, e.g., [23], is also related to the use of points. The particle systems of Reeves and Blau [18] are in the spirit of our work, however not in an interactive context. In [26], an explicit level of detail mechanism is applied in which leaves become points and then disappear, resulting in effects similar to ours for trees, but from a completely different standpoint.

Interactive display using ray-tracing approaches is also related to our work; examples include the Utah interactive ray-tracing environment [14] and the Render Cache [24]. Image-based rendering techniques share several problems with points based methods, in particular for hole filling. Some of the solutions developed, for example layered depth-images e.g., [22, 8] and the work of Max for trees [9] are in a similar vein to those developed for Surfels for example.

In what follows, we will be using procedural models, often based on the noise function [15]. We have used or been inspired by several models described in [11, 7]. The procedural and other geometric modifiers we use are inspired by the work of Neyret [12] and Dischler e.g., [2]. The approach of Meyer and Neyret [10] in particular permits interactive viewing of similar kinds of procedural objects; The generation of slices however requires quite sophisticated hole filling techniques. The initial idea of line-based occlusion culling for which we use for terrains can be found in [5].

The Reyes [1] rendering architecture is close in spirit to our approach. Objects are tessellated into polygons, until their size is under some predefined threshold. The major differences are that their system stays in the polygonal world, and the emphasis there is high quality rendering rather than interactivity; the choices and tradeoffs are thus very different from our own.

A very recent paper partially covers similar ideas for the rendering of complex static scenes [25], in the context of a walkthrough system.

3 $\sqrt{5}$-Sampling: adaptive point generation

As mentioned in the introduction, procedural objects like displaced surfaces will require adaptive sampling. The $\sqrt{5}$-sampling scheme is a hierarchical object-space sampling which allows us to efficiently treat displacement mapped objects, procedural geometry modifiers and terrains.

We start with an initial set of samples for each object, with each sample corresponding to a region of surface A ("sample area") on the object (Fig. 2(a)). The union of these regions entirely covers the object. The projection of the region A in image space is $A' \approx A \frac{cos\alpha}{d^2}$, where α is the angle of the surface normal to the viewing direction, and d is the distance of the surface element to the eye (Fig. 2(a)).

If we were to compute the exact projections A' of the sample regions onto the image plane, we would have an image of the object without holes. Since our goal is interactive rendering, we instead project the center of the sample to the image, and draw a simple primitive around it in image space (a hardware accelerated disk in practice). To avoid

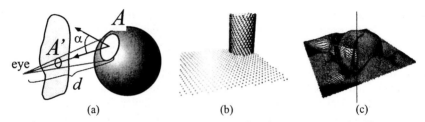

Fig. 2. (a) The basic point sample geometry in world and image space. (b) Object curvature results in denser sampling as we approach silhouettes. Projective foreshortening results in denser image space sampling further in the distance. (c) After displacement, holes appear in the steep parts (left). With adaptive insertion of new samples, these holes are filled (right),

holes, this primitive should have an image space area which is roughly the size of A'. The size of these primitives provides a user-controlled tradeoff between speed and quality. The user defines a threshold A'_{min}, which is the desired image size of a projected sample region. For example if A'_{min} is 4, a sample will cover 2x2 pixels on average in the image. Thus for larger values of A'_{min}, fewer samples will be generated, resulting in faster display. This is similar to the approach used in Q-splat [19], for controlling display speed.

Clearly, a uniform sample density in object space does not always result in a uniform density in image space, as illustrated in Fig. 2(b)-(c). Displacement mapping makes this worse. In what follows, we present a sampling scheme which increases sample density where required for such objects.

3.1 The Hierarchical Sampling Scheme

When choosing the initial points, we try to capture all essential object features by choosing a sufficiently dense set of points. For certain classes of procedural objects, we can use a priori information about the frequencies used to generate them. If probable undersampling is detected during evaluation of a point, new samples are created locally in the neighbourhood, which can in turn recursively spawn new samples. Appropriate sampling of a displaced surface, for instance, should increase sample density in steep regions.

To guide the refinement process, we define the *undersampling factor* $F = A'/A'_{min}$ which is a measure of how well the current set of samples represents the object, given the users choice of sample size A'_{min}. If $F = 1$ we meet the user define A'_{min} criterion. If $F < 1$ too many samples were initially created and finally if $F > 1$ more samples are needed, thus spawning additional refinement.

We assume that we have an (u, v) parameterisation of the object considered. Initially, we create a uniform grid of points in the parameter domain. The grid step size is h; we can consider $u_0 = (h, 0)$ and $v_0 = (0, h)$ to be the initial *spawning vectors*, Fig. 3(a). When denser sampling is required locally, we *refine* or *subdivide* single grid points. To refine an initial grid point, four new points are inserted at relative positions:

$$u_1 = 2u_0/5 + v_0/5, \qquad v_1 = -u_0/5 + 2v_0/5, \tag{1}$$

as well as $-u_1$ and $-v_1$ (see Fig. 3(c)).

Thus, after each initial point has been refined, the initial and refined points form a new uniform grid of step size $h/\sqrt{5}$ (Fig. 3(b)). The new grid is spawned by vectors u_1

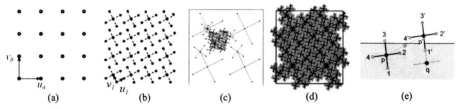

Fig. 3. $\sqrt{5}$ sampling. (a) initial grid with vectors v_0, u_0 (b) once subdivided and rotated grid spanned by vectors v_1, u_1 (c) adaptively refined sample set (d) fractal covered by generated samples (e) resolving boundary problems

and v_1 and it is *rotated* by an angle of $\alpha = \arctan 1/2 \approx 26.6^o$.

This refinement procedure can also be applied to the new grid, using offset vectors $u_2 = 2u_1/5 + v_1/5$, $v_2 = -u_1/5 + 2v_1/5$, $-u_2$ and $-v_2$ and so forth. The grid at level i has grid size $\sqrt{5}^{-i}$ and a rotation angle of $i\alpha$. Note that this refinement process can be done locally, resulting in increased sample density where needed (see Fig. 3(c)). All descendants of a single grid point form a fractal, Fig. 3(d), which is very similar to the dragon fractal [21].

The computational effort required for $\sqrt{5}$ sampling is minimal, since we can pre-compute vectors u_i, v_i. In order to subdivide (u, v) at level i, we simply insert new points at $(u, v) + u_i$, $(u, v) + v_i$, $(u, v) - u_i$, $(u, v) - v_i$. The samples form a forest, with one tree per initial sample, which are "root", Fig. 3(d). Each node has 5 children, four with an offset according the level in the tree and a self copy.

Consider the 2x2 grid shown in Figure 3(d), which has been subdivided globally several times. Some regions, shown in white in the figure, are never reached, due to the fractal like nature of our construction. Our solution is to also examine neighbours during subdivision. When subdividing a point p, we always look at its neighbours; if a neighbour p' lies outside, but one of its children lies inside, we attach it as a child to p, Fig. 3(e). Note that these neighbours do not exist in the initial grid or its subdivisions. Care has to be taken since other neighbours of p may then have the same children attached. For example, $1'$ and $4'$ are attached to p' and also to q in Fig. 3(e). The solution is to attach such "boundary children" of p' to a single neighbour of p'. We choose the neighbour which is inside the boundary and is closest to the child being considered.

This sampling scheme has nice properties. Due to its uniformity and its lack of randomness new samples are well positioned in between other samples resulting in little overlap. The scheme is purely hierarchical, i.e., every point has exactly one parent in a previous level. Two other schemes with this property are a corresponding $\sqrt{2}$-subdivision scheme ($u_0 = v_0 = 1/2$) or a $\sqrt{9}$-subdivision scheme ($\{u_i, v_i\} = \{-1/3, 0, 1/3\}^2 \setminus (0,0)$. The former has a very directional nature: when refining a sample, only one new sample is created, and it is always offset in a certain direction. The latter scheme has a large branching factor of 9.

3.2 Displacement mapping

Displacement mapping is a way to add very rich visual detail to otherwise simple models. However, the sample density problems mentioned above become worse when displacement mapping is applied.

Define A to be the sample area of the undisplaced surface, and A_d the sample area

156

of the displaced surface. Also, A'_d is the projected area on the image plane of A_d, with α the angle between the the undisplaced and the displaced surface normals, and β the angle between the viewing direction and the displaced surface normal, Fig. 4(a). Thus,

$$A_d = \frac{A}{cos\alpha}, \quad A'_d = \frac{A_d \, cos\beta}{d^2} = \frac{cos\beta}{cos\alpha \, d^2}A \tag{2}$$

The geometry of these quantities is illustrated in Fig. 4(a)-(c).

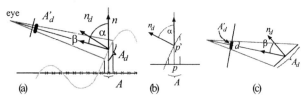

Fig. 4. Undersampling factor determination.

We select the number of initial samples n_s by assuming that all points have distance $\tilde{d}$ (later on, we will account for the error due to this assumption automatically):

$$n_s = \frac{A_{total}}{A'_{min}\tilde{d}^2} \Rightarrow A = A'_{min}\tilde{d}^2, \tag{3}$$

where A_{total} is the total area of the object. After displacement we have:

$$A_d = \frac{A}{cos\alpha} = \frac{A'_{min}\tilde{d}^2}{cos\alpha}, \tag{4}$$

and after image projection:

$$A'_d = A_d\frac{cos\beta}{d^2} = A'_{min}\frac{\tilde{d}^2}{d^2}\frac{cos\beta}{cos\alpha} = A'_{min}F, \tag{5}$$

which determines the undersampling factor for displacement.

3.3 Procedural Geometry Modifiers

Interpreting scene objects as point sample generators allows for procedural geometry manipulation beyond simple displacement, which can be very complicated with a surface based object representation. We attach a callback function to each object, which processes each sample point created. The function can then modify this point, remove it, or create several new points.

An example is the WickerWork-modifier (see Fig. 7). For each point sample the modifier tests whether the sample is (a) in a hole of the wickerwork ($\rightarrow$ remove it), (b) in the region where two strings overlap ($\rightarrow$ create two points, one with positive, one with negative elevation), or (c) it is in the region of a single string, in which case it is just displaced accordingly. For each modified point, a new undersampling factor is computed, using Eq. (5). The Wickerwork-modifier returns a value larger than 1 only in case (c). Another example of modifiers are Holes in the sphere of Fig. 1.

3.4 Terrains

Terrains are different in that they are infinite, so we cannot start with a uniform sampling. Nevertheless, it is possible and effective to represent them as point sets since their image is finite. Furthermore, their heightfield nature also enables efficient occlusion culling, explained below. In the following we assume the terrain is a heightfield on the $z = 0$ plane. The elevation is positive, with maximum value z_{max}.

Base Plane Sampling. Obviously, it is sufficient to sample a sector of the base plane with the projection of the camera as its apex and an opening angle which is sufficient to contain all visible points. We use a parameterisation that leads to a sufficiently uniform sampling of the sector's projection onto the image plane. We first describe how the sector is computed and then define a mapping of $[-1,1] \times [0,1]$ to the sector.

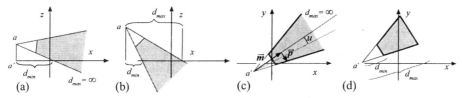

Fig. 5. Side view: (a) horizon is visible and thus $d_{max} = \infty$, (b) horizon invisible, d_{max} is finite. Top view: (c) Paramterization of a sector, (d) v parameter.

The medial axis of the sector is the projection of the camera's viewing direction onto the base plane. Its opening angle is determined such that it contains all visible base plane points. We can parameterise this sector using a normalised medial axis vector $\vec{m}$ and a perpendicular vector $\vec{p}$. The sector point defined by parameters (u,d) is $(\vec{m} + u\vec{p})d$ (Figure 5(c)).

We scale p so that u is in the range $[-1,1]$. For d a possibly infinite interval $[d_{min}, d_{max}]$ is needed to address the entire visible sector. If the horizon is visible, d_{max} equals infinity (Fig. 5(a)), otherwise it can be obtained from the intersection of the viewing frustum with the base plane (Fig. 5(b),(d)). The value d_{min} can be determined accordingly (Fig. 5(a)-(b)), however it usually has to be decreased further since invisible base plane points are likely to be elevated into the viewing frustum.

For the parameterisation of the interval $[d_{min}, d_{max}]$ we consider the typical case where the viewing direction is parallel to the base plane. In this case, the y_i-coordinate of a projected point is proportional to $1/d$, if the horizon is at $y_i = 0$. Consequently, we compute $d(v) = (1/d_{min} - v(1/d_{max} - 1/d_{min}))^{-1}$, where $v \in [0,1]$. Note that for $d_{max} = \infty$ we can set $1/d_{max} = 0$. Thus, we parameterise the sector by $p(u,v) = (\vec{m} + u\vec{p})d(v)$, where $u \in [-1,1]$ and $v \in [0,1]$ (Fig. 5(d)).

Fig. 6(a) shows a uniform $(u,v) - grid$ of this parameterisation, projected to image space. If the viewing direction is parallel to the base plane (Fig. 6(a)), the grid remains uniform, if the viewing direction moves up or down (Fig. 6(b)), the projected pattern becomes less uniform. However, this is just an initial pattern; if critical undersampling is detected, we automatically insert new samples.

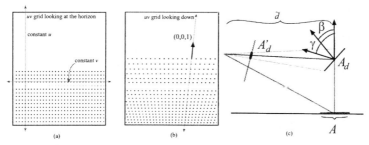

Fig. 6. (a) If we look straight at the horizon, the projected grid is uniform. (b) If we look down, there is distortion. The elevation occurs along the constant u line in image space, facilitating occlusion culling. (c) Undersampling factor F geometry. (d) Occlusion culling for terrains.

158

Another alternative would be to directly parameterise the image plane with (u, v) and map these to the base plane point visible through this image point. Our parameterisation however fits well with our occlusion culling method described below.

Terrain Generation. We generate a set of points on the base plane sector using a uniform grid of valid (u, v) values. Due to our choice of parameterisation, the image projections of these points on the base plane are approximately uniform. By elevating these points, the sampling on the image plane becomes non-uniform, resulting in the same kind of undersampling as for finite displaced objects.

If (u, v) are sampled uniformly with step sizes $(\Delta u, \Delta v)$, the base plane area A represented by this sample is approximately (see Fig. 6(c)):

$$A \approx \left| \frac{\partial p(u, v)}{\partial u} \right| \left| \frac{\partial p(u, v)}{\partial v} \right| \Delta u \Delta v \approx d(v)^3 (1/d_{\max} - 1/d_{\min}) \Delta u \Delta v. \qquad (6)$$

Elevating this area (A_d, Fig. 6(c)-(d)) and projecting it onto the image plane results in

$$A'_d \approx \frac{d(v)^3 (1/d_{\max} - 1/d_{\min}) \cos\gamma \, \Delta u \, \Delta v}{\cos\beta \, d'^2}, \qquad (7)$$

so the undersampling factor $F = A'_d / A_{\min}$. Note that this factor accounts for under- and oversampling due to non-optimal sector sampling as well as due to the displacement.

Occlusion culling. The sector parameterisation has a nice property for occlusion culling: if we consider base plane lines with constant u, their projection also forms a line in image space. By elevating these points, their image is only moved along this line (see Figure 6(b)). Consequently, a point at (u, v) can only be hidden by a point (u, v'), where $v' < v$. This property is reportedly used in computer games and has been used before e.g., in [5].

As a result, we can render the terrain line by line, where each line has constant u. The line $u = u_l$ is rendered from front to back, uniformly sampling v in the interval $[0, 1]$. The current horizon point is the point on the line that currently has the maximum y-coordinate in the image. A later point at $v' > v$ is hidden if it is below the horizon. We do this occlusion test twice: first we test whether the point would be visible with maximum elevation. If it cannot be rejected trivially, the real elevation z is computed and the test is repeated with z, avoiding many costly elevation computations.

We only perform occlusion culling for initial sample points. Child samples have different u and violate the strict ordering along v. A point only spawns samples if it is not occluded. Nonetheless, an initial point can be occluded, while one of its children is not. We account for this by approximating the maximum elevation of the point and its children by extrapolating the elevation to the children using the terrain gradient at the point. We only discard points if none of its children could be visible, based on this computation.

4 Complex Geometry

Point based rendering is also a highly efficient means for the rendering of complex geometry, e.g., defined by polygons. Others have investigated this approach very successfully (QSplat [19], Surfels [16]), using precomputed samples.

To achieve rapid sample generation for complex geometry, we create a vector of point samples for every object, randomly distributed over the object. There is no spatial order within the vector. We generate this vector by addressing all surface points with (u,v)-coordinates and sampling the object using quasi random numbers, in our case the first two Halton-sequences [13]. This way, we can create an arbitrarily long vector and, more importantly, we can extend this efficiently when needed.

Due to our construction, any prefix of the vector contains samples which are quite evenly distributed over the object's surface. At each frame, we determine how many samples n_s are necessary to obtain adequate image sample density. If the current vector has fewer elements, it is filled to size n_s, by using subsequent samples of the Halton sequence. Only the first n_s samples are rendered, since the vector may be longer.

To determine n_s, we compute the minimum distance $\bar{d}$ of the object's bounding box to the camera. If the object's surface area is A, we select $n_s = A/\bar{d}^2 A'_{min}$. Note that this neglects the cosine of the surface normal to the camera, so n_s reflects the "worst" case of an object directly facing the viewer.

Our approach provides straightforward *level-of-detail* (LOD) control. By selecting n_s, we have an almost continuous degree of accuracy. Objects with m polygons can be rendered with good quality even with $n_s < m$ samples. Since we always render the prefix of a list up to a certain number, the overall appearance of the object will not change quickly from frame to frame, and flickering or popping artifacts are diminished, compared to traditional LOD approaches.

Finally, simple time dependent object modifications can be performed on-the-fly, for example the movement of trees in a turbulent breeze. For each point sample of a tree we precompute the distance to the stem. According to this distance the point is moved in the current wind direction. Wind directions are defined by a turbulence function. We compute the wind direction for each object at its center and use this direction for the entire object. We do not insert additional samples to fill potential resulting holes, as a display speed/computation tradeoff.

5 System Issues

5.1 Sample distance and splat size

Almost continuous and predictable quality control are a major advantage of point based rendering methods. Very fast images can be obtained by rendering few, large points, whereas many small points require more time, but give accurate results. In our implementation the user can steer this tradeoff by defining the desired sample density in the rendered image: the average distance in pixels between samples. Using this size, the point radius is selected automatically, such that holes are almost always avoided.

Alternatively, the user can select a desired frame rate. The time needed for rendering each frame is measured and the sample density parameter is adapted continuously. During motion, the user might see coarse, approximate solutions at high frame rates, which refine quickly as soon as motion stops. This is illustrated in Fig 8, and in the accompanying movie (see the publications page at http://www-sop.inria.fr/reves).

5.2 Caching of $\sqrt{5}$-sampled Points

If we consider the samples obtained by the $\sqrt{5}$ scheme as a forest, the depth of some trees changes from frame to frame, but the upper parts in the hierarchy remain the same. It is thus natural to store the forest computed in each frame and to reuse it for the next frame. Such a forest is stored per object.

The cached forest can then be traversed top down: for each node the refinement criterion is reevaluated considering the new camera. If a leaf in the cache needs to be refined, new children are computed. If an inner node is classified as a leaf in the new frame, all the children in the cache are skipped. This caching mechanism can significantly reduce the sample computations; the subdivision criterion however has to be evaluated for every sample at every frame.

5.3 OpenGL issues

For point rendering we simply use OpenGL GL_POINTS. Evidently, higher quality rendering could be achieved by using ellipsoidal splats as in the Surfels approach [16]. The current implementation of hardware supported points limits our ability to correctly treat texture and transparency. Use of a Surfels-type rendering method would resolve these problems.

The rendering of unmodified complex geometry is accelerated using OpenGL's glVertexPointer-calls, where an entire array of points can be passed to OpenGL in one call. If the object is composed of different materials, we generate random points on the object, but store these in different vectors, one for each material. Then n_s is distributed over the arrays, and each material's sample vector is rendered separately with the according material properties, reducing expensive OpenGL material switches.

5.4 Parallelism

Point sample generation is a perfect candidate for parallelisation. No neighbourhood or coherence between samples is considered, so samples can be generated on parallel processors or remote machines. The $\sqrt{5}$ subdivision scheme leads to a forest of completely independent trees, which can be computed independently on parallel processors.

6 Results

We have tested our system in three different scenarios. The first is an indoors procedural design test, where we add procedural objects to the scene, and interactively select their parameters. The second is the design of an outdoors world, in which we choose procedural parameters for the terrain. Finally, we have a VR- or game-style scenario, where the user can move around and interact with the scene.

The indoor design example is illustrated in Fig. 7, including an indoor plant moving in the wind of a fan, a procedural wicker work basket and a rock paperweight. The user can move in this scene at 13 frames per second (fps)[1]. Modifications of the procedural objects as shown in the figure can be done at 8 fps for the paperweight, and 4 fps for the basket. During modification of the paperweight object 8% of the time is spent on the base object sample generation, 75% on the displacement computation, and 3.5% on the refinement decisions. When the user moves around the unchanged object, rendering becomes dominant. The time needed for refinement goes up to 30%, whereas the generation of new samples requires limited resources.

For the outdoor design and VR scenarios, we use procedural terrains based on fractal turbulence functions generated by Poisson events [7]. In order to give higher regions a rougher appearance, we start with only a small number of turbulence octaves (e.g., 3). If the resulting height is above a user-defined threshold, additional octaves are blended

---

[1] All timings are on a Pentium III PC at 733 Mhz (Sgi 330), with a VR3 (NVidia Quadro) graphics card.

in, resulting in smooth valleys and rocky mountains (this effect can also be obtained with multifractals [3]). By applying an exponential function, the valleys can be made wider and the mountains steeper. Since we know the area represented by each sample, we stop this evaluation process for detail that is too small to be represented by the sample. This avoids computation for unnecessary or even undesired detail. The model is fast enough for on-the-fly terrain generation but as a more efficient alternative, we can replace it by a tiled, precomputed terrain texture. We also implemented the sky model of [17], which is precomputed and mapped to a dome around the scene, adding further realism to our outdoors views.

An example of an interactive design session for an outdoors scene in illustrated in Fig. 8, where we add mountains and trees. The center right image is rendered with 280,000 points, 23,000 of which are the online evaluated terrain. Without occlusion culling the number of terrain samples is 40,000. The trees can be moved at 14 fps, if the view point does not change and thus the terrain does not require recomputation. The rightmost image is obtained by increasing sample density, resulting in 3.3 million points, which took 2 seconds. The terrain is always computed by an additional thread on the second processor.

In the VR- or game-like scenario, the user moves around in a coast scene. All terrain points below water level are replaced by lake surface samples, which in turn is displaced according to a procedural wave function (e.g., the ripples in the accompanying video). For the images in Fig. 9 we use a precomputed terrain stored in a texture. Again 1,000 trees were added. The trees are moving in the wind, the user can create ripples in the lake by throwing virtual stones. At 400x400 resolution we obtain about 8 fps.

7 Conclusion and Discussion

We have presented a novel sampling approach, which generates samples for procedural and complex geometry efficiently. The approach, coupled with caching mechanisms, is fast enough for interactive viewing on todays PC graphics hardware. Our object-space sampling is based on a user-controlled speed/quality threshold A'_{min}, namely the desired minimum image space coverage of a sample. This in turns controls the sample density.

For procedural objects, we introduced $\sqrt{5}$-sampling. Local refinement is controlled by an undersampling factor, defined by the A'_{min} threshold. We showed how this factor is computed for displacement maps and other procedural modifiers. For terrains, we introduced a suitable parameterisation, also allowing occlusion culling. Complex unmodified geometries such as trees can also be sampled efficiently with Halton sequences. Samples are stored in vectors which can be efficiently and incrementally updated.

Evidently, there are certain cases where point-based representations are not the best choice. Insufficient point densities or rendering techniques lead to visible holes in continuous surfaces. Our method strives to address this problem by choosing sample densities based on the current viewpoint. Furthermore, coherence over smooth surfaces cannot be exploited. Clearly, polygons are more efficient when they cover many pixels on the screen, but when this is not the case, point representations become the natural choice.

The main limitation of our approach is currently the expense of generating points. Using a hierarchy on very complex objects and a more general occlusion culling approach for all objects would reduce the number of samples generated. Hardware accelerated noise functions would also greatly improve the performance of our method. Better hardware support of point rendering could improve the quality of our images. Other directions include rendering with shadows or more sophisticated illumination models.

162

8 Acknowledgements

Thanks to F. Durand, F. Neyret, and J. Stewart for providing comments on an early draft. The sky model integration was done by M. Weber, based on code of B. Smits. The first author is supported by a Marie-Curie postdoctoral Fellowship. iMAGIS is a joint research project of CNRS/INRIA/UJF/INPG.

References

[1] R. L. Cook, L. Carpenter, and E. Catmull. The Reyes image rendering architecture. *Computer Graphics (SIGGRAPH '87)*, 21(4):95–102, July 1987.

[2] J-M. Dischler. Efficient rendering macro geometric surface structures with bi-directional texture functions. In *Rendering Techniques '98*, EG workshop on rendering, pages 169–180. Springer-Verlag, 1998.

[3] D. Ebert, K. Musgrave, D. Peachey, K. Perlin, and S. Worley. *Texturing and Modeling: A Procedural Approach*. Academic Press, 1994.

[4] J. P. Grossman and W. J. Dally. Point sample rendering. In *Rendering Techniques '98*, EG workshop on rendering, pages 181–192. Springer-Verlag, 1998.

[5] C-H. Lee and Y. G. Shin. An efficient ray tracing method for terrain rendering. In *Pacific Graphics '95*, August 1995.

[6] M. Levoy and T. Whitted. The use of points as a display primitive. TR 85-022. CS Department, University of North Carolina at Chapel Hill, January 1985. http://www-graphics.stanford.edu/papers/points/.

[7] J. P. Lewis. Algorithms for solid noise synthesis. *Computer Graphics (SIGGRAPH '89)*, 23(3):263–270, July 1989.

[8] D. Lischinski and A. Rappoport. Image-based rendering for non-diffuse synthetic scenes. In *Rendering Techniques '98*, EG workshop on rendering, pages 301–314. Springer-Verlag, 1998.

[9] N. Max and K. Ohsaki. Rendering tree from precomputed Z-buffer views. In *Rendering Techniques '95*, EG workshop on rendering, pages 74–81. Springer-Verlag, 1995.

[10] A. Meyer and F. Neyret. Interactive volumetric textures. In *Rendering Techniques '98*, EG workshop on rendering, pages 157–168. Eurographics, Springer Wein, July 1998.

[11] F. K. Musgrave, C. E. Kolb, and R. S. Mace. The synthesis and rendering of eroded fractal terrains. *Computer Graphics (SIGGRAPH '89)*, 23(3):41–50, July 1989.

[12] F. Neyret. Modeling animating and rendering complex scenes using volumetric textures. *IEEE Trans. on Visualization and Computer Graphics*, 4(1), January–March 1998.

[13] H. Niederreiter. *Random Number Generation and Quasi-Monte Carlo Methods*, volume 63 of *CBMS-NSF regional conference series in Appl. Math*. SIAM, Philadelphia, 1992.

[14] S. Parker, B. Martin, P.-P. J. Sloan, P. Shirley, B. Smits, and C. Hansen. Interactive ray tracing. In *Proc. of I3D Symp.'99*, pages 119–126, April 1999.

[15] K. Perlin. An image synthesizer. In *Computer Graphics (SIGGRAPH '85)*, volume 19:3, pages 287–296, July 1985.

[16] H. Pfister, M. Zwicker, J. van Baar, and M. Gross. Surfels: Surface elements as rendering primitives. pages 335–342. Proc. ACM SIGGRAPH, 2000.

[17] A. J. Preetham, P. Shirley, and B. Smits. A practical analytic model for daylight. pages 91–100. Proc. ACM SIGGRAPH, 1999.

[18] W. T. Reeves and R. Blau. Approximate and probabilistic algorithms for shading and rendering structured particle systems. In *Computer Graphics (SIGGRAPH '85)*, volume 19(3), pages 313–322, July 1985.

[19] S. Rusinkiewicz and M. Levoy. QSplat: A multiresolution point rendering system for large meshes. pages 343–352. Proc. ACM SIGGRAPH, 2000.

[20] G. Schaufler and H. Wann Jensen. Ray tracing point sampled geometry. In *Rendering Techniques 2000*, EG workshop on rendering, pages 319–328. Springer-Verlag, 2000.

[21] M. Schroeder. *Fractals, Chaos, and Power Laws*. Freeman, New York, 1991.

[22] J. W. Shade, S. J. Gortler, L. He, and R. Szeliski. Layered depth images. pages 231–242. Proc. ACM SIGGRAPH, July 1998.

[23] R. Szeliski and D. Tonnesen. Surface modeling with oriented particle systems. In *Computer Graphics (SIGGRAPH '92)*, volume 26:2, pages 185–194, July 1992.

[24] B. Walter, G. Drettakis, and S. Parker. Interactive rendering using the Render Cache. In *Rendering Techniques '99*, EG workshop on rendering, pages 19–30. Springer-Verlag, 1999.

[25] M. Wand, M. Fischer, I. Peter, F. Meyer auf der Heide, and W. Starsser. The randomized z-buffer algorithm: Interactive rendering of highly complex scenes. Proc. ACM SIGGRAPH, 2001. to appear.

[26] J. Weber and J. Penn. Creation and rendering of realistic trees. In *Computer Graphics (SIGGRAPH '95)*, pages 119–128, August 1995.

Editors' Note: see Appendix, p. 334 for colored figures of this paper

Point-Based Impostors for Real-Time Visualization

Michael Wimmer, Peter Wonka, François Sillion

iMAGIS - GRAVIR/IMAG-INRIA, Vienna University of Technology

Abstract. We present a new data structure for encoding the appearance of a geometric model as seen from a viewing region (view cell). This representation can be used in interactive or real-time visualization applications to replace a complex model by an impostor, maintaining high quality rendering while cutting down rendering time. Our approach relies on an object-space sampled representation similar to a point cloud or a layered depth image, but introduces two fundamental additions to previous techniques. First, the sampling rate is controlled to provide sufficient density across all possible viewing conditions from the specified view cell. Second, a correct, antialiased representation of the plenoptic function is computed using Monte Carlo integration. Our system therefore achieves high quality rendering using a simple representation with bounded complexity. We demonstrate the method for an application in urban visualization.

1 Introduction

Fig. 1. A scene from an urban walkthrough. Geometry in the red region has been replaced by a point-based impostor, providing for fast, antialiased rendering of the far field.

A general and recently quite popular approach to handle the interactive display of complex scenes is to break down the view space into cells (*view cells*) and compute optimizations separately for each view cell. A typical example is region visibility, which calculates the potentially visible set (PVS) of objects from a specific view cell.

In this paper we address the problem of simplifying distant geometry (the far field) for view cells (see Fig. 1). This is an important problem because rendering distant geometry often leads to aliasing artifacts and, even after visibility calculations, the amount of geometry remaining in the PVS is often overwhelming for current graphics accelerators.

We begin by defining our goals in this process. First, we set out to build a representation that provides a high-quality rendered image for all views from a specific view cell. This means that we try to avoid artifacts such as holes, aliasing or missing data, and that we require high fidelity in the rendering of view-dependent appearance changes. Second, we insist that our representation be as compact as possible, while being amenable to hardware acceleration on consumer-level graphics hardware.

Distant geometry has some peculiarities resulting from its complexity that make simplification difficult:

- One aspect is that because of limited image resolution and perspective projection, typically several triangles project to a single pixel. This makes antialiasing and filtering an important issue.
- Another aspect is that we can not rely on surfaces to drive the simplification process: the triangles that project to one pixel can stem from disconnected surfaces and even from different objects. This means, for example, that there is no well-defined normal for such a pixel.

Generally, simplification can be based either on geometric criteria as in most level-of-detail approaches, or on image-based representations. Geometric simplification is useful for certain models, but has its limitations. Scenes with alpha textures, regular structures as found in buildings, chaotic disconnected structures as found in trees, or new shading paradigms such as pixel and vertex shading are not easy to deal with even in recent appearance-based simplification methods. We will therefore concentrate on image-based simplification approaches.

We observe, however, that none of the simplified representations proposed to date meets all the goals defined above:

- Layered depth images (LDIs) and similar representations introduce bias in the sampling patterns, and cannot accommodate situations in which many primitives project onto each pixel of a view. In the presence of such *microgeometry*, we also have to be aware that appearance can change with the viewing direction. This requires a representation with directionally dependent information, such as a light field.
- Light field approaches are powerful enough to cope with complex and directionally dependent appearance. However, geometric information needs to be incorporated into the light field in order to obtain acceptable quality within a reasonable amount of storage space [3]. A possible starting point to build an impostor would therefore be a surface lightfield [28], but as the name of this primitive already indicates, this requires a surface (and its parameterization).

In this paper we introduce a new representation for a complex geometric model that is especially useful to build impostor objects to replace the far field for a given view cell. The proposed representation effectively decouples the geometry, represented as a set of 3D points, and the appearance, represented as a simplified light field computed from the original model. In our algorithm, the points are selected from a number of viewpoints, chosen so as to approach a minimal sampling criterion in image space, across the entire view cell. Therefore our sampling mechanism prevents the appearance of holes. In the context of very complex models composed of a great many independent primitives, 3D points can not be considered as representatives of a well-defined surface, as in the surfel or QSplat techniques [20, 21]. In contrast, we define a proper characterization of the radiance contribution to the image from these points, which can be computed using Monte Carlo integration, and is encoded as a texture map to model view-dependent effects. The resulting representation is compact, renders quickly using existing graphics hardware, produces a high quality image with little aliasing, has no missing or disappearing objects as the viewpoint moves, and correctly represents view-dependent changes within the view cell (such as occlusion/disocclusion effects or appearance changes).

The paper is organized as follows: after reviewing previous work in section 2, we present an overview of the proposed representation, its construction and its usage in section 3. We then provide in section 4 an in-depth analysis of the point-sampled rendering primitive, its meaning in terms of appearance modeling and theoretically founded means of representing image radiance information at these points. Section 5 presents the details of the current implementation, which computes impostor representations for the far field. Results are presented and discussed in section 6.

2 Previous Work

Our work can be seen in the context of image-based rendering. The idea of image-based rendering is to synthesize new views based on given images. Ideally, we would like to replace distant geometry by one image, an alpha texture map, because it is very fast to render [14]. Schaufler et al. [22] and Shade et al. [24] used this idea to build a hierarchical image cache for an online system, with relaxed constraints for image quality. However, to properly capture parallax effects of the replaced geometry, it would be necessary to precalculate many alpha texture maps for several viewpoints in the view cell and to blend between them dependent on the viewing position. This is basically equivalent to storing the five-dimensional plenoptic function (the function that encodes all possible environment maps from any point in the scene [17]) and requires too much memory if high image quality is desired. A more efficient solution is a 4D parameterization of the plenoptic function, the light field [11], which can be seen as a collection of images taken from a regular grid on a single plane. At runtime it is possible to synthesize images for new viewpoints not only on this plane, but also for all viewpoints within a certain view cell behind the plane. Gortler et al. [9] independently developed a similar parameterization. They additionally use depth information for better reconstruction. Depth information can also be added as a triangle mesh to create surface light fields [19, 28]. Shum et al. [3] study the relationship between depth and (spatial) spectral support of the light field in more detail and add depth information to the light field in layers. Although light fields can be rendered interactively, memory consumption and calculation times make it hard to use them for most real-time rendering applications.

Starting from the texture map idea, depth information can be added to make an image usable for a larger number of viewpoints, for example by using layers [18, 23]. These layers can be rendered quickly on existing hardware, but they contain a strong directional bias which can lead to image artifacts, especially in complex scenes. Several authors have added depth information to images using triangles [1, 7, 8, 15, 26]. While a (layered) depth mesh can be calculated and simplified for one viewpoint, the representation is undersampled for other viewpoints, leading to disocclusion artifacts or blurring effects. The calculation of an equally sampled high quality triangle mesh remains an open problem. Finally, depth can be added per point sample. In particular, layered depth images (LDI) [16, 25] provide greater flexibility by allowing several depth values per image sample. However, warping the information seen from a view cell into the image of a single viewpoint again leads to a sampling bias. To overcome this problem, several LDIs have to be used [4, 13].

As an alternative, point-based rendering algorithms were investigated by Levoy et

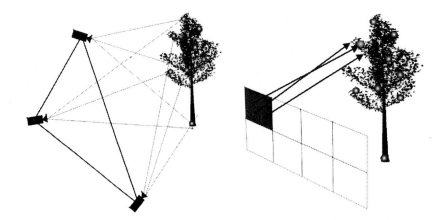

Fig. 2. *Left:* Geometry is sampled using three perspective LDI cameras from a view cell. *Right:* Rays are cast from the view cell to calculate a Monte Carlo integral. A texture map on the sampling plane records contributions for different view cell locations.

al. [12], Grossman et al. [10] and Pfister et al. [20]. These algorithms are currently not implemented in hardware and especially hole filling is a challenging problem. For faster rendering, warping can be replaced by hardware transformation together with a splatting operation [21]. The main argument for the use of points is their simplicity. However, in the context of complex geometry, points can no longer be seen as point samples on a surface [20, 21]. Therefore, our work stands in contrast to previous point rendering techniques and we will derive a characterization of points that differs fundamentally from those approaches.

3   Overview of the algorithm

We propose a rendering primitive based on points to replace geometry as seen from a view cell. The system implements the following pipeline:

- Sampling geometry: we calculate sample points of the geometry using three perspective LDIs to obtain a dense sampling for a view cell (Fig. 2, left). We call the plane defined by the three camera locations the *sampling plane*.
- Sampling appearance: The antialiased appearance of each point is calculated for different view cell locations using Monte Carlo integration. We shoot rays from a rectangular region which is contained in the triangle formed by the three cameras (see Fig. 2, right). Each point is associated with a texture map which encodes the appearance contributions for different view cell locations.
- Real-time display: point-based impostors make full use of existing rendering hardware for transforming each point as well as shading it with its associated texture map depending on the current viewer location. No additional software calculations are necessary.

4 Point-Based Impostors

4.1 Complexity of appearance

The plenoptic function $P(s, \varphi)$ completely models what is visible from any point s in space in any given direction φ. Rendering is therefore the process of reconstructing parts of the plenoptic function from samples. Both geometry and appearance information of scene objects contribute to the plenoptic function. Current rendering algorithms usually emphasize one of those aspects:

- Light fields record rays regardless of geometric information, even if they all hit the same diffuse surface.
- Other, geometric approaches usually model appearance only to a degree allowed by their lighting model. They cannot account for *microgeometry*, i.e., geometry that projects to less than a pixel. Microgeometry can have different appearance when viewed from different angles (see Fig. 3, left). This usually results in aliasing artifacts or is dealt with by blurring, thereby discarding possibly important information.

Our point-based representation contains both geometric information (the 3D location) and directionally dependent appearance information. It therefore captures all of these aspects:

- Point sampling can easily adapt to unstructured geometry in the absence of surfaces or a structured model.
- A point on a diffuse, locally flat surface which projects to more than a pixel has the same appearance from all directions and can be encoded with a single color.
- Objects with view-dependent lighting effects (e.g. specular lighting) show different colors when viewed from different angles.
- Microgeometry is also view dependent and is encoded just like lighting effects.

4.2 Geometric sampling

The first step in the creation of a point-based rendering primitive is to decide on the geometric location of the sample points. The points encode the part of the plenoptic function defined by the view cell and the geometry to be sampled. To allow hardware reconstruction, there should be no holes when projecting the points into any possible view from the view cell.

A sufficient criterion that a point-sampled surface will have no holes in a projection is that the projected points can be triangulated so that the maximum projected edge-length is smaller than the side length of a pixel [10].

It is in general difficult to prove that a particular point-based representation fulfills this criterion. For unit magnification and orthographic viewing, three orthogonal LDIs provide such an adequate sampling [13]. Although this sampling strategy works with our method, it is not well suited for far-field objects because the sampling density is not adapted to the possible viewing directions from the view cell and typically results in a large number of point samples. Therefore, our method chooses perspective LDIs to better distribute the samples with respect to the view cell.

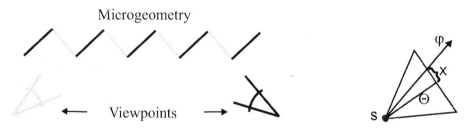

Fig. 3. *Left:* Microgeometry: if the structure in the figure projects only to a pixel for the view cell, directional appearance information is required to let it appear shaded light in the left camera and dark in the right camera. *Right:* The figure shows the relation of the plenoptic function and plenoptic image function parameters.

4.3 Appearance: the plenoptic image function

The geometric sampling step results in a set of n points $p_1, \ldots, p_n$ with fixed locations in 3D space. In this section, we derive a method to determine color values for each of these points. We examine the meaning of a point in light of our goal: for each viewing location and camera position in a view cell, the image obtained by rendering all points $p_1, \ldots, p_n$ should be a correctly filtered image of the far field objects (i.e., one slice of the plenoptic function $P(s, \varphi)$. Our derivation will show that several colors per point are needed for that.

Most rendering algorithms use a z-buffer or depth ordering to determine the visibility of the primitives they render. A point, however, is infinitely small. Its meaning is mainly determined by its reconstruction. In many reconstruction methods (as, for example, in hardware rendering) only one point is visible per pixel and determines the color of the pixel. Due to finite image resolution, a point can be visible or occluded depending only on the viewing camera orientation. The plenoptic function is not powerful enough to model this form of occlusion.

Consequently, we introduce the *plenoptic image function PIF(s, θ, x)*. The parameter s represents the 3D viewer position, θ is a camera orientation, and x is a 2D pixel coordinate in the local camera coordinate system. Fig. 3 (right) illustrates how the domains of the *PIF* and the plenoptic function relate to each other: any pair (θ, x) corresponds to one ray orientation $\varphi(\theta, x)$ from the plenoptic function, so under ideal conditions (i.e., infinitely precise displays etc.), the *PIF* is related to the plenoptic function P via

$$PIF(s, \theta, x) = P(s, \varphi(\theta, x))$$

Note that this mapping is many to one. The *PIF* with its additional parameters will allow us to incorporate the visibility term inherent to current reconstruction techniques directly into our calculations.

We now interpret points via the images they produce (their image functions) when rendered with a specific rendering algorithm—in our case, z-buffered hardware rendering.

If we consider only one point p_j alone, the point defines an image function $r_j(s, \theta, x)$. This function specifies a continuous image for each set of camera parameters (s, θ). Each of those images is set to the typical reconstruction filter of a monitor, a Gaussian centered at the pixel which the point projects to (see Fig. 4, top). However, it is very crucial to see a point p_j in relation to the other points in the point set. We have to take

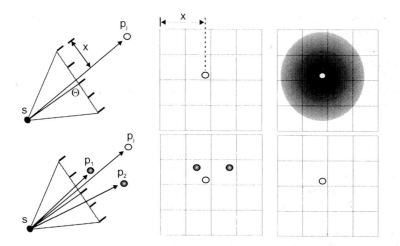

Fig. 4. These figures explain the image function of a point p_j and the influence of visibility. The left column shows a 2D cross-section for fixed camera parameters (s, θ). Note that we only show one component of the 2D image coordinates x. The central column shows the point p_j in the resulting image. The top right figure shows the image function $r_j(s, \theta, x)$. While the top row considers only point p_j, in the bottom row, two additional points p_1 and p_2 have been added. Here, the point p_1 occludes the point p_j due to the z-buffer, causing the visibility term $v_j(s, \theta)$ of point p_j to be 0. Therefore, $Q_j(s, \theta, x)$ (in the bottom right figure) is 0 for all image coordinates x.

into account a visibility term v_j which evaluates to 1 if the point p_j is visible in the image defined through the camera parameters (s, θ) and 0 otherwise. This gives us the actual image function Q_j of a point (see Fig. 4, bottom):

$$Q_j(s, \theta, x) = v_j(s, \theta) r_j(s, \theta, x)$$

From an algebraic point of view, we can regard the functions $Q_j, 1 \leq j \leq n$, as basis functions spanning a finite dimensional subspace of the space of all *PIF*s. One element PIF_{finite} of this finite dimensional subspace can be written as a weighted sum of the basis functions of the points:

$$PIF_{finite}(s, \theta, x) = \sum_j c_j Q_j(s, \theta, x)$$

Note that the weight c_j is the color value assigned to the point p_j. The weights c_j should be chosen so as to make PIF_{finite} as close as possible to PIF. This can be achieved by minimizing $\|PIF_{finite} - PIF\|$ (with respect to the Euclidean norm on the space of functions over (s, θ, x)), and the resulting weights can then be found via the dual basis functions as

$$c_j = \iiint q_j(s, \theta, x) PIF(s, \theta, x) ds \, d\theta \, dx$$

where $q_j(s, \theta, x)$ is the dual basis function (the dual basis functions are defined via $\langle q_j, Q_k \rangle = \delta_{jk}$).

This representation only assigns one color value per point, regardless of the location s in the view cell. However, because of view-dependent shading effects and micro-geometry as discussed in section 4.1, a point might need to show very different appearance from different viewing locations. Thus, we make the model more powerful by replacing the weights c_j by functions $c_j(s)$. In order to represent those functions, they are discretized with respect to the space of possible viewing locations (this is similar in spirit to the camera aperture necessary when sampling light fields). Given a basis $B_i(s)$ for this space, we can write each $c_j(s)$ in terms of this basis, with coefficients found via the dual basis $b_i(s)$:

$$c_j(s) = \sum_i c_{ij} B_i(s), \text{ where } c_{ij} = \int c_j(s) b_i(s) ds$$

One possible choice for the basis $B_i(s)$ is to use a regular subdivision of a plane with a normal directed from the view cell towards the objects. The weights c_{ij} for each point p_j can then be stored in a texture map. This means that $c_j(s)$ will be looked up in a texture map, which is typically reconstructed with a bilinear kernel, so $B_i(s)$ is actually just a bilinear basis.

Putting all parts together, the rendering process is described with the formula

$$PIF_{finite}(s, \theta, x) = \sum_{i,j} c_{ij} Q_j(s, \theta, x) B_i(s)$$

and the weights to make the PIF_{finite} resemble most closely the PIF are calculated as

$$c_{ij} = \iiint PIF(s, \theta, x) q_j(s, \theta, x) b_i(s) ds\, d\theta\, dx \qquad (1)$$

The final task is finding the dual basis functions. If our basis functions $Q_j B_i$ were orthogonal, we would have $q_j = Q_j$ and $b_i = B_i$ (apart from normalization issues). In the non-orthogonal case, however, calculating the real duals is tedious: geometric occlusion means each one would be different; one would really have to invert a large matrix for each one to find a (discretized) version of the dual. We have opted for an approximate approach inspired by signal theory: both the bilinear basis B_i and the monitor reconstruction filter r_j can be regarded as an approximation to the ideal (and orthogonal) reconstruction filter, a sinc-function. As is common practice, we approximate the ideal lowpass filter (the signal-theoretic version of dual basis functions) using Gaussians.

The integral (1) can be estimated using Monte Carlo integration with b_i and q_j as importance functions. Samples $PIF(s, \theta, x) = P(s, \varphi(\theta, x))$ are calculated with a simple ray tracer.

5   Implementation

In this section we describe the choices made in our particular implementation of the method.

5.1   Obtaining geometric samples

To place the three LDI cameras used to obtain geometric samples, a sampling plane is chosen to parameterize viewer positions within the view cell: as in light fields, we use a plane oriented from the view cell towards the far field. Then, we calculate the intersection of the supporting planes of the view cell and the far field with the sampling plane. We select three cameras on a triangle that tightly bounds the resulting polygon (i.e., the triangle with minimum circumference).

In order to determine the LDI resolution necessary to avoid holes in the reprojection of the sampled points, our method offers a sampling mechanism based on a 2D observation: suppose we have two cameras on both ends of a segment of possible viewing locations in 2D, and a short edge viewed by the two cameras. These two cameras are used to sample the endpoints of the edge. Resampling happens from a camera placed anywhere on the segment between the two cameras. It can now be shown that the "worst" discrepancy between the resampling angle and the sampling angle appears if the edge is parallel to the segment joining the two cameras, and if the center of the edge is equidistant to both cameras.

Inspired by this, we have developed a heuristic in 3D which takes the following effects into account:

- Movement within the view cell: for three cameras looking at a plane parallel to the sampling plane, the worst mutual sampling resolution occurs at the point on the plane that is equidistant from the three cameras. This point is the circumcenter of the triangle defined by the three cameras, projected on the plane in question. The sampling angle of the three cameras has to be chosen so that neighboring samples project to less than a pixel when viewed directly from the circumcenter (where the maximum projection occurs).
- Perspective: perspective cameras have varying angular resolutions in space: a feature (e.g., a triangle) projects to more pixels at the border of the viewing frustum than in the center when seen under the same viewing angle. The sampling resolution has to be increased accordingly by the factor between angular resolution in the center of the camera and at the border of the viewing frustum. For a field of view of $45°$ for example, this factor is about 1.17.
- Sampling pattern orientation: if perspective cameras are used for sampling, the sampling pattern on objects in space is tilted with respect to the viewing camera. Therefore, given a minimum sampling angle from a point, the resolution has to be calculated from the pixel diagonal and not the pixel edge. This accounts for a factor of $\sqrt{2}$.

Sampling resolution is chosen according to these factors. In practice, we employ a simple heuristic to reduce the number of points: many points are sampled sufficiently already by a single camera. This means that a triangulation of the sampling pattern from this camera in a small neighborhood contains no edge which projects to more than a pixel in any view. If a point recorded by one camera lies in a region which is sampled better and sufficiently by another camera, we remove it. This typically reduces the number of points by 40–60%, leading to a ratio of about 2–3 points projected to a screen pixel.

5.2 Monte Carlo integration of radiance fields

The goal of the Monte Carlo integration step is to evaluate integral (1) to obtain the weights c_{ij} of the reconstruction basis functions. The domain in s is a rectangle on the sampling plane. The index c_{ij} corresponds to one point p_j and one rectangle on the sampling plane represented by a texel t_i in the texture map for point p_j.

We select a viewpoint s on this rectangle (according to $b_i(s)$, a Gaussian distribution), a random camera orientation θ in which the point is in the frustum, and shoot an occlusion ray to test whether this point is visible in the selected camera (this corresponds to an evaluation of $v_j(s, \theta)$). If it is visible, we select a ray according to $q_j(s, \theta, x)$ (a Gaussian distribution centered over the pixel which the point projects to in the selected camera) and add its contribution to t_i. Rays are shot until the variance of the integral falls below a user-selectable threshold.

5.3 Compression and Rendering

Points are rendered with z-buffered OpenGL hardware. For each point, the directional appearance information is saved in a texture, parameterized by the sampling plane. The texture coordinates of a point are calculated as the intersection of a viewing ray to the point with the sampling plane. This can also be interpreted as the perspective projection of the sampling point into a viewing frustum where the apex is defined by the viewpoint and the borders of the projection plane by the four sides of the bounding rectangle on the sampling plane.

Perspective projections can be expressed using the 4x4 homogeneous texture-matrix provided by OpenGL. However, since switching textures for every point is costly, we pack as many point textures into one bigger texture as the implementation allows. This requires adding a fixed offset per point to the final texture coordinate, which, although not available in standard OpenGL, can be done using the vertex program extension [5].

Interpolation between the texture samples (which corresponds to the basis function $B_i(s)$) is done using bilinear filtering. A lower quality, but faster preview of the representation can be rendered by using only one color per point and no texture. However, directional information will be lost in this case.

To compress our representation, we calculate the variance of the color information of a texture to identify points that only require one color for the whole view cell. Further compression can be obtained by using hardware supported vector quantization [6], which provides for a fixed compression ratio of 8:1. Note that this adapts to the scene complexity: regions with low perceived geometric complexity will always be represented by simple colored points.

6   Results

We used an 800 MHz Pentium III with a GeForce II GTS graphics card for our tests. The vertex program used to calculate texture coordinates is simulated in software. To give an impression of the expected performance of a hardware implementation, we also rendered simple textured points.

Three different test scenes are used to demonstrate the behavior of point-based impostors. Table 1 shows results for each scene, based on an output screen resolution of 640x480 pixels. It includes the number of points in the impostor, the approximate number of pixels covered by the impostor for a view in the center of the view cell (based on the screen bounding box), and the resulting number of points per projected pixel. The table also shows the time required for computing the impostor, and the memory requirements. The last two rows represent average frame rates achieved for some positions within the view cell.

Generally, it can be observed that it takes about 75,000 points to cover a screen area of about 300x100 pixels.

Although we are using an unoptimized ray tracer, preprocessing times are still reasonable. For each point, an 8x2 texture map was found to sufficiently capture view-dependent effects for the view cells considered (determining the size of the texture

Results	scene1	scene2	scene3
#points	80,341	87,665	31,252
#points/screen pixel	2.35	2.42	2.8
approx. #screen pixels	34,000	36,000	11,000
Preproc. time (min)	22	41	31
Memory (MB)	1.6	1.75	0.6
Rendering performance SW (Hz)	36	32	98
Rendering performance HW (Hz)	60	54	160

Table 1. The table shows results from impostors of three scenes, calculated for a screen resolution of 640x480 pixels. Hardware rendering is emulated by rendering simple textured points.

Fig. 5. The figure shows the impostor from scene 3 placed in the city. The view cell shown in the dark rectangle is 63 meters wide and 120 meters long. The impostor shown in the light polygon is about 700 meters long and placed 200 meters from the view cell.

map automatically would warrant further investigation). The memory requirements are listed without applying the variance-based reduction of textures to single colors.

One of the strong points of our representation is high rendering quality in the presence of detailed geometry. Fig. 7 (see also appendix) shows the filtering of many thin tree branches in front of a moving specular highlight. Fig. 6 (see also appendix) demonstrates correct antialiasing even for extreme viewing angles on building fronts.

Fig. 8 (appendix, bottom) shows how a point-based impostor can be used to improve the rendering quality of the far field in an urban scene which contains several polygons per pixel. It should be noted that the improvement over geometry is even more noticeable when moving the viewpoint. Furthermore, the impostor in Fig. 8 (bottom) replaces a geometric model of about 95,000 vertices, but consists only of about 30,000 points. This shows that the impostor not only improves the rendering quality of the far field, but also reduces the rendering load on the graphics hardware. Fig. 5 shows the placement of this impostor and its view cell in the city model and gives an impression of the typical relative sizes of view cells and impostors.

In the current experimental system, view cells are formed from street segments, and impostors placed at the ends of street segments, in a fashion similar to previous impostor systems [8, 26]. Our test scene is 4 square kilometers large and consists of

174

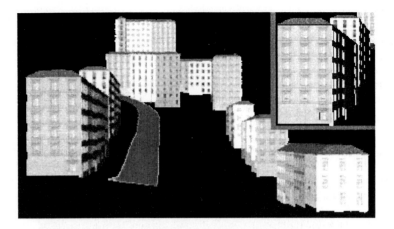

Fig. 6. An impostor for a number of buildings. The inset shows the aliasing that would result if geometry were used.

Fig. 7. Note the correct filtering of the trees against the building front and the specular highlight in the windows for the impostor (top), and severe aliasing in the trees for geometry (bottom).

2.1 million polygons. After the application of a conservative region-visibility algorithm [27], we identified view cells with too many visible polygons [2]. A rough estimate of the memory requirements using a brute force impostor placement strategy results in about 165 MB used for 437 impostors. Note, however, that the development of good impostor placement strategies is not straightforward and subject to ongoing research. Our future work also aims at reducing memory requirements by sharing information between neighboring view cells, and finding guarantees to ensure a minimum frame rate.

7 Conclusions

We have introduced point-based impostors, a new high-quality image-based representation for real-time visualization.

The value of this representation lies in the separation between the geometric sampling problem and the representation of appearance. Sampling is performed by combining layered depth images to obtain proper coverage of the image for the entire view cell. Based on the mathematical analysis of point-based models, we compute the rendering parameters using Monte Carlo integration, eliminating most of the aliasing artifacts. Rendering information is compactly encoded and can be rendered on contemporary hardware. Point-based impostors show great promise for all situations in which a geometrically very complex model constitutes the far field, such as in urban walkthroughs of detailed models. The rendering times indicate that this representation is applicable to real-time visualization applications, where frame times above 60 Hz are required.

Acknowledgements

This research was supported by the EU Training and Mobility of Researchers network (TMR FMRX-CT96-0036) "Platform for Animation and Virtual Reality" and by the Austrian Science Fund (FWF) contract no. P13867-INF.

References

1. Daniel Aliaga, Jon Cohen, Andrew Wilson, Eric Baker, Hansong Zhang, Carl Erikson, Keny Hoff, Tom Hudson, Wolfgang Stürzlinger, Rui Bastos, Mary Whitton, Fred Brooks, and Dinesh Manoclia. MMR: An interactive massive model rendering system using geometric and image-based acceleration. In *1999 Symposium on interactive 3D Graphics*, pages 199–206, 1999.
2. Daniel G. Aliaga and Anselmo Lastra. Automatic image placement to provide a guaranteed frame rate. *Computer Graphics*, 33:307–316, 1999.
3. Jin-Xiang Chai, Xin Tong, Shing-Chow Chan, and Heung-Yeung Shum. Plenoptic sampling. In *Siggrapph 2000, Computer Graphics Proceedings*, pages 307–318, 2000.
4. Chun-Fa Chang, Gary Bishop, and Anselmo Lastra. LDI tree: A hierarchical representation for image-based rendering. In *Siggraph 1999, Computer Graphics Proceedings*, pages 291–298. ACM Siggraph, 1999.
5. NVIDIA Corporation. Nv_vertex_program extension specification, 2000. available at http://www.nvidia.com/Marketing/Developer/DevRel.nsf/Pro-grammingResourcesFrame.
6. NVIDIA Corporation. Using texture compression in opengl, 2000. available at http://www.nvidia.com/Marketing/Developer/DevRel.nsf/WhitepapersFrame.
7. Lucia Darsa, Bruno Costa Silva, and Amitabh Varshney. Navigating static environments using image-space simplification and morphing. In *1997 Symposium on Interactive 3D Graphics*, pages 25–34, 1997. ISBN 0-89791-884-3.

8. Xavier Decoret, François Sillion, Gernot Schaufler, and Julie Dorsey. Multi-layered impostors for accelerated rendering. *Computer Graphics Forum*, 18(3):61–73, 1999. ISSN 1067-7055.

9. Steven J. Gortler, Radek Grzeszczuk, Richard Szeliski, and Michael F. Cohen. The lumigraph. In *SIGGRAPH 96 Conference Proceedings*, pages 43–54, 1996. held in New Orleans, Louisiana, 04-09 August 1996.

10. J. P. Grossman and William J. Dally. Point sample rendering. In *Rendering Techniques '98*, pages 181–192, 1998.

11. Marc Levoy and Pat Hanrahan. Light field rendering. In *SIGGRAPH 96 Conference Proceedings*, pages 31–42, 1996. held in New Orleans, Louisiana, 04-09 August 1996.

12. Marc Levoy and Turner Whitted. The use of points as a display primitive. Technical Report TR 85-022, University of Carolina at Chapel Hill, 1985.

13. Dani Lischinski and Ari Rappoport. Image-based rendering for non-diffuse synthetic scenes. In *Rendering Techniques '98*, pages 301–314, 1998.

14. P. Maciel and P. Shirley. Visual navigation of large environments using textured clusters. *SIGGRAPH Symposium on Interactive 3-D Graphics*, pages 95–102, 1995.

15. William R. Mark, Leonard McMillan, and Gary Bishop. Post-rendering 3D warping. In *1997 Symposium on Interactive 3D Graphics*, pages 7–16, 1997. ISBN 0-89791-884-3.

16. Nelson Max. Hierarchical rendering of trees from precomputed multi-layer Z-buffers. In *Eurographics Rendering Workshop 1996*, pages 165–174, 1996. ISBN 3-211-82883-4.

17. Leonard McMillan and Gary Bishop. Plenoptic modeling: An image-based rendering system. In *SIGGRAPH 95 Conference Proceedings*, pages 39–46, 1995. held in Los Angeles, California, 06-11 August 1995.

18. Alexandre Meyer and Fabrice Neyret. Interactive volumetric textures. In *Rendering Techniques '98*, pages 157–168, 1998.

19. Gavin Miller, Steven Rubin, and Dulce Ponceleon. Lazy decompression of surface light fields for precomputed global illumination. In *Rendering Techniques '98*, pages 281–292, 1998.

20. Hanspeter Pfister, Matthias Zwicker, Jeroen van Baar, and Markus Gross. Surfels: Surface elements as rendering primitives. In *Siggraph 2000, Computer Graphics Proceedings*, pages 335–342, 2000.

21. Szymon Rusinkiewicz and Marc Levoy. QSplat: A multiresolution point rendering system for large meshes. In *Siggraph 2000, Computer Graphics Proceedings*, pages 343–352, 2000.

22. G. Schaufler and W. Stürzlinger. A three-dimensional image cache for virtual reality. In *Proceedings of EUROGRAPHICS'96*, 1996.

23. Gernot Schaufler. Per-object image warping with layered impostors. In *Rendering Techniques '98*, pages 145–156, 1998.

24. Jonathan Shade, Dani Lischinski, David Salesin, Tony DeRose, and John Snyder. Hierarchical image caching for accelerated walkthroughs of complex environments. In *SIGGRAPH 96 Conference Proceedings*, pages 75–82, 1996. held in New Orleans, Louisiana, 04-09 August 1996.

25. Jonathan W. Shade, Steven J. Gortler, Li-wei He, and Richard Szeliski. Layered depth images. In *SIGGRAPH 98 Conference Proceedings*, pages 231–242, 1998. ISBN 0-89791-999-8.

26. François Sillion, G. Drettakis, and B. Bodelet. Efficient impostor manipulationfor real-time visualization of urban scenery. *Computer Graphics Forum*, 16(3):207–218, 1997. Proceedings of Eurographics '97. ISSN 1067-7055.

27. Peter Wonka, Michael Wimmer, and Dieter Schmalstieg. Visibility preprocessing with occluder fusion for urban walkthroughs. In *Rendering Techniques 2000*, pages 71–82, 2000.

28. Daniel N. Wood, Daniel I. Azuma, Ken Aldinger, Brian Curless, Tom Duchamp, David H. Salesin, and Werner Stuetzle. Surface light fields for 3D photography. In *Siggraph 2000, Computer Graphics Proceedings*, pages 287–296, 2000.

Editors' Note: see Appendix, p. 335 for colored figure of this paper

Opacity Shadow Maps

Tae-Yong Kim   Ulrich Neumann

taeyongk@usc.edu   uneumann@usc.edu

Computer Graphics and Immersive Technology Laboratory

Integrated Media Systems Center

University of Southern California

Abstract

Opacity shadow maps approximate light transmittance inside a complex volume with a set of planar opacity maps. A volume made of standard primitives (points, lines, and polygons) is sliced and rendered with graphics hardware to each opacity map that stores alpha values instead of traditionally used depth values. The alpha values are sampled in the maps enclosing each primitive point and interpolated for shadow computation. The algorithm is memory efficient and extensively exploits existing graphics hardware. The method is suited for generation of self-shadows in discontinuous volumes with explicit geometry, such as foliage, fur, and hairs. Continuous volumes such as clouds and smoke may also benefit from the approach.

1. Introduction

Rendering self-shadows inside volumetric objects (hair, fur, smoke, and cloud) is an important but hard problem. Unlike solid objects, a dense volume made of many small particles exhibits complex light propagation patterns. Each particle transmits and scatters rather than fully blocks the incoming rays. The strong forward scattering properties as well as the complex underlying geometry make the shadow generation difficult. However, self-shadows are crucial to capture effects such as backlighting.

Two techniques are generally used for volumetric shadows[1]; shadow maps [10, 12, 13] and ray tracing [5, 6]. In traditional depth-based shadow maps (DBSM), the scene is rendered from the light's point of view and the depth values are stored. Each point to be shadowed is projected to the light's camera and the point's depth is checked against the depth in the shadow map. In ray tracing, a ray is shot from a scene point to the light. If the ray intersects any particle on its way, shadows are detected and accumulated. Despite its accuracy, a complete ray tracing of dense volumetric objects can be prohibitive in terms of rendering time. In practice, shadow maps are often used in conjunction with ray tracing for efficiency.

A good property of DBSM is that it can be accelerated with hardware by rendering the scene and storing the depth buffer. However, severe aliasing artifacts can occur with small semi-transparent objects. In a dense volume made of small primitives, depths can vary radically over small changes in image space. The discrete nature of depth sampling limits DBSM in handling such objects. Moreover, small particles are often semi-transparent due to forward scattering. The binary decision in depth testing inherently precludes such transparency. Thus, DBSM is unsuited for dense volumes.

Rendering volumetric objects requires a precise measure of a transmittance function for any point in space. The transmittance $\tau(p)$ of a light to a point p can be written as

---

[1] For other types of shadows, refer to [14] and survey sections in [10, 15] for more recent ones.

$$\tau(p) = \exp(-\Omega), \text{ where } \Omega = \int_0^l \rho(l')dl' \tag{1}$$

In (1), l is the optical depth from the light to the point, ρ is an extinction (or a density) function along the path [1, 6, 10], and Ω is the *opacity* value at the point[2].

In the deep shadow maps (DSM) [10], each pixel stores a piecewise linear approximation of the transmittance function instead of a single depth, yielding more precise shadow computation than DBSM. Despite the compactness and quality, however, DSM requires a significant amount of data initialization time. When the volume changes in time with regard to the light (e.g. hair animation or moving lights), the generation cost can cancel out the computational benefit of the algorithm.

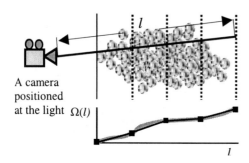

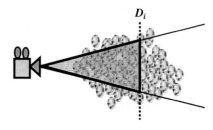

Fig. 1. The opacity function $\Omega(l)$ shown in a solid gray curve is approximated by a set of opacity maps.

Fig. 2. The volume is rendered on each opacity map, clipped by the map's depth (D_i). The transparent region illustrates the clipped volume.

Opacity shadow maps (OSM) use a set of parallel opacity maps oriented perpendicular to the light's direction (Figure 1). By approximating the transmittance function with discrete planar maps, opacity maps can be efficiently generated with hardware. On each opacity map, the scene is rendered from the light's point of view, clipped by the map's depth (Figure 2). Instead of storing depth values, each pixel stores Ω, the line integral of densities along the path from the light to the pixel. The opacity values from adjacent maps are sampled and interpolated during rendering.

Although OSM resembles volume rendering [3, 8], a major distinction is that OSM uses a volume of explicit geometry primitives (points, lines, and polygons) instead of a sampled scalar-field (voxels). Thus, it does not incur high memory requirements for a full voxel data array. Also, OSM maintains the object space accuracy of the scene model unlike volume rendering where precision is subject to sampling density.

The idea of opacity maps was exploited in feature films. For example, in the movie *'Mission to Mars'*, a software renderer was used to render the sand-vortex sequence using an SGI origin machine with 16 processors [9]. These attempts did not consider hardware acceleration and hence the rendering took a substantial amount of time (about an hour per frame). To our knowledge, none of these techniques were published.

---

[2] For brevity, we use the term *opacity* to denote the accumulative extinction function. Note that the term opacity is often used to denote the actual shadow. Thus, more precise term for Ω will be *opacity thickness* as described in [11].

2. Algorithm

Opacity shadow maps heavily rely on graphics hardware and operate on any bounded volumes represented by standard primitives such as points, lines and polygons. (For example, hairs can be represented as a cluster of lines.) The volume is sliced with a set of opacity map planes perpendicular to the light's direction. The scene is rendered to the alpha buffer, clipped by each map's depth. Each primitive contributes its associated alpha value. [3] Each pixel in the map stores an alpha value that approximates the opacity relative to the light at the pixel's position. The opacity values of adjacent maps are sampled and linearly interpolated at the position of each shadow computation point, to be used in a shadowed shading calculation.

The pseudo code below uses the following notation. P is the set of all the shadow computation sample points (or simply *shadow samples*). N is the number of maps and M is the number of shadow samples. D_i is the distance from the opacity map plane to the light ($1 \leq i \leq N$). P_i is a set of shadow samples that reside between D_i and D_{i-1}. p_j is j_{th} shadow sample ($1 \leq j \leq M$). *Depth*(p) returns a distance from p to the light. $\Omega(p_j)$ stores the opacity at p_j. $\tau(p_j)$ is the transmittance at p_j and $\Phi(p_j)$ is the computed shadow. B_{prev} and $B_{current}$ are the previous and current opacity map buffers.

Pseudo Code

```
1.      D₀= Min (Depth(pⱼ)) for all pⱼ in P (1 ≤j ≤M)
2.      for (1 ≤i ≤N)                                              (Loop 1)
3.          Determine the opacity map's depth Dᵢ from the light (Figure 3).
4.          for each shadow sample point pⱼ in P (1 ≤j ≤M)        (Loop 2)
5.              Find i such that Dᵢ₋₁≤ Depth(pⱼ) < Dᵢ
6.              Add the point pⱼ to Pᵢ.
7.      Clear the alpha buffer and the opacity maps Bₚᵣₑᵥ, B_current.
8.      for (1 ≤i ≤N)                                              (Loop 3)
9.          Swap Bₚᵣₑᵥ and B_current.
10.         Render the scene clipping it with Dᵢ₋₁ and Dᵢ.
11.         Read back the alpha buffer to B_current.
12.         for each shadow sample point pₖ in Pᵢ                 (Loop 4)
13.             Ω prev = sample(Bₚᵣₑᵥ , pₖ)
14.             Ω current = sample(B_current , pₖ)
15.             Ω = interpolate (Depth(pₖ), Dᵢ₋₁, Dᵢ, Ω prev, Ω current)
16.             τ(pₖ) = e⁻ᵏΩ
17.             Φ(pₖ) = 1.0 - τ(pₖ)
```

In loop 1, the depth of each map is determined. Uniform slice spacing is reasonable for evenly distributed volumes (Figure 3a). When the structure of the volume is known, adaptive slicing (1D BSP) can be used such that tighter spacing is used in denser or more detailed regions (Figure 3b). Considering that regions farther from the light have ever-decreasing variations of shadows, a nonlinear partition conforms to perceptual sensitivity analogous to gamma correction (Figure 3c).

---

[3] The alpha value is a user-controllable parameter that depends on the size (thickness) and the optical property (albedo) of the primitive. It also depends on the resolution of the opacity maps.

180

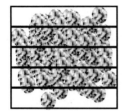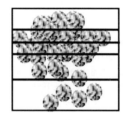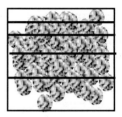

Fig. 3. Choice of slicing schemes. (a) Uniform slicing (b) Density based slicing (1D BSP) (c) Non-uniform slicing similar to Gamma Correction [4].

Prior to shadow rendering, shadow samples are produced for the primitives. In volumetric clusters, the primitives tend to be very small and thus the end points of lines and the vertices of polygons often suffice. More samples can be taken if needed. When many samples are required for each primitive, it may be useful to pre-compute the visibility and use only the visible points as shadow samples as in [15]. Loop 2 prepares a list of shadow samples that belong to each buffer. The procedure makes the shadow computation time linear in the number of samples.

Each pixel in the map stores the opacity value, which is a summation that produces the integral term Ω in equation (1). Thus each primitive can be rendered antialiased with hardware support in any order[4]. The alpha buffer is accumulated each time the volume is drawn with the OpenGL blend mode *glBlendFunc(GL_ONE,GL_ONE)*. The depth buffer is disabled. Clipping in line 10 ensures correct contribution of alpha values from the primitives and culls most primitives, speeding up the algorithm.

As loop 3 and 4 use only two opacity map buffers at a time, the memory requirement is independent of the total number of opacity maps computed. In loop 4, the shadow is computed only once for each sample. So, the amortized cost of the algorithm is linear in the number of samples. The overall complexity is *O(NM)* since the scene is rendered for each map, but the rendering cost is low with hardware acceleration.

The sample function in loop 4 can be any standard pixel sampling function such as a box filter, or higher-order filters such as a Bartlett filter and a Gaussian filter [4]. We use a 3x3 averaging kernel. Such filtering is possible because alpha values are stored instead of depths. The sampled opacity values Ω_{prev}, $\Omega_{current}$ are linearly interpolated for each point $\mathbf{p_k}$[5]. A higher order interpolation may be used. For example, four buffers will be needed for a cubic-spline interpolation.

A volume turns opaque as the opacity Ω reaches infinity. The quantization in the alpha channel limits the maximum amount of opacity that a pixel can represent. A constant κ in line 16 controls the scaling of opacity values such that $e^{-\kappa} = 2^{-d}$, where d is the number of bits per pixel (for example, κ is about 5.56 for 8 bit alpha buffer). Thus, an opacity value of 1.0 represents a complete opaqueness. The transmittance function for an opaque surface is a step function [10]. Although step functions are

---

[4] The order can be arbitrary due to the commutative nature of addition (or integral).

[5] $\Omega(p_k) = t\Omega_{current} + (1.0 - t)\Omega_{prev}, t = (Depth(p_k) - D_{i-1})/(D_i - D_{i-1})$

approximated with a large number of maps, the integration of opaque objects is more efficiently achieved by adding a traditional depth buffer shadow map (Figure 5).

3. Results

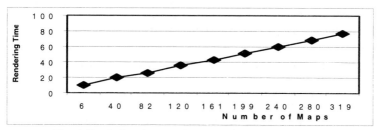

Fig. 4. Rendering time as a function of the number of maps

The performance of the algorithm is tested with a hair model of about 340,000 lines (Plate 1). Opacity maps are created at a resolution of 512 x 512 with uniform slicing scheme. The rendering time is linear in the number of the maps (Figure 4). Loop 3 and 4 account for most of the calculation time. Other steps such as the bounding box calculation (0.09 sec), assigning shadow samples to the maps (2.21 sec), and object shadow map generation (0.24 sec) use constant time. The slope of the graph in Figure 4 indicates the hardware's performance. About 4 opacity maps per second are computed using an SGI 540 NT Workstation with a 550Mhz Pentium CPU that can render about five million triangles per second. Figure 5 shows selected opacity maps. Plate 2 shows the images of a hair model of about 500,000 lines at various lighting conditions. Each hair strand is shaded using a lighting model in [7].

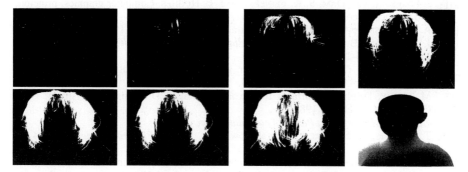

Fig. 5. Opacity shadow maps. Each ith map is shown from left to right, top to bottom (i = 1,6,14,26,40,52,60). The last figure shows a depth map for the opaque head and torso.

4. Discussion and Conclusion

Opacity shadow maps (OSM) provide a fast and memory efficient solution to rendering time-varying volumetric self-shadows without requiring any expensive preprocessing. Well suited for discontinuous volumes with explicit geometry (hair, fur, grass, and particle systems), it may be also used for continuous volumes (clouds and smoke) that are often sampled in voxel grids or implicitly defined. For example, clouds can be represented with independently moving point samples. Smoke can be

182

represented with a set of lines that vary their thickness and length in time.

A tradeoff between the speed and the quality is achieved by varying the number of maps. In complex geometry, the self-shadowing procedure can be viewed as a convolution of two high frequency signals, one from the geometry, and the other from the shadows. The study of the human visual system indicates that humans do not easily separate one signal from such mixed signals [2]. OSM mimics a low-pass filter for shadow signals. Due to the perceptual effects of visual masking, the degradation in perceived quality may be lower than quantitative measures might predict (Plate 3).

The opacity map farthest from the light can be used to compute shadows cast from the volume to other scene objects. A scene with many volumes can be spatially partitioned and the opacity maps can be composited. Instead of drawing every volume, the line 7 of the algorithm can be rewritten as 'Load the stored alpha buffer for the volumes closer to the light'. The partitioning scheme can improve the performance and reduce memory requirements for the scene graph. The simplicity of OSM may also allow further acceleration with multi-texture or 3D-texture hardware.

Acknowledgement

This work was funded by DARPA and the Annenberg Center at USC. Funding and research facilities were also provided from the NSF through its ERC funding of the Integrated Media Systems Center. The authors thank anonymous reviewers for many valuable comments.

References

[1]   J. F. BLINN, Light reflection functions for simulation of clouds and dusty surfaces, *SIGGRAPH Proceedings*, Vol. 16, pp. 21-29, 1982.

[2]   M. BOLIN AND G. W. MEYER, A frequency based ray tracer, *SIGGRAPH Proceedings*, Vol. 29, pp. 409-418, 1995.

[3]   R. DREBIN, L. CARPENTER, AND P. HANRAHAN, Volume rendering, *SIGGRAPH Proceedings*, Vol. 22, pp. 65 – 74, 1988.

[4]   J. FOLEY, A. VAN DAM, S. K. FEINER, AND J. F. HUGHES, Computer graphics, principles and practice, Second Edition, *Addison-Wesley*, July, 1995.

[5]   A. S. GLASSNER, An introduction to ray tracing, *Academic Press,* 1993

[6]   J. KAJIYA AND B. P. HERZEN, Ray tracing volume densities, *SIGGRAPH Proceedings*, Vol. 18, pp. 165-174, 1984.

[7]   J. KAJIYA AND T. KAY, Rendering fur with three dimensional textures, *SIGGRAPH Proceedings*, Vol. 23, pp. 271-280, 1989.

[8]   M. LEVOY, Display of surfaces from volume data, Ph.D. thesis, University of North Carolina at Chapel Hill, 1989.

[9]   J. P. LEWIS, *Disney TSL, Personal communication.*

[10] T. LOKOVIC AND E. VEACH, Deep shadow maps, *SIGGRAPH Proceedings*, Vol. 34, pp. 385-392, 2000.

[11] S. N. PATTANAIK AND S. P. MUDUR, Computation of global illumination in a participating medium by Monte Carlo simulation, *The Journal of Visualization and Computer Animation*, Vol. 4(3), pp. 133-152, John Wiley & sons, 1993.

[12] W. T. REEVES, D. H. SALESIN, AND R. L. COOK, Rendering antialiased shadows with depth maps, *SIGGRAPH Proceedings*, Vol. 21, pp. 283-291, 1987.

[13] L. WILLIAMS, Casting curved shadows on curved surfaces, *SIGGRAPH Proceedings,* Vol. 12, pp. 270-274, August, 1978.

[14] A. WOO, P. POULIN, AND A. FOURNIER, A survey of shadow algorithms, *IEEE Computer Graphics and Applications, 10(6),* pp. 13-32, November, 1990.

[15] H. ZHANG, Forward shadow mapping, *Rendering Techniques '98*, Vol. 9, pp. 131-138, Springer-Verlag, 1998.

Editors' Note: see Appendix, p. 336 for colored figures of this paper

Interactive Rendering of Trees
with Shading and Shadows

Alexandre Meyer   Fabrice Neyret   Pierre Poulin

{Alexandre.Meyer|Fabrice.Neyret}@imag.fr   poulin@iro.umontreal.ca
iMAGIS-GRAVIR/IMAG-INRIA   LIGUM

Abstract. The goal of this paper is the interactive rendering of 3D trees covering a landscape, with shading and shadows consistent with the lighting conditions. We propose a new IBR representation, consisting of a hierarchy of Bidirectional Textures, which resemble 6D lightfields. A hierarchy of visibility cube-maps is associated to this representation to improve the performance of shadow calculations.

An example of hierarchy for a given tree can be a small branch plus its leaves (or needles), a larger branch, and the entire tree. A Bidirectional Texture (BT) provides a billboard image of a shaded object for each pair of view and light directions. We associate a BT for each level of the hierarchy. When rendering, the appropriate level of detail is selected depending on the distance of the tree from the viewpoint. The illumination reaching each level is evaluated using a visibility cube-map. Thus, we very efficiently obtain the shaded rendering of a tree with shadows without loosing details, contrary to mesh simplification methods. We achieved 7 to 20 fps fly-throughs of a scene with 1000 trees.

Keywords: Real-time rendering, natural scenes, forests, IBR, levels of detail, billboards

URL: http://www-imagis.imag.fr/Publications/2001/MNP01/index.html

1 Introduction

Walk- and fly-throughs of natural landscapes with the best possible visual quality have been a continuous challenge since the beginning of Computer Graphics. In real-time applications such as simulators and games, users want ever more convincing realism (*i.e.,* more trees, better looking trees). In off-line applications such as impact studies and special effects, users want the rendering software to compute more rapidly.

The rendering of tree covered landscapes is especially demanding, because of the total amount of details, the complex lighting situation (shading of small shapes, shadows, sky illumination), and the complex visibility situation (there are no large blockers that can be efficiently exploited).

Fortunately, trees also have interesting properties. Their complexity of appearance is counterbalanced by significant redundancy of elements, and their structure is naturally hierarchical. Trees are composed of a trunk and main branches, which group small branches together. Boughs are made of leaves or needles; and leaves, needles, boughs, branches, and even trees resemble each other. These properties allow many modeling simplifications: elements of a family can be represented as instances of a few base models, and complex objects as a collection of similar, simpler, objects.

In this paper, we exploit this notion by considering alternate and hierarchical representations and techniques to efficiently render trees, including shading and shadows.

184

Our goal is to render large landscapes covered with dense forests of trees with good image quality.

To achieve this level of efficiency and quality, we introduce a hierarchical bidirectional texture (HBT), inspired by recent image-based rendering (IBR) representations. It encodes the appearance of a tree model using several levels of detail relying on the hierarchy described above, for many view and illumination directions. This allows for fast rendering adapted to the amount of detail required.

The same hierarchical organization of a tree is also exploited for the visibility computation occuring within the elements of a hierarchical level. Combining the occlusions by traversing the shadowing structure upwards provides efficient and appropriate soft shadows within the tree itself, and also between different trees. This allows for the real-time calculation of shadows while the light source is moving.

All these techniques have been implemented in hardware rendering using OpenGL 1.2, and results are presented and discussed.

This paper is organized as follows. In Section 2 we review several approaches related to the rendering of natural scenes. In Section 3 we describe our representation, the *Hierarchy of Bidirectional Textures* (HBT). We explain in Section 4 how to render an object using this representation, then we provide in Section 5 the global algorithm for the rendering of the scene. Once the use of the representation is clear, we detail in Section 6 how to built it from an existing object (*e.g.,* a polygonal tree model). We describe our implementation, show our results, and give performance measures in Section 7, before concluding.

2 Previous Work

In early fight simulators, trees and other objects (*e.g.,* buildings) were painted on the floor, represented by very simple polyhedrons (pyramids, cubes), or using the very first IBR representation, the sprite. Billboards, another early IBR representation, can be seen as an extension to sprites, since they always face the observer but are attached to a 3D frame. These are still used in current simulators [17] and off-line video productions on a short schedule. Games in the mid-80's to the mid-90's, *i.e.,* before the arrival of 3D graphics boards, extensively used sprites and billboards to produce interactive fake 3D environments, *e.g.,* for car races. With the generalization of hardware-accelerated 3D and textures, workstations and home PC started using *cross-trees*, made of 2 to 3 orthogonal faces textured with a transparent image, thus behaving like 3D objects. This has been generalized in applications up to a dozen textured faces or more, used to represent foliage.

Several early papers have described methodologies to model the shape of trees. We do not discuss these here, since we concentrate on efficient rendering. Numerous methods have been progressively introduced to precompute polygonal levels of detail or simplify meshes on the fly. These are also beyond the scope of this discussion, as they do not behave very well for trees, suffering numerous artifacts during a geometric simplification. Nonetheless, an hybrid solution dedicated to trees [32] achieved nice results, but is still not sufficient for our quality and real-time goals.

The most interesting solutions result from the use of representations other than meshes, proposing a way to efficiently achieve both quality and quantity. An early example was particle systems [23, 24], in which geometry is replaced by strokes, thus producing the first dense forest images. Although originally too slow, the approach is now used in real-time applications.

Since 1995, the creativity in the field of alternate representations has exploded, following different tracks:

- IBR reuses real or synthetic views of objects [10, 27, 29, 8, 1], and in particular lightfields [9, 6], storing the color for the various possible rays hitting an object. While it can capture and redisplay most views of a tree, including under different views, the shading and shadowing remain fixed, and lightfields are very memory intensive. They have been applied to surfaces [16, 34] to incorporate some shading effects, however memory requirements are still too large to represent good quality trees.
- In a dual manner, textures have been extended to reproduce the view angle dependency with directional texture functions or relief textures [4, 20], or even to simulate objects in volumes with layered impostors, volumetric textures, and LDI [25, 15, 28]. Between these last techniques and the early cross-trees, Max *et al.* have combined Z-buffers used as a representation in various ways [13, 11, 12], with different orientations, organized in a level of detail hierarchy, or more recently with multilayers. Some of these methods have been used explicitly for trees: volumetric textures [15, 19], and the work of Max *et al.*
- A totally different approach lies in point-based rendering, such as surfels [21]. To date, it is not adapted to sparse geometry like foliage, but we think it might be a promising technique.

Bidirectional reflection distribution functions (BRDF) [18] encode the proportion of reflected light given a pair of incident and reflected (view) directions. They are thus used in high quality rendering, and represent precisely the aspect lacking in usual IBR and textural encodings. BTFs, and to a certain extent surface lightfields, are a way to introduce this missing dimension.

Our representation shares various aspects with the BTFs [4, 3], the hierarchical IBR of Max *et al.* [12], billboards, and lightfields. Like Max *et al.* [12], we manage levels of detail using a hierarchy of alternate representations: an alternate object type encodes a set of smaller objects, which can be themselves standard geometry or alternate representation. Depending on the apparent screen size, we use either the large object or the collection of smaller ones, depending on the level. Our alternate representation is a BTF, instead of layered Z-buffer as for Max *et al.* [11, 12]. These BTFs are precomputed using multiple local pre-renderings as [4], but using the 6 degrees of freedom of [3, 2]: position on texture, view direction, and light direction. Indeed, we sample all these directions because we want to encode 3D objects, while [3, 2] sample only 3 of the 4 degrees of freedom, since their purpose is the encoding of surface materials, not 3D objects; in case of anisotropy, they simply add a second sample set. As for lightfield and BRDF representations, we have to manage the sampled representation of a 4D direction space. However, our structure is much more compact despite its 6D nature, as we use it only for distant objects that appear small on the screen. Using billboards, we share the representation of 3D objects with textures which adapt to the point of view.

The auxiliary representation we introduce to accelerate the shadows was inspired by horizon maps [14, 31] and visibility precomputed for cells [5, 26], in a more approximate fashion. On the other hand it is 3D since all directions are valid, and also hierarchical, since it is connected to the HBT representation. We detail this representation in the next section.

3 Our Representation

There are 3 elements in our representation:

- The **BTF encoding** of an object, which is an alternate representation that produces similar images of this object even when varying the observer and light locations. This is explained in Section 3.1 and illustrated by Fig. 1.
- The **HBT structure** associated to a complex object, treated in Section 3.2, which extends the existing hierarchical scene graph of this object with level of detail information (see Fig. 5): a BTF is associated to each level. Reciprocally, most of the objects contained in a given level have an associated BTF. Since this work focuses on trees, these objects are basically organized as multiple instances of one similar base object (*e.g.*, a branch), plus possibly one mesh object (*e.g.*, a piece of trunk). This greatly reduces the total number of different BTFs, we use 3 per each kind of tree in our implementation.
- The structure for shadows, *i.e.*, the **hierarchy of visibility cube-maps**, that is described in Section 3.3 and illustrated by Fig. 2.2.

3.1 Bidirectional Texture Functions

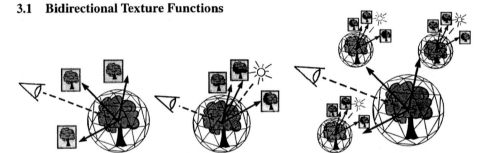

1.1: A billboard is reconstructed from a given view direction by combining the 3 closest images stored in the sampled sphere of view directions.

1.2: A billboard is reconstructed from a given light direction by combining the 3 closest images stored in the sampled sphere of light directions.

1.3: The complete BTF allows the reconstruction of a billboard for given view and light directions by combining up to 9 stored images (in our implementation).

Fig. 1. The Bidirectional Texture Function representing a tree.

The principle of the representation is to associate a billboard representing an object with each pair of view and light directions (see Fig. 1 and Fig. 6), much like a BRDF associates a color with a pair of such directions. If we limit ourselves to objects that are not pathological shading-wise, only a small set of directions will be necessary. Moreover, these billboards are targeted to replace the detailed 3D representation of objects appearing small on the screen, and therefore their texture resolution can be very coarse (*e.g.*, 32×32 or 64×64 in our implementation). At rendering time, we reconstruct an image for given view and light directions by interpolating between the closest precomputed billboards. We detail the rendering in Section 4 and the BTF construction in Section 6.

It is better to avoid mixing in the same billboards the effects of sun illumination and ambient (sky) light, otherwise it would not be possible to separately tune their colors and intensities, or to consider several light sources. As an example, we would like to deal with the weather becoming overcast (showing only ambient term), the sun turning red while the sky remains light blue, or extra light sources such as helicopter headlights. Thus we store separately "ambient" billboards associated with each view direction. Note that this "ambient light" differs from classical Phong ambient since it takes occlusions into account.

In practice we use either 6, 18, 66, or 258 samples for the view directions, evenly distributed on a sphere. For each sample direction, we associate a similar sampled sphere for light directions.[1] A small color texture with transparencies is stored for each pair of directions. To efficiently determine the closest 3 samples at rendering time, a precomputed table gives the 3 closest sampled directions for any given vector.

The instances of the obtained BTFs are associated with a local frame of reference and a scale factor, much like standard objects.

3.2 Hierarchy of BTFs (or HBTs)

We rely on the existing scene graph hierarchy, knowing that for trees this hierarchy typically contains several levels and massive instancing.

A BTF is associated to each level in the hierarchy (Fig. 2.1 and Fig. 5), representing its coarse level of detail. A level consists of a set of objects. Each of them can be unique or an instance of a given base object, located and oriented using its frame of reference. Most base objects should have an associated BTF, except if their shape is very simple. At rendering time, either the level's BTF or the set of objects will be used, depending on the distance.

Please note that in this paper, we call "highest" the coarsest level, representing the entire object.

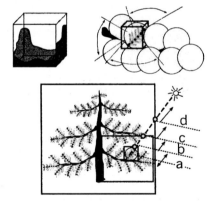

2.1: Hierarchy of BTFs. *Top:* a typical tree model, showing a natural hierarchy (leaves or needles, small branches, main branches, trunk). *Bottom:* 3 BTFs associated to 3 levels of the hierarchy. For instance, the main branch (middle) is composed of instances of small branches (left).

2.2: Hierarchy of visibility cube-maps. *Top:* a visibility cube-map is associated to each instance, here a small branch on a main branch. It registers the occlusion (represented by grey zones on the cube-map) generated by its environment in every direction. *Bottom:* to obtain the total visibility in a given direction, we combine the corresponding values in the cube-maps of the higher levels, *e.g.*, b, c, d for the small branch. Self-shadows (a) are already encoded in the branch BTF.

---

[1]The number of samples can be different on the 2 spheres. In practice, the quality of interpolation is more sensitive to the view directions than to the light directions.

3.3 Hierarchy of Visibility Cube-maps for Shadows

Since we are using hardware rendering we cannot rely on it to compute shadows, and because the scene is complex we cannot evaluate it on the fly using shadow rays. [2] Thus we use precomputation information, but we still want the light direction to change in real-time. As we cannot afford a per-pixel shadow evaluation, we will evaluate the visibility at the billboard corners, and let the hardware interpolate.

Note that self-shadows are already represented in the BTF associated with the object (*i.e.*, the current level of detail), thus we only have to account for shadowing caused by occluders outside the object (*i.e.*, at the upper levels). We store the visibility around the current object (Fig. 2.2(top)), using cube-maps. The idea is analog to the horizon maps [14, 31] (except that those are 1D while we need 2D), or to visibility precomputed per cell [5, 26]. A cube-map represents the visibility at a given location. For each light direction, we precompute the total amount of light reaching this location, which gives the amount of occlusion in this direction, stored in the corresponding pixel of the visibility cube-map. [3] For an object, we sample the visibility at several locations, and the visibility at any location is estimated by interpolating the cube-maps. [4] In our implementation, we used the 8 corners of the bounding volume. In the following, the "visibility cube-map" associated to an object refers to this set of cube-maps, and its value for a given direction refers to the interpolation of the corresponding value in the cube-maps within the set. The pixel values correspond to opacities in the range [0,1], and are used at rendering time to modulate the color of the billboard in order to get the shadows. Note that the dynamic nature of this occlusion value allows for transparent objects, antialiasing, and soft shadows.

Computing and storing a different cube-map for every instance of objects in our scene would be excessively costly, given the total number of small branches in the forest. Instead, we rely on a hierarchical structure following the HBT hierarchy, and separate the occlusions occuring inside one level from the occlusions occuring outside: for a given level in the hierarchy, a visibility cube-map is associated to each instance of the objects in the set. It only represents the occlusions caused by the objects within the set. At rendering time, the illumination received by an object from a given light direction is modulated by combining the values of the cube-maps at the current and higher levels of the hierarchy, as shown on Fig. 2.2(bottom).

The status of shadows is thus as follows:

- self-shadowing is encoded in the BTF (represented by a in Fig. 2.2);
- a visibility cube-map encodes the blocking of light between its associated object and the cube-map associated to the entire hierarchy level (corresponding to b and c in Fig. 2.2);
- the cube-map at the highest level of the hierarchy encodes the blocking of light coming from outside, within the entire scene (stored in d in Fig. 2.2).

Therefore a different cube-map has to be stored for every instance of the highest level objects in the scene. In contrast, for an intermediate hierarchy level, since the cube-maps of objects handle only the visibility within this level (and not relatively to the entire scene), we only need one cube-map per instance of an object in the level. For instance, each main branch constituting a tree has its own cube-map, but as the trees

---

[2]A global shadowmap cannot be used either because the objects are partly transparent.

[3]The visibility cube-map is thus the dual of a shadowmap, which encodes the visibility of every location in the scene for one single light direction.

[4]We use software interpolation when the value is needed at a given vertex, and hardware interpolation when rastering a billboard.

in the landscape are instances of one single tree, we do not need to consider a new visibility cube-map for each branch in the scene. In our implementation, the maps are $32 \times 32 \times 6$, and the highest level corresponds to a tree, so the total required memory is acceptable (see Section 7). If necessary, we could add an extra level consisting of a group of trees.

We also precompute the average value of each cube-map, that gives the ambient visibility (*i.e.*, the sky occlusion); this will be used to evaluate the ambient illumination.

4 Rendering an HBT

To render an HBT, first we need to determine the appropriate level of detail according to its apparent size in the image. This is done by using the level whose billboard pixels projection is close to the screen pixels size. Then all the objects in the 'opened' levels of the hierarchy, either polygonal meshes or BTF, are rendered from back to front. To render a BTF, we reconstruct a billboard for the current observer and light directions, and then compute its illumination taking into account light color, sky color, and shadows.

4.1 Reconstructing an Image from a BTF

Formally, the reconstruction problem is mainly the same as for a BRDF: we have to sum weighted values of the closest samples. Three classical issues are then: how to choose the best samples and weights, how many samples, and how to find them efficiently.

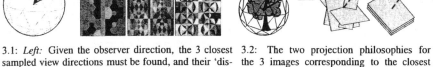
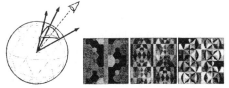

3.1: *Left:* Given the observer direction, the 3 closest sampled view directions must be found, and their 'distance' to the current direction calculated. *Right:* The 3 tables giving the precalculated 3 closest sampled directions (the colors encode the sample ids).

3.2: The two projection philosophies for the 3 images corresponding to the closest view directions: cross-tree like (middle), and billboard-like (right).

Our implementation is straightforward regarding these issues. As we separate the 4D table into a sampled sphere for view directions and another one for light directions, we have to find in which cell bounded by 3 samples a given direction falls (Fig. 3.1(left)). To be more efficient, we construct a precomputed table that directly provides the 3 sample directions for any given direction (Fig. 3.1(right)). The blending coefficients correspond to the barycentric coordinates within the cell on the sphere. Since the 3 billboards corresponding to the 3 samples from the view direction result themselves from the blend of the 3 samples from the light direction, we get 9 billboards to blend. The blending coefficients are the products of the barycentric coordinates relative to the view cell and to the light cell. However 9 can be considered a bit high.[5] To reduce this number, we do not consider samples associated to coefficients below a given threshold and we renormalize the other coefficients. It might be possible to reduce this number even further using some similarity criteria, considering only the samples that add enough information.

---

[5]Especially when noticing that directly considering a 4D-sphere for directions would have yielded 5-vertex cells, *i.e.*, the shape of a 4D-simplex.

As we deal with images instead of scalars in BRDFs, there are 2 extra issues: how to project each image onto the screen, and how to blend them together, knowing that we want to use the hardware Z-buffer that is not totally compliant with transparent images (see Appendix).

Two main choices exist to address the projection onto the screen, depending whether the billboard or the cross-textured philosophy is preferred for trees (Fig. 3.2):

- considering each image as a projected slice, that should then keep its original orientation;
- considering each image as a billboard, that are consequently mapped at the same location, *i.e.*, facing the eye.

The first solution provides more parallax effects especially if very few directions are available. The drawback is that the bounding volume depends on the angle of view, and that the opacity is poorly distributed, *i.e.*, we get a higher density where the images superimpose. The second solution is well adapted for objects having cylindrical or spherical symmetry: as the image is always facing the observer, the bounding volume is more stable and the opacity better distributed. Note that with more sampled directions, the two solutions are closer, so it is better to use the simplest one, *i.e.*, billboards. For a low number of samples (*e.g.*, 6 directions), it is probably better to choose the strategy depending on the look of objects: in such case, we used the standard cross-images.

4.2 Shadowing an Object

An object has to be modulated by the received illumination before it is drawn. The amount of light is simply obtained by combining the opacity values for the current light source direction in the visibility cube-maps (VCM) associated to the current object and all the levels above (Fig. 2.2). Combining two opacity values is done with the following scheme $Opacity_{combined} = 1 - (1 - Opacity_{levelB}) \times (1 - Opacity_{levelA})$. This value is multiplied by the light source intensity and color, then used as the polygon color when drawing the billboards as described above. We can also consider a cloud map to modulate the sun intensity:

$$illumination_L = C_L \prod_{level\ k} 1 - VCM_k(L)$$

To handle multiple light sources, we iterate the process above, yielding a maximum of 9 new passes per light source with our implementation. We could potentially exploit the fact that any additional light source in a landscape should have a more limited visual impact on the entire forest (*e.g.*, helicopter headlights) and therefore treat it only for the closer trees.

The last component is the ambient term: to consider diffuse illumination not directly due to the sun, namely, sky illumination, we have to sum another image corresponding to the ambient contribution. Since it does not depend on light direction, we only have to combine 3 billboards, associated to the view direction sampled sphere. The "ambient shadowing" is obtained by multiplying the average visibility associated to the cube-maps and the average cloud transparency.

$$illumination_{amb} = C_{sky} \prod_{level\ k} 1 - average\_VCM_k$$

So $C = \sum_{light\ s} HBT(V, L_s)\ illumination_L + HBT_{amb}(V)\ illumination_{amb}$
where V is the view direction and L_s the direction of the light source s.

As stated in Section 3.3, all these computations are done in software using the various precomputed tables, and evaluated at the 4 billboard corners (or possibly only once at the billboard center, for small details). The hardware interpolates these values when rasterising the billboard.

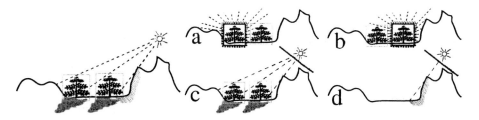

Fig. 4. The 4 kinds of shadow interaction between trees and terrain. *Left*: desired effects. *a,b*: The visibility cube-maps of each tree take into account the presence of both the mountain (and ground) and the other trees (self-shadows are included in the BTFs and in the cube-maps down in the hierarchy, see Fig. 2.2). *c*: The alpha-shadowmap accounts for the soft shadows of the trees on the ground. *d*: The Z-shadowmap (or *depth map*) accounts for the self-shadows of the mountain (any of the numerous shadowing algorithms for terrain could be used instead).

5 Rendering the Landscape

The global scene rendering algorithm is simple: first we render the terrain (and possible extra opaque objects), then we consider all the objects at their highest level (*i.e.*, trees) from back to front, culling those that are clearly not visible (outside the view frustum, and if possible behind the mountains, using a conservative occlusion technique [35, 5, 26], or extending techniques dedicated to terrains [14, 30, 31]). The rendering of HBT objects is then processed as described in Section 4.

The last issue is the shading and shadowing of the terrain. We could use the same principle described in Section 4.2, applied at the vertices of the terrain mesh. But the resolution of the shadows would probably be too coarse, and a visibility cube-map would have to be stored at each vertex which is probably too much. We prefer to simply use shadowmaps [33, 7], recomputed when the light direction changes.[6] In fact, two different kinds of shadowmaps have to be combined: one dealing with transparent objects (the trees), and the other with opaque objects (the terrain), as illustrated in Fig. 4(bottom). These shadowmaps are built by rendering the scene from the sun location.[7] For the first shadowmap, only the trees transparency is drawn (*i.e.*, we considere only the alpha value of textures), as a grey level. The terrain is drawn invisible (*i.e.*, white): it should not produce a shadow, but it should hide the trees behind the mountains. For the second shadowmap, which takes into account the terrain self-shadowing (*e.g.*, the shadow of a mountain on the valley), a depth map is used. Note that any terrain shadowing technique such as horizon map [14, 30] could be used instead, which is provided in hardware on the SGI *Infinite Reality*.

6 Building the Data

Our scenes are mainly composed of a terrain and many instances of one or more tree models. We need to encode an existing tree model into our representation, as transparently as possible for the user. Our only assumption is that instances are massively used to design a tree: *e.g.*, a tree is composed of numerous instances of a few branch models, which are composed of numerous instances of small branches and leaves (or needles).

---

[6]Here a shadowmap can be used because the terrain is opaque (while trees are not).

[7]Unfortunately building these 2 shadowmaps takes a significant amount of time using current SGI hardware. When the light direction moves, it is thus better not to update these at each frame.

We rely on this existing hierarchy to organize our levels of detail.

We have two hierarchical structures to built: the BTFs encoding the appearance of each subset of a tree (including the tree itself), and the visibility cube-maps encoding how the environment modulates the received illumination of each element.

The entire scheme and structure are illustrated by Fig. 5.

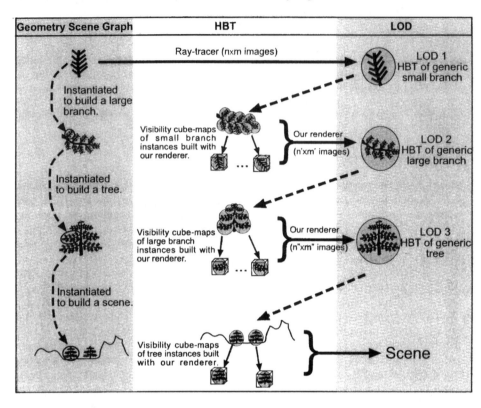

Fig. 5. Building the data.

6.1 Building an HBT

A BTF is a collection of images of a shaded object from various view directions and light directions (Fig. 6). We proceed in the same spirit as [4], adding the loop for light directions. We have two kinds of objects:

- The lowest level of the hierarchy is composed of standard objects. We use a ray-tracer to produce the views of mesh models even though final rendering is with a Z-buffer algorithm. Ray tracing allows us to easily get self-shadowing, antialiasing, transparencies, and to use complex shaders (*e.g.*, the shading of needles can be analytically integrated [?], while the cylinders should be discretized if a Z-buffer were used).
- The higher levels of the hierarchy are mainly composed of BTFs, plus possibly a few simple polygonal meshes (*e.g.*, for the trunk). We use the hardware Z-buffer to produce the views of these higher levels, in order to guarantee a consistent shading when either the lower or the higher level of detail is used during the

interactive rendering. Indeed, we use the same rendering algorithm as for interactive rendering, which provides us with shadows cast between the elements using the visibility cube-map structure.

In addition to the light-dependent BTFs, we also have to build the small set of light-independent BTFs corresponding to the ambient term, which are used for the sky illumination. They are currently produced by rendering the object with the ambient term only, taking into account ambient visibility. In our implementation, the views are 32×32 or 64×64 RGBA images.

6.2 Building the Visibility Hierarchy

A visibility cube-map associated to an object encodes the light occlusion in every direction due to the environment, but limited to the elements in the hierarchical level it belongs to or the entire scene for the highest level.

Thus for each pixel of the cube-map, the energy transfer between the light source (the sun) in the corresponding direction and the bounding volume of the object (taking occlusions into account) should be evaluated, and the amount of occlusion should be stored. As a cube-map has to be computed for each instance of a tree model in the scene taking into account a complex environment, this precomputation can be costly.

We implemented an approximative, yet very efficient simplification, using our OpenGL-based rendering algorithm. We place the camera at the center of the cube, and render the appropriate environment (in fact, only its transparency, as a grey level) in the 6 directions. This corresponds to the illumination received at the center, instead of the average value received by the object.

Once the cube-map is built, we need to compute its average value, that is used to evaluate the ambient (*i.e.,* sky) illumination.[8] Note that the cube-map is a generalization of the horizon map [14], while the average value is equivalent to an accessibility (or exposure) map.

7 Results

In our implementation, billboard images are 32×32 or 64×64 RGBA textures. Observer and light directions spheres are discretized with 6 or 18 evenly distributed samples. Thus regular BTFs are $32 \times 32 \times 4 \times 6 \times 6$ (144 Kb), $32 \times 32 \times 4 \times 18 \times 6$ (432 Kb), or $32 \times 32 \times 4 \times 18 \times 18$ (1.3 Mb), and ambient BTFs are $32 \times 32 \times 4 \times 6$ (24 Kb) or $32 \times 32 \times 4 \times 18$ (72 Kb). Our tree models are produced by an L-system [22]; we used 2 kinds of pine-trees and a prunus tree for our tests. We consider 3 hierarchical levels: a small branch with leaves or needles, a main branch made of instances of small branches, and a tree made of main branches. The pine-tree has 30 main branches, 300 boughs, and 30,000 needles. The whole HBT thus consists of 3 BTFs (0.5 to 4 Mb), plus the same scene graph as the tree with standard geometry.

The scene contains 1000 trees, so there are $8 \times (1000 + 30 + 10)$ visibility cube-maps. The cubes are $32 \times 32 \times 6$ luminance textures (6 Kb), thus the visibility structure represents roughly $8 \times 6 \times 1000$ Kb = 48 Mb. If this is unacceptable,[9] one could easily introduce a fourth hierarchical level consisting of a cluster of a dozen trees, which would divide the memory expense by the same amount.

Precalculation time is about 75 minutes using an $Onyx^2$ *Infinite Reality*, 2/3 for visibility and 1/3 for the HBT.

---

[8] See effect on Fig.7(middle).

[9] However, note that this data structure lies in main memory, and is never loaded on the graphics board.

194

Our global rendering algorithm is straightforward: we cull only the trees completely outside the view frustum, we sort the trees, then the parts of the trees for 'opened' levels of detail. We consider sun and sky illuminations, *i.e.*, one light source plus ambient. Our optimization for billboard combination requires on average 5 images instead of 9. In the worst case we have to draw 15 billboards per object,[10] which requires a high fill rate. The SGI we use has no multitexturing ability. However recent graphics boards such as Nvidia or ATI do have this feature, which allows us to decrease the number of passes to 5 (or 3, if the billboards of low contribution are eliminated).

We produced animations of 640×480, using an $Onyx^2$ *Infinite Reality*, showing a fly over a scenery covered by 1000 trees. The frame rate is 7 to 20 fps. We observed a 20% gain using an Nvidia board on a PC, without using multitexturing. Using this feature, we should gain another factor of 2 to 3.

A pine tree represented by a polygonal mesh is about 120k polygons. Using the lowest level of detail (*i.e.*, maximum resolution) yields a gain of 8 in the rendering time. Switching to the middle level gives an extra gain of 18. With the highest (*i.e.*, coarsest) level, we have another gain of 30.

8 Conclusion

We have introduced a new IBR representation for trees, which allows for very efficient quality rendering with complex effects such as shading, shadows, sky illumination, sun occlusion by clouds, and motion of the sun. Our naive implementation runs at 7 to 20 fps on an $Onyx^2$ *Infinite Reality* on a scenery containing 1000 trees.

The HBT representation consists of a hierarchy of bidirectional textures, which provides a billboard for each given observer and light directions, plus a visibility hierarchical structure for self- and cast-shadows. Despite the 6 degrees of freedom of the BTF, the required memory of a few tens of Mb is acceptable. Our representation is efficient in memory as long as hierarchy and instancing exist in the data, which is often the case for trees. It should thus also apply to other kind of scenes (*e.g.*, city, crowd, ...).

Specularities, BRDF, and transmission are also handled by our method, but precision is limited by the sampling density of view and light directions. The sampling of directions and of cube-map locations potentially yield artifacts, as linear interpolation does not perfectly reconstruct the data. This issue disappears with higher sampling rates, at the cost of memory. Thus there is a trade-off between visual quality *vs.* memory used. However, results show that nice real-time fly-overs can be produced with reasonable memory, even when using several kinds of trees.

A far more efficient global rendering algorithm could be implemented, using grids and smart culling methods, thus allowing the interactive visualization of much larger landscapes. Various different implementation choices could be made on the HBT rendering and construction. For instance, a more accurate visibility evaluation could be precomputed.

It would be interesting to see how the future graphics boards will include features easing the rendering process: SGI *Infinite Reality* implements 4D textures; Nvidia chips should do the same soon. Once 4D textures will be treated like any texture interpolation, filtering and compression wise, lightfields will be directly available in hardware. If 6D textures are also managed some day, BTFs will be directly available as well...

---

[10] 3 for darkening the background, 9 for direct illumination, 3 for ambient (*i.e.*, sky) illumination.

Appendix: Images weighted summation with hardware

We want to combine images by weighted summation, which is different than blending them together by alpha compositing which would depend on the order of operation. On the other hand, we want to blend the result with the background image already on screen by compositing.

$$C = \sum_{i,j} \alpha_i \beta_j \, \mathrm{BTF}_a(i,j) \, \mathrm{BTF}_{rgb}(i,j) \, ,$$
$$A = \sum_{i,j} \alpha_i \beta_j \, \mathrm{BTF}_a(i,j) \;=\; \sum_i \alpha_i \mathrm{BTF}_a(i) \, ,$$
$$C_{pixel} = C + (1 - A)C_{pixel},$$

where α_i and β_j are the barycentric coordinates of the view and light directions.

Another problem is that we do not want the depth test of the Z-buffer to reject fragments that might appear behind a transparent fragment, especially when drawing intersecting billboards. A costly solution would be to process the reconstruction in a separate buffer (without a Z-test), and to use the result as a texture to be blended with the image on screen. To simulate this process, while maintaining the pipe-line, we first darken the background according to the cumulated transparency of the billboards. As the same transparency occurs for the 3 images corresponding to one view direction sample, we only have 3 transparency maps to consider. "Darkening" is done using the ADD blending equation of the OpenGL API with (0 , 1-SRC_ALPHA) blending coefficients. The weight α_i is encoded in the alpha of the underlying polygon.

Then we draw the weighted textures (the polygon alpha is set to $\alpha_i\beta_j$), using (SRC_ALPHA , 1) blending coefficients. Thus we have a total of 12 passes if all the billboards are to be drawn. To avoid Z-interactions, the Z values are stored only in the last pass.[11]

This yields the following pseudo-algorithm:

```
Draw scene from back to here
Disable Z-write
BlendCoeff(0,1 − SRC_ALPHA)
Darken screen according to object transparency (3 passes)
BlendCoeff(SRC_ALPHA,1)
Draw the object (9 passes) (enable Z-write before the last pass)
```

Acknowledgments : We wish to thank Patricio Inostroza and George Drettakis for proofreading this paper. Pierre Poulin is currently at REVES/Inria Sophia-Antipolis as part of his sabbatical.

---

[11]As the objects are sorted, storing the Z values of trees is not very useful anyway, as long as possible extra opaque objects are drawn first (the Z-test remains enabled).

References

1. S.E. Chen. Quicktime VR - an image-based approach to virtual environment navigation. In *SIGGRAPH 95 Conference Proceedings*, pages 29–38, August 1995.
2. K. Dana, B. van Ginneken, S. Nayar, and J. Koenderink. Columbia-utrecht reflectance and texture database, http://www.cs.columbia.edu/cave/curet/.index.html.
3. K.J. Dana, B. van Ginneken, S.K. Nayar, and J.J. Koenderink. Reflectance and texture of real-world surfaces. *ACM Transactions on Graphics*. 18(1):1–34, January 1999.
4. J.-M. Dischler. Efficiently rendering macrogeometric surface structures using bi-directional texture functions. In *Eurographics Workshop on Rendering 98*, pages 169–180, 1998.
5. F. Durand, G. Drettakis, J. Thollot, and C. Puech. Conservative visibility preprocessing using extended projections. In *SIGGRAPH 2000, Computer Graphics Proceedings*, pages 239–248, 2000.
6. S.J. Gortler, R. Grzeszczuk, R. Szeliski, and M.F. Cohen. The lumigraph. In *SIGGRAPH 96 Conference Proceedings*, pages 43–54, August 1996.
7. A. LeBlanc, R. Turner, and D. Thalmann. Rendering hair using pixel blending and shadow buffers. *Journal of Visualization and Computer Animation 2(3)*, pages 92–97, 1991.
8. J. Lengyel and J. Snyder. Rendering with coherent layers. *Proceedings of SIGGRAPH 97*, pages 233–242, August 1997.
9. M. Levoy and P. Hanrahan. Light field rendering. In *SIGGRAPH 96 Conference Proceedings*, pages 31–42, August 1996.
10. P.W.C. Maciel and P. Shirley. Visual navigation of large environments using textured clusters. *1995 Symposium on Interactive 3D Graphics*, pages 95–102, April 1995.
11. N. Max. Hierarchical rendering of trees from precomputed multi-layer Z-buffers. In *Eurographics Workshop on Rendering 1996*, pages 165–174, June 1996.
12. N. Max, O. Deussen, and B. Keating. Hierarchical image-based rendering using texture mapping hardware. In *Eurographics Workshop on Rendering 99*, pages 57–62, 1999.
13. N. Max and K. Ohsaki. Rendering trees from precomputed Z-buffer views. In *Eurographics Workshop on Rendering 1995*, June 1995.
14. N.L. Max. Horizon mapping: shadows for bump-mapped surfaces. *The Visual Computer*, 4(2):109–117, July 1988.
15. A. Meyer and F. Neyret. Interactive volumetric textures. In *Eurographics Workshop on Rendering 1998*, pages 157–168, July 1998.
16. G.S.P. Miller, S. Rubin, and D. Ponceleon. Lazy decompression of surface light fields for precomputed global illumination. *Eurographics Workshop on Rendering 1998*, pages 281–292, June 1998.
17. J. Neider, T. Davis, and M. Woo. *OpenGL Programming Guide*. Addison-Wesley, 1993.
18. F.E. Nicodemus, J.C. Richmond, J.J. Hsia, I.W. Ginsberg, and T. Limperis. Geometric considerations and nomenclature for reflectance. October 1977.
19. T. Noma. Bridging between surface rendering and volume rendering for multi-resolution display. In *Eurographics Workshop on Rendering 1995*, pages 31–40, June 1995.
20. M.M. Oliveira, G. Bishop, and D. McAllister. Relief texture mapping. *Proceedings of SIGGRAPH 2000*, July 2000.
21. H. Pfister, M. Zwicker, J. van Baar, and M. Gross. Surfels: Surface elements as rendering primitives. *Proceedings of SIGGRAPH 2000*, pages 335–342, July 2000.
22. P. Prusinkiewicz, A. Lindenmayer, and J. Hanan. Developmental models of herbaceous plants for computer imagery purposes. In *Computer Graphics (SIGGRAPH '88 Proceedings)*, volume 22, pages 141–150, August 1988.
23. W.T. Reeves. Particle systems – a technique for modeling a class of fuzzy objects. *ACM Trans. Graphics*, 2:91–108, April 1983.
24. W.T. Reeves and R. Blau. Approximate and probabilistic algorithms for shading and rendering structured particle systems. In *Computer Graphics (SIGGRAPH '85 Proceedings)*, volume 19(3), pages 313–322, July 1985.
25. G. Schaufler. Per-object image warping with layered impostors. In *Eurographics Workshop on Rendering 98*, pages 145–156, 1998.
26. G. Schaufler, J. Dorsey, X. Decoret, and F.X. Sillion. Conservative volumetric visibility with occluder fusion. In *SIGGRAPH 2000, Computer Graphics Proceedings*, pages 229–238, 2000.
27. G. Schaufler and W. Stürzlinger. A three dimensional image cache for virtual reality. *Computer Graphics Forum*, 15(3):227–236, August 1996.
28. J. Shade, S.J. Gortler, L. He, and R. Szeliski. Layered depth images. *Proceedings of SIGGRAPH 98*, pages 231–242, July 1998.
29. J. Shade, D. Lischinski, D. Salesin, T. DeRose, and J. Snyder. Hierarchical image caching for accelerated walkthroughs of complex environments. *Proceedings of SIGGRAPH 96*, pages 75–82, August 1996.
30. A.J. Stewart. Hierarchical visibility in terrains. In *Eurographics Workshop on Rendering 97*, June 1997.
31. A.J. Stewart. Fast horizon computation at all points of a terrain with visibility and shading applications. *IEEE Transactions on Visualization and Computer Graphics*, 4(1):82–93, March 1998.
32. J. Weber and J. Penn. Creation and rendering of realistic trees. In *Computer Graphics (SIGGRAPH '95 Proceedings)*, pages 119–128, August 1995.
33. L. Williams. Casting curved shadows on curved surfaces. In *Computer Graphics (SIGGRAPH '78 Proceedings)*, volume 12(3), pages 270–274, August 1978.
34. D.N. Wood, D.I. Azuma, K. Aldinger, B. Curless, T. Duchamp, D.H. Salesin, and W. Stuetzle. Surface light fields for 3D photography. In *SIGGRAPH 2000, Computer Graphics Proceedings*, pages 287–296, 2000.
35. H. Zhang, D. Manocha, T. Hudson, and K.E. Hoff III. Visibility culling using hierarchical occlusion maps. In *SIGGRAPH 97 Conference Proceedings*, pages 77–88, August 1997.

Editors' Note: see Appendix, p. 337 for colored figures of this paper

Combined Rendering of Polarization and Fluorescence Effects

Alexander Wilkie

Institute of Computer Graphics and Algorithms
Vienna University of Technology

Robert F. Tobler

VRVis Research Center for Virtual Reality and Visualization

Werner Purgathofer

Institute of Computer Graphics and Algorithms
Vienna University of Technology

Abstract. We propose a practicable way to include both polarization and fluorescence effects in a rendering system at the same time. Previous research in this direction only demonstrated support for either one of these phenomena; using both effects simultaneously was so far not possible, mainly because the techniques for the treatment of polarized light were complicated and required rendering systems written specifically for this task.

The key improvement over previous work is that we use a different, more easily handled formalism for the description of polarization state, which also enables us to include fluorescence effects in a natural fashion. Moreover, all of our proposals are straightforward extensions to a conventional spectral rendering system.

1 Introduction

For the purposes of truly predictive photorealistic rendering it is essential that no effect which contributes to the interaction of light with a scene is neglected. Most aspects of object appearance can be accounted for by using just the laws of geometric optics, comparatively simple descriptions of surface reflectivity, tristimulus representations of colour and light, and can nowadays be computed very efficiently through a variety of common rendering algorithms. However, several physical effects, namely fluorescence, diffraction, dispersion and polarization, are still rarely – if at all – supported by contemporary rendering software.

1.1 Polarization

Polarization has received particularly little attention because – while of course being essential for specially contrived setups that e.g. contain polarizing filters   it seemingly does not contribute very prominent effects to the appearance of an average scene. This misconception is in part fostered by the fact that the human eye is normally not capable of distinguishing polarized from unpolarized light[1].

---

[1]Contrary to common belief trained observers *can* distinguish polarized from unpolarized light with the naked eye. Named after its discoverer, the effect is known as *Haidinger's brush* and is described by Minnaert in his book about light in outdoor surroundings [7].

One of the main areas where it in fact does make a substantial difference are outdoor scenes; this is due to the usually quite strong polarization of skylight, as one can find documented in G. P. Können's book [6] about polarized light in nature. But since such scenes are currently still problematical for photorealistic renderers for a number of other, more obvious reasons (e.g. scene complexity and related global illumination issues), this has not been given a lot of attention yet. Other known effects which depend on polarization support are certain darkening or discolourization patterns in metal objects and their reflections, and the appearance of faceted transparent objects, such as crystals.

1.2 Fluorescence

Some of the reasons for the small amount of work fluorescence has received are different from those which have made polarization a fringe topic. Firstly, although it causes very prominent effects, these can also be faked comparatively easily through custom shaders at a fraction of the effort involved in actually simulating the real process. Secondly, measurements of fluorescent pigments are very hard to obtain, virtually no publicly accessible data of this kind exists, and designing such spectra by hand is tedious. The third main reason is shared between fluorescence and polarization: they ought to be done using a spectral rendering system, which still rank as comparatively exotic and expensive to use.

2 Previous Work

2.1 Raytracing with Polarization Parameters

Physics has long achieved a very thorough understanding of light polarization; a classic introduction is e.g. to be found in the book of Born and Wolf [1]. In the computer graphics literature there are two publications about it; one by Wolff and Kurlander [16], who demonstrated polarization–aware image synthesis for the first time, and one by Tannenbaum et al. [14], who concentrated on the rendering of anisotropic crystals and extended the techniques used by Wolff et al.

The main goal of these efforts was that of finding an appropriate way to describe, and perform calculations with, polarized light; both groups of authors settled for a notation suggested by standard reference texts from physics literature.

Coherency Matrices. The formalism to describe polarized light used by both Wolff and Tannenbaum is that of *coherency matrices* (CM for short); this technique was introduced by Born and Wolf [1]. As derived in detail by Tannenbaum et al. [14], the coherency state of a monochromatic wave can be expressed in a matrix J of the form

$$J = \begin{pmatrix} J_{xx} & J_{xy} \\ J_{yx} & J_{yy} \end{pmatrix} = \begin{pmatrix} \langle E_x E_x^\star \rangle & \langle E_x E_y^\star \rangle \\ \langle E_y E_x^\star \rangle & \langle E_y E_y^\star \rangle \end{pmatrix}$$

where E_x and E_y are the E–field vectors for the X and Y directions, respectively, and $E_x^\star$ denotes the complex conjugate of E_x. The main diagonal elements – J_{xx} and J_{yy} – are real valued, and the trace $T(J) = J_{xx} + J_{yy}$ of the matrix represents the total light radiation of the wave, while the complex conjugates J_{xy} and J_{yx} represent the correlation of the X and Y components of E. For fully polarized light, these components are fully correlated and $|J|$ vanishes.

Coherency Matrix Modifiers. Besides being able to describe a ray of light, it is also necessary to process the interaction of light with a medium or surface. Such *filtering operations* (or *filters* for short) on polarized light described by a coherency matrix can be performed by using *coherency matrix modifiers*, or CMM. Tannenbaum et al. brought this approach, which was originally introduced by Parrent et al. [8], to the computer graphics world for use in their rendering system.

CMMs have the form of a complex–valued 2×2 matrix. If all participating elements have the same reference coordinate system, such a matrix M_p can be applied to a given coherence matrix J in the sequence of $J_p = \mathcal{M}_p J \mathcal{M}_p^\dagger$, where $\mathcal{M}_p^\dagger$ signifies the conjugate transpose of $\mathcal{M}_p$. If the modifier and the coherency matrix are not in the same coordinate system, an appropriate transformation – as discussed in section 2.3 of the full version of Tannenbaum et al. [14] (to be found on the proceedings CD–ROM) – has to be applied first.

2.2 Reflection Models which take Polarization into Account

Apart from the modified Cook–Torrance model used by Wolff et al., only one other surface model proposed so far, namely that of He et al. [5], attempts to consider polarization effects. As could be inferred from the results section of this paper, the high complexity of their surface model apparently led the authors to only implement a simpler, non–polarizing version in practice, and to contain themselves with just providing the theoretical derivation of the polarization–aware model in the text.

2.3 Rendering of Fluorescence Effects

So far Glassner has apparently been the only graphics researcher who investigated the rendering of fluorescence phenomena [3]. The main focus of his work was centered around the proper formulation of the rendering equation in the presence of phosphorescence and fluorescence, and he provided striking results generated with a modified version of the public domain raytracer *rayshade*. Sadly, this work was not followed up, nor was the modified version of rayshade made public. Also, we are not aware of any work that aims at considering the inclusion of fluorescence effects in sophisticated reflectance models.

3 A Combined Renderer

We first introduce an alternative notation that can be used for polarization support, and then show how this formalism can easily be combined with fluorescence support.

3.1 Alternative Polarization Support

A description for polarized radiation which due to its simpler mathematical characteristicsis is better suited for use in raytracing–based rendering systems is that of *Stokes parameters*. This description, while equivalent to coherency matrices, has the advantage of using only real–valued terms to describe all polarization states of optical radiation, and has an – also noncomplex – corresponding description of ray weights in the form of Müller matrices [11].

It has to be kept in mind that – similar to coherency matrices – both Stokes parameters and Müller matrices are meaningful only when considered within their own local reference frame; the main effect of this is that in a rendering system not only light, but also filters are *oriented* and have to store an appropriate reference in some way. However, for the sake brevity this spatial dependency is omitted in our following discussion except in the section about matrix realignment.

Stokes Parameters. Apart from coherency matrices, the polarization state of an electromagnetic wave of a given frequency can also be described in several other ways. Three real–valued parameters are required to describe a general polarization ellipse, but the *Stokes vector* notation defined by

$$
\begin{aligned}
E_{n,0} &= \kappa(V_x^2 + V_y^2) \qquad [W \cdot m^{-2}]\\
E_{n,1} &= \kappa(V_x^2 - V_y^2)\\
E_{n,2} &= \kappa(2V_x^2 \cdot V_y^2 \cdot \cos\gamma)\\
E_{n,3} &= \kappa(2V_x^2 \cdot V_y^2 \cdot \sin\gamma)
\end{aligned}
\tag{1}
$$

(in the notation used by Shumaker [11]) has proven itself in the optical measurements community, and has the key advantage that the first component of this 4–vector is the unpolarized intensity of the light wave in question (i.e. the same quantity that a non-polarizing renderer uses). Components 2 and 3 describe the preference of the wave towards linear polarization at zero and 45 degrees, respectively, while the fourth encodes preference for right–circular polarization. While the first component is obviously always positive, the values for the three latter parameters are bounded by $[-E_{n,0}, E_{n,0}]$; e.g. for an intensity $E_{n,0} = 2$, a value of $E_{n,3} = -2$ would indicate light which is totally left circularly polarized.

The – at least in comparison to coherency matrices – much more comprehensible relationship between the elements of a Stokes vector and the state of the wavetrain it describes is, amongst other things, very beneficial during the debugging stage of a polarizing renderer, since it is much easier to construct verifiable test cases.

Müller Matrices. Müller matrices (MM for short) are the data structure used to describe a filtering operation by materials that are capable of altering the polarization state of incident light represented by a Stokes vector. The general modifier for a 4–vector is a 4×4–matrix, and the structure of the Stokes vectors implies that the elements of such a matrix correspond to certain physical filter properties. As with Stokes vectors, the better comprehensibilty of these real–valued data structures is of considerable benefit during filter specification and testing.

The degenerate case of MM is that of a nonpolarizing filter; this could equally well be described by a simple reflection spectrum. For such a filter the corresponding MM is the identity matrix. A more practical example is the MM of an ideal linear polarizer T_{lin}, where the polarization axis is tilted by an angle of ϕ against the reference coordinate system of the optical path under consideration, and which has the form of

$$
T_{lin}(\phi) = \frac{1}{2}
\begin{bmatrix}
1 & \cos 2\phi & \sin 2\phi & 0\\
\cos 2\phi & \cos^2 2\phi & \sin 2\phi \cdot \cos 2\phi & 0\\
\sin 2\phi & \sin 2\phi \cdot \cos 2\phi & \sin^2 2\phi & 0\\
0 & 0 & 0 & 0
\end{bmatrix}.
$$

For the purposes of physically correct rendering it is important to know the MM which is caused by evaluation of the Fresnel terms; for this we use the notation from [16].

For a given wavelength and intersection geometry (i.e. specified index of refraction and angle of incidence), the resulting terms $F_\perp$, $F_\parallel$, $\delta_\perp$ and $\delta_\parallel$ have to be used as

$$T_{Fresnel} = \begin{bmatrix} A & B & 0 & 0 \\ B & A & 0 & 0 \\ 0 & 0 & C & -S \\ 0 & 0 & S & C \end{bmatrix},$$

where $A = (F_\perp + F_\parallel)/2$, $B = (F_\perp - F_\parallel)/2$, $C = \cos(\delta_\perp - \delta_\parallel)$ and $S = \sin(\delta_\perp - \delta_\parallel)$; $\delta_\perp - \delta_\parallel$ is the total retardance the incident wavetrain is subjected to.

Filter Rotation. In order to correctly concatenate a filter chain, as effectively first described by Hall et al. in [4] (which basically amounts to matrix multiplications of the MMs in the chain), we have to be able to re–align a MM to a new reference system, which amounts to rotating it along the direction of propagation to match the other operands.

Contrary to first intuition, directional realignment operations are *not* necessary along the path of a concatenated filter chain; the retardance component of a surface interaction is responsible for the alterations that result from changes in wavetrain direction.

Since in the case of polarized light a rotation by an angle of ϕ can only affect the second and third components of a Stokes vector (i.e. those components that describe the linear component of the polarization state), the appropriate rotation matrix $M(\phi)$ has the form of

$$M(\phi) = \begin{bmatrix} 1 & 0 & 0 & 0 \\ 0 & \cos 2\phi & \sin 2\phi & 0 \\ 0 & -\sin 2\phi & \cos 2\phi & 0 \\ 0 & 0 & 0 & 1 \end{bmatrix}. \tag{2}$$

Matrices of the same form are also used to rotate Müller matrices. In order to obtain the rotated version of a MM $T(0)$, $M(\phi)$ has to be applied in a way similar to that shown for CMMs, namely $T(\phi) = M(-\phi) \cdot T(0) \cdot M(\phi)$.

Apart from being useful to re–align a filter through rotation, the matrix M given in equation (2) is also the MM of an ideal *circular retarder*. Linearly polarized light entering a material of this type will emerge with its plane of polarization rotated by an angle of ϕ; certain materials, such as crystal quartz or dextrose, exhibit this property, which is also referred to as *optical activity*.

3.2 Rendering of Fluorescence Effects

Since fluorescence is a material property, its description only affects the filter data structure. Specifically, for a system which uses n samples to represent spectra, filter values of fluorescent substances have to be a re–radiation matrix (RRM) of $n \times n$ elements.

The fact that fluorescence only ever causes light to be re–radiated at *lower* wavelengths than those at which it is absorbed allows us to only consider the lower half of this matrix. In practice, we use the same reflection spectra as for normal materials, only augmented with a data structure that holds the area below the main diagonal. All filtering operations were adapted to handle the presence of this crosstalk component as a sticky property; even if only one filter in a concatenation chain has an off–diagonal component, the overall result has to be also fluorescent.

202

3.3 Combining Fluorescence and Polarization

Similar to the previous section, this is a problem which only concerns the filtering operations. Specifically, the question is in which way nonpolarizing $n \times n$ (or n plus sub–diagonal crosstalk of $(n \times (n-1))/2$) re–radiation matrix filters and $n \times (4 \times 4)$ reflectance spectra with Müller matrices as samples can be properly mixed.

Practical Considerations. Fortunately, the solution is straightforward. The key observation here is that light which is re–emitted by fluorescent molecules can be considered to be unpolarized for our purposes, since this kind of light interaction with pigments usually has no directional character. This means that, while the full combination of the two properties would require the rather unwieldy construct of a data structure with $n \times n \times 4 \times 4$ entries (a MM for each RRM entry), we can get by with using a much smaller entity.

Our combined filter data structure uses the same nonpolarizing crosstalk component as the plain fluorescence–aware filter described in the previous section, and just replaces the main diagonal reflection spectrum with its polarizing counterpart.

The only area where this change causes a considerable increase in the complexity of a rendering system are the filter manipulation methods, which now have to account for four possible states of each operand (fluorescent yes/no, polarizing yes/no) in each procedure.

4 Results

We implemented the proposed dual polarization and fluorescence support in the public domain rendering software under development at our institute, the Advanced Rendering Toolkit (ART for short).

Filters and Light. The first task was to introduce the distinction between filters and light – as described in the previous sections – throughout the raytracing code of ART; the previously used polymorphous colour data type had to be appropriately replaced by filter and light structures. As an unasked–for fringe benefit of this quite substantial task it transpired that the entire rendering code became much clearer semantically through the introduction of this distinction; this might serve as an encouragement for others who face the same task.

Fluorescence. The filters were then extended so that they also became capable of encoding fluorescence information as described in section 3.2. The main work during this step was the alteration of the filter manipulation routines and development of specialized storage classes for fluorescent reflection data.

Polarization. In order to be able to make meaningful performance comparisons, and also to keep the option of using a faster renderer without polarization capabilities for the majority of users who do not need the feature, polarization support was implemented as a compile–time option in ART. For the non–polarizeable renderer the procedures for polarization support expand to NOPs, so no overhead is incurred, and for the polarization–aware renderer they are expanded as inline funtions.

Apart from additional large changes to the light and filter manipulation code – which had already been fleshed out and pushed into one module during the first step – the major changes in this stage involved the introduction of the capability to store and manipulate the orientation of light and filter data structures during rendering processes. Three sample images obtained with this hybrid renderer are shown in figure 1 in the colour plate section.

Optimization. The only computational optimization with respect to polarization that has been implemented in ART so far is that each instance of the light and filter data structures is tagged as to whether it actually describes polarized light or a polarizing filter. This makes it possible to use faster routines if both operands in a calculation involving lights and/or filters are not polarized (specifically, multiplication of the samples instead of matrix operations). If one of the operands is polarized or polarizing, then so is the result of the computation: polarization is a sticky property of light and filters.

This simple optimization leads to a polarization–aware renderer which is on average only $10 - 30$ percent slower than its plain counterpart for scenes which do not contain any polarizing surfaces, lightsources or materials. Since practically all scenes contain at least a certain percentage of objects and lightsources that do not exhibit any polarized or polarizing property, this shortcut actually improves the performance of the polarization–aware renderer for all but extreme scenes.

For scenes with large amounts of polarizing objects – like e.g. the example scene shown in figure 1 – the slowdown of the polarizeable version compared the plain renderer is naturally higher and depends strongly on the scene. The example in figure 1 exhibits a fairly typical slowdown of around 500 percent (30 vs. 150 seconds rendering time); in some rare cases we have observed even larger performance drops. This drastic increase in rendering time is the price one has to pay for increased physical accuracy, although we estimate that some additional performance could be gained from aggressive global optimization of the numeric code in our rendering system.

5   Conclusion

We presented a practical way to implement combined polarization and fluorescence support in the context of a modern rendering system. The key improvements over previous approaches are

- The use of Stokes vectors to describe both unpolarized an polarized light with a single, intuitive formalism.
- The use of Müller matrices to describe the polarizing effect of materials and surfaces in an understandable way that is complementary to Stokes vectors.
- The combination of these formalisms with fluorescence information into a single rendering system.

Our future research will concern itself with the efficiency of spectral rendering in general, and in particular the choice of the most suitable spectral representation for photorealistic rendering; this is a question for which a good answer that is generally valid has yet to be given. In the course of these investigations we plan to also investigate if both polarization and fluorescence can be represented even more efficiently, and investigate whether and how the usually large similarity in polarization state amongst samples in a given light spectrum can be safely exploited to reduce storage and computation requirements.

204

Acknowledgements

We are grateful to Labsphere Inc. for generously making measurements of fluorescent samples available. We also want to thank Ferdinand Bammer, Thomas Theußl and Katharina Horrak for valuable discussions.

References

1. Max Born and Emil Wolf. *Principles of Optics*. The Macmillan Company, 1964.
2. R. L. Cook and K. E. Torrance. A reflectance model for computer graphics. *Computer graphics, Aug 1981*, 15(3):307–316, 1981.
3. Andrew Glassner. A model for fluorescence and phosphorescence. In *Fifth Eurographics Workshop on Rendering*, pages 57–68, Darmstadt, Germany, June 1994. Eurographics.
4. Roy A. Hall and Donald P. Greenberg. A testbed for realistic image synthesis. *IEEE Computer Graphics and Applications*, 3(8):10–20, November 1983.
5. Xiao D. He, Kenneth E. Torrance, François X. Sillion, and Donald P. Greenberg. A comprehensive physical model for light reflection. *Computer Graphics*, 25(4):175–186, July 1991.
6. G. P. Können. *Polarized Light in Nature*. Cambridge University Press, 1985.
7. M. Minnaert. *Light and Color in the Open Air*. Dover, 1954.
8. G. B. Parrent and P. Roman. On the matrix formulation of the theory of partial polarization in terms of observables. *Il Nuovo Cimento (English version)*, 15(3):370–388, February 1960.
9. Mark S. Peercy. Linear color representations for full spectral rendering. In James T. Kajiya, editor, *Computer Graphics (SIGGRAPH '93 Proceedings)*, volume 27, pages 191–198, August 1993.
10. Gilles Rougeron and Bernard Péroche. An adaptive representation of spectral data for reflectance computations. In Julie Dorsey and Philipp Slusallek, editors, *Eurographics Rendering Workshop 1997*, pages 127–138, New York City, NY, June 1997. Eurographics, Springer Wien. ISBN 3-211-83001-4.
11. John B. Shumaker. Distribution of optical radiation with respect to polarization. In Fred E. Nicodemus, editor, *Self–Study Manual on Optical Radiation Measurements, Part 1: Concepts*. Optical Physics Division, Institute for Basic Standards, National Bureau of Standards, Washington, D.C., June 1977.
12. Robert Siegel and John R. Howell. *Thermal Radiation Heat Transfer, 3rd Edition*. Hemisphere Publishing Corporation, New York, NY, 1992.
13. Yinlong Sun, F. David Fracchia, and Mark S. Drew. A composite model for representing spectral functions. Technical Report TR 1998-18, School of Computing Science, Simon Fraser University, Burnaby, BC, Canada, November 1998.
14. David C. Tannenbaum, Peter Tannenbaum, and Michael J. Wozny. Polarization and birefringency considerations in rendering. In Andrew Glassner, editor, *Proceedings of SIGGRAPH '94 (Orlando, Florida, July 24–29, 1994)*, Computer Graphics Proceedings, Annual Conference Series, pages 221–222. ACM SIGGRAPH, ACM Press, July 1994. ISBN 0-89791-667-0.
15. Turner Whitted. An improved illumination model for shaded display. *IEEE Computer Graphics & Applications*, 23(6):343–349, June 1980.
16. Lawrence B. Wolff and David Kurlander. Ray tracing with polarization parameters. *IEEE Computer Graphics & Applications*, 10(6):44–55, November 1990.

Editors' Note: see Appendix, p. 338 for colored figure of this paper

Hardware-accelerated from-region visibility using a dual ray space

Vladlen Koltun[1], Yiorgos Chrysanthou[2], Daniel Cohen-Or[1]

[1] School of Computer Science, Tel Aviv University, Tel Aviv, Israel
{vladlen,dcor}@tau.ac.il
[2] Department of Computer Science, University College London, London, UK
y.chrysanthou@cs.ucl.ac.uk

Abstract. In this paper a novel from-region visibility algorithm is described. Its unique properties allow conducting remote walkthroughs in very large virtual environments, without preprocessing and storing prohibitive amounts of visibility information. The algorithm retains its speed and accuracy even when applied to large viewcells. This allows computing from-region visibility on-line, thus eliminating the need for visibility preprocessing. The algorithm utilizes a geometric transform, representing visibility in a two-dimensional space, the *dual ray space*. Standard rendering hardware is then used for rapidly performing visibility computation. The algorithm is robust and easy to implement, and can trade off between accuracy and speed. We report results from extensive experiments that were conducted on a virtual environment that accurately depicts 160 square kilometers of the city of London.

1 Introduction

In a remote walkthrough scenario, a large three-dimensional virtual environment is stored on a server. The client performs an interactive walkthrough, via a remote network connection, with no a priori information regarding the environment. The client is assumed to possess the computational resources equivalent to those of a personal workstation, not being able to render a significant portion of the environment in real time, nor even fit it into its memory.

This scenario brings about the need for *selective transmission*, the crux of which is that the server monitors the client's (virtual) location during the walkthrough, and transmits the relevant portions of the scene to the client. A selective transmission scheme must carefully balance between the necessity of not causing errors or visual artifacts on the client's side, and the desirability of real-time frame rates.

To keep the client's frame-rate high, the server has to ensure that the set of objects displayed by the client is as close to the set of visible objects as possible. Unfortunately, the ideal situation in which the client always renders only the visible objects is computationally infeasible. However, *conservative* visibility algorithms can be employed, which ensure that the client renders all the visible objects, as well as some occluded ones. Conservative visibility algorithms that perform well in practice have been the subject of intensive study for the past decade.

Fig. 1. The results of the algorithm for a viewcell of size 50x50x2 meters that partly lies on London's Oxford street. The model is shown on the left and the results are visualized on the right. The algorithm has detected that the whole length of Oxford street is visible (blue) from the viewcell (green), and was able to mark the immediately surrounding areas as occluded (red). The tall green wireframe box is drawn in order to mark the viewcell's location. Results for this viewcell are shown in Figure 6(a) as well.

From-point visibility algorithms [5, 12, 14, 30] are not suitable for remote walk-throughs, since they necessitate transmitting visibility changes every frame, giving rise to unacceptable communication lags, no matter how fast the visibility is computed. To avoid the problem of lag, from-region visibility [4, 8, 15, 22, 25, 29] can be used. The idea behind from-region visibility is to partition the space into a grid of viewcells. For each viewcell, the set of objects visible from at least one point inside the viewcell is conservatively estimated, yielding a *Potentially Visible Set* (PVS) that is associated with the viewcell.

While the client is in a certain viewcell, the server transmits the PVS of the adjacent viewcells. This alleviates lag, since the client does not have to wait every frame for updates from the server. Rather, the set of objects displayed by the client changes only when a viewcell boundary is crossed. By the time the client leaves a viewcell, the PVS of the next viewcell has already been transmitted, and the walkthrough proceeds smoothly.

This approach does not come without cost. Since the PVS of each viewcell contains information about the visibility of the whole scene (from that viewcell), and there is a large number of viewcells, the overall amount of visibility information that has to be stored on the server is enormous. Although compression schemes have been developed specifically to tackle this problem [11, 27], it is still very relevant and prohibitive for large scenes such as urban models.

The space problem is exacerbated by the fact that previous approaches to from-region visibility computation are efficient primarily when dealing with relatively small viewcells (with the exception of [9, 25, 26], which are dedicated to in-doors walkthroughs). This implies that large scenes have to be partitioned into tens of thousands of viewcells, the Potentially Visible Sets of which have to be computed and stored.

Another bothersome aspect concerning small viewcells is the fact that the time it takes the client to cross one viewcell is short. If during that time the server cannot complete the transmission of the visibility change required for proceeding into an adjacent viewcell, visually disturbing errors occur. This is essentially the same problem of lag that occurs if the server uses from-point visibility computation. Note that the difference in visibility from two adjacent viewcells can be very significant, even if they are small.

In this paper, we introduce a different approach to computing from-region visibility, which eliminates the need for preprocessing and storing prohibitive amounts of visibility information, and does not introduce lag. The speed and accuracy of our from-region visibility algorithm are retained for very large viewcells. This allows utilizing from-region visibility computation on-line. While the client traverses one (large) viewcell, the server computes the visibility information for adjacent viewcells. The speed of the algorithm allows computing and transmitting this visibility information before the client reaches the next viewcell, and its accuracy (see Figure 1) ensures that the PVS is small enough to be displayed by the client in real time.

The next section surveys previous approaches to from-region visibility computation, and outlines the specific properties of our approach. Section 3 gives an overview of our algorithm, which is then developed in Sections 4 and 5. Implementation decisions and experimental results are reported in Section 6, and we conclude in Section 7.

2 From-region visibility

Detecting the objects that are visible from at least one point in a three-dimensional viewcell is inherently a non-linear four-dimensional problem [7, 24]. Exact solutions to the from-region visibility determination problem are considered impractical. In fact, no such solutions have explicitly appeared in computer graphics literature, with the exception of [7, 24]. Instead, researchers have concentrated on providing practical conservative algorithms that overestimate the set of visible objects.

For general scenes, conservative methods were introduced that take into account only the occlusion of individual large convex occluders [4, 21]. It was shown that such methods are only effective if the viewcells are smaller than the occluders [18]. For large viewcells, occlusion may arise out of the combined contribution of several objects. Often, a "cluster" of small objects occludes a large portion of the scene, while the individual occlusion of each object is insignificant.

New techniques have recently emerged that attempt to perform occlusion fusion, that is, capture occlusion caused by groups of objects [8, 15, 22, 29]. Durand et al. [8] perform from-region visibility computation by placing projection planes behind occluders, and projecting objects onto these planes. Koltun et al. [15] "slice" the scene and aggregate occlusion inside each slice to form large virtual occluders. Schaufler et al. [22] discretize the scene into a hierarchy of voxels and determine occlusion by testing the voxels against the umbrae of the occluders. Wonka et al. [29] prove that after the occluders are appropriately "shrunk", sampling the visibility at discrete locations on the boundary of the viewcell provides a conservative estimate of the visibility from the viewcell. Further discussion on these recent techniques can be found in [3].

The from-region visibility algorithm presented in this paper utilizes a geometric transform that maps rays in object-space to points in image-space. This alternative representation of visibility allows the problem to be conservatively discretized and solved rapidly, using standard rendering hardware. The resolution of the discretization can be adjusted to trade off between accuracy and speed. The algorithm has been successfully applied to viewcells that are much larger than individual occluders (see Figure 6(b)). Its accuracy and speed allow computing from-region visibility on-line, eliminating the need for visibility preprocessing. It thus provides inherent support for dynamic removal and addition of objects.

3   Overview

The algorithm processes a model that is represented by a hierarchical space subdivision; we use a kd-tree. Each node of this space subdivision is associated with an axis-aligned bounding box, and with the objects that are (perhaps partially) contained in this box. The bounding box associated with a node is completely contained in the bounding box associated with the node's parent.

For a given viewcell, our algorithm hierarchically traverses this subdivision in a top-down fashion. For each subdivision node, the algorithm determines whether the bounding box of the node is visible from the viewcell. When an occluded node is reached, the recursion terminates, since the children of that node are guaranteed to be occluded. This early termination strategy contributes to the speed of the algorithm, by allowing large portions of the scene to be culled after just one visibility determination query.

The cell-to-cell visibility determination algorithm is the core of the system. Denote the axis-parallel boxes corresponding to the viewcell and to some subdivision node by $\mathcal{A}$ and $\mathcal{B}$, respectively. Denote a collection of occluding objects by $\mathcal{S}$. The algorithm determines whether $\mathcal{A}$ and $\mathcal{B}$ are mutually visible among $\mathcal{S}$. $\mathcal{A}$ and $\mathcal{B}$ are said to be mutually visible if there exists a line segment with one end-point in $\mathcal{A}$ and another in $\mathcal{B}$ that is disjoint from all objects of $\mathcal{S}$. The cell-to-cell visibility determination algorithm operates by first reducing the problem to planar visibility determination as described in Section 4, and then solving this planar problem as described in Section 5.

Simplifying assumptions. There is no known rapid from-region visibility algorithm that is also exact. This does not seem likely to change due to the four-dimensional nature of the problem, and the complex geometric structure of visibility events [7]. Practical conservative algorithms [4, 8, 15, 22, 29] necessarily discretize or simplify the problem in some way. One common strategy, which is adopted here as well, is to assume that the input scene (more accurately, the set of occluders) is 2.5D [4, 15, 29].

Clearly, one can construct a scene in which this assumption is too restrictive for any significant occlusion to be detected. Such a scene may be, for example, a randomly generated "soup" of long and slim triangles. We consider such scenes to be of relatively little interest to the practical uses of the presented algorithm. A common type of input scenes for walkthrough systems is urban environments, where the most important occluders are buildings, large parts of which are 2.5D due to engineering constraints. In

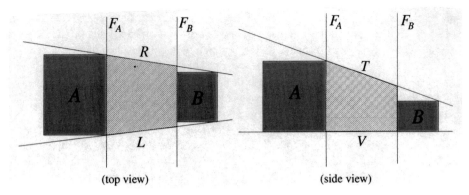

Fig. 2. The construction involved in the reduction to a planar problem. The shaft $\mathcal{AB}$ is shown filled.

architectural scenes, much of the occlusion is also caused by 2.5D objects. Even if a virtual environment is not specifically designed to model a city, a building, or a landscape, it is rare to come across a commercial virtual environment that is not largely 2.5D.

Moreover, "good" occluders can be synthesized from arbitrary input objects. Synthesis of large convex occluders was studied by Andujar et al. [1], and similar techniques can be applied to synthesize 2.5D occluders.

4 Reduction to a planar problem

The algorithm has to decide whether two axis-parallel boxes $\mathcal{A}$ and $\mathcal{B}$ are mutually visible. We now show how this problem can be reduced to *planar* visibility determination. We start with a simple observation. Denote the edges bounding the upper face of $\mathcal{A}$ ($\mathcal{B}$) by $\mathcal{A}_i$ (respectively, $\mathcal{B}_i$), for $1 \leq i \leq 4$.

Observation 1 *$\mathcal{A}$ and $\mathcal{B}$ are mutually visible with respect to $\mathcal{S}$ if and only if $\mathcal{A}_i$ and $\mathcal{B}_j$ are mutually visible with respect to $\mathcal{S}$, for some $1 \leq i, j \leq 4$. In other words, $\mathcal{A}$ and $\mathcal{B}$ are mutually visible if and only if their upper rims are.*

Proof. It is obvious that $\mathcal{A}$ and $\mathcal{B}$ are visible if their upper rims are. We thus concentrate on the "only if" part, stating that if $\mathcal{A}$ and $\mathcal{B}$ are mutually visible then their upper rims also are. $\mathcal{A}$ and $\mathcal{B}$ are mutually visible if and only if there is a visibility segment s between them. s is disjoint from $\mathcal{S}$ and has one end-point in the interior of $\mathcal{A}$ and another in the interior of $\mathcal{B}$. Consider the semi-infinite vertical "wall" defined as the union of upward vertical rays originating from s. Since the occluders are 2.5D and are disjoint from s, they are also disjoint from this wall. Also, the wall must contain at least one point belonging to the upper rim of $\mathcal{A}$ and another point belonging to the upper rim of $\mathcal{B}$. Since it is convex, it also contains the segment connecting these two points. Thus, there exists a segment connecting the upper rims of $\mathcal{A}$ and $\mathcal{B}$ that is disjoint from $\mathcal{S}$. $\square$

We now define the term *shaft*; the definition is illustrated in Figure 2. Let L and R be the two vertical planes that support $\mathcal{A}$ and $\mathcal{B}$. Let F_A and F_B be two parallel vertical planes that separate $\mathcal{A}$ and $\mathcal{B}$, such that F_A contains a face of $\mathcal{A}$ and F_B contains a face of $\mathcal{B}$. Let T be a plane that contains two parallel horizontal edges, one of $\mathcal{A}$ and one of $\mathcal{B}$, and supports $\mathcal{A}$ and $\mathcal{B}$ from above. (In general, there are two such planes.) Let V be the plane that supports $\mathcal{A}$ and $\mathcal{B}$ from below. The shaft $\mathcal{AB}$ is the area bounded by L, R, F_A, F_B, T, and V. (Notice that our definition of a shaft is different from that in [13].)

Observation 1 implies that there exists a visibility ray between $\mathcal{A}$ and $\mathcal{B}$ inside the shaft $\mathcal{AB}$ only if there exists a visibility ray on the "ceiling" of $\mathcal{AB}$. More precisely, let a_1 denote the point $T \cap F_A \cap L$, and let a_2 denote the point $T \cap F_A \cap R$. Similarly, $T \cap F_B \cap L$ is denoted by b_1, and $T \cap F_B \cap R$ is denoted by b_2. Also, denote by $\mathcal{S}_T$ the collection of intersections of the polygons of $\mathcal{S}$ with T, which is a collection of segments on T. $\mathcal{A}$ and $\mathcal{B}$ are mutually visible among $\mathcal{S}$ only if the segments (a_1, a_2) and (b_1, b_2), both lying on the plane T, are mutually visible among $\mathcal{S}_T$. We have thus reduced the problem to planar visibility determination on T.

5 Planar visibility determination

Given two segments s_1 and s_2 in the plane, and a collection of occluding segments O, we wish to determine whether s_2 is visible from s_1. We first provide a simple analytic algorithm for this problem, which is then converted into a rapid hardware-assisted one.

5.1 Exact analytic algorithm

We define a bounded two-dimensional space, the *dual ray space*, such that every ray originating on s_1 and intersecting s_2 corresponds to a point in this space. Our algorithm "marks" all points in the ray space that represent rays that pass through occluding segments. Visibility is then detected by checking whether there is at least one point that has not been "marked".

More precisely, parameterize s_1 and s_2 as $\{s_1(t) | 0 \leq t \leq 1\}$ and $\{s_2(t) | 0 \leq t \leq 1\}$, respectively. Let $\mathcal{RS}$ be the unit square $\{(x, y) | 0 \leq x, y \leq 1\}$, such that a point (x, y) in $\mathcal{RS}$ corresponds to the ray originating at $s_1(x)$ and passing through $s_2(y)$.

Define a mapping $\mathcal{T} : \mathbb{R}^2 \rightarrow \mathcal{RS}$ that maps each point $p \in \mathbb{R}^2$ to the collection of points in $\mathcal{RS}$ that correspond to rays passing through p. For any $p \in \mathbb{R}^2$, $\mathcal{T}(p)$ is a line segment in $\mathcal{RS}$. For a segment $v \in O$, parameterized as $\{v(t) | 0 \leq t \leq 1\}$, $\mathcal{T}(v)$ is defined to be the continuous collection of segments $\{\mathcal{T}(v(t)) | 0 \leq t \leq 1\}$. This collection is bounded by the segments $\mathcal{T}(v(0))$ and $\mathcal{T}(v(1))$ that correspond to the end-points of v. In general, it forms either a trapezoid (Figure 3(a)) or a double-triangle (Figure 3(b)), depending on whether the line containing v intersects the interior of s_1 or not.

This implies a simple exact algorithm for determining whether s_2 is visible from s_1: Map each segment $v \in O$ to $\mathcal{RS}$ and compute the union of the resulting trapezoids and double-triangles (i.e. $\bigcup_{v \in O} \mathcal{T}(v)$). This computation can be performed in worst-case optimal $O(n^2)$ time without employing complex data structures [6]. If s_1 and s_2 are mutually visible, there is a point $p_o \in \mathcal{RS}$ that is not contained in this union. The point p_o corresponds to a visibility ray (see Figures 3(c) and 3(d)).

The dual ray space mapping $\mathcal{T}$ bears similarities to other duality transforms, such as the standard duality transform in computational geometry [6] and the Hough transform,

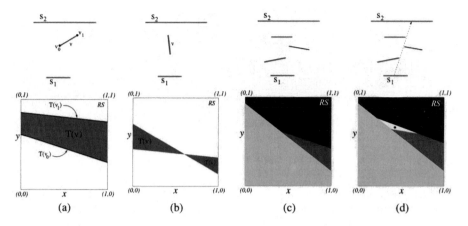

Fig. 3. Simple scenes (top) and their dual ray space (bottom). In this figure, each trapezoid in the ray space has the color of the segment it corresponds to. (a) and (b) each show an occluding segment. s_2 is occluded from s_1 in (c) and is visible in (d); the black point in the ray space of (d) corresponds to the dashed visibility ray.

which is used for line detection in image analysis [16]. However, the dual ray space is a bounded region (as opposed to the infinite dual planes of the above-mentioned transforms) that can be efficiently discretized. This is a crucial advantage that served as the main motivation for the current definition of the dual ray space. In this sense, the dual ray space is similar to the lumigraph [10] and the light field [17]. (Notice that Gortler et al. [10] also use the term "ray space".) In the context of related work in computational geometry, our exact algorithm corresponds to local computation of one face of the *visibility complex* [20]. The visibility complex has been previously applied to ray-tracing [2] and radiosity [19].

5.2 Hardware-accelerated algorithm

We wish to determine whether $\bigcup_{v \in O} \mathcal{T}(v)$ covers the unit square $\mathcal{RS}$. This can be accomplished conservatively by discretizing $\mathcal{RS}$ into a bitmap and rendering all $\mathcal{T}(v)$ onto this bitmap using graphics hardware. All $\mathcal{T}(v)$ are drawn in white, without z-buffering or shading, onto an initially black background. If a black pixel remains, the segments s_1 and s_2 are reported to be mutually visible. This algorithm avoids the complex analytic computation of the union and alleviates robustness problems common in geometric algorithms.

The default behavior of OpenGL is to color a pixel if its *center* is inside a drawn polygon. This may cause inaccuracy, since our algorithm is conservative provided that only the pixels that are *completely* covered by $\bigcup_{v \in O} \mathcal{T}(v)$ are colored white. This behavior is ensured by "shrinking" the double-triangles and trapezoids prior to rendering. Their edges are moved inward by $\sqrt{2}a$, where a is half the pixel size (see Figure 4). The center of a pixel is inside $\mathcal{T}(v)$ after shrinking, only if the pixel was completely covered by it prior to shrinking [28].

212

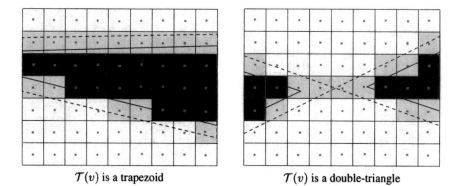

| $\mathcal{T}(v)$ is a trapezoid | $\mathcal{T}(v)$ is a double-triangle |

Fig. 4. The green pixels are properly contained in $\mathcal{T}(v)$ (shown dashed), and their centers are contained in the "shrunk" $\mathcal{T}(v)$ (shown solid). The yellow pixels are only partially covered by $\mathcal{T}(v)$, but their centers are contained in $\mathcal{T}(v)$; shrinking prevents them from being colored.

The process of checking whether there are any black pixels left after rendering is accelerated using the OpenGL minmax operation, part of the OpenGL 1.2 standard. The minmax operation allows a quick determination of the minimal (or maximal) pixel color in the frame buffer. It can therefore be used for deciding whether the buffer is fully white or contains a black pixel.

The image-space nature of the described algorithm allows it to be applied hierarchically, in a manner similar to [30]. We can use a low-resolution bitmap to represent $\mathcal{RS}$, and rapidly render all $\mathcal{T}(v)$ onto it. If the resulting bitmap is not fully white, a bitmap of higher resolution is used to refine the test, yielding a less conservative PVS.

6 Results

The algorithms described in this paper were implemented, and tested on an IBM A20p laptop with a 750Mhz Pentium III CPU and an ATI Rage Mobility graphics card. The exact planar visibility algorithm (Section 5.1) was also implemented, for the sake of comparison. Our test model accurately depicts 160 sq. km. of London. It was created using Ordnance Survey data, and comprises of about 1.7 million polygons [23].

One goal of our experiments was to determine an effective resolution for the discretization of the dual ray space. There is a clear trade-off involved. Higher resolution yields a less conservative PVS, at the cost of computation speed. Another goal was determining an effective viewcell size. Small viewcells induce lag, but prohibitively large portions of the scene are visible from viewcells that are too large.

We have tested the algorithm with viewcells of sizes ranging from 50x50 meters to 300x300 meters, and with discretization resolutions ranging from 16x16 to 256x256. All the viewcells were 2 meters high. The average time to compute the PVS is shown in Table 1, for a sample of viewcell sizes and discretization resolutions. Table 1 also shows the impact of the discretization resolution on the overestimation of the PVS. The

Resolution	Time (sec.)			Overestimation (%)		
	Viewcell Size			Viewcell Size		
	50x50	100x100	300x300	50x50	100x100	300x300
16x16	0.4	0.5	1.8	0.391	0.518	1.192
32x32	0.6	0.7	2.7	0.335	0.436	0.901
64x64	0.9	1.1	4.1	0.185	0.240	0.533
128x128	2.1	2.5	7.8	0.012	0.026	0.106
256x256	6.6	7.9	24	0.001	0.005	0.019

Table 1. The effect of the discretization resolution on the speed and overestimation of the algorithm.

overestimation is given by

$$\frac{P_E - P_C}{P_E} \cdot 100\%,$$

where P_E is the size of the occluded areas, as computed using the exact planar algorithm, and P_C is the size of the occluded areas, as computed using the conservative planar algorithm. One of the advantages of this measure is its independence from the depth complexity of the model.

Table 1 shows that the speed of the algorithm directly depends on the discretization resolution. Hence, using better graphics hardware can further accelerate the visibility computation. This indicates that we have made the from-region visibility determination problem hardware intensive.

Based on our experiments, we have chosen to work with viewcells of size 100x100 meters and discretization resolution of 128x128. The PVS of a 100x100 viewcell in the London model consists of on average 8K polygons (0.5% of the model). This means that a client using a personal workstation can render the PVS in real time.

Before the walkthrough begins, the server computes and sends the PVS of the initial viewcell and the eight viewcells adjacent to it. During the walkthrough, the server ensures that the client receives the PVS of a viewcell before reaching it. Since the server does not know in advance which viewcell the client will enter next, this necessitates computing and transmitting the PVS of up to five adjacent viewcells while the client traverses a single viewcell, as shown in Figure 5. Assuming average walkthrough speed of 6km/h, such computation takes 12.5 seconds on average (Table 1), which leaves 47 seconds for transmitting the five visibility changes to the client, considering the fact that crossing a single 100x100 viewcell at this speed takes about one minute.

Even in the case of a slow network connection, this clearly shows that remote walkthroughs can be conducted unhindered by network lag. The large size of the viewcells gives the server enough time to compute and transmit the visibility information. The algorithm's speed allows performing visibility computation on-line. Finally, the accuracy of the algorithm ensures that the PVS is small enough to be displayed by the client in real time.

7 Conclusion

We have presented a novel from-region visibility algorithm. Its central idea is an alternative representation of visibility in the *dual ray space*, which allows utilizing standard

214

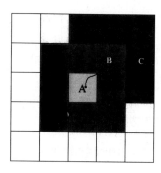

Fig. 5. A client's path in the model is shown in red. When the client commences the walkthrough at viewcell A, it has the PVS of A and the green viewcells. Upon the client's arrival at viewcell B, the server starts computing the PVS of the blue viewcells. Experiments show that the client will receive the PVS of all the blue viewcells before reaching any one of them. In similar fashion, the server ensures throughout the walkthrough that the client never reaches a viewcell before its PVS is received by the client.

rendering hardware for visibility determination. The algorithm is simple to implement, is robust due to working primarily in image-space, and can trade off between accuracy and speed. It was shown to be efficient even when applied to large viewcells. This allows remote walkthroughs to be conducted without preprocessing and storing a priori visibility information.

Acknowledgements

This work was supported by grants from the Israeli Academy of Sciences (center of excellence), and from the Israeli Ministry of Sciences. The London model was generated by the COVEN ACTS project on the Cities Revealed data from the GeoInformation Group.

References

1. C. Andujar, C. Saona-Vazquez, and I. Navazo. LOD visibility culling and occluder synthesis. *Computer Aided Design*, 32(13):773–783, November 2000.
2. F. S. Cho and D. Forsyth. Interactive ray tracing with the visibility complex. *Computer & Graphics*, 23(5):703–717, 1999.
3. D. Cohen-Or, Y. Chrysanthou, and C. Silva. A survey of visibility for walkthrough applications. *SIGGRAPH 2000 'Visibility: Problems, Techniques, and Applications' course notes*.
4. D. Cohen-Or, G. Fibich, D. Halperin, and E. Zadicario. Conservative visibility and strong occlusion for viewspace partitioning of densely occluded scenes. *Computer Graphics Forum*, 17(3):243–254, 1998.
5. S. Coorg and S. Teller. Real-time occlusion culling for models with large occluders. *1997 Symposium on Interactive 3D Graphics*, pages 83–90, April 1997.
6. M. de Berg, M. van Kreveld, M. Overmars, and O. Schwarzkopf. *Computational Geometry: Algorithms and Applications*. Springer-Verlag, Berlin, 1997.

7. F. Durand. *3D Visibility: analytical study and applications*. PhD thesis, Université Joseph Fourier, Grenoble I, July 1999.
8. F. Durand, G. Drettakis, J. Thollot, and C. Puech. Conservative visibility preprocessing using extended projections. *Proceedings of SIGGRAPH 2000*, pages 239–248, July 2000.
9. T. Funkhouser. Database management for interactive display of large architectural models. *Graphics Interface*, pages 1–8, May 1996.
10. S. J. Gortler, R. Grzeszczuk, R. Szeliski, and M. F. Cohen. The lumigraph. *Proceedings of SIGGRAPH 96*, pages 43–54, August 1996.
11. C. Gotsman, O. Sudarsky, and J. Fayman. Optimized occlusion culling. *Computer & Graphics*, 23(5):645–654, 1999.
12. N. Greene and M. Kass. Hierarchical z-buffer visibility. *Proceedings of SIGGRAPH 93*, pages 231–240, 1993.
13. A. E. Haines and J. R. Wallace. Shaft culling for efficient ray-traced radiosity. *2nd Eurographics Workshop on Rendering*, pages 122–138, 1994.
14. T. Hudson, D. Manocha, J. Cohen, M. Lin, K. Hoff, and H. Zhang. Accelerated occlusion culling using shadow frusta. In *Proceedings of the 13th Symposium on Computational Geometry*, pages 1–10, June 1997.
15. V. Koltun, Y. Chrysanthou, and D. Cohen-Or. Virtual occluders: An efficient intermediate PVS representation. *11th Eurographics Workshop on Rendering*, pages 59–70, 2000.
16. V. F. Leavers. Which Hough transform? *Computer Vision and Image Understanding*, 58(2):250–264, 1993.
17. M. Levoy and P. Hanrahan. Light field rendering. *Proceedings of SIGGRAPH 96*, pages 31–42, August 1996.
18. B. Nadler, G. Fibich, S. Lev-Yehudi, and D. Cohen-Or. A qualitative and quantitative visibility analysis in urban scenes. *Computer & Graphics*, 23(5):655–666, 1999.
19. R. Orti, S. Riviére, F. Durand, and C. Puech. Radiosity for dynamic scenes in flatland with the visibility complex. *Computer Graphics Forum*, 15(3):237–248, August 1996.
20. M. Pocchiola and G. Vegter. The visibility complex. *International Journal on Computational Geometry and Applications*, 6(3):279–308, 1996.
21. C. Saona-Vazquez, I. Navazo, and P. Brunet. The visibility octree: A data structure for 3D navigation. *Computer & Graphics*, 23(5):635–644, 1999.
22. G. Schaufler, J. Dorsey, X. Decoret, and F. X. Sillion. Conservative volumetric visibility with occluder fusion. *Proceedings of SIGGRAPH 2000*, pages 229–238, July 2000.
23. A. Steed, E.Frecon, D. Pemberton, and G. Smith. The london travel demonstrator. In *Proceedings of the ACM Symposium on Virtual Reality Software and Technology (VRST-99)*, pages 150–157, Dec. 1999.
24. S. J. Teller. Computing the antipenumbra of an area light source. *Computer Graphics (Proceedings of SIGGRAPH 92)*, 26(2):139–148, July 1992.
25. S. J. Teller. *Visibility cmputations in dnsely ocluded plyhedral evironments*. PhD thesis, Dept. of Computer Science, University of California, Berkeley, 1992.
26. S. J. Teller and P. Hanrahan. Global visibility algorithms for illumination computations. *Proceedings of SIGGRAPH 93*, pages 239–246, August 1993.
27. M. van de Panne and J. Stewart. Effective compression techniques for precomputed visibility. *10th Eurographics Workshop on Rendering*, pages 305–316, 1999.
28. P. Wonka and D. Schmalsteig. Occluder shadows for fast walkthroughs of urban environments. *Computer Graphics Forum*, 18(3):51–60, September 1999.
29. P. Wonka, M. Wimmer, and D. Schmalstieg. Visibility preprocessing with occluder fusion for urban walkthroughs. *11th Eurographics Workshop on Rendering*, pages 71–82, 2000.
30. H. Zhang, D. Manocha, T. Hudson, and K. Hoff. Visibility culling using hierarchical occlusion maps. *Proceedings of SIGGRAPH 97*, pages 77–88, August 1997.

Editors' Note: see Appendix, p. 339 for colored figure of this paper

Real-Time Occlusion Culling with a Lazy Occlusion Grid

Heinrich Hey[1]   Robert F. Tobler[2]   Werner Purgathofer[1]
[1]Vienna University of Technology   [2]VRVis
{hey,rft,wp}@cg.tuwien.ac.at

Abstract. We present a new conservative image-space occlusion culling method to increase the rendering speed of very large general scenes on today's available hardware without time-expensive preprocessing. The method is based on a low-resolution grid upon a conventional z-buffer. The occlusion information in the grid is updated in a lazy manner. In comparison to related methods this significantly reduces the number of pixels that have to be read from the z-buffer. The grid allows fast decisions if an object is occluded or potentially visible. It is used together with a bounding volume hierarchy that is traversed in a front-to-back order and which allows to cull large parts of the scene at once. A special front-to-back traversal is used if no pixel-level query for the furthest z-value of an image area is available. We show that the method works efficiently on today's available hardware and we compare it with related methods.

1 Introduction

Complex scenes may consist of millions of polygons, much more than available graphics hardware can render at interactive frame-rates if only hierarchical view frustum culling and back face culling [11] is used. Occlusion culling methods try to determine which parts of the scene are occluded so that they do not have to be drawn.

In this paper we present a new conservative image-space occlusion culling method for general scenes. It does its occlusion calculations on the fly during rendering. It does not require time-expensive visibility-preprocessing which makes it suited for applications that need to display the scene instantly after the user has modified it, eg. for interactive changes in animations or virtual environments, or for scenes where dynamic objects are important occluders.

The image is subdivided into a low-resolution grid of tiles. Each tile stores occlusion information that shows if the tile is occluded by already drawn objects, and a flag that shows if this occlusion information is outdated. A tile's outdated-flag is set when an object is drawn and the projection of the object's bounding volume (BVol) onto the image plane intersects the tile's area. The tile's occlusion information is not immediately updated after the object has been drawn.

Occlusion of an object is determined by testing if its BVol is occluded in all tiles that intersect the BVol's projection on the image plane. The BVol's occlusion test returns that it is potentially visible if the first tile is found where the BVol is not occluded. First those up-to-date tiles are tested where the occlusion can be determined fast by means of the tiles' occlusion information. This avoids that the z-values of all the pixels of these tiles have to be tested. Only if the BVol is occluded in all these tiles then the occlusion information of outdated tiles has to be updated so that the BVol can be tested against them. The update of a tile's occlusion information is done with a pixel-level query that tests the z-values of the tile's pixels.

This image-space occlusion test is used on a bounding volume hierarchy that is traversed in a front-to-back order. If a bouding volume is rated as occluded then it is culled without having to process its sub-objects and sub-BVols. This way a large part of the scene can be culled at once. The occlusion test can be done in two different versions:

- The *occlusion state-version* is for systems that provide a pixel-level query which returns if all pixels in a given image area are occluded (their z-values are less than z_{max}, z_{max} corresponds to an unoccluded pixel). This query is already available on some of today's hardware [8,12]. The cost of this query compared to the cost of drawing primitives varies between different hardware [13]. On other systems the query can be implemented in software if the hardware provides fast reading access to the z-buffer. Each tile's occlusion information consists of an occlusion state that can be *free* (completely unoccluded), *partially occluded*, or *full* (completely occluded), and a flag that shows if the state is outdated. A special front-to-back traversal of the BVols is used so that objects are occlusion-tested and drawn in an order that guarantees correct occlusion. If an arbitrary front-to-back traversal would be used then BVols could be falsely occluded by already drawn objects behind them. Note that no primitive-wise front-to-back sorting is needed because the exact visibility of the primitives is solved by drawing them with the z-buffer hardware.

- The z_{far}-*version* is for systems that provide a pixel-level query which returns the furthest z-value of all pixels in the z-buffer in a given image area [3]. On systems where this query is not available in hardware (unfortunately this is commonly the case today) it can be implemented in software if the hardware provides fast reading access to the z-buffer. Each tile's occlusion information consists of the furthest z-value (z_{far}) of its pixels rendered so far, and a flag that shows if z_{far} is outdated. Any appoximative front-to-back traversal [5] can be used because the z_{far}-version allows to test the occlusion of a BVol after objects behind it have been drawn.

We have chosen a flat grid instead of a pyramid [5,6,14] because of the low average number of tiles that have to be tested per BVol, as can be seen in our results. The optimal number of pixels per tile that gives the best overall-performance is system-dependent and can be determined by testing typical scenes of the desired application with different numbers of pixels per tile.

A major feature that distinguishes our method from related methods like the hierarchical z-buffer [5] is that we update the occlusion information of a tile only when it is queried and if it is currently marked as outdated (*lazy update*) instead of updating it every time after an object has been drawn in its image area. Therefore a significantly lower number of pixels must be read from the z-buffer because:

- an object is potentially visible if the first unoccluded tile is found in its image area. Therefore up-to-date tiles are queried first which reduces the chance that outdated tiles have to be queried and updated.

- often several objects draw into a tile's area before the tile is queried and updated.

In section 2 we review existing occlusion culling techniques with special emphasis on image-space methods. Section 3 and 4 describe the occlusion state-version and the z_{far}-version in more detail. In section 5 we describe our implementation and present our results and a comparison with related methods. Section 6 finally presents our conclusions.

2 Previous work

For a static scene occlusion information can be precomputed by subdividing the scene into cells and calculating the potentially visible set (PVS) of each cell [2] which usually requires between several minutes and several hours depending on the scene complexity. The advantage of precomputed PVSs is that the display-phase is usually very fast because the objects in the PVS of the viewpoint's cell can be rendered without any further occlusion culling-overhead. Therefore these methods are often used eg. in games [1] where the frame-rate is the major criterion and the time-expensive precomputation is secondary.

Methods that, like our new method, do their occlusion calculations on the fly during rendering [10] have the advantage that they do not need a time-expensive precomputation, but of course the occlusion calculation during rendering produces some overhead. The hierarchical z-buffer (HZB) [5] is an image-space method that does occlusion culling on the fly with a pyramid of z-values. An octree subdivision is used for hierarchical culling of the scene. An improved version of the HZB [7] reduces the required memory traffic, but currently there is no hardware implementation of the HZB available. Hierarchical coverage masks [6] use a pyramid that contains an occlusion state instead of a z-value. Table-lookups and bit-operations are used instead of traditional scanline-rasterization. Geometry is traversed in exact front-to-back order. Currently available graphics-hardware can only be used for texturing and shading. Hierarchical occlusion maps (HOM) [14] work with a pyramid of occlusion-values which is initially build for a few heuristically chosen occluders. This assumes that they occlude large parts of the scene. HOM support non-conservative culling which speeds up the computation but which does not guarantee that all visible objects are drawn. A simple occlusion test can be done with an available hardware accelerated occlusion query [8,12] that rasterizes a BVol without modifying any buffer and that returns whether any fragment passed the z-test. This query is used eg. in the conservative prioritized-layered projection algorithm [9] to cull occluded cells from the front. Extended hardware accelerated occlusion queries have been suggested that return additional occlusion information [4] and that also work in parallel [3].

3 Occlusion state-version

In the occlusion test of a BVol we classify the tiles that intersect the BVol into two types, as shown in fig. 1:
• *Internal tiles* are those which are completely covered by the BVol.
• *Border tiles* are those which only partially intersect the BVol.
We do this to be able to do a pixel-level query to determine if the part of the BVol that intersects a border tile is occluded if the tile is only partially occluded.

Initially (before any object is drawn or any BVol is tested) the z-buffer is cleared and all tiles are set to free-state. The occlusion test of a BVol works as follows:
• Test if one of the BVol's up-to-date internal tiles is not in full-state. If this is true then the BVol is potentially visible.
• After that, but only if we not already have potential visibility, test if one of the BVol's up-to-date border tiles is in free-state. If this is true then the BVol is potentially visible.

- Next, but only if we not already have potential visibility, test each outdated internal tile of the BVol with a pixel-level query in the tile's whole area whether the tile is full or partially occluded, and set the tile's state. If one of these tiles is partially occluded then the BVol is potentially visible.
- At last, but only if we not already have potential visibility, test each border tile of the BVol which is outdated or in partially occluded-state with a pixel-level query in the intersection area of the tile and the BVol. If the pixel-level query returns that the intersection area is not occluded then the BVol is potentially visible.

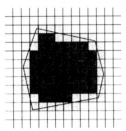

Fig. 1. Border tiles (light grey) and internal tiles (dark grey) of the tested BVol.

Fig. 2. Front-to-back traversal for the occlusion state-version: z_{near}-sorted BVols (white) are occlusion-tested before z_{far}-sorted potentially visible objects (black) that are not completely in front of them are drawn. z_{near}/z_{far} is marked at each BVol/object.

The approximate front-to-back traversal of the occlusion state-version is illustrated in fig. 2. It uses two lists:

- BVols that are not occlusion-tested yet are sorted by their respective nearest z-value (z_{near}). Initially this *test-list* contains the root BVol of the scene.
- BVols that are already rated as potentially visible and that have objects as direct children are sorted by their respective furthest z-value (z_{far}). Initially this *draw-list* is empty. In fig. 2 the objects are shown instead of the BVols of the draw-list.

If the z_{far} of the frontmost BVol of the draw-list is smaller than the z_{near} of the frontmost BVol of the test-list then the frontmost BVol of the draw-list is removed from the list and its object is drawn. Otherwise the frontmost BVol of the test-list is removed from the list and is occlusion-tested. If it is occluded then it is culled, otherwise its sub-BVols are inserted into the test-list and the BVol is inserted into the draw-list if it has an object as direct child.

4 Z_{far}-version

The z_{far}-version works similar to the occlusion state-version. Initially (before any object is drawn or any BVol is tested) the z-buffer is cleared and all tiles' z_{far} are set to z_{max}. In contrast to the occlusion state-variant the z_{far}-version compares if the nearest z-value (z_{near}) of the BVol is greater than the tile's z_{far} to determine if the BVol is occluded or potentially visible in a tile's area. An outdated tile's z_{far} is updated with a pixel-level query that returns the furthest z-value of all pixels in the tile's area.

5 Implementation and Results

We have implemented and tested occlusion culling with the lazy occlusion grid on a PC with a 900 MHz Thunderbird CPU and a GeForce2 GTS graphics card under

OpenGL. We had no access to graphics hardware that supports pixel-level occlusion queries, therefore we implemented the pixel-level queries in software by reading the hardware z-buffer, which is done with the glReadPixels function. The size of the grid's tiles is 32x32 pixels per tile and has been determined heuristically as described in section 1. Of course on other systems the optimal tile-size may be different. We have measured that our hardware does 34,783 glReadPixels of 32x32 z-values (35,617,792 pixels) per second without flushing the rendering pipeline. For our scenes (fig. 3-5, see appendix) we have used a hierarchy of axis-aligned bounding boxes (BBox), but any other kind of BVol could also be used. The image area of a BBox is approximated by its bounding rectangle in the image. The traversal of the BBoxes hierarchy incorporates hierarchical view frustum culling [11] which is implemented by clipping the BBoxes' polygons in software. The BBoxes hierarchy is initially built for the given set of objects of the scene. In the forest scene each tree is an object with an own bounding box. In the city scene each triangle is a primitive object and the scene is hierarchically subdivided into bounding boxes until each bounding box contains no more than 1500 triangles. This generation of the bounding boxes hierarchy takes less than one second for our scenes. The forest scene contains 1,694,426 triangles and the city scene contains 34,034,176 triangles. We tested each of these scenes with a walkthrough that was rendered with occlusion culling

- with the occlusion state-version of the lazy occlusion grid (LOG).
- with the occlusion state-version of the occlusion grid, but each tile is immediately updated after an object has been drawn into its image area if the tile has not already been marked as full (busy occlusion grid (BOG)).
- with occlusion culling with the HZB [5]. After an object has been drawn the conventional z-buffer in the image area of the BBox is read to update the HZB.
- with occlusion culling solely with a pixel-level query per BBox (PQ) that tests all pixels in the image area of the BBox.

and finally without occlusion culling (no OC), but still with hierarchical view frustum culling. The scenes were rendered at 640x480 as well as 1280x960 pixels to show to what extent image resolution affects the rendering time and the number of pixels that are read from the z-buffer. The average rendering time per frame, the average number of drawn triangles per frame (this means that they are sent to OpenGL, backface culling is done by OpenGL), and the average number of pixels that are read from the z-buffer per frame are shown in table 1. We have measured that with our hardware 38-52% of the total rendering time is spent for the glReadPixels calls when we use the LOG and 54-69% when we use the BOG. The average number of tiles that are tested per BBox with the LOG (including those tiles where no pixel-level query is done) is 14.6 in the forest scene and 17.7 in the city scene at 640x480. The average frame-rate with the LOG is 2.1 to 6.9 times faster than with the BOG, which shows the importance of the lazy update. In the moderately large forest scene rendering without occlusion culling is even faster than most of the occlusion culling methods.

6 Conclusion

We have shown that the lazy occlusion grid considerably reduces the number of pixels that have to be read on today's available z-buffer hardware to determine occlusion, and that this significantly increases performance. Future work includes utilization of temporal coherence and support of parallel pixel-level occlusion queries.

222

Table 1. Average time, no. drawn triangles and no. read pixels per frame of walkthrough.

forest 640x480	LOG	BOG	HZB	PQ	no OC
time [s]	0.018	0.073	0.162	0.152	0.045
no. drawn triangles	7,009	7,009	7,009	7,009	147,969
no. read pixels	198,621	2,288,217	2,682,035	5,880,310	-

forest 1280x960	LOG	BOG	HZB	PQ	no OC
time [s]	0.031	0.216	0.632	0.611	0.052
no. drawn triangles	7,510	7,510	7,510	7,510	147,969
no. read pixels	424,713	6,844,437	10,729,627	23,495,623	-

city 640x480	LOG	BOG	HZB	PQ	no OC
time [s]	0.021	0.045	0.087	0.158	0.741
no. drawn triangles	11,981	11,981	11,981	11,981	1,964,918
no. read pixels	283,306	1,272,965	1,361,715	6,032,486	-

city 1280x960	LOG	BOG	HZB	PQ	no OC
time [s]	0.033	0.138	0.328	0.630	0.742
no. drawn triangles	11,775	11,775	11,775	11,775	1,964,918
no. read pixels	312,053	4,230,168	5,417,068	24,042,029	-

Acknowledgments

This work has been supported by the Austrian Science Fund (FWF) project P13600-INF. Thanks to M. Wimmer and P. Wonka for the original version of the city model.

References

1. M. Abrash. Inside Quake: Visible Surface Determination. *Dr. Dobb's Sourcebook* January/February 1996 pp. 41-45
2. J. Airey, J. Rohlf, F. Brooks Jr. Towards Image Realism with Interactive Update Rates in Complex Virtual Building Environments. *Symposium on Interactive 3D Graphics 90* p. 41
3. D. Bartz, M. Meißner, T. Hüttner. Extending Graphics Hardware For Occlusion Queries In OpenGL. *EUROGRAPHICS/SIGGRAPH workshop on graphics hardware 98* pp. 97-103
4. D. Bartz, M. Meißner, T. Hüttner. OpenGL-assisted Occlusion Culling for Large Polygonal Models. *Computers & Graphics* 23 (1999) pp. 667-679
5. N. Greene, M. Kass, G. Miller. Hierarchical Z-Buffer Visibility. *SIGGRAPH 93* p. 231
6. N. Greene. Hierarchical Polygon Tiling with Coverage Masks. *SIGGRAPH 96* pp. 65-74
7. N. Greene. Occlusion Culling with Optimized Hierarchical Buffering. *SIGGRAPH 99 Sketches & Applications* p. 261
8. Hewlett-Packard. OpenGL Implementation Guide. www.hp.com/workstations/support/documentation/manuals/user_guides/graphics/opengl/ImpGuide/01_Overview.html#OcclusionExtension, 2000
9. J. T. Klosowski, C. T. Silva. Efficient Conservative Visibility Culling Using The Prioritized-Layered Projection Algorithm. *SIGGRAPH 2000* Course Notes 4
10. D. Luebke, C. Georges. Portals and Mirrors: Simple, Fast Evaluation of Potentially Visible Sets. *Symposium on Interactive 3D Graphics 95* pp. 105-106
11. T. Möller, E. Haines. *Real-Time Rendering* pp. 192-200, 1999
12. N. Scott, D. Olsen, E. Gannett. An Overview of the VISUALIZE fx Graphics Accelerator Hardware. *Hewlett-Packard Journal* May 1998 pp. 28-34
13. K. Severson. *VISUALIZE Workstation Graphics for Windows NT*. Hewlett-Packard product literature, 1999
14. H. Zhang, D. Manocha, T. Hudson, K. Hoff III. Visibility Culling using Hierarchical Occlusion Maps. *SIGGRAPH 97* pp. 77-88

Editors' Note: see Appendix, p. 340 for colored figures of this paper

Perceptually Driven Simplification for Interactive Rendering

David Luebke, Benjamin Hallen
University of Virginia

Abstract

We present a framework for accelerating interactive rendering, grounded in psychophysical models of visual perception. This framework is applicable to multiresolution rendering techniques that use a hierarchy of local simplification operations. Our method drives those local operations directly by perceptual metrics; the effect of each simplification on the final image is considered in terms of the contrast the operation will induce in the image and the spatial frequency of the resulting change. A simple and conservative perceptual model determines under what conditions the simplification operation will be perceptible, enabling imperceptible simplification in which operations are performed only when judged imperceptible. Alternatively, simplifications may be ordered according to their perceptibility, providing a principled approach to best-effort rendering. We demonstrate this framework applied to view-dependent polygonal simplification. Our approach addresses many interesting topics in the acceleration of interactive rendering, including imperceptible simplification, silhouette preservation, and gaze-directed rendering.

1 Introduction

Interactive rendering of large-scale geometric datasets continues to present a challenge for the field of computer graphics. Despite tremendous strides in computer graphics hardware, the growth of large-scale models continues to outstrip our capability to render them interactively. A great deal of research has therefore focused on algorithmic techniques for managing the rendering complexity of these models. *Polygonal simplification* algorithms offer a powerful tool for this task. These methods, also known as *level of detail* or *LOD* techniques, hinge on the observation that most of the complexity in a detailed 3-D model is unnecessary when rendering that model from a given viewpoint. These methods simplify small, distant, or otherwise unimportant portions of the scene, reducing the rendering cost while attempting to retain visual fidelity. Visual fidelity has traditionally been measured using geometric criteria. Often, however, the most important measure of fidelity is not geometric but perceptual: does the simplification *look* like the original?

We describe an LOD framework guided directly by perceptual metrics. These metrics derive from the *contrast sensitivity function* or *CSF*, a simple measure of low-level perceptibility of visual stimuli. Testing local simplification operations against a model of the CSF provides a principled approach to the fidelity/performance tradeoff. Our approach addresses several interesting problems in regulating level of detail:

- **Imperceptible simplification:** We evaluate simplification operations by the "worst-case" contrast and spatial frequency they induce in the image, and apply only those operations judged imperceptible. We show that the resulting simplified model is indistinguishable from the original.

- **Best-effort simplification:** Often we wish to render the best image possible within time or polygon constraints. Ordering simplification operations according to the viewing distance at which their effect on the image becomes perceptible provides a principled framework for simplifying to a budget.
- **Silhouette preservation:** Silhouettes have long been recognized as visually important, but how important? Our model quantifies silhouette importance by accounting for their increased contrast, and preserves them accordingly.
- **Gaze-directed rendering:** If the system can monitor the user's gaze, the image may be simplified more aggressively in the visual periphery. We can extend our model to incorporate *eccentricity*, or the falloff of visual acuity in the periphery.

Our framework applies to any rendering system based on hierarchical approximations, such as polygonal mesh reduction, texture-based imposters, and some forms of image- and point-based rendering. In this paper, we explore the application of this framework to view-dependent polygonal simplification. Our key contribution is a technique for evaluating the worst-case perceptibility of local simplification operations, each removing a few polygons from the mesh, according to the contrast and spatial frequency they induce.

2 Background and Previous Work

2.1 The Contrast Sensitivity Function

A large body of perceptual psychology literature focuses on the perceptibility of visual stimuli. The simplest relation established in this literature is *Weber's law*, which predicts the minimum detectable difference in luminance between a test spot on a uniform visual field. At daylight levels, this threshold difference in luminance increases linearly with background luminance. Interesting scenes are not uniform, however, but contain complex frequency content. Outside a small frequency range, the threshold sensitivity predicted by Weber's law drops off significantly. Many perception studies have therefore examined the perceptibility of *contrast gratings*,

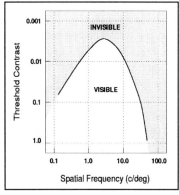

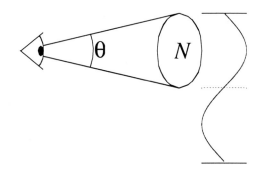

Figure 1: The *contrast sensitivity function* measures the perceptibility of visual stimuli (sinusoidal gratings) in terms of their contrast and spatial frequency (cycles per degree). Courtesy Martin Reddy.

Figure 2: The lowest spatial frequency that can be affected by a node spanning $\theta°$ of visual arc has one cycle per $2\theta°$.

sinusoidal patterns that alternate between two extreme luminance values L_{max} and L_{min} [3]. Contrast grating studies use *Michaelson contrast*, defined as $(L_{max} - L_{min}) / (L_{max} + L_{min})$, and *spatial frequency*, defined as the number of cycles per degree of visual arc. The *threshold contrast* at a given spatial frequency is the minimum contrast that can be perceived in a grating of that frequency, and *contrast sensitivity* is defined as the reciprocal of threshold contrast. The *contrast sensitivity function* (CSF) plots contrast sensitivity against spatial frequency, and so describes the range of perceptible contrast gratings [Figure 1].

Of course, interesting images are more complex than the simple sinusoidal patterns used in contrast gratings. To a first approximation, however, perceptibility of complex signals can be determined by decomposing a signal into sinusoidal components using Fourier analysis [4]. In particular, if no frequency component of a signal is perceptible, the signal will not be perceptible.

The CSF predicts the maximum perceptibility of a stationary grating at the center of view. Other factors can lower contrast sensitivity further, including *eccentricity*, or angular distance from the direction of gaze. The *fovea* is the region of highest sensitivity on the retina, occupying the central 1° or so of vision. *Visual acuity*, measured as the highest perceptible spatial frequency, is significantly lower in the visual periphery than at the fovea [25]. Extending our perceptual model to incorporate eccentricity lets us predict peripheral visibility for gaze-directed rendering.

2.2 Perceptually Based Offline Rendering

Many researchers have worked on perceptually based rendering algorithms, such as Walter et al [29], Bolin and Meyer [2], and Ramasubramanian et al [23]. The latter two both include good surveys of the field. These algorithms take advantage of the limitations of human vision to avoid rendering computation where the result will be imperceptible. Unlike our work, which seeks to accelerate interactive rendering, almost all previous perceptually based rendering approaches have addressed realistic offline rendering approaches such as ray and path tracing. Since image creation times in such approaches are typically measured in seconds or minutes, these algorithms use sophisticated perceptual models that are costly to evaluate by interactive rendering terms. For example, Ramasubramanian et al take several seconds to evaluate a 512x512 image. This is clearly unsuitable for interactive rendering, which measures frame time in milliseconds.

2.3 Perceptually Based LOD Selection

Regulating scene complexity by simplifying small or distant objects was first proposed in Clark's seminal 1976 paper [5], and several recent surveys examine the current state of the art [10][17][22]. The basic approach described by Clark remains the most common approach today: create several versions of each object, at progressively coarser levels of detail (called *LODs*), and choose at run-time which LOD will represent the object.

Comparatively few systems have attempted to guide this process with explicit perceptual metrics. Funkhouser and Sequin used a cost-benefit estimate to pick the best levels of detail within a specified time budget [9]. Their system used ad hoc weighting factors to account for eccentricity and *velocity*, the speed at which the image of an object moves across the retina. Ohshima et al described a system for gaze-directed stereoscopic rendering [21]again using heuristic models of eccentricity, velocity, and convergence to guide selection of precomputed LODs.

Reddy was the first to attempt an LOD selection system guided throughout by a principled perceptual model [24]. Using images rendered from multiple viewpoints, Reddy analyzed the frequency content of objects and their LODs, A model of the visual acuity, defined as highest perceptible spatial frequency, guided LOD selection: if a high-resolution and a low-resolution LOD differed only at frequencies beyond the visual acuity of the viewer, the system used the low-resolution LOD. Scoggins et al analyzed the frequency content more thoroughly, transforming a prerendered reference image to frequency space [28]. Scoggins et al then applied the CSF as a modulation transfer function and used the resulting mean-squared error to decide which LOD was appropriate.

2.4   View-Dependent Polygonal Simplification

One difficulty with all these approaches is their reliance on a few discrete levels of detail to represent each object. This limits the degree to which perceptual metrics can be applied, since the entire object must be simplified uniformly. For example, silhouette details tend to be more perceptible than interior details because of higher contrast, so the entire object must be treated as if it were on the silhouette. *View-dependent* simplification methods offer a solution. Rather than calculating a series of static LODs, view-dependent systems build a data structure from which a desired level of detail may be extracted at run time. Objects in a view-dependent algorithm may span multiple resolutions; for example, portions of the object under the viewer's gaze can be represented at higher fidelity than portions in the peripheral vision.

Several researchers have proposed view-dependent algorithms, including Hoppe, Luebke, and Xia [11][16][30]. These algorithms use a hierarchy of *vertex merge* operations that can be applied or reversed at run-time. Our chief contribution is a method for evaluating the perceptibility of a vertex merge. We have implemented our system using *VDSlib*, a public-domain library that allows users to plug in custom callbacks for building, culling, simplifying, and rendering the model [19]. We first augment VDSlib with some perceptual data (described below), then at run time, our callback examines possible simplifications, using contrast, spatial frequency, and possibly eccentricity to decide which vertices VDSlib should merge. Before describing the details of this process, we briefly review the VDSlib algorithm and notation.

The main data structure of VDSlib is the *vertex tree*, a hierarchical clustering of vertices. Leaf nodes of the tree represent a single vertex from the original model; interior nodes represent multiple vertices clustered together, and the root node represents all vertices from the entire model, merged into a single cluster. In VDSlib parlance, a node **N** *supports* a vertex **V** if the leaf node associated with **V** descends from **N**. Similarly, **N** *supports* a triangle **T** if it supports one or more of the corner vertices of **T**. The set of triangles in the model supported by a node is called the *region of support* of the node.

Each node stores a representative vertex called the *proxy*. For leaf nodes, the proxy is exactly the vertex of the original model that the node represents; for interior nodes, the proxy is typically some average of the represented vertices. *Folding* a node merges all of the vertices supported by that node into the node's single proxy vertex. In the process, triangles whose corners have been merged together are removed, decreasing the overall polygon count of the scene. Since folding a node is the core simplification operation of VDSlib, to apply our perceptual framework we must evaluate the contrast and spatial extent of the change in the rendered image induced by a fold.

3 Overview of our approach

Our main contribution is a way to map the change resulting from a local simplification operation to a *worst-case* contrast grating, meaning a grating with the most perceptible possible combination of contrast and frequency induced by the operation. This gives us a bound on the perceptibility of that simplification operation. For example, for imperceptible simplification we apply only those operations whose corresponding gratings we would not expect to be visible, while for best-effort simplification we order the simplification operations according to the perceptibility of their gratings.

3.1 Determining the Worst Case

We wish to characterize the frequency and contrast induced in the rendered image by a simplification operation, but this induced change will generally have a non-trivial spectrum, with multiple frequencies present at different amplitudes. Since the CSF is non-linear, it does not obviously follow that the frequency component with the greatest amplitude is the most perceptible. Performing a Fourier transform of the image in the neighborhood of each local operation and modulating the resulting frequencies by the CSF could evaluate the most perceptible frequency, but this is clearly too expensive. We argue below that if all induced frequencies were present at equal amplitudes, the *lowest* frequency would be the most perceptible. Furthermore, a conservative estimate

Figure 3: The original Stanford Bunny model (69,451 faces) and a simplification by our perceptually driven system (29,866 faces). In this view the user's gaze is 29° from the center of the bunny...equivalent to looking at the top of this page from a distance of 29 cm. Note that the silhouette is well preserved, along with strong interior details (the line of the haunch, the shape of the eye, etc.) while subtle bumps on the surface are simplified. The bunny and other models used here are courtesy of the Stanford 3-D Scanning Repository.

of the induced contrast establishes a lower bound on the amplitude of any frequency component. Thus our key observation: the perceptibility of a change induced by simplification can be conservatively equated to the perceptibility of the *lowest frequency* induced by that change, at the *maximum contrast* induced by that change.

To show this, we make some conservative simplifying assumptions. We observe that the peak contrast sensitivity occurs at approximately 2-4 cycles per degree, and that most local simplification operations on a complex model only affect much higher frequencies. We therefore assume that contrast at lower spatial frequencies is more perceptible than at higher frequencies, and ensure this assumption holds by clamping our worst-case frequency to be no lower than the point of peak sensitivity. The minimum frequency component of a region in the image spanning n degrees of the user's angular field of view is one cycle per $2n$ degrees. Put another way, the maximum wavelength needed to represent a region of the image is twice the maximum spatial extent of that region [Figure 2]. Consequently, we can reduce finding the worst-case frequency induced by a simplification to finding the screen-space extent of the affected region.

For the worst-case contrast, we determine a bound on the maximum change in luminance among all the pixels affected by the simplification. The worst-case contrast of a simplification operation is thus the maximum contrast between an image of the affected region at full resolution and an image of the region simplified. For 3-D models, there are two basic cases:

- The entire affected region lies interior to a surface that entirely faces the viewer. This is the simplest case: the contrast between the original region and the folded region is completely determined by the luminance of the local surface before and after the fold.

- The affected region includes a silhouette or visual contour. This expands the possible contrast incurred by the simplification to include the portion of the scene *behind* the affected region, since simplifying the surface may expose a very bright or very dark feature occluded before simplification.

Consequently, silhouette regions of the object are simplified less aggressively—exactly the behavior we should expect in a perceptually driven simplification algorithm. Note, however, that even at these higher contrast levels silhouette regions can still be simplified if they represent very fine details (high spatial frequencies) or are in the viewer's peripheral vision (high eccentricity).

3.2 An Empirical Perceptual Model

Many researchers have characterized the contrast sensitivity function. In early work, Kelly derived an abstract relationship for the perceptibility of sinusoidal gratings over a narrow range [13]. A broader range was described by the equation of Mannos and Sakrison [20]. More recent and accurate CSF models, such as the models given by Barten [1] and Daly [7], are used in current advanced global illumination algorithms [23][2]. Modern perceptual theory attributes the shape of the CSF to the combined response curves of multiple bandpass mechanisms in the visual system, each processing only a small range of the visible spatial frequency spectrum. This multiscale visual processing can be emulated with a Laplacian pyramid for spatial decomposition [15]. Current perceptual rendering techniques also account for *contrast*

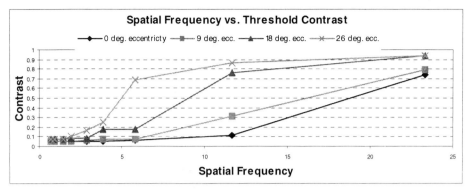

Figure 4: We use a simple model of contrast sensitivity based on an empirical calibration procedure. Shown here are results from one user's calibration.

masking, which represents the visual system's decreased contrast sensitivity in the presence of strong patterns. This can further increase the allowable error in an image [23][2][8].

Unfortunately, these sophisticated perceptual models, which employ the latest advances in understanding perception, are far too costly for the interactive framework we propose. In our framework, thousands of simplification operations must be considered every second, leaving less than a millisecond to evaluate the induced contrast and frequency. Clearly, we must forego the state-of-the-art perceptual models used in current global illumination work for a simple, fast, and conservative model.

We have had promising results using a simple mathematical model of the CSF, namely Rushmeier's simplification of Daly's equation [26]. However, for the results shown here we chose to take an empirical approach that allows us to achieve simplicity and speed, while still accounting for real-world factors (such as ambient light) that affect perception. Recall our hypothesis: a simplification operation, mapped to a "worst-case" contrast grating, can be performed imperceptibly if that grating would not be perceptible. We build our perceptual model directly from contrast grating tests performed under the same conditions—room illumination, monitor, etc—under which our final system will run. A calibration procedure tests the ability of a user to detect contrast gratings, recording threshold contrast over a wide range of spatial frequency and eccentricity. We then build a lookup table from the resulting CSF curves and use linear interpolation at runtime to determine whether the user can perceive a given contrast at a given spatial frequency and eccentricity. As mentioned in Section 3.1, we ensure conservative behavior by clamping threshold contrast below the frequency of peak sensitivity.

This model could certainly be improved, but we chose to focus on developing a framework for driving interactive rendering with a perceptual model, rather than on developing the model itself. Our empirical model is simple to implement and works well in practice. Figure 4 shows example CSF curves determined from a typical calibration procedure. Note that we must calibrate the monitor to map OpenGL intensities to luminance. We used a photometer, but simple gamma correction would suffice if less precision were required.

3.3   Evaluating the fold operation

Folding a node in VDSlib can affect the rendered image in complex ways. As the vertices and triangles supported by the node merge and shift, features in the image may shrink, stretch, or disappear completely. Shifting triangles on the silhouette may expose previously occluded features. To analyze the effect of folding a node, we should consider all of these changes. One possibility, recently demonstrated by Lindstrom and Turk for static LOD generation, is to render the scene before and after the operation and analyze the resulting images [14]. At present, however, the requisite rendering and image processing appears too expensive for dynamic simplification. Instead, we want a conservative worst-case bound on the changes in the image caused by folding the node. As discussed, this worst case bound can be reduced to finding the minimum frequency and the maximum contrast.

Spatial Frequency: Estimating Extent

Recall that the minimum frequency induced by a simplification is determined by the spatial extent of the resulting change in the image. Notice that features in the image affected by a fold consist of triangles connecting vertices involved in the fold. The largest feature that can be removed or exposed by geometric distortion upon folding a node is therefore constrained by the distance vertices move during the fold. Thus, the problem of computing the minimum frequency induced by folding a node reduces to computing the screen-space extent of all vertices supported by the node.[1] We use bounding spheres to estimate this extent, associating with each node a tight-fitting sphere that contains all vertices in the node's region of support. The angular extent of these bounding spheres, as seen from a given viewpoint, can be calculated very quickly. The minimum frequency affected by folding a node is then one cycle per two degrees of angular extent spanned by the node's bounding sphere [Figure 2].

Contrast: Estimating Intensity Change

Determining the precise contrast induced by folding a node would be as expensive as rendering the unfolded geometry. Instead, we want a conservative lower bound, which could be computed several ways. For simplicity, we currently assume pre-lit Gouraud-shaded meshes, and obtain a conservative bound by comparing the intensities of all the vertices the node supports in the original model with the intensities of the vertices in the simplified surface. The greatest difference between the intensities of the surface vertices before folding and after folding bounds the maximum contrast between the simplified surface and the original surface, since in a Gouraud-shaded model extremes of intensity always occur at the vertices. This test may overestimate the contrast induced by folding, but will not underestimate it.

When the node's region of support includes a silhouette, we must be even more conservative. Lacking knowledge about what lies behind the region, we must assume the worst: moving a silhouette edge might expose the darkest or brightest object in the scene, including the background. Hence we must compare the range of vertex

---

[1] Technically, this holds when the model is flat shaded; for Gouraud-shaded models, adjacent vertices should also be included. However, we have not found this necessary in practice.

intensities of the node's region of support against the brightest and darkest intensities in the scene, and use the maximum possible difference in intensity for calculating the contrast induced by the fold.

Determining Silhouette Nodes

Since nodes affecting silhouette edges must be treated differently, we require an efficient method for identifying such nodes. For a given view, we define *silhouette nodes* as those nodes supporting both front-facing and back-facing triangles in the original mesh. One possibility would use the normal cone hierarchies of Johnson and Cohen [12], but we currently use a bitwise approach inspired by the rapid backface culling technique of Zhang and Hoff [31]. We quantize the Gauss sphere of normal space to a *normal cube* whose faces are tiled into cells, and store a per-node *normal mask*, or bit vector representing the normals of all its supported triangles. The silhouette test may then be implemented with simple bitwise operations. This technique is fast and accurate, though it requires more storage (we use 48 bytes/node) than the normal cone hierarchies.

Putting It All Together: Imperceptible Simplification

Given these elements, imperceptible simplification is easily implemented. A VDSlib traversal visits each node in the hierarchy top-down, applying our custom simplification criterion as a callback at each node. The callback evaluates the worst-case frequency based on the screen-space size of the node, and then looks up the threshold contrast for that frequency in our empirical CSF model. If the contrast induced by folding is less than the threshold contrast, the callback allows VDSlib to fold the node, otherwise the node is left unfolded and traversal continues.

3.4   Perceptually Guided Best-Effort Rendering

We can also use our model for best-effort simplification. VDSlib supports *triangle budget simplification*, which lets the user specify how many triangles the scene should contain. Using a user-specified error metric, VDSlib applies a greedy algorithm to

Figure 5: Perceptually driven best-effort simplification. Both images show the horse model (originally 96,966 faces) reduced to 18,000 faces using triangle budget rendering in VDSlib. Left, the default VDSlib error metric uses screenspace node size, leading to unnecessarily even tesselation. Right, our perceptually driven metric uses fewer polygons in interior and low-contrast regions.

minimize the total error induced by all folded nodes, while staying within this triangle budget constraint. We must therefore generate a sound perceptual measure of the error introduced by folding a node. The key is to recast our metric for evaluating the perceptibility of fold operations: rather than a binary perceptible/not perceptible decision, we need a scalar to express *how* perceptible a fold operation could be.

Unfortunately, the CSF provides only threshold information, and cannot be used directly to evaluate suprathreshold perceptibility. In other words, the CSF can tell us whether a fold operation is perceptible, but cannot tell us which of two perceptible folds is more objectionable. We therefore chose to cast the question in terms of distance: how far would the viewer have to be from the screen before the node could be folded imperceptibly? The answer can be computed from our current perceptual model, in effect by inverting our lookup tables. Rather than computing the spatial frequency of a node and looking up the threshold contrast at which folding is perceptible, we use the precomputed contrast induced by folding and look up the threshold spatial frequency. From this we can compute the distance at which folding the node would be perceptible, and sort nodes to be folded according to this distance. We then order folds based on the viewing distance at which they become perceptible and stop when the budget is reached. This provides an intuitive physical measure of the fidelity achieved, since the system can report the distance at which a simplification should be imperceptible.

3.5 Results

All results given are on an 866 MHz Pentium III computer with NVidia GeForce[2] graphics. Figure 3 shows a model simplified imperceptibly while accounting for eccentricity. Since we are guaranteeing imperceptible simplification, the reductions in polygon count may seem modest. However, these results and our user study (below) clearly show that perceptually driven simplification can reduce model complexity without visual effect.

Perceptually driven best-effort rendering may be of more use to many 3-D applications. Figure 5 compares our results to VDSlib's built-in triangle budget rendering, which orders fold operations only by screen-space size of the node. Note that the perceptually driven algorithm preserves more triangles near silhouettes, and simplifies more aggressively in regions of low contrast.

We have performed a preliminary user study to determine whether our simplifications are indeed imperceptible from the original model. The study tested whether 4 subjects in 200 trials could perceive any difference between a rendering of a full-resolution model and a rendering of a model simplified with our algorithm. The study, which we do not describe in detail here, confirmed that subjects' ability to discern the simplification was no better than chance. For a full description of the study, please see our technical report [18].

4 Summary And Discussion

Perceptually guided interactive rendering is a broad and difficult topic. Our system shows the feasibility and potential of imperceptible view-dependent simplification, but many avenues for further research remain. Below we summarize our contribution and results, and address what we see as pressing and interesting directions for future work.

4.1 Summary

We have demonstrated a novel approach to reducing model complexity that is directly driven by perceptual criteria. Our principle contribution is a practical framework for perceptually guided interactive rendering that equates local simplification operations to worst-case contrast gratings whose perceptibility we can evaluate. We have demonstrated this framework in the context of view-dependent polygonal simplification. Our approach addresses several interesting problems, including silhouette preservation and imperceptible simplification. An optional gaze-directed component uses eye tracking to obtain further simplification by reducing fidelity in the viewer's peripheral vision.

4.2 Ongoing and Future Work

We have demonstrated our perceptual framework applied to view-dependent polygonal simplification, but the framework also applies to many other rendering schemes. We are experimenting with a perceptually driven version of the *Qsplat* point-rendering system by Rusinkiewicz and Levoy [27], which provides a completely different model representation and rendering paradigm. We believe this is an excellent testimonial to the flexibility and generality of our framework.

The current system is far from perfect; we see this work as the first step rather than the last word in perceptually guided interactive rendering. Our chief problem: the system is overly conservative. In practice, we find that our models could be reduced two to three times further in polygon count without perceptible effect. We attribute this primarily to our highly conservative estimate of spatial frequency, and are exploring more accurate ways to compute the induced frequencies.

Incorporating dynamic lighting into the contrast calculation is an obvious extension; this should be quite possible given the node normal masks. Incorporating texture mapping is an exciting area for future work, and could both increase and decrease the amount of simplification possible. The distortion of a texture on a simplified surface being simplified could increase the perceptibility of the simplification, but the frequency content of the texture could potentially be analyzed in a preprocess to account for visual masking effects that would decrease perceptibility of simplification. We are investigating integrating the texture deviation metric of Cohen's *appearance-preserving simplification* [6] to account for these factors. Like other perceptually driven rendering algorithms (e.g., [23][2]) we model perceptibility of static stimuli; we believe that the field as a whole needs to begin incorporating measures of *temporal contrast sensitivity* to address possible flicker artifacts in interactive or animated rendering. Finally, we would like to exploit the reduced visual acuity caused by velocity across the retinal field, which Reddy's work suggests provides a promising opportunity for further simplification [24].

5 References

[1] Barten, Peter. "The Square-Root Integral", In *Human Vision, Visual Processing, and Digital Display*, vol. 1077, Proceedings SPIE (1989)

[2] Bolin, Mark. and G. Meyer. "A Perceptually Based Adaptive Sampling Algorithm", *Computer Graphics*, Vol. 32 (SIGGRAPH 98).

[3] Campbell, F., Gubisch, R. "Optical Quality of the Human Eye", *Journal of Physiology* 186.

[4] Campbell, F.W. and Robson, J.G. "An Application of Fourier Analysis to the Visibility of Contrast Gratings", *Journal of Physiology*, 187 (1968)

[5] Clark, James H. "Hierarchical Geometric Models for Visible Surface Algorithms," *Communications of the ACM*, Vol. 19, No 10, pp 547-554.

[6] Cohen, J, M. Olano, and D. Manocha. "Appearance-Preserving Simplification," *Computer Graphics*, Vol. 32 (SIGGRAPH 98).

[7] Daly, S. "Visible differences predictor: An algorithm for the assessment of image fidelity," *Digital Images and Human Vision* (A. Watson, ed.), pp 179--206, MIT Press (1993).

[8] Ferdwada, James, S. Pattanaik, P. Shirley, and D. Greenberg. "A Model of Visual Masking for Realistic Image Synthesis", *Computer Graphics*, Vol. 30 (SIGGRAPH 96).

[9] Funkhouser, Tom, and C. Sequin. "Adaptive display algorithm for interactive frame rates during visualization of complex virtual environments", *Computer Graphics*, Vol. 27.

[10] Heckbert, Paul, and M. Garland. "Survey of Polygonal Surface Simplification Algorithms", SIGGRAPH 97 course notes (1997).

[11] Hoppe, Hughes. "View-Dependent Refinement of Progressive Meshes", *Computer Graphics*, Vol. 31 (SIGGRAPH 97).

[12] Johnson, David, and E. Cohen. "Spatialized Normal Cone Hierarchies", *Proceedings ACM Symposium on Interactive 3D Graphics* (2001).

[13] Kelly, D.H. "Spatial Frequency Selectivity in the Retina", *Vision Research*, 15 (1975).

[14] Lindstrom, Peter. and Turk, G. "Image-Based Simplification", *ACM Transactions on Graphics*, July 2000 (2000).

[15] Lubin, Jeffery. "A Visual Discrimination Model for Imaging System Design and Evaluation", *Vision Models for Target Detection and Recognition*, World Scientific (1995).

[16] Luebke, David, and C. Erikson. "View-Dependent Simplification of Arbitrary Polygonal Environments", *Computer Graphics*, Vol. 31 (SIGGRAPH 97).

[17] Luebke, David. "A Developer's Survey of Polygonal Simplification Algorithms", *IEEE Computer Graphics & Applications* (May 2001). See tech report CS-99-07, U of Virginia.

[18] Luebke, David, and B. Hallen. "Perceptually-Driven Interactive Rendering". Technical report CS-2001-01, University of Virginia (2000).

[19] Luebke, David. See *http://vdslib.virginia.edu*.

[20] J. L. Mannos, D. J. Sakrison, "The Effects of a Visual Fidelity Criterion on the Encoding of Images", *IEEE Transactions on Information Theory*, pp. 525-535, Vol. 20, No 4, (1974).

[21] Oshima, Toshikazu, H. Yamammoto, and H. Tamura. "Gaze-Directed Adaptive Rendering for Interacting with Virtual Space", *Proceedings of VRAIS 96* (1996).

[22] Puppo, Enrico, and R. Scopigno. "Simplification, LOD and Multiresolution—Principles and Applications", *Eurographics '97 Tutorial Notes*, PS97 TN4 (1997).

[23] Ramasubramanian, Mahesh, S. Pattanaik, and D. Greenberg. "A Perceptually Based Physical Error Metric for Realistic Image Synthesis", *Computer Graphics*, Vol. 33.

[24] Reddy, Martin. "Perceptually-Modulated Level of Detail for Virtual Environments", Ph.D. thesis, University of Edinburgh, 1997.

[25] Rovamo, J. and Virsu, V. "An Estimation and Application of the Human Cortical Magnification Factor", *Experimental Brain Research*, 37 (1979)

[26] Rushmeier, H., G. Ward, C. Piatko, P. Sanders, and B. Rust. "Comparing Real and Synthetic Images: Some Ideas About Metrics," In *Rendering Techniques '95*, pp 82-91, Springer-Verlag (1995).

[27] Rusinkiewicz, S. and Levoy, M. "QSplat: A Multiresolution Point Rendering System for Large Meshes", *Computer Graphics*, Vol. 34 (SIGGRAPH 2000).

[28] Scoggins, Randy, R. Machiraju, and R. Moorhead. "Enabling Level-of-Detail Matching for Exterior Scene Synthesis", *Proceedings of IEEE Visualization 2000* (2000).

[29] Walter, Bruce, P. M. Hubbard, P. Shirley, and D. Greenberg. "Global Illumination using Local Linear Density Estimation", *ACM Transaction on Graphics* (1997).

[30] Xia, Julie and Amitabh Varshney. "Dynamic View-Dependent Simplification for Polygonal Models", *Visualization 96*.

[31] Zhang, Hansong, and K. Hoff. "Fast Backface Culling Using Normal Masks", *Proceedings of ACM Symposium on Interactive 3D Graphics* (1997).

Measuring the Perception of Visual Realism in Images

Paul Rademacher [†‡]   Jed Lengyel [‡]   Edward Cutrell [‡]   Turner Whitted [‡]

[†] University of North Carolina at Chapel Hill   [‡] Microsoft Research

Abstract. One of the main goals in realistic rendering is to generate images that are indistinguishable from photographs – but how do observers decide whether an image is photographic or computer-generated? If this perceptual process were understood, then rendering algorithms could be developed to directly target these cues. In this paper we introduce an experimental method for measuring the perception of visual realism in images, and present the results of a series of controlled human subject experiments. These experiments cover the following visual factors: shadow softness, surface smoothness, number of light sources, number of objects, and variety of object shapes. This technique can be used to either affirm or cast into doubt common assumptions about realistic rendering. The experiments can be performed using either photographs or computer-generated images. This work provides a first step towards objectively understanding why some images are perceived as photographs, while others as computer graphics.

1   INTRODUCTION

One of the goals in computer graphics research since its inception has been to generate computer images *indistinguishable from photographs*. The most realistic results emerge from special effects studios, which typically forego physically-accurate rendering methods, relying instead on the visual skills of their artists. These artists have a keen understanding of *how an image must look for it to be perceived as real*. They operate in a continual loop of generating images, evaluating them for realism, and then making adjustments as necessary. However, the average practitioner in computer graphics does not precisely understand what makes some images look photographic and others computer-generated, and is unable to create fully-realistic imagery.

If the perceptual criteria by which people evaluate whether an image is real were understood, then one could build new rendering algorithms to directly target the necessary visual cues. Furthermore, one could optimize the rendering budget towards those visual factors that have the greatest impact, without wasting effort on elements that will not noticeably improve the realism of an image.

In this paper we demonstrate that the perception of visual realism in images can be studied using techniques from experimental psychology. We present an experimental method that directly asks participants whether an image is real (photographic) or not real (CG). We conducted experiments to explore several

Figure 1. Is this a photograph or CG? What visual factors affect your decision?

visual factors, including shadow softness, surface smoothness, number of objects, variety of object shapes, and number of light sources. The resulting data confirmed some common assumptions about realistic rendering, and contradicted others. We found that while shadow softness and surface smoothness played a significant role in determining an image's perceived realism, increasing the number of light sources did not. Also, increasing the number of objects in a scene, or the variety of object shapes, did not increase an image's likelihood to be perceived as real / photographic. Our method can be conducted using exclusively photographs, or using exclusively computer-generated images. We ran duplicate experiments using both photographs and computer-generated images, with similar and consistent results between the two.

2   PREVIOUS WORK

There have been several approaches to the creation of realistic images. One is to analyze, measure, approximate, and simulate the various physical processes that form a real-world image (light transport, surface BRDFs, tone mapping, and more). This approach has met with only limited success. Furthermore, the few projects that *have* created images indistinguishable from specific target photographs (such as the Cornell Box [Patt97]) do not reveal which visual factors a viewer expects in order to perceive the image as real.

Another approach to realism is image-based rendering [Leng98], which has created synthetic images which are nearly indistinguishable from photographs. This is to be expected, of course, since image-based rendering works by rearranging image samples taken directly from photographs. What was it about the original photographs that made them realistic in the first place?

There exists an enormous amount of previous work on human vision and classical perception. [Bruc96] and [Gord97] are good introductions. Work in these fields includes low-level vision, classical psychophysics, object recognition, scene understanding [Hage80], and more. However, the direct question of how people distinguish photographs from computed-generated images has not been raised in the classical perceptual literature. Indirectly, works such as [Parr00], which analyzes the approximate $1/f$ frequency spectrum of natural images, provide clues as to the nature of real-world imagery. An informal essay on how visual realism in computer graphics was given by [Chiu94]. [Barb92] describes limitations of display technologies when trying to simulate *direct* vision.

There are several recent works in the computer graphics literature dealing with human visual perception (e.g., applications of psychophysics in [Ferw98], [Vole00], [Rama99]). [Chal00] describes various image quality metrics. [Rush95] proposed perceptually-based image metrics to differentiate between a pair of images, in order to evaluate the accuracy of synthetic renderings of real-world scenes. In [Thom98], shadows and other visual cues are tested against subjects' ability to discern properties such as object orientation or proximity. [Horv97] measures subjects' response to various settings of image quality, to guide an efficient renderer. [Mcna00] compares computer-generated images with real, physical scenes (viewed directly) to evaluate the perceptual fidelity of the renderings, in a manner similar to [Meye86]. None of these perceptually-based research efforts directly studied the visual causes for the perception of some images as photographic and others as synthetic.

We conclude that while many areas of classical perception, realistic rendering, and perceptually-based rendering have been thoroughly studied, the central problem of determining what about an image tells a person whether it is photographic or computer-generated remains largely unexplored.

3   DESIGNING A PERCEPTUAL TEST OF VISUAL REALISM

The goal of this project is to study the perception of realism in images using techniques adapted from classical human visual perception. The ultimate goal of this line of research is to gain a full understanding of exactly what cues tell observers that an image is photographic or computer-generated, so that rendering algorithms can be built to directly target these cues. While this end result is still far away, our intent in this work is to frame the problem in perceptual terms, and to develop methods by which observers can be objectively tested, and meaningful analyses performed.

3.1   Experimental question and task

Our strategy for finding out what visual cues matter for realism is to ask experimental participants to directly rate a series of controlled images as either "real" or "not real" – but how do we communicate to the participants what we mean by "real"?

One of the difficulties is that it would appear that subjects need a clear definition of what is meant by "realism" in order to properly perform the experiment and not yield invalid data. Yet the reason these experiments are being conducted in the first place is because we *do not* have a clear definition of what makes an image realistic – we want *them* to tell *us* what makes an image look real. The more we tell subjects about our notion of realism or the context under which we are studying it, the more their responses will be biased towards what they are told.

Our solution is to give the participants minimal instructions: they are only told that some of the images are "photographic / real" while others are "computer-generated / not real," and that their job is to differentiate between the two (see Appendix for full written instructions). We therefore present the context of photographs versus CGI, but offer no guidance on how to actually evaluate the two. It is the subjects' job to interpret these keywords and respond accordingly (thereby providing an *operational definition* [Levi94] of realism).

Although one might worry that the variability inherent in these sparse instructions could lead to invalid results, the exact purpose of this experimental method is to see whether different participants converge to similar responses, given only a few keywords.

Another potential concern is whether the subjects' responses are more a reflection of the forced-choice nature of the experiment, rather than of the perceived realism of the images. The design of the experiment does force participants to make a choice, but if a given visual factor has no effect whatsoever on a participant's interpretation of "real" versus "not real," then the resulting responses will be completely uncorrelated with the factor levels. If there *is* a correlation, and one which holds across the majority of participants, then the analysis will yield a statistically-significant result, and we can claim that the visual factor does influence subjects' interpretation of "real" versus "not real." In our experiments we found that some visual factors did correlate with subjects' responses (they measurably influenced subjects' interpretation of "real") while other visual factors did not.

3.2 Controlled image factors

We use a common experimental technique in which subjects are presented with sets of controlled images which vary only along some predetermined dimensions, with all other image factors held as constant as possible [Levi94]. We then analyze the pattern of responses across these dimensions of interest. If there is a statistically-significant change in the response, then we can claim the existence of a *causal relationship* between the visual factor and the subjects' responses (since the images are controlled against extraneous factors).

It is important to note that because of this design, we actually do not mix photographs and computer-generated images in a single experiment. If they were mixed, then unless the CG images exactly matched the corresponding photographs, there would be confounding factors which would interfere with the analysis. For a single experiment, therefore, *the images should be either all photographs or all computer-generated*. That is, they should be from the same source. A consequence of this is that these experiments actually have no notion of "correctness" – it is not appropriate to think of the responses as hits, misses, false positives, false negatives, etc. It only matters how the subjects' response pattern changes across the dimensions of interest.

3.3 Types of images

The images in these experiments consisted of very simple scenes, containing only blocks, spheres, and egg-shapes, in grayscale and without motion. We chose this approach to limit the number of factors to contend with in these early studies. An initial concern when using simple scenes was that the simplicity itself might cause a strong sense of *un*realism, which could obscure any true effect of other visual factors. This proved not to be the case, as we did observe statistically-significant effects based on certain visual factors. The issue of scene simplicity is further addressed in Section 6, where we present a series of experiments on number of objects, variety of object shapes, and number of light sources.

3.4   Experiment methodology

All the experiments followed the same format. A series of images was presented to each subject, who rated each as either "real" or "not real." The images were all of simple objects. They varied according to some visual factors under investigation – either shadow softness, surface smoothness, number of objects, variety of object shapes, or number of lights. For example, in the first experiment the shadows were at one of five possible levels, ranging from very sharp to very soft.

The experimental method asks for only a binary "real / not real" response (rather than a multi-point scale) to simplify the task for each subject (who only needs to maintain a single internal differentiation threshold), and to reduce problems of scale interpretation across subjects.

The proportion of "real" responses for a particular level of a factor is the **realism response rating** for that level (which we denote by $\Re$). If we assign the numerical value of one to "real," and zero to "not real," then the $\Re$ value is simply the mean of all numerical responses for a given level. For example, if 37 out of 60 images at the sharpest shadow level were rated as real, then we say that $\Re = .62$ for sharp shadows. In the analysis stage, we infer the effect of the various visual factors on realism by testing for statistically-significant changes in $\Re$.

All image presentation and data collection was automated, and the order of presentation was fully randomized for each subject at run-time. Subjects ran all their image trials in one sitting (with short breaks). The average completion time was 1¼ hours.

The 21" monitors were set to 1152×864, and each image was 800×600. Subjects sat approximately two feet from the screen, giving a subtended viewing angle of the images of approximately 30 degrees. The experiments were all conducted under controlled illumination.

Subjects all gave informed consent, and were naïve to the study's purpose, non-experts in computer graphics or related visual fields, aged 20 to 50, with normal or corrected-to-normal vision.

3.5   Creating the images

For the photographic experiments, we acquired images with an Olympus 3030Z digital camera, at 800×600. The green channel (least noisy) was used to create a grayscale image. The camera was locked into place for all the images. The objects were wooden cubes and spheres (5 centimeters in height), and 7-cm wooden egg-shapes. They were all painted with white acrylic paint. In all the images, the objects are set against a large draped sheet of white paper.

For the CG experiments, we used 3D Studio Max, with raytraced soft shadows. The CG experiments used only blocks (no spheres or egg-shapes), and the texture maps were acquired by orthographically photographing our physical wooden blocks, and normalizing the resulting textures. The background texture map was taken from a photograph of our physical stage. No indirect illumination was computed. Since the CG images were all batch-rendered from the same dataset, the CG version of the experiments had very precise experimental control.

To reduce the dependence on any single spatial arrangement of objects (position and orientation), we used several spatial arrangements in each experiment. For example, in the shadow softness experiment, we placed the objects in a given spatial layout, then gathered the images at each of the five shadow levels (keeping the positions and orientations *constant across shadow levels* for each "scene"). We then rearranged the objects and gathered images again at each shadow level, and so on. Since the "scenes" are orthogonal to the main visual factors under investigations, they do not in any way confound the analysis of the factors, but only reduces bias towards any single spatial arrangement.

The images were all generated with the light source on the right side. As the experiments ran, images were randomly flipped horizontally, so that half of them appeared to have the light source on the right side, and half on the left side (chosen randomly at run-time for each image presentation). This was done to reduce bias towards a particular light direction, and to reduce fatigue on the participants by increasing the image variety. Since the two image directions were evenly and randomly distributed, they have no impact on the analysis (they cancel out).

3.6 Analysis method

The appropriate method of statistical analysis was dictated by two design elements. First, because the response variable was binary, standard linear regression models or analysis of variance (ANOVA) are not appropriate (they are only valid on continuous data from normal distributions). Instead, the correct analysis is *logistic regression* [Wine91], an extension of linear regression for binary data. Logistic regression computes the correlation between a manipulated factor (e.g., level of shadow softness) and a binary response variable ("real" vs. "not real").

Second, because each subject ran many trials (and the responses are therefore not all independent), a *repeated measures* analysis [Wine91] was called for, to take into account the correlation between responses by the same subject. We used the commercial statistics package SUDAAN [Shah96], which handles repeated measures logistic regression designs.

A concern when subjects run many trials is that time-dependent/training effects may emerge. That is, as the experiment progresses, responses could begin to drift towards one end of the response scale. We tested for this by computing the regression between trial number and subjects' responses, and found no presence of time-dependent/training effects.

The subjects' response times were also measured. An analysis showed no correlation between the subjects' response times and their response values. This indicates that subjects did not respond any faster to images they rated as real than to those rated as not real.

3.7 Additional experimental details

A blank gray screen was displayed for approximately one second between images. Subjects chose between "real" and "not real" by pressing one of two keys. They were free to change their responses (visual feedback was given) and they confirmed their current response and advanced to the next image by pressing the spacebar.

To prevent regression to the mean – where responses degenerate as the experiment progresses due to the lack of a fixed reference point – the images were presented in groups of eight. In a first pass the images in each group were only previewed, and in a second pass the subjects actually rated them. This provided an internal reference point for subjects throughout each experiment. At the start of each experiment, a number of images (sixteen) were presented, to allow the subject to become acquainted with the experiment. The responses for these were excluded from analysis.

4 SHADOW SOFTNESS

In this first experiment, we were interested in whether subjects' realism response would change significantly as a result of varying the shadow softness. It is typically taken for granted that very sharp shadows are seen as unrealistic, yet not much is known about how realism is affected when shadows are not perfectly sharp. For example, if softening a shadow makes an image more realistic, does softening it twice as much double the increase in realism?

4.1 Setup: Shadow Softness

There were five levels of shadow softness. The lowest (sharpest) level was created with a focused 300W spotlight, at 2.3 meters from the scene. The next two levels were created with a clear incandescent 300W light bulb, at 2.0 and 1.0 meters from the scene, respectively. The last (softest) two shadow levels were created with the same light bulb, but now diffused, at 1.0 and .2 meters. The resulting penumbral spread angles were .39°, 1.5°, 2.5°, 5.2°, and 10.3°. Close-ups of some shadows from this experiment are shown below. Note that the images are nearly identical except for the shadows.

There were twelve scenes (different spatial arrangements), and each scene was photographed at each of the five shadow levels. That is, there were 12 sets of 5 images, where the five within each set *were nearly-identical except for their shadow softness*. The total number of images presented to each subject was therefore $12 \times 5 = 60$ images.

240

Because the different shadow levels were generated using lights at different distances, the images varied slightly in brightness and contrast. They were manually adjusted to account for any obvious exposure differences. The remaining differences were small and randomly distributed, and therefore should not affect the analysis. This slight loss of experimental control when using photographs is one of the motivations for performing experiments using computer-generated images (as described in Section 7), which offer precise experimental control.

We measured the penumbra angles for the shadows in all of the images, and averaged these to get a single penumbra angle measurement for each of the five shadow levels, as shown below.

Figure 2. Detail of images from shadow softness experiment. Average penumbra angles for the five shadow levels were .39°, 1.5°, 2.5°, 5.2°, and 10.3°.

4.2 Results: $\Re$ vs. Shadow Softness

The experiment was run with 18 subjects. The graph shows $\Re$ vs. shadow softness (the proportion of "real" responses for each shadow level). The error bars show the inter-subject variability in $\Re$ – i.e., the standard error of the set of $\Re$ values, one from each subject, for the given shadow level.

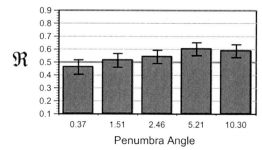

Figure 3. $\Re$ vs. shadow softness for photographic experiment. (*note:* the x-axis is not evenly scaled). The increase in $\Re$ rating becomes statistically significant when the shadow penumbra reaches 5.21 degrees. There is no statistical difference between the last two levels of shadow softness.

The first question we ask is whether the subjects' responses varied significantly due to shadow softness. To test this, we fit a repeated measures logistic regression model to the data, using shadow softness as the independent variable, and the binary "Real / Not Real" response as the dependent variable. Shadow softness was found to be a statistically-significant predictor of realism ($\chi^2 = 4.31$, df = 1, p = .0379)[1]. Indeed, the subjects' reported visual realism varied as a result of shadow softness.

Clearly the sharpest shadows (leftmost level) were rated the lowest in realism. This agrees with the common notion in computer graphics that sharp shadows are unrealistic. By performing pair-wise comparisons in a repeated measures logistic regression analysis between the sharpest shadow level and each of the four remaining shadow levels, we found that a statistically significant difference was found beginning at the 4th shadow level (5.21 degrees penumbra). The test was ($\chi^2 = 5.39$, df = 1, p = .0203). This indicates that at 5.21 degrees, we begin to see a measurable change in reported realism. Furthermore, there is no statistical difference between the last two (softest) shadow levels ($\chi^2 = 2.64$, df = 1, p = .1043). From all this we can conclude that in this set of images, perceived realism was maximized with respect to shadow softness in the neighborhood of 5.21 degrees of penumbra angle. Any additional increase in softness had

---

[1] A p-value of .05 or less denotes a statistically significant effect.

diminishing returns. Rendering soft shadows is an expensive computation, so knowing how people will respond to various shadow qualities can result in significant savings during rendering.

5   SURFACE SMOOTHNESS

It is often said in the computer graphics folklore that for an image to look realistic, "surfaces should not be too smooth." Roughing up the surfaces, for example, was one of the major efforts in the creation of Toy Story [Stre95]. Certainly, with computer graphics it is easy to create surfaces with no surface variation whatsoever – something unlikely to be encountered in real life. Nevertheless, in the real world we *do* find objects with all degrees of surface smoothness. A freshly-painted wall is much smoother than a cork bulletin board, for example – but is a smooth *real-world surface* really seen as less realistic than a rough real-world surface? In this experiment we tested this by comparing the realism response for photographs of smooth-textured objects versus photographs of rough-textured objects.

5.1   Setup: Surface Smoothness

We presented subjects with a series of photographs, where half the images contained smooth-textured cubical blocks, and the other half contained rough-textured blocks. The smooth textures were created by painting the cubes with white spray-paint, which gave a smooth, even coat. The rough blocks were created by painting them white with a rough-bristled brush, which yielded strongly-noticeable brush marks on the surface.

There were thirty scenes, with each scene in both rough-texture and smooth-texture form. The total number of images presented to each subject was therefore 30×2 = 60 images.

Figure 4. Detail of two images from surface smoothness experiment. The smooth, spray-painted blocks, such as on the left, rated much lower in realism ($\Re$ = .39) than the rough, brush-painted blocks ($\Re$ = .71)

5.2   Results: $\Re$ vs. Surface Smoothness

This experiment was run on 18 subjects. We found that there was a very strong difference in realism for the two types of surfaces. As shown in the graph, the rough-painted blocks rated much higher than the spray-painted ones ($\Re$ = .71 vs. $\Re$ = .39). This effect was stronger than the effect due to shadow softness.

We tested for statistical significance using surface type as the independent variable, and the "real / not real" response as the binary dependent variable. The effect was strongly statistically significant (χ^2 = 13.04, df = 1, p = .0003). This indicates that the smoothness of surface textures was undoubtedly a determinant of realism – which backs up the common graphics folklore that says that surfaces should not be "too smooth."

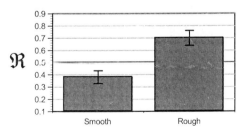

Figure 5. $\Re$ vs. surface smoothness. There was a strong effect due to surface type.

It is worthwhile to point again that this experiment was conducted using *only photographs*. When presented with the question of whether the images were real (photographic), the smooth textures ranked low, even though they were, in fact, physically-real surfaces. This has implications for areas of rendering such as global illumination research, where untextured objects are typically used to report results. This experiment suggests that these untextured images may never look highly realistic – no matter how good the lighting algorithm. As one critiques the results of an advanced lighting algorithm, it is therefore worth remembering that if the surfaces are untextured, then this alone may cause a much stronger decrease in realism than any error in the light transport computation.

As a final point, this experiment only demonstrates that there was a difference in realism between the two surface types, but does not characterize what it was about the rougher surface that made it look more real. As seen in the fields of texture synthesis and BRDF measurement, there are many ways to analyze the properties of surfaces, and it remains as future work to discover exactly which of these are important.

6 NUMBER OF OBJECTS, VARIETY OF OBJECT SHAPES, AND NUMBER OF LIGHT SOURCES

In this set of experiments we looked at what happens to the reported realism as we manipulated three factors: the number of objects in the scene, the variety of object shapes, and the number of light sources. One might expect and assume that the subjects' responses would increase as more objects are added to a scene, the types of objects varied, or the number of light sources increased. But since these increases consume more memory and rendering time, it would be useful to first verify what effect these increases will have on the realism of an image.

6.1 Setup: Number of Objects / Variety of Object Shapes

Figure 6. The horizontal axis increases the number of objects, and the vertical axis varies the object shapes (blocks-only above, versus blocks, spheres, and egg-shapes below). There was no statistically-significant difference in perceived realism along either axis.

We tested the effect of increasing the number and types of objects in a scene with a single two-factor experiment. The first factor was the number of objects – each image either contained 2, 4, 8, or 30 objects. The second factor was the variety of object shapes, with two levels: each image consisted either of only cubical blocks, or of half blocks and half curved objects (spheres and egg-shapes). For example, an image might have 8 objects which are all blocks, or it might have 30 objects with mixed shapes (15 blocks and 15 spheres and egg-shapes). Crossing the two factors yields 4×2 = 8 images. Subjects were shown five different sets of images, each set fully representing the crossed factors (for a total of 4×2×5 = 40 images).

6.2   Setup: Number of Light Sources

Before presenting the results of the previous setup, we describe the setup for the experiment on the number of light sources. There were three levels for the main factor: one light, two lights, and four lights. To create images with accurate exposure and light source control, we radiometrically blended photographs containing a single light each.

The same scene was repeatedly photographed, each time with a single light source placed at four different locations along a 120° arc around the scene. Then, to generate a new image with two light sources, for example, our custom image-assembly utility randomly picked two light source positions, and blended these images to create a single new image that appears to be lit by two lights. The camera was locked into place and operated via remote control to eliminate any camera shake, so that the images would blend well. Also, the aperture and exposure settings were locked across all the original images.

The blend operation was radiometrically correct. We first computed our digital camera's CCD response curve using the *mkhdr* software tool ([Diuk98], based on [Debe97]). We then mapped each image into radiometric space (mapped from camera pixel intensities to irradiance), summed in that space (simulating the additive nature of light), adjusted the exposure (multiplied the summed image by either 1/2 or 1/4, depending on the number of lights), and then mapped from radiometric space back to camera space to yield the final image.

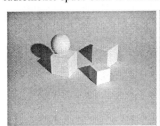 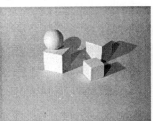 

Figure 7. Images from experiment on number of light sources.

Because blending images decreases camera noise, we actually acquired *four* photographs from each of the four light source positions (i.e., 4×4 = 16 photographs per scene). The final images were all created by blending exactly four images out of sixteen (e.g., blending four photographs with the same light position to create an image with "one" light), so they all had the same level of camera noise present.

Note that it is not possible to keep all other factors absolutely constant when we increase the number of light sources. The light on each surface will change, the overall contrast will diminish, and so forth. However, these are all physically-dictated byproducts of increasing the number of lights (the primary factor under investigation), and are accepted since they have a small visual effect compared to the very distinct increase in number of shadows.

Finally, in addition to number of light sources, we also co-varied the shadow softness, to reduce the bias on any particular shadow type. The above process was repeated for each scene, once with a spotlight and once with a diffuse light source.

There were 6 scenes, 2 shadow types per scene (soft and sharp), and 3 numbers of lights per shadow type (1 light, 2 lights, or 4 lights). Thus, this experiment consisted of 6×2×3 = 36 images.

244

6.3 Results: $\mathfrak{R}$ vs. Number of Objects / Variety of Object Shapes / Number of Lights

Ten subjects ran the experiment on number of objects and variety of object shapes, and seven subjects ran the experiment on number of light sources. One can immediately see in the graphs below that the realism response did not increase due to either number of objects, variety of object shapes, or number of lights. In fact, the graphs appear to indicate that there was actually a *decrease* in reported realism when the number of objects and the number of lights was increased.

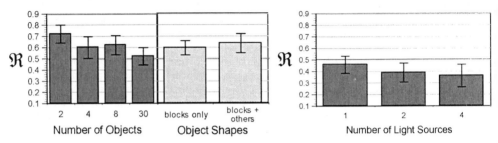

Figure 8. $\mathfrak{R}$ vs. Number of objects / Variety of object shapes / Number of lights. None of the effects were statistically significant.

We tested for significance in all three cases. For number of light sources, no significant effect was found ($\chi^2 = .56$, df = 1, p =.4546). For variety of object shapes (blocks-only versus blocks, spheres, and egg-shapes), there was also no significant effect ($\chi^2 = .58$, df = 1, p =.4454).

For the number of objects, the results varied depending on how the analysis is performed. If we perform the analysis using the *level number* as the independent variable (taking on the values 1, 2, 3, and 4), then we see a borderline-significant effect ($\chi^2 = 3.55$, df = 1, p = .0597). This is because, as we can see in the graph, the response at the first level is indeed higher than at the last. If, however, we perform the analysis using the actual *number of objects* as the independent variable (taking on the values 2, 4, 8, and 30), then the regression is *not* considered significant ($\chi^2 = 2.43$, df = 1, p = .1193). The interpretation of these two results is that while the low-endpoint case (only two objects) indeed rated higher than the rest, the overall effect is not significant when the large scale of the axis is considered (i.e., there was no significant difference between four objects and thirty objects).

These were unexpected results. Despite the tremendous visual difference between images with only four objects and images with thirty, subjects did not respond any differently to them. Furthermore, subjects were no more convinced by an image with several light sources and shadows than they were by an image with only one, nor were they any more convinced by images that showed a variety of objects types rather than only blocks.

These results have implications for computer graphics rendering. For example, if an image of a simple scene (such as those often found in conference proceedings) appears unrealistic, it is not necessarily because of its simplicity. There may be other factors which are causing the low realism (e.g., sharp shadows or "too smooth" textures), which should be addressed first. Furthermore, these results suggest that in a rendering application, it may be better to spend time on generating proper soft shadows and adequate textures, rather than adding more of the same lights or objects, or simply adding new objects for variety.

6.4 Ramifications of negative results

These negative, non-significant results have important implications for our experimental technique.

One concern before these experiments were conducted was that the subjects might be able to simply "decode" the experimental factors under investigation. For example, if they notice that the only difference between images is the shadow softness, then they may simply give every sharp-shadowed image one response, and every soft-shadowed image the opposite response. We would still be able to learn something from this, since at least we would know which end of the softness spectrum they considered "real" and which "not real," and what they considered to be the boundary point. However, this decoding is still not ideal, since we want to learn about subjects' true internal perception of the images, and we want each image to be evaluated fairly.

However, because we have negative, non-significant results for these previous three experiments – despite the strong, obvious visual differences in the images – we have evidence to support the claim that subjects were *not*, in fact, simply decoding or "figuring out" the experimental factors, but rather were responding with a true measure of their perception of realism for each image. Otherwise, we would have seen significant changes in $\Re$ for the previous three experiments, just as we did for shadow softness and surface smoothness.

7   EXPERIMENTS USING COMPUTER GENERATED IMAGES

All the experiments presented thus far have employed photographs exclusively. As explained in Section 3.3, it is not important where the images come from, as long as they only differ along a particular dimension of interest, with all other visual factors held as nearly constant as possible. However, we can clearly achieve a higher level of control using computer-generated images than using photographs. Furthermore, with CGI we can easily manipulate certain dimensions that would be difficult to do with photographs (e.g., secondary illumination).

It would be useful, therefore, to know whether our experimental methodology is valid in the CG case. If, for example, we found that the results from some all-CG experiments, mimicking the photographic experiments above, yielded only responses of $\Re = 0$ (all images rated as "not real"), or had response curves that were qualitatively different than the curves for the photographic cases, then we would lose confidence in the robustness of the experimental method. To test this, we replicated the shadow softness and surface texture experiments using CG images exclusively. We hoped to find the response curves to be similar to those from the photographic cases, allowing for differences in scaling, offset, and noise.

We rendered images using 3D Studio Max, with raytraced soft shadows, and object textures extracted from intensity-normalized orthographic photographs of the wooden cubes. Seven subjects ran the computer-generated experiments. These were different subjects from those that ran the photographic experiments, so there was no crossover effect between the two types of images.

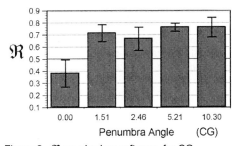

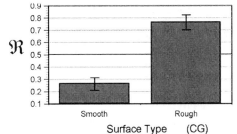

Figure 9. $\Re$ vs. shadow softness, for CG images. Note the sharp increase between the first two levels. This may be because with CG we could achieve a perfect point light source (smaller than our physical spotlight).

Figure 10. $\Re$ vs. surface texture, for CG images. We used textures obtained from photographs of our wooden blocks. The CG results match the earlier photo-based results closely.

By comparing the CG graphs to their photographic counterparts from the previous sections, we see that the computer-generated version of these experiments yields qualitatively similar data. In the surface texture experiment, the smooth texture is still much lower in $\Re$ than the rough texture. In the shadow softness case, the $\Re$ curve ascends as it did with the photographs. There is a difference here compared to the photographic case, however, in that the jump between the sharpest and the second-sharpest shadows is much more pronounced for the CG case than for the photographic case. This may be due to the fact that in the CG renderer we were able to create a true point light source, and so the sharpest shadow level in the CG case actually causes a sharper, much more "unrealistic" penumbra than with the photographic spotlight.

We now perform tests for significance, by applying the same repeated measures logistic regression analysis as before. The test yielded significance for both the computer-generated shadow softness experiment ($\chi^2 = 4.92$, df = 1, p=.0265) and for the computer-generated surface smoothness experiment ($\chi^2 = 20.51$, df = 1, p < .0001).

Since the all-CG experiments yielded qualitatively-similar data to the photographic experiments, and were statistically significant (as were the photographic experiments), we claim that our experimental methodology indeed yields valid results using only computer-generated images. For completeness, the remaining three photographic experiments should also be replicated in CG form – we leave this for future work.

Of course, if the rendered CG images had some artifacts that were extremely fake-looking, this could have pulled the response curve down to zero, and the effect of the variable under investigation would have been lost. Nonetheless, by having the option of running experiments using only CG images, we open up the possibility of much more complicated experiments than what could be done with photographs – e.g., investigations of global illumination, BRDF models, tessellation / simplification techniques, and more.

8 CONCLUSION

A crucial component for the creation of realistic imagery is an objective understanding of the perceptual criteria by which viewers decide if images are real or not. While much research has been invested into physics-based rendering, the experiments presented in this paper have shown that even *photographs* (which are, by definition, "photo-real") are not all equally realistic. Physics, therefore, is not the only key to realism. Once the graphics community understands how different visual factors determine whether an observer perceives an image as photographic, then new rendering algorithms can be developed to specifically target these visual cues.

In this paper we have presented an early step towards understanding this perceptual process, with an experimental technique that directly asks subjects about the realism of images. The method was shown to be capable of affirming common assumption in graphics, of providing quantitative data , and also of casting into doubt certain common notions about realistic rendering. Furthermore, these experiments can be conducted using either photographs or computer generated images, which greatly expands the range of hypotheses that can be tested.

As more visual factors are investigated using this experimental method and future techniques for measuring the perception of realism in images, we will eventually have a full understanding of what it really means for an image to look like a photograph or like computer graphics.

REFERENCES

[Barb92] Christopher Barbour and Gary Meyer. Visual Cues and Pictorial Limitations for Computer Generated Photorealistic Images. In *The Visual Computer*, vol 9, pp. 151-165. 1992.

[Bruc96] Vicki Bruce, Patrick Green, and Mark Georgeson. Visual Perception: Physiology, Psychology, and Ecology. East Sussex, UK, 1996. Psychology Press

[Chal00] Alan Chalmers, Scott Daly, Ann McNamara, Karol Myszkowski, and Tom Troscianko. Image Quality Metrics. *SIGGRAPH 2000 Course Notes #14.* July, 2000. ACM.

[Chiu94] Kenneth Chiu and Peter Shirley. Rendering, Complexity, and Perception. In *Proc of the 5th Eurographics Rendering Workshop.* SpringerWien, New York, NY. 1994.

[Debe97] Paul E. Debevec and Jitendra Malik. Recovering High Dynamic Range Radiance Maps from Photographs. In *Proc of SIGGRAPH 97*, August 1997. ACM.

[Diuk98] H.P Duiker, Tim Hawkins, and Paul Debevec. Mkhdr. *www.debevec.org/FiatLux/mkhdr*

[Ferw98] James Ferwerda. Visual Models for Realistic Image Synthesis. Ph.D. thesis, Cornell, 1998.

[Gord97] Ian Gordon. Theories of Visual Perception. John Wiley & Sons, New York, NY, 1997.

[Hage80] Margaret Hagen. The Perception of Pictures. New York, 1980. Academic Press.

[Horv97] Eric Horvitz and Jed Lengyel. Perception, Attention, and Resources: A Decision-Theoretic Approach to Graphics Rendering. In *Proc of Thirteenth Conf on Uncertainty in AI*, pp. 238-249. Providence, 1997.

[Leng98] Jed Lengyel. The Convergence of Graphics and Vision. In *IEEE Computer*, July 1998.

[Levi94] Gustave Levine and Stanley Parkinson. Experimental Methods in Psychology. Hillsdale, New Jersey, 1994. Lawrence Erlbaum Associates.

[Mcna00] Ann McNamara, Alan Chalmers, Tom Troscianko, and Iain Gilchrist. Comparing Real & Synthetic Scenes using Human Judgement of Lightness. In *Proc of Eurographics Workshop on Rendering*. Springer-Verlag 2000.

[Meye86] Gary Meyer, Holly Rushmeier, Michael Cohen, Donald Greenberg, and Kenneth Torrance. An Experimental Evaluation of Computer Graphics Imagery. In *Transactions on Graphics, 5 (1)*, pp. 30-50. New York, 1986. ACM.

[Parr00] Alejandro Parraga, Tom Troscianko, David Tolhurst. The Human Visual System Is Optimized For Processing The Spatial Information In Natural Visual Images. In *Current Biology, 10*, pp. 35-38. 2000.

[Patt97] Sumanta Pattanaik, James Ferwerda, Kenneth Torrance, and Donald Greenberg. Validation of Global Illumination Solutions Through CCD Camera Measurements. In *Proc of 5th Color Imaging Conf, Soc for Imaging Sci and Tech*, pp. 250-253, 1997.

[Rama99] Mahesh Ramasubramanian, Sumanta Pattanaik, and Donald Greenberg. A Perceptually Based Physical Error Metric for Realistic Image Synthesis. In *Proc of SIGGRAPH 99*. New York, 1999. ACM.

[Rush95] Holly Rushmeier, G. Larson, C. Piatko, P. Sanders, and B. Rust. Comparing Real and Synthetic Images: Some Ideas About Metrics. In *Proc of Eurographics Rendering Workshop 1995*. SpringerWien, New York, NY. 1995

[Shah96] Babubhai Shah, Beth Barnwell, and Gayle Bieler. SUDAAN User's Manual, Release 7. Research Triangle Institute, RTP, NC.

[Stre95] Rita Street. Toys Will be Toys: Toy Story. Cinefex, issue 64. 1995.

[Thom98] William Thompson, Peter Shirley, Brian Smits, Daniel Kersten, and Cindee Madison. Visual Glue. University of Utah Technical Report UUCS-98-007, March 12, 1998 .

[Vole00] Vladimir Volevich, Karol Myszkowski, Andrei Khodulev, and Edward Kopylov. Using the Visual Differences Predictor to Improve Performance of Progressive Global Illumination Computation. In *Transaction on Graphics*, 19(1), pp. 122-161. New York, 2000. ACM.

[Wine91] B. J. Winer, Donald Brown, and Kenneth Michels. Statistical Principles in Experimental Design, 3rd ed. New York, 1991. McGraw-Hill.

APPENDIX: INSTRUCTIONS TO SUBJECTS

These are the written instructions that were provided to each subject at the beginning of an experimental session. Aside from user-interface instructions for entering their responses, no other guidance was given.

Today we are interested in gathering some information about how people perceive images. In the tasks that follow, you will see a number of images and we will ask you to evaluate what you see. There is no "right" or "wrong" answer to any response; we just want to know what you think. As you look at these images, try not to "think too much" about what you see. Go with your first impression.

In this experiment we will show you a number of images, one shown right after the other. Some of these images are photographs of real objects, and others are computer-generated. For each image, we want to know whether you think it is real or not real. Sometimes it may be a close call, but just do the best you can.

A Perceptually-Based Texture Caching Algorithm for Hardware-Based Rendering

Reynald Dumont   Fabio Pellacini   James A. Ferwerda

Program of Computer Graphics, Cornell University

Abstract: The performance of hardware-based interactive rendering systems is often constrained by polygon fill rates and texture map capacity, rather than polygon count alone. We present a new software texture caching algorithm that optimizes the use of texture memory in current graphics hardware by dynamically allocating more memory to the textures that have the greatest visual importance in the scene. The algorithm employs a resource allocation scheme that decides which resolution to use for each texture in board memory. The allocation scheme estimates the visual importance of textures using a perceptually-based metric that takes into account view point and vertex illumination as well as texture contrast and frequency content. This approach provides high frame rates while maximizing image quality.

1. Introduction

Many important graphics applications require complex scenes to be rendered at interactive rates (simulation, training systems, virtual environments, scientific visualization, games). Hardware-based rendering is currently the best solution for these interactive applications. Performance increases in hardware-based graphics accelerators have enabled significant improvements in rendering capabilities, but concurrent increases in user requirements for realism, complexity and interactivity mean that computational demands will continue to outstrip computational resources for the foreseeable future. For example, the performance of current graphics hardware strongly depends on the number of primitives drawn as well as the number and resolution of the textures used to enrich the visual complexity of the scene. While much work has been done to try to reduce the number of primitives displayed (see [12] for a good summary), little research has been devoted to optimizing texture usage.

Current graphics accelerators employ fast memory for texture storage. To achieve the best possible framerate, all the textures should reside in texture memory. While textures might be dynamically loaded from main memory, this remains a slow operation that causes drastic framerate reductions (even with fast AGP buses). Hardware developers are trying to address this problem by constantly incrementing the amount of texture memory available, by speeding up texture swapping operations and by employing hardware texture compression techniques. However such improvements do not solve the problem when the total size of textures exceeds the capacity of the board memory. In such conditions, it is often impossible to allocate on-board memory quickly enough to load the textures needed to render the scene.

A few software texture caching systems have been presented in the past to address this problem. Some of them optimize texture swapping with respect to no image degradation. While these algorithms ensure image quality, they provide framerates which are strongly dependent on the size of the original texture set. Other approaches guarantee target framerates by allowing image degradation. Unfortunately, the metrics employed to measure image degradation are too simple and do not guarantee that the rendered image has the best possible quality for the given target framerate.

In this paper, we present a new algorithm for texture caching that allows fast and predictable framerates while maximizing image quality on current low-end graphics hardware. The algorithm employs a resource allocation scheme that decides which resolution to use for each texture in board memory. The resolution is chosen depending on the current view-point and illumination conditions as well as texture contrast and frequency content. This naturally led us to employ a perceptual metric. Unlike previous approaches, the texture content is analyzed to provide the best decisions on the chosen resolutions. Depending on the texture content, the allocation scheme allows more or less reduction in resolution for the texture to save on-board memory.

In the following sections, we first review previous work and then outline our texture caching algorithm before describing some of the implementation details. Finally, we present the results produced by the algorithm, before concluding and discussing future work.

2. Related work

Hardware texture compression is now frequently used to increase the effective size of texture memory in graphics hardware. A simple lossy scheme presented by S3 [18] can now be found in most off-the-shelf graphics boards. Talisman [19] is an example of non-standard graphics pipeline that employs a hardware-based compression scheme similar to JPEG. A texture compression algorithm based on vector quantization has been proposed to be used in hardware in [1].

Software caching schemes try to address texture memory limitations by only using a subset of the original texture set to render the current frame. A good portion of the texture caching algorithms described in the literature uses specialized caching schemes to address specific applications. For examples, Quicktime VR [4] cuts texture panoramas into vertical strips for caching purposes. Many simple metrics, based on viewing distance and viewing angle, have been proposed in terrain visualization applications [2][6][10][15]. A progressive loading approach has been presented in [5] and applied to terrain visualization; this caching scheme tolerates image degradation to ensure framerate during its progressive loading steps.

While these approaches have proven to be fairly effective, either they do not guarantee framerate, or when they do, they cannot guarantee that the image generated is the best possible one since their metrics do not take perceptual effects into account. In this paper we will show that a caching stategy that maximizes image quality by using a perceptual metric is better than standard load/unload priority schemes.

3. Texture cache formulation

3.1. Problem statement

We consider that the color at each pixel of each rasterized polygon is the product of the Gouraud interpolated vertex color multiplied by the color of the trilinearly interpolated texture applied to the polygon (using a pyramidal mip-mapping scheme for each texture). We can write the shading equation for each pixel (x,y) as:

$$C^{x,y} = V^{x,y} \cdot T^{x,y} \qquad (1)$$

where C is the pixel color, V the Gouraud interpolated vertex color and T is the trilinearly interpolated texture color.

In order to maximize the framerate, we have to ensure that the texture set in use is smaller than the texture memory on the graphics board. When this is not possible, the scene should be displayed with a texture set that maximizes perceived image quality, while respecting texture memory constraints. To obtain this set, we can use the mip-map pyramids and only load a subpart of each original pyramid (called from now on subpyramid) on the board.

In order to solve this resource allocation problem, we developed an algorithm based on a cost/benefit analysis, following the formalism presented in [8]. We define a texture tuple as (T_i, j_i) to be the instance of a texture mip-map pyramid T_i rendered using a subpyramid starting at level j_i (higher values of j_i correspond to lower resolution). For each texture subpyramid we also define a cost function c_i and a benefit function q_i. The cost of a subpyramid is its size, while its benefit is computed by our perceptually-based error metric which predicts the expected visual degradation between the image rendered by the texture subpyramid (T_i, j_i) and the one for the high-resolution "gold standard" texture pyramid (T_i, v_i) $(0 \le v_i < j_i)$. Our resource allocation scheme maximizes the total benefit Q, while keeping the total cost C smaller than texture memory limits. Using this formalism we can state our resource allocation problem as

Maximize: $$Q = \sum_i q_i \qquad (2)$$

Subject to: $$C = \sum_i c_i \le texture\_memory \qquad (3)$$

3.2. Resource allocation algorithm

In general the problem of maximizing the total benefit under the cost constraint is NP-complete, so it cannot be solved in real time even for a small number of textures. While approximation algorithm exists [17], they are computationally inadequate for a real-time implementation. After trying various approaches, we settled on an improved greedy algorithm.

We first sort all the possible texture subpyramids with respect to $\Delta q_i(j_i, j_{i+1}) / \Delta c_i(j_i, j_{i+1})$ (estimated degradation between level j_i and j_{i+1} divided by memory saved while using level j_{i+1} instead of level j_i). Starting with the full texture set, we keep reducing its size by discarding the texture levels that have smaller $\Delta q_i(j_i, j_{i+1}) / \Delta c_i(j_i, j_{i+1})$ until the size of the set is smaller than the allowed size (i.e board texture memory).

3.3. Perceptually-based benefit function

The major contribution of our work is the metric used to estimate the benefit function. Given the current viewpoint, we would like this metric to accurately measure the perceived visual difference between the current subpyramid and the texture pyramid used in the gold standard. We believe that a metric based on a psychophysical model of the human visual system is best suited to accurately measure visual differences in images. In the past this approach has been employed very successfully to speed up offline algorithms [3][13][14][16]. Unfortunately the computational cost of such metrics prohibits their use for real time applications.

However, our application does not require the same level of generality in perceptual metrics as the ones presented before, since we are specifically interested in computing the visible difference caused by decreasing the resolution of a texture. This means that we can derive a computationally efficient metric by tailoring the metric to the needs of our application without losing the predictability and accuracy of the perceptually-based metrics previously given in the literature.

Our benefit function is based on two aspects of the human visual system: *visual saliency* (α_i) and *perceived error* (ε_i). Intuitively, the benefit q_i of a rendered texture is proportional to the probability α_i that we are focusing our attention to this specific texture, and the visual degradation ε_i that may occur by reducing its resolution. We can formally write this as:

$$q_i = \alpha_i \cdot (-\varepsilon_i) \qquad (4)$$

In our formulation, the maximum benefit is 0 when we are using the gold standard texture pyramid and it decreases when we use lower resolution subpyramids.

Following [10], we model visual saliency as proportional to the pixel coverage of the texture in the current frame. This is a statistical model based on the premise that we are focusing our attention on each part of the image with equal probability. We can simply write

$$\alpha_i \propto A_i \qquad (5)$$

where A_i is the area in pixel covered by texture T_i.

More advanced saliency models might avoid cases where small areas present strongly perceivable errors. Metrics for visual saliency are a new area of research in computer graphics. [20] has introduced a sophisticated metric based on low-level visual processing and a model of attention. However this metric is currently too computationally expensive to be used in interactive systems.

The perceived error term ε_i measures the apparent visual difference between the image rendered using the gold standard texture pyramid and the one rendered using a subpyramid. In order to estimate the response of the human visual system, we use a formulation based on a Visible Difference Predictor, VDP [7]. The VDPs predict the per-pixel probability that an observer will detect a difference between two images rendered using different approximations. Using this model of the human visual system, the perceivable error can be written as the product of the VDP times the physical error. We can write the perceived error as:

$$\varepsilon_i = \frac{1}{A_i} \cdot \sum_{v_i \leq m < j_i} \left(A_{i,m} \cdot f(m, j_i) \right) \qquad (6)$$

where v_i is the lowest mip-map level visible in the current frame for texture T_i (finest resolution used), m is the m-th mip-map level (m is greater than v_i), A_i is the area covered in the gold standard image by texture i, $A_{i,m}$ is the area covered in the gold standard image by m, and $f(m,j_i)$ computes the error using a filtered texture j_i (with a lower resolution) versus a higher resolution one, m. Intuitively the error produced by using j_i is the weighted average of the perceived error in the regions drawn using the different mip-map levels m, this takes into account the fact that if a mip-map level is only used in a small region, the corresponding change in visual quality will be small.

For the levels when $v_i \leq m < j_i$ (the ones that need to be drawn but are not in the subpyramid (T_i, j_i)), the error can be estimated as:

$$f(m, j_i) = \frac{1}{A_{i,m}} \cdot \sum_{x,y \in A_{i,m}} \left[\left(\Delta_{images}^{j_i,m} C \right)^{x,y} \cdot VDP^{x,y} \right] \qquad (7)$$

Here, $f(m,j_i)$ is equal to the difference Δ in color C using mip-map level j_i instead of m multiplied by the probability of detection of the error (VDP), normalized by the pixel coverage. The differences are taken in the CIELAB perceptually uniform color space.

To compute the probability of detection, we chose the *VDP* presented in [16] for its accuracy and computational efficiency[1].
This *VDP* is defined as:

$$VDP = \frac{1}{TVI \cdot Elevation} \qquad (8)$$

Threshold vs. intensity function (*TVI*), describes the luminance sensitivity of the visual system as a function of background luminance, modeling visual adaptation. The *Elevation* term describes the changes in sensitivity caused by the frequency content of the image. It is based on the contrast sensitivity function (*CSF*), which describes variations in sensitivity for patterns of various spatial frequencies, corrected by a masking function to capture the visual system's nonlinear response to pattern contrast. In this formulation, the luminance dependent *TVI* component can be computed in real-time once per frame, but the spatially-dependant *Elevation* component one cannot, which makes this VDP too slow to be used in our system.

The insight that allows us to speed up the evaluation of this metric is the fact that our application does not require a VDP that is accurate for each pixel but only for each texture. Since the most expensive part of the computation is evaluating the spatial contribution *(Elevation)*, we will separate it from the computation of the luminance contribution *(TVI)* by decoupling the two components. By taking this conservative approximation, we obtain a VDP formulation that is efficient enough for real-time applications, while accurately predicting the perceived error for each texture. The function $f(m, j_i)$ becomes:

$$f(m, j_i) = \text{LuminanceContribution} \cdot \text{SpatialContribution}$$

$$= \left[\frac{\overline{V}_{i,m} \cdot \overline{T}_{i,m}}{TVI(\overline{V}_{i,m} \cdot \overline{T}_{i,m})} \right] \left[\frac{1}{n_{texels} \cdot \overline{T}_{i,m}} \cdot \sum_{u,v \in T_{i,m}} \frac{\left(\Delta_{texel}^{j_i,m} T \right)^{u,v}}{Elevation(T_{i,m})^{u,v}} \right] \qquad (9)$$

where $\overline{V}_{i,m}$ is the average of the Gouraud interpolated vertex colors in the area covered by mip-map level m of texture i and $\overline{T}_{i,m}$ the average color of mip-map level m of texture i. Note that the differences are taken only on the texture values T (and not the color ones C as before). Figure 1 illustrates the computation of the spatial contribution. The efficiency of this new metric derives from evaluating the spatial contribution as a pre-process (which can be done during mip-map pyramid creation), and by evaluating the simpler luminance component on the fly.

Example: $j_i=3, m=0$

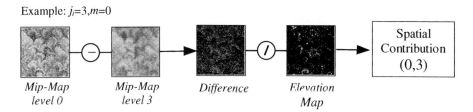

| Mip-Map level 0 | Mip-Map level 3 | Difference | Elevation Map | Spatial Contribution (0,3) |

Figure 1: Computation of the spatial contribution of the benefit function.

---

[1] The reader should consult [16] for implementation details and theoretical justification of the computational model presented.

4. Implementation details

4.1. System overview

We implemented our texture caching algorithm in a real time walkthrough application written using standard OpenGL. The scene vertex colors are produced by a mesh simplification algorithm performed on a tone mapped hierarchical radiosity solution. Any global illumination algorithm can be used to provide these per vertex color values. If no global illumination solution is available, the direct illumination provided by the hardware shading could be used by our metric. The system is composed of off-the-shelf PC components: a Pentium III processor with a GeForce II Ultra graphics board with 64 MB of video RAM.

The resource allocation algorithm runs asynchronously and with lower priority than the display loop, to ensure that the frame rate will not be affected by the execution of the algorithm itself. After the computation of the benefit function (as detailed in the next section), the resource allocation algorithm determines the best possible texture set to use when drawing the scene. It then loads the specified subpyramids in texture memory by using OpenGL texture priorities and loading only textures that are needed but do not reside yet in texture memory. This ensures a minimum number of texture switching operations. We also decided to amortize the total cost by distributing the computation steps over time, especially the switching of textures to avoid large demands on the hardware at the same time. By doing this, the overhead per frame does not exceed a couple of milliseconds.

4.2. Benefit function evaluation

In order to evaluate our benefit function we need to compute the area covered by each mip-map level of each texture and the average color $\overline{V}_{i,m}$ in each of those regions. To compute these values, we need the following per-pixel information: V, *textureID* and *mip-map level*. We obtain this information with a single display pass called *TextureIDMap*, where for each polygon, the R, G, B values of the vertices are set as:

$$R_P=V, \quad G_P=\text{TextureID}, \quad B_P=1 \tag{10}$$

To determine the mip-map levels required when rendering with the high-resolution gold standard texture set, we render the polygons with a special mip-mapped texture, whose values are constant over the texels. This encodes the mip-map pyramid levels:

$$R_T=1, \quad G_T=1, \quad B_T=\text{mip-map level} \tag{11}$$

The combination of the polygon color and this texture (with blending operation) fills the frame-buffer with all the required information. After this step, all per-pixel information has been calculated.

Treatment of the frame-buffer values now provides the final information required (e.g. pixel coverage per texture and mip-map level - A_i, and $A_{i,m}$ -, color values $\overline{V}_{i,m}$...). Since the allocation algorithm runs asynchronously, we use a prediction camera placed slightly behind the location of the actual viewing camera to anticipate the appearance of previously non-visible textures.

This *TextureIDMap* predicts mip-map level usage while solving the occlusion problem. If a textured polygon is occluded by another one its texture quality q_i is reduced (eventually to zero). Unlike previous approaches our metric takes occlusion events into account. This allows us to handle both open environments such as terrains and cluttered environments such as architectural walkthroughs. The *TextureIDMap* is illustrated in Fig. 2 (here the contrast of each map has been enhanced to facilitate reading the figure).

5. Results

We tested our algorithm on a highly textured architectural scene containing approximately 100,000 radiosity elements after mesh simplification. Figure 3-A shows the variation over time of the values of the benefit function (q_i), for each texture i present in this environment. As the observer moves into the scene, new parts of the scene become visible (or occupy more space on the screen), while others go out of view. As a result, the evaluation of the quality function varies with time. Figure 3-B presents the evolution of the active texture set over time for the same scene during the walkthrough. This graph shows the minimum mip-map levels that are loaded onto the graphics board for each texture present in the scene. As one can observe, in this walkthrough, most of the time the minimum mip-map levels used are 1 or 2 except between the 50th second and 65th second of the walkthrough where dramatic changes in the rendering state occur, since the observer has moved toward a picture on the wall to see it in greater detail. As he moves toward the picture, the resource allocator gives more memory to this particular texture to permit rendering it at full resolution (level 0). As a result, this affects the approximations chosen for the other textures and some of them are almost completely removed from the board memory.

We also tested this scene with high resolution textures (1024 by 1024) to greatly overload the board memory (the set of textures was 4 times bigger than the memory allowed by our system). Under these conditions, the rendering system ran at 3 frames per second. With the framework presented in this paper the framerate remains above 40 frames per second as shown in Figure 3-C.

Note that we also compared our algorithm with a load/unload priority scheme that used a visibility heuristic. In many circumstances this texture management heuristic will fail. Indeed, if in one frame all the visible textures overload the board memory, this heuristic will preserve image quality but at the price of a dramatic reduction in frame rate. In our test we found that in some cases, this method could only produce 4 frames per second while our algorithm yielded rates above 60 frames per second. Progressive loading as in [5] would solve this problem but without any guarantee on image quality.

Some snapshots from the walkthrough scene are shown in Figure 4. In these images the diagram in the left indicates the approximation chosen for each texture (the longer the bar, the coarser the approximation). The graphs indicate that the optimal texture set is different for each location. The image on the lower right shows the scene when the observer has moved toward the picture.

6. Conclusion

In this paper we presented a texture caching algorithm that provides high framerates while maximizing image quality on current commodity graphics hardware. Unlike previous approaches, our algorithm uses an efficient perceptual metric to determine where lower resolution textures can be used without reducing the visual quality of the resulting images. It relies on a textureIDMap to solve the visibility problem and estimate mip-map level usage. The algorithm should be useful in a variety of interactive rendering scenarios and could be incorporated and optimized for graphics APIs like Performer, Direct3d or OpenGL to improve the performance of PC rendering applications.

This texture caching algorithm may be employed on top of main memory and disk based texture management schemes (as in [5]) and is compatible with geometric simplification approaches (LOD, culling, impostors…) used to reduce the demands on the graphics pipeline.

The benefit function that drives our algorithm is of general utility and can be integrated in various other applications. For example, it could be used to prioritize network bandwidth in client/server rendering for telecollaboration or shared virtual environments. It could also be used to automate the laborious hand-tuning of texture and environment maps currently done in memory-constrained console gaming applications by treating main memory as a limited resource.

In the future we would like to develop more advanced perception metrics to further increase the efficiency and effectiveness of our algorithm, for example, by taking the perceptibility of color differences into account. We would also to extend our algorithm to handle additional map-based shading methods (e.g. shadow maps, light maps, environment maps, multitexturing) to increase the realism and performance of interactive rendering applications.

7. Bibliography

[1]   A. C. Beers, M. Agrawala and N. Chaddha. *Rendering from Compressed Textures.* SIGGRAPH '96 Conference Proceedings.

[2]   J. Blow. *Implementing a Texture Caching System.* Game Developer, April 1998.

[3]   M. R. Bolin and G. Meyer. *A Perceptually Based Adaptive Sampling Algorithm.* SIGGRAPH '98 Conference Proceedings.

[4]   S. E. Chen. *Quicktime VR – An image-Based Approach to Virtual Environment Navigation.* ACM SIGGRAPH '95 Conference Proceedings.

[5]   D. Cline and P. K. Egbert. *Interactive Display of Very Large Textures.* IEEE Visualization '98 Conference Proceedings.

[6]   D. Cohen-Or, E. Rich, U. Lerner and V. Shenkar. *A Real-Time Photo-Realistic Visual Flythrough.* IEEE transaction on Visualization and Computer Graphics, 1996.

[7]   S. Daly. *The Visual Difference Predictor : An Algorithm for the Assessment of Visual Fidelity.* Digital Image and Human Vision, MIT Press, 1993.

[8]   T. A. Funkhouser and C. H. Sequin. *Adaptive Display Algorithms for Interactive Frame Rates During Visualization of Complex Virtual Environments.* SIGGRAPH '93 Conference Proceedings.

[9]   I. Homan, M. Eldridge, K. Proudfoot, *Prefetching in a Texture Cache Architecture.* Proc. 1998 Eurographics/Siggraph workshop on graphics hardware

[10]   E. Horvitz and J. Lengyel. *Perception, Attention, and Resources: A Decision-Theoretic Approach to Graphics Rendering.* Proceedings of the Thirteenth Conference on Uncertainty in Artificial Intelligence, 1997.

[11]   P. Lindstrom, D, Koller, L. F. Hodges, W. Ribarsky, N. Faust and G. Turner. *Level-of-Detail Managements for Real-Time Rendering of Photo-Textured Terrain.* GIT-GVU Technical Report, 1995.

[12]   T. Möller and E.Haines. *Real-Time Rendering.* AK Peters, 1999.

[13]   K. Myszkowski. *The Visible Differences Predictor : Applications to Global Illumination Problems.* Eurographics Rendering Workshop '98 Proceedings, 1998.

[14]   K. Myszkowski, P. Rokita and T. Tawara. *Perceptually-informed accelerated rendering of high quality walkthrough sequences.* Eurographics Rendering Workshop '99 Proceedings, 1999.

[15]   S. M. Oborn. *UTAH: The Movie.* Master's Thesis, Utah State University, 1994.

[16]   M. Ramasubramanian, S. N. Pattanaik and D. Greenberg. *A Perceptually Based Physical Error Metric for Realistic Image Synthesis.* ACM SIGGRAPH '99 Conference Proceedings.

[17]   Sahn. *Approximate algorithms for the 0/1 knapsack problem.* ACM Publication.

[18]   *S3TC DirectX 6.0 Standard Texture Compression.* S3 Inc., 1998.

[19]   J. Torborg and J. T. Kajiya. *Talisman: Commodity Realtime 3D Graphics for the PC.* SIGGRAPH '96 Conference Proceedings.

[20]   H. Yee, S. N. Pattanaik and D. P. Greenberg. *Spatio-Temporal Sensitivity and Visual Attention in Dynamic Environments,* accepted for publication in ACM Transactions on Computer Graphics (2001).

Editors' Note: see Appendix, p. 341 for colored figures of this paper

Path differentials and applications

Frank Suykens, Yves D. Willems

Department of Computer Science, K.U.Leuven, Belgium
Frank.Suykens@cs.kuleuven.ac.be

Abstract. Photo-realistic rendering algorithms such as Monte Carlo ray tracing sample individual paths to compute images. Noise and aliasing artefacts are
usually reduced by supersampling. Knowledge about the neighborhood of the
path, such as an estimated footprint, can be used to reduce these artefacts without
having to trace additional paths. The recently introduced ray differentials estimate such a footprint for classical ray tracing, by computing ray derivatives with
respect to the image plane. The footprint proves to be useful for filtering textures locally on surfaces. In this paper, we generalize the use of these derivatives
to arbitrary path sampling, including general reflection and refraction functions.
Sampling new directions introduces additional partial derivatives, which are all
combined into a footprint estimate. Additionally the path gradient is introduced;
it gives the rate of change of the path contribution. When this change is too steep
the size of the footprint is reduced. The resulting footprint can be used in any
global illumination algorithm that is based on path sampling. Two applications
show its potential: texture filtering in distributed ray tracing and a novel hierarchical approach to particle tracing radiosity.

1 Introduction

The traditional image pipeline processes the scene primitives one by one and renders
them on screen. Ray tracing on the other hand takes point samples on the image plane,
and traces infinitely thin rays through the scene. This allows an easy simulation of
reflection and refraction effects. Extensions such as Monte Carlo ray tracing handle
arbitrary bidirectional reflection functions (BRDF's) for even more photo-realistic images.

These methods still use ray tracing as the engine to compute light transport. Because a ray (and a path) is a point sample, with no information about its neighborhood,
these algorithms are prone to aliasing or noise. The common solution is supersampling,
averaging the evaluation of many paths. This is expensive, and researchers have tried
to exploit coherence in the neighborhood of the rays to reduce aliasing or noise.

Beam tracing [6], Cone tracing [1] and pencil tracing [11] all extend a ray to a
finite width. Lighting calculations can be done coherently over the extent of the ray,
but intersection, reflection and refraction calculations are much more difficult. The
combination of physically based BRDF's with these methods is a difficult problem.

Collins [4] explicitly maintains connectivity between neighboring paths when they
are traced through the scene. The distance to neighboring rays serves as a kernel size
for splatting in a caustic lightmap. Connectivity is lost, however, when adjacent rays hit
different objects leading to different ray trees. Stochastic sampling is possible but may
diverge the ray trees even more.

One particularly interesting approach presented by Igehy [7] computes ray differentials, partial derivatives of a ray with respect to the position on the image plane. The

footprint of a ray is approximated by the differential vectors: the partial derivatives multiplied by a finite distance on the image plane. The differentials give an idea about the distance to neighboring rays. This proves to be very effective for filtering textures locally over the footprint. Only perfectly specular reflections and refractions are supported, limiting the technique to classical ray tracing. The use of derivatives alleviates many of the problems of previously mentioned techniques. Because differential calculus is used, a ray or path stays infinitely thin.

Chen and Arvo [3] present another interesting use of path derivatives. They compute first and second order derivatives of specular reflection paths. These derivatives allow an efficient computation of small path perturbations, that accurately approximate neighboring paths. An application uses perturbations of a sparse set of known paths to efficiently approximate reflections on implicit surfaces.

In this paper we extend the concept of ray differentials to arbitrary sampled paths, including arbitrary reflection and refraction functions and area light source sampling. A key observation is that the sampling of BRDF's or light sources introduces new degrees of freedom in the generation of the path. This gives rise to extra partial derivatives and differential vectors that must all be combined into a useful estimate of the paths footprint. We will show how to compute the new partial derivatives and present a simple heuristic to derive a useful footprint from these derivatives.

We also propose to track *path evaluation* derivatives, that tell us how fast the (image) contribution changes over the differential vectors. This *path gradient* is used to refine the footprint estimate; a smaller footprint is used for large gradients.

The combined result forms a convenient footprint estimate for arbitrary sampled eye-paths and light-paths. Therefore our techniques can be applied to any global illumination algorithm that is based on path sampling.

Two applications demonstrate the potential of the method:

- **Texture Filtering:** A classical ray tracer is extended with glossy reflections and refractions. Textures are filtered locally over the estimated footprint to reduce noise.
- **Particle Tracing:** A hierarchical refinement criterion for particle tracing radiosity is presented. The estimated footprint of single paths is sufficient to determine an appropriate level of subdivision.

Many other applications are possible. Some possibilities are discussed in the conclusions (Section 5).

Section 2 explains the framework for computing partial derivatives and differentials for arbitrary sampled paths. Section 3 shows how to compute the path gradient and Section 4 demonstrates applications.

2 Path differentials

2.1 Path sampling and path footprint

Stochastic ray tracing constructs paths by sampling. Newly sampled directions (or vertices) depend on the previous directions and vertices and possibly on some new variables. Figure 1 shows a short eye path where $\mathbf{D}_1$ and $\mathbf{V}_1$ depend on variables x_1, x_2, a position on the image plane. The reflected direction $\mathbf{D}_2$ depends on x_1, x_2 as well, but also on new variables x_3, x_4 determined by the BRDF sampling. In stochastic ray tracing random numbers are used to instantiate the variables and corresponding paths.

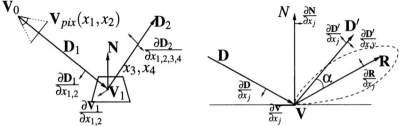

Fig. 1. Tracing an eye ray and a scattered ray introduces new variables x_j in the path, for which partial derivatives need to be computed.

Fig. 2. Partial derivatives for phong lobe sampling. $\mathbf{D}'$ has derivatives for previous sampling variables x_j but also for new variables x, y from BRDF sampling

For a certain vertex $\mathbf{V}$ (or a direction) in the path one can say that:

$$\mathbf{V} = g(x_1, x_2, \ldots, x_k) = g(X_k) \tag{1}$$

with g the *path generation function*, and k the number of variables that $\mathbf{V}$ depends on.

A small perturbation ε_j applied to a variable x_j slightly moves vertex $\mathbf{V}$:

$$\mathbf{V} + \delta\mathbf{V}_j = g(x_1, \ldots, x_j + \varepsilon_j, \ldots, x_k) \tag{2}$$

This change can be approximated by a first order Taylor expansion:

$$\delta\mathbf{V}_j \approx \frac{\partial g(x_1, \ldots, x_j, \ldots, x_k)}{\partial x_j} \varepsilon_j \tag{3}$$

The magnitude of the partial derivative determines the sensitivity of $\mathbf{V}$ in terms of x_j. Simultaneous perturbation of several variables corresponds to a $\delta\mathbf{V} = \sum_j \delta\mathbf{V}_j$.

If we consider all perturbations $\varepsilon_j \in [-\Delta x_j/2, \Delta x_j/2]$ then the set of perturbed vertices $\delta\mathbf{V}_j$ forms a line segment defined by a vector centered around $\mathbf{V}$:

$$\Delta\mathbf{V}_j = \frac{\partial g(x_1, \ldots, x_k)}{\partial x_j} \Delta x_j \tag{4}$$

We will call these the *differential vectors*.

Given a perturbation interval Δx_j for each variable and allowing simultaneous perturbation of the variables, the set of all possible perturbed vertices $\mathbf{V} + \delta\mathbf{V}$ forms an area[1]. We call this area *the footprint* of the path for vertex $\mathbf{V}$.

The shape of the footprint is a polygon with the differential vectors as edges (see 2.5). In Igehy's approach only two variables exist, the image plane coordinates. The footprint is a parallelogram formed by the two differential vectors.

Given the perturbation intervals Δx_j, the footprint estimates the region of influence or the sensitivity of the path in a vertex $\mathbf{V}$. A suitable choice for Δx_j should ensure coherence over the footprint while being large enough to reduce noise and aliasing (see 2.4 and 3). The computation the partial derivatives themselves is detailed in 2.3.

Other definitions of a path footprint are also possible. For instance a filter kernel could be defined for each differential vector. The resulting 'footprint' filter would be the convolution of these filter kernels. Using Gaussian kernels turns out to be interesting as the convolution of elliptic Gaussians is again an elliptic Gaussian [2].

---

[1]Partial derivatives of a vertex do lie in a plane perpendicular to the surface normal due to ray transfer computation (see 2.3)

2.2 Sampling Domain

The set of variables x_j determines the domain of all possible paths. We choose a unit interval $[0,1]$ as the domain of each x_j, corresponding to the random numbers that are used in stochastic sampling. Importance sampling can be used to transform variables with a different, desired distribution.

The domain of all possible paths with M degrees of freedom $(g(X_M))$ is the M-dimensional unit hypercube. A point in the domain determines a path. Such a uniform domain will simplify the choice of Δx_j's when constructing differentials from the partial derivatives (see 2.4).

2.3 Partial derivatives

Tracing paths involves sampling of new directions and vertices. For stochastic sampling a certain probability density function (pdf) determines the distribution of the new direction or vertex. Importance sampling [9] is a well known procedure to sample according to a given pdf. In general sampling a new direction (or vertex) with an importance sampling procedure h derived from the pdf gives:

$$\mathbf{D}' = h(\mathbf{D}, \mathbf{V}, x, y) \qquad (5)$$

where $\mathbf{D}'$ is a new direction dependent on the previous direction and vertex (if these exist) and some new random variables x, y (a 2D sampling in most cases). Partial derivatives of $\mathbf{D}'$ can be computed by simply deriving h for all random variables x_j, x, y. Note that $\mathbf{D}$ and $\mathbf{V}$ depend on previous x_j. We will briefly describe all relevant sampling events. More details on the derivative computation can be found in [13].

Pixel sampling: The initial vertex $\mathbf{V}_0$ of a path is the eye. (This could already be a sampling event, but is not considered as such here.) Pixel sampling generates a ray direction $\mathbf{D}_1$ based on a randomly chosen point in a certain pixel. Computation of the two derivatives of $\mathbf{D}_1$ is given in [7].

Transfer: Transfer computes a new point in the path by tracing a ray: $\mathbf{V}' = \mathbf{V} + t\mathbf{D}$, with t the traveled distance. No new sampling occurs, so existing derivatives of $\mathbf{V}$ and $\mathbf{D}$ are used to computed $\frac{\partial \mathbf{V}'}{\partial x_j}$. All partial derivatives of $\mathbf{V}'$ lie in the plane perpendicular to the geometric normal. See [7] for a detailed computation.

Scattering: Scattering in a vertex $\mathbf{V}$ given an incoming direction $\mathbf{D}$ determines a new direction $\mathbf{D}'$. The pdf for direction sampling is usually chosen proportional to the BRDF or 'BRDF $\times$ cosine'. Partial derivatives of the resulting sampling procedure must be computed.

An example for a glossy phong BRDF is shown in figure 2. The new direction $\mathbf{D}'$ is distributed according to $cos^S\alpha$ around the perfectly reflected direction $\mathbf{R}$. Since $\mathbf{D}'$ depends on $\mathbf{R}$ and $\mathbf{R}$ on $\mathbf{D}$, $\frac{\partial \mathbf{D}'}{\partial x_j}$ can be different from zero.

The new derivatives $\frac{\partial \mathbf{D}'}{\partial x, y}$ depend on the specific sampling procedure. For example for uniform sampling of a hemisphere:

$$\phi = 2\pi x, \ cos(\theta) = 1 - y$$
$$\mathbf{D}' = h(x, y) = (cos(\phi)sin(\theta), sin(\phi)sin(\theta), cos(\theta)) \qquad (6)$$

Partial derivatives of $h(x, y)$ are easily computed.

For perfectly specular reflection or refraction (deterministic!) no new random variables are introduced. This case was handled in [7].

Light sampling: When light paths are constructed, a starting point must be chosen on a light and a light direction must be sampled. Again partial derivatives of the specific sampling procedure are easily computed.

Any other sampling event not covered here, can usually be easily derived from the sampling procedure.

2.4 Choice of Δx_j

Given a vertex $\mathbf{V}$ we have computed a number of partial derivatives $\frac{\partial \mathbf{V}}{\partial x_j}$. In this section we will derive a heuristic for choosing intervals Δx_j that correspond to the expected distance to a neighboring sample (the closest sample $(x_1 \ldots x_k)$ differing only in x_j).

Multiplying the deltas with the corresponding derivative results in differential vectors that approximate the expected distance to a neighboring similar path. For example differential vectors from sampling a Lambertian reflection will usually be larger compared to a glossy Phong reflection, because the partial derivatives are larger while the deltas are the same. The rays get 'spread out' more.

The footprint is inversely proportional to the expected density of similar paths around a vertex.

For classical ray tracing [7] only two differential vectors have to be considered: those with respect to the position on the image plane. The deltas are chosen to be the size of a pixel, the distance to the next sample on the image plane.

In our case we have to make a choice for each x_j possibly coming from very different sampling events. As said, each variable has a unit interval domain. We consider two approaches for choosing deltas.

Local deltas: Each Δx_j depends on the number of samples that was used in the sampling event that introduced x_j. For example if N samples per pixel are traced, these samples are distributed over the unit square. Δx_0 should be chosen as an approximate distance to a neighboring sample. For regular sampling this distance is $1/\sqrt{N}$ for both Δx_0 and Δx_1 and we have found this distance to be useful for stochastic sampling also.

If extra information about the sampling process is known (e.g. nonuniform stratification), different values for Δx_0 and Δx_1 may be better.

For scattering, a 2D sampling, a splitting factor N' determines how many scattered samples are spawn. Again we choose deltas to be $1/\sqrt{N'}$. If many samples are spawn, the corresponding differentials will be smaller.

Global deltas: The previous approach does not work well with path tracing, where a large number of samples per pixel is used, but the splitting factor is 1.

In this case we consider the complete M-dimensional domain of a path, and considerer the samples evenly distributed over the domain. An estimate of the distance to a neighboring sample in one dimension is now given by $1/\sqrt[M]{N}$. All Δx_j are chosen equally large.

Longer paths will have a larger delta, as N samples have to be distributed over a higher dimensional domain.

Russian roulette, an unbiased way to limit the length of paths, can be incorporated in this approach. Absorption probabilities P_{rr} are accumulated along the path, and deltas

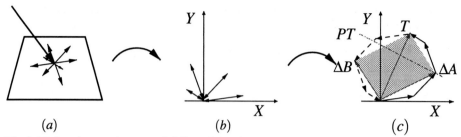

Fig. 3. Each path vertex has several differential vectors lying in the same plane (a). These vectors describe the footprint of the path. By transforming to the $X - Y$ plane (b), this polygonal footprint can be constructed by combining the vectors in a particular order (c). A good approximation is given by vectors ΔA and ΔB.

are computed as $1.0/ \sqrt[M]{N \times \prod_i P_{rr}(\mathbf{V}_i)}$. Thus the number of samples for 'this kind of path' is decreased by the absorption probabilities, and deltas grow larger.

This approach works well for path tracing and also particle tracing as demonstrated in the second application.

2.5 Differential vectors to footprint

Consider a vertex $\mathbf{V}$ and its (planar) differential vectors $\Delta \mathbf{V}_j$ (Fig. 3). As said the footprint of the path in $\mathbf{V}$ is the area reachable by perturbation of the path within the chosen Δx_j's.

This area can be constructed from the line segments defined by the differential vectors. Any perturbed vertex $\mathbf{V}'$ is a combination of points on the line segments. The area defined by a set of line segments is the Minkowski sum ($\oplus$) of these segments (centered around $\mathbf{V}$):

$$\bigoplus_j \Delta \mathbf{V}_j = \{\mathbf{V}' = \sum_j \gamma_j \Delta \mathbf{V}_j| - 0.5 < \gamma_i < 0.5\} \tag{7}$$

For two differentials this sum is a parallelogram formed by the two vectors. In general the Minkowski sum forms a polygon where each vector appears twice as an edge. This polygon can be constructed as follows (see fig. 3):

- Transform the differential vectors to the 2D $X - Y$ plane. (a to b)
- Sort the segments according to the angle made with X (b)
- Add the sorted vectors one by one as edges of the polygon (reaching the top of the polygon) (c solid)
- Add edges by subtracting the vectors in the same order, starting at the top of the polygon (c dashed)

To perform operations such as texture filtering over the footprint, a convenient representation is needed. For more than two differential vectors the area expression becomes impractical. Therefore we compute two representative vectors ΔA and ΔB that give a good approximation of the covered area (see 3 (c)):

- T = the sum of all differential vectors
- PT = a vector perpendicular to T
- ΔA = sum of all vectors $\Delta \mathbf{V}_j$ that have $\Delta \mathbf{V}_j \cdot PT > 0$
- $\Delta B = T - \Delta A$

Constructing the representative vectors processes all differential vectors twice (For T and ΔA; no sort is needed). This is a linear operation in terms of the number of differentials.

ΔA and ΔB now provide a convenient estimate of the footprint of the path in $\mathbf{V}$.

3 Path gradient

In the previous section, Δx_j were chosen to approximate the distance to neighboring samples. In this section we propose an alternative choice for Δx_j based on the rate of change of the path contribution when perturbations are applied.

Any function defined on a path is a function of the generating variables x_j. In this section we compute partial derivatives of the path evaluation, the function that determines the contribution to the quantity (e.g. pixel flux) we want to compute.

We present the technique for eye paths, but it is equally applicable to light paths.

3.1 Rendering equation

The light flux reaching the eye $\mathbf{V}_0$ through a certain pixel is given as an integral of a pixel weighting function W_e and the incoming radiance (see fig. 1 for notations):

$$\Phi_{pix} = \int_{A_{pix}} dA_{pix} W_e(\mathbf{V}_0 \to \mathbf{D}_1) L(\mathbf{V}_0 \leftarrow \mathbf{D}_1) \tag{8}$$

L is unknown and can be expanded using the rendering equation:

$$\Phi_{pix} = \int_{A_{pix}} dA_{pix} \int_\Omega d\omega \, W_e(\mathbf{V}_0 \to \mathbf{D}_1) f_r(\mathbf{D}_1, \mathbf{V}_1, \mathbf{D}_2) cos(\theta_1) L(\mathbf{V}_1 \leftarrow \mathbf{D}_2)$$

with f_r the BRDF and $cos(\theta_1) = \mathbf{N}_1 \cdot \mathbf{D}_2$.

Each new reflection or refraction introduces an f_r and cosine factor. To simplify notation we define the potential function W_i of a path of length i as the product of W_e and all subsequent f_r and cosine factors. Now the *path evaluation F* (the integrand) of a path is simply:

$$F = W_i(\mathbf{V}_i \to \mathbf{D}_{i+1}) \cdot L(\mathbf{V}_i \leftarrow \mathbf{D}_{i+1}) \tag{9}$$

And W_{i+1} is:

$$W_{i+1} = W_i(\mathbf{V}_i \to \mathbf{D}_{i+1}) f_r(\mathbf{D}_{i+1}, \mathbf{V}_{i+1}, \mathbf{D}_{i+2}) cos(\theta_{i+1}) \tag{10}$$

Actual contributions to the image are made when a light source is hit or by direct sampling of the light sources.

3.2 Relative partial derivatives

The partial derivatives of a path evaluation are:

$$\frac{\partial F}{\partial x_j} = \frac{\partial W_i}{\partial x_j} L + W_i \frac{\partial L}{\partial x_j} \tag{11}$$

We compute *relative partial derivatives* by dividing this expression by F:

$$\frac{\partial F}{\partial x_j}/F = \frac{\partial W_i}{\partial x_j}/W_i + \frac{\partial L}{\partial x_j}/L \tag{12}$$

This expression gives the relative rate of change of F in terms of x_j.

Because common factors cancel out it also provides a convenient way for tracking partial derivatives of W_i when extending a path:

$$\frac{\partial W_{i+1}}{\partial x_j}/W_{i+1} = \frac{\partial W_i}{\partial x_j}/W_i + \frac{\partial f_r}{\partial x_j}/f_r + \frac{\partial cos(\theta)}{\partial x_j}/cos(\theta)$$

Just the relative partial derivatives of the individual factors must be added to the known $\frac{\partial W_i}{\partial x_j}/W_i$. To start a path $\frac{\partial W_e}{\partial x_j}$ must be computed, which is 0 for constant W_e.

The computation of these derivatives is straightforward, as the BRDF evaluation and the cosine factor can be expressed in terms of $\mathbf{V}_i$, $\mathbf{D}_i$ and $\mathbf{N}_i$ for which derivatives have already been computed for the differential vectors. Consider for example the cosine factor:

$$\frac{\partial cos\theta_i}{\partial x_j} = \frac{\partial(\mathbf{N}_i\mathbf{D}_{i+1})}{\partial x_j} = \frac{\partial\mathbf{N}_i}{\partial x_j}\mathbf{D}_{i+1} + \mathbf{N}_i\frac{\partial\mathbf{D}_{i+1}}{\partial x_j}$$

Both derivatives of $\mathbf{N}_i$ and $\mathbf{D}_{i+1}$ were computed before.

When an actual radiance contribution from a light source is computed, $\frac{\partial L}{\partial x_j}/L$ must be added to $\frac{\partial W_i}{\partial x_j}/W_i$ to get $\frac{\partial F}{\partial x_j}/F$. Computation depends on the light source sampling. Currently we consider the change of the light source contribution to be constant, so that its derivative is zero. For moderately distant light sources, this approximation is well acceptable.

3.3   Choosing Δx_j

When a perturbation Δx_j is applied to a path X, the relative change of the contribution $F(X)$ can be approximated as:

$$\Delta FR_j \approx [\frac{\partial F}{\partial x_j}(X)/F(X)] \cdot \Delta x_j \tag{13}$$

For example a gradient ΔFR_j of 300% means the contribution of the perturbed path is approximately three times higher (or lower) than $F(X)$.

Now consider a vertex $\mathbf{V}$ in a path. The differential vectors $\Delta\mathbf{V}_j = \frac{\partial\mathbf{V}}{\partial x_j}\Delta x_j$ define a maximal allowed perturbation of $\mathbf{V}$ when changing x_j. Since the same Δx_j is used as in equation 13, this maximal perturbation corresponds to the relative change ΔFR_j of the path contribution.

In our applications we consider the contribution F to be constant over the differential vectors. Of course F does change and ΔFR_j indicates how much. By constraining the relative change ΔFR_j to be smaller than a maximum threshold ΔFR_{max}, deltas can be computed from equation 13:

$$\Delta x_j = \frac{\Delta FR_{max}}{\frac{\partial F}{\partial x_j}/F} \tag{14}$$

Using these deltas for the vertex differential vectors results in smaller vectors (and resulting footprint) when the gradient is large. The threshold controls the allowable error.

A very small gradient, however, can lead to arbitrary large footprints. We use the local or global delta heuristic (Section 2.4) as an upper limit for the deltas computed using the gradient. This gives good results, but the choice of $\Delta F R_{max}$ (that controls over the error) is not obvious.

3.4 Discussion

Other functions of a path can also be candidates for derivative computation. The *score function* of a path $\mathcal{P}$ in Monte Carlo integration is $F(\mathcal{P})/p(\mathcal{P})$, where p is the pdf used for generating the path. It is in fact the score function that is evaluated and averaged when computing pixel fluxes with Monte Carlo ray tracing. This could be an interesting choice for tracking derivatives.

Usually pdf's for direction sampling are chosen proportionally to the BRDF or the cosine. These factors cancel out and the score function only contains factors not used in path sampling.

We have chosen to compute derivatives of F itself so that these path sampling factors are explicitly included. It can be shown that (for separable pdf's) derivatives of these factors are related to the second order derivative of footprint. However, a full analysis is beyond the scope of this paper.

Both choices do include factors not present in the path sampling, so that bad path sampling is countered with large ΔF_j.

For classical ray tracing $W_{i+1} = W_i \cdot f_s$ with f_s the *constant* specular reflection or refraction coefficient. Derivatives of f_s are zero so the path gradient does not yield any extra information for the method presented by Igehy.

4 Applications

The differentials, gradients and footprint estimation were implemented in RenderPark. Derivatives are supported for diffuse reflection, phong reflection and refraction, area light sources and pixel sampling.

4.1 Texture Filtering

In a first application we extend a ray tracer with glossy reflections and refractions. The computed footprint is used for filtering textures locally on surfaces to reduce noise.

Igehy presented the same application for classical ray tracing. Comparison with other filtering approaches can be found in [7]. We use trilinear interpolated mipmapped textures and anisotropic filtering. The smallest representative vector in the footprint determines the mipmap level, and several samples are averaged along the larger axis. We used a box filter, but weighted filtering might give even better results.

The scene contains several textured surfaces; the two 'playing pieces' consist of a squashed sphere on a diffuse base. One is reflective, the other refractive. Both use a glossy phong lobe for scattering. For all but the reference image we used one sample per pixel and 4 stratified samples for each scattering.

Figure 5 shows standard distributed ray tracing. The reflections and refractions show a lot of noise, as 4 is a low sampling rate.

Figure 6 shows filtering with the *local delta* heuristic (2.4). Using only 4 scattering samples, the estimated distance to a neighboring ray is quite large The filtering reduces the noise of the glossy scatterings, but it sometimes over-blurs, especially for the multiple refractions in the glass object.

Fig. 4. Hierarchical particle tracing radiosity (400k paths) using the area defined by the path differentials as a refinement oracle.

For **figure 7** the path gradient was used for estimating deltas. Over-blurring is reduced because the glossy phong lobes give rise to high gradients. The noise still remains a lot lower as in image 5. The threshold value FR_{max}, that restricts relative changes over the differential vectors, was chosen to be 70%. This choice was not very critical, anything from 50% to 100% worked well.

A reference image using 81 samples per pixel is given in figure 8.

Note that only textures are filtered; 'edge' noise due to scattered rays hitting different objects is not reduced (e.g. the table edge seen in the metal piece). An adaptive sampling scheme could direct more samples towards edges, but not towards varying textures.

The overhead introduced by differential computation was relatively small ($< 10\%$ for this example). Computing BRDF differentials is about as expensive as sampling and evaluating the BRDF itself. As a path grows longer, however, more differentials have to be computed, and the overhead is not negligible. Reducing the differential vectors to a few representatives before prolonging the path, keeping the amount of tracked differentials constant, could be an interesting line of research.

4.2 Particle tracing

Particle tracing constructs paths starting from the light sources. This Monte Carlo simulation of light transport is used in many global illumination algorithms, e.g. radiosity [5, 10], density estimation [12] and photon map construction [8].

We present a hierarchical radiosity application to demonstrate the usefulness of path differentials for particle tracing, but it can be used as well for the other algorithms.

A hierarchical version of particle radiosity was presented in [5] and [14]. Both methods accumulate the hits (the radiance) on elements and subdivide if the variation over the element is too large. In [14] hits are stored simultaneously on the two lower levels of the hierarchy. Some remarks that are valid for both algorithms:

- While the radiosity solution is hierarchical, the light transport itself is not. All particles contribute to the most detailed or the two most detailed levels in the hierarchy.
- When subdivision occurs, the radiance information of the discarded level is thrown away, because it is equal (and inadequate) for its children.

We use path differentials to estimate a footprint for each individual particle. The area defined by the two representative vectors ($\Delta A \times \Delta B$) gives an idea about the density of similar paths in the neighborhood.

Our refinement oracle looks for the largest element that is just smaller than the footprint, subdividing as necessary. The contribution is made to this element in the hierarchy. The level in the hierarchy can be different for each particle so the light transport is hierarchical. No previous paths are thrown away.

While this refinement oracle based on a single particle has interesting advantages, we do not claim it to be the best oracle in existence. The main purpose is to show the behavior and usefulness of the path differentials for particle tracing.

The implementation of our radiosity algorithm uses clustering and constant basis functions. We used the gradient to determine deltas and the global deltas as an upper bound.

Figure 4 shows the radiosity solution for a simple room with a table, a diffuse and a glossy refractive ball (phong exponent 40). Note that the refractive ball shows up black as it has no diffuse component.

Several interesting things to note in the image:

- A correct caustic is visible on the table. The fine subdivision is due to a large gradient (and small delta). Merely using the global delta heuristic barely shows the caustic. The overall subdivision due to direct light and diffuse interreflection is less influenced by the gradient. The gradient for these paths is small and the global delta upper limit is used (except in corners).
- Only 400,000 paths were traced, resulting in a relatively noiseless solution. This is because global deltas depend on the number of samples. Only where the gradient is used (e.g. the caustic) more noise can be seen.
- The ceiling is lit by diffuse interreflection. A diffuse reflection (using $cos\theta$ sampling) results in relatively large derivatives for the sampled direction. Transfer to the ceiling results in a large footprint and thus a coarser subdivision. Near the bright spot on the back wall though a finer subdivision can be seen and some color bleeding.

5 Conclusions

In this work ray differentials are generalized to arbitrarily sampled paths, including general BRDF's. Each sampling introduces new partial derivatives that are all combined in a footprint estimate.

We also introduced the computation of a path gradient, the change of the path contribution over the differential vectors. It is used to restrict the footprint in case of high gradients.

We successfully used the footprint estimation for texture filtering in ray tracing with glossy materials and in a novel refinement oracle in hierarchical particle tracing radiosity.

Since our framework allows arbitrary sampling many other methods can benefit from path differentials, in particular Monte Carlo global illumination methods:

- In photon maps the footprint of eye paths can determine the area over which photons must be considered for illumination reconstruction. If too few photons are found the path can be extended.
- Importance calculations can also be performed. The footprint of an eye ray indicates the density of similar paths. A small footprint indicates a high importance,

for example by magnification through glass.

Another interesting line of research would be to introduce visibility into the framework. As the footprint is still based on a point sample, nearby visibility changes are ignored. It would be interesting to adjust the footprint by selective visibility tests.

We explored only one possible definition of a path footprint: the area made up by a set of perturbed vertices. Other interesting approaches are possible such as using a convolution of kernel filters defined over the differential vectors.

6 Acknowledgments

Many thanks to Vincent Masselus for modeling the scenes and to all the people that made useful suggestions. This research was partly supported by FWO Grant #G.0263.97.

References

1. John Amanatides. Ray tracing with cones. *Computer Graphics*, 18(3):129–135, July 1984.
2. Philippe Bekaert. *Personal Communication*. 2001.
3. M. Chen and J. Arvo. Perturbation methods for interactive specular reflections. In Hans Hagen, editor, *IEEE Transactions on Visualization and Computer Graphics*, volume 6 (3), pages 253–264. IEEE Computer Society, 2000.
4. Steven Collins. Adaptive Splatting for Specular to Diffuse Light Transport. In *Fifth Eurographics Workshop on Rendering*, pages 119–135, Darmstadt, Germany, June 1994.
5. Paul S. Heckbert. Adaptive radiosity textures for bidirectional ray tracing. *Computer Graphics*, 24(4):145–154, August 1990.
6. Paul S. Heckbert and Pat Hanrahan. Beam tracing polygonal objects. *Computer Graphics*, 18(3):119–127, July 1984.
7. Homan Igehy. Tracing ray differentials. *Computer Graphics*, 33(Annual Conference Series):179–186, 1999.
8. Henrik Wann Jensen. Global illumination using photon maps. In Xavier Pueyo and Peter Schröder, editors, *Eurographics Rendering Workshop 1996*, pages 21–30, New York City, NY, June 1996. Eurographics, Springer Wien. ISBN 3-211-82883-4.
9. M. Kalos and P. Whitlock. *Monte Carlo Methods, Volume 1: Basics*. J. Wiley, New York, 1986.
10. S. N. Pattanaik and S. P. Mudur. Computation of global illumination by monte carlo simulation of the particle model of light. *Third Eurographics Workshop on Rendering*, pages 71–83, May 1992.
11. Mikio Shinya, Tokiichiro Takahashi, and Seiichiro Naito. Principles and applications of pencil tracing. *Computer Graphics*, 21(4):45–54, July 1987.
12. Peter Shirley, Bretton Wade, Philip M. Hubbard, David Zareski, Bruce Walter, and Donald P. Greenberg. Global Illumination via Density Estimation. In P. M. Hanrahan and W. Purgathofer, editors, *Rendering Techniques '95 (Proceedings of the Sixth Eurographics Workshop on Rendering)*, pages 219–230, New York, NY, 1995. Springer-Verlag.
13. F. Suykens. Path differentials and applications. Technical Report CW307, Department of Computer Science, K.U. Leuven, Leuven, Belgium, May 2001.
14. Robert F. Tobler, Alexander Wilkie, Martin Feda, and Werner Purgathofer. A hierarchical subdivision algorithm for stochastic radiosity methods. In Julie Dorsey and Philipp Slusallek, editors, *Eurographics Rendering Workshop 1997*, pages 193–204, June 1997.

Editors' Note: see Appendix, p. 342 for colored figures of this paper

Interleaved Sampling

Alexander Keller[1], Wolfgang Heidrich[2]

[1] University of Kaiserslautern, keller@informatik.uni-kl.de
[2] The University of British Columbia, heidrich@cs.ubc.ca

Abstract. The known sampling methods can roughly be grouped into regular and irregular sampling. While regular sampling can be realized efficiently in graphics hardware, it is prone to inter-pixel aliasing. On the other hand these artifacts can easily be masked by noise using irregular sampling which, however, is more expensive to evaluate as it lacks the high coherence of a regular approach. We bridge this gap by introducing a generalized sampling scheme that smoothly blends between regular and irregular sampling. By interleaving the samples of regular grids in an irregular way, we preserve the high coherence and efficiently reduce inter-pixel aliasing thus significantly improving the rendering quality as compared to previous approaches.

1 Introduction

Sampling of functions is one of the most fundamental tasks in computer graphics. It has to be performed for applications as diverse as anti-aliased scan-conversion of scenes, illumination from area light sources, cameras with depth-of-field effects, motion blur, and volume rendering. The existing sampling schemes for these applications can be grouped into regular and irregular methods.

On the one hand, sampling on regular grids is efficient and simple, and also well suited for hardware rasterization. Unfortunately, the signals that need to be sampled in computer graphics typically are not band limited and often can contain arbitrarily large frequencies. Therefore some amount of aliasing is unavoidable, and sampling by regular grids emphasizes these artifacts.

On the other hand, Monte Carlo methods use randomized sample positions instead thus masking the aliasing artifacts by noise that is more visually pleasing. However, per pixel irregular sampling does not exhibit the kind of coherence known from regular sampling. Consequently, these methods are more expensive and not well suited for hardware implementations.

The new sampling scheme of *interleaved sampling* allows to smoothly blend between regular and irregular sampling thus yielding the best and most efficient compromise. To this end we interleave samples taken from a number of independent regular grids, and merge them into a single sampling pattern. The relative positions of the regular grids are determined by irregular offsets. Each regular grid can be interpreted as a low resolution image of the scene that can be rendered using the efficient rasterization algorithms. The samples of all regular grids are interleaved such that in the final high-quality, high-resolution image adjacent pixels are not correlated. Only minimal changes to existing hardware algorithms such as the Accumulation Buffer or multisampling allow to exploit the benefits of the new sampling scheme.

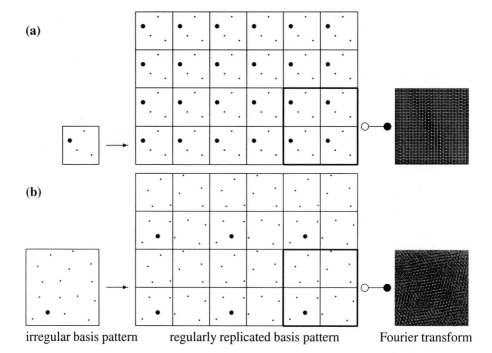

(a)

(b)

irregular basis pattern   regularly replicated basis pattern   Fourier transform

Fig. 1. The principle of interleaved sampling illustrated by example: In **(a)** the classical Accumulation Buffer is illustrated. The same sampling pattern is repeated for all pixels. The Fourier transform of this repeated pattern clearly shows a high potential for inter-pixel aliasing. In **(b)** a 2 × 2 pixel basis pattern is replicated. Thus the sampling patterns in adjacent pixels are different by interleaved sampling and the Fourier transform reveals a much reduced potential for inter-pixel aliasing. To illustrate the regular grids involved, one sample from the irregular basis pattern is emphasized as well as its corresponding replications. Also note that both approaches require exactly the same number of samples.

2 The Algorithm

The basic idea of interleaved sampling is intriguingly simple and instantly becomes obvious from Figure 1: in the Accumulation Buffer method [HA90] the irregular sampling pattern is affixed to *one pixel* and in consequence periodically repeated for all pixels such bearing a high potential for inter-pixel aliasing (see Figure 1a). For interleaved sampling an irregular offsetting pattern is chosen that covers *multiple pixels*. By periodically repeating this pattern regular grids still persist as emphasized in Figure 1b, however adjacent pixels are sampled by different patterns. Note that although the number of regular grids involved is increasing the inter-pixel aliasing potential is effectively decreased and the total number of samples remains the same.

2.1 Blending between Regular and Irregular Sampling

In a first step an arbitrary irregular sampling pattern is selected. By periodically tiling the image plane, each sample of the irregular basis pattern generates a regular grid. In a second step the pixel resolution is fixed. Visually spoken this means to superimpose the pixel graphpaper onto the periodic sampling pattern. Each regular grid then is rendered using a fast rasterization algorithm, and its samples are accumulated in the pixels determined by the superposition of the graphpaper. Finally each pixel is averaged by a box filter over the number of samples that fell inside.

By interleaving the regular grids by an irregular basis pattern, a high level of coherence is preserved and can still be exploited by raster graphics hardware, yet the high risk of local aliasing, i.e. inter-pixel aliasing, is reduced drastically since adjacent pixels use different sampling patterns.

Note that this general interleaving scheme does not require an integer ratio of the number of pixels covered by the irregular basis pattern as in the example of Figure 1. Depending on the irregular basis pattern and the graphpaper resolution it may also happen, that the pixels have different oversampling rates. The ratio of the support of a pixel and the support of the irregular basis pattern determines the amount of correlation. We can blend between two limit cases (see also Figure 4): In the first the basis pattern consists of only one sample, which results in correlated sampling on one regular grid. For the second case the size of the basis pattern is chosen as large as the image graphpaper which corresponds to the completely uncorrelated case where no regular grid structure is present.

2.2   Theoretical Considerations

The method of dependent tests [Sob62, FC62] was introduced as a generalization of the Monte Carlo method of integration. The basic idea was to use the *same* set of samples for the estimation of multiple integrals instead of using a new realization of the set of samples for each integral.

The Accumulation Buffer is the best example for the realization of the method of dependent tests: the same sampling pattern is used for all pixel integrals. However due to the repetition of the sampling pattern for each pixel, adjacent pixels can be highly correlated causing inter-pixel aliasing (see the periodogram in Figure 1a). This effect is not observed in the uncorrelated approach as taken by e.g. a software ray tracer that is applying a different sampling pattern to each pixel. The specific sampling pattern for the method of dependent tests can be chosen from a wide variety of different methods (for a survey see [Gla95]). A summary of the approaches that have been used for graphics hardware can be found in a report by Goss and Wu [GW99]. We use samples with blue noise characteristics that perfectly tile periodically and are generated by a relaxation scheme similar to the one introduced in [MF92].

By interleaving the method of dependent tests adjacent pixels are sampled in an uncorrelated way. The periodicity by the replication of the irregular basis pattern is much reduced as compared to the per pixel approach. Thus the inter-pixel aliasing potential is attenuated, and lower sampling rates as compared to the Accumulation Buffer can be used. This partially was recognized in [DW85], however without the awareness of the method of dependent tests and consequently without exploiting the coherence induced by the grid structure. Interleaved sampling is a generalization of the method of dependent test considering spectral issues.

3   Applications

Interleaved sampling as introduced above can be applied to a number of different sampling tasks, in particular those for which the Accumulation Buffer [HA90] has been used before. This includes soft shadows based on the method by Brotman and Badler [BB84], limited depth-of-field [HA90, KHM95, HSS97], and Instant Radiosity [Kel97].

Fig. 2. On the left we see the standard Accumulation Buffer approach for anti-aliasing at 4 samples per pixel as depicted in Figure 1a. Using the interleaved approach (see Figure 1b) on the right, the aliasing artifacts are spatially separated yielding a more visually pleasing appearance.

In addition to these applications, we will also consider interleaved sampling for texture based volume rendering along the lines of Cabral et al. [CCF94].

3.1 Anti-Aliasing by Supersampling

The first application we will look at is supersample anti-aliasing along the lines of multisampling [Ake93] and the Accumulation Buffer [HA90]. Existing multisampling implementations can be interpreted as a special case for interleaved sampling. If we consider only the ith sample of every pixel in an image, we see that all these samples are located on a regular grid with a spacing that is identical to the spacing of the pixels (see the emphasized sample in Figure 1a). Therefore, efficient incremental scan-conversion algorithms can be applied on this grid for rasterizing geometric primitives.

With interleaved sampling we stretch out the grid spacing of the samples so that they are no longer identical to the pixel spacing. Therefore, every sample on a particular grid corresponds to a different sub-pixel position in one of the pixels (see the emphasized sample in Figure 1b). Stretching out the grid spacing also stretches out aliasing structures thus very much improving the visual quality as can be seen in Figure 2.

There are different ways of implementing interleaved sampling in hardware rendering applications:

- **Modification of Multisample Hardware.** The most generally applicable way would be to add direct hardware support for interleaved sampling in a similar fashion multisampling is supported today. The hardware for scan conversion does not need to be modified for this. The only difference to multisampling is that not all the pixels will have the same sub-pixel masks, but the mask is one of a predetermined and implementation-specific number of masks. With these modifications the geometry only needs to be processed once, while individual scan converters take care of rasterizing the regular grids.

  The relative positions of the regular grids, which also determine the masks for the individual pixels, would be an implementation-specific arrangement that could be wired into the hardware. These positions would be generated in the design phase of the hardware. Since interleaved sampling is composed of regular grids, the hardware implementation will be less expensive than the 3Dlabs Wildcat multisample extension [3Dl], which randomizes the sample selection on a higher resolution grid.

- **Implementation on Current Hardware.** Another way to implement interleaved sampling is to individually render lower resolution images corresponding to the regular grids, and to then interleave the samples obtained this way by hand. To this end, the individual regular grids (low resolution images) are rendered directly into a texture map (an operation that is supported on many contemporary platforms). With these regular grids as textures, we can then render full-screen polygons while a second texture or a screen-space stipple pattern is used to mask out the pixels that should not be affected by the regular grid.

If the whole application is bounded by fill rate, then rendering multiple copies of the geometry will not degenerate the rendering performance. In this case, the method introduces only a constant overhead for interleaving the samples after the low-resolution regular grids have been rendered. The cost of this process does not depend on the shading complexity of every sample in the image. Thus, if the application is limited by the rasterization performance, this algorithm has only a constant overhead over supersampling with the same sampling pattern for each pixel. It is therefore a feasible algorithm that is interesting for applications that have high shading costs for each individual sample, such as complex procedural shaders [POAU00], or volume rendering (also see Section 3.3).

3.2 Motion Blur

The basic concept of interleaved sampling can easily be extended to arbitrary dimensions. For example, by simply assigning each of the interleaved images one moment in time, the above algorithm can support motion blur: then the irregular basis sampling pattern is 3-dimensional, where the first two dimensions are used for interleaving and the third dimension specifies the moment in time. Interleaved sampling so enables efficient and correct motion blur simulation for e.g. the REYES architecture [CCC87] or the photon map [JC98] using a very small set of different time samples (i.e. just the samples in the basis pattern), where each image to be interleaved is rendered by the original algorithm, however for the specified moment in time.

In Figure 4 the results of a motion blur simulation at 16 samples per pixel are shown. Using uncorrelated random samples no aliasing artifacts are visible, whereas the standard correlated Accumulation Buffer technique exhibits visible artifacts. Using a 2×2 interleaved irregular basis pattern of 64 samples with blue noise characteristics (yielding 16 samples per pixel as in the other cases), we blend between uncorrelated and correlated sampling and are able to exploit rasterization on regular grids. Despite the low sampling rate the aliasing artifacts are clearly reduced at the same amount of sampling work.

3.3 Volume Rendering

The next application we consider is texture-based volume rendering as described by Cabral [CCF94]. This algorithm uses a simple emission-absorption model for the volume, so that the rendering is reduced to a 1D integration along the viewing ray for every pixel in the final image. The texture-based approach for computing this 1D integral works as follows: the volume is sliced with equidistant planes. These are sorted back-to-front and blended together in the framebuffer. As a result of this algorithm, we obtain a sampling pattern that corresponds to a regular 3D grid in clip coordinates (i.e. after the projective transform).

Typically, on the order of 100 slices are used for this kind of application, and each slice yields a polygon that covers a large portion of the screen and is textured with a

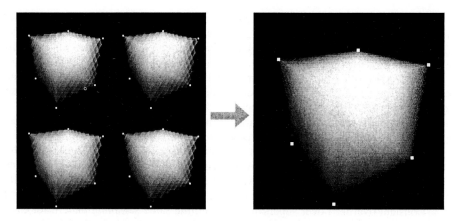

Fig. 3. For volume rendering, we combine a collection of small resolution images with slightly offset sample planes into a large resolution image by interleaving the samples from the smaller images. Except for a final combining operation, the fill rate required is the same as for rendering a large image in the first place, but the rendering quality is much better.

3D texture with tri-linear interpolation. Thus, the fill-rate required by this method is quite high, while the cost of geometric transformations is negligible. But even with 100 slices, there are often still some serious aliasing artifacts left. After all, modern medical imaging devices can generate data sets in the order of 512^3, and therefore 100 slices would result in an undersampling of a factor of 5. On the other hand it is not possible to increase the number of slices arbitrarily, both because of the performance implications and because of the limited depth of the framebuffer that results in quantization artifacts when using alpha blending. This could be avoided by hierarchical summation, which however requires additional framebuffers for the intermediate results and in consequence cannot be realized efficiently.

Interleaved sampling can be used to improve on this situation. Since we do not have the fill rate to do supersampling at interactive rates, we are only going to interleave the samples in one dimension; the z-coordinate in camera space. Interleaving in that dimension corresponds to varying the offsets for the samples in z direction. These offsets will be different for adjacent pixels, but since we are using interleaved sampling, they will repeat after a number of pixels, thus providing us with the coherence we need for exploiting graphics hardware. The method can be considered as a hardware implementation of the equidistant ray marcher from [PKK00] with interleaved jittered offsets.

Using existing hardware, the method then proceeds similarly to the method described in Section 3.1. First, we use the traditional texture-based volume rendering algorithm [CCF94] to render lower resolution regular grids (i.e. images), each with the sampling planes slightly offset compared to the other regular grids. The cost of this operation is identical to the original texture-based volume rendering algorithm, since volume rendering is completely determined by the rasterization cost.

As described in Section 3.1, we then combine the low-resolution regular grids into a high-resolution image using stipple patterns or 2D textures to mask out the pixels that are not affected by the individual regular grid. Figure 3 illustrates this method for the configuration with 4 regular grids. The cost of this second step is constant, that is, it does not depend on the number of sampling planes. During our tests with an SGI Octane VPro, we found this constant cost to be about the same as rendering 8 additional planes with the original method. The quality improvements we can achieve with interleaved sampling are much higher than the improvements we get by adding this number of additional samples.

Figure 5 shows a comparison of the algorithm with and without interleaved sampling for 20, 60, and 120 sampling planes. Since we are not supersampling in this application, interleaved sampling replaces the aliasing effects with noise that resembles the patterns known from ordered dithering. Note, however, that we are jittering sample locations instead of dithering color values.

On an Octane VPro, the frame rate for the 20 plane version is > 30 frames per second both with and without interleaving. For the 120 plane version we get around 18 frames per second in the interleaved case, and 20 frames per second in the non-interleaved case. Note that even for the 120 plane version there is still some aliasing left, and the 60 plane version with interleaved sampling looks better than the 120 plane version without. Also note that renderings with 120 sample planes already exhibit quite serious quantization artifacts due to the limited depth of the framebuffer. Thus, further increasing the number of sampling planes will not improve the quality.

Some more comparisons between the traditional volume texture-based volume rendering and interleaved sampling can be found in Figure 6.

3.4 Other Applications

The basic techniques of interleaved sampling presented in this paper naturally generalize to all Accumulation Buffer [HA90] and multi-pass frame-buffer [POAU00] techniques while preserving the good spectral properties and the fast convergence. So it is straightforward to apply interleaved sampling to weighted sampling [HA90], to the simulation of extended light sources using deep shadow maps [LV00], and to global illumination simulations [Kel97, HDKS00]. Here interleaved sampling can replace the N-shadows-artifact by noise. Finally it is very appealing to apply interleaved sampling to CCD-chip designs.

4 Conclusion

We have presented a new sampling scheme called *interleaved sampling* that exhibits excellent spectral behavior and yields excellent quality especially at low sampling rates, while at the same time it is simple and efficient to implement.

The fundamental idea of the new method is to interleave samples from several regular grids to form a locally irregular sampling pattern. By stretching out the periodicity of the per-pixel sampling pattern, aliasing structures are spread out, too, and in consequence much less perceivable. The high coherence of the involved regular grids allows for very efficient implementations in software, and in new as well as current hardware. The feasibility of interleaved sampling has been demonstrated by a number of examples ranging from supersampling over motion blur to volume rendering.

Acknowledgements

For the image in Figure 6 we used an MR data set kindly provided by Christoph Rezk-Salama, University of Erlangen-Nürnberg. Part of this work was done in August 2000, while both authors stayed at the Max-Planck-Institut für Informatik in Saarbrücken,

276

Germany. We would like to thank Hans-Peter Seidel for granting the research stay of the first author, who was also supported by mental images, Germany.

References

3Dl.   3Dlabs, *Wildcat: SuperScene Antialiasing*, http://www.3dlabs.com/product/technology.

Ake93.   K. Akeley, *RealityEngine Graphics*, Computer Graphics (SIGGRAPH '93 Conference Proceedings), 1993, pp. 109–116.

BB84.   L. Brotman and N. Badler, *Generating Soft Shadows with a Depth Buffer Algorithm*, IEEE Computer Graphics and Applications **4** (1984), no. 10, 71–81.

CCC87.   R. Cook, L. Carpenter, and E. Catmull, *The Reyes Image Rendering Architecture*, Computer Graphics (SIGGRAPH '87 Conference Proceedings), 1987, pp. 95–102.

CCF94.   B. Cabral, N. Cam, and J. Foran, *Accelerated Volume Rendering and Tomographic Reconstruction Using Texture Mapping Hardware*, 1994 Symposium on Volume Visualization, October 1994, pp. 91–98.

DW85.   M. Dippé and E. Wold, *Antialiasing through Stochastic Sampling*, Computer Graphics (SIGGRAPH '85 Conference Proceedings), 1985, pp. 69–78.

FC62.   A. Frolov and N. Chentsov, *On the calculation of certain integrals dependent on a parameter by the Monte Carlo method*, Zh. Vychisl. Mat. Fiz. **2** (1962), no. 4, 714 – 717, (in Russian).

Gla95.   A. Glassner, *Principles of Digital Image Synthesis*, Morgan Kaufmann, 1995.

GW99.   M. Goss and K. Wu, *Study of Supersampling Methods for Computer Graphics Hardware Antialiasing*, Tech. report, HP Labs, 1999.

HA90.   P. Haeberli and K. Akeley, *The Accumulation Buffer: Hardware Support for High-Quality Rendering*, Computer Graphics (SIGGRAPH '90 Conference Proceedings), 1990, pp. 309–318.

HDKS00.   W. Heidrich, K. Daubert, J. Kautz, and H.-P. Seidel, *Illuminating Micro Geometry Based on Precomputed Visibility*, Computer Graphics (SIGGRAPH '00 Conference Proceedings), 2000, pp. 455–464.

HSS97.   W. Heidrich, Ph. Slusallek, and H.-P. Seidel, *An Image-Based Model for Realistic Lens Systems in Interactive Computer Graphics*, Graphics Interface '97, May 1997, pp. 68–75.

JC98.   H. Jensen and P. Christensen, *Efficient Simulation of Light Transport in Scenes with Participating Media using Photon Maps*, Computer Graphics (SIGGRAPH '98 Conference Proceedings), 1998, pp. 311–320.

Kel97.   A. Keller, *Instant Radiosity*, Computer Graphics (SIGGRAPH '97 Conference Proceedings), 1997, pp. 49–56.

KHM95.   C. Kolb, P. Hanrahan, and D. Mitchell, *A Realistic Camera Model for Computer Graphics*, Computer Graphics (SIGGRAPH '95 Conference Proceedings), 1995, pp. 317–324.

LV00.   T. Lokovich and E. Veach, *Deep Shadow Maps*, Computer Graphics (SIGGRAPH '00 Conference Proceedings), 2000, pp. 385–392.

MF92.   M. McCool and E. Fiume, *Hierarchical Poisson Disk Sampling Distributions*, Proceedings of Graphics Interface '92, May 1992, pp. 94–105.

PKK00.   M. Pauly, T. Kollig, and A. Keller, *Metropolis Light Transport for Participating Media*, Rendering Techniques 2000 (Proc. 11th Eurographics Workshop on Rendering), Springer, 2000, pp. 11–22.

POAU00.   M. Peercy, M. Olano, J. Airey, and J. Ungar, *Interactive Multi-Pass Programmable Shading*, Computer Graphics (SIGGRAPH '00 Conference Proceedings), 2000, pp. 425–432.

Sob62.   I. Sobol, *The use of w^2-distribution for error estimation in the calculation of integrals by the Monte Carlo method*, U.S.S.R. Comput. Math. and Math. Phys. **2** (1962), 717 – 723.

Editors' Note: see Appendix, p. 343 for colored figures of this paper

Interactive Distributed Ray Tracing of Highly Complex Models

Ingo Wald, Philipp Slusallek, Carsten Benthin

Computer Graphics Group,
Saarland University, Saarbruecken, Germany
{wald,slusallek,benthin}@graphics.cs.uni-sb.de

Abstract. Many disciplines must handle the creation, visualization, and manipulation of huge and complex 3D environments. Examples include large structural and mechanical engineering projects dealing with entire cars, ships, buildings, and processing plants. The complexity of such models is usually far beyond the interactive rendering capabilities of todays 3D graphics hardware. Previous approaches relied on costly preprocessing for reducing the number of polygons that need to be rendered per frame but suffered from excessive precomputation times — often several days or even weeks.

In this paper we show that using a highly optimized software ray tracer we are able to achieve interactive rendering performance for models up to 50 million triangles including reflection and shadow computations. The necessary preprocessing has been greatly simplified and accelerated by more than two orders of magnitude. Interactivity is achieved with a novel approach to distributed rendering based on *coherent ray tracing*. A single copy of the scene database is used together with caching of BSP voxels in the ray tracing clients.

1 Introduction

The performance of todays graphics hardware has been increased dramatically over the last few years. Today many graphics applications can achieve interactive rendering performance even on standard PCs. However, there are also many applications that must handle the creation, visualization, and manipulation of huge and complex 3D environments often containing several tens of millions of polygons [1, 9]. Typical examples of such requirements are large structural engineering projects that deal with entire buildings and processing plants. Without special optimization techniques these environments will stay well below interactive rendering performance.

In the past these models were usually handled on a component by component basis, as the sheer data volume prohibited any interactive visualization or manipulation of the models as a whole. However,

Fig. 1. Four copies of the UNC power-plant reference model with a total of 50 million triangles. In this view a large fraction of the geometry is visible. At 640x480 pixels the frame rate is 3.4 fps using seven networked dual Pentium-III PCs.

there are several scenarios that require the interactive visualization and manipulation of entire models. For instance, design reviews and simulation-based design must often deal with the complex interrelations between many components of the model, such as a large processing plant involving many industrial robots and transport devices. Many interactive tasks benefit greatly from the ability to instantly inspect any aspect of the entire model, such as walking or flying around the model as a whole and then zooming in on relevant details.

A minimum requirement for achieving interactivity is the spatial indexing of the geometry. This allows to limit rendering to visible parts of the model by using view frustum and occlusion culling (e.g. [4, 22]). Unless the model has been organized in such a way already, spatial indexing requires sorting the geometry spatially in a relatively simple and efficient preprocessing phase.

Beyond spatial indexing rendering can be improved by performing additional precomputation: computing and rendering only the potentially visible set (PVS) of geometry, creating and selecting levels-of-detail (LOD), simplifying the geometry, and replacing distant geometry using image-based methods. Aliga et al. [1] created a framework using all these methods to achieve interactive performance for our reference power-plant model (see Figure 1).

This advanced preprocessing, however, is very costly and for most cases cannot be fully automated yet. Preprocessing time was estimated to be 3 weeks for the complete model of only a single power-plant from Figure 1.

Because of this tremendous overhead, alternatives need to be found that do not require such costly preprocessing in order to achieve interactivity. Ray tracing is an obvious candidate as it only relies on spatial indexing for efficient rendering and features built-in view frustum and occlusion culling. It is known to have logarithmic scalability in terms of models size and also scales well with available computational resources due to being "embarrassingly parallel".

However, ray tracing is known for its high computational cost and is not usually associated with interactive rendering. Fortunately, this situation is changing rapidly as highly optimized ray tracing implementations become available [20, 14].

1.1 Interactive Ray Tracing on Standard PCs

The *coherent ray tracing* approach by Wald et al. [20] achieves high rendering speed both through a new ray tracing algorithm and low-level optimizations. The latter include simplifying and optimizing code paths, optimizing data structures for caching, and using SIMD extensions (Single Instruction – Multiple Data, such as Intels SSE [6]) for data-parallel implementations of basic ray tracing algorithms. This implementation is limited to triangles only but offers arbitrary shading computations through dynamically loadable modules.

The new algorithm improves on basic recursive ray tracing by making significantly better use of coherence through reordering rays and tracing, intersecting, and shading them in packets of four or more rays in SIMD fashion. This is similar in spirit to [16]. It reduces the memory bandwidth proportionally to the number of rays in a packet because data needs to be fetched only once for the whole packets instead of once for each ray. It also improves caching behavior through better data locality.

By tracing rays in packets the usual depth-first ray tracing algorithm is essentially reordered to be breadth-first within each packet. This reordering can exploit the coherence among adjacent eye rays as well as among shadow and other secondary rays.

With all these optimization the coherent ray tracing algorithm runs almost completely within the data caches of the CPU, thus achieving speedup factors between 11 to 15 (!) compared to conventional ray tracers. It challenges the performance of high-end graphics hardware already for scene complexities of more than half a million triangles and moderate screen resolutions of 512^2 using only a single Intel Pentium-III CPU [20].

1.2 Interactive Distributed Ray Tracing

Due to the "embarrassingly parallel" nature of ray tracing these results scale well with the use of multiple processors as long as they all get the necessary bandwidth to the scene database. However, contrary to other approaches [10, 14, 1] our target platform is not an expensive shared-memory supercomputer but the inexpensive cluster of workstations (CoW) that is commonly available everywhere. Unless the complete data base is replicated on each machine the bandwidth of the network limits the performance for distributed ray tracing in this scenario.

We use the classic setup for distributed ray tracing using a single master machine responsible for display and scheduling together with many working clients that trace, intersect, and shade rays. The main challenges of this approach are efficient access to a shared scene data base that can contain several GB of data, load balancing, and efficient preprocessing.

We solve these issues with a novel approach that is again based on exploiting coherence using the same basic ideas as in [20] but on a coarser level. Our main contributions are:

Scene subdivision In a preprocessing step a high-level BSP-tree is built while adaptively subdividing the scene into small, self-contained voxels. Since preprocessing is only based on the spatial location of primitives it is simple and fast. Each voxel contains the complete intersection and shading data for all of its triangles as well as a low-level BSP for this voxel. These voxels form the basis for our explicit cache management.

Scene cache management The complete preprocessed scene is stored on a server only once and all clients request voxels on demand. The clients explicitly manage a cache of voxels, thus exploiting coherence between rays (within the rays of a single packet and between multiple adjacent packets) and in time (between similar rays in subsequent frames).

Latency hiding By reordering the computations we hide some of the latencies involved in demand loading of scene data across the network by continuing computations on other rays while waiting for missing data to arrive. This approach can easily be extended by prefetching data for future frames based on rays coarsely sampling a predicted new view.

Load balancing We use the usual task queue approach based on image tiles for load balancing. Instead of randomly assigning image tiles to clients we try to assign tiles to clients that have traced similar rays in previous frames. This approach maximizes cache reuse across all clients. Ideally this leads to the working set (visible geometry) being evenly distributed among the caches of all clients.

The paper is organized as follows: we start with a review of related work in the next section before presenting and discussing the main issue of distributed data management in Section 3. Section 4 describes our preprocessing algorithm, which is followed by a discussion of our load balancing algorithm in Section 5. Results are presented in Section 6 before we conclude and offer suggestions for future work in Section 7.

2 Related Work

Regarding the visualization of large models, the most closely related previous work is the UNC "Framework for Realtime Walkthrough of Massive Models" [1]. In particular we have chosen to directly compare our results with the performance published in this paper. The UNC framework focuses on walkthroughs using high end graphics hardware and a shared-memory multiprocessor machine. It consistently achieves interactive frame rates between 5 and 15 frames per second on an early SGI Onyx with four R4400 and an InfiniteReality graphics subsystem.

The UNC framework uses a combination of different speedup techniques. The largest effect is due to the replacement of distant geometry by textured depth meshes [1, 19, 3], which results in an average reduction of rendered polygons by 96%. This reduction is due to occlusion as well as sparse resampling of the environment with image-based methods. Both effects are implicit in ray tracing, even though the resampling in ray tracing is dynamic and uses the original geometry instead of rendering a smaller simplified scene. The resulting scintillations or temporal noise can at least partially be resolved by a temporal coherent sampling strategy [8].

Another reduction by 50% each resulted from view frustum and level-of-detail (LOD) selection. While the first is again an implicit feature of ray tracing, we do not implement LODs even though they could easily be used once they are generated [5]. This is a typical time/image quality trade-off because not using LOD increases aliasing but avoids the long preprocessing times for LOD creation.

Finally, occlusion culling based on hierarchical occluder maps (HOM) [22] for the near geometry reduces the number of rendered polygons by another 10%. Again occlusion culling is implicit in a ray tracer and does not require additional preprocessing.

The main drawback of the UNC approach is the tremendous preprocessing time — estimated to be three weeks for a single copy of the power-plant model. The technique is also less scalable both in terms of model size (the preprocessing is apparently super-linear) and graphics performance, where performance of ray tracing can easily be scaled by adding more client PCs.

Recently Parker et al. [14, 12, 13] demonstrated that interactive frame rates could also be achieved with a full-featured ray tracer on a large shared-memory supercomputer. Their implementation offers all the usual ray tracing features, including parametric surfaces and volume objects, but is carefully optimized for cache performance and parallel execution in a non-uniform memory-access environment. They have proven that ray tracing scales well in the number of processors in a shared memory environment, and that even complex scenes of several hundred thousand primitives could be rendered at almost real-time frame rates.

A similar system has been realized by Muuss [9, 10]. It used CSG objects as its primitives, which makes direct comparisons difficult. It also uses an optimized general ray tracer and was able to render highly complex models at a few frames per second on high-end shared-memory supercomputers with up to 96 CPUs. However, both this and the Utah system require an expensive shared-memory machine, while we concentrate our effort on low cost PCs in standard network environments.

Memory coherent ray tracing by Pharr et al [15] has also been able to efficiently render highly complex objects by exploiting coherence between rays. In addition to basic ray tracing their system also implements global illumination effects through path tracing [7].

We share the basic idea of splitting the scene into smaller voxels and using these for manual caching. However, our usage of the voxel structure is quite different, as

Pharr et al. performs significantly more reordering and scheduling of computations. In their system intersection computations are scheduled based on voxels: all rays that have entered a voxel so far are intersected in batches with the geometry in this voxel and rays are forwarded to adjacent voxels if there is no hit. The intersection computations for a voxels are scheduled based on the number of rays waiting, their weight, the amount of geometry, the state of the geometry cache, and other factors.

The system made it possible to ray trace scenes of up to 50 million triangles, but was far from realtime with rendering times still in the order of several hours for images of moderate size. On the other hand this system was mainly designed for generality and not for highest performance.

Another difference to our approach is the regular structure of the scheduling grid and the local forwarding of rays. The first issue results in large numbers of voxels even in empty regions of the scene (particularly relevant in the power-plant model) and the second has a significant overhead in tracing individual rays through empty space. By tracing packets of rays in parallel until they all terminate we eliminate this overhead while our BSP hierarchy better adapts to the local structure of the scene.

Of course, there has been a tremendous amount of previous work on parallel and distributed ray tracing in general. Detailed surveys can be found in [2, 18, 17]. Most of the techniques used in our ray tracing engine have been proposed in one or another way in previous publications, but never in the combination and with the optimizations as presented here. To our knowledge this is the first time anything close to interactive performance has been reported for distributed ray tracing with models of this size.

3 Distributed Data Management

The main problem we had to deal with for highly complex scenes are related to file size, limited address space, network distribution of the model data, and stalls due to demand loading. File size is not really a problem any more as most platforms (Linux in particular) are now supporting file sizes beyond 2 GB. More problematic is the limited virtual address space on 32 bit architectures such as Intel's Pentium CPUs.

In the original implementation of coherent ray tracing [20] we created a single binary file containing the model. It used the main memory layout so that we could directly map the entire file into our address space using the Unix mmap-facilities. However this is no longer possible with files larger than the supported address space. One possible solution would be to map only parts of a larger file and change the mappings on demand (essentially using a cache of mappings).

On the other hand we did not want to replicate the entire model of several GB on each of our client machines. This means that demand loading of mapped data would be performed across the network with its low bandwidth and large latency. While this approach is technically simple by using mmap across an NFS-mounted file system, it drastically reduces performance for large models. For each access to missing data the whole ray tracing process on the client is stalled while the operating system reads a single memory page across the network.

Even stalling for a few milliseconds due to network latency is very costly for an interactive ray tracer: Because tracing a single ray costs roughly one thousand cycles [20], we would lose several thousand rays for each network access. Instead we would like to suspend work on only those rays that require access to missing data. The client can continue working on other rays while the missing data is being fetched asynchronously. However, this approach is not possible with the automatic demand loading facilities of the operating system unless large numbers of threads would be used, which would be

282

infeasible.

3.1 Explicit Data Management

Instead of relying on the operating system we had to explicitly manage the data ourselves. For this purpose we decompose the models into small voxels. Each voxel is self-contained and has its own local BSP tree. In addition, all voxels are organized in a high-level BSP tree starting from the root node of the entire model (see Figure 2). The leaf nodes of the high-level BSP contain additional flags indicating whether the particular voxel is in the cache or not.

If a missing voxel is accessed by a ray during traversal of the high-level BSP, we suspend this ray and notify an asynchronous loader thread about the missing voxel. Once the data of the voxel has been loaded into memory by the loader thread, the ray tracing thread is notified, which resumes tracing of rays waiting on this voxel. During asynchronous loading, ray tracing can continue on all non-suspended rays currently being processed by the client. More latency could still be hidden by deferring shading operations until all rays are stalled or a complete tile has been traced. We use a simple least-recently-used (LRU) strategy to manage a fixed size geometry cache.

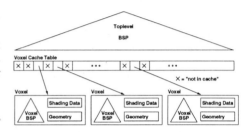

Fig. 2. The data structure used to organize the model data. Voxels are the smallest entity for caching purposes. Their average compressed size is roughly 75 KB.

3.2 Compressed Data

We had to come up with a reasonable compromise between the file size of voxels and the overhead through replication of triangle data. That compromise resulted in an average file size of voxels of 250 KB. With files of this size the voxel loading time is strongly dominated by the amount of data transfered over the network. This means that reducing the file size would also reduce the loading time. We pack our voxels using a method that allows fast and space/cache efficient decompression using the LZO compression library [11].

Though this compression is more optimized towards speed, its compression ratio is approximately 3:1 for our voxel data. Decompression performance is significantly higher than the network bandwidth, taking at most a few hundred microseconds, thus making the decompression cost negligible compared to the transmission time even for compressed voxels.

3.3 Shared Voxel Cache

All the PCs in our system are dual-processor PCs and run two ray tracing threads in parallel. In addition to a good price/performance ratio, it offers the additional advantage that network bandwidth can be reduced by up to a factor of two: whenever data is loaded, it is made available to both threads. Of course, this requires that both threads share the same voxel cache. In order to keep overhead as low as possible all cache management functionality is bundled in a third cache management and voxel fetcher thread, which shares the address space with the rendering threads.

4 Preprocessing

The total size of a single power-plant model is roughly 2.5 GB after preprocessing including BSP-trees, replicated triangles, and shading data. Due to this large data size we need an out-of-core algorithm to spatially sort and decompose the initial model.

The algorithm reads the entire data set once in order to determine its bounding box. It then recursively determines the best splitting plane for the current BSP node and sorts all triangles into the two child nodes. Triangles that span both nodes are replicated. Note that the adaptive decomposition is able to subdivide the model finely in highly populated areas and generates large voxels for empty space. At this stage each node is a separate file on disk in a special format that is suitable for streaming the data through the preprocessing programs.

Once the size of a BSP node is below a given threshold we create a voxel and store it in a file that contains its data (triangles, BSP, shading data, etc.). This is a binary file format that is suitable for directly reading it into memory. In order to avoid large directories with the associated lookup cost on some file systems, the files are automatically sorted into a directory hierarchy.

This preprocessing algorithms is easy to set up as it has only two parameters that need to be set: the number of triangles in a voxel and the maximum depth of the BSP trees. The rendering speed is fairly insensitive to the exact setting of these parameters as long as the minimum size of voxels is reasonably small. However, the size of the generated data set increases steadily with smaller voxel size and larger BSP depth. It is still unclear if there is an automatic way to determine good values for these two parameters.

The cost of preprocessing algorithms has a complexity of $O(n \log n)$ in the model size. Preprocessing is mainly I/O bound as the computation per triangle is minimal. We are currently using a serial implementation, where each step in the recursive decomposition is a separate invocation of a single program. Currently, the resulting files are all located on a single machine acting as the model server.

With a little more programming effort we could significantly speed up preprocessing by distributing the triangle data to multiple machines. A master process would control the decomposition, distribute the load across the machines, and build the high-level BSP tree. Storing the data base on several machines would have the additional benefit that access is distributed across all data base servers, thus making better use of the available bandwidth in a fully switched network. Of course, once the data set of a node is small enough an in-core algorithm should be used for better preprocessing performance.

5 Load Balancing

The efficiency of distributed/parallel rendering depends to a large degree on the amount of parallelism that can be extracted. We are using demand driven load balancing by subdividing the image into tiles of a fixed size (32 by 32 pixels). As the rendering time for different tiles can vary significantly (e.g. see the large variations in model complexity in Figures 1 and 7), we must distribute the load evenly across all client CPUs. This has to be done dynamically, as the frequent camera changes during an interactive walkthrough make static load-balancing impossible.

We employ the usual dynamic load balancing approach where the display server distributes tiles on demand to clients. The tiles are taken from a pool of yet unassigned tiles, but care is taken to maintain good cache locality in the clients. Currently, the scheduler tries to give clients tiles they have rendered before, in order to efficiently reuse the data in their geometry caches. This approach is effective for small camera movements but fails to make good use of caches for larger movements.

This simple assignment can be improved using an idea from image-based rendering — essentially a simplified RenderCache [21, 8]. For each traced ray the 3D intersection points would be stored together with its rendering cost and the client that computed it. This information can then reprojected into the next frame. For each new tile, its cost is estimated by averaging the cost over all the intersection points reprojected to this tile.

Additionally, for each tile a *client affinity value* is estimated based on the fraction of reprojected samples computed by a particular client. Tiles are then assigned to clients primarily based on affinity in order to maximize cache reuse. Additionally we hand out costly tiles first in order to minimize load imbalance towards the end of a frame.

In order to avoid idle times while the clients are waiting for the next task from the master each client buffers one additional task. This way, when a client has completed its current tile, it can immediately proceed working on the next tile without having to wait for the servers reply. In a similar way, we double-buffer workload in the server: If all tiles from the current frame have been assigned to clients, the server starts assigning tiles from the next frame while waiting for the last frame to complete.

6   Implementation and Results

Our current setup uses two servers — one for display and one for storing and distributing the preprocessed models. Both machines are connected via Gigabit Ethernet to a Gigabit Ethernet switch. These fast links help in avoiding network bottlenecks. In particular we require a high bandwidth connection for the display server in order to deal with the pixel data at higher resolutions and frame rates. The bottleneck for the model data could be avoided by distributing it among a set of machines as mentioned above.

For our experiments we have used seven dual P-III 800-866 MHz machines as ray tracing clients. These clients are normal desktop machines in our lab but were mostly unused while the tests were performed. The client machines are connected to a FastEthernet switch that has a Gigabit uplink to the server switch.

The model server has two very fast striped disks for storing the preprocessed model data. The disks can sustain a bandwidth of roughly 55 MB/s, which almost exactly matches the maximum measured Gigabit network bandwidth. We use NFS with large read and write buffers to access the model data from the clients. Each client is able to almost saturate the full bandwidth of its network connection, such that our potential bottleneck is now the connection to the model server. The display and scheduling server runs at a very light computational load but must handle a large and constant stream of pixels from all clients.

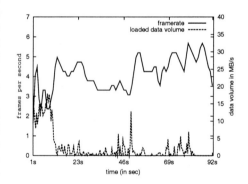

Fig. 3. Frame rate and transfered data rate after decompression during a walkthrough heading from the outside to the inside of the powerplant building. The frame rate is pretty constant around 4-5 fps unless large amounts of data are transfered (at the beginning where the whole building is visible). The frame rate is achieved without the SIMD optimization, which should the frame rate by at least a factor a two to 6–12 fps.

We have tested our setup with the power-plant model from UNC [1] to allow for a direct comparison with previous work. This also provides for a comparison of algorithms based on rasterization versus ray tracing.

The power-plant test model consists of roughly 12.5 million triangles mostly distributed over the main building that is 80 meter high and 40 by 50 meters on either side (see Figure 1). Each triangle of the model also contains vertex normals that allow smooth shading and reflection (see below).

Preprocessing including conversion from the original PLY-files into our format as well as voxel decomposition took roughly 2.5 hours, with our unoptimized, sequential implementation. This already is significantly faster than the preprocessing required in [1]. That approach required 17 hours for a partial preprocessing that did only allow for interactive movements in a small fraction of the overall model. Their preprocessing time for the whole model was estimated to take three weeks [1]. We estimate that once parallel preprocessing is fully implemented, our preprocessing time could be reduced to less than half an hour.

Figure 3 gives a compact summary of our overall results. It shows the frame rate achieved by our system as well as the amount of geometry fetched over the course of a walk through the model. All images in this paper are computed at 640 by 480 resolution. The total time of the walkthrough is 92 seconds using all seven clients. Note that we only trace primary rays for this test in order to allow direct comparison with the results from [1]. We only show the results of a single walkthrough, as they closely match those from other tests.

The walkthrough starts outside the main building while sweeping the view across most of the power-plant. This is very demanding as the building is mostly open and allows to see much of the complex inside structure. A lot of geometry needs to be loaded, which saturates the network connection to the model server at up to 17 MB/s of geometry (uncompressed) for a single client only.

We then move inside the main building. The working set is much lower here, but can change very quickly as we move past a large occluder. During this time we still fetch an average of 1–2 MB/s of geometry data (with spikes up to 13 MB/s). However, the latency of those transfers can mostly be hidden by our asynchronous fetching approach. We do not yet perform any form of prefetching, even though this would help even more in avoiding network effects.

With seven dual CPU machines we achieve a pretty constant frame rate of 3–5 fps. However, all numbers are computed with plain C++ code, as the SIMD code was still being adapted to the new distributed algorithm. Early tests of the SIMD optimized ray tracing code has consistently achieved speedups by a factor greater than 2. This brings our frame

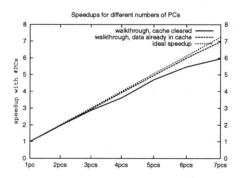

Fig. 4. The system shows almost perfect scalability from 1 to 7 dual CPU PCs if the caches are already filled. With empty caches we see some network contention effects with 4 clients but scalability is still very good. Beyond 6 or 7 clients we start saturating the network link to the model server.

rate up to 6–12 fps, which is about the same as achieved in [1]. Note that we still render the original model with all details and not a simplified version of it.

Fig. 5. Two images showing show the structure of the high-level BSP tree by color coding geometry in each voxel (bottom image). Voxels are relatively large for the walls but become really small in regions with lots of details.

Figure 5 visualizes the BSP structure that is built by our preprocessing algorithm. The voxel size decreases significantly for areas that have more geometric detail.

The original model does not provide material information other than some meaningless surface colors. In order to test some of the advanced features of ray tracing, we added a distant light source to the model and made some of the geometry reflective (see Color Plate 6). Of course, we see a drop in performance due to additional rays being traced for shadows and reflections. However, the drop is mostly proportional to the number of traced rays, and shows little effect due to the reduced coherence of the highly diverging rays that are reflected off the large pipe in the front as well as all the tiny pipes in the background.

We also tested the scalability of our implementation by using one to seven clients for rendering exactly the same frames as in the recorded walkthrough used for the tests above and measured the total runtime. The experiment was performed twice — once with empty caches and once again with the caches filled by the previous run. The difference between the two would show network bottlenecks and any latencies that could not be hidden. As expected we achieved almost perfect scalability with filled caches (see Figure 4), but the graph also shows some network contention effects with 4 clients and we start saturating the network link to the model server beyond 6 or 7 clients. Note, that perfect scalability is larger than seven because of variations in CPU clock rates.

Because we did not have more clients available, scalability could not be tested beyond seven clients. However, our results show that scalability is mainly bound by the network bandwidth to the model server, which suggests that a distributed model data base would allow scalability well beyond our numbers. Of course we could also replicate the data — space permitting.

Color Plate 7 shows some other views of the power-plant showing some of the complexity hidden in this huge test model.

For a stress test of our system we have placed four copies of the power-plant model next to each other resulting in a total model complexity of roughly 50 million triangles (see Figure 1). Preprocessing time increased as expected, but the frame rate stayed almost identical compared to the single model. Essentially the depth of the higher-level BSP tree was increased by two, which hardly has any effects on inside views.

However, for outside views we suffer somewhat from the relatively large voxel granularity, which results in an increased working set and accordingly longer loading times that can no longer be completely hidden during movements. When standing still the frame rates quickly approach the numbers measured for a single copy of the model.

7   Conclusions and Future Work

Previously, interactive rendering performance for highly complex models with tens of millions of polygons and more could only be achieved with high-end graphics hardware on supercomputers and required very expensive preprocessing techniques that makes the technique mostly infeasible.

In this paper, we have shown that using a software ray tracing approach, interactive rendering performance can be achieved for more complex models even on inexpensive clusters of workstations. We use a two–level, adaptive scene decomposition with BSP trees that allows explicit data management for caching and reordering purposes.

We have shown that a high degree of parallelism can be extracted from such systems by using efficient load balancing and paying careful attention to network bandwidth and latencies. Stalling due to network latencies can be avoided to some degree by reordering the computations within the clients.

Even though our system already achieves interactive rendering performance by using only seven rendering clients, there are many ideas for further improvements:

Obviously, faster computers and networks are already available. They would allow for almost twice the performance while being only slightly more expensive.

The other obvious extension to the system is to increase speed by fully activating the SIMD extensions and prefetching methods as described in [20]. Also a distributed scene data base would avoid the server bottleneck and allow for even more rendering clients.

More computational resources would allow us to spend more effort on illumination and shading computations. In particular, anti-aliasing and more complex shading computations, like programmable shading, would be interesting. It would also be interesting to implement more complex global illumination algorithms and deal with the reduced coherence for illumination rays.

Bandwidth could be reduced further by separating BSP, geometry, and shading information into separately loadable entities. This would prevent loading shading data even for voxels that never generate an intersection. Similarly, we need to avoid the increased file size due to replicating information for geometry contained in multiple voxels.

Finally, as is the case with all algorithms working on a fixed spatial decomposition, we are limited to static environments. New algorithms and data structure that can deal with complex dynamic environments are desperately needed for interactively ray tracing.

8   Acknowledgements

We thank the the Computer Graphics Group at the University of North Carolina and Anselmo Lastra in particular for providing the power-plant model. Georg Demme and Marcus Wagner provided invaluable help and support with programming and system setup. We also thank the anonymous reviewers for the helpful comments.

References

1. D. Aliaga, J. Cohen, A. Wilson, E. Baker, H. Zhang, C. Erikson, K. Hoff, T. Hudson, W. Strzlinger, R. Bastos, M. Whitton, F. Brooks, and D. Manocha. MMR: An interactive massive model rendering system using geometric and image-based acceleration. In *1999 ACM Symposium on Interactive 3D Graphics*, pages 199–206, Atlanta, USA, April 1999.
2. Alan Chalmers and Erik Reinhard. Parallel and distributed photo-realistic rendering. In *SIGGRAPH 98 Course*, pages 425–432. ACM SIGGRAPH, Orlando, July 1998.
3. Lucia Darsa, Bruno Costa, and Amitabh Varshney. Navigating static environments using image-space simplification and morphing. In *ACM Symposium on Interactive 3D Graphics*, pages 25–34, Providence, RI, 1997.
4. Ned Greene, Michael Kass, and Gavin Miller. Hierarchical Z-buffer visibility. *Computer Graphics*, 27(Annual Conference Series):231–238, 1993.
5. Homan Igehy. Tracing ray differentials. *Computer Graphics*, 33(Annual Conference Series):179–186, 1999.
6. Intel Corp. *Intel Pentium III Streaming SIMD Extensions*. http://developer.intel.com/vtune/-cbts/simd.htm.
7. James T. Kajiya. The rendering equation. *Computer Graphics*, 20(4):143–150, August 1986.
8. William Martin, Steven Parker, Erik Reinhard, Peter Shirley, and William Thompson. Temporally coherent interactive ray tracing. Technical Report UUCS-01-005, Computer Graphics Group, University of Utah, 2001.
9. Michael J. Muuss. Towards real-time ray-tracing of combinatorial solid geometric models. In *Proceedings of BRL-CAD Symposium '95*, June 1995.
10. Michael J. Muuss and Maximo Lorenzo. High-resolution interactive multispectral missile sensor simulation for atr and dis. In *Proceedings of BRL-CAD Symposium '95*, June 1995.
11. Markus Oberhume. LZO-compression library. available at http://www.dogma.net/-DataCompression/LZO.shtml.
12. Steven Parker, Michael Parker, Yaren Livnat, Peter Pike Sloan, Chuck Hansen, and Peter Shirley. Interactive ray tracing for volume visualization. *IEEE Transactions on Computer Graphics and Visualization*, 5(3):238–250, July-September 1999.
13. Steven Parker, Peter Shirley, Yarden Livnat, Charles Hansen, and Peter Pike Sloan. Interactive ray tracing for isosurface rendering. In *IEEE Visualization '98*, pages 233–238, 1998.
14. Steven Parker, Peter Shirley, Yarden Livnat, Charles Hansen, and Peter Pike Sloan. Interactive ray tracing. In *Interactive 3D Graphics (I3D)*, pages 119–126, april 1999.
15. Matt Pharr, Craig Kolb, Reid Gershbein, and Pat Hanrahan. Rendering complex scenes with memory-coherent ray tracing. *Computer Graphics*, 31(Annual Conference Series):101–108, August 1997.
16. E. Reinhard and F. W. Jansen. Rendering large scenes using parallel ray tracing. In *Eurographics Workshop of Parallel Graphics and Visualization*, pages 67–80, September 1996.
17. Erik Reinhard. *Scheduling and Data Management for Parallel Ray Tracing*. PhD thesis, University of East Anglia, 1995.
18. Erik Reinhard, Alan Chalmers, and F.W. Jansen. Overview of parallel photorealistic graphics. In *Eurographics '98, State of the Art Reports*. Eurographics Association, August 1998.
19. Francois SIllion, George Drettakis, and Benoit Bedelet. Efficient imposter manipulation for real-time visualization of urban scenery. *Computer Graphics Forum, Proceeding Eurographics '97*, 16(3):207–218, September 1997.
20. Ingo Wald, Carsten Benthin, Markus Wagner, and Philipp Slusallek. Interactive rendering with coherent ray tracing. *Computer Graphics Forum (Proceedings of EUROGRAPHICS 2001*, 20(3), 2001. available at http://graphics.cs.uni-sb.de/ wald/Publications.
21. Bruce Walter, George Drettakis, and Steven Parker. Interactive rendering using the render cache. *Eurographics Rendering Workshop 1999*, 1999. Granada, Spain.
22. Hansong Zhang, Dinesh Manocha, Thomas Hudson, and Kenneth E. Hoff III. Visibility culling using hierarchical occlusion maps. *Computer Graphics*, 31(Annual Conference Series):77–88, August 1997.

Editors' Note: see Appendix, p. 344 for colored figures of this paper

Realistic Reflections and Refractions on Graphics Hardware With Hybrid Rendering and Layered Environment Maps

Ziyad S. Hakura[*], John M. Snyder[**]

[*]Stanford University, [**]Microsoft Research

Abstract.
We introduce hybrid rendering, a scheme that dynamically ray traces the local geometry of reflective and refractive objects, but approximates more distant geometry by hardware-supported environment maps (EMs). To limit computation, we use a greedy ray path shading model that prunes the binary ray tree generated by refractive objects to form just two ray paths. We also restrict ray queries to triangle vertices, but perform adaptive tessellation to shoot additional rays where neighboring ray paths differ sufficiently. By using layered, parameterized EMs that are inferred over a set of viewpoint samples to match ray traced imagery, we accurately handle parallax and view-dependent shading in the environment. We increase robustness of EMs by inferring them simultaneously across multiple viewpoints and including environmental geometry that is occluded from the viewpoint sample but is revealed in nearby viewpoints. We demonstrate realistic shiny and glass objects with a user-controlled viewpoint.

1 Introduction

Z-buffer hardware is well-suited for rendering texture-mapped 3D geometry but inadequate for rendering reflective and refractive objects. It rasterizes geometry with respect to a constrained ray set – rays emanating from a point and passing through a uniformly parameterized rectangle in 3D. Reflective and refractive objects create a more general lens system mapping each incoming ray into a number of outgoing rays, according to a complex, spatially-varying set of multiple ray "bounces". Environment maps (EMs) [2] extend hardware to simulate reflections from an infinitely distant environment, but ignore all but the first bounce and so omit self-reflections and refractions. On the other hand, ray tracing [22] generates these effects but is unaccelerated and incoherently accesses a large scene database. Nevertheless, modern CPUs are powerful enough to perform limited ray tracing during real-time rendering.

We combine the benefits of both systems by tracing ray paths through reflective/refractive objects to compute how the local geometry maps incoming rays to outgoing. To encapsulate more distant geometry, we use the outgoing rays as indices into a previously-inferred EM per object, allowing efficient access and resampling by graphics hardware. We call this *hybrid rendering*.

We begin by segmenting reflective/refractive scene geometry into a set of *local lens objects*. Typically each glass or shiny object forms a single local lens object, but multiple objects can be combined if they are close or one contains or surrounds another. Because rays are traced through a system of only one or a few objects, the working set is smaller and memory access more coherent than with traditional ray tracing. To make the approach practical, we also initially limit the number of ray casts to polygon vertices, adaptively shooting additional rays only where necessary. We also prune the ray tree (binary for refractive objects where an incoming ray striking an interface generates child reflection and refraction rays) ignoring all but a few ray paths that still approximate the full ray traced rendering well (see Figure 2).

290

Each local lens object's EM is different from traditional ones: it is *inferred, layered,* and *parameterized.* Inferred means our EMs are computed as a least-squares best match to a pre-computed, ray traced image at a viewpoint *when applied as an EM in a rendering by the target graphics system.* The alternative of sampling a spherical image of incident radiance at a point (typically the lens

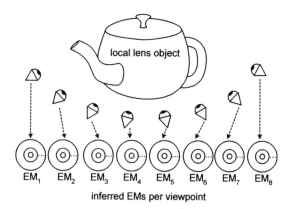

Figure 1: A PEM is a sequence of EMs recorded over a set of viewpoints for each local lens object. Each EM_i consists of layered shells at various distances from the local lens object's center.

object's center) ignores view-dependent shading in the environment and produces a less accurate match at the viewpoint. Layered means that we use multiple environmental shells to better approximate the environment. Parameterized means we compute an EM per viewpoint over a set of viewpoints (Figure 1) to provide view-dependent shading on imaged objects and reduce the number of layers needed for accurate parallax. Our examples use a 1D viewpoint subspace that obtains accurate results over that subspace and plausible results for any viewpoint.

Our contributions include the hybrid rendering shading model and its combination of dynamic ray tracing with hardware-supported EMs. We improve on the parameterized EMs (PEMs) described in [8] by generalizing to more than two layers and providing tools for determining their placement. In addition, we handle self-reflections by ray tracing the local geometry rather than representing it as an EM, and so achieve good results with as much as ten times sparser sampling of EMs compared with [8]. The method of [8] also has the problem that its inferred EMs represent only the part of the environment imaged at one viewpoint, resulting in disocclusions from nearby viewpoints. We ensure completeness in our layered EMs by matching to a layered image that includes occluded surfaces, as well as simultaneously over multiple nearby viewpoints or direct images of the environment. Results show our method supports rendering of realistic reflective and refractive objects on current graphics hardware.

2   Previous Work

2.1   Reflections

Several efforts have been made to exploit fast graphics hardware to produce realistic reflections. Diefenbach [5] simulates planar reflections by mirroring the viewpoint about the reflection plane. Ofek and Rappoport [20] extend the idea to curved objects, requiring careful decomposition of objects with mixed convexity or saddle regions.

Image-based rendering (IBR) methods [6][14] can tabulate view-dependent shading effects like reflections. Surface light fields [19][23] are a variant that parameterize the radiance field over surfaces rather than views. These methods visit an irregular scattering of samples over the entire 4D light field to reconstruct a particular view, and lack hardware acceleration. They also require very high sampling densities to reconstruct specular objects, a problem we address by ray tracing and tabulating EMs over simpler 1D viewpoint subspaces.

Cabral et al. [3] store a collection of view-dependent EMs where each EM pre-integrates a BRDF with a lighting environment. The lighting environments are generated using standard techniques and thus ignore local reflections and refractions.

Lischinski and Rappoport [16] ray trace through a collection of view-dependent LDIs for glossy objects with fuzzy reflections, and three view-independent LDIs representing the diffuse environment. Bastos et al. [1] reproject LDIs into a reflected view for rendering primarily planar glossy surfaces in architectural walkthroughs. Our approach succeeds with simpler and hardware-supported EMs rather than LDIs, resorting to ray tracing only for the local "lens" geometry where it is most necessary.

Hakura et al. [8] introduce parameterized and layered environment maps to simulate local reflections including self-reflections. We make use of these ideas for the more distant geometry, but use local ray tracing to more accurately simulate self-reflections and extend to refractive objects. We also improve their EM inference to handle disocclusions and produce more accurate parallax.

2.2   Refractions

Heidrich et al. [10] attempt to handle refractive as well as reflective objects using a light field to map incoming view rays into outgoing reflected or refracted rays. These outgoing rays then index either a static environment map, which ignores local effects further from the object, or another light field, which is more accurate but also more costly. Though our hybrid rendering similarly partitions local and distant geometry, we obtain sharper, more accurate reflections and refractions using local ray tracing rather than light field remapping. We also exploit the texture-mapping capability of graphics hardware using layered EMs for the more distant environment rather than light fields.

Chuang, et. al. [4], and Zongker et. al. [24] capture the remapping of incident rays for real and synthetic reflective/refractive objects, but only for a fixed view. Kay and Greenberg [12] simulate refractive objects with a simple, local model restricted to surfaces of uniform thickness.

Adaptive sampling has been used in ray tracing since it was first described [22]. To decouple local and distant geometry, our adaptation is based on ray path, not color or radiance, differences. Kajiya's idea of ray paths rather than trees [13] forms the basis of our local model. Finally, the caching and ray intersection reordering of Pharr et. al. [21] is another, completely software-based approach for memory-coherent access to the scene database.

3   Shading Model And Overview

Ray tracing simulates refractive objects by generating child reflective and refractive rays whenever a ray strikes a surface interface. The relative contribution of these children is governed by the Fresnel coefficients [9], denoted $\hat{F}_R$ and $\hat{F}_T$ for reflected and transmitted (refracted) rays, respectively. These coefficients depend on the ray's angle of incidence with respect to the surface normal and the indices of refraction of the two media at the interface. Purely reflective objects are simpler, generating a single child reflected ray modulated by $\hat{F}_R$ but can be considered a special case with $\hat{F}_T = 0$.

Rather than generating a full binary tree for refractive objects which can easily extend to thousands of ray queries, we use a two-term model with greedy ray path propagation. When a ray from the viewpoint first strikes the refractive object, we consider two paths: one beginning with an initial reflection and the other with an initial refraction. These paths are then propagated until they exit the local object by selecting the child ray having the greatest Fresnel coefficient. The result is two terms whose sum approximates the full binary tree. Reflective objects require

292

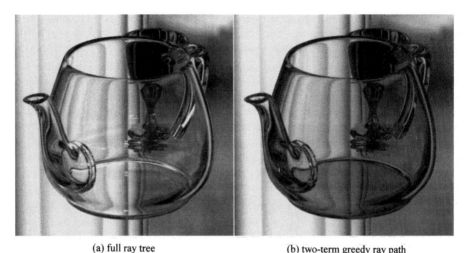

(a) full ray tree   (b) two-term greedy ray path

Figure 2: Shading Models. The full ray tree (a) requires 5 times more ray queries than our greedy ray path model (b).

only a single term but use the same ray propagation strategy in case the local system contains other refractive objects. Figure 2 compares the quality of this approach with a full ray tree simulation.

Our model also includes a simple transparency attenuation factor, G, which modulates the ray color by a constant for each color channel raised to a power depending on the thickness of glass traversed between interfaces [12]. The resulting model is

$$T F_T G_T + R F_R G_R$$

where respectively for the refracted and reflected ray paths: T and R are radiances along exit ray, F_T and F_R multiply the Fresnel coefficients along the path, and G_T and G_R multiply the transparency attenuation along the path (see Figure 3).

As a preprocess, for each viewpoint sample, we use a modified ray tracer to compute the two terms of this model as separate images. We then infer an EM that produces the best least-squares match to both terms simultaneously. The result is a viewpoint-dependent sequence of inferred EMs. Each viewpoint's EM is layered by segmenting the environmental geometry into a series of spherical shells.

At run-time, we dynamically trace rays through each vertex of the local geometry according to our ray path model to see where they exit the local system and intersect the EM shells. We select the EM corresponding to the viewpoint closest to the current view or blend between the

refraction term   reflection term   result

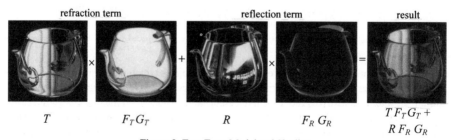

T $F_T G_T$ R $F_R G_R$ $T F_T G_T + R F_R G_R$

Figure 3: Two-Term Modulated Shading.

two closest. A separate pass is used for each term and then summed in the framebuffer. The Fresnel and transparency attenuation factors are accumulated on-the-fly as the path is traced, and produce per-vertex terms that are interpolated over each triangle to modulate the value retrieved from the EM. A better result can be achieved using 1D textures that tabulate highly nonlinear functions such as exponentiation [11].

While our current system neglects it, a diffuse component can be handled as an additional view-independent diffuse texture per object that is summed into the result. Such textures can be inferred to match ray traced imagery using the technique of [7].

4   Layered EMs

A local lens object is associated with a layered EM per viewpoint in which each layer consists of a simple, textured surface. We use a nested series of spherical shells sharing a common origin for the geometry because spheres are easy to index and visibility sort. Other kinds of simple geometry, such as finite cubes, cylinders, and ellipsoids, may be substituted in cases where they more accurately match the actual geometry of the environment. A layer's texture is a 4-channel image with transparency, so that we can see through inner shells to outer ones where the inner geometry is absent. At run-time, we perform hybrid rendering to compute outgoing rays and where they intersect the layered EMs. We use the "over" blending mode to composite the layers L_i in order of increasing distance before modulating by the Fresnel and transparency attenuation terms, F and G, via

$$(L_1 \text{ over } L_2 \text{ over } ... \text{ over } L_n) \, F \, G$$

for each term in the two-term shading model.

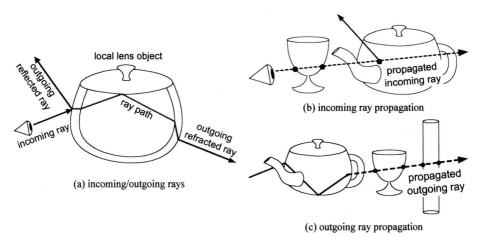

(a) incoming/outgoing rays

(b) incoming ray propagation

(c) outgoing ray propagation

Figure 4: Incoming/Outgoing Rays and Ray Propagation.

4.1   Compiling the Outgoing Rays

To build layered EMs, the ray tracer compiles a list of intersections which record the eventual *outgoing rays* exiting the local lens object and where they hit the more distant environment. These intersections are generated from *incoming rays* originating from a supersampled image at a particular viewpoint including both terms of the shading model (reflection and refraction), each of which generates different outgoing rays (Figure 4a). Between incoming and outgoing rays, the ray paths are propagated using the model of Section 3. The intersection record also stores the image position of the incoming ray and color of the environment at the outgoing ray's intersection.

To avoid disocclusions in the environment as the view changes, we modified the ray tracer to continue rays through objects to reach occluded geometry. For each outgoing ray, we record all front-facing intersections with environmental geometry along the ray, not just the first (Figure 4c). Once the layer partitions are computed (Section 4.2), we then discard all but the first intersection of each outgoing ray with that layer. This allows reconstruction of parts of the environment in a distant layer that are occluded by a closer one. We also continue incoming rays in a similar fashion (Figure 4b) so that occluded parts of the lens object still generate intersection records. For example, we continue incoming rays through a cup to reach a glass teapot it occludes.

4.2   Building Layered EM Geometry

To speed run-time performance, we seek a minimum number of layers. But to approximate the environmental geometry well, we must use enough shells and put them in the right place.

We use the LBG algorithm [15] developed for compression to build vector quantization codebooks. The desired number of layers is given as input and the cluster origin is computed as the centroid of the local object. The LBG algorithm is run over the list of intersections, clustering based on distance to this origin. This algorithm begins with an initial, random set of cluster distances and assigns each intersection to its closest cluster. It then recomputes the average distance in each cluster, and iterates the assignment of intersection to closest cluster. Iteration terminates when no intersections are reassigned.

When partitioning geometry into layers, parts of coherent objects should not be assigned to different layers. This can cause incorrect tears in the object's reflected or refracted image. Our solution assigns whole objects only to the single cluster having the most intersection records with that object. The clustering algorithm should also be coherent across the parameterized viewpoints. This is accomplished by clustering with respect to all viewpoints simultaneously. Figure 7 shows clustering results on an example scene in which our algorithm automatically segments a glass teapot's environment into three layers.

Layer shells are placed at the average distance of intersections in the cluster, where "continued ray" intersections are represented only by their frontmost cluster member.

Layer Quads Often a spherical shell is only sparsely occupied. In that case, to conserve texture memory we use a simple quadrilateral impostor for this geometry rather than a spherical one. To define the impostor quadrilateral, we can find the least-squares fit of a plane to the layer's intersection points. A simpler, but less optimal, scheme is to find the centroid of the layer's intersection points and define the normal of the plane as the direction from the lens object center to the centroid. The plane's extent is determined from a rectangular bounding box around points computed by intersecting the outgoing rays associated with the layer's intersection records with the impostor plane. One complication is that during run-time, outgoing rays may travel away from the quad's plane, failing to intersect it. This results in an undefined texture access location. We enforce intersection for such rays by subtracting the component of the ray direction normal to the impostor plane, keeping the tangential component but scaling it to be very far from the impostor center.

Texture maps for spherical shells or quads are computed using the same method, described below.

4.3 Inferring Layered EM Texture Maps

As in [7][8], we base our EM inference on the observation that a texel contributes to zero or more display pixels. Neglecting hardware quantization effects, a texel that is twice as bright contributes twice as much. Hardware rendering can thus be modeled as a linear system, called the *rendering matrix*, mapping texels to display pixels. To find the rendering matrix, we perform test renderings that isolate each texel's display contribution. Given the rendering matrix, A, we then find the least-squares best EM, x, which when applied matches the ray tracer's segmented incident radiance layer, b. This results in the linear system $Ax=b$, which we solve using conjugate gradient. Details about the rendering matrix inference and linear system solution are found in [7].

There are two advantages of this inference method over a simple projection of the environment onto a series of shells. By matching a view-dependent ray traced image, it reproduces view-dependent shading on reflected or refracted objects, like a reflective cup seen through a glass teapot. It also adjusts the EM to account for the geometric error of approximating environmental objects as simpler geometry, such as a spherical shell. The result is better fidelity at the ray traced viewpoint samples.

We infer each layer of the layered EM independently, but simultaneously over both terms of the shading model (Figure 7). After performing the layer cluster algorithm on samples from a supersampled image, each layer's samples are recombined into a single image and filtered to display resolution to form two images b_R and b_T, corresponding to the two terms of the shading model. Only a single image is needed for reflective objects. These images have four channels – the alpha channel encodes the fraction of supersampled rays through a given pixel whose outgoing ray hit environmental geometry in that layer, while the rgb channels store the color of the environment intersected by those outgoing rays. We infer the two rendering matrices, A_R and A_T, corresponding respectively to hybrid rendering (Section 5) with an initial reflection or refraction. We then find the least-squares solution to

$$A_R x = b_R$$
$$A_T x = b_T \tag{1}$$

to produce a single EM for the layer, x, matching both terms. Figure 7 shows an example of these b terms and resulting inferred EM, x, for each of three layers.

It is possible for the ray tracer to generate widely diverging rays when sampling a single output pixel, causing noise in the environment map solution. We therefore modified the ray tracer to generate a confidence image. The per-pixel confidence value is computed as a function of the maximum angle between the directions of all ray pairs contributing to the particular pixel. More precisely, we use the formula

$$1 - \min(\theta_m^2, \theta_c^2)/\theta_c^2$$

where θ_m is the maximum angle between ray pairs and $\theta_c = 5°$ is an angular threshold. We multiply the confidence image with both sides of equation (1) prior to solving for x.

To conserve texture memory, it is beneficial to share more distant EM layers between local lens objects. To do this, we can add more equations to the linear system (1) corresponding to multiple lens objects and simultaneously solving for a single EM x.

As observed in [8], choosing the proper EM resolution is important to preserve frequency content in the imaged environment. A very conservative approach generates test renderings to determine the most detailed EM MIPMAP level actually accessed by the graphics system. Texture memory bandwidth and capacity limitations may dictate the use of lower resolutions.

Simultaneous Inference Over Multiple Viewpoints A difficulty with this inference technique is that the lens objects can fail to image all of its environment. For example, a flat mirror does not image geometry behind it and a specular fragment images only a small part of its environment from a particular viewpoint. These missing portions can appear in a view near but not exactly at the pre-rendered viewpoint. We solve this problem by inferring EMs that simultaneously match ray traced images from multiple views. The views can be selected as a uniform sampling of a desired viewspace centered at the viewpoint sample.

To compute simultaneous viewpoint inference, outgoing rays are compiled for each of these multiple viewpoints. A single EM layer, x, is then inferred as a least-squares simultaneous match at all viewpoints, using the system of equations (1) for each viewpoint. Although this blurs view-dependent shading in the environment, good results are achieved if the set of viewpoints matched are sufficiently close.

An alternative method to fill in the missing portions in the environment map is to infer it using extra rays in addition to the ones that exit the lens object. These additional rays can be taken from the object center as in traditional environment maps. They can also be taken from the viewpoint, but looking directly at the environment (i.e., without the lens object), to approximate view-dependent shading in the environment. Direct images from the lens object center tend to work better for reflective objects while direct images from the viewpoint are better suited for refractive (transparent) objects.

We use the confidence-weighted, least-squares solution method in (1), but solve simultaneously across images of the lens object from the viewpoint as before (*lens object images*), combined with direct images of the environment without the lens object (*direct images*). In these direct images, per-pixel confidence is computed as a function of the likelihood that the pixel represents a missing portion of the environment. We compute this via distance of the direct image ray's intersection with its closest point in the intersection records of the lens object images. The advantage of this scheme is that it fills in the missing portions of the environment with a fixed, small number of extra images, regardless of the size of the viewspace around a viewpoint sample.

5 Hybrid Rendering

Adaptive Tessellation Performing ray tracing only at lens object vertices can miss important ray path changes occurring between samples, producing very different outgoing rays even at different vertices of the same triangle. Our solution is to perform adaptive tessellation on the lens object based on two criteria: the ray path "topology" and a threshold distance between outgoing rays. Using topology, ray paths are considered different if their path lengths are different, or the maximum coefficient at an interface changes between reflection and refraction. Using outgoing ray distance, they are different if the angle between their directions is more than 3°.

Figure 5: Adaptive Tessellation.

Figure 5 illustrates adaptive tessellation using an example image shaded darker with increasing subdivision level. Places where rays go through more interfaces or where the surface is highly curved require more sampling.

When the ray paths at a triangle's vertices are too different, the triangle is subdivided at the midpoints of each of its edges in a 1-to-4 subdivision, and the metric is recursively applied. The process is continued until the three ray paths are no longer different or the triangle's screen-projected edge lengths are less than a threshold, τ. We also allow 1-to-3 and 1-to-2

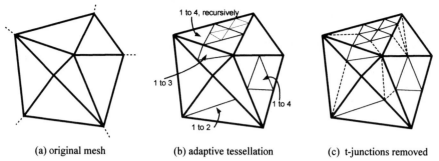

| (a) original mesh | (b) adaptive tessellation | (c) t-junctions removed |

Figure 6: The original mesh, (a), is adaptively subdivided when ray paths at the vertices are sufficiently different, (b). The resulting t-junctions are removed by additional tessellation of adjacent triangles, (c), illustrated with dotted lines, to form a triangular tessellation.

subdivision in cases where some of the triangle edges are already small enough (see Figure 6). We adapt the tessellation simultaneously for both terms of the shading model, subdividing a triangle if either ray path is considered different. We ignore differences in subdivision between neighboring triangles, fixing the resulting "t-junction" tessellation as a postprocess. A hash table on edges (vertex pairs) returns the edge midpoint if it has already been computed from a more highly subdivided neighboring triangle. Recursive querying yields all vertices along the edge.

Given all the boundary vertices, it is simple to compute a triangular tessellation that avoids t-junctions. The hash table is also used to quickly determine whether a triangle vertex ray has already been computed, thus avoiding redundant ray queries.

To avoid unnecessary ray tracing and tessellation in occluded regions, we compute whether each vertex is directly visible from the viewpoint using a ray query. If all three vertices of a triangle are occluded, we do not subdivide the triangle further, but still compute correct texture coordinates for its vertices via ray tracing in case some part of its interior is visible. Another optimization is to avoid ray tracing at vertices whose triangles are all backfacing. Using a pass through the faces, we mark each triangle's vertices as "to be ray traced" if the triangle is front-facing; unmarked vertices are not ray traced.

Multipass Rendering with Layered EM Indexing Assuming we have a refractive object with n layers in its EM, we perform n passes for its refractive term, and n passes for the its reflective term. We multiply each term by the $F G$ function interpolated by the graphics hardware across each triangle. The texture index for each term/layer pass is generated by intersecting the outgoing ray with the layer's geometric impostor, such as a sphere. Taking this point of intersection and subtracting the EM origin point yields a vector that forms the hardware EM index, recorded with the vertex. As in [8], we use a hardware-supported cube map spherical parameterization which doesn't require normalization of this vector. Note that the texture indices change per layer since the distances to the EM spheres are different and the outgoing rays do not emanate from the EM origin.

When rendering from a viewpoint away from a pre-rendered sample, a smoother result is obtained by interpolating between the two closest viewpoints. Thus, we perform $4n$ passes, $2n$ for each viewpoint, blended by the relative distance to each viewpoint. Ray tracing, adaptive tessellation, and texture coordinate computation are performed just once per frame. Ray tracing is performed with respect to the actual viewpoint, not from the adjacent viewpoint samples.

Each layer is computed in a separate pass because of texture pipeline limitations in the current graphics system (Microsoft Direct3D 7.0 running on an Nvidia GeForce graphics accelerator).

298

To begin the series of compositing passes for the second of the two summed shading terms, the framebuffer's alpha channel must be cleared. This is accomplished by rendering a polygon that multiplies the framebuffer's rgb values by 1 and its alpha by 0. We then render its layers from front to back, which sums its contribution to the result of the first term's passes. With the advent of programmable shading in inexpensive PC graphics hardware and the ability to do four simultaneous texture accesses in each pass, it will be possible to reduce those $4n$ passes to n and avoid the alpha clear step [17][18].

6 Results and Discussion

We tested a scene containing a glass teapot, a reflective cup, a ring of columns, and distant walls. EMs were parameterized by viewpoints circling around the teapot in $8°$ increments. The scene contains two lens objects, a teapot and cup; we used our clustering algorithm to select 3 EM layers for the teapot and 2 for the cup. A quadrilateral impostor was used for the sparsely-occupied cup environmental layer of the teapot (Figure 7, top), a cylindrical shell for the columns environmental layer of the teapot (Figure 7, middle), and spherical shells for all other layers. We also tried a solution that was constrained to a single EM layer for each lens object, still using the clustering algorithm to determine placement of the single shell.

Figure 8 compares the quality of our results for two novel views: one in the plane of the circle of viewpoints (a), and one above this plane (b). Using multiple EM layers, we achieve quality comparable to the ray tracer. Reconstruction using a single layer is noticeably blurry because of conflicts where different points in the environment map to identical ones in the spherical shell approximation. Moreover, the video results for the single layer solution show significant "popping" when switching between viewpoint samples. The multi-layer solution better approximates the environment, providing smooth transitions between viewpoints.

Together, we call the method of ray continuation to reach occluded geometry from Section 4.1, and the simultaneous solution across multiple viewpoints from Section 4.3, *EM disocclusion prevention*. Figure 9 and our video results show the effectiveness of these methods in eliminating environmental disocclusions which would be obvious otherwise.

To measure performance, we tried two different adaptive subdivision thresholds of $\tau = 3$ and $\tau = 5$ (measured in subpixels) in a 3×3 subsampled 640×480 resolution rendering. Performance was measured in seconds on a 1080MHz AMD Athlon with Nvidia GeForce graphics card; reduction factors are with respect to ray tracing without hybrid rendering. For comparison, the ray tracer required 480 seconds to render each frame, using 6,153,735 rays and 168,313,768 triangle intersection tests. The

	$\tau = 3$	$\tau = 5$
Ray tracing at vertices	13.48	7.82
Texture coord. generation	0.71	0.38
Tessellation	2.11	0.83
Other (inc. rendering)	2.57	1.45
Total frame time	18.87	10.48
Time reduction factor	25.4	45.8
Ray count	1,023,876	570,481
Ray reduction factor	6	10.8
Triangle intersection tests	11,878,133	6,543,993
Intersection red. factor	14.2	25.7

version with τ=3 is shown in Figure 8; the two versions are compared in Figure 10. The faster τ=5 achieves good quality but suffers from some artifacts when animated. The difference is discernible in the still image in Figure 10 as slightly increased noise along edges such as the bottom of the teapot and where the spout joins the body.

Hybrid rendering was 25-45 times faster than a uniformly-sampled ray tracing, though both used identical ray casting code and the greedy ray path shading model. (Using a full tree shading model would incur an additional factor of 5.) This is not entirely accounted for by the reduction of roughly a factor of 6-11 in ray queries or 14-25 in triangle intersection tests obtained by hybrid rendering. The reason for our increased performance is the increased locality we achieve by ray tracing only through the lens object's geometry, and the hardware acceleration of texture map access. Although adaptive sampling reduces triangle intersection tests and ray queries by roughly the same factor, triangle intersection tests (which include ray misses as well as actual intersections) are reduced by an additional factor because the environment is approximated with simple spherical shells.

Though our performance falls short of real-time, significant opportunity remains both to optimize the software and parameters (like the initial lens object's tessellation), and to tradeoff greater approximation error for higher speed. We note that more complicated environmental geometry will increase the benefit of our use of approximating shells. To speed up ray tracing, it may be advantageous to exploit spatial and temporal coherence, possibly combined with the use of higher-order surfaces rather than memory-inefficient polygonal tessellations. In any case, we believe that future improvement to CPU speeds and especially support for ray tracing in graphics hardware will make this approach ideal for real-time rendering of realistic shiny and glass objects.

7   Conclusion

Hybrid rendering combines ray tracing, which simulates complicated ray bouncing off local geometry, with environment maps which capture the more distant geometry. This exploits the hardware's ability to access and resample texture maps to reduce the number of ray casts and consider them in a memory-coherent order. By inferring layered EMs parameterized by viewpoint, we preserve view-dependent shading and parallax effects in the environment without performing unaccelerated ray casts through its complicated geometry. With these techniques, we obtain a realistic simulation of highly specular reflective and refractive objects that would be impractical with light field based methods.

A major benefit of this work is to make the cost of ray tracing *low* and *predictable* without sacrificing quality. Lower cost, but probably not higher predictability, results from our adaptive ray tracing algorithm. Two of our other techniques enhance both. We avoid large variations in the ray tree of refractive objects from one pixel to the next by substituting two ray paths. We also substitute a fixed set of simple shells for arbitrarily complex environmental geometry.

One area of future work is to study the effect of hybrid rendering on compression of parameterized image spaces. We expect that PEMs should better capture the coherence in image spaces compared with parameterized texture maps that are statically mapped on objects [7]. Another possible application of this work is in speeding up the rendering of realistic animations. Hybrid rendering could be used to interpolate between ray traced key frames at which view-dependent layered environment maps are inferred.

References

[1] BASTOS, R., HOFF, K., WYNN, W., AND LASTRA, A. Increased Photorealism for Interactive Architectural Walkthroughs. Interactive 3D Graphics 1999, pp.183-190.

[2] BLINN, J. F., NEWELL, M. E. Texture and Reflection in Computer Generated Images. Comm. ACM, 19(10), Oct. 1976, pp.542-547.

[3] CABRAL, B., OLANO, M., AND NEMEC, P. Reflection Space Image Based Rendering. SIG-GRAPH 99, pp.165-170.

[4] CHUANG, Y., ZONGKER, D., HINDORFF, J., CURLESS, B., SALESIN, D., AND SZELISKI, R., Environment Matting Extensions: Towards Higher Accuracy and Real-Time Capture, SIG-GRAPH 2000, pp.121-130.

[5] DIEFENBACH, P. J. Pipeline Rendering: Interaction and Realism through Hardware-based Multi-Pass Rendering. PhD thesis, University of Pennsylvania, June 1996.

[6] GORTLER, S., GRZESZCZUK, R., SZELISKI, R., AND COHEN, M. The Lumigraph. SIG-GRAPH 96, pp.43-54.

[7] HAKURA, Z., LENGYEL, J., AND SNYDER, J. Parameterized Animation Compression. Euro-graphics Rendering Workshop 2000, pp.101-112.

[8] HAKURA, Z., SNYDER, J, AND LENGYEL, J. Parameterized Environment Maps. Interactive 3D Symposium 2001, March 2001, pp. 203-208.

[9] HECHT, E., Optics, Second Edition, Addison-Wesley, 1987.

[10] HEIDRICH, W., LENSCH, H., COHEN, M. F., AND SEIDEL, H. Light Field Techniques for Reflections and Refractions. Eurographics Rendering Workshop 1999, pp.195-375.

[11] HEIDRICH, W., SEIDEL, H. REALISTÍC, Hardware-Accelerated Shading and Lighting. SIG-GRAPH 99, pp.171-178.

[12] KAY, D., AND GREENBERG, D., Transparency for Computer Synthesized Images, Siggraph 1979.

[13] KAJIYA, J., The Rendering Equation, SIGGRAPH '86, Aug. 1986, pp.143-150.

[14] LEVOY, M., HANRAHAN, P. Light Field Rendering. SIGGRAPH 96, pp.31-41.

[15] LINDE, Y., BUZO, A., AND GRAY, R. M., An algorithm for Vector Quantizer Design, IEEE Transactions on Communication COM-28, 1980, pp. 84-95.

[16] LISCHINSKI, D., RAPPOPORT, A., Image-Based Rendering for Non-Diffuse Synthetic Scenes. Eurographics Rendering Workshop 1998, pp.301-314.

[17] MICROSOFT DIRECTX8.0, http://www.microsoft.com/directx/.

[18] MICROSOFT XBOX, http://www.xbox.com/xbox/flash/specs.asp.

[19] MILLER, G., RUBIN, S., AND PONCELEON, D. Lazy Decompression of Surface Light Fields for Precomputed Global Illumination. Eurographics Rendering Workshop 1998, pp.281-292.

[20] OFEK, E., RAPPOPORT, A. Interactive Reflections on Curved Objects. SIGGRAPH 98, pp.333-341.

[21] PHARR, M., KOLB, C., GERSHBEIN, R., AND HANRAHAN, P., Rendering Complex Scenes with Memory-Coherence Ray Tracing, SIGGRAPH 97, pp.101-108.

[22] WHITTED, T. An Improved Illumination Model for Shaded Display. Communications of the ACM, 23(6), June 1980, pp.343-349.

[23] WOOD, D. N., AZUMA, D. I., ALDINGER, K. ET AL. Surface Light Fields for 3D Photogra-phy. SIGGRAPH 2000, pp.287-296.

[24] ZONGKER, D., WERNER, D., CURLESS, B., AND SALESIN, D., Environment Matting and Composition, SIGGRAPH 99, pp.205-214.

Editors' Note: see Appendix, p. 345f. for colored figures of this paper

Texture and Shape Synthesis on Surfaces

Lexing Ying, Aaron Hertzmann, Henning Biermann, Denis Zorin

New York University

http://www.mrl.nyu.edu

Abstract. We present a novel method for texture synthesis on surfaces from examples. We consider a very general type of textures, including color, transparency and displacements. Our method synthesizes the texture *directly* on the surface, rather than synthesizing a texture image and then mapping it to the surface. The synthesized textures have the same qualitative visual appearance as the example texture, and cover the surfaces without the distortion or seams of conventional texture-mapping. We describe two synthesis methods, based on the work of Wei and Levoy and Ashikhmin; our techniques produce similar results, but directly on surfaces.

1 Introduction

Computer graphics applications increasingly require surfaces with highly detailed reflective properties, geometry and transparency. Constructing such detailed appearances manually is a difficult and tedious task. A number of techniques have been proposed to address this problem; procedural synthesis techniques are among the most widely used. A number of recent techniques [4, 13, 2] make it possible to synthesize textures from examples.

Creating a surface with a complex appearance can be viewed as synthesis of a collection of functions on an arbitrary two-dimensional domain. These functions include color, transparency, normals and coordinates of surface points. We will refer to all such functions as textures. The textures can be thought of as continuous and defined directly on surfaces, although they will be represented as samples in implementation. In this view, previously proposed example-based texture synthesis algorithms synthesize attributes for a special kind of surfaces, i.e. flat rectangles.

In this paper, we extend synthesis from examples to arbitrary surfaces. The obvious approach to the problem, synthesizing a texture on a rectangle and mapping it to an arbitrary surface, is likely to result in artifacts (e.g. seams or shape distortion); typically, creating high-quality maps requires considerable user intervention. Performing synthesis directly on a surface avoids many of the these problems.

Existing texture synthesis methods rely on the presence of identical, regular sampling patterns for both the example and the synthesized texture. Therefore, it is impossible to apply such methods directly to surfaces. In this paper, we regard the example and the synthesized texture as continuous functions that happen to be represented by samples, but not necessarily laid out in identical patterns. Whenever necessary, we resample either the example or the synthesized texture on a different pattern.

We describe two specific synthesis methods, based on the methods of Wei and Levoy [13] and Ashikhmin [2]. As with image synthesis, the choice of algorithm depends primarily on the texture.

The main contributions of this paper are: generalizations of existing image texture synthesis methods to synthesis on surfaces; synthesis of surface texture maps independent of parameterization; efficient and accurate neighborhood sampling operations; and synthesis of texture, transparency, and displacements.

2 Related Work

Recently, several nearest-neighbor methods have been shown to produce textures of good quality. De Bonet [3] demonstrates a coarse-to-fine procedure that fills in pixels in an output texture image pyramid by copying pixels from the example texture with similar coarse image structure. Efros and Leung [4] create texture using a single-scale neighborhood. Wei and Levoy [13] combine the methods of [3, 4] by using a neighborhood that contains both coarse-scale and same-scale pixel information, and use Tree-structured vector quantization (TSVQ) [5] to accelerate the search for the nearest neighbor. Ashikhmin [2] produces high-quality textures by copying contiguous texture patches when possible.

Neyret and Cani [10] texture a surface isotropically by tiling from a small collection of tileable example texture triangles. Praun et al. [11] extend this by placing oriented texture patches over an independent parameterization of a surface. Although these methods produce high-quality results for many textures, they have some drawbacks: they cannot use texture patches that are large with respect to the surface shape, they cannot capture low-frequency texture without sacrificing high-frequency randomness, and the texture patches do not necessarily line up exactly, which requires careful selection of the patch shapes, and blending to hide discontinuities between patches.

In work concurrent to our own, Wei and Levoy [14] and Turk [12] develop methods for texture synthesis on surfaces. These methods also generalize Wei and Levoy's multiscale image texture synthesis algorithm [13]. We believe that our approach has several advantages. First, we define a fast method for neighborhood sampling that guarantees that there will not be any folds in the sampling grid, in contrast to relaxation [14] and surface marching [12]. Second, we synthesize directly to surface texture maps rather than to a densely tesselated mesh, meaning that our algorithm will be faster and require much less memory. However, we do require that the surface be covered with texture maps, and that charts can be constructed. Finally, we also generalize Ashikhmin's algorithm, which gives good results for many textures that are handled poorly by the multiscale synthesis algorithms.

3 Overview

Given a 2D example and a 3D surface, our goal is to create a texture that "looks like" it came from the same process that generated the example. We make the assumption that this is equivalent to requiring the texture on every small surface neighborhood to "look like" the texture on some neighborhood in the example.[1] The example and synthesized textures will be discretized into samples, although not necessarily with the same sample density. The texture may be from any domain: in particular, we explore image textures, transparency textures and geometric textures. For brevity, we refer to the synthesized texture as *target*.

---

[1] This formulation is based on the *Markov condition* assumption on the texture: we assume that the texture has local statistics (the value at a point depends only on its local neighborhood), and stationary statistics (the dependence is the same for every point). These assumptions imply that the the surface texture will "look like" the example texture if this joint density of texture values is the same for the surface as for the example.

Review of image texture synthesis: We now briefly review image texture synthesis algorithms; see the relevant papers for details. Efros and Leung [4] synthesize a texture in scan-line order. For each pixel, the already-synthesized values in neighborhood of the target pixel x are collected, and the example texture is searched to find pixel y with the neighborhood that matches the target neighborhood as closely as possible. The value of the pixel y is copied to the pixel x. Wei and Levoy [14] synthesize a Gaussian pyramid from coarse to fine. Each level of the pyramid is synthesized as in the Efros-Leung algorithm, except that samples are collected from the neighborhood at both the current scale and the coarser scale, and that TSVQ is used to accellerate the nearest-neighbors search.

Ashikhmin [2] synthesizes a texture in the same manner as Efros-Leung, except that only a restricted range of candidates for each pixel is tested. When synthesizing a value for a pixel x, we first consider each already-synthesized pixel y_i adjacent to x. Some source pixel y_i' in the example texture was previously copied to y_i. If we were to continue copying from the same patch of the example texture used for y_i', then x would get the value at location $y_i' + (x - y_i)$; this location is used as a candidate for x. Each y_i generates a candidate. We compare the neighborhood of each candidate to the neighborhood of x, and copy the color from the closest match y_i to x.

Texture representation: For simplicity, we assume that the example texture is resampled on a rectangular sampling grid, i.e. that it is an image. The target texture is represented by samples on the surface (i.e. by texture maps). We assume that there is a collection of rectangular images mapped to the surface and the texture samples will be stored in these images.

An important feature of our approach is that the synthesis process is independent of the choice of the texture-mapping parameterization: given a parameterization, our method will synthesize a texture without distortion on the surface. However, parametrization distortion may result in blurry textures in some areas.

Idea of our algorithms: For each sample of the target texture, we consider the previously-synthesized texture within a small neighborhood of the sample. Then we locate a similar neighborhood in the example and copy the value of the texture in the center of the neighborhood to the target sample.

Several issues need to be addressed to make this idea practical:

- how to pick a neighborhood of samples from the target texture,
- how to compare neighborhoods in the target and example,
- how to find similar neighborhoods in the example.

The two methods that we describe use somewhat different approaches to these problems. Each method has its strengths and weaknesses, illustrated in Section 6. Both methods use a common sampling pattern for the example and target textures to make the comparison possible, but use different approaches to resampling as discussed below.

Surface orientation: As most interesting textures are anisotropic, orientation must be established on the surface. We use a vector field to specify the correspondence between orientation on the surface and orientation in the domain of the example texture. A pair of orthogonal tangent vector fields v_1 and v_2 is used for this purpose. To compare the texture on the surface neighborhood centered at x to a neighborhood centered at y in the example texture we establish a map between the neighborhoods, mapping x to y and v_1 and v_2 to the coordinate directions in the example.

The field v_1 is computed using the method described in [7][2]. The field v_2 is computed as the cross-product of v_1 and the oriented surface normal. The field could also be specified interactively, as in [11, 12].

Synthesis methods: Our first method is based on [13] and described in Section 4. For each generated sample x, we attempt to find the neighborhood in the entire example texture that matches the neighborhood of x as closely as possible. The sampling pattern of the example is used to resample the neighborhood of the target. As the example is a regularly sampled image, the fixed sampling pattern makes it possible to accelerate the search with standard nearest-neighbors algorithms, such as TSVQ.

The second method, based on [2] (Section 5), selects candidate values only from example neighborhoods that are spatially close in the example with some already-synthesized sample near x (*coherent synthesis*). This makes it necessary to keep track of the source of each generated sample. In this method, we use the target sampling pattern for comparison of neighborhoods, which is simpler than resampling the target. Acceleration (such as with TSVQ) is unnecessary in this method, because only a few neighborhoods will be tested.

4 Multiscale Synthesis

Our first method is based on the multiscale image synthesis procedure of Wei and Levoy [13]. In this method, we first synthesize a coarse version of the surface texture and then perform coarse-to-fine refinement. This method allows us to efficiently capture both coarse and fine-scale statistics, while performing several iterative refinements to the texture.

Our algorithm requires that the surface is covered by an atlas of sufficiently large overlapping charts. A chart is a map from a part of a surface into the plane; every point should be in the interior of a chart. Charts allow us to efficiently sample small neighborhoods of points.

Chart construction is relatively easy for a large class of texture-mapped surfaces, including polygonal meshes. If a surface is tiled with quadrilateral or any other polygonal texture maps, we can construct vertex charts from the texture maps. The texture maps themselves form a mesh on the surface. We can create a chart for each vertex of the mesh by flattening the collection of texture-mapped regions sharing the vertex to the plane, as explained below. Clearly, the resulting charts cover the whole surface, and any point on the surface is in the interior of one of the charts.

Chart construction is particularly simple for multiresolution subdivision surfaces, which we use in our implementation. There are several methods available for converting an arbitrary mesh to this representation [8, 6, 15], but we emphasize that this is not essential for our algorithm; as long as a tiling of the surface with texture maps is available, any representation can be used.

Our algorithm begins by creating a Gaussian pyramid for the example image and for each of the target texture maps. Every level of the hierarchy will be synthesized, from coarse-to-fine.

---

[2]Since we are optimizing a vector field, and do not desire 90°-invariance as in [7], the optimization formula is of the form $\sum \cos((\theta_i - \varphi_{ij}) - (\theta_j - \varphi_{ji}))$ instead of $\sum \cos 4((\theta_i - \varphi_{ij}) - (\theta_j - \varphi_{ji}))$.

Our synthesis methods iterate over the surface texture maps in breadth-first order. Within each texture map, we synthesize in scan-line order, starting from a scan-line that is adjacent to an already-synthesized texture.

We use a brute-force search to synthesize the coarsest level. In order to synthesize a sample x, we sample the previously synthesized target texture in a neighborhood of x using the regular pattern of the example, and the surface marching technique described in the next section. Then we exhaustively search the example to find the nearest match under a weighted l^2-norm. We then copy the central sample from the best-matching neighborhood to x. Samples are weighted with a Gaussian kernel in image space. We sample texture values by bilinear interpolation of the four nearest neighboring values from the target texture maps. However, if some of these values have not yet been generated, then instead we use the nearest already-generated neighbor. If none of the values are available, then no sample value is generated at that location. This brute-force search is inefficient, but the coarse-level synthesis is nonetheless fast because there are very few samples to search over or to synthesize at the coarsest level of the pyramids.

We synthesize each of the remaining levels using a two-pass algorithm based on Wei and Levoy's [13] hole-filling algorithm. In the first pass, we synthesize each sample of a level of the hierarchy using a 5×5 neighborhood that contains only samples from the coarser level of the pyramid. In the second pass, we refine the texture at the current level using the composition of the 9×9 neighborhood from the current level and a 5×5 one from the coarser level. This means that all samples in each neighborhood have already been synthesized, allowing us to use TSVQ [5] or Approximate Nearest Neighbors [1] to accelerate the nearest-neighbors searches in both passes. The best match found during these searches is copied to the target sample. We also introduce some randomness into the search, with the same randomization used in [3, 13]: we locate the eight nearest matches found during the TSVQ traversal with backtracking, discard all matches that have a distance worse than the best match by a factor of 0.1, and then randomly pick one of the remaining matches by uniform random sampling.

We use two different methods for sampling neighborhoods on a surface. For the coarsest levels of the image hierarchy, we use *surface marching*, in which we traverse over smoothed geometry to locate sample points. For the remainder of the image hierarchy, we perform *chart sampling*, in which we construct sampling neighborhood patterns in a globally-defined parametric domain. In our experiments, chart sampling performs twice as fast; marching is only used for coarse levels where chart sampling cannot be used (for reasons described below).

4.1 Surface Marching

In the surface marching algorithm, we collect a grid of sample locations that corresponds to a grid of locations in the plane (Figure 1), using a tesselated mesh representation of the surface. For each sample point, we compute the angle and distance in the plane to the point. We then draw a straight path from the center surface point in the computed distance and direction (with respect to the orientation field on the mesh) to find the corresponding surface sample point. When the path intersects a mesh edge, the line is continued on the adjacent face, at the same angle to the mesh edge as on the previous face.

Note that other choices of path shape could be used to march from the center point to the target sample point. In particular, Turk [12] uses a path that corresponds to marching up or down in the texture domain, then left or right to find the sample point. In general, however, each of these paths may reach different parts of the surface. We

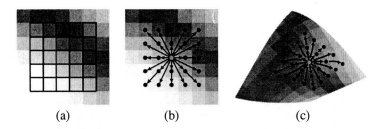

(a)	(b)	(c)

Fig. 1. Surface marching for neighborhood sampling. (a) A 5 × 5 rectangular surface neighborhood pattern on an image. (b) Each sample location in the neighborhood may be reached by a straight line from the center pixel. (b) A corresponding sampling pattern on a surface. From the center sample, we "march" over the surface, in directions corresponding to the straight-line directions in the image plane. This gives us a set of surface sample locations. Values at each location are determined by bilinear sampling from the texture map. The orientation of the pattern is determined by the surface vector field.

believe that the diagonal path described above is preferable, because it is the shortest such path, and thus least prone to distortion due to irrelevant features.

Regardless of which path we use, there are several problems with the surface marching approach. First, it is not guaranteed to give even sampling of a surface neighborhood in irregular geometry. Second, the sampling pattern is numerically unstable, as minute surface variations can cause substantial variations in the pattern. Finally, this method is relatively slow, because of the many geometric intersection and projection operations required.

4.2 Chart Sampling

Rather than trying to move on the surface from one face to the next, one can take advantage of a suitable surface parameterization. Recall that our goal is to be able to sample the texture at (approximately) regularly spaced locations around a sample x. Suppose a sufficiently large part of the surface around x is parameterized over a planar domain V. Then we can sample in the parametric domain V, choosing the sampling pattern in such a way that the corresponding sample points on the surface form the desired approximately regular arrangement (Figure 2). This can be achieved by using the Jacobian of the map from V to distort the sampling pattern in V.

The crucial assumption of the method is that the size of the neighborhood to be sampled is sufficiently small, so that the parameterization for the neighborhood is sufficiently close to linear and each neighborhood fits on the image of one *chart* $g(V)$. When this does not hold, as happens at the coarsest levels of synthesis, chart sampling cannot be used and we perform marching instead.

Chart sampling in detail: To explain more precisely how chart sampling is performed we need some additional notation. Let U_i be rectangular texture domains on which the surface is parameterized and f_i be the parameterizations (Figure 2). In practice, f_i are represented by piecewise-linear approximations defined by arrays of vertices, but it is convenient to consider f_i and other maps as continuous for now. Note that the images of boundaries of the rectangular domains form a mesh on the surface, with images of corners of the rectangles corresponding to vertices of the mesh.

We define overlapping charts, each corresponding a mesh vertex. The chart map g is defined implicitly by specifying maps Φ_i^v for each vertex, mapping each U_i into a

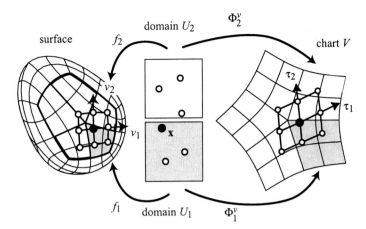

Fig. 2. Chart sampling. In order to sample the texture in the neighborhood of x, we construct its sampling pattern in the chart. The pattern is distorted in the chart such that it will be aligned with the surface orientation field (v_1 and v_2) and roughly square.

common planar domain V. The maps Φ_i^v should agree on the boundaries of the domains U_i which map to the same curves on the surface. Then g is taken to be $g = f_i \circ (\Phi_i^v)^{-1}$ on $\Phi_i^v(U_i) \subset V$.

The maps Φ_i^v should be defined using the same procedure as is used to define the parametrizations f_i, in order to ensure that the chart maps are smooth. For example, if an optimization process was used to define f_i, the same process should be used to define Φ_i^v, for some choice of the values for the images of the boundaries. We explain how we defined chart maps for subdivision surfaces at the end of this section.

In addition to parametrizations and chart maps, we assume orthogonal unit tangent vector fields v_1 and v_2 are defined on all U_i. These fields specify local orientation for synthesized anisotropic textures, and may be discontinuous.

We use the notation Dh to denote the differential of a map $h : R^s \to R^t$, which is a linear map given by the matrix $(\partial h^i / \partial x^j)_{ij}$.

Now we are ready to define the procedure to compute samples. Given a sample x in the domain U_1, we wish to compute a set of samples x_{lm} in domains U_i such that their corresponding surface points $f_i(x_{lm})$ form a pattern approximating a square grid with step δ in each direction, centered at $f_1(x)$. The samples are computed in several steps (Figure 2):

1. Map x to the chart domain V: $y = \Phi_1^v(x)$.
2. Compute chart domain vectors τ_1 and τ_2 that correspond to v_1 and v_2, respectively. For this, we require that the differential $Df_1(D\Phi_1^v)^{-1}$ maps τ_1 to v_1 and τ_2 to v_2. As v_1 and v_2 are tangent vectors, they can be written as $v_j = Df_1 w_j$ $j - 1, 2$, for some two-dimensional w_j. Then $\tau_j = D\Phi_1^v w_j$, $j = 1, 2$.
3. Compute sample locations in the chart domain: $y_{lm} = y + l\tau_1\delta + m\tau_2\delta$, for $l, m = -4..4$ (for a 9×9 sampling pattern).
4. Map the sample locations back to one of the parametric domains U_i, depending on which part $\Phi_i^v(U_i)$ of the chart domain V they are located: $x_{lm} = (\Phi_i^v)^{-1}(y_{lm})$.
5. Sample the texture values from the texture maps. For each sample location, the location x_{lm} is sampled by bilinear interpolation in texture map i, where i is determined by the parametric domain used in the previous step.

This procedure takes advantage of the assumption that the sampling neighborhood is small enough that various maps can be replaced by their linearized versions.

The maps f_i and Φ_i^v are represented as samples at vertex locations. To find a value of a map at an arbitrary point of a domain U_i, we use bilinear interpolation; to invert a map, we use point location and bilinear interpolation.

Chart sampling for subdivision surfaces: For a subdivision surface, we use one domain (and, thus, one texture map) per face of the control mesh. To compute chart maps Φ_i^v, we proceed as follows. For a vertex with valence k, we assign coordinates of the vertices of a regular planar k-gonal star as initial values of Φ_i^v to the corners of each rectangular domain U_i. We assign the coordinates of the center of the star to the corner of each U_i corresponding to v. Next, we extend the k-gonal star with an extra layer of similar quads. Finally, we apply subdivision to the two-dimensional coordinates to obtain values of Φ_i^v everywhere on U_i. This procedure is similar to computation of the *characteristic map*; in fact, values of the characteristic map also can be used as chart maps. See [15] for further details on characteristic maps and how they can be computed.

5 Coherent Synthesis

We now describe the *coherent synthesis* algorithm, based on Ashikhmin's algorithm for image texture synthesis [2]. This algorithm is based on the observation that the l^2-norm is an imperfect measure of perceptual similarity. Instead, it attempts to copy large coherent regions from the example texture, since such regions are guaranteed to have the appearance of the example texture, although there might be seams between them. This method runs much faster than the other methods and produces higher-quality results for many textures. The chart representation used in the previous section is not necessary here, nor is any multiresolution representation. However, like Ashikhmin's algorithm, this method does not work well for some smoothly varying textures.

This method runs in a single pass over all samples on the surface. For each synthesized sample, we record the floating point coordinates in the texture map that this sample was copied from. To synthesize a sample x, we find nearby samples which are already synthesized and use them to look up corresponding locations in the example texture. We displace these locations in order to obtain candidate source samples for x. These candidates are chosen so that they correspond to continuations of the samples already copied from the example. For each candidate, we collect a neighborhood of the same connectivity as the original target neighborhood, and compare it to the target neighborhood. We copy the value of the closest-matching candidate to x. Note that only a few candidates are considered, so no search acceleration is necessary. This makes it possible to resample the example texture rather than the target.

Now we describe the algorithm in greater detail. We treat the example texture as continuous, and use bilinear interpolation to evaluate between texture samples. The algorithm is illustrated in Figure 3.

1. To synthesize a sample x coming from an texture map I, we collect all synthesized samples x_i, $i = 0 \dots m$ in the texture map I which are no more than 2 samples away from x. In the interior of the texture map, this corresponds to a 5×5 neighborhood of pixels in the texture domain. If x is less than two samples away from the texture map boundary, we also retrieve samples in the texture map sharing the boundary with I. Finally, if x is less than two samples away from a corner of an texture map, we also collect adjacent samples from all texture maps

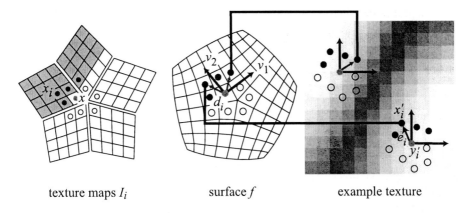

| texture maps I_i | surface f | example texture |

Fig. 3. Coherence synthesis. In order to synthesize a texture value for a point x, we examine each of its already-synthesized neighbors x_i (filled circles). In the figure, we show a point x that occurs at a "corner" where five texture maps meet on the surface. (The open circles indicate unsynthesized pixels, which are ignored during this step.) Each neighbor proposes a candidate location y_i' from the example, based on its own location in the example and its distance from x on the surface. Each y_i' corresponds to the texture location for x *if* we were to continue the texture patch used for x_i to x. The best candidate is computed by comparing the candidate neighborhoods with l^2.

    sharing the corner. If no synthesized samples are located, a random value from the example texture is selected.

2. For each collected sample x_i, we compute the 3D displacement $d_i = f(x_i) - f(x)$ to the target surface point, and project d_i into the tangent plane at $f(x)$ to obtain tangent displacements d_i^t. The tangent displacements can be represented in the local coordinate system (v_1, v_2) by 2D vectors e_i: $d_i^t = e_i^1 v_1 + e_i^2 v_2$.

3. Our next goal is to locate candidate locations for x in the example texture. For each of the neighboring samples x_i, we look up the corresponding location x_i' in the example texture. We use these samples to generate candidate locations $y_i' = x_i' - e_i$, i.e. by looking up the value which is located in the example in the same way with respect to x_i' as x is with respect to x_i. Note that, unlike in Ashikhmin's method, the location and the displacement should be represented as floating point numbers in order to prevent errors due to round-off.

4. Now we need to choose which of the candidates is used to get the value for the target. To do this, we compare neighborhoods of y_i' with the neighborhood of x. We use the same set of displacements e_i to get samples around y_i' which are arranged in the same pattern as x_i around x, i.e. we consider neighborhoods $N(y_i')$ consisting of samples $y_{ij}' = y_i' + e_j$. Undefined values are discarded when the distance is computed. Among these neighborhoods we choose the one for which the l^2 distance from the the neighborhood of x is minimal

6   Experiments

In Figure 4, we demonstrate coherent synthesis of a nut texture on a cow model. Note that the texture maps appear distorted, because they are synthesized to appear undistorted on the surface. With coherent synthesis, the texture has high quality, but some small discontinuities are visible. Figures 5 and 6 show the transparency and displacement maps created with multiscale synthesis. In Figure 7, different scales of the same texture were synthesized with multiscale synthesis and the same vector field. Figure 8 compares the multiscale and coherent algorithms. The quality of the results is very similar to those of the 2D algorithms when applied to these textures. In our experience, one can predict the results of the surface synthesis by running the 2D algorithms. Figure 9 demonstrates synthesis of transparency maps. The results of coherent synthesis on complex models are displayed in Figure 10.

Timings for these experiments were as follows:

Mesh	Texels		Example size		Method		Time (min)	
Cow (Fig 4)	369,664		96 × 96		C		3	
3D Cross (Fig 5)	399,360		64 × 64		M		10	
Ball (Fig 6)	98,304		64 × 64		M		2.5	
Dog (Fig 7)	696,320	174,080	64 × 64	64 × 64	M	M	18	5
Torus (Fig 8)	114,688		64 × 64	64 × 64	M	C	1.5	0.5
			192 × 192	192 × 192	M	C	290	0.5
Ball (Fig 9)	98,304		64 × 64		M		2.5	
Cow (Fig 10)	289,792		128 × 128		C		2	
Horse (Fig 10)	275,968		128 × 128		C		2	

For meshes with multiple results, the positions in the table correspond to the positions in the figures. The second column shows the total number of samples that were synthesized in texture maps for each result. The fourth column shows the synthesis method used: "M" for multiscale or "C" for coherent. These timings compare favorably with those reported by Wei and Levoy [14] and Turk [12]; our multiscale synthesis appears to be about 3 times faster for generating a comparable number of samples with a given example size. Our coherent synthesis is dramatically faster than multiscale synthesis or the other methods. It appears that the multiscale synthesis does not scale well when both the example size and neighborhood size grow; the flower texture on the torus (Figure 8) took nearly five hours to compute. This time can be reduced to a few minutes by reducing the neighborhood size to 5 × 5 (as done by Turk [12]), by reducing the example texture size, or by using coherent synthesis.

7 Discussion and Future Work

We have presented efficient methods for synthesizing a texture onto a 3D surface from a 2D example texture. These methods produce textures with similar quality and speed to their 2D counterparts. This means that those textures that work well with Ashikhmin's algorithm work well with our coherence algorithm. Hence, there is reason to hope that these strategies may be applied to future 2D texture synthesis algorithms as well.

There are a number of directions for future work. All of our sampling operations use either point sampling or bilinear sampling. However, since texels represent area averages of a function, weighted area integrals should be used instead.

Surface reflectance functions and material properties, such as BRDFs or fur [9], can be synthesized, perhaps via straightforward extensions of the ideas presented here.

Real-time procedural shaders for example-based texture synthesis would allow complex surface textures to be generated in real time. However, this appears difficult because the samples generated by the algorithms are interdependent.

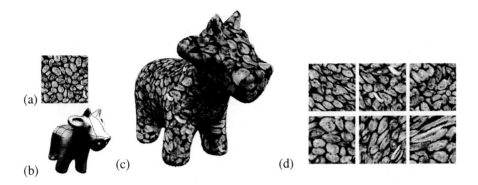

Fig. 4. Surface texture synthesis. (a) Example texture, obtained from VisTex database and down-sampled to 96 × 96. (b) Cow model, showing edges corresponding to edges of top-level faces. (c) Synthesis result using coherent method based on Ashikhmin's algorithm [2]. (d) Representative texture maps generated during the process. Variations in surface shape appear as distortions in the texture maps. The surface is covered by a total of 50 texture maps.

References

1. Sunil Arya, David M. Mount, Nathan S. Netanyahu, Ruth Silverman, and Angela Y. Wu. An Optimal Algorithm for Approximate Nearest Neighbor Searching in Fixed Dimensions. *Journal of the ACM*, 45(6):891–923, 1998.
2. Michael Ashikhmin. Synthesizing natural textures. *2001 ACM Symposium on Interactive 3D Graphics*, pages 217–226, March 2001.
3. Jeremy S. De Bonet. Multiresolution sampling procedure for analysis and synthesis of texture images. *Proceedings of SIGGRAPH 97*, pages 361–368, August 1997.
4. Alexei Efros and Thomas Leung. Texture Synthesis by Non-parametric Sampling. *7th IEEE International Conference on Computer Vision*, 1999.
5. Allen Gersho and Robert M. Gray. *Vector Quantization and Signal Compression*. Kluwer Academic Publishers, 1992.
6. Igor Guskov, Kiril Vidimče, Wim Sweldens, and Peter Schrder. Normal meshes. *Proceedings of SIGGRAPH 2000*, pages 95–102, July 2000.
7. Aaron Hertzmann and Denis Zorin. Illustrating smooth surfaces. *Proceedings of SIGGRAPH 2000*, pages 517–526, July 2000.
8. Aaron W. F. Lee, Wim Sweldens, Peter Schröder, Lawrence Cowsar, and David Dobkin. Maps: Multiresolution adaptive parameterization of surfaces. *Proceedings of SIGGRAPH 98*, pages 95–104, July 1998.
9. Jerome E. Lengyel, Emil Praun, Adam Finkelstein, and Hugues Hoppe. Real-time fur over arbitrary surfaces. *2001 ACM Symposium on Interactive 3D Graphics*, pages 227–232, March 2001.
10. Fabrice Neyret and Marie-Paule Cani. Pattern-based texturing revisited. *Proceedings of SIGGRAPH 99*, pages 235–242, August 1999.
11. Emil Praun, Adam Finkelstein, and Hugues Hoppe. Lapped textures. *Proceedings of SIGGRAPH 2000*, pages 465–470, July 2000.
12. Greg Turk. Texture Synthesis on Surfaces. *Proc. SIGGRAPH 2001*, August 2001. To appear.
13. Li-Yi Wei and Marc Levoy. Fast Texture Synthesis Using Tree-Structured Vector Quantization. *Proceedings of SIGGRAPH 2000*, pages 479–488, July 2000.
14. Li-Yi Wei and Marc Levoy. Texture Synthesis Over Arbitrary Manifold Surfaces. *Proc. SIGGRAPH 2001*, August 2001. To appear.
15. D. Zorin, P. Schröder, T. DeRose, L. Kobbelt, A. Levin, and W. Sweldens. Subdivision for modeling and animation. SIGGRAPH 2000 Course Notes.

312

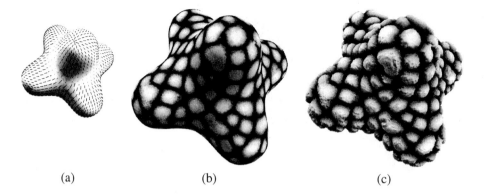

(a)   (b)   (c)

Fig. 5. (a) Surface with orientation field. Note the singularity of the field at the top of the model. (b) Synthesized texture using multiscale synthesis of the first texture from Figure 8 in grayscale. The texture appears consistent at the singularity. (c) Texture mapping and displacement mapping with the same texture.

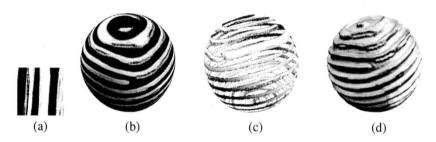

(a)   (b)   (c)   (d)

Fig. 6. Textured sphere generated with multiscale synthesis. (a) Example texture. (b) Synthesized texture. (c) Texture mapping plus transparency mapping (using the same texture). (d) Displacement mapping.

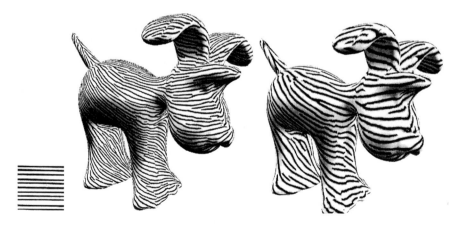

Fig. 7. Zebra dog, generated with multiscale synthesis. Varying the scale parameter creates a texture with a different size on the surface.

Real-Time High-Dynamic Range Texture Mapping

Jonathan Cohen, Chris Tchou, Tim Hawkins, and Paul Debevec

University of Southern California Institute for Creative Technologies
13274 Fiji Way, Marina del Rey, CA 90292
{jcohen,tchou,timh,debevec}@ict.usc.edu

Abstract. This paper presents a technique for representing and displaying high dynamic-range texture maps (HDRTMs) using current graphics hardware. Dynamic range in real-world environments often far exceeds the range representable in 8-bit per-channel texture maps. The increased realism afforded by a high-dynamic range representation provides improved fidelity and expressiveness for interactive visualization of image-based models. Our technique allows for real-time rendering of scenes with arbitrary dynamic range, limited only by available texture memory.

In our technique, high-dynamic range textures are decomposed into sets of 8-bit textures. These 8-bit textures are dynamically reassembled by the graphics hardware's programmable multitexturing system or using multipass techniques and framebuffer image processing. These operations allow the exposure level of the texture to be adjusted continuously and arbitrarily at the time of rendering, correctly accounting for the gamma curve and dynamic range restrictions of the display device. Further, for any given exposure only two 8-bit textures must be resident in texture memory simultaneously.

We present implementation details of this technique on various 3D graphics hardware architectures. We demonstrate several applications, including high-dynamic range panoramic viewing with simulated auto-exposure, real-time radiance environment mapping, and simulated Fresnel reflection.

1 Introduction

Real-world scenes usually exhibit a range of brightness levels greatly exceeding what can be accurately represented with 8-bit per-channel images. This is typical in outdoor scenes where some surfaces are in sunlight and others are in shadow, in environments with both interior and exterior areas, or in unevenly illuminated interior environments. Previous work has described techniques for acquiring high-dynamic range (HDR) images of real world scenes, and for representing such images efficiently. Other work has described techniques for visualizing high-dynamic range images by compressing the dynamic range into the 8 bits of dynamic range that most display systems will accept.

We propose a technique for visualizing HDR image-based scenes in graphics hardware without compressing the dynamic range. Borrowing from real imaging devices, we add an "exposure level" parameter to the virtual camera model. The exposure level can be dynamically adjusted to map a particular section of the full dynamic range of the scene to the displayable dynamic range of the output device. Our technique is similar in motivation to the dynamic visual adaptation work recently presented by Pattanaik *et al.* [22], but focuses on how such visual adaptation can be accomplished in real time using current graphics hardware. Central to our technique is the use of high-dynamic range texture maps (HDRTMs) for real-time rendering of HDR image-based environments. Our implementations of HDRTMs use standard 8-bit per-channel texture memory to store 8-bit sections of arbitrary bit-depth textures.

In image-based rendering, texture maps often store the exitant radiance from a surface rather than albedo. Since light can be arbitrarily intense, standard clamped 8-bit textures have limited usefulness for image-based rendering. HDRTMs, on the other hand, allow us to store arbitrarily large radiance values in texture maps. During rendering, these radiance values are scaled according to the camera's exposure level and any light attenuation due to reflection or transmission, and then clamped to the valid range of the display device. Thus HDRTMs are an appropriate technique for visualizing global illumination solutions interactively and properly simulating bright lights reflected in dark surfaces.

Most devices display images with 8 bits per-channel, employing a nonlinear mapping between pixel values and brightness levels. This mapping is typically described by a *gamma curve*, in which the intensity i displayed on the monitor for a pixel with value p is computed as $i = (p/255)^\gamma$. In this work, we create texture maps that have a greater number of bits per pixel than the display device, allowing for increased dynamic range. For example, a texture map with 16 bits per pixel allows us to represent 256 times the displayable pixel value range, and with a $\gamma = 2.2$ mapping[1] the maximum representable intensity increases by $256^{2.2}$, or nearly a factor of 200,000. This dynamic range is enough to represent bright outdoor scenes and darker indoor regions in the same texture map, and is therefore adequate for most applications.

2 Related work

An early source of high-dynamic range (HDR) images in computer graphics were the renderings produced by radiosity and global illumination algorithms. As a particular example, Greg Ward's RADIANCE synthetic imaging system [32] outputs each of its renderings in Ward's "Real Pixels" [31] high-dynamic range Red-Green-Blue-Exponent format, representing HDR images in just 32 bits per pixel. Schlick [27] later presented a nonlinear mapping process to encode color HDR in 24 bits per pixel, and Ward has presented two other formats based on separating high-dynamic range luminance from perceptually represented chrominance as the LogLuv extension to the TIFF image format [15]. HDR images of real-world radiance may also be acquired using standard digital cameras as demonstrated in [4]. We use HDR images acquired with this technique in this paper.

Displaying HDR images on low-dynamic range (LDR) devices such as video monitors and has been studied in the context of *tone reproduction* [29]. [10] performed this process through quantization, [16] through histogram adjustment, and [30] through a form of anisotropic diffusion. [21] modeled the effect of visual adaptation in viewing high-dynamic range images, and later work [22] modeled global time-dependent effects. [30] discussed a foveal display program in which the exposure of a high-dynamic range image was adjusted according to user mouse input, but was implemented in software only. [26] presented a technique for performing Ward's tone reproduction algorithm interactively to visualize radiosity solutions.

Texture mapping has been used in scan line renderers, ray tracers, and hardware-accelerated computer graphics applications for over two decades. A survey of applications of texture mapping is presented by Haeberli and Segal in [11]. We take advantage

---

[1] 2.2 is a typical value for γ on PC monitors.

of the powerful new additions to the texturing pipeline that allow for programmable texture preprocessing such as NVidia's register combiner and texture shader architectures [19].

Of particular relevance to our work is the use of texture mapping for real-time image-based rendering [5, 7, 17, 24]. Most applications of these techniques have been limited to reproducing scenes with low-dynamic range, such as flatly illuminated room interiors or cloudy outdoor environments. This paper provides a way to extend these techniques to environments with dramatic lighting, such as both interior and exterior areas, by allowing high-dynamic range images to be used as texture maps.

[3] used high-dynamic range images of incident illumination to render synthetic objects into real-world scenes. This work used non-interactive global illumination rendering to perform the lighting calculations. Significant work has been done to approximate these full lighting calculations in real-time using graphics hardware. For example, [1] and [12] described how texture prefiltering and standard texture mapping could be used to interactively render convincing approximations to the illuminated objects in [3], while [13, 14, 23] use multi-pass rendering methods to simulate arbitrary surface reflectance properties. This paper presents a potential step towards extending these techniques by allowing high-dynamic texture maps to be rendered with hardware acceleration and used for hardware-based lighting calculations. An alternate implementation by Simon Green uses the new two-channel 16-bit HILO texture format available in the NVidia GeForce3 architecture [8] to perform similar calculations.

3 Representation and rendering of HDRTMs

3.1 General technique

Most graphics hardware allows only 8-bit per-channel color values to be used in texture maps.[2] However, many graphics cards allow texels from multiple textures to be combined during texture fetching or in the framebuffer to produce the final rendered color. In our technique, we use multiple textures to represent high-dynamic range textures. These textures are then combined in hardware to produce a correct 8-bit texture for any exposure setting.

Consider a 16-bit texture that stores values directly proportional to the exitant radiance from a surface. We simulate the appearance of the surface as seen by a linear-response camera with a given exposure value and white point by computing:

$$I(v) = clamp(ev).$$

Here e is a virtual exposure level that may take on any non-negative value, and the *clamp* function simply clamps the result to 8 bits, that is, to a pixel value of 255. To provide for hardware computation of $I(v)$, we can represent the 16-bit texture v as two 8-bit textures, storing the low bits into v_0 and the high bits into v_1. We then have

$$
\begin{aligned}
I(v) &= clamp(e(v_0 + 256v_1)) \\
&= clamp(ev_0 + 256ev_1) \\
&= clamp(clamp(ev_0) + clamp(256ev_1)) \quad (1)
\end{aligned}
$$

where the last equality follows from the observation that for $a, b \geq 0$, $clamp(a+b) = clamp(clamp(a) + clamp(b))$. This is demonstrated graphically in Figure 1.

---

[2]The newest GeForce3 cards from NVidia allow for a two-channel 16 bit per-channel format.

316

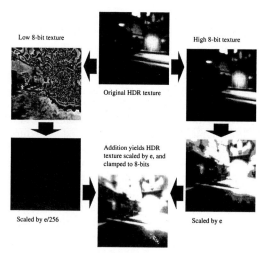

Fig. 1. Overview of HDRTM pipeline.

Many graphics systems have multitexturing that supports texture computations of the form of Equation 1, although all systems we have investigated have required some modifications to accommodate limitations such as restricted ranges for operands (e.g. multiplication by values greater than 1 is not supported).

It should be noted that when $e < 1/256$, any regions that were clamped (saturated) in the 16-bit texture will begin to dim incorrectly. Similarly, when $e > 1$, the low 8 bits of the texture will be amplified and the displayed texture will begin to appear quantized for lack of sufficient low-order bits. This means that restricting e to the range $[256^{-1}, 1]$ allows the 16-bit texture to be viewed without visible artifacts.

For textures with greater than 16 bits, we can modify Equation 1 by adding one term to the sum for each additional 8 bits. However, adding many textures together during rendering may impact performance. By precomputing and storing additional texture maps, we can compute Equation 1 by adding only two 8-bit textures together. We illustrate this with an example. Consider a 24-bit texture value v. From v we compute $x = v/256$, which is representable in 16 bits. We also compute $y = clamp_{(2^{16}-1)}(v)$ which clamps v to the 16-bit maximum. We split the 16-bit values x and y into 8-bit textures x_0, x_1 and y_0, y_1 as above. For a given value of e, we compute $I(v)$ as follows. If $e \in [256^{-1}, 1]$, $I(v) = clamp(clamp(ey_0) + clamp(256ey_1))$, as in Equation 1. If $e \in [256^{-2}, 256^{-1}]$, $I(v) = clamp(clamp(256ex_0) + clamp(256^2ex_1))$. In general, the number of textures required to store a texture of bit depth $8n$ with $n \geq 2$ is $2n - 2$. Note that for an $8n$-bit texture, the useful exposure range is $[256^{1-n}, 1]$.

3.2 Gamma-corrected textures

Most display devices apply a gamma curve to the output intensities as described in Section 1. To produce the correct display values, we must therefore gamma correct an HDRTM by exponentiating the radiance values by $1/\gamma$.

Let $v' = v^{1/\gamma}$ be a gamma-corrected texture value. To apply our technique to gamma-corrected values, we need only observe that gamma-correcting the result of scaling radiance value v by e is equivalent to scaling v' by $e^{1/\gamma}$. If we let $e' = e^{1/\gamma}$, this implies that

$$I(v)^{1/\gamma} = clamp(v'e') = clamp(clamp(e'v'_0) + clamp(256e'v'_1)). \tag{2}$$

Thus, provided the values in the HDRTM are gamma-corrected before they are converted to 8-bit textures, we can correctly render this HDRTM by gamma-correcting the exposure level as well. Note that this extends the effective exposure range of the texture map to $[1/256^\gamma, 1]$. The downside is that we can not correctly add two gamma-corrected HDRTMs using the standard addition operator, for example to render diffuse and specular passes as shown in Figure 3e.

3.3 Implementation on SGI

We can implement HDRTMs using the hardware-accelerated pixel transfer pipeline operations on SGI systems. Assuming gamma-corrected 16-bit texture values, we first render the high 8 bits of the texture into the framebuffer, v'_1. We turn off blending, set the pixel transfer function to scale all color channels by $256e'$, and call glCopyPixels to read the framebuffer back onto itself and apply the scale factor. Next, we turn on additive blending, set the current color to be (e', e', e'), set the texture environment mode to modulate the texture values by the current color, and render the least-significant portion of the texture into the framebuffer, v'_0. This directly computes the quantity as in Equation 2. On an Onyx3 Infinite Reality, this runs in full screen mode (1280 x 1024 resolution) at 30 Hertz.

3.4 Implementation on NVidia GeForce2

We have also implemented HDRTMs using the programmable texture combiner system in NVidia's GeForce2 and TNT architectures. This is inherently difficult because these architectures do not directly support multiplying textures by values greater than one. Texture combiners process texture values after they have been fetched from memory before they are written into the framebuffer. The GeForce2 contains two texture combiners, each of which can take 4 inputs (A, B, C, D) interpreted as 8-bit fixed point numbers between 0 and 1 and generate the output $A*B+C*D$. The inputs to the combiners can be either the value 0, the value 1, the current texel color, a constant color, an interpolated color, or the result of a previous texture combiner. Finally, the output of the combiner can be multiplied by 1, 2, or 4, with the result clamped back to the 8-bit range. The details of this operation may be found in [19, 25].

Within this architecture, we can compute $clamp(ex_0 + 16ex_1))$ for any value of e between 0 and 1 as follows:

Exposure Range	Combiner Name	A	B	C	D	Final Multiplier
$e \in [\frac{1}{2}, 1]$	TC0	x_1	1	x_1	1	x4
	TC1	TC0	e	x_0	$e/2$	x2
$e \in [\frac{1}{4}, \frac{1}{2}]$	TC0	x_1	1	x_1	1	x2
	TC1	TC0	$2e$	x_0	$e/2$	x2
$e \in [\frac{1}{8}, \frac{1}{4}]$	TC0	x_1	1	x_1	1	x1
	TC1	TC0	$4e$	x_0	$e/2$	x2
$e \in [0, \frac{1}{8}]$	TC0	x_1	1	0	0	x1
	TC1	TC0	$8e$	x_0	$e/2$	x2

We carefully set up the combiners so that if a value has been clamped at any point in the pipeline, future computations will never multiply the resulting number by less than $1/2$. This correctly ensures that the final output of TC1 after the multiplication by 2 will be 255 if any previous computations clamped.

If the texture combiners performed calculations in 8-bits of precision, the x2 multiplier at the end of TC1 would result in the low bit of the output always being zero. In the TNT2 and later architectures, however, all texture calculations are performed in 9 bits (although this is not guaranteed by the specifications), so we do not lose precision.

The ability to modulate a texture value by up to a factor of 16 implies that we can store 8-bit sections of an n-bit texture with each successive 8-bit chunk shifted 4 bits from the previous. Thus with two textures, we can store a 12-bit texture map. We may chain these 12-bit sections to achieve higher bit depth as in Section 3.1. Since we can only multiply by up to 16, however, this representation requires $4n - 4$ textures to represent an $8n$-bit texture map. Again, only two textures are ever used simultaneously.

With this method, a 16-bit texture would usually require 4 textures; however, in this particular case it is actually possible to use a trick to reduce the number of textures required to only 3. We start with two 8-bit textures, x_0 and x_1, representing the least-significant and most significant 8 bits of a 16-bit texture as in Equation 1. We then precompute a third texture $z = clamp(16 \cdot clamp(x_1))$. Since we can scale a texture by up to 16, we can obtain $clamp(256x_1)$ using $clamp(16z)$. In the case that $e > 1/16$, we replace x_1 with z in the above texture combiner setup. If $e \leq 1/16$, we multiply e by 16, divide the scale factors in variables B and D in the TC1 stage by 16, and use x_1 as described in the table. This is the technique we used to create the images in this paper.

4 Applications

4.1 Visualizing HDR scenery

We have implemented a high-dynamic range panoramic image viewer using hardware-accelerated HDRTMs, similar to panoramic image viewers like Quicktime VR [2]. Our viewer is implemented with hardware-accelerated cube-based environment mapping, where we render a cube that surrounds the viewpoint with the panoramic texture appropriately mapped onto it. The user can change the viewpoint by rotating and zooming, as in Quicktime VR. Our viewer has an extra degree of freedom, however, since the user can additionally set the exposure level at which the panorama is rendered. The system is demonstrated in Figure 2.

The exposure can be set either by a slider or with an "auto-exposure" mode. In auto-exposure mode, the system samples pixels near the center of the visible portion of the panorama. The system then adjusts the exposure level to correctly expose the image for these pixel values, similar to [28, 22]. To keep the exposure from fluctuating in an unpleasant manner, we do not adjust exposure directly, but model it as a high friction spring system, where the rest state is set to the desired exposure. More sophisticated models of adaptation as in [28, 22] could also be investigated.

4.2 Lighting

We can also use HDRTMs to correctly model sharp specular reflections of bright environments from dark objects. We demonstrate this with high-dynamic range environment mapping of a teapot and simulating Fresnel reflection from the polished surface of a dark monolith.

Perfect specular reflection of convex objects can be simulated using graphics hardware by environment mapping techniques [9, 11] or by changing the camera's projection matrix according to the position of the reflector, as in [6] and [20]. While these techniques correctly calculate the position at which reflected objects appear on the surface of the reflector, [3] notes that the intensity of the reflected light will be incorrect unless the reflected color is computed in full dynamic range before being clamped to the range of the display device.

For a point s on a perfectly specular surface, the reflected imaging function $I_s(r)$ calculates the value to render to the framebuffer given incident environment radiance r along the ray that is reflected towards the camera about s. Assume s modulates incident radiance by specular coefficient ϕ, where $\phi \in [0, 1]$. To display the result of the reflection, we compute $I_s(v) = clamp(e\phi v)$. Thus we set our exposure level to $e \cdot \phi$ and render the value v that is stored in a HDRTM. To account for a gamma curve we must actually set the exposure level to be $(e\phi)^{1/\gamma}$ and use the texture value v'. An example using this technique for real-time environment mapping is shown for a dark polished teapot in Figure 3a; the specular reflection produces an image of the environment $1/8^{th}$ of the environment's brightness. Figure 3b shows the same result using just standard 8-bit texture maps incorrectly clamped at the exposure level seen in the background environment.

We can also simulate glossy materials with a two-pass technique shown in Figure 3e. First, we render the object with a pre-convolved diffuse environment map. Then we render the object with a darker specular environment map and add the results in the framebuffer. Note that we cannot correctly add gamma-corrected pixel values in the framebuffer, so the result is not physically correct, although it looks plausible. Figure 3f shows the correct result, obtained by compositing the two passes in software.

Most real-world polished surfaces will behave as near-perfect mirrors ($\phi = 1$) at glancing angles, while dropping to as low as $\phi = 0.05$ at angles normal to the surface (the so-called "Fresnel effect"). Because the reflectivity can change by a factor of 20, the environment map must have dynamic range of at least 20 times that of the display device. Figures 3c-d show the wide dynamic range seen by rotating about a polished black monolith in a bright environment. To model Fresnel effects on curved surfaces efficiently, we would need a way of continuously varying the exposure level at which the HDRTM is rendered over the surface. This may be possible using different hardware-based techniques on newer architectures such as the GeForce3 [8].

5   Conclusion and Future Work

We have demonstrated that high-dynamic range texture maps can be stored and rendered efficiently using current hardware texturing architectures by storing high and low bits in different texture maps and recombining them during rendering. While native support for high-dynamic range would be ideal, the relatively small memory and processor overhead in our implementations on the SGI Onyx3 and NVidia GeForce2 systems suggest that HDRTMs could be applied in real applications on current hardware.

While the applications to lighting and scene visualization demonstrated in this paper are useful, we believe that much more work could be done in this area. We would like to experiment with performing hardware lighting calculations in full dynamic range and using these results to illuminate textured surfaces, which may be possible with the latest geometry and lighting engine on NVidia's GeForce3 cards [18]. Other applications include high-dynamic range lightfields and image-based models, as well as interaction techniques that exploit the ability to adjust exposure level. The addition of direct support for arbitrary multiplication of texture values in the texture fetching stage, and the ability to correctly add gamma corrected values in the framebuffer and multitexturing units would enable more physically realistic real-time lighting simulation. We leave this as future work in the area of hardware design.

320

Acknowledgements

We thank Simon Green from NVidia for his helpful comments. This work was supported by funds from the University of Southern California and the United States Army but does not necessarily reflect any corresponding positions or policies and no official endorsement should be inferred.

References

1. CABRAL, B., OLANO, M., AND NEMEC, P. Reflection space image based rendering. *Proceedings of SIGGRAPH 99* (August 1999), 165–170.
2. CHEN, S. E. Quicktime VR - an image-based approach to virtual environment navigation. *Proceedings of SIGGRAPH 95* (August 1995), 29–38. ISBN 0-201-84776-0. Held in Los Angeles, California.
3. DEBEVEC, P. Rendering synthetic objects into real scenes: Bridging traditional and image-based graphics with global illumination and high dynamic range photography. In *SIGGRAPH 98* (July 1998).
4. DEBEVEC, P. E., AND MALIK, J. Recovering high dynamic range radiance maps from photographs. In *SIGGRAPH 97* (August 1997), pp. 369–378.
5. DEBEVEC, P. E., YU, Y., AND BORSHUKOV, G. D. Efficient view-dependent image-based rendering with projective texture-mapping. In *9th Eurographics workshop on Rendering* (June 1998), pp. 105–116.
6. DIEFENBACH, P. *Pipeline Rendering: Interaction and Realism through Hardware-based Multi-Pass Rendering.* PhD thesis, University of Pennsylvania, 1996.
7. GORTLER, S. J., GRZESZCZUK, R., SZELISKI, R., AND COHEN, M. F. The Lumigraph. In *SIGGRAPH 96* (1996), pp. 43–54.
8. GREEN, S. Personal communication, May 2001.
9. GREENE, N. Environment mapping and other application of world projections. *IEEE Computer Graphics and Applications 6*, 11 (November 1986), 21–29.
10. HAEBERLI, P., AND SEGAL, M. Quantization techniques for visualization of high dynamic range pictures. In *Fourth Eurographics Workshop on Rendering (Paris, France)* (June 1993), pp. 7–18.
11. HAEBERLI, P., AND SEGAL, M. Texture mapping as A fundamental drawing primitive. In *Fourth Eurographics Workshop on Rendering* (June 1993), M. F. Cohen, C. Puech, and F. Sillion, Eds., Eurographics, pp. 259–266.
12. HEIDRICH, W., AND SEIDEL, H.-P. Realistic, hardware-accelerated shading and lighting. *Proceedings of SIGGRAPH 99* (August 1999), 171–178. ISBN 0-20148-560-5. Held in Los Angeles, California.
13. KAUTZ, J., AND MCCOOL, M. D. Approximation of glossy reflection with prefiltered environment maps. *Graphics Interface* (2000), 119–126. ISBN 1-55860-632-7.
14. KAUTZ, J., AND MCCOOL, M. D. Interactive rendering with arbitrary BRDFs using separable approximations. *Eurographics Rendering Workshop 1999* (June 1999).
15. LARSON, G. W. Logluv encoding for full-gamut, high-dynamic range images. *Journal of Graphics Tools 3*, 1 (1998), 15–31. ISSN 1086-7651.
16. LARSON, G. W., RUSHMEIER, H., AND PIATKO, C. A visibility matching tone reproduction operator for high dynamic range scenes. *IEEE Transactions on Visualization and Computer Graphics 3*, 4 (October - December 1997), 291–306.
17. LEVOY, M., AND HANRAHAN, P. Light field rendering. In *SIGGRAPH 96* (1996), pp. 31–42.
18. LINDHOLM, E., KILGARD, M., AND MORETON, H. A user-programmable vertex engine. In *SIGGRAPH 2001* (2001).
19. NVIDIA CORPORATION. NVIDIA OpenGL extension specifications. Tech. rep., NVIDIA Corporation, 2001.
20. OFEK, E., AND RAPPOPORT, A. Interactive reflections on curved objects. *Proceedings of SIGGRAPH 98* (July 1998), 333–342. ISBN 0-89791-999-8. Held in Orlando, Florida.
21. PATTANAIK, S. N., FERWERDA, J. A., FAIRCHILD, M. D., AND GREENBERG, D. P. A multiscale model of adaptation and spatial vision for realistic image display. *Proceedings of SIGGRAPH 98* (July 1998), 287–298.
22. PATTANAIK, S. N., TUMBLIN, J. E., YEE, H., AND GREENBERG, D. P. Time-dependent visual adaptation for realistic image display. *Proceedings of SIGGRAPH 2000* (July 2000), 47–54. ISBN 1-58113-208-5.
23. PEERCY, M. S., OLANO, M., AIREY, J., AND UNGAR, P. J. Interactive multi-pass programmable shading. *Proceedings of SIGGRAPH 2000* (July 2000), 425–432. ISBN 1-58113-208-5.
24. PULLI, K., COHEN, M., DUCHAMP, T., HOPPE, H., SHAPIRO, L., AND STUETZLE, W. View-based rendering: Visualizing real objects from scanned range and color data. In *Eighth Eurographics Workshop on Rendering* (June 1997), pp. 23–34.
25. ROGERS, D. TNT 8-stage setup in Direct3D. Tech. rep., NVIDIA Corporation, 2001.
26. SCHEEL, A., STAMMINGER, M., AND SEIDEL, H.-P. Tone reproduction for interactive walkthroughs. In *Eleventh Eurographics Workshop on Rendering* (2000).
27. SCHLICK, C. High dynamic range pixels. *Graphics Gems IV* (1994), 422–429.
28. TUMBLIN, J., HODGINS, J. K., AND GUENTER, B. K. Two methods for display of high contrast images. *ACM Transactions on Graphics 18*, 1 (January 1999), 56–94. ISSN 0730-0301.
29. TUMBLIN, J., AND RUSHMEIER, H. E. Tone reproduction for realistic images. *IEEE Computer Graphics & Applications 13*, 6 (November 1993), 42–48.
30. TUMBLIN, J., AND TURK, G. Lcis: A boundary hierarchy for detail-preserving contrast reduction. *Proceedings of SIGGRAPH 99* (August 1999), 83–90. ISBN 0-20148-560-5. Held in Los Angeles, California.
31. WARD, G. Real pixels. *Graphics Gems II* (1991), 80–83.
32. WARD, G. J. The RADIANCE lighting simulation and rendering system. In *SIGGRAPH 94* (July 1994), pp. 459–472.

Editors' Note: see Appendix, p. 348 for colored figures of this paper

Scheel et al. (pp. 1–12)

Fig. 6. Results. Upper small image: number of samples (red: visib., green: formfactor). Lower small image: radiosity solution. Images sizes (top to bottom): 424 × 363, 512 × 384, 427 × 363

Stark and Riesenfeld (pp. 13–24)

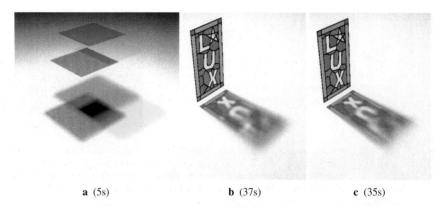

a (5s)   b (37s)   c (35s)

Fig. 7. Shadows of **a** purely transparent polygons, **b** a stained glass window under a large triangular source and **c** the source rotated 45 degrees; note the differences in the fine structure of the shadow

a 20 facets (8.6s)   b 180 facets (19s)

c 20 facets (17s)   d dispersion

Fig. 8. a, b Purely reflective objects. **c** Transmission through a glass icosahedron. **d** Dispersion

Chen and Avo (pp. 25–38)

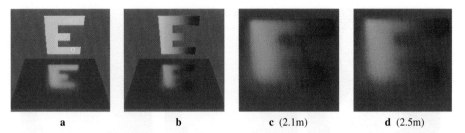

a   b   c (2.1m)   d (2.5m)

Fig. 2. A simple test scene of analytical glossy reflection involving a glossy surface with a Phong exponent of 200 and an E-shaped luminaire whose radiant exitance is uniform (**a**) and linearly-varying with respect to position (**b**). The closeup images of the reflection on the floor were computed analytically (**c**) and by Monte Carlo method with approximately the same amount of time, using stratified and importance sampling and 64 samples per pixel (**d**)

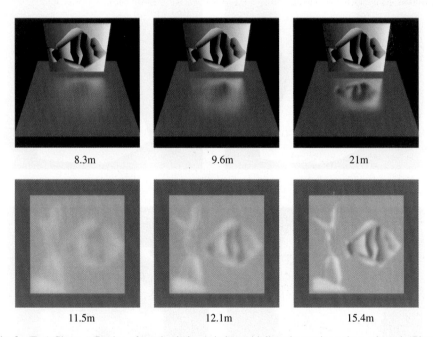

8.3m   9.6m   21m

11.5m   12.1m   15.4m

Fig. 3. (Top) Glossy reflection of a stained glass window with linearly-varying colors, where the Phong exponents are 15, 50 and 300 from left to right. (Bottom) Glossy transmission through a frosted glass fish tank, where the tropical fish and the seaweed are superimposed with linearly-varying colors. From left to right, the Phong exponents are 5, 15, and 65, respectively. Refraction is not considered here. The numbers beneath each image indicate the computation time in minutes

Stam (pp. 39–52)

a Comparison of our shader (right) with a Lambertian shader (left) and the Hanrahan-Krueger model (center)

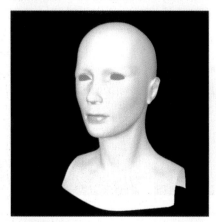

b Head under different lighting conditions. Flash-like area source (left) and two area light sources (right)

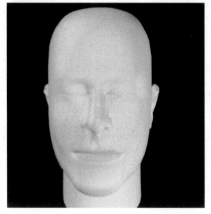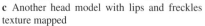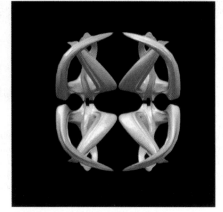

c Another head model with lips and freckles texture mapped   **d** Another application of our model

Fig. 6. Renderings created using our new skin shader

Haro et al. (pp. 53–62)

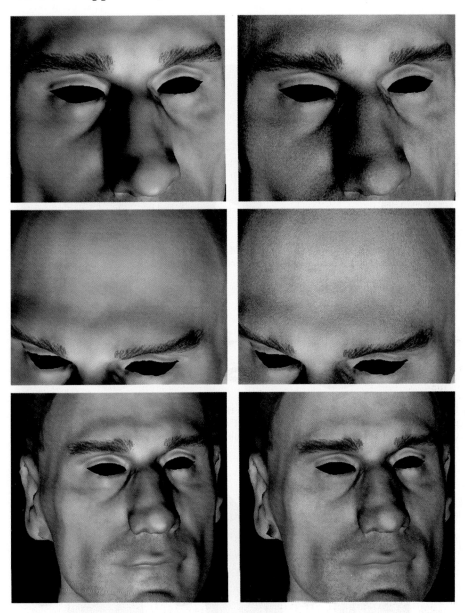

Fig. 7. Left: skin rendered without fine scale structure. Right: skin rendered with fine scale structure

Daubert et al. (pp. 63–70)

Fig. 4. a A dress rendered with BRDFs consisting of only one lobe. **b** Left: Aliasing artifacts are clearly visible if no mip-mapping is used. Right: Using several mip-mapping layers

Fig. 5. The fabric patterns displayed on the models (left and right) were both computed from the micro geometry in the middle. In contrast to the right BRDF model, the left one does not include a lookup table. Clearly this BRDF is not able to capture the color shift to red for grazing angles, nicely displayed on the right

Fig. 6. Different fabric patterns on the same model. Left: plain knit, middle: loops with different colors, right: perl loops

Durand et al. (pp. 71–82)

Fig. 9. Sanguine style (red chalk)

328

Gooch et al. (pp. 83–88)

Fig. 3. The rules of thirds and fifths are examples of heuristic compositional rules. Linear elements often run along these lines and key features often occur at line intersections (Banjo Lesson, Henry Tanner, oil on canvas.)

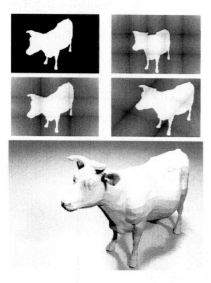

Fig. 4. Top left: initial viewpoint. Top right: combined rules of fifths and thirds. Middle left: rule of thirds. Middle right: angled rule of thirds. Bottom: rendered cow from angled rule of thirds

Fig. 5. Top: toy plane with rule of thirds layout and views from below and above. Bottom: toy plane rendered with view from above

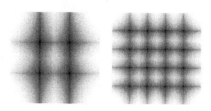

Fig. 6. Two images that guide layout optimization. The dark areas attract silhouette edges. The edges will tend to fall "downhill" toward these dark regions

Fig. 7. Left: Bunny overlaid on a portrait format, combined rule of thirds and fifths template. Right: The resulting shaded image

Raskar et al. (pp. 89–102)

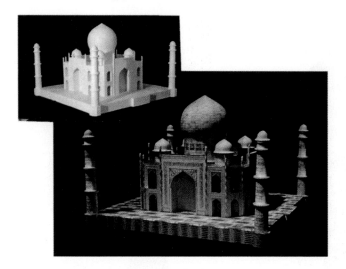

Fig. 1

Fig. 4

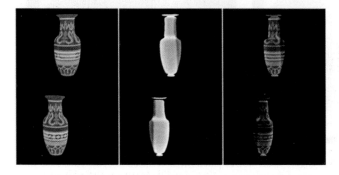

Fig. 6. Intensity weights using feathering methods

Fig. 7

Lensch et al. (pp. 103–114)

Fig. 5. A bronze bust rendered with a spatially varying BRDF, which was acquired with our reconstruction method

Fig. 6. This image shows the bird with the spatially varying BRDF determined by projecting each lumitexel into a basis of BRDFs. Note the subtle changes of the materials making the object look realistic

Fig. 7. Left: Photograph of model. Right: Model with acquired BRDF rendered from the same view with similar lighting direction. The difference in the hair region is due to missing detail in the triangle mesh

Matusik et al. (pp. 115–125)

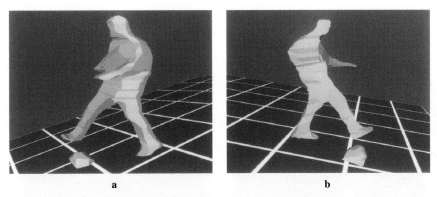

Fig. 6. Two flat-shaded views of a polyhedral visual hull

Fig. 7. Two view-dependently textured views of the same visual hull model. The left rendering uses conservative visibility computed in real-time by our algorithm. The right view ignores visibility and blends the textures more smoothly but with potentially more errors

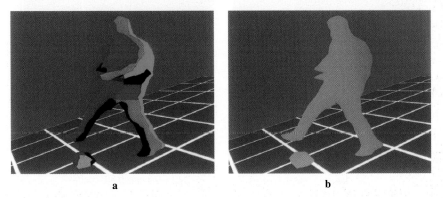

Fig. 8. Two visualizations of the camera blending field. The colors red, green, blue, and yellow correspond to the four cameras in our system. The blended colors demonstrate how each pixel is blended from each input image using both **a** visibility and **b** no visibility

Peter and Straßer (pp. 127–138)

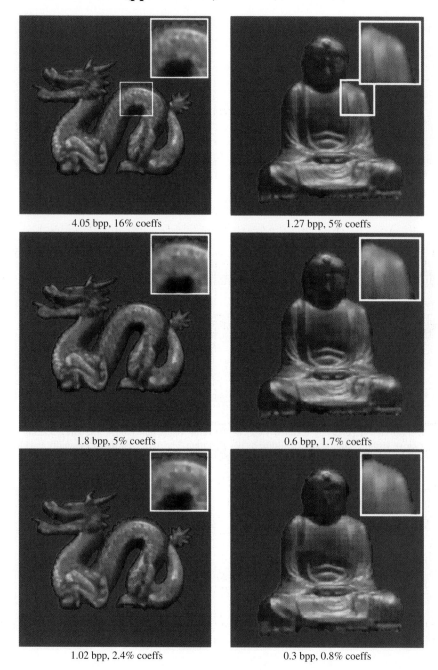

Fig. 10. Dragon and Buddha Light Field with magnified detail for different compression ratios: With increasing compression ratio, the obtained image quality decreases only slightly

333

Kalaiah and Varshney (pp. 139–150)

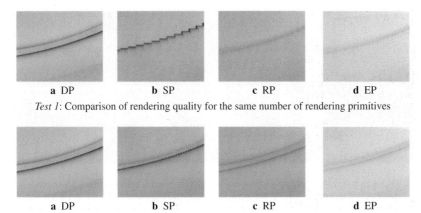

| a DP | b SP | c RP | d EP |

Test 1: Comparison of rendering quality for the same number of rendering primitives

| a DP | b SP | c RP | d EP |

Test 2: Approximately similar rendering quality achieved with different sampling frequency

Fig. 6. Selected areas of rendering of the teapot model for the two test cases: **a** Differential points. **b** Square primitive. **c** Rectangle primitive. **d** Elliptical primitive

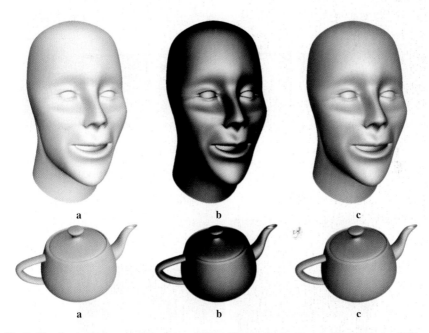

Fig. 7. Illumination and per-pixel shading: **a** Diffuse illumination. **b** Specular illumination. **c** Diffuse and specular illumination

Stamminger and Drettakis (pp. 151–162)

Fig. 7. Interactive design of an interior environment. To a radiosity solution of an office rendered with polygons, we added a complex tree, a wicker work basket and a paper weight, all displayed with 75,000 points. After turning on the fan, the tree is moving in the wind (center, 13 fps at 400×400). The images on the right show the interactive change of parameters of procedural objects. Top row: changes at 4 fps, bottom row: 8 fps, the last one at 1.5 fps

Fig. 8. Interactive design of an outdoors scene (resolution 400×400). We start with a simple terrain (left: 23,000 points, 6 fps), add 1000 chestnut trees made of 150,000 triangles each and add two clouds (280,000 points, 5 fps). If we increase accuracy, we get the right image using 3,300,000 points after 2 sec

Fig. 9. Two snapshots of an interactive session in a dynamic procedural virtual world. The user navigates at about 8 fps. The trees are moving in the wind and the user "throws rocks" into the lakes. The terrain is precomputed and stored in a texture

Wimmer et al. (pp. 163–176)

Fig. 8. Top: An impostor for a number of buildings (inset: geometry). Center: Filtering of tree for impostor (top) against geometry (bottom). Bottom: Impostor for a city walkthrough. Note the correct filtering of the impostor (top) compared to geometry (bottom)

Kim and Neumann (pp. 177–182)

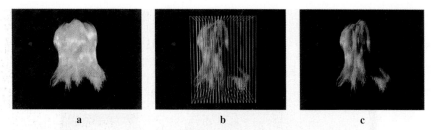

Plate 1. a Hair rendering without self-shadows. **b** Each opacity map is illustrated as a green rectangle. **c** Shadowed hair model (about 340,000 lines)

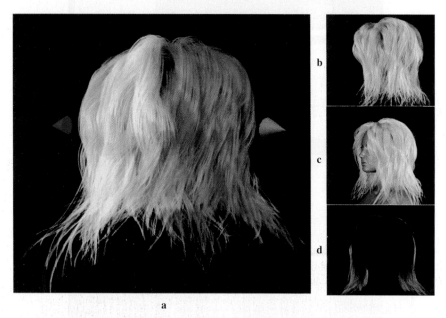

Plate 2. a A hair model lit by three lights (N = 80). **b** Different view of the model of about 500,000 lines. **c** The opaque head and torso is shown. **d** Backlighting effect

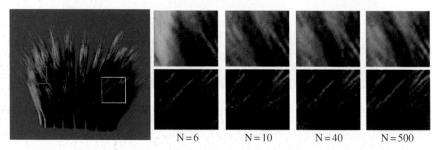

Plate 3. A fur model rendered with 500 maps (left). One light is positioned at the left side of the image. Close-up views are shown on the right side, upper rows for a bright area (blue rectangle) and lower rows for a dark area (yellow rectangle). Note that artifacts are visible at brighter regions, but only with relatively small numbers of maps

Meyer et al. (pp. 183–196)

Fig. 6. The BTF associated to the highest level (horizontal axis: 18 view directions, vertical axis: 6 light directions, 64×64 resolution per billboard, with colors and transparencies)

Fig. 7. Left to right: a pine tree with shadows, without shadows, amount of shadow. The pine with only ambient, the ambient visibility coefficient, the billboards used at the lowest level of detail. A prunus tree drawn at 3 levels of detail

Fig. 8. 4 views in a forest (1000 trees on a landscape, with shading, shadows, and fog). The frame rate is 7 to 20 fps on our test machine. Note the detailed trees in the foreground

338

Wilkie et al. (pp. 197–204)

Fig. 1. Example renderings of polarization effects combined with fluorescent objects. The left and right columns show similar setups under two different illuminations – at the left D65, and at the right UV blacklight. The scene shows several metal spheres (gold, copper, silver) and a nonfluorescent object (the biplane model) which float over a diffuse floor with fluorescent properties, and which are reflected in a large block of a dielectric material (glass). The reflection is viewed well below Brewster's angle in order to increase its intensity; because of this, the polarizing filters which are placed in front of the camera in the two lower images (horizontal polarizer in the middle, vertical at the bottom) do not affect the entire reflected energy. For comparison purposes, the topmost two images have a 50 percent neutral grey filter instead of a polarizer placed in front of the camera. These images can also be viewed in higher resolution at http://www.artoolkit.org/Gallery/Fluorescence/

Koltun et al. (pp. 205–215)

a A viewcell of size $50 \times 50 \times 2$

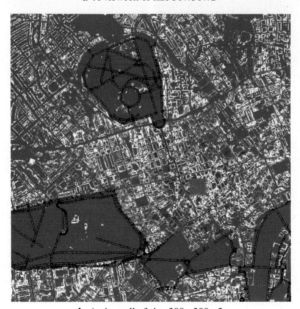

b A viewcell of size $300 \times 300 \times 2$

Fig. 6. Results of two experiments. Overviews of 25 square kilometers of the London model are shown, with outlines of the buildings in white. The algorithm has classified the red areas as occluded from the green viewcell, which is $50 \times 50 \times 2$ meters large in **a**, and $300 \times 300 \times 2$ meters large in **b**. Discretization resolution of 128×128 was used

Hey et al. (pp. 217–222)

Fig. 3. Actually rendered image

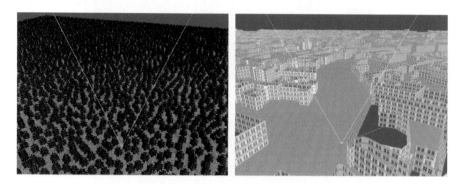

Fig. 4. View from above. The view frustum of Fig. 3 is visualized as wireframe

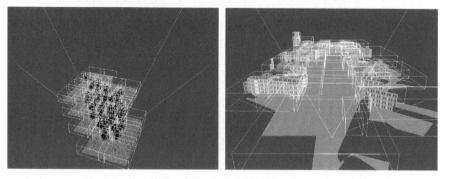

Fig. 5. Only the objects that pass the occlusion test and that are therefore drawn (sent to OpenGL) in Fig. 3, their leaf-bounding boxes and the view frustum

Dumont et al. (pp. 249–256)

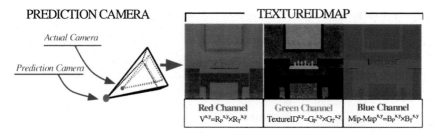

PREDICTION CAMERA

Actual Camera

Prediction Camera

TEXTUREIDMAP

Red Channel	**Green Channel**	**Blue Channel**
$V^{x,y}=R_P^{x,y}\times R_T^{x,y}$	$TextureID^{x,y}=G_P^{x,y}\times G_T^{x,y}$	$Mip\text{-}Map^{x,y}=B_P^{x,y}\times B_T^{x,y}$

Fig. 2. TextureIDMap computation

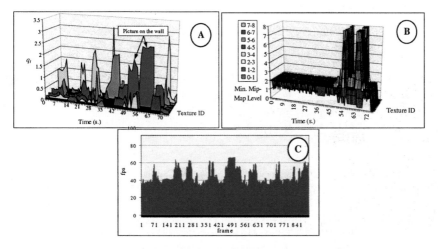

Fig. 3. Variation of q_i (**A**), subpyramids loaded (**B**), frames per second (**C**) along time

Fig. 4. Walkthrough of an architectural scene (performance with our caching strategy is 40 fps, without is 3 fps)

Suykens and Willems (pp. 257–268)

Fig. 5. Image of a scene with glossy materials without the use of texture filtering. Glossy reflections and refractions are noisy

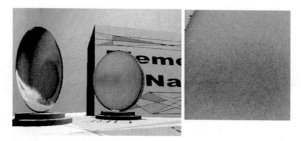

Fig. 6. For this image texture filtering is used, based on the footprint of the path. In some regions the footprint is over-estimated, causing too much blurring (especially the glossy transparent squashed sphere, as shown in the magnification)

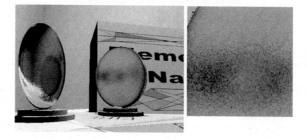

Fig. 7. For this image the path gradient was used to reduce over-estimated footprints and the excessive blurring is effectively reduced

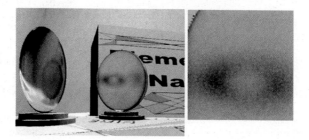

Fig. 8. Reference image using many more samples

Keller and Heidrich (pp. 269–276)

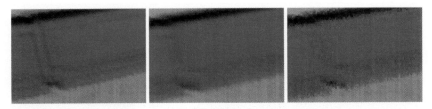

Fig. 4. Blending between regular and irregular sampling for the example of motion blur. In all images we use 16 samples per pixel. From left to right: method of dependent tests (Accumulation Buffer), interleaved sampling, and for illustration independent random samples

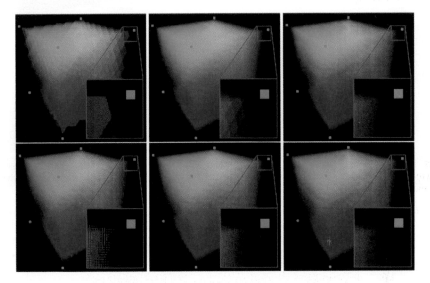

Fig. 5. A comparison of interleaved sampling for volume rendering (bottom) with the traditional texture-based approach described by Cabral et al. [CCF94] (top). From left to right: 20, 60, and 120 planes. Note that in the 120 plane example quantization artifacts due to the limited dynamic range of the framebuffer start to appear. To avoid these artifacts, smaller numbers of planes have to be used, in which case interleaved sampling produces much better results than the original algorithm

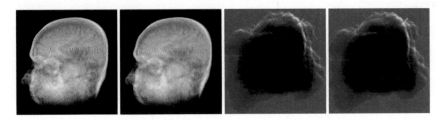

Fig. 6. Illustration of our volume rendering algorithm with real data sets. Left of pair: traditional texture based method exhibiting aliasing artifacts that show up as ringing structures. Right of pair: interleaved sampling with drastically reduced depth aliasing

Wald et al. (pp. 277–288)

Fig. 6. Shadow and reflection effects created with ray tracing using one light source. The performance drops roughly proportional to the number of total rays traced but the size of the working set increases. Note the reflections off all the small pipes near the ground. Diffuse case: 1 ray per pixel, 4.9 fps, with shadow and reflection (multiple of 2 rays): 1.4 fps

Fig. 7. Two complex views of the power-plant. Both still render at 4.9 and 3.9 fps, respectively

Hakura et al. (pp. 289–300)

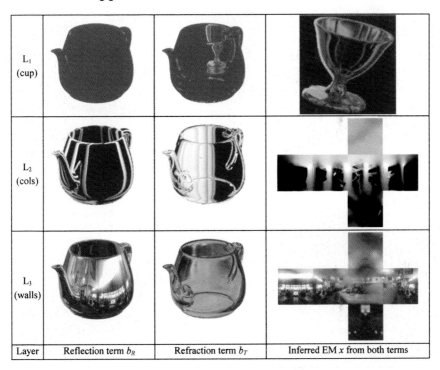

Fig. 7. Layered EMs inferred at a viewpoint sample for a glass teapot (three layers). A quadrilateral was used for the L_1 layer, a cylindrical shell for L_2, and a spherical shell for L_3. Shells are parameterized by a six-faced cube map. Entire MIPMAPs are inferred; only the finest level is shown

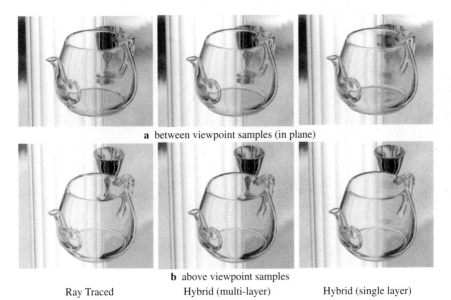

Fig. 8. Hybrid rendering results. The right two columns were generated by a PC graphics card

a full ray tree   **b** two-term greedy ray path

Fig. 2. Shading models. The full ray tree (**a**) requires 5 times more ray queries than our greedy ray path model (**b**)

a with prevention

b without prevention

Fig. 9. EM disocclusion

ray traced (480s/frame)

hybrid slower, $\tau = 3$ (19s/frame)

hybrid faster, $\tau = 5$ (10s/frame)

Fig. 10. Quality comparison

Ging et al. (pp. 301–312)

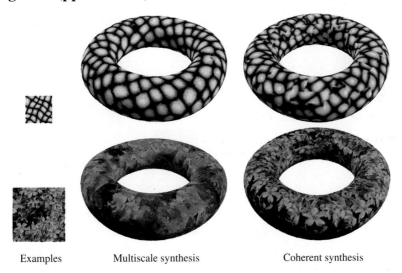

Examples   Multiscale synthesis   Coherent synthesis

Fig. 8. Comparison of multiscale (based on Wei-Levoy [13]) and coherent algorithms (based on Ashikhmin [2]). The results are comparable to those of the image texture synthesis algorithms

Fig. 9. Transparency mapping. Left: Example textures. Middle: Wicker ball, generated from first texture by multiscale synthesis. Right: Bronze cow, generated by coherent synthesis from second texture blended with a green surface color

Fig. 10. Chia cow and sea horse, generated with coherent synthesis

Cohen et al. (pp. 313–320)

Fig. 2. Screen snapshots from our high-dynamic range panorama viewer. The viewer implements our HDRTM technique allowing these results to be rendered interactively at 50 Hertz at 640 × 480 pixels with 4 × antialiasing. The exposure changes by a factor of 100 over these 5 images

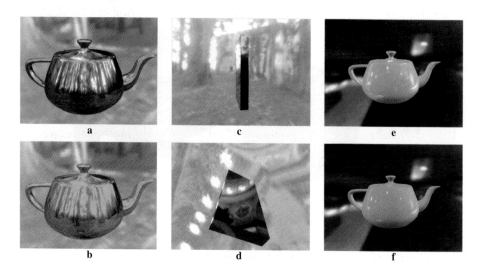

Fig. 3. a Environment mapping with a specular coefficient of $\phi = 0.125$ using HDRTMs. **b** Environment mapping with 8-bit per-channel texture maps. The attenuation due to reflection is not displayed correctly. **c** and **d** Simulated Fresnel reflection on a monolith in two environments. For the faces seen at glancing angles, the monolith is a near-perfect mirror. For the faces viewed more directly, the specular reflectance drops to just 5 percent, revealing the colors of the bright light sources: **e** A colored glossy material is simulated by adding a diffuse enviromnent map to a specular environment map with $\phi = 0.08$. Because the textures have been gamma-corrected, the result of compositing in the framebuffer is incorrect. **f** The simulated correct result

EXTERNAL REVIEWERS

Maneesh Agrawala
Daniel Aliaga
Michael Ashikhmin
Kavita Bala
Philippe Bekaert
Marc Bolin
Stefan Brabec
Pere Brunet
Chris Buehler
Patrick Callet
Min Chen
Jonathan Cohen
Michael Cohen
Satyan Coorg
Brian Curless
Cyrille Damez
Katja Daubert
Jeremy De Bonet
Georg Demme
Reynald Dumont
Fredo Durand
Philip Dutre
David Ebert
Sergey Ershov
Marcos Fajardo
Tao Feng
James Ferwerda
Shachar Fleishman
Tom Funkhouser
Michael Garland
Michael Goesele
Amy Gooch
Edward Groeller
Brian Guenter
Joerg Haber
Sven Havemann
Aaron Hertzmann
Nicolas Holzschuch
Hugues Hoppe
Isabelle Icart
Homan Igehy
Masa Inakage
Victoria Interrante
Thouis Jones
Jan Kautz
Konstantin Kolchin
Vladlen Koltun

David Kurlander
Paul Lalonde
Greg Larson-Ward
Anselmo Lastra
Justin Legakis
Henrik Lensch
Ming Li
Tom Lokovic
Andrzej Lukaszewski
Marcus Magnor
Lee Markosian
Steve Marschner
Ignacio Martin
Wojciech Matusik
Leonard McMillan
Ann McNamara
Radomir Mech
Gary Meyer
David Mould
Isabel Navazo
Fabrice Neyret
Marc Olano
Manuel Oliveira
Peter Lindstrom
Sebastien Paquet
Steven Parker
Frederic Perez-
Cazorla
Hanspeter Pfister
Matt Pharr
Marc Pollefeys
Andreas Pomi
Pierre Poulin
Jan Prikryl
Przemyslaw
Prusinkiewicz
Jacek Raczkowski
Przemyslaw Rokita
Christian Roessl
Szymon Rusinkiewicz
Pedro Sander
Mateu Sbert
Gernot Schaufler
Andreas Schilling
Peter Schroeder
Marc Segal
Hans-Peter Seidel

Steve Seitz
Jonathan Shade
Annette Sheel
Hartmut Schirmacher
Harry Shum
Mel Slater
Peter-Pike Sloan
Philipp Slusallek
Laszlo Szirmay-Kalos
John Snyder
Cyril Soler
Marc Stamminger
Michael Stark
James Stewart
Wolfgang Sturzlinger
Frank Suykens
Marco Tarini
Robert Tobler
Jack Tumblin
Greg Turk
Amitabh Varshney
Christian Vogelgsang
Jens Vorsatz
Ingo Wald
Bruce Walter
Harold Westlund
Alexander Wilkie
Andrew Willmott
Michael Wimmer
Tien-Tsin Wong
Peter Wonka
Dane Wood
Yizhou

AUTHOR INDEX

SpringerComputerScience

Thomas Driemeyer

Rendering with mental ray®

Second revised edition
2001. XI, 535 pages.
Numerous figures, partly in colour. With CD-ROM.
Softcover DM 116,–, öS 815,–, EUR 59,20*⁾
(Recommended retail prices)
*⁾ All prices are net-prices subject to local VAT,
Euro-price valid as of January 2002.
ISBN 3-211-83663-2. mental ray Handbooks, Volume 1

mental ray is the leading rendering engine for generating photorealistic images, built into many 3D graphics applications. This book, written by the mental ray software project leader, gives a general introduction into rendering with mental ray, as well as step-by-step recipes for creating advanced effects, and tips and tricks for professional users. A comprehensive definition of mental ray's scene description language and the standard shader libraries are included and used as the basis for all examples.

The second edition was extended to cover the new generation of mental ray, version 3.0, throughout the book. A CD with a fully programmable demo version of the software together with example scene data and shaders that are described in the book is enclosed. The software permits experimentation on a wide variety of supported computer platforms.

 **Springer**WienNewYork

A-1201 Wien, Sachsenplatz 4–6, P.O.Box 89, Fax +43.1.330 24 26, e-mail: books@springer.at, Internet: **www.springer.at**
D-69126 Heidelberg, Haberstraße 7, Fax +49.6221.345-229, e-mail: orders@springer.de
USA, Secaucus, NJ 07096-2485, P.O. Box 2485, Fax +1.201.348-4505, e-mail: orders@springer-ny.com
Eastern Book Service, Japan, Tokyo 113, 3–13, Hongo 3-chome, Bunkyo-ku, Fax +81.3.38 18 08 64, e-mail: orders@svt-ebs.co.jp

SpringerComputerScience

David Ebert,

Jean M. Favre, Ronald Peikert (eds.)

Data Visualization 2001

Proceedings of the Joint Eurographics – IEEE TCVG Symposium
on Visualization in Ascona, Switzerland, May 28-30, 2001

2001. XI, 364 pages. 212 figures, partly in colour.
Softcover DM 118,–, öS 830,–, EUR 59,90*)
(Recommended retail prices)
*) All prices are net-prices subject to local VAT,
Euro-price valid as of January 2002.
ISBN 3-211-83674-8. Eurographics

This book contains 33 papers presented at the Third Joint Visualization
Symposium of the Eurographics Association and the Technical
Committee on Visualization and Graphics of the IEEE Computer
Society.
The main topics treated are
• visualization of geoscience data
• multi-resolution and adaptive techniques
• unstructured data, multi-scale and visibility
• flow visualization
• biomedical applications
• information visualization
• object representation
• volume rendering
• information visualization applications
• automotive applications

SpringerWienNewYork

A-1201 Wien, Sachsenplatz 4–6, P.O. Box 89, Fax +43.1.330 24 26, e-mail: books@springer.at, Internet: **www.springer.at**
D-69126 Heidelberg, Haberstraße 7, Fax +49.6221.345-229, e-mail: orders@springer.de
USA, Secaucus, NJ 07096-2485, P.O. Box 2485, Fax +1.201.348-4505, e-mail: orders@springer-ny.com
Eastern Book Service, Japan, Tokyo 113, 3–13, Hongo 3-chome, Bunkyo-ku, Fax +81.3.38 18 08 64, e-mail: orders@svt-ebs.co.jp

SpringerComputerScience

Bernd Fröhlich, Joachim Deisinger, Hans-Jörg Bullinger (eds.)

Immersive Projection Technology and Virtual Environments 2001

Proceedings of the Eurographics Workshop
in Stuttgart, Germany, May 16-18, 2001

2001. XI, 284 pages. 150 figures, partly in colour.
Softcover DM 110,–, öS 770,–, EUR 55,90*)
(Recommended retail prices)
*) All prices are net-prices subject to local VAT,
Euro-price valid as of January 2002.
ISBN 3-211-83671-3. Eurographics

17 papers report on the latest scientific advances in the fields of immersive projection technology and virtual environments. The main topics included here are human computer interaction (user interfaces, interaction techniques), software developments (virtual environment applications, rendering techniques), and input/output devices.

 **Springer**WienNewYork

A-1201 Wien, Sachsenplatz 4–6, P.O. Box 89, Fax +43.1.330 24 26, e-mail: books@springer.at, Internet: **www.springer.at**
D-69126 Heidelberg, Haberstraße 7, Fax +49.6221.345-229, e-mail: orders@springer.de
USA, Secaucus, NJ 07096-2485, P.O. Box 2485, Fax +1.201.348-4505, e-mail: orders@springer-ny.com
Eastern Book Service, Japan, Tokyo 113, 3–13, Hongo 3-chome, Bunkyo-ku, Fax +81.3.38 18 08 64, e-mail: orders@svt-ebs.co.jp

SpringerComputerScience

G. Alefeld, Xiaojun Chen (eds.)

Topics in Numerical Analysis

With Special Emphasis on Nonlinear Problems

2001. Approx. 250 pages.
Softcover DM 168,–, öS 1180,–, EUR 85,–*)
Reduced price for subscribers to "Computing"
DM 151,20, öS 1062,–, EUR 76,50*)
(Recommended retail prices)
*) All prices are net-prices subject to local VAT.
Euro-prices valid as of January 2002.
ISBN 3-211-83673-X
Computing, Supplement 15

This collection of papers on numerical analysis with special emphasis on nonlinear problems covers a broad spectrum of fields. Several papers are involved in applying numerical methods for proving the existence of solutions of nonlinear problems, e.g. of boundary problems or of obstacle problems.
Naturally the solution of linear and nonlinear problems by iterative methods is the subject of a couple of papers. Here topics like the fast verification of solutions of monotone matrix equations, the convergence of linear asynchronous iteration with spectral radius of modulus one or aggregation and disaggregation methods for p-cyclic Markov chains are treated. On the other hand papers involved in optimization problems can be found. Nearly all fields of modern numerical analysis are touched by at least one paper.

 SpringerWienNewYork

A-1201 Wien, Sachsenplatz 4–6, P.O. Box 89, Fax +43.1.330 24 26, e-mail: books@springer.at, Internet: **www.springer.at**
D-69126 Heidelberg, Haberstraße 7, Fax +49.6221.345-229, e-mail: orders@springer.de
USA, Secaucus, NJ 07096-2485, P.O. Box 2485, Fax +1.201.348-4505, e-mail: orders@springer-ny.com
Eastern Book Service, Japan, Tokyo 113, 3–13, Hongo 3-chome, Bunkyo-ku, Fax +81.3.38 18 08 64, e-mail: orders@svt-ebs.co.jp